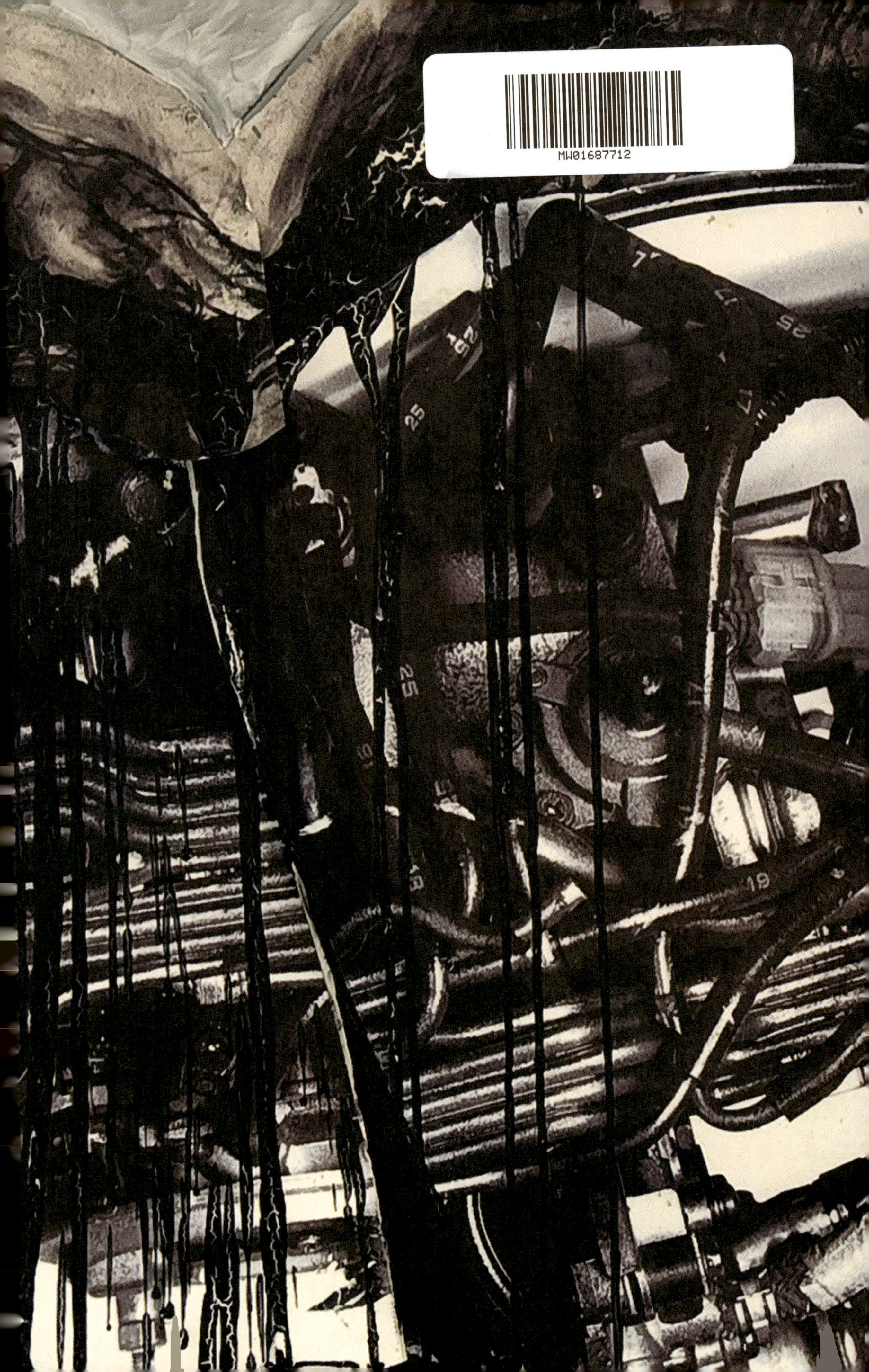

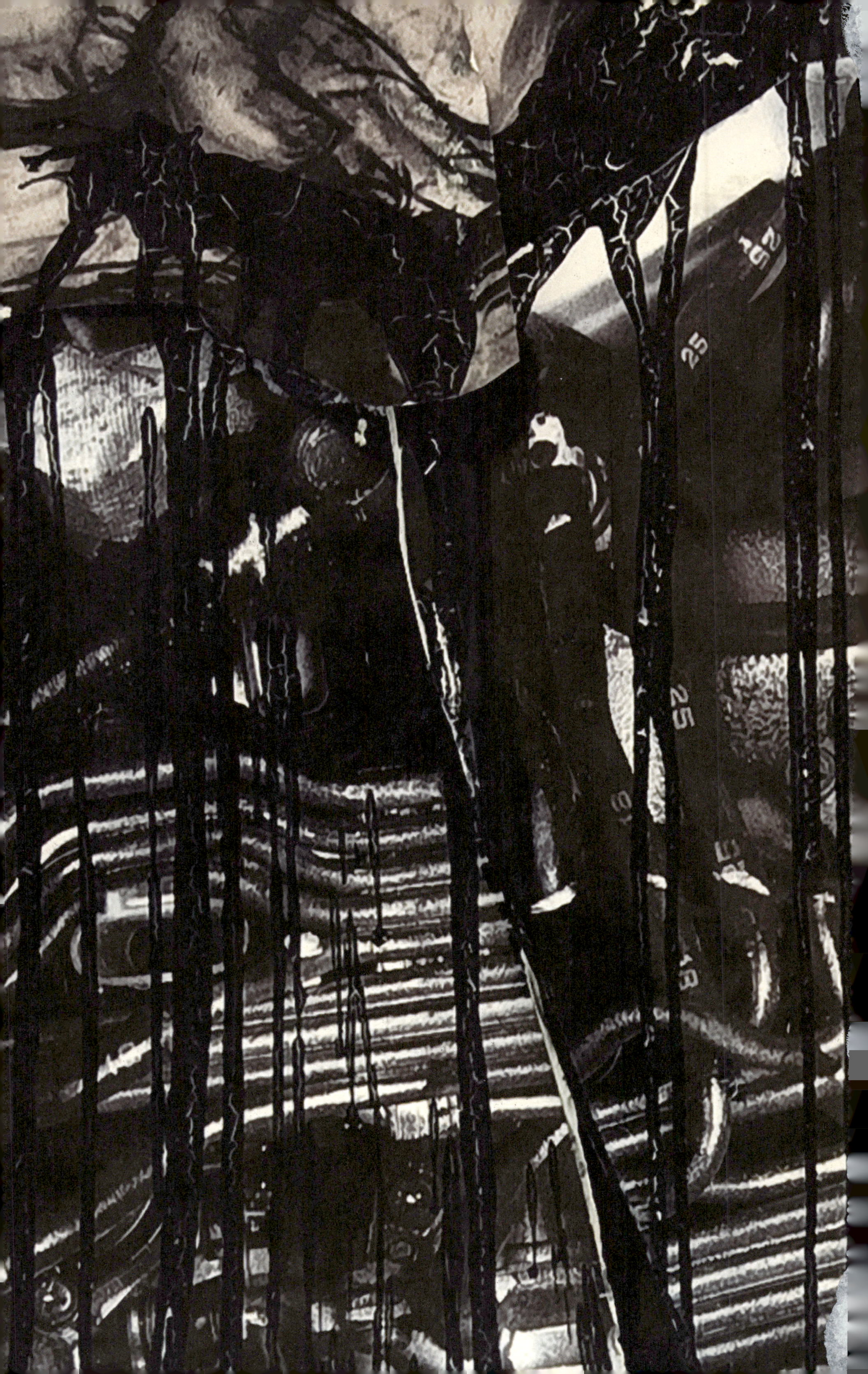

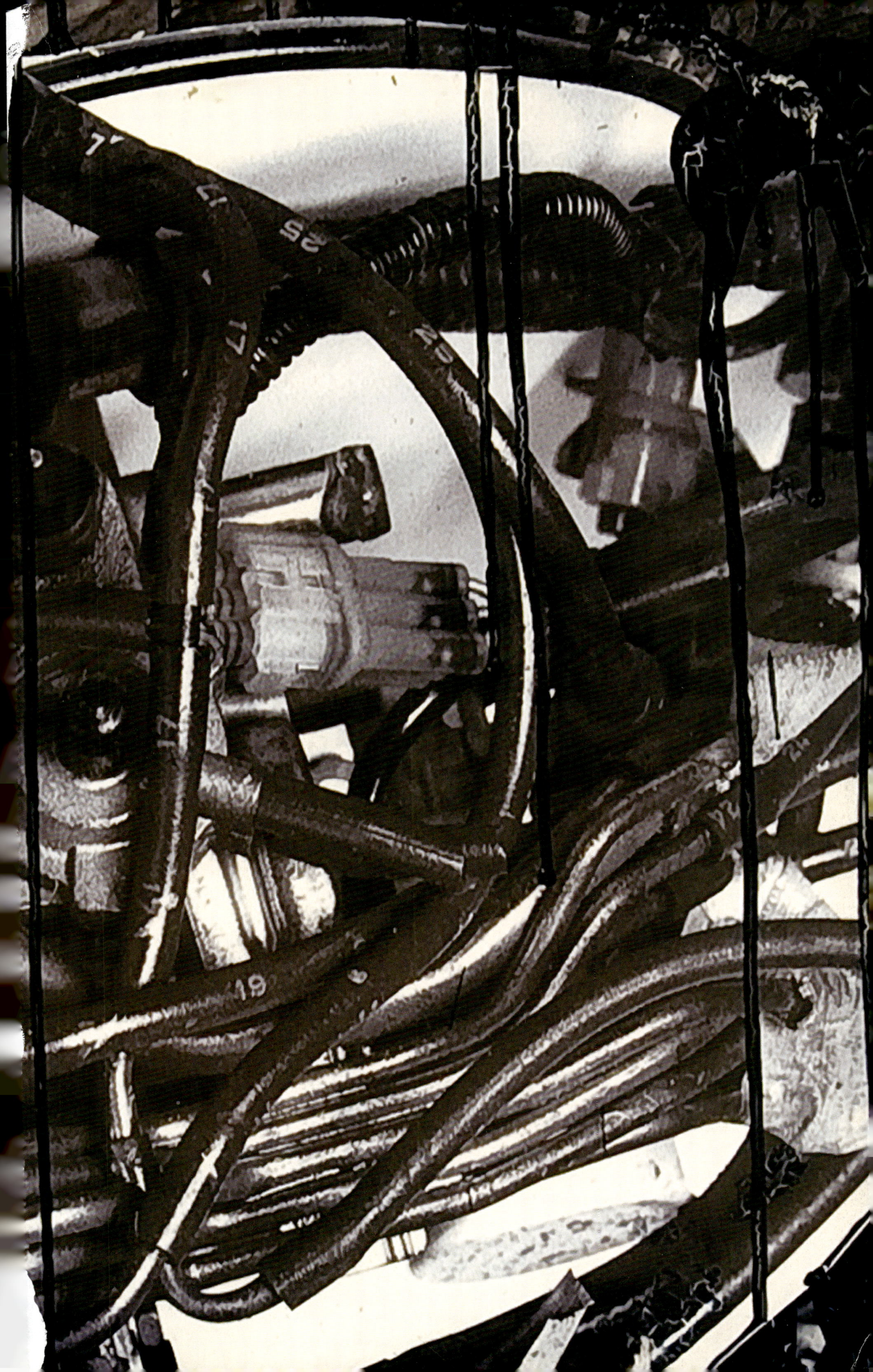

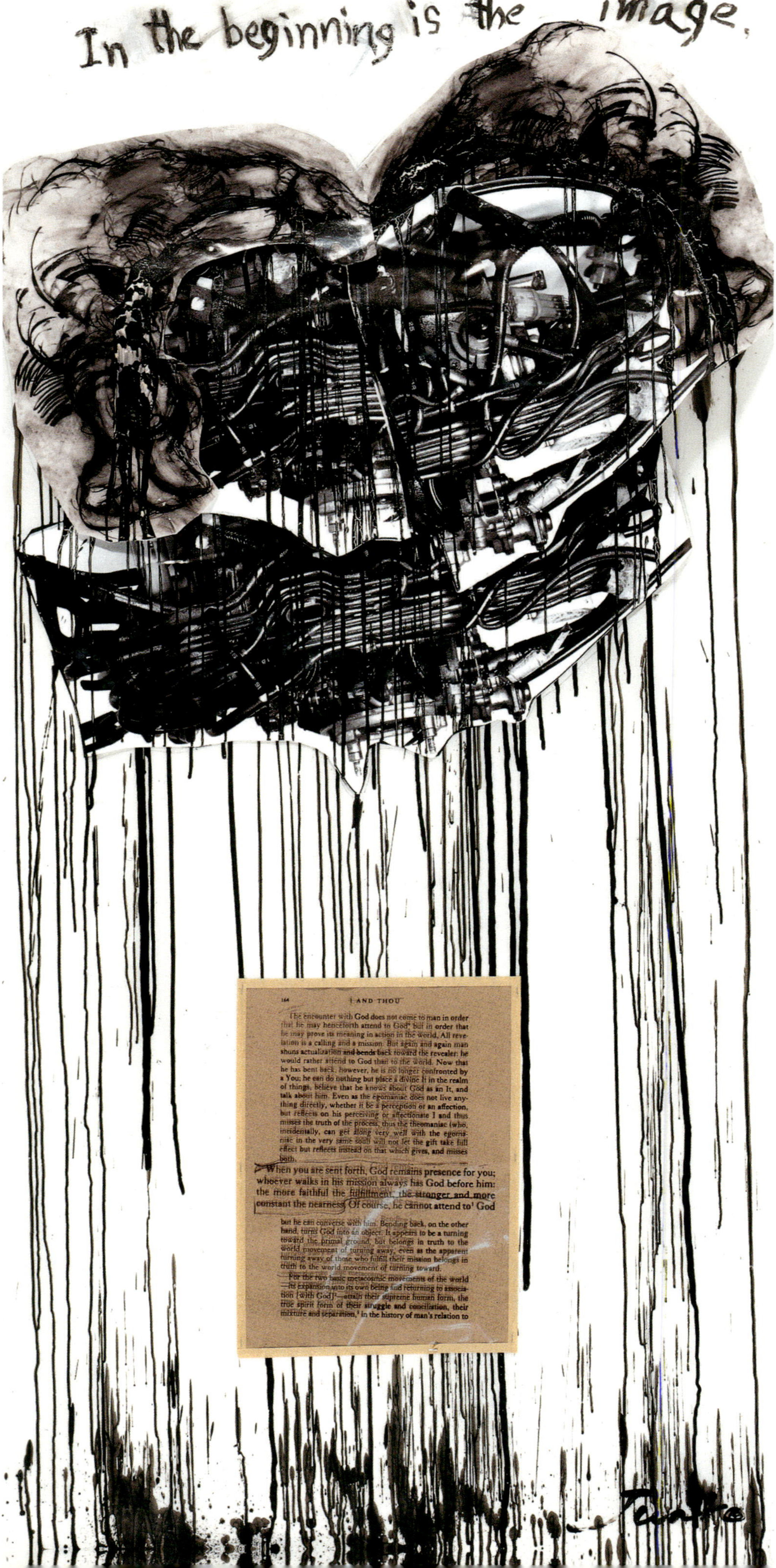
In the beginning is the image.
164
I AND THOU
The encounter with God does not come to man in order that he may henceforth attend to God but in order that he may prove its meaning in action in the world. All revelation is a calling and a mission. But again and again man shuns actualization and bends back toward the revealer: he would rather attend to God than to the world. Now that he has bent back, however, he is no longer confronted by a You; he can do nothing but place a divine It in the realm of things, believe that he knows about God as an It, and talk about him. Even as the egomaniac does not live anything directly, whether it be a perception or an affection, but reflects on his perceiving or affectionate I and thus misses the truth of the process, thus the theomaniac (who, incidentally, can get along very well with the egomaniac in the very same soul) will not let the gift take full effect but reflects instead on that which gives, and misses both.
When you are sent forth, God remains presence for you; whoever walks in his mission always has God before him: the more faithful the fulfillment, the stronger and more constant the nearness. Of course, he cannot attend to[1] God
but he can converse with him. Bending back, on the other hand, turns God into an object. It appears to be a turning toward the primal ground, but belongs in truth to the world movement of turning away, even as the apparent turning away of those who fulfill their mission belongs in truth to the world movement of turning toward.
For the two basic metacosmic movements of the world—its expansion into its own being and returning to association [with God][2]—attain their supreme human form, the true spirit form of their struggle and conciliation, their mixture and separation,[3] in the history of man's relation to

WHY ON EARTH DOES GOD HAVE TO PAINT?

CENTRIPETAL ART

by RAFAEL CHODOS

Junko

Based on Selected Works and Writings of

JUNKO CHODOS

Why on Earth Does God Have to Paint? / Centripetal Art
by Rafael Chodos

First print edition

Published by
Giotto Multimedia
P.O. Box 995
Malibu, CA 90265
United States of America

www.giottomultimedia.com

ISBN 10: 0-9704042-8-X
ISBN 13: 978-0-9704042-8-2

Library of Congress information on file with Publisher

Printed in Canada

AUTHOR'S PREFACE

How can we understand the power of contemporary art to move people, to reach into the viewers' souls and transform their lives?

Over the last fifty years we seem to have forgotten that art can have such power. In our museums we see people streaming through the contemporary galleries admiring the works, finding them beautiful, or interesting, smiling at them. The artists are praised for being talented, or skilled, or witty, or simply for being authentic representatives of this or that culture or subculture. Museums assess their performance by counting their traffic and they are managed by people whose overriding mandate is to attract supporters and pander to them.

In commercial galleries, too, the whole setup is calculated to flatter the viewers, to reassure them that they are intelligent, educated, sophisticated, and affluent. "This art looks empty but you are clever enough to see its real worth. *Won't you have another glass of wine?* The artist has quite a following in his own country. You are seeing his work now before many people have heard of it. By coming here you have shown yourself to be a member of the real elite!" If the flattery succeeds, the viewers might even purchase the works and hang them on their living room walls where their friends can admire them.

We will not blame anyone for this regrettable situation: museums and galleries have to earn a living like everyone else and the patrons have the right to feel good about themselves. But we will not forget what they seem to have forgotten.

There is a kind of art that has the power to reach the viewer's soul. Before this kind of art the viewer will stand with tears in his eyes; he will move slowly through the gallery and as he responds to the emanations he senses from each work, his life will start to change. Though he may be standing in a huge gallery with hundreds of other viewers, he feels himself enclosed in a space so private that he is afraid lest anything disturb it. Standing before the work, he realizes that there is something ineffable in it, something we will speak of as a divine presence[1]; and he realizes that this same presence is in him, and that the work has summoned it up from his innermost part. Later he will not say that he saw the art: he will say that he *encountered* it.

This book is about that kind of art. Such art is created out of the belief that the most personal thing can become the most universal because the center, the innermost world, is a place beyond gender, beyond ethnicity, and beyond any religious denomination. By making the journey to the center of the self—a journey which may lead through darkness and danger, a journey on which every step must be taken with honesty, with discipline, and with courage—the artist strives to reach divine presence. When the artist's journey is successful the viewer can experience it and participate in it, and this participation can help the viewer make his own journey.

It is a special kind of art, and particularly in the postmodern age—an age in which detachment from universal values was elevated to a principle—not every artist aspired to creating it. Let us call it "centripetal art:" art which seeks the center. Even among those artists who share an impatience with the surface—the artists who might be called "subjective" to distinguish them from the many kinds of "objective" artists[2]—the aspiration toward divine presence is unusual. It is a new kind of art, post-postmodern, which involves the most serious issues and processes in the lives of both the artist and the viewer.

This book is a document of the artistic journey of my wife, JUNKO CHODOS, whose paintings and writings established this new concept of art: centripetal art. As a child born in Japan and growing up there during World War II, surviving the allied

Cover:
Detail from
CONCERNING ART
AND RELIGION,
No. 6 (2003)

Frontispiece:
CONCERNING ART
AND RELIGION,
No. 7 (2003)
"In the beginning
is the image"
Paper, acetate and
acrylic on mylar
84 x 42 in.
(213.4 x 106.7 cm.)
Opening and
closing spreads:
details from this work.

bombings, Junko lived through a period of the darkest destruction, cruelty, and death. It became her spiritual project, as it did for many philosophers, psychologists, and serious thinkers of that age, to transcend that darkness—not only as a victim, but as a responsible representative of humanity. So this book is also about spirituality, and religion, and mysticism, and psychology.

Junko chose to emigrate to the United States when she was in her late twenties and soon afterward she married me, the son of a rabbi. So this book includes a personal account of my own multicultural experience—that is to say, of the cross-cultural dimensions of my marriage to Junko. The Japanese say that you cannot graft a tree onto bamboo, which means that there can be no satisfactory resolution of the conflict between Eastern and Western cultural ideals and that the best that can be hoped for is compromise and mutual tolerance. This may be true as long as the cultural categories are taken as fixed and immutable. But compromise and tolerance lead inevitably to frustration and anger, and they are incompatible with the love and intimacy which married people share. Something more radical and much deeper is required: something which involves a transcending of the cultural givens. I want my book to document the ways in which the tree and the bamboo can be transformed so that they grow together.

We are just emerging from that postmodern period, an age after the death of God, and of Art.[3] But to speak of "death" in this context, as in our deepest dreams, is actually to embark upon a phase of radical growth: death is a metaphor for an ending, a release, and a new birth. After the death of God, I want to show how Junko's centripetal art relates passionately to divine presence. I want to show how, in the age after the postmodern, art can function as a matrix of spiritual growth for both the artist and the viewer.

Topanga Canyon, California
Spring 2009

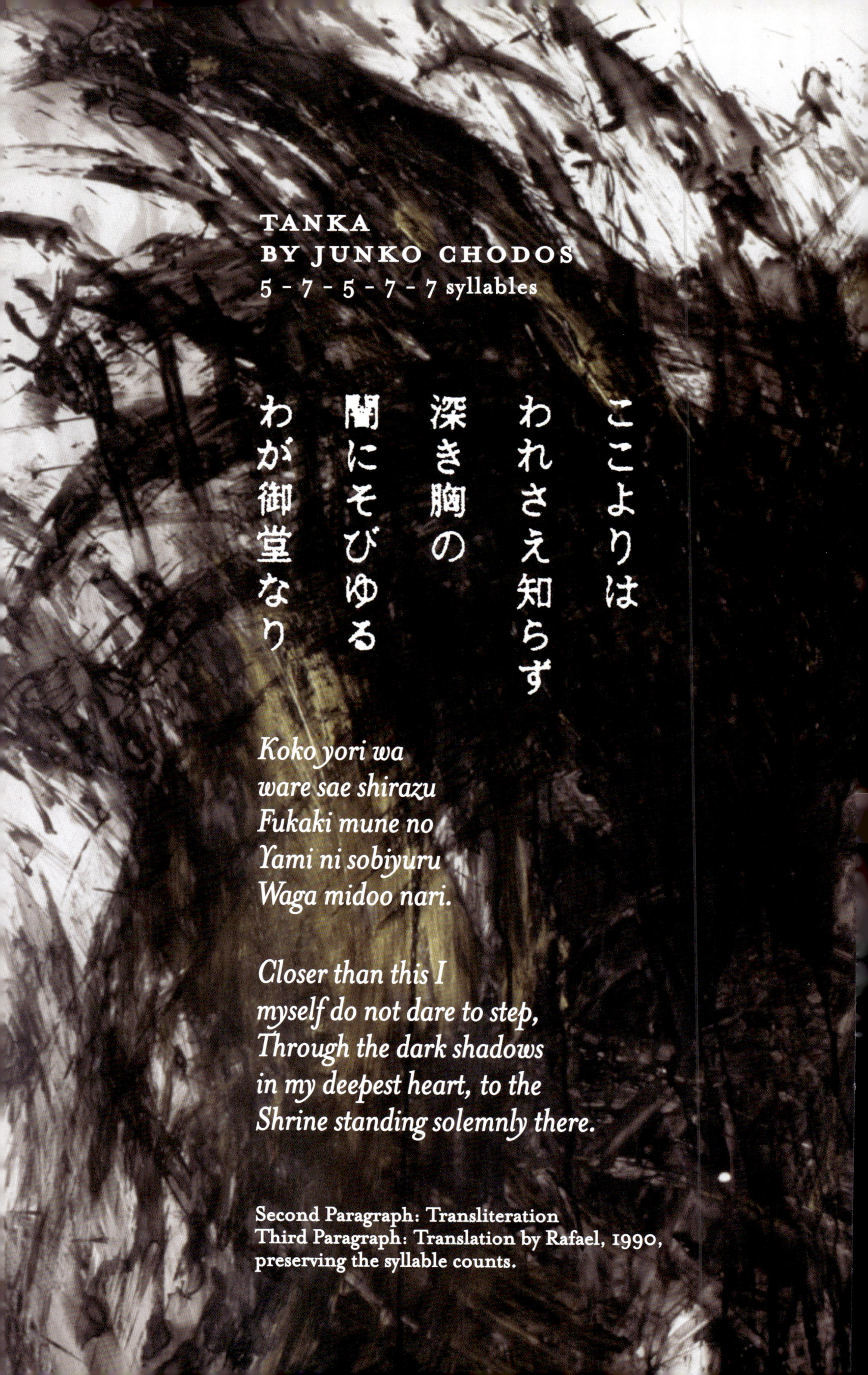

TANKA
BY JUNKO CHODOS

5 - 7 - 5 - 7 - 7 syllables

ここよりは
われさえ知らず
深き胸の
闇にそびゆる
わが御堂なり

Koko yori wa
ware sae shirazu
Fukaki mune no
Yami ni sobiyuru
Waga midoo nari.

Closer than this I
myself do not dare to step,
Through the dark shadows
in my deepest heart, to the
Shrine standing solemnly there.

Second Paragraph: Transliteration
Third Paragraph: Translation by Rafael, 1990, preserving the syllable counts.

ACKNOWLEDGMENTS

Many people have helped me to carry this book over a long and difficult road from its conception to its present form.

My thanks go to the early set of "beta readers" who saw my first complete draft for what it was and were good enough friends to tell me so: Dennis MacDonald, Lothar van Falkenhausen, and Albert Walton. Special thanks go to my friend Bruce Kerner, who read the first draft and made detailed comments, and then took the time to make many useful suggestions to me all the way through my process of revision.

About eight months later, I gave review copies of a second draft to Barbara Wells, Hannah Chodos, Saul Takahashi, Karl Morrison, Paul Young, and Rolf Knierim. All of these readers gave me constructive criticisms and detailed responses which were most helpful.

In addition to those beta readers who gave me detailed responses to the second draft, I want to thank several other people who read all or part of the book and gave me their general reactions: Joy Johnson, Robert Primes, George Gereby, John Schott, and Joe Matza. Their comments helped me to think more deeply about the purpose of this book.

In April of 2008, an electronic version of this book was published under the title, "Centripetal Art / Matrix of Growth." That version includes four essays by outside contributors, and remains the "mother lode" of the ideas presented here. The eBOOK is searchable, and incorporates something called "Discussion Notes"—a feature which enables readers to make comments on the text and respond to each other's comments. I am grateful to the essayists whose contributions to that form of the book remain helpful and provocative: George Gorse, Terrence Dempsey, J. Harold Ellens, and Karen Torjesen.

But the eBOOK version seemed excessively academic and hard to read. Junko and I both thank Rachel Resnick, who read the eBOOK carefully and advised us to make the transition from the eBOOK to this printed form. We thank also Catherine Madsen for taking the time to read and comment on this final draft. And we thank Mark Devendorf for his comments.

I give special thanks to the designer, Jeanette Hsu, without whose patient and skillful help I myself could never have visualized the end product. Thanks also to Brian Forrest, the skilled photographer to whom Junko and I have turned for high-quality images of her artworks for many years. And I thank the copy editors, Maurene Goo, Linda Ellis-Stiewing, and Terry Allen, each of whom made improvements to the text for which I am grateful.

Finally I thank Junko herself for having the patience, and the self-control, to read my manuscript as a third party might read it, suppressing her desire to write this book herself and supporting me in my effort to write it. At my request, she made many selections from her own writings and translated them out of Japanese so that I could incorporate them. She also served as editor on the final draft, and even though English is her second language, her editorial inputs were surprisingly sharp. For these contributions, I thank her.

March 2009

TABLE OF CONTENTS

AUTHOR'S PREFACE I

Definition of centripetal art. — Its place in art history: after the postmodern period. — Introducing the subject matter: one centripetal artist's journey. — The relationship with multiculturalism. — After the death of God and of art.

ACKNOWLEDGMENTS V

FOREWORD 1

How the author's connection with his wife's art grew more intimate over the years. — Learning in marriage. — "*Why on earth does God have to paint?*" — Marriage and the sense of mission. — **The Structure of this Book.** (7) — **The Artist Inside and Out** (9)

PART ONE: THE SURFACE LAYERS

CHAPTER ONE — OBJECTS AS VISITANTS 11

The artist's relationship to her subject matter: before and after modern art. — Encounter. — Visitants.

[Section One] Individual Visitants 15

— **Dead Flowers and Root.** (15) — **Root.** (21) — **Engine.** (26) — **Horseshoe Crab.** (35) — **Curtains.** (39) — **Lungs and Rib Cage.** (48) — **Burls and Tree Spirits.** (52) — **Birds and the Decanter.** (56) — **Human Figures and Dance.** (62) — **Deformed Babies.** (67) — The Story of St. Christopher.

[Section Two] Visitants Transforming: Burls Becoming Horrific Gods 70

Two aspects of the deity: gods as wrathful, gods as bestowers of bliss. — Tracing the process by which the visitant is transformed. — *FATHOM*: the figure of Kuukai.

CHAPTER TWO — BIOGRAPHY AND CULTURAL INFLUENCES 85

Birth and early childhood: living through the Allied bombing of Japan. —The executed bird. — Gakushûin. —Early art: painting in secret. — Klee and Rilke. — First marriage. Bride of the Church. — Shigetaro Akashi. — Teaching Sunday School. — Flower arrangement. — First trip to America: Starr-King School. — Divorce. — Waseda University. — Shigeo Ueda and Buber. Marxism. — Marriage to the author. Difficulty of living in a foreign country. — Encounter with Masahisa Goi, spiritual teacher in Japan. — First professional exhibitions.

CHAPTER THREE — TECHNIQUES AND STYLES 115
Pen and ink. (116) — Pencil and Charcoal Pencil. (119) — Collage. (120) — Xerox. (124) — Smears. (126) — Clorox. (128) — Cannibalization/Recycling. (128) — Mylar. (128) — Photography. (134) — Computer Manipulation. (137) — Charcoal and Acrylic. (142) — Styles. (145) — Orientation: Vertical and Horizontal. (145) — Time - Gesturality. (147) The story of the samurai. Kuukai's shipwreck. — **Images, Narratives, and Reflections. (154)** — Relationship between image and text.

PART TWO: THE DEEPER LAYERS

CHAPTER FOUR — NARRATIVE: RESOLUTION AND TRANSCENDENCE 161
Relationship between the images in the centripetal artist's works and the images she sees in her dreams. — Understanding the images as parts of narratives. — Different kinds of narrative: illustration distinguished from centripetal narrative. — **Childhood illustration - *Kamishibai* (164) — Centripetal Narratives: Requiem and Forest. (165) — Requiem for an Executed Bird (167) — The Viewer's Participation (178) — In the Forest of Amida Buddha (179) — Mixed Genre: FATHOM. (184) — Resolution and Transcendence. (191)**

CHAPTER FIVE — A VITAL SPIRITUALITY 197
The vital question: How is this art spiritual? —Why this art could not have been created earlier. — Echoes of the spiritual artists of the early 20th century. — Five "motivations" that transformed the consciousness of the 20th Century into the consciousness of the 21st Century:

TABLE OF CONTENTS

— **The Impact of Psychology. (198) — The Impact of Multiculturalism. (201) — The Impact of World War II and Fascism. (203) — The Impact of Existentialism: the Total Absence of Complacency. (206) — The Impact of the Atomic Bomb; Ecological Concerns. (209) — Markers for Spirituality (211) — Centripetal Art Overflows the Studio. (212)** — Forcing the author to rethink his relationship to Judaism. — **A New Kind of Spirituality. (214)** Transcending stereotypes and disappointing our expectations.

CHAPTER SIX — A COMPLEX SPIRITUALITY 219

Spirituality of the 21st Century. — **Formative Experience: Destruction. (220) — Formative Experience: Performance versus creation. (225) — Individuation. (229)** Erich Fromm's analysis of Fascism. — Art and the process of individuation. — **Individuation through a Legal Dispute (236) — Organic/Inorganic. (240) — Altered States. (245)** Coping with the altered state: The story of Tsu (Japanese folklore). — Feeling comfortable with the altered state.

CHAPTER SEVEN — THE ROLE AND MISSION OF THE ARTIST 261

What contribution does this kind of artist make to the community? — Junko's answer. How this answer locates her art in the 21st Century. — **The Artist's Mission in the 21st Century. (263) — The Artist's Contribution: Modelling integrity. (266)**

AFTERWORD — THE FURNACE 271

Polytheism and monotheism in the artwork. — Goethe's aphorism. — Marriage and the alchemist's furnace. — Answers to the question with which we started: *Why does God have to paint?*

PART THREE: THE PHYSIOLOGY OF THIS BOOK

CURRICULA VITAE

Artist: Junko Chodos 283

Author: Rafael Chodos 291

ENDNOTES 295
BIBLIOGRAPHY 305
LIST OF CITATIONS TO WRITINGS OF JUNKO CHODOS 309
JAPANESE TERMS USED IN THIS BOOK 312
ALPHABETICAL IMAGE TABLE 315
SERIES LIST: CHRONOLOGICAL 330
GENERAL INDEX 332
THEMES IN SERIES 1973/2006 (FOLD-OUT) AFTER 336

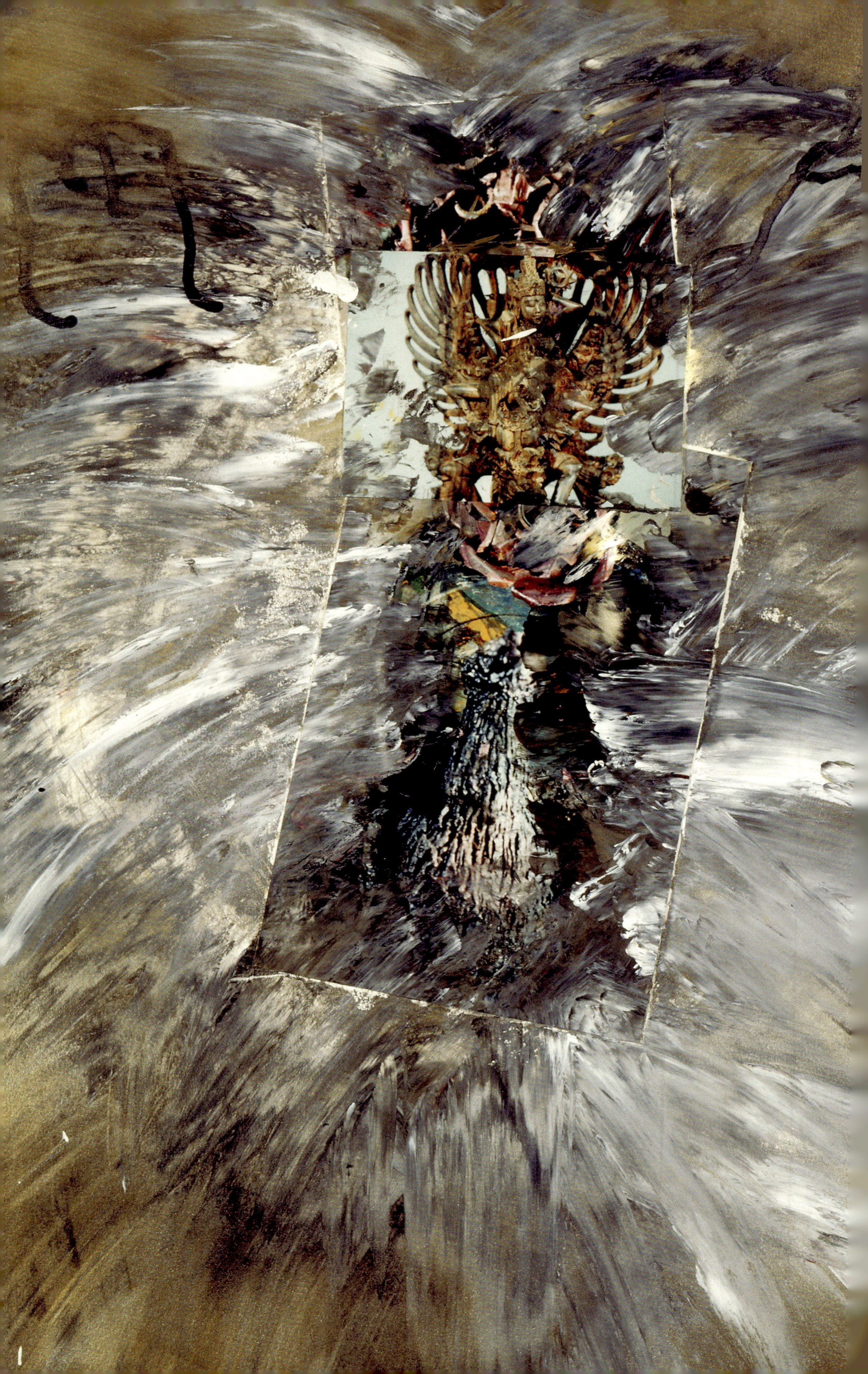

FOREWORD

Over the course of the last thirty-seven years, as my marriage to the artist JUNKO CHODOS has lasted longer and become deeper, my relationship with her art has intensified. From the outset I encouraged her to dedicate herself to her art, but this was only out of respect for her own passionate connection to it. I had no idea whether her work was any good and I could not know whether it would have meaning to anyone else in the world but her. At the time, I identified myself as a person who knew nothing about art and had no interest in it. My creative interests lay in computers and law, in literature and philosophy, and in music: art was something for other people. So when I saw that Junko identified herself as an artist I wanted to support her and encourage her, but I had to do that from the outside. It was always more than just financial support: I often researched art materials and went with her to the art supply stores and I insisted that the largest and best-lit space in our home should always be her studio. But most important, we agreed that we would construct our new life together in such a way that she would have as much time as she wanted in her studio, free from interruptions.

This was a second marriage for both of us and we were eager to identify what was most important to us and to construct our life together consciously. Junko was better at this than I was: having lived all her life in Japan, she had already decided to leave her homeland behind her and live as an immigrant in America. That required a level of conscious decision-making which had never been required of me. I was still trying hard in those days to build a bridge between my inner and outer worlds and I had not yet found a pathway into my inner world. Junko already had an urgent need to paint and knew it. So although we agreed that we would construct our life together to support her commitment, the fact is that when

Opposite:
Detail from
REQUIEM FOR AN
EXECUTED BIRD,
No. 42 (1991)
Mixed media on paper

we married I could not even understand the full extent of Junko's commitment to her art.

Two years after we married, she started working on her *Dead Flower Series*. She would spend ten hours or more in her studio every day, staring at a vase of dead flowers and making sketches, every single day. I thought I was familiar with commitment to artistic endeavor: my older brother is a classical pianist and throughout his childhood he spent many hours a day practicing. I had always admired that kind of diligent, steady work but the quality of Junko's commitment to her art was something quite different. She did not go into her studio out of any sense of discipline or diligence—she was compelled to go there, and while she was there she was in a state of mind quite outside the range of what is normal. I began to realize that her compulsion to paint and her access to her inner world were far beyond anything I had known.

A year later she began her *Root Series* collages and as those works emerged from her studio, one per month, even I sensed that there was something very special about them. When she exhibited that series at a museum in Tokyo, I saw hundreds of people a day walk meditatively through the gallery and stare at the works with evident emotion. I saw many people weep at the works, and the newspapers were full of commentary about them. I saw one man return, day after day, and draw up a chair in front of one of the works, *Root Series, No. 16, Mandala,* and meditate silently until the gallery closed. This experience has repeated itself every time Junko exhibits her art: in Boston, in New York, in California, among her viewers there are always some who are so deeply moved that they seek Junko out to tell her their reactions to her work—and usually, to share their innermost secrets with her. After one slideshow lecture Junko gave in Northern California, a woman came up to her to tell her that she was dying of AIDS and that she was ready to die in peace now that she had seen Junko's art. She said that she realized that her own life, personal as it was, had universal meaning. Junko's art had made a bridge for her from the very personal to the universal. I was amazed to see that art has such a mysterious power to reach people's souls and that something in Junko's art unlocks the hearts even of strangers.

Opposite:
ROOT SERIES No. 16,
Mandala (1979)
Mixed media collage
on paper
21 x 16.5 in.
(53.3 x 41.9 cm.)

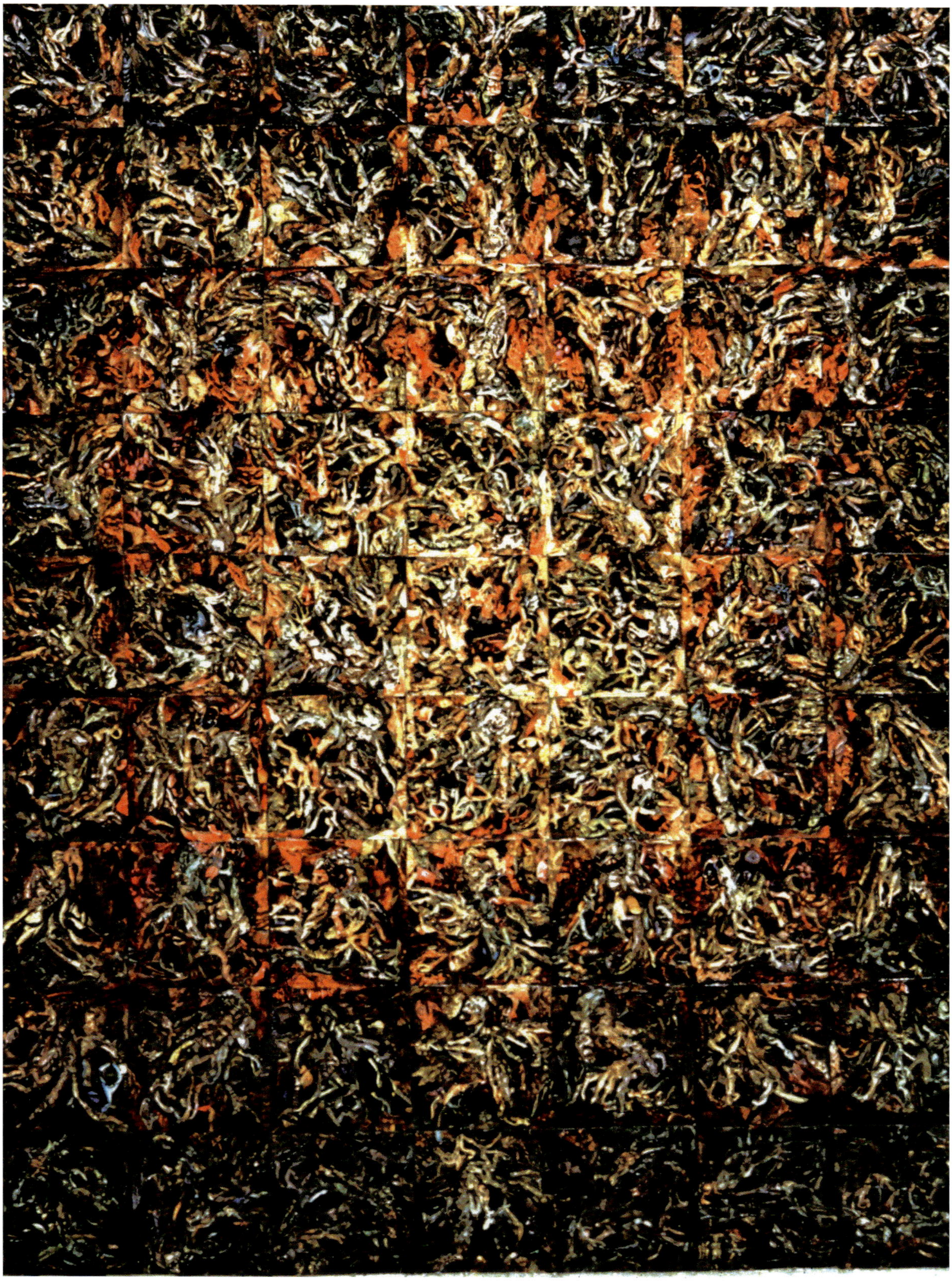

Married people learn from each other whether they want to or not. In those early years, Junko would sit with me on our couch and we would look together at reproductions of art works she admired. She would show me drawings by Rembrandt, and call my attention to the brush strokes, the "breathing," and how each work could be "read." She did the same with paintings she admired by Klee, Rouault, de Kooning, and others, showing me how honest their lines were to their inner worlds. Then she showed me masterworks of Japanese art, and showed me how to look at them. This was not by any means a systematic course in art appreciation, but it was the kind of steady teaching, administered in small doses by a loved one, that makes the deepest change in the student. Just as they say that drops of water can melt stone if they are sustained over a period of time, in that way my own identity as one who had no interest in art was melted away and I began to be interested in art and to identify myself as someone who was interested in it. At the same time, I began to find a way into my own inner world. I decided to leave the computer business as a lifework and to devote myself to law which I saw then as a more direct way of helping people and affirming eternal values.

But I am jumping ahead of myself: it was before these things, when we came into contact with a spiritual and psychic teacher in Japan, that both Junko's attitude toward her art, and my attitude toward her art and my own life, underwent a transformation. This is discussed more fully in Chapter Two. Before he ever saw Junko or any reproductions of her art, this teacher told an acquaintance of Junko's that he saw Junko's art psychically and that God was painting through her. The acquaintance relayed this information to us and both of us were surprised and mystified. *"Why on earth does God have to paint?"* Junko whispered. She intended this as a slightly humorous way of asking, what is essentially important about art? Her art had been a secret thing, a dark thing, a way of resolving her innermost suffering. She saw her art, in a word, as *ugly*. The idea that God was painting through her struck her as a great irony. But very quickly, the question caused her to see her art as the gateway to a world of more focused mystical experience. For me, coming as I do from a Judaeo-Christian background, Junko's question seemed more literal, as if it were an invitation to inquire into the motives of a personal God. But even though the question resonated differently for the two of us at first, we both took it very seriously. As we talked about it we both came to understand it as a question about the nature of art and for many years we searched earnestly for an answer to it.

We were in our thirties in those days, and both of us were asking ourselves, with great intensity, what was the meaning of our lives. By then I was already a lawyer and I asked myself often whether there was any need for lawyers in heaven—and if not, what was the good of being a lawyer on earth? Up to that time I had viewed my own work as a form of "self-expression" and, as I said, Junko had viewed her art as dark, inward, and secret. But through pondering the question why God has to paint, Junko came to realize that darkness is not merely an opposite of light: that darkness, as it is, embraces the light.[1] She started being aware of the possibility that transcending her suffering ego through art was something that might radiate light in the world. And for myself, I came to have a deeper concept of my own mission as a lawyer and a writer. Gradually both of us came to feel strongly that the real purpose of our marriage was to help each other accomplish our missions and that our missions were deeply intertwined. So it became part of my own mission to help Junko create her art and share it with others.

In order to pursue our mission, we made serious sacrifices. We decided not to have children because we both knew well that we could not handle the creation of art in the way that Junko works and the raising of children at the same time.

Over the years, I continued to support her as before but my involvement became more ramified. As she exhibited her art more widely it became necessary for her to write and speak about it. Because English is her second language I became her editor, correcting her language errors and putting her writings into final shape. In 1992, on the occasion of my fiftieth birthday, Junko allowed me to curate a showing of her series, *Requiem for an Executed Bird* [see Chapter Four]. My unique curatorial approach to the installation of the works in the gallery, as well as Junko's art, were both very favorably reviewed.[2] A few years later, I took Junko to a meeting of computer graphics specialists at the Los Angeles Convention Center. There she saw in person what computers could do with imaging, and she immediately asked me to help her incorporate those capabilities into her art. We began to compile a digital catalog of her works, and I took the major responsibility for that function. My role as Junko's computer helper grew over the years until finally, in 2005 and 2006, she invited me into her studio to help her create her *FATHOM* series: forty giant mylar panels of collaged computer prints. I was responsible for generating those prints, under her supervision, and for nearly half a year I went with her to the studio every day—except when I was in trial and had to be in court. We worked on the images from early morning to early evening without interruption. That work was completed in mid-2006, and it was then that I turned my mind in earnest to writing this book.

I want to offer my readers as deep an analysis as I can of the meaning of Junko's art and to try to say what it is in Junko's art that moves people so. I know that many—particularly those who consider themselves sophisticated in art—believe that the only way to understand a work of art is to look at it and that whatever one says about a work, no matter how well-intentioned, detracts from it. But my own experience has been to the contrary. Junko herself speaks and writes most eloquently about her art, and I know of no one who has heard her speak, or who has read what she has written, who does not feel his appreciation of her work deepened and refined. And it is through Junko's words about the works of other artists that my own eyes were opened and I gained access to a world that was closed to me before.

The fact is that Junko's art is the result of a deep, intense, and wide-ranging process of thinking and interior growth. Its implications reach far beyond the merely visual realm into the realms of psychology, mysticism, and religion. To understand this requires more than merely looking at the works— it requires some understanding of how the works came to be created.

The Structure of This Book

The corpus of Junko's work is large and growing. As I write, it includes more than one thousand works either catalogued or waiting to be catalogued, and many hundreds more that she does not include in her catalogue. So her art has to be seen as a living thing. Because it integrates so many layers, her work is after all at once physical and metaphysical, spiritual and worldly. The subjects and themes are drawn from the realm of what is organic and what is inorganic, what is natural and what is artificial, what is earthly and what is otherworldly. These realms are conjoined here and the artist finds passageways that lead—like time warps, or trap doors—miraculously quickly from one realm to another. This layered quality lends Junko's art an unusual kind of spirituality—not by virtue of its subjects or themes, but by virtue of the way the subjects and themes are handled.

So I have presented my discussion in layers. In **Part One**, which I subtitle "The Surface Layers" and which comprises Chapters One, Two, and Three, I present what I would say are matters of fact. These are things that would appear to anyone who had the opportunity and took the time to become closely acquainted with Junko's work, with her biography, and with her writings. In **Part Two**, which I subtitle "The Deeper Layers" and which comprises Chapters Four, Five, Six, and Seven, I invite you to consider the deeper themes and issues which lie below the surface of Junko's art. This part concludes with an Afterword in which I talk about the ways in which all the elements discussed earlier work together to form the special kind of spirituality which is the focus of the entire book. And in **Part Three**, my readers will find the apparatus: the endnotes, bibliography, tables of images, the sources and the relationships among them, which worked together to form the exposition in the first two Parts.

Chapter One addresses the question, What is the relationship between Junko and the subjects she paints? In order to answer that question, I include a selection of images of Junko's works and quotations from Junko's own writing about those works. Centripetal art grows out of Junko's life experience so **Chapter Two**

presents a biographical account of Junko, together with selections from her own writings which show how her life experience formed her attitude toward art. Through selections from her notebooks and diaries, I trace the development of "centripetal art" from her earliest childhood, untangling the many threads which are all brought together in her mature work. In **Chapter Three** I present a survey of the many techniques that Junko has used over the years—most but not all of which she has invented—and I discuss some of the stylistic features of her art. At the end of Chapter Three I describe the three major groupings of Junko's art: images, narratives, and reflections.

In Part Two, I revisit the themes that are presented in Part One—but at a deeper level. Many of the themes in this book, particularly the most important ones, crop up twice, or three or four times. This is intentional: each occurrence is pitched at a different level and as each theme reappears, it is explored from a different perspective.

Chapter Four deals with narrative in Junko's art and with the themes of resolution and transcendence. While the notion of narrative is suggested in Chapter One, mentioned in Chapter Two, and defined in Chapter Three, it is explored more deeply in Chapter Four. **Chapter Five**, titled "A Vital Spirituality," includes a discussion of why I call Junko a spiritual artist for the twenty-first century. Tracing the roots of her aesthetic into the early decades of the twentieth century, I show how her centripetal art incorporates the life-changing experiences of the last half of that century and so becomes unavoidably twenty-first century. **Chapter Six**, titled "A Complex Spirituality," treats of several other deeper issues which all of Junko's works engage: the childhood experiences which I believe proved formative (and these were presented in a more matter-of-fact way in Chapter Two), the notion of individuation, the connection between the organic and the inorganic, and the special frame of mind in which Junko works. I call this frame of mind an "altered state of consciousness" and it comes up many times throughout the book. Junko's diaries and notebooks record her movements in and out of that altered state, and in this chapter

I talk about the impact the altered state has had on our lives. **Chapter Seven** discusses the role of the artist in society—how it is reminiscent of the role of the shaman in ancient times, but how it has additional dimensions in the twenty-first century. That chapter begins with a question: What contribution does an artist like Junko make to society?

The Artist Inside and Out

Junko's own writings are as much a part of Junko's art as her paintings. Both are traces on paper of her diligent and ceaseless effort to understand her own work and her own life, and to wrestle with the ideas and issues discussed in this book. The inseparability of Junko's writing from her art, and the deep entanglement of both her writing and her art with the issues she deals with in her inner life, is one of the central themes of this book.

I incorporate Junko's writings into my own exposition because my book presents Junko, deliberately, from two points of view: from the outside looking in, and from the inside, looking out. Junko herself adopts both these points of view, because she considers it important to maintain the "observing ego"[3] even in the midst of her most turbulent creative process. In the deliberate oscillation between these two points of view, the reader can participate in Junko's creative process. It is partly in order to facilitate this oscillation that my presentation departs—quite consciously—from academic norms of style and structure.

I hope that my book will give my readers some insight into the essence of centripetal art and that it will succeed in its attempt to analyze Junko's centripetal art and characterize its unusual kind of spirituality. I hope too that it will prove interesting even to readers such as I used to be, who identify themselves as people not interested in art at all. And I dare to hope that this book will offer at least one convincing answer to the question with which Junko and I struggled for so many years: *Why on earth does God have to paint?*—an answer which may provoke my readers to find their own convincing answers.

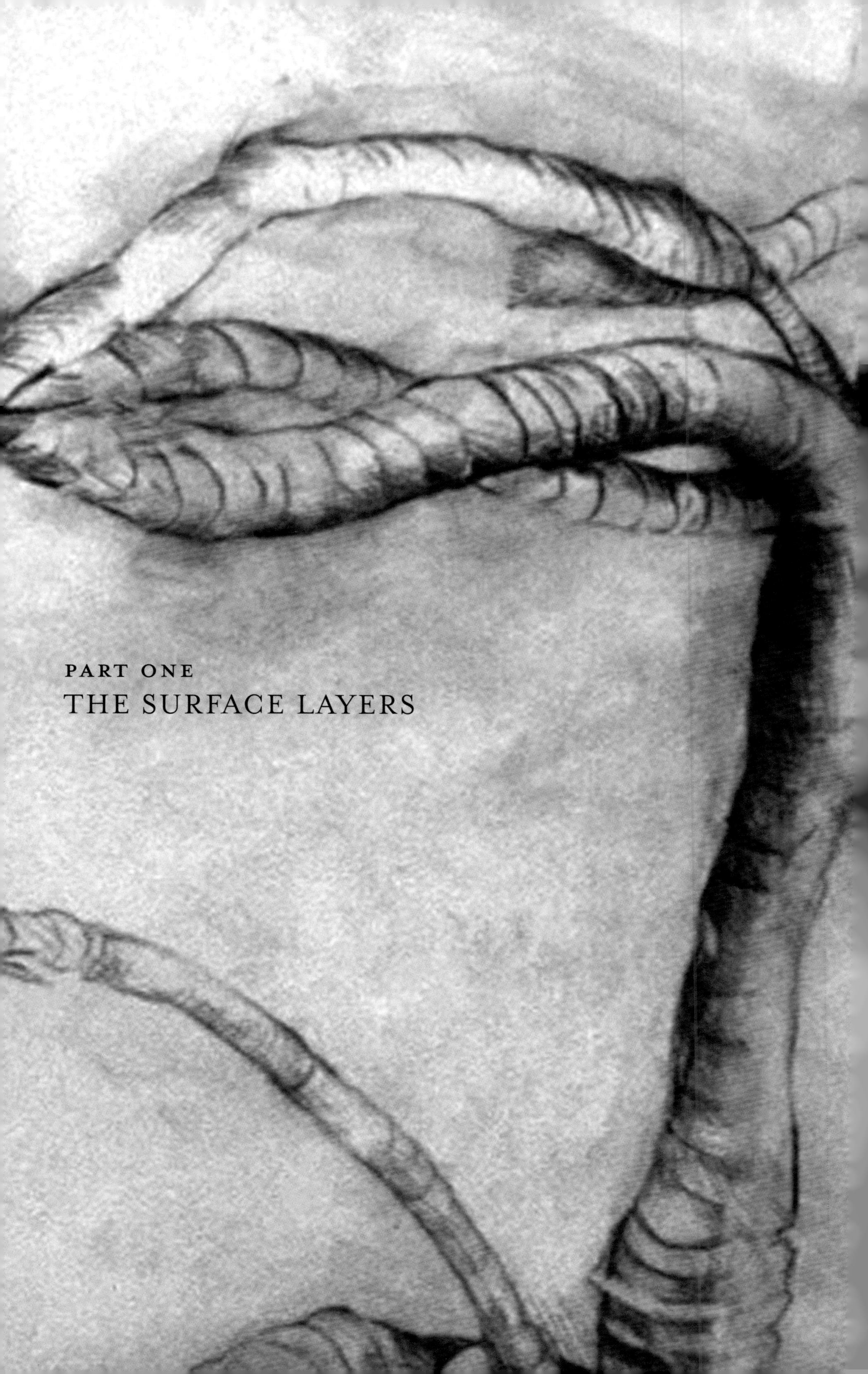

PART ONE

THE SURFACE LAYERS

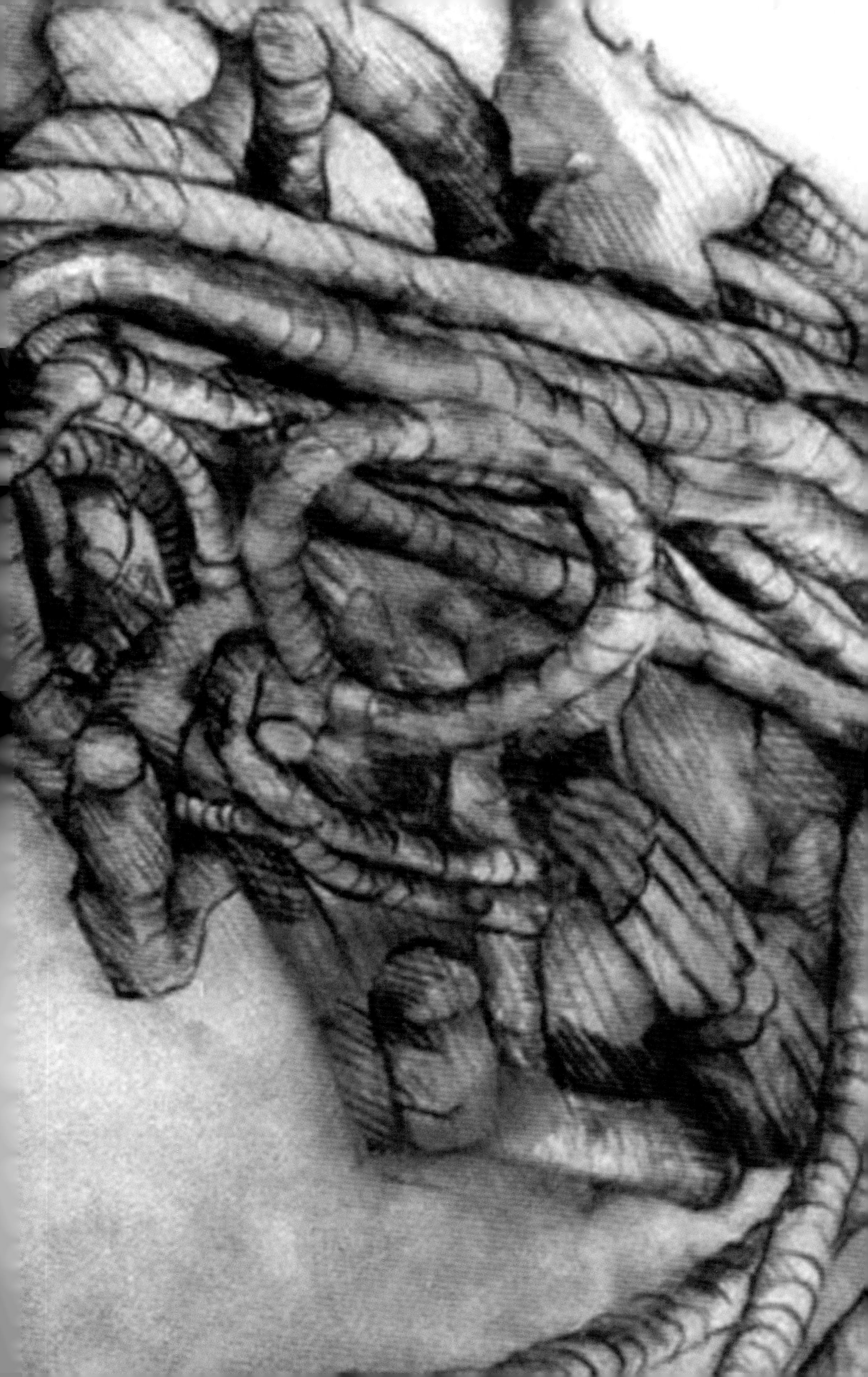

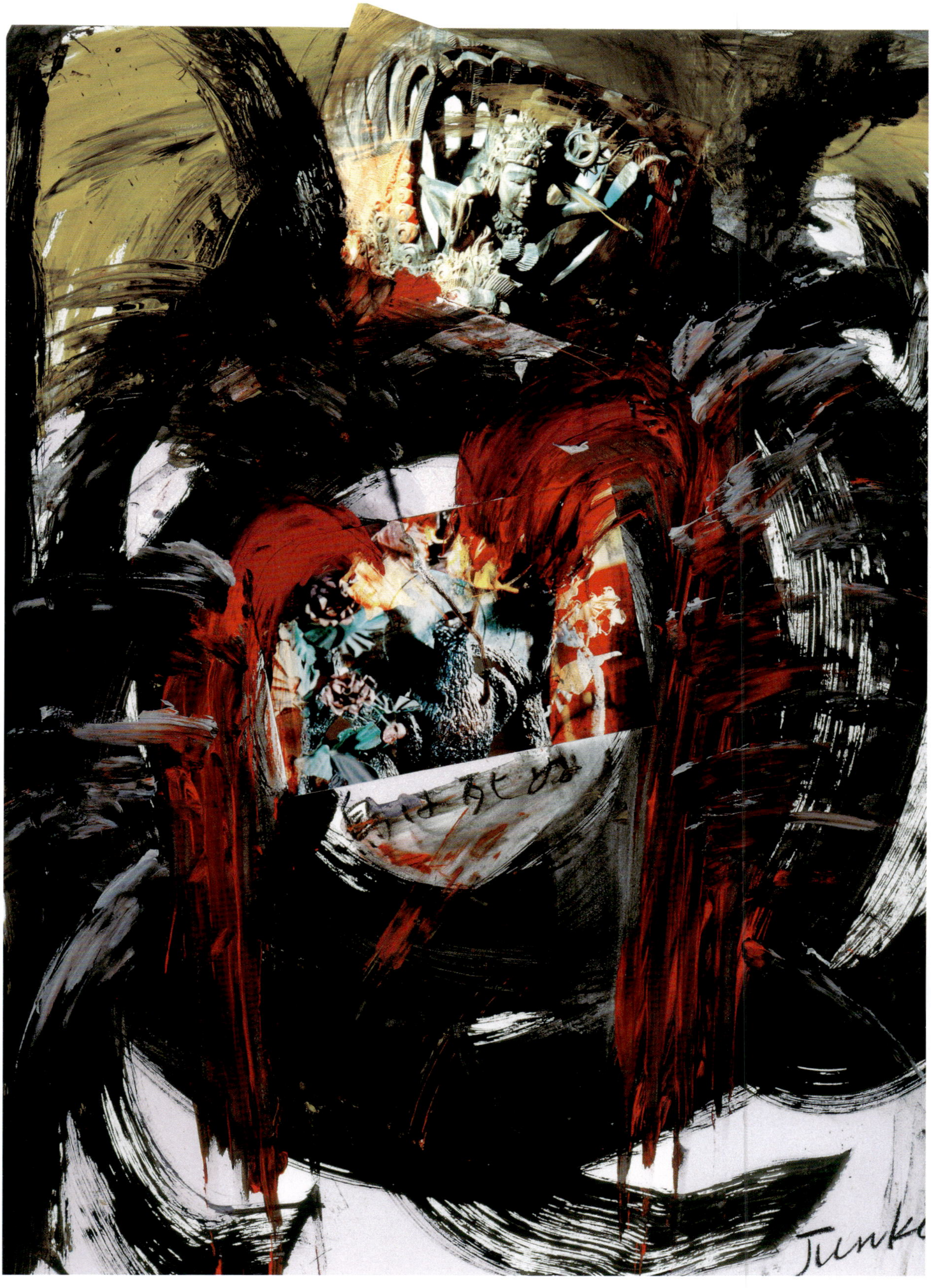

CHAPTER ONE
OBJECTS AS VISITANTS

It has been a hundred years since artists stopped feeling compelled to paint glorious subjects. One of the breakthroughs of so-called "modern art"—the art of the early twentieth century—was that the greatest artists began to refuse to pander to the narcissism of the aristocracy and of the church. Instead of painting heroic scenes of war showing uniformed generals on horseback, Picasso painted *Guernica*—an entirely different image of war. The grand cathedrals of earlier centuries gave way to the blurry facades of Rouen Cathedral as painted by Monet, or to the humble structure of van Gogh's *Church Tower at Nuenen*. Instead of the clean-faced Christ so familiar from earlier times, Rouault gave us a distraught, jumbled *Head of Christ*, drawn with confused lines that show him as sorrowful, not glorious. Even the human figure was seen in a different way: instead of Michelangelo's *David*, we got the strange figures of Henry Moore and Giacometti. And artists began to paint things that had never been painted before: van Gogh painted peasants at their dinner table—as if it were a Last Supper; he painted an old worn-out pair of shoes with great intensity. And artists began to paint abstracts—compositions that had no referents outside themselves.

When the artist is showing us a great cathedral, or the figure of Christ on the cross, or a beautiful woman, or a wondrous landscape, we know why he is painting it and we know what we are expected to feel. The painting reaffirms values which the artist believes we share, and we are expected to admire the art to the extent that we are persuaded that the artist has done justice to his subject. But when the subject is something other than intrinsically noble or glorious we have to ask, Why is the artist painting this? What justice can one do to an old weather-beaten pair of shoes? What values can we affirm as we look at the abstracts of Kandinsky or the figures of de Kooning?

Opposite:
REQUIEM FOR AN EXECUTED BIRD, No. 21 (1991)
Mixed media on paper
40 x 32 in.
(101.6 x 81.3 cm.)

In Junko's case, these questions present themselves to us with particular urgency. For most of the objects that move Junko to paint are objects that no one else might consider even worth looking at: dead flowers, roots, burls, parts of broken engines—commonplace things in which Junko finds a creative force yearning for expression. In this chapter, we explore the intense relationship between Junko and her subjects—a relationship which I call "encounter": it grows out of a connection between qualities in the objects and qualities in Junko which attract and transform each other. It goes beyond mere interest or even fascination: it is a personal kind of interaction between Junko and her subjects which could not possibly have been understood before this time in history, for to understand it requires a modern psychological consciousness. Without such a consciousness, Junko's viewers could not appreciate her radical rejection of all forms of malignant narcissism nor recognize her frequent evocation of Jungian archetypes. Nor could her art have been appreciated before Western viewers were exposed to Eastern styles of empathy which arise from the awareness of a spirit inside everything.

The dead flowers, roots, and burls that Junko paints are commonplace things which can be found almost anywhere—but to find them is not yet to encounter them. Other objects that she paints—her found objects—are less common but still hardly exalted: a broken wine decanter, purchased in a junk shop, launched her into her first narrative series, *Requiem for an Executed Bird* (1991, forty-five works, see Chapter Four). A model of a deformed alien creature made for a science fiction movie figured in her *Esoteric Buddhism* series, both in the preparatory drawings (2000) and in the actual works (2001). And often she recycles fragments of her own drawings, as in *Meditations on Dance* (1987), which uses body parts from her figure drawings; and in *Esoteric Buddhism* and *Concerning Art and Religion*, both of which recycle her own drawings of engines and birds.

Because the same objects keep recurring in Junko's work, she calls them "visitants": entities that appear and reappear and demand to be encountered. They do not include only specific objects: there are certain generic things that also keep recurring, such as lungs and rib cages, curtains hanging in the air, and figures both human and "monstrous." In this chapter you will find photographs of the tangible visitants. After those photographs, you will find examples of them first in Junko's sketches and then in her finished works.

My purpose in this chapter is to present as deep and accurate a picture as I can of the encounter between Junko and her subjects, so I have included many selections from Junko's own writings: from the "series statements" she made on the first occasion that the works in question were exhibited; from her studio notebooks made at the time she was painting; and from her correspondence, essays, lectures, notebooks, and memoirs made years after she had completed the works in question. Before any object can become a powerful symbol in Junko's painting, she has to experience it on many levels. Although Junko's art works are the highest realization of her encounter with her subjects, her study, thinking, and writing about them are another important part of that encounter. From these selections you can see how Junko's involvement with her visitants becomes deeper and more personal over the years: that is why they keep reappearing in her works.

The visitants arrive sometimes in groups—not always singly. As the following pages show, each of the visitants has brought its own cluster of issues and concerns, but for Junko, every one of them is a portal between this world and the spirit world. These portals allow Junko to travel in both directions, and even when she refers to the spirit world as "death," the visitants—and her art—insist that she travel from death to life as easily as she moves from life to death.

The relationship between Junko and her visitants goes beyond even encounter. In Section Two of this chapter, I trace the metamorphosis of one of Junko's visitants, the burls, into something else—something quite different and totally unexpected.

One unusual feature of Junko's art is the way the visitants appear in her images and writings over a period of many years — often over decades. In Part Three of this book, there is a fold-out chart, "Themes in Series 1973-2006," which traces the visitants' appearances in Junko's images over the course of the last thirty-five years. In this chapter, I give specific examples of what is reflected in that chart, visitant by visitant, one by one.

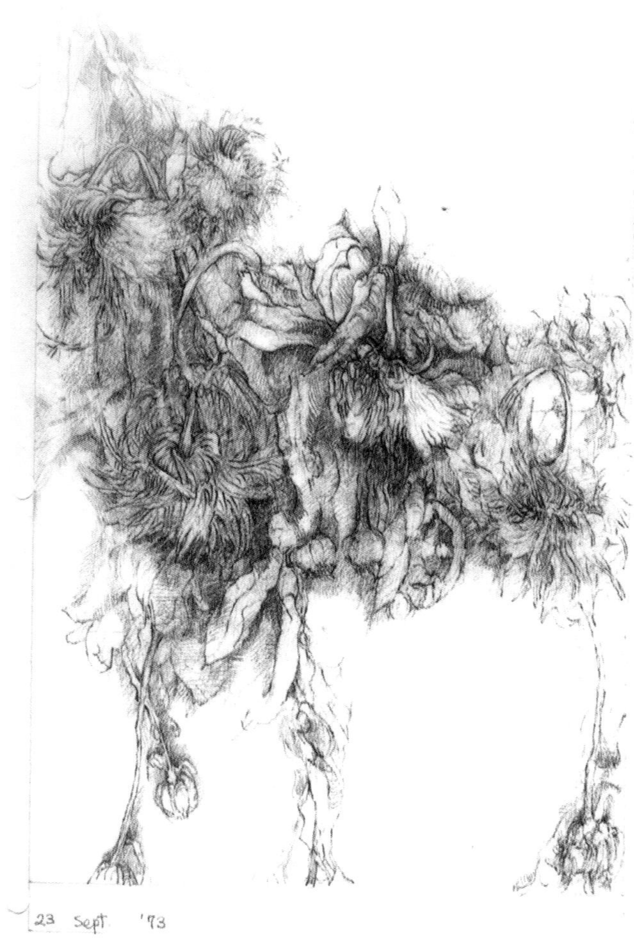

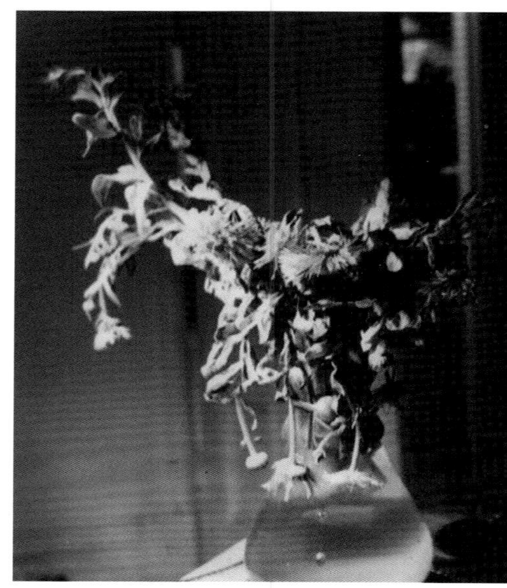

Left:
Dead Flowers Sketch
Sept. 25, 1973
8 x 10 in.
(20.3 x 25.4 cm.)

Right:
Dead Flowers sitting
on Junko's studio
table in 1973

SECTION ONE
INDIVIDUAL VISITANTS

DEAD FLOWERS AND ROOT

Series Statement "Dead Flowers," 1973

Flowers standing in a vase were gradually dying and I found them beautiful. I stared at them for one year and drew them in all their stages of death. Soon I saw a radiant light shining out from them, and the light began to take the shape of a thousand Buddhas welling up from among the dry leaves and flowers. The flowers were reborn in front of my eyes.

Ten years later, Junko was still thinking about the dead flowers, and about the way the thousand Buddhas welled up from among them.

Studio Notebook, 1983

During the days that I was staring at the dead flowers and working on drawing them many hours every day, death approached very close to me. A dark and dangerous time started. I heard a voice in my dream saying, "There is a dead one who pulls your hand from underground: be strong, stand up firmly." The voice repeated this a few times, and the dark urgent feeling continued for several days and nights. But as I kept working on the drawings in my studio, it seemed that my body gradually was losing its sense of weight, and my eyes seemed to have changed their gaze: the eyes that were gazing at the dead flowers were floating up higher and were lifted into a height from which I was to able to look down at the dead flowers. The gaze of myself looking at death turned into the gaze of death looking at me. I did not have to lift my eyes up in order to look at heaven: heaven was looking down at the tiny me standing far below on the earth and I had become one with death. The broad scope of the bird's eye view was spread out underneath me.

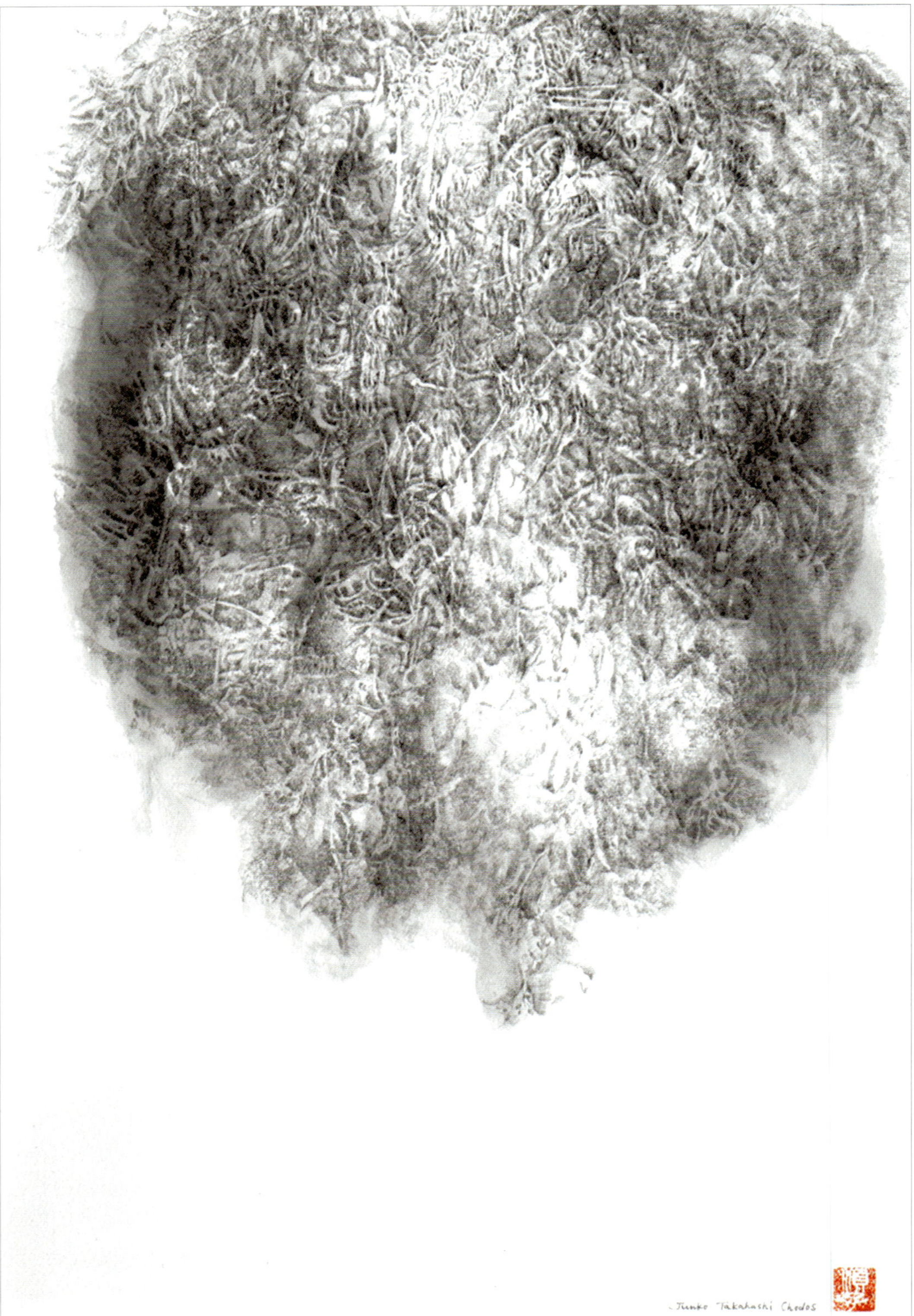
Junko Takahashi Chodos

The delightful memory of those days has revived in me again and again and comes to me still now—days in which the little figures of Buddha sprang up in my art and spilt over the edge of the paper one after another. Those Buddhas floated into my dreams, and after I awaken they are still floating in the air and they surround me.

At that time I went through a dark forest where I almost lost my way. By continuing to work with the pen, stroke by stroke on my paper, I was able to walk through one of the most dangerous times in my life.

Junko spent one year drawing the dead flowers and then she found the root—shown on the next pages. These two visitants are both organic and seemingly "dead," yet both revealed a special kind of life to Junko. While the differences between them are significant—the flowers, drawn with innumerable strokes of a pen, seem to be hanging down, gauze-like, while the root, drawn with countless fragments of paper from science and art books, seems more muscular and gives the impression of rising up—the root must be seen as related to the flowers, and it replaced them in Junko's later works.

Opposite:
DEAD FLOWER SERIES, No. 7 (1973)
Pen and ink with wash on Arches paper
Overall 40 x 66 in. (101.6 x 167.6 cm.)

This page:
DETAIL FROM DEAD FLOWERS No. 8, *Byoobu*

Following page:
DEAD FLOWER SERIES, No. 8, *Byoobu* (1973)
Pen and ink with wash on Arches paper
Overall 40 x 66 in. (101.6 x 167.6 cm.)
Collection of the Pacific Asia Museum

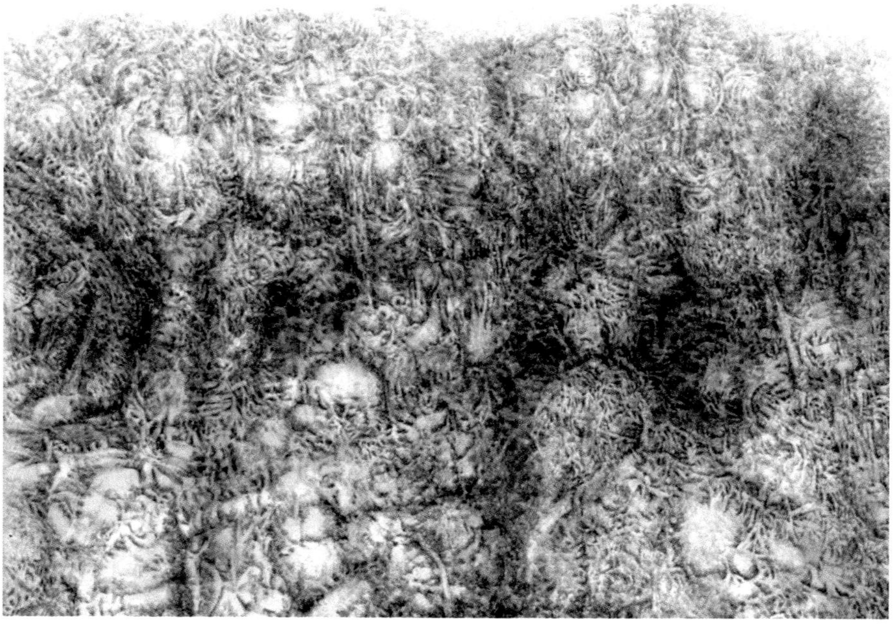

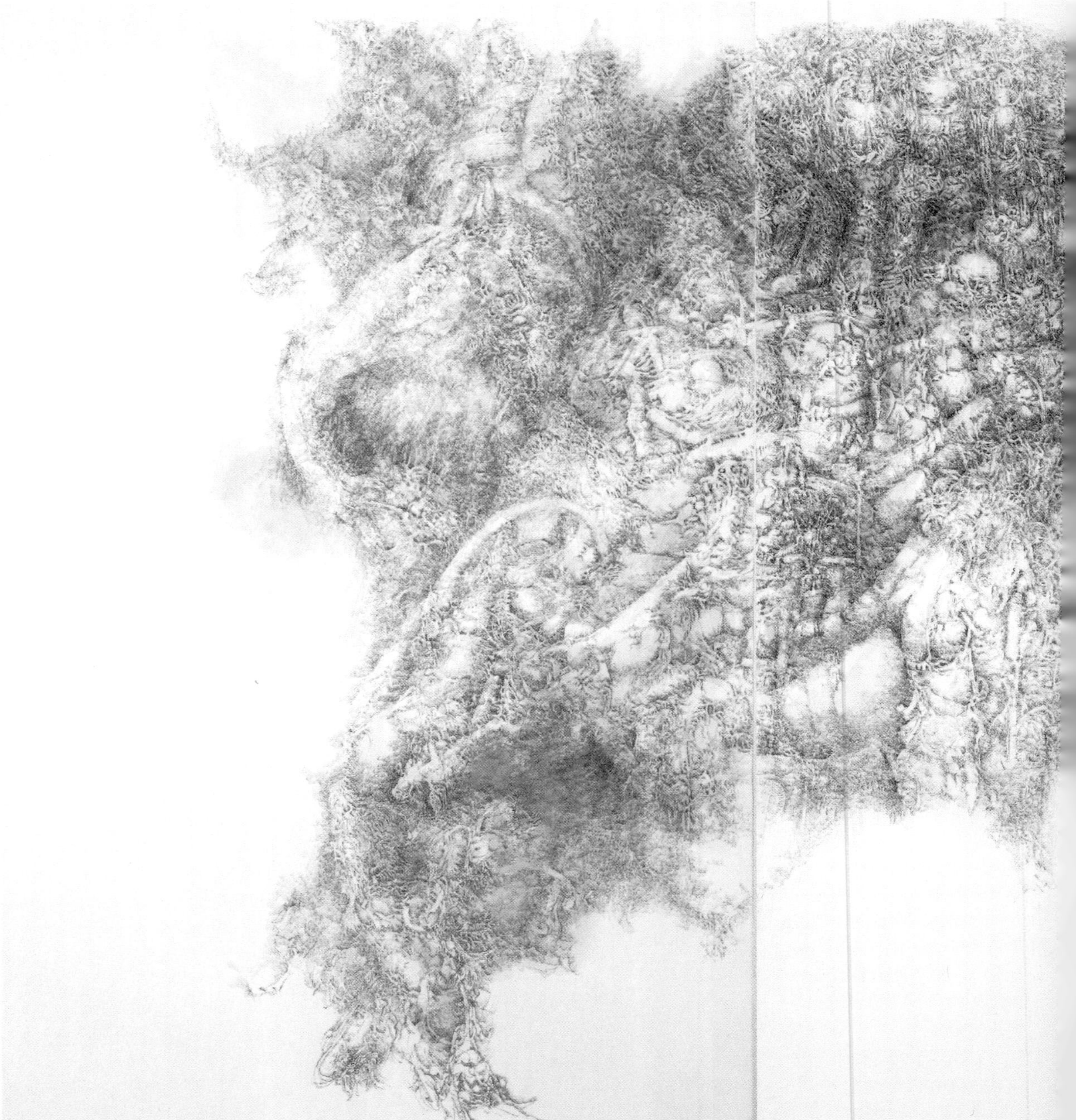

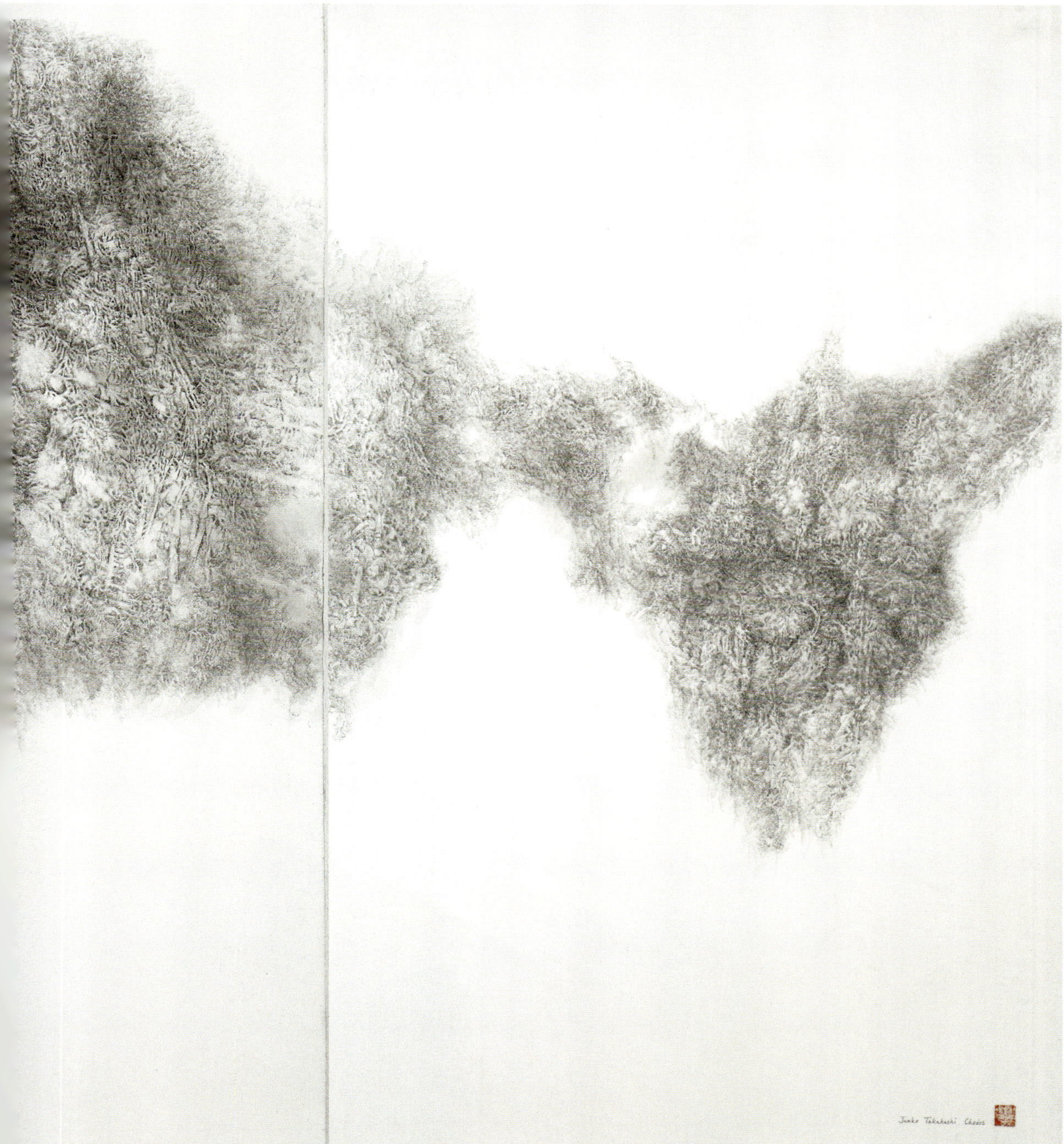
Junko Takahashi Chaos

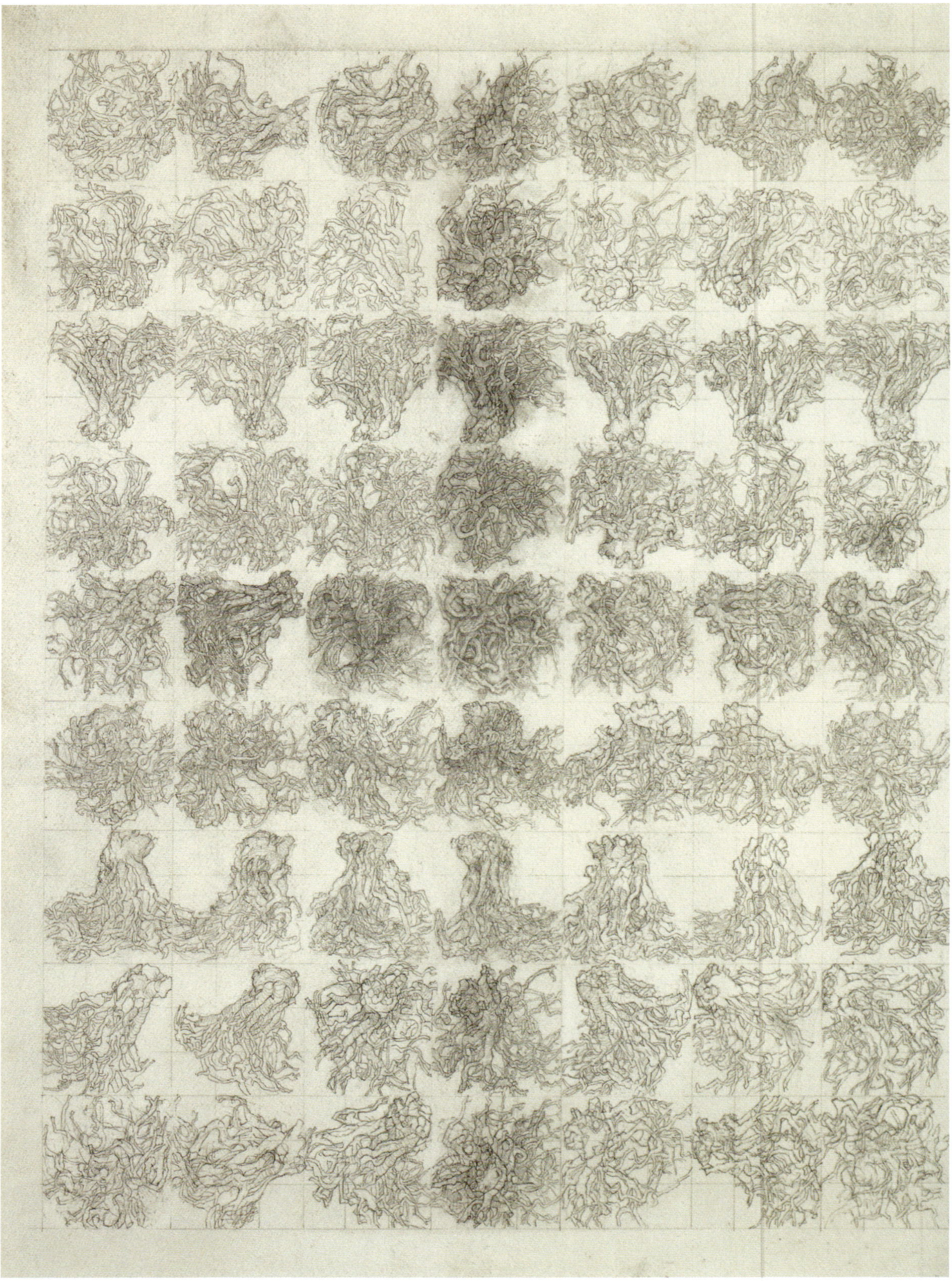

ROOT

Series Statement "Roots," 1979

I was overwhelmed by the beauty of a root which was dug up from the ground. In a dark place, silently, a powerful force had been working to make a tree and I was attracted by that force. While I was struggling with this tremendously complicated figure, which seemed at first to be totally confused, I started to find in it a mysterious, hidden order. Since then the root loomed before me like the whole universe itself. I set that universe in front of me and spent more than five years working on it.

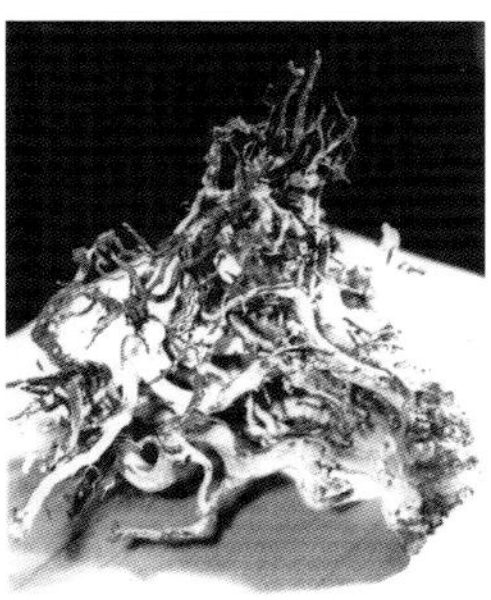

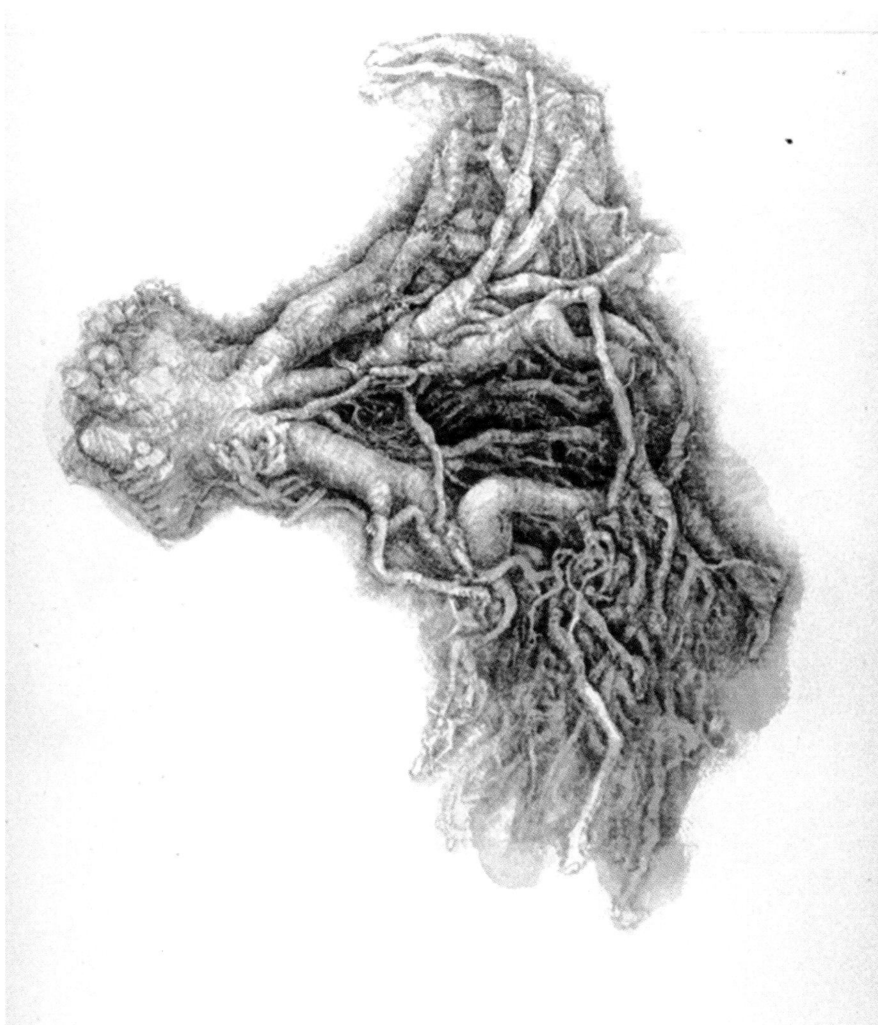

Above:
Photograph of the root sitting on Junko's studio table in 1974

Right:
ROOT STUDY (1975)
Pen and ink on paper
22.5 x 16 in.
(57.2 x 40.6 cm.)

Opposite:
Preparatory Work, ROOT SERIES No. 16, *Mandala* (1979)

Next page:
ROOT SERIES No. 1 (1975)
Mixed media collage on paper
22.5 x 16 in.
(57.2 x 40.6 cm.)
Also preparatory pencil sketch.

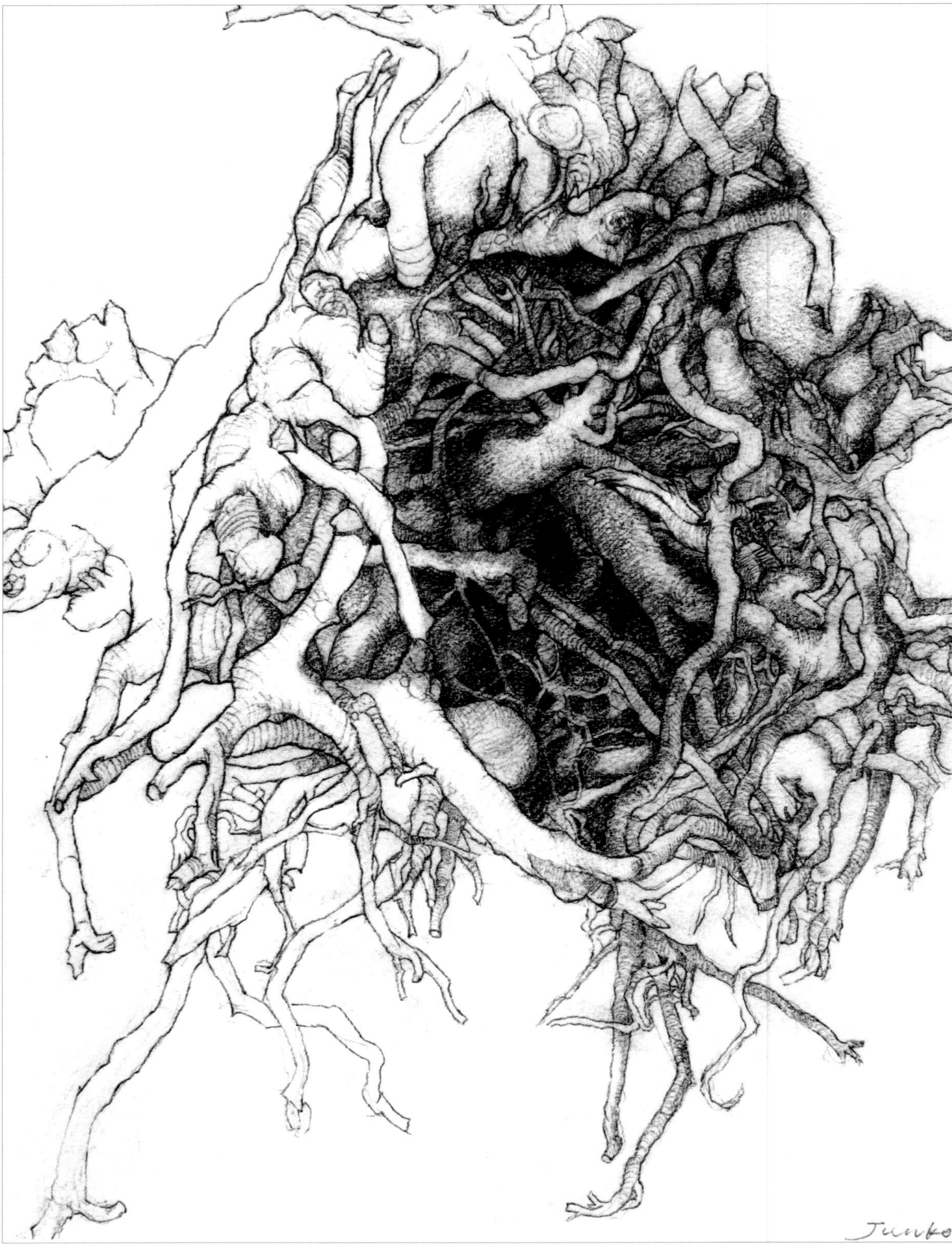
Junko

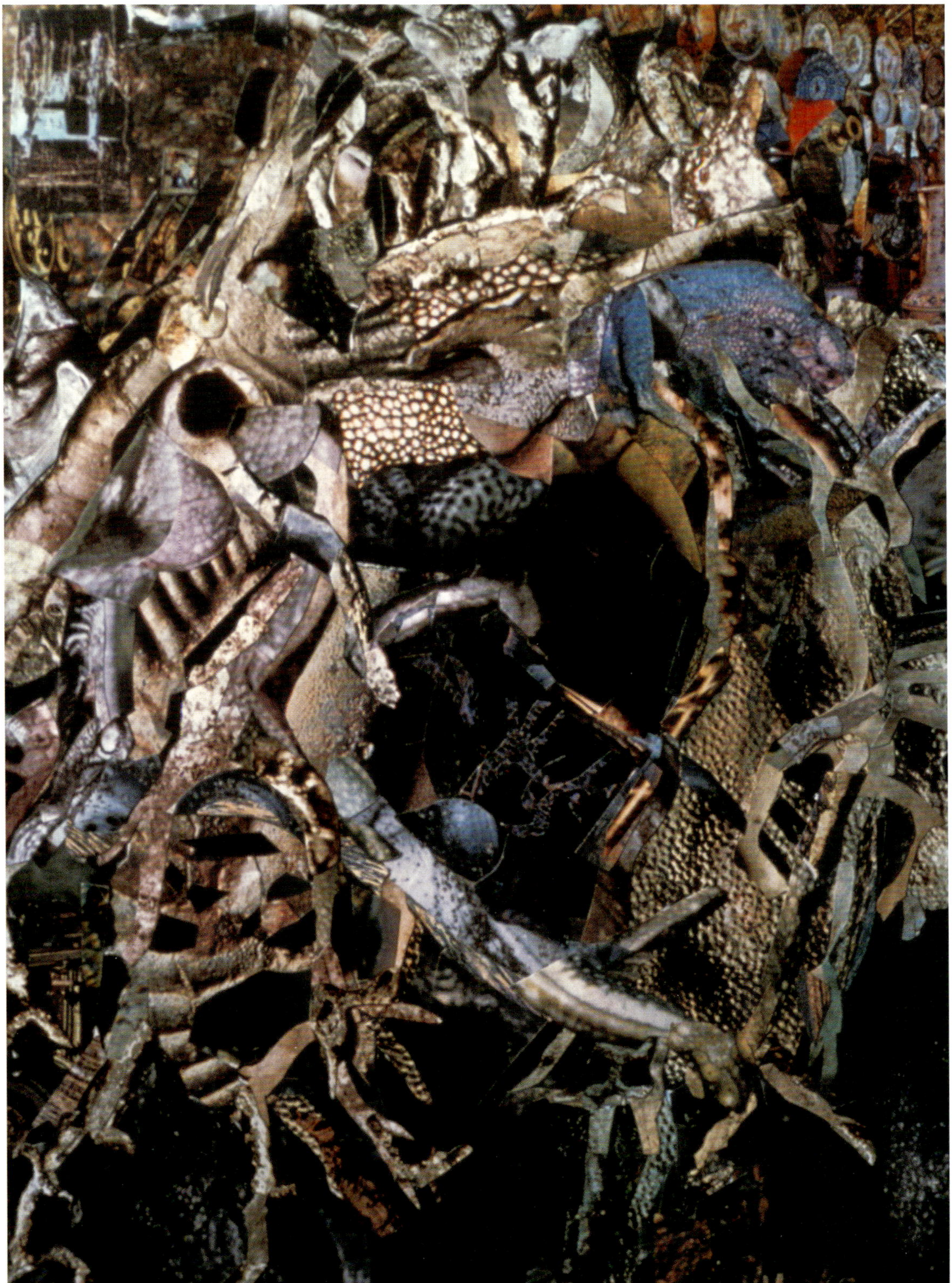

Twenty-two years later, Junko wrote to a friend about the mandala she had created from the root. And five years after that, she incorporated images of the root into some of her giant mylar FATHOM panels.

Letter to a Friend, 2001

"He tried to explore sexuality by putting it on the desk in front of him as if it were some tangible object." Ryotaro Shiba, the Japanese writer, in his book, *The Landscape of Kuukai,*[1] describes how Kuukai, the ninth century Japanese priest of Esoteric Buddhism, treated sexuality. This remark really made me smile because it reminds me of what I did with the root which was dug out of the ground still soiled: a dark, sensual color remained. I put it on the desk in front of me (in my case the desk was a turntable which has four secure wheels on in its feet) and explored it, drawing it from every angle every day for more than five years. Later Kuukai created the most solemn philosophical structure of the universe based on his exploration of sexuality, that huge, mysterious force, the often uncontrollable vitality of the human psyche which makes us gravitate towards life and often towards death. Such intense philosophical structure is quite exceptional in the history of Japanese thought. Shiba points out that many mandalas were created in order to explain and interpret Kuukai's philosophy. Again that makes me smile because I too ended up creating a mandala after a tenacious exploration, after I had made many intricate drawings and collages of the root. The root is a looming universe all by itself, and yet when sixty-three images of the root are turning, each displaying a different angle at the same time, it turns into a map of the cosmos itself. (See *Mandala*, pg. 3.)

Opposite:
Two Trees from
FATHOM:
COMMUNICATNG WITH
NATURE (2006)
Collage of computer
prints on mylar
Each 10 ft. x 42 in.
(304.8 x 86.7 cm.)
See pp. 44-45 for a
full image of this work,
with dancers.

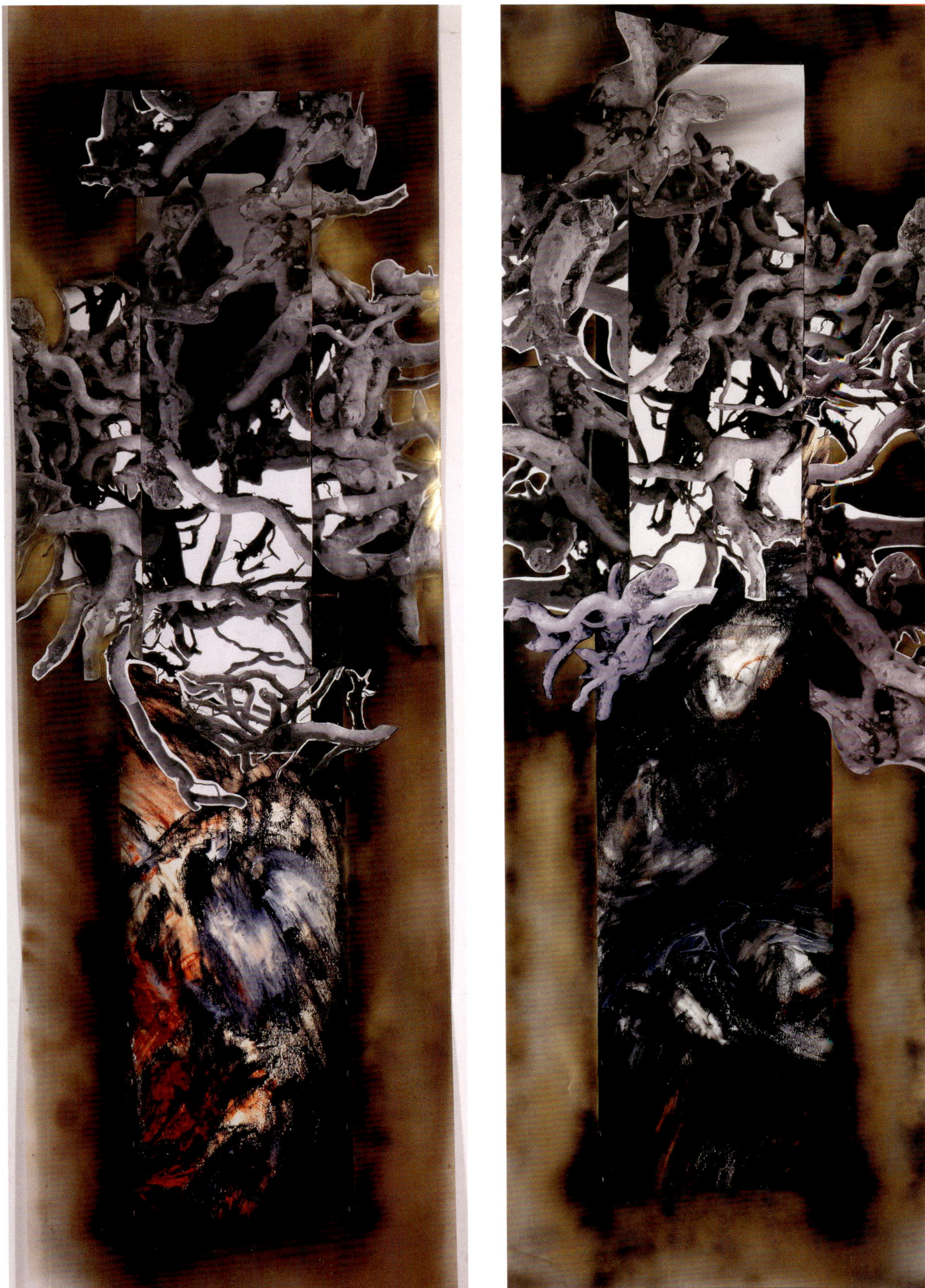

ENGINE

Series Statement "Engines," 1982

The innards of a Rolls Royce engine seemed to me like the exposed organs of a body, vulnerable, disconnected from the system in which they are intended to function. Something which is supposed to be a source of power is now crying out in anguish. And the engine seemed also like a huge structure, or cathedral, with light streaming through it.

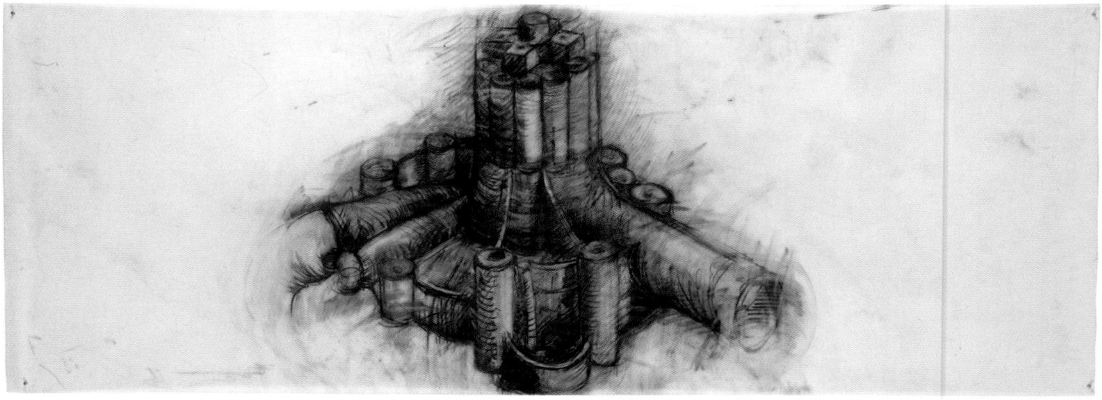

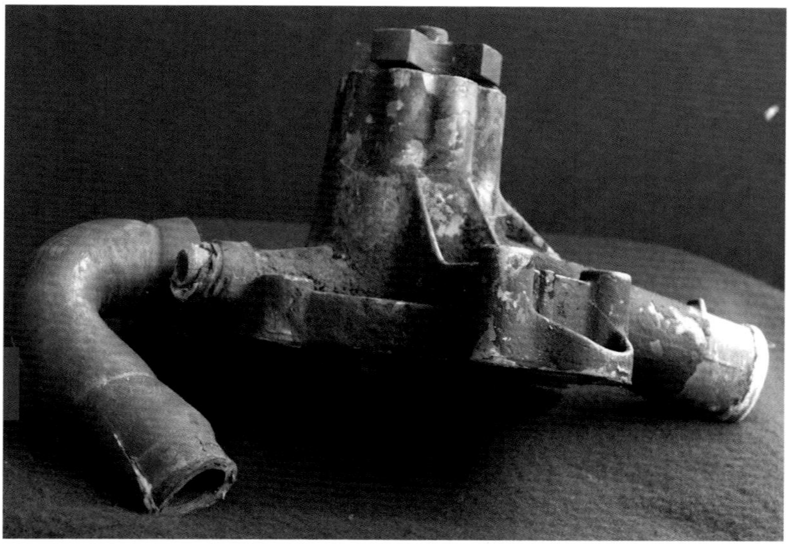

Above:
GIANT SKETCHBOOK, ENGINE DRAWING No. 1 (1997)
Charcoal on mylar
42 x 118 in.
(106.7 x 29.7 cm.)

Below:
Photograph of an engine part in Junko's studio, 1995

All these engines and engine parts figure in Junko's works.

Opposite:
ENGINE SERIES No. 2 (1981)
Pencil on paper
10 x 8 in.
(25.4 x 20.3 cm.)

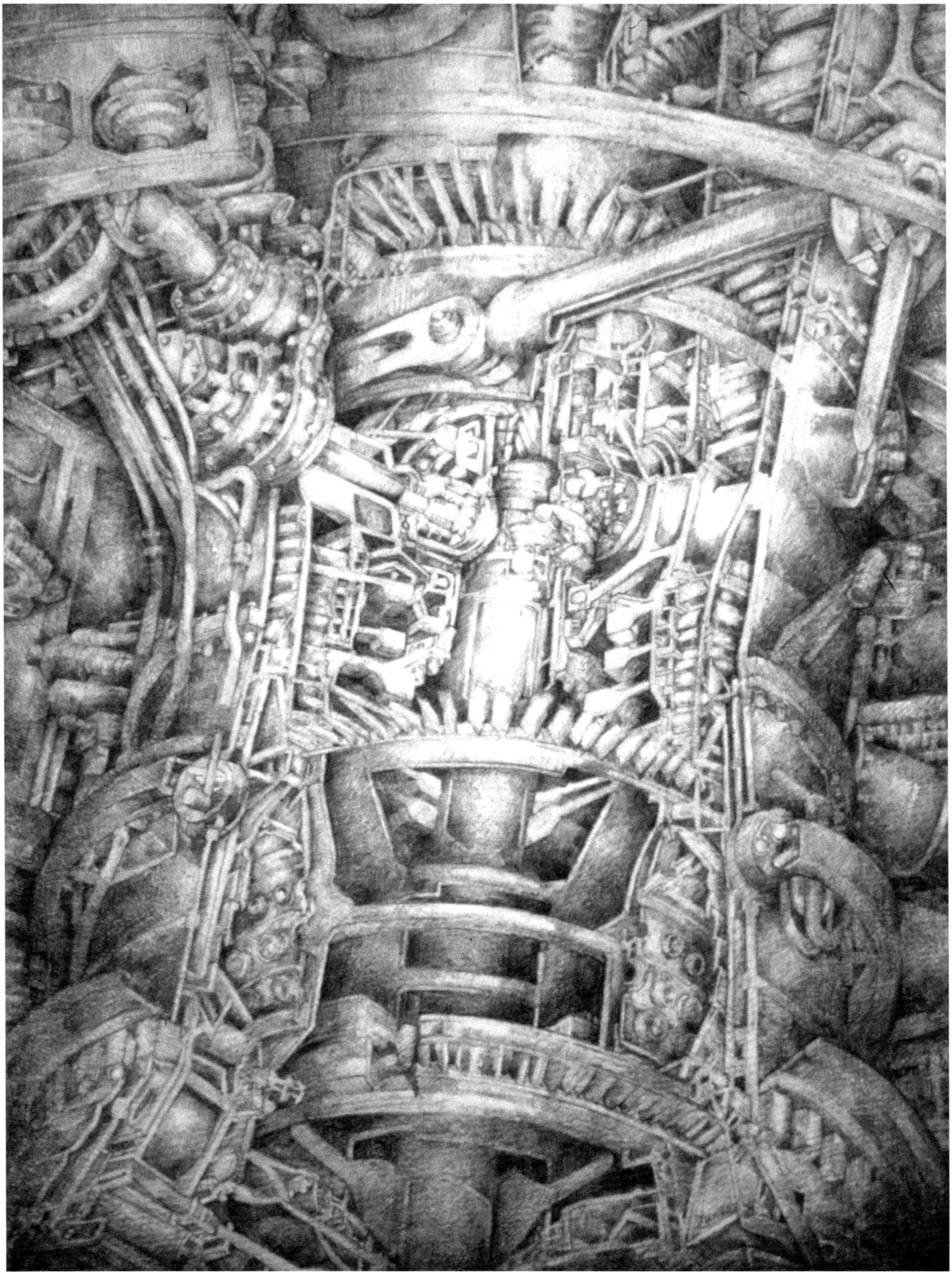

Studio Notebook, 2000

The compelling idea that this engine is a heart that was cut off at its arteries and veins occupied my mind. All the rubber tubes that stick out from this engine looked exactly like arteries. They are cut off with sharp knives, isolated from the rest of the body, lonely and beautiful. This morning I started to draw it again on the back of a huge piece of drum computer printer paper. The image of the cut-off heart was so vivid and urgent, I felt acute pain in my heart, I had to rest many times. The image appeared with a special tone: printed on the back of film it almost looked transparent. When I wiped it with water, it looked as if the air surrounding the heart had itself disappeared and the heart is now floating in a vacuum.

Letter to a Friend, 2001

Anything that is supposed to be covered and is yet exposed evokes strong emotion in the viewer. Organs exposed by surgery, injury, crime, autopsy, or even X–rays bring some emotional reaction: skinned animals, featherless birds are the same. My urgent emotion which was evoked by this engine was pain: the pain of being vulnerable which is caused by being exposed. If Jesus in the Crucifixion were fully clothed, the image would have not evoked that much

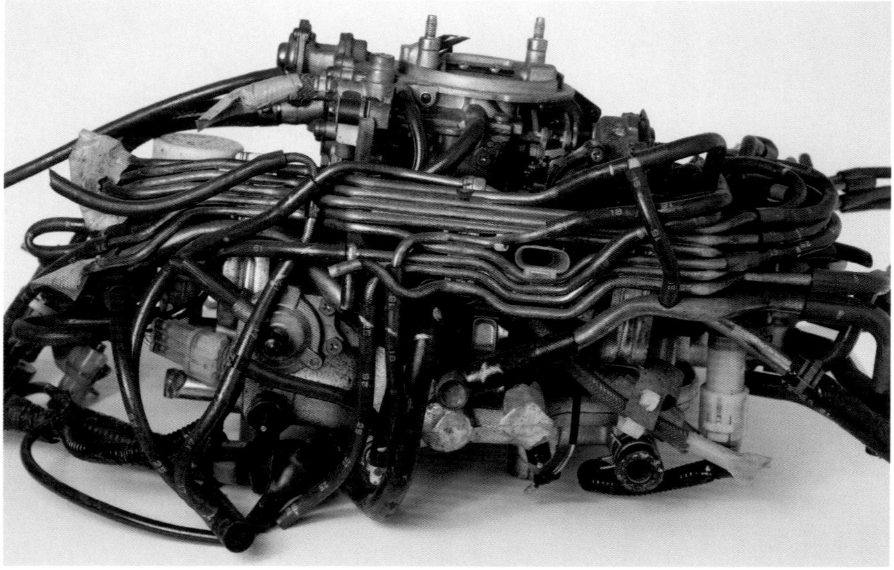

Left:
Photograph of used engine purchased from an auto parts store, 1995

Opposite:
ESOTERIC BUDDHISM, PREPARATORY No. 5 (2000)
Charcoal on industrial mylar, computer processed
Virtual size

Next page:
INTERPLANETARY ICON No. 11 (1990)
Mixed media on paper
Irregular shape:
23 x 19.5 in.
(58.4 x 49.5 cm.)

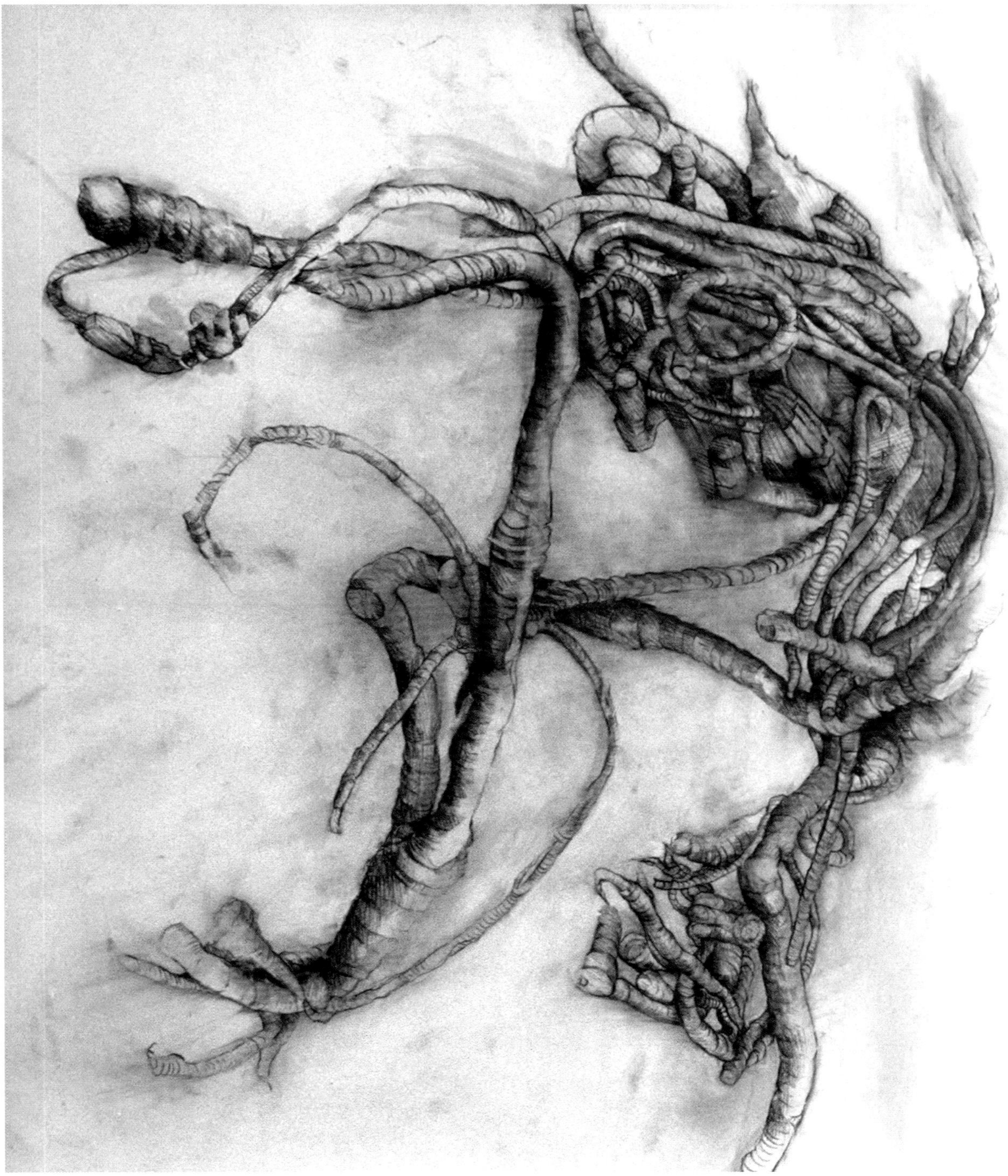

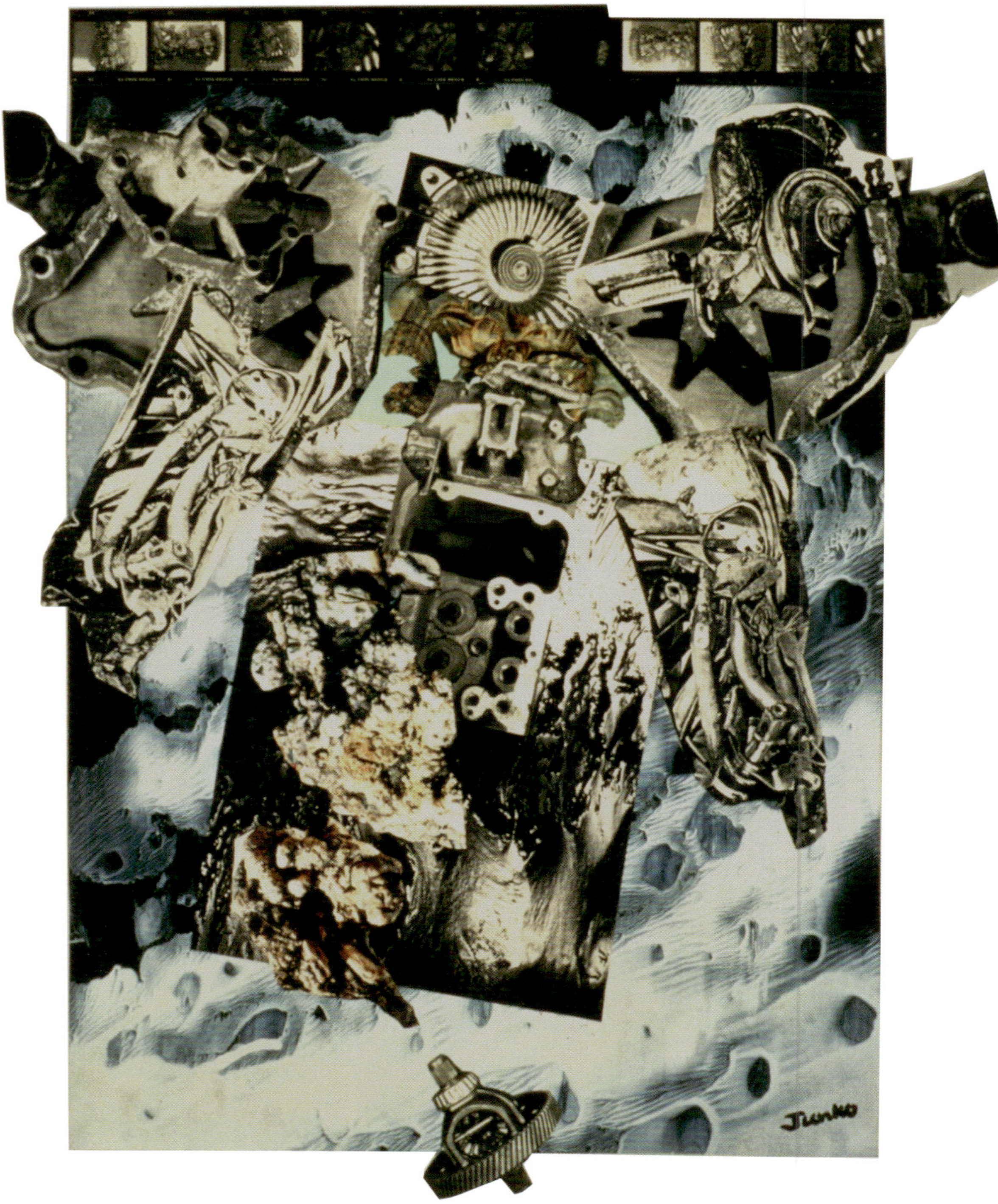
Junko

pain in us: the great sense of tragedy in the painting of the Crucifixion has much to do with his nakedness. But to talk about the impact of the image of Jesus in the Crucifixion on the same level as the image of injury, or surgery of skinned animals, is too much of an understatement.

The impact which the Crucifixion evokes in us does not come from the same place as the impact of a crime scene or of a medical description. Torture, violence, blood, and death are involved but those images are impregnated with great irony. When this irony is captured by the artist in the depths of his honesty the painting reveals the true sense of tragedy. If the artist fails to do that, for any reason, Jesus remains looking like an ordinary victim of crime, and the painting will never gain the power to transcend the viewer and the images remain just shocking and painful.

Of this engine we can say the same thing. In this broken, exposed engine I see a great irony; radiance still yet deeply sealed. If I fail to bring this radiance to the drawing, then my work will become just another technical drawing of a machine.

Essay "Esoteric Buddhism" 2001

I was working on these pieces reflecting a faint red glow on my body, in the middle of my studio floor almost buried under images of the engine—the engine, cut off from the car whose driving force it was created to be in the first place, not functioning, not connected in the universe now, images of it spread out and printed on big rolls of computer printing paper, dark, passionate, painful images. My engine is a symbol of sexuality—not of sexual organs, but of the life force, pain, and mortality.

A month later, the engine had gained life in my painting. It looked still wounded, still bleeding, but it had placed itself in the right place in my painting. It was working, functioning in the universe as a perfect part, and as a strong driving force in my painting. It was even radiating its oxidized gold light, and illuminating the whole painting with its own glow. The engine was reborn and made a living participant in the Big Desire, the sexual energy of the universe.

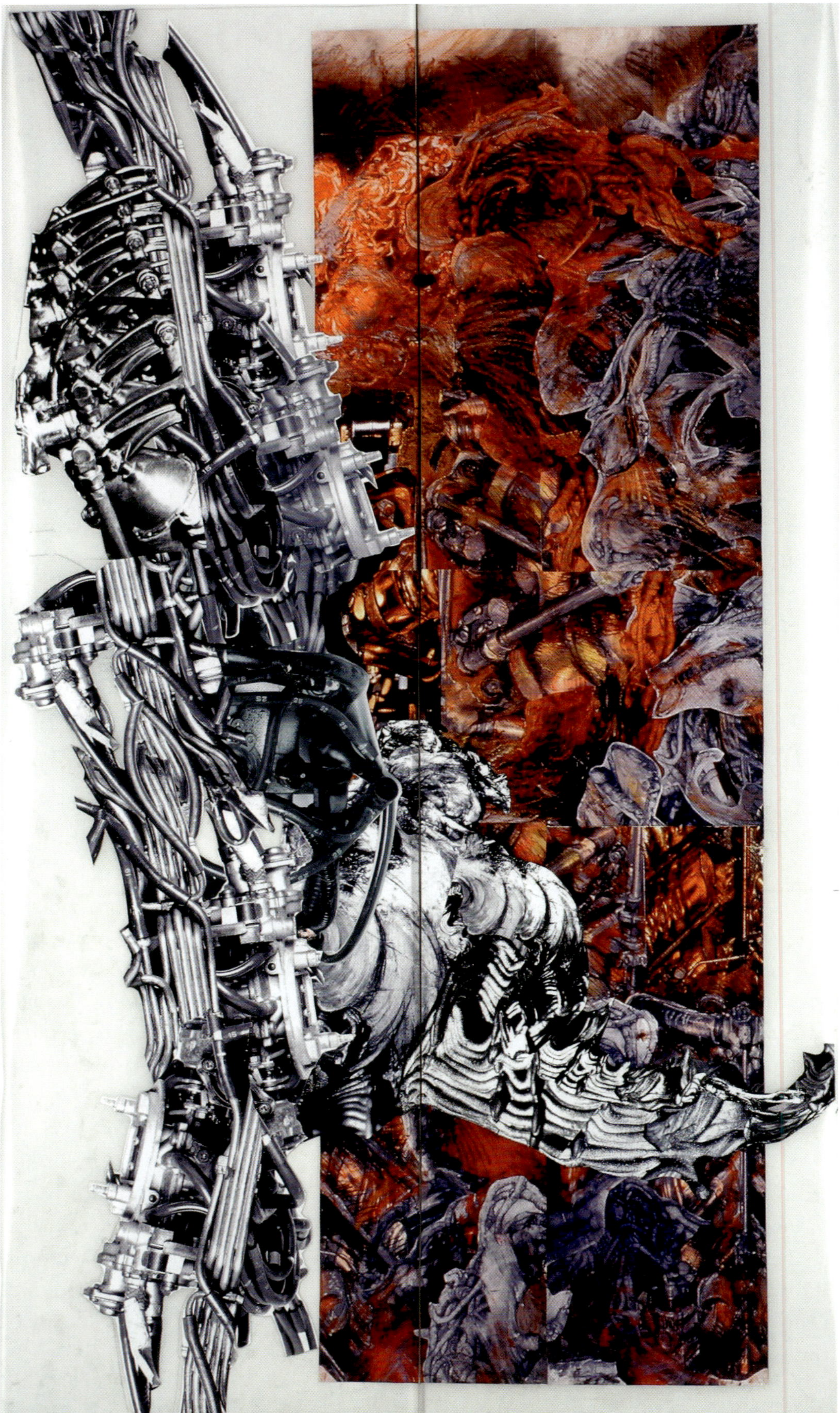

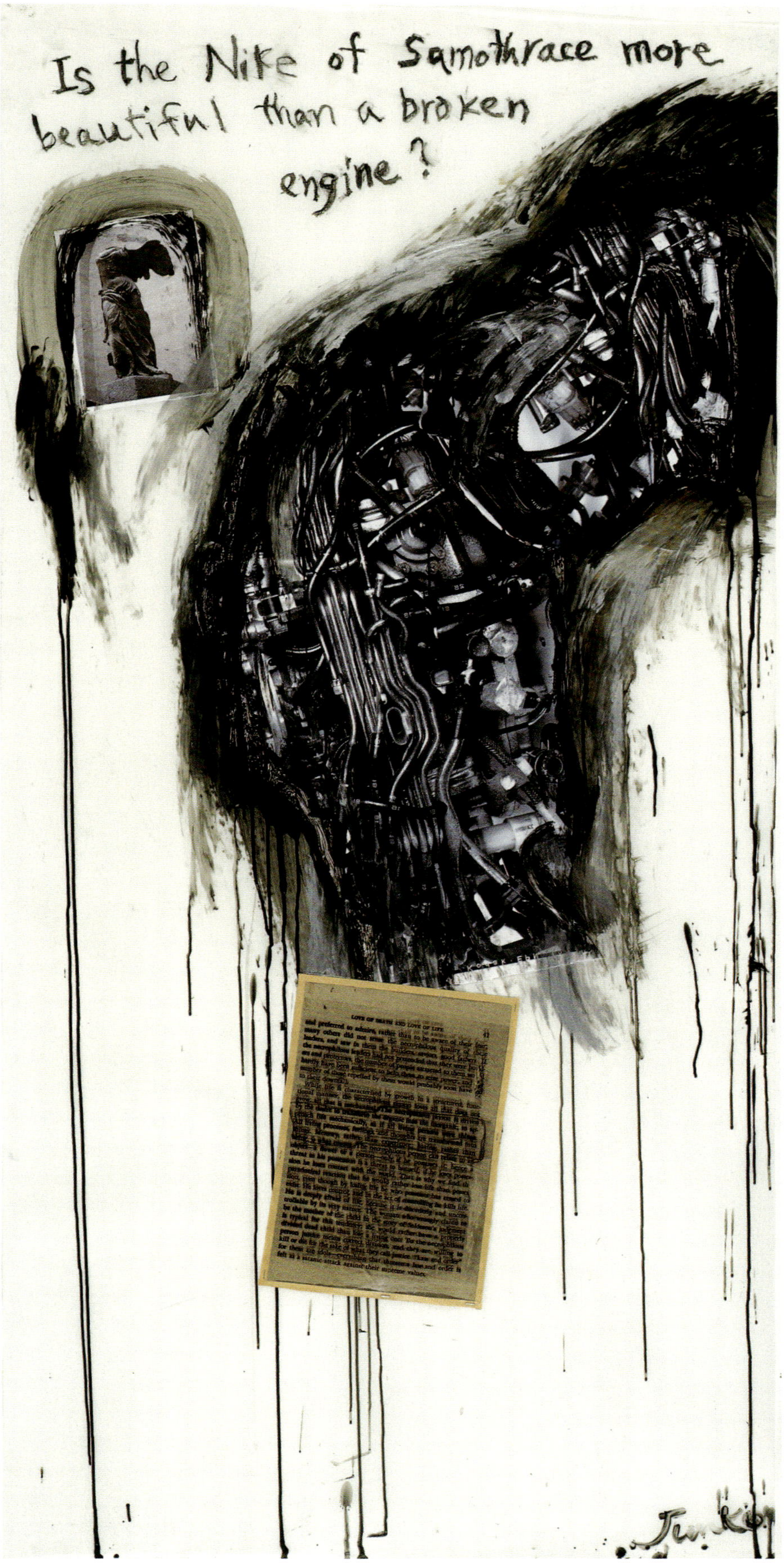

Junko parodies a phrase from Marinetti's Futurist Manifesto (1909)[2]: instead of expressing unrestrained enthusiasm for technology, she reveals some scepticism of it. This engine is "broken," and yet it is eroticized in ways Marinetti could never have envisioned.

This page:
CONCERNING ART AND RELIGION, No. 3 (2004)
"IS THE NIKE OF SAMOTHRACE MORE BEAUTIFUL THAN A BROKEN ENGINE?"
Computer prints and collage on mylar
80 x 42 in.
(203.2 x 106.7 cm.)

Opposite:
FATHOM: MANDALA No. 2 (2006)
The Engine Embraces the Flame
Collage of computer prints on mylar
12 ft. x 84 in.
(365.8 x 213.4 cm.)

The engine came to Junko after the *Root Series* had been completed. It represented an entirely different kind of portal to the other world; it was mechanical rather than organic but Junko empathized with its organic qualities: vulnerability and disconnectedness. She sees her art as a way of redeeming this visitant.

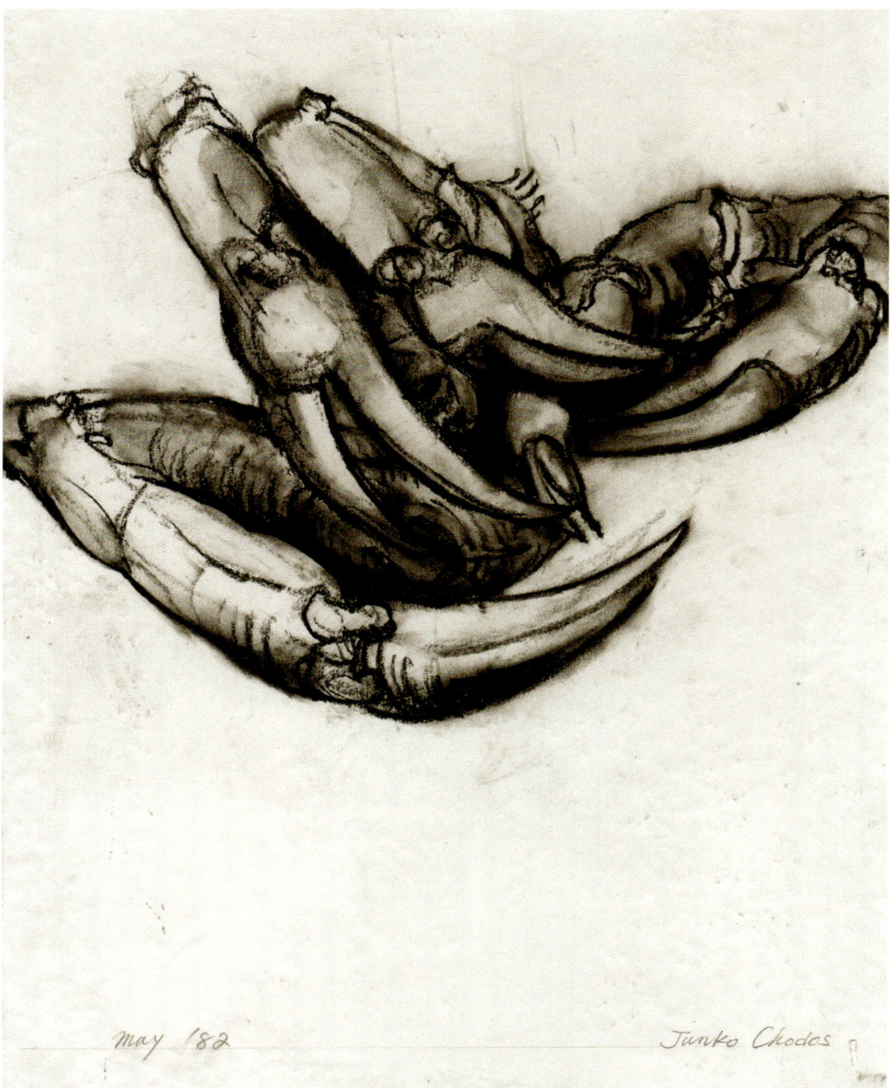

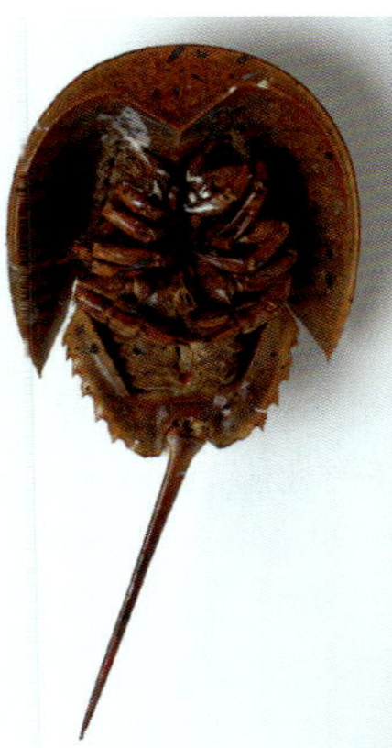

Above:
Photograph of
horseshoe crab

Left:
HORSESHOE CRAB
SERIES, No. 1 (1983)
Charcoal on paper
9 x 7 in.
(22.9 x 17.8 cm.)

HORSESHOE CRAB

Series Statement "Horseshoe Crab," 1983

The horseshoe crab is a personal symbol of vulnerability. Its vulnerability is protected with a coarse strong armor of shell. But at the same time it is a symbol of the suppression of vitality, and it has to explode in order to become itself. This symbol was sketched many times in my sketchbooks, and it appeared in my *Engine* series, and it would appear again in my *Celestial Curtain*.

Studio Notebook, 2003

The corpse of the horseshoe crab finally fell apart today. The tightly folded and confined hands inside of the amber colored shell got loosened. From that loosened crevice, yellow powder spilt out ceaselessly. Was it all internal organs and liquid before it became powder? It is a creature that has been playing the inspiration part for me for more than twenty years. With a sharp knife, I cut its shell decisively into two pieces, and put it into my laboratory glass jar and placed it on the shelf in my studio. It still radiates its power inside of the glass.

I saw a horseshoe crab for the first time in my life in a dark underground aquarium window. It appeared suddenly in front of my eyes as I proceeded to the next display window. He was sitting on the floor of sand motionlessly, covered with his own heavy hard armor. I was struck with big emotion, and tears fell from my eyes. Did such a life ever exist? It was one afternoon during the honeymoon of my first marriage in Japan almost half a century ago. I was eighteen years old. I saw over my newly wedded husband's firm shoulder that my own vulnerability was guarded, my own vitality and freedom were repressed tightly underneath this amber armor. This horseshoe crab cannot keep his life inside of this armor forever. A vision of it exploding followed. I thought I foresaw something—the most frightening thing in my future.

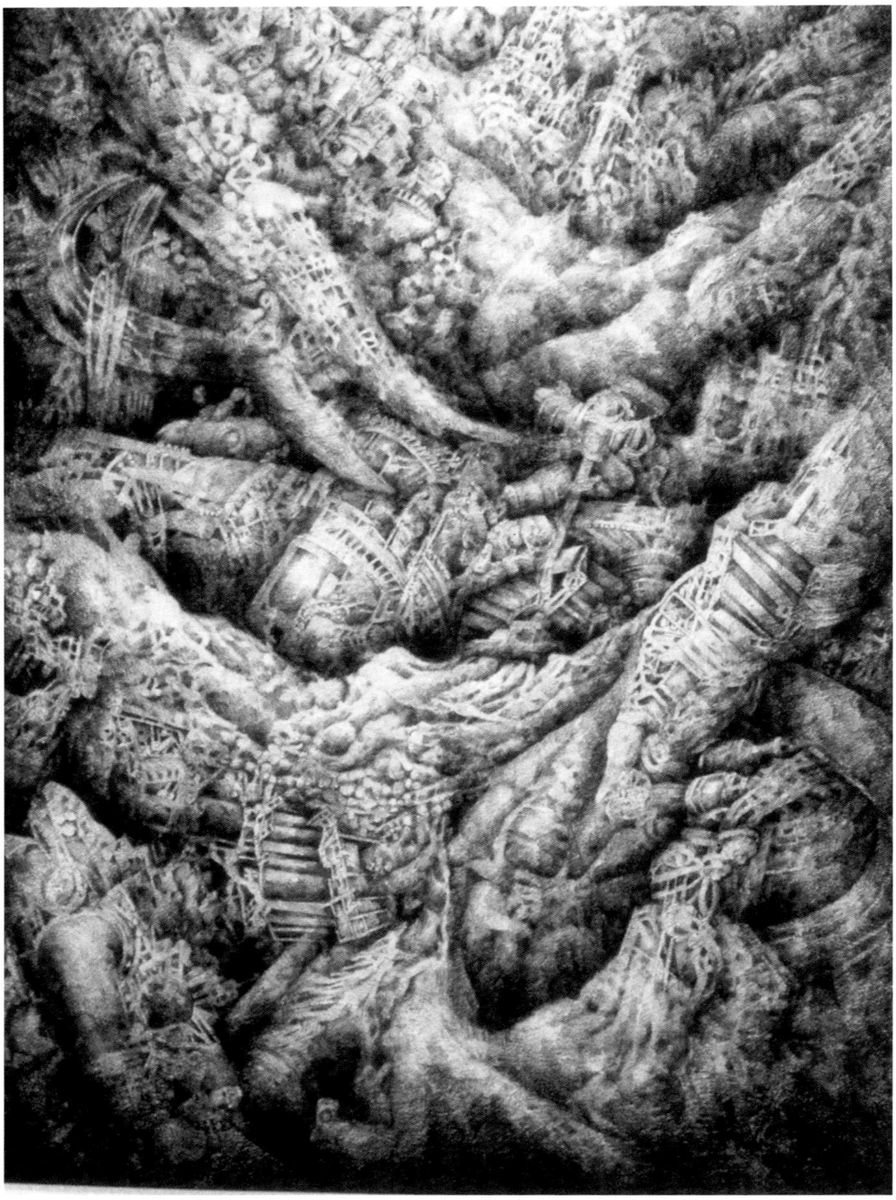

ENGINE SERIES,
No. 4 (1983)
Pencil on paper
13.25 x 10.5 in.
(33.7 x 26.7 cm.)

Opposite:
REQUIEM FOR AN
EXECUTED BIRD,
No. 23 (1991)
Mixed media on paper
40 x 32 in.
(101.6 x 81.3 cm.)

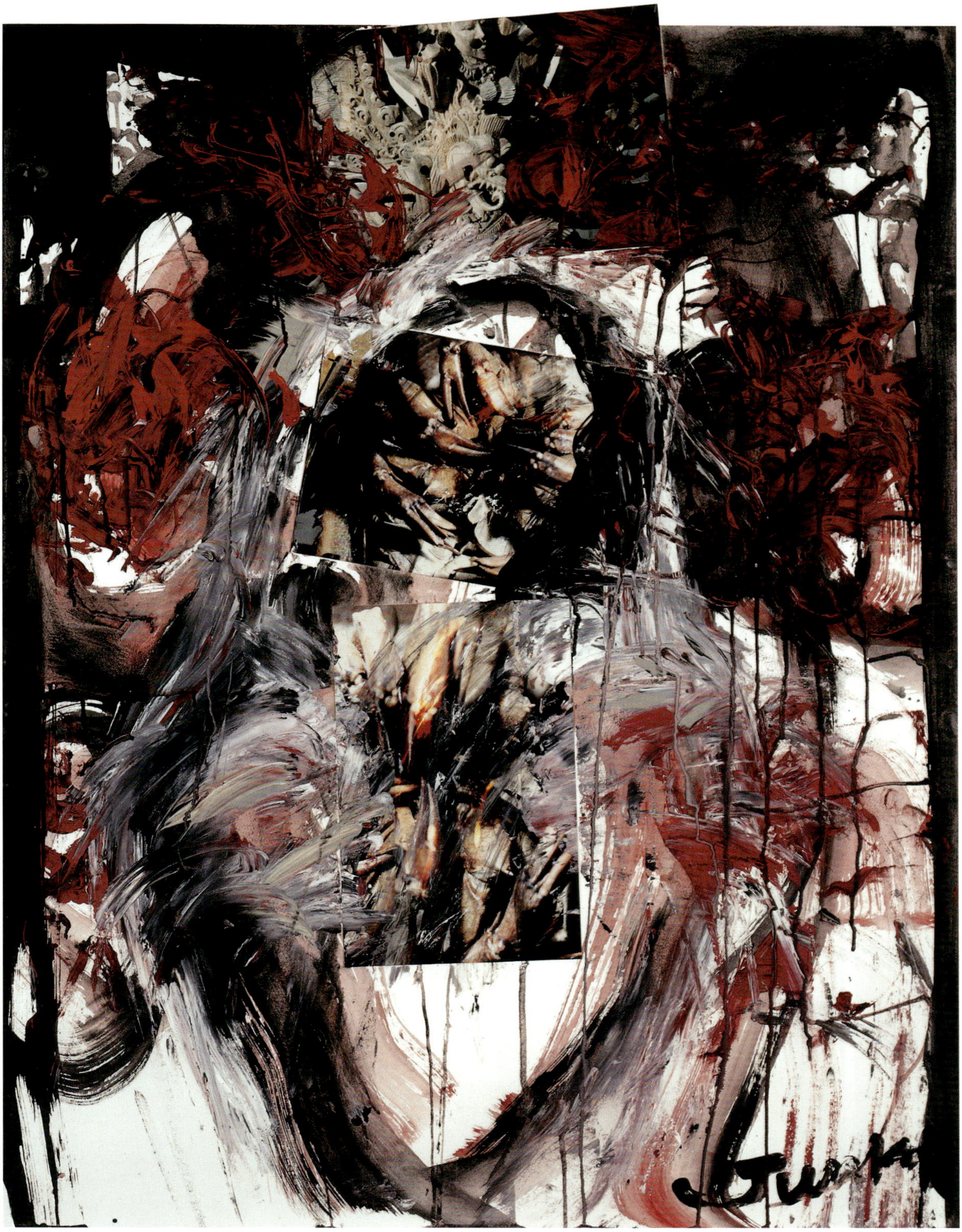

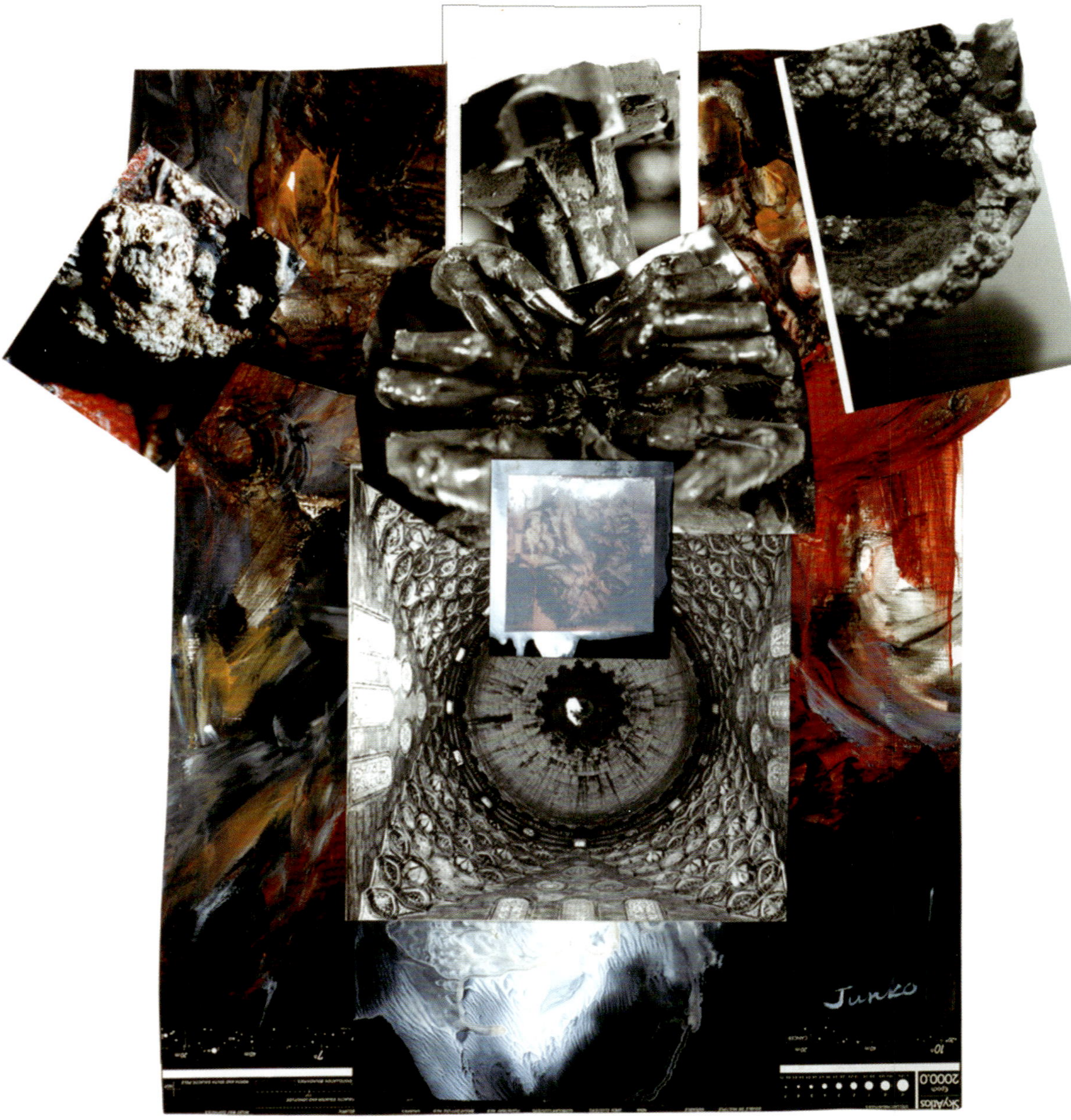

INTERLANETARY ICON,
No. 12 (1990)
Mixed media on paper
Irregular shape:
21 5 x 21.25 in.
(54.61 x 54.0 cm.)

CURTAINS

Series Statement "Curtains," 1988

When I was driving along the Pacific Coast Highway, suddenly I saw a vision of a huge curtain hanging in the faraway sky. It came down in front of my car as if it were a command from God. "Oh, no!" I said, "I am not strong enough to create this. Such a task would be too much for me, too difficult. Please do not command me to create that work." My car went through that curtain, but then I could see yet another one far ahead.

I created other works for many years since then. But one day, while I was working on a particular drawing in my studio, that drawing began changing rapidly into the image of the heavenly curtain I had seen seven years earlier. It became *Celestial Curtain, No. 1*. After that, I created three smaller works showing what I had seen behind the Celestial Curtain, and then, still not released from the command, I created *Celestial Curtain, No. 2*.

The theme of the curtain runs through Junko's work from the very beginning. It is not only the works specifically titled "Curtains" that exhibit this theme: the "*byoobu*"—the last work in her *Dead Flower* series—is a curtain, and her hanging mylars are all curtain-like. The *Giant Burls* are reminiscent of *noren*, the Japanese curtains that hang at the entrance to restaurants and retail stores.

By the time she started work in 2005 on her *FATHOM* series which hung on stage as backdrops for a dance performance, the curtain theme was already a regular part of Junko's work.

The curtain is drawn to hide something and it is raised, or drawn back, to reveal something. Yet it may itself become an object of attention—as when we sit in a theater staring at it and waiting for it to rise.

Letter to a Friend, 2001

My art works in the studio are doing remarkably well so far. Everybody around me is panicked because I have not produced the last big work that I promised for the show. I don't blame them because they cannot see the work hanging in a high place above me. The work is awesome: it is a rich, powerful, dignified image and in the image are the words, "Sexual ecstasy, clean and pure—this too is the realm of the boddhisatva," the words of the seventh century sutra. It moves in the breeze, it reflects the light in different ways at different times of the day. I am moved by it, intrigued by it, and I feel joy in it. I cannot see it in detail until it is manifested in my art, and that frustration keeps me working hard in the studio.

I glimpsed the scene of a beetle being stepped on by the heavy shoe of a man in a science-fiction movie on TV which Rafael mindlessly turned on when he came back from work at midnight the other day. The beetle was crushed and splashed all his yellow liquid and sticky entrails on the floor and made an ugly pile there, and it strangely started growing on the floor. "This is it, this is what I should be doing, the honeymoon in the studio is over," I thought. The image I call "curtain" is always breathtakingly beautiful when it is far away in heaven, but when it comes down it is like a giant shoe. I am squeezed by it and my whole liquid is splashed out. And then I have to work on the ugly pile of my own internal organs spread out on the floor. From the next morning, every single day was a revolutionary day since then. I fought, I could not believe that I was able to go through so many fights at one time. I was literally crawling on the middle of my own artwork which was spread on the floor, all my body covered with sticky materials, acrylic, and oil pastels. It was a dark, frightening time. But I am still in one piece and I will soon be finishing my work.

Images drawn on hanging curtains are important to Junko's art in another way. They relate closely to her "altered state of consciousness," discussed in Chapter Six.

Opposite:
CELESTIAL CURTAIN, No. 1 (1988)
Mixed media on paper
77 x 64 x 3 in.
(195.6 x 162.6 x 7.6 cm.)

Collection of the Long Beach Museum of Art

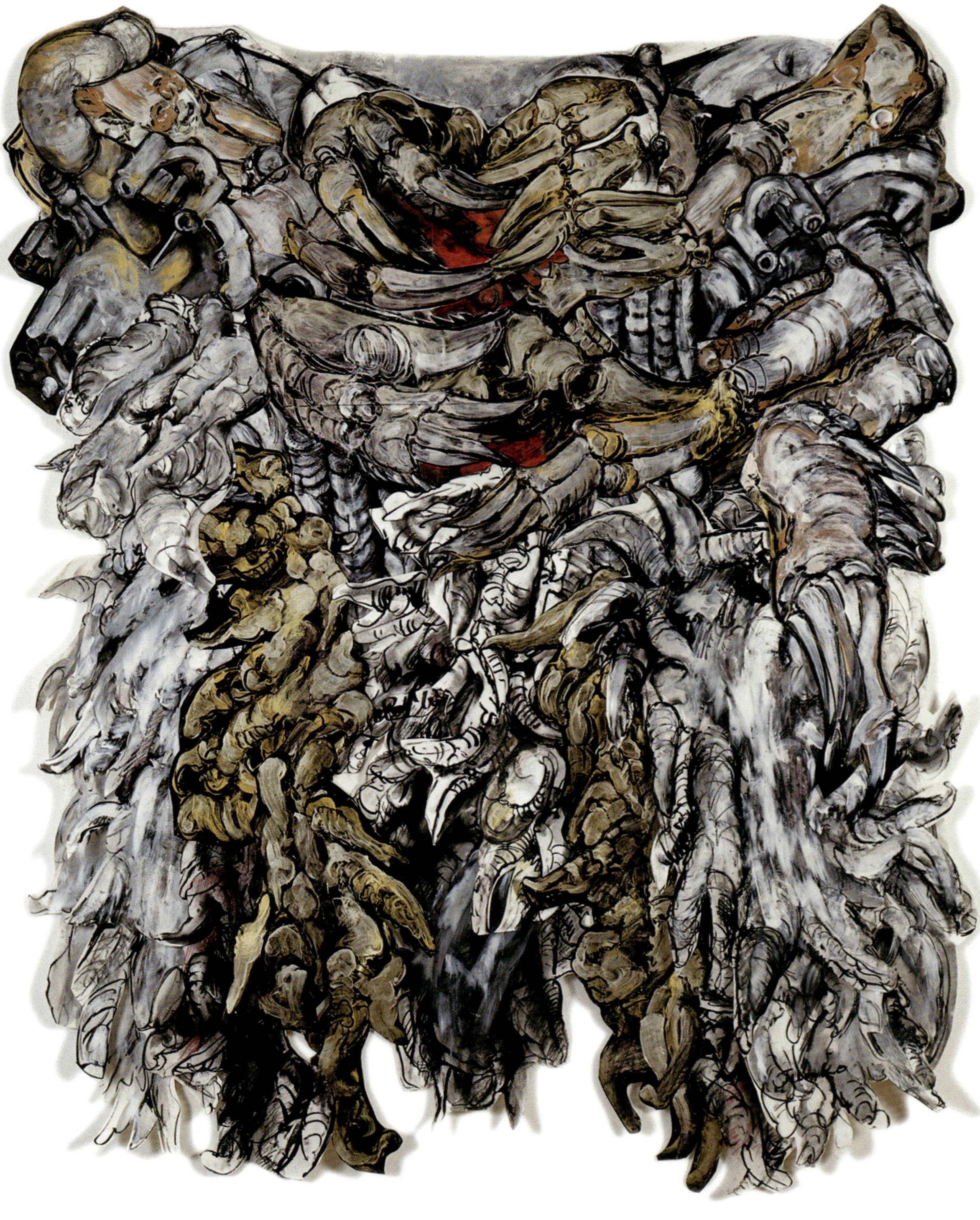

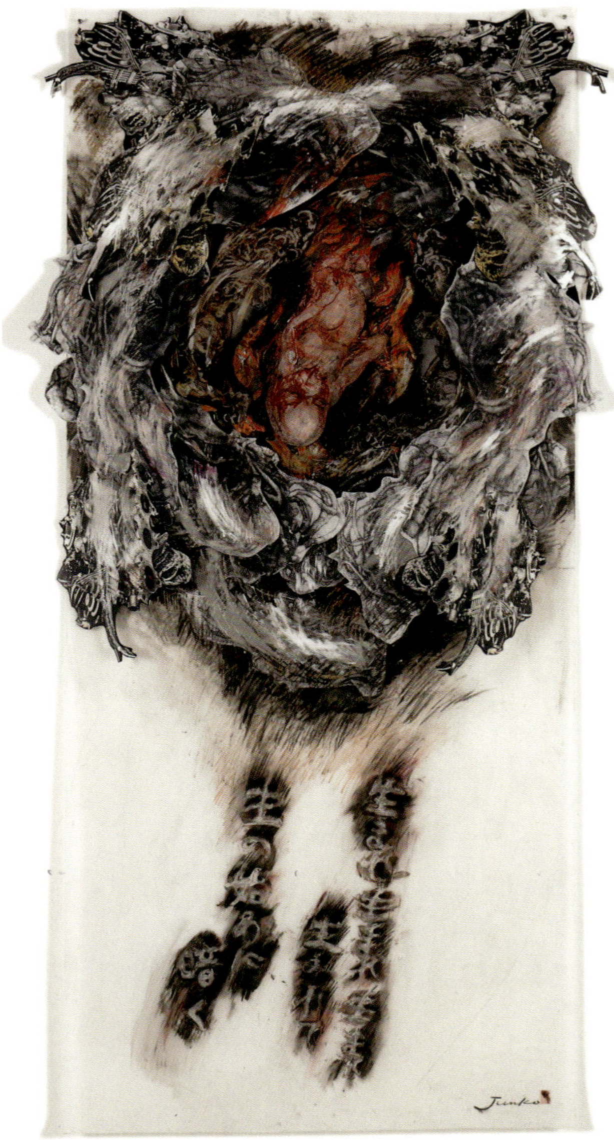

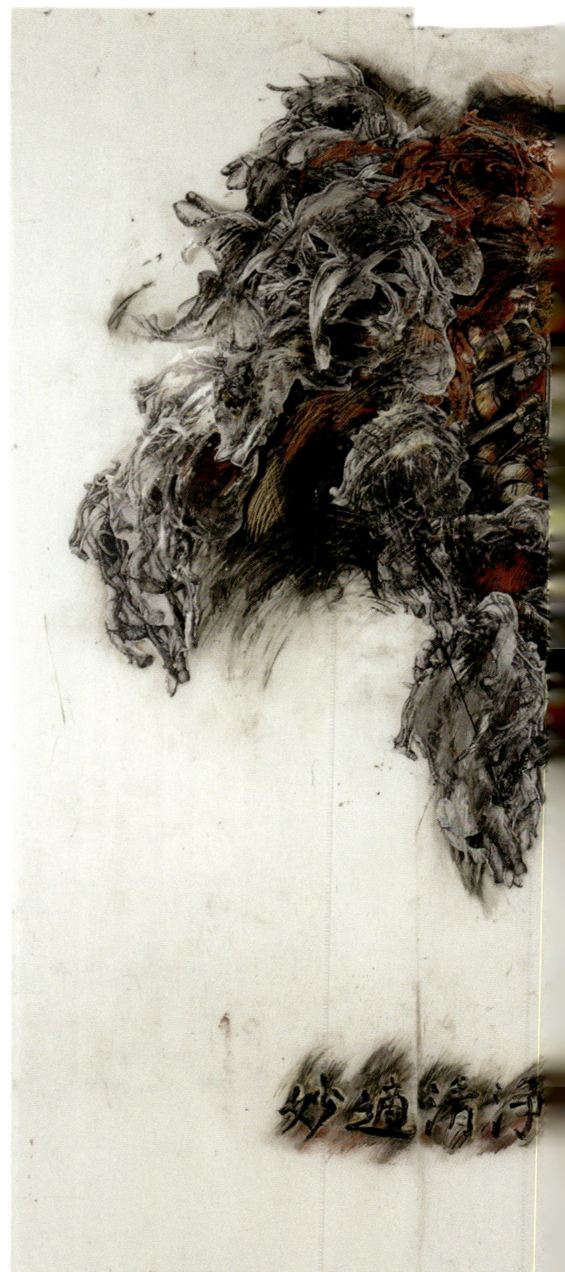

No. 1: *Birth* (2001)
Mixed media collage mounted on mylar
90 x 42 x 1 in. (228.6 x 106.7 x 2.5 cm.)
Translation of inscription:
"Born, reborn, and born yet again, in the cycle of reincarnation, in darkness." – Kuukai

ECSTASY: Translation of inscription:
"Sexual ecstasy, clean and pure — this too is the realm of the boddhisatva." – *Risshukyo* (Esoteric Buddhist sutra).

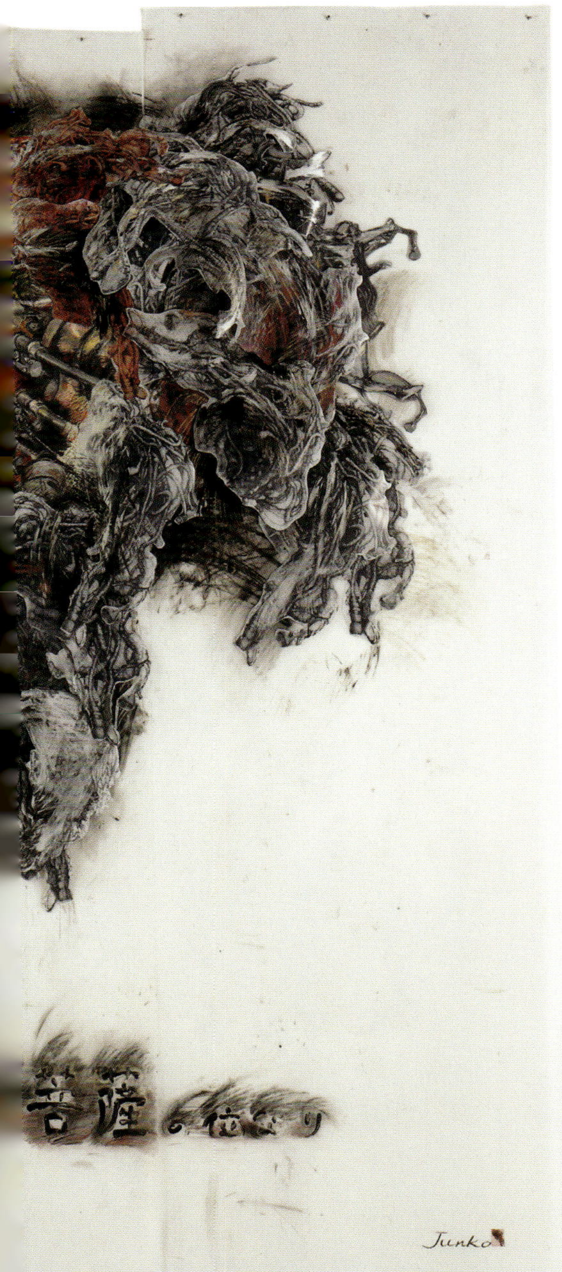

ESOTERIC BUDDHISM SERIES,
No. 2: *Ecstasy* (2001)
Mixed media collage on film mounted on mylar
Three panels
Overall 132 x 126 x 1 in.
(325.3 x 320 x 2.5 cm.)

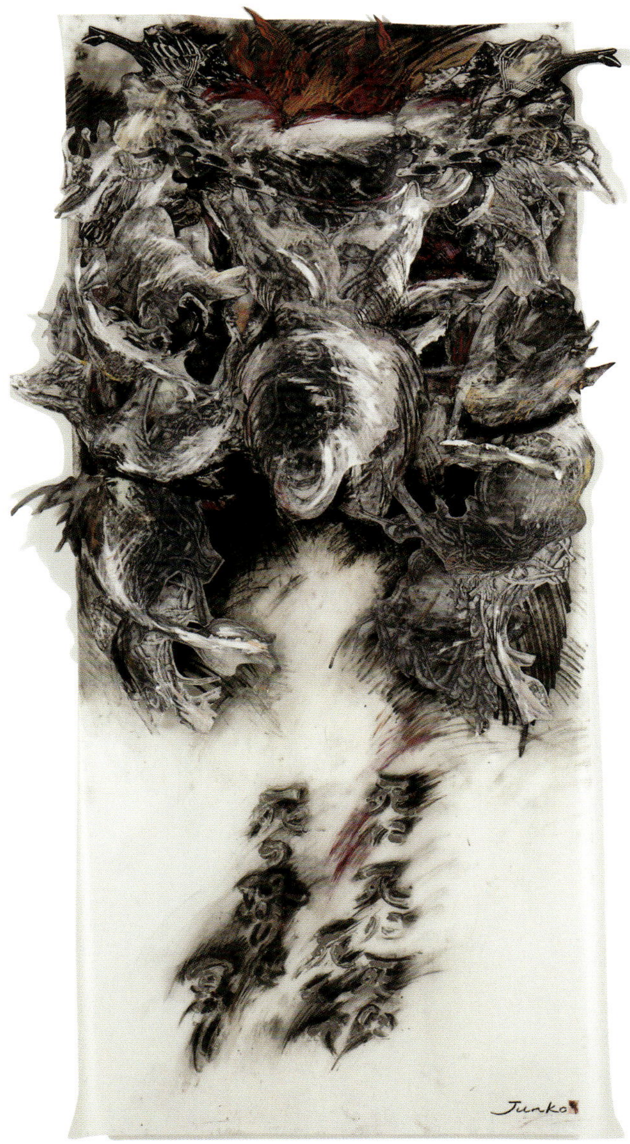

No. 3: *Death* (2001)
Mixed media collage mounted on mylar
90 x 42 x 1 in. (228.6 x 106.7 x 2.5 cm.)
Translation of inscription:
"Dying, dying, and dying yet again, in the cycle of reincarnation, in darkness." – Kuukai

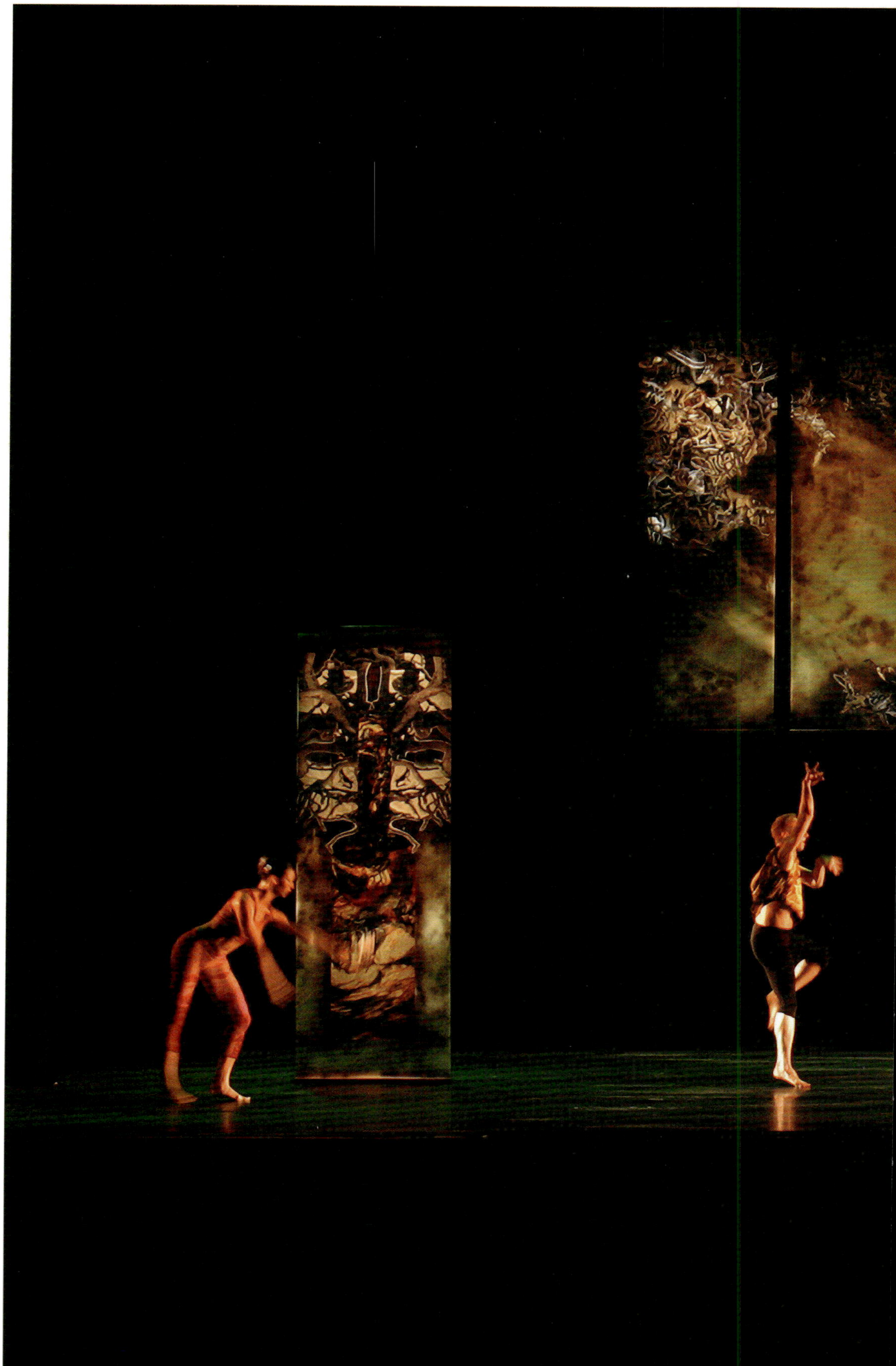

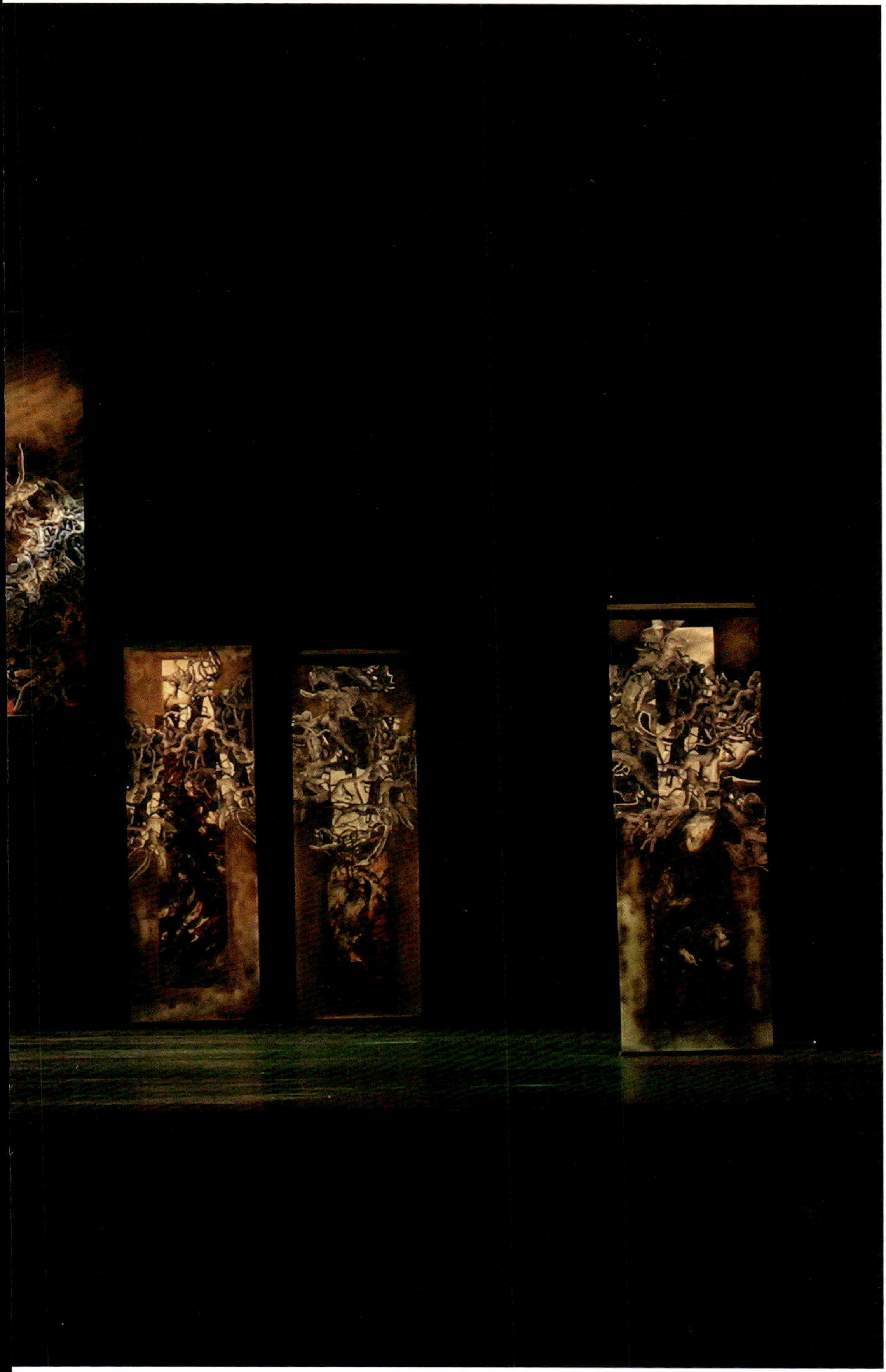

Studio Notebook, 2003

Today I read *The Mind in the Cave*, by David Lewis-Williams.[3] The author hypothesizes that Upper Paleolithic people possessed two kinds of consciousness: primary consciousness and higher-order consciousness which is like my own altered state of consciousness. The development of this higher-order consciousness enabled them to experience shamanistic trances and have visions, and it was this that drove them into dark, dangerous caves to paint vivid images on the cave walls. They used that imagery as a means of defining the individual self, and of forming social relationships and establishing their society.

What hit me most strongly was that the author pointed out that the images of those lively animals on the walls have no hoofs. They are depicted as if they are hanging or sometimes as if they are floating in the air rather than standing on the ground. He believes this is because the images were created in the altered state of consciousness: the artists saw visions on the screen of their own minds first and then tried to translate those images onto the wall.

This insight struck me as profoundly sharp. This is exactly what I experience when I am in the altered state of consciousness. The screen of my mind is the "curtain" for me. It hangs between this world and the spirit world from which the vision comes. Imagery on paper or mylar (in their case, on the cave wall) often seems to be hanging or floating and this is what so upset all my authoritative art teachers when I was young. They would say, "This image is not standing on the ground!" But I have always been attracted to the paintings of Lascaux and Altamira and other caves. And now I feel that those artists saw the "curtain" the same way I see it: they saw the incredible mystery of the life force probably even more vividly than I ever saw it, there in the dark, narrow, dangerously winding passages of the caves. They are truly my ancestors!

Art is about how you experience space—the space you see internally, and the space you see physically are translated into the limited physical pictorial space. There are many kinds of perspective in different cultures all over the world. But when the outer scientific eye, the "primary consciousness," became dominant, mainstream, and authoritative in history, countless images that were painted in the altered state of consciousness—in the "higher-order consciousness"—must have been lost, and that special way of experiencing space was lost. Along with it, man lost the ability to perceive visions. The curtain disappeared, and the sensitivity to the tremendous magic power that the artist had conjured up into the pictorial space from the dark, unknown terrain—that disappeared altogether as well.

Of course Picasso "broke" scientific perspective and since his time, Renaissance perspective has not been the artist's only choice and much freedom of style resulted. But cubism was still a new expression of rational consciousness, and even though it developed into a series of new "styles" it was not a return to the higher-order consciousness of the cave painters. As long as rational consciousness remains the primary way of seeing the world, we will miss the visions that are accessible only to the higher-ordered consciousness—the altered state.

The day may come when we will write an entirely different history of perspective from the one we know now. The matter of perspective in art history is a serious issue for all the spiritual and intellectual endeavors of mankind.

Previous page:
FATHOM:
COMMUNICATING
WITH NATURE (2006)
Collage of computer
prints on mylar
Each panel:
120 x 42 in.
(304.8 x 106.7 cm.)

LUNGS AND RIB CAGE

Series Statement "Relic," 1984

The rib cage has some special meaning for me. It reminds me of the little wooden crucifix I saw when I was a young girl, which shocked me so violently. It reminds me of the tuberculosis I suffered when I was eight years old. It has become for me a symbol of life's vulnerability. But at the same time, it is sacred, full of blood, flesh, and color.

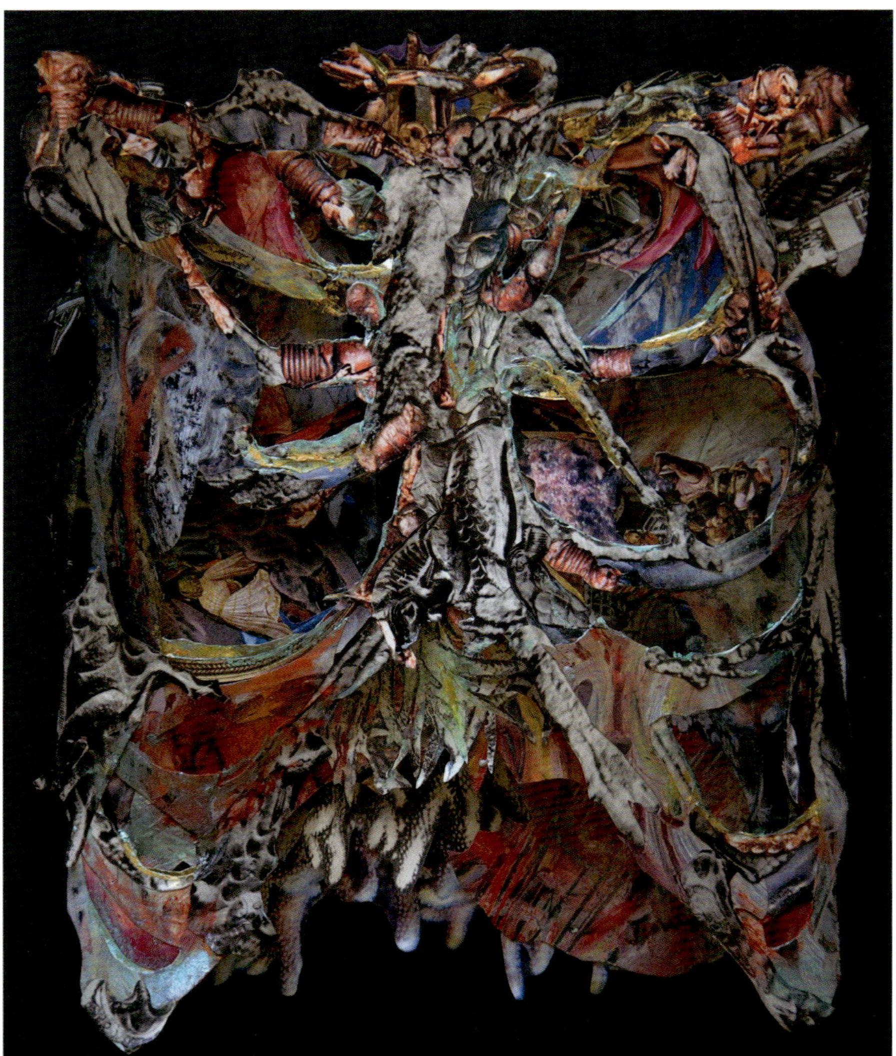

This page:
RELIC (1984)
Collage and acrylic
on paper,
3-dimensional:
11 x 9.125 x 2 in.
(27.9 x 23.2 x 5 cm.)

Opposite:
DEAD FLOWER SERIES
No. 5 (1973)
Pen and ink on paper,
with wash
22.5 x 16 in.
(57.2 x 40.6 cm.)

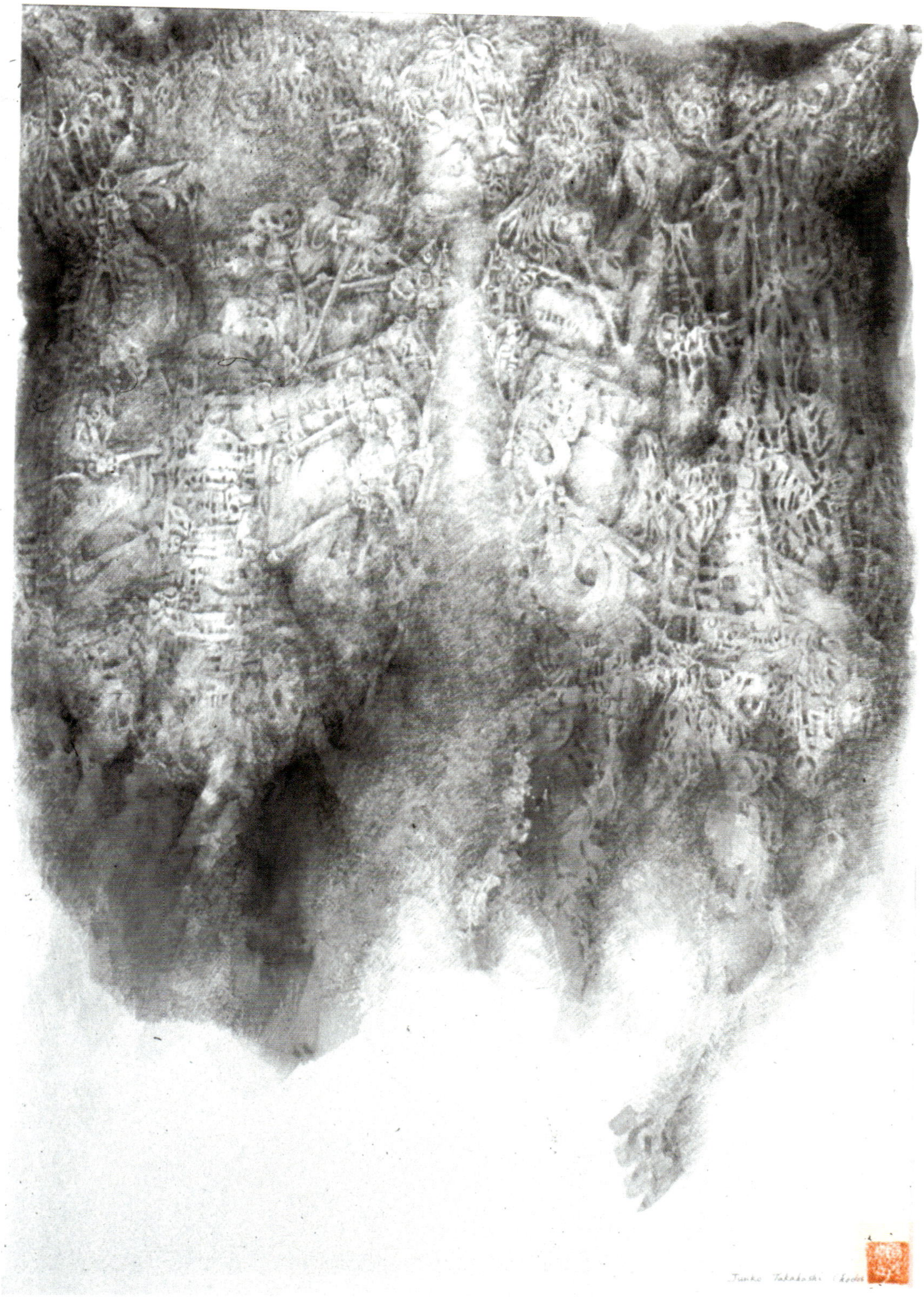

Studio Notebook, 2001

Tuberculosis was still a disease of terror and shame in postwar Japan when I was contaminated with this sickness, and severe malnourishment during the war contributed to the erosion of my lungs. People were terrified of this contagious disease, just like pestilence or leprosy in medieval times and AIDS in our own time. After the war was finally over, I had to confront my own death. I was not allowed to laugh or cry in order to avoid excess use of my lungs—crying especially could bring death. So I listened to my own inner scream and cry echoing in my rib cage silently. Not allowed to take any kind of bath, I looked like a filthy, dark, dried up, smelly little corpse. I laid my skeleton-like body on the thin *futon* on the floor in my home for nearly one year. That was the time when all of Japan finally got out of the everyday threats of death, of war, and started vigorously building a new life in the burnt fields. I was left out, a threat to others, an abhorred omen. Shame was deep among the people around me—no one told me what was wrong with me, even to utter the name of the sickness itself was a dark taboo.

Death was finally internalized in me after having experienced death as an outer phenomenon during the war. I recognized that the seed of death was planted in my rib cage at the age of 8. I started feeling God's presence around me and in me, and I started to talk to Him alone in silence, day and night, asking about death, about the meaning of my sickness, about the meaning of my life. When I felt strong enough, I put paper on my chest and I wrote my words to Him lying on the *futon*. I could not see my writing well as I was writing since it was prohibited for me to sit up. Those were prayers and now that I think of it, some might have been written very likely by a kind of automatic writing. I wrote them without being taught how to pray or how to recite prayers. I did not even know there were people who could have taught me that. But I became happy being alone with God. I was always aware that death and God were both quietly growing in my rib cage.

Junko *empathized* with the dead flowers, roots, engine, and horseshoe crab. But she *identifies* with the lungs and rib cage: they are part of herself in a more direct way than the other visitants. This accounts for the wide range of images she draws from them.

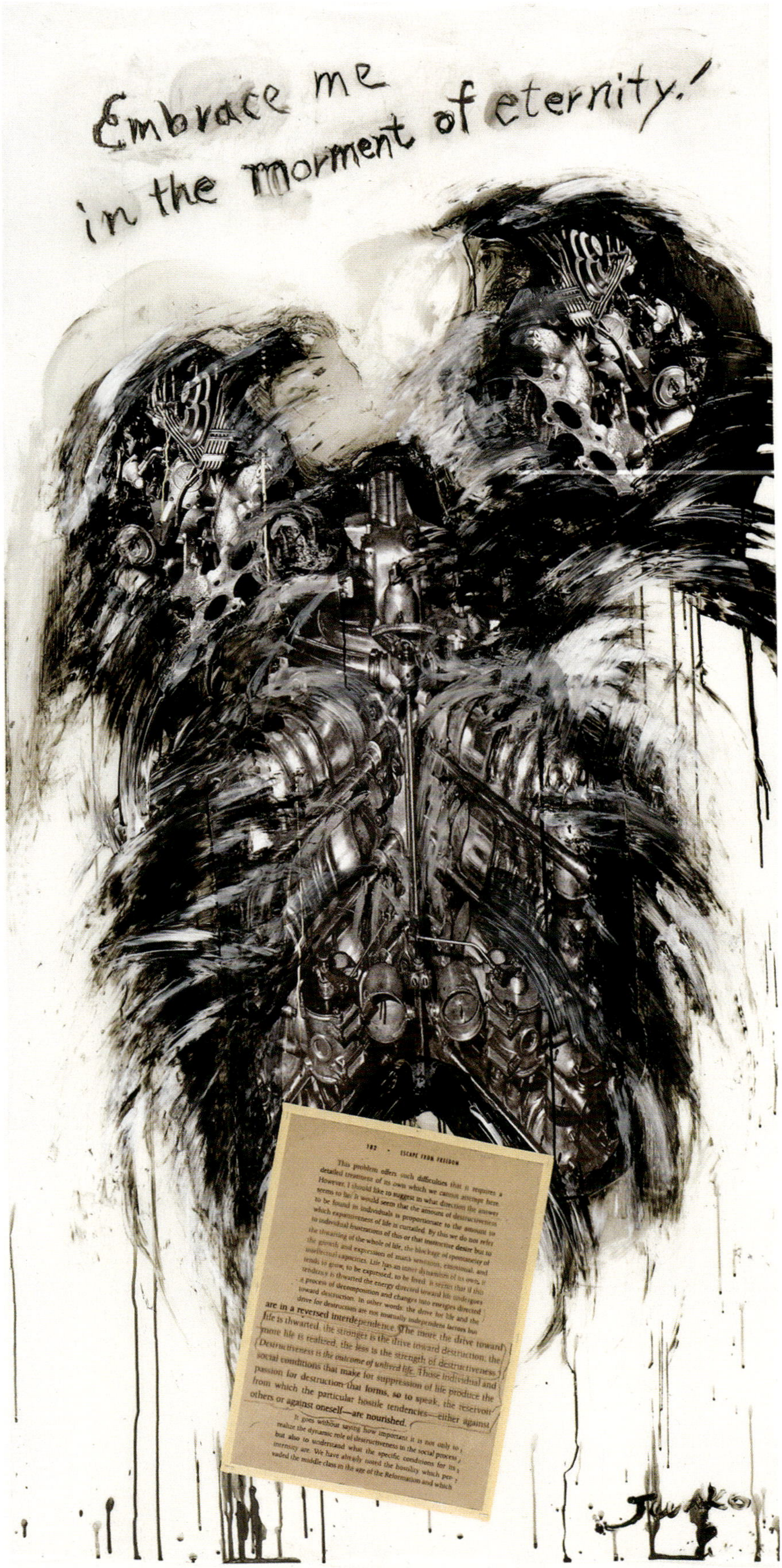

CONCERNING ART AND RELIGION, No. 8 (2003)
"EMBRACE ME IN THE MOMENT OF ETERNITY!"
Collage of computer prints on mylar
84 x 42 in.
(213.36 x 106.68 cm.)

Series Statement "Burls," 1989

Swollen and twisted, amputated from their trees, red, dark and radiant, cast down in front of me like corpses, dead burls imprison the still living spirits of trees.

Those spirits cried out to me and I said to them, "It is time for you to leave your pain and be released from your struggling. Come out of the burls and I will grieve with you. Toss yourselves into the air and I will dance with you."

Studio Notebook, 1989

A new art work rose up in my studio today. Suddenly burls started breathing in my pictorial space. It is surprising; these are the same burls I have been working on for days and days and anguished over for more than three months. Many works of burls were born and died during those days. Their breath is so subtle that I almost cannot hear them: only through all the pores of my body, my skin can hear them. It might be possible that this work can be the first work preceding a long series of works, I secretly thought. Their breath pushed the air away and created a new space around them in my work. The space is intense and powerful. Inside of that space they started faintly moving, and quietly dancing. And then their dance became wild, and twenty-one works of "Tree Spirits" followed one after another over the next few months.

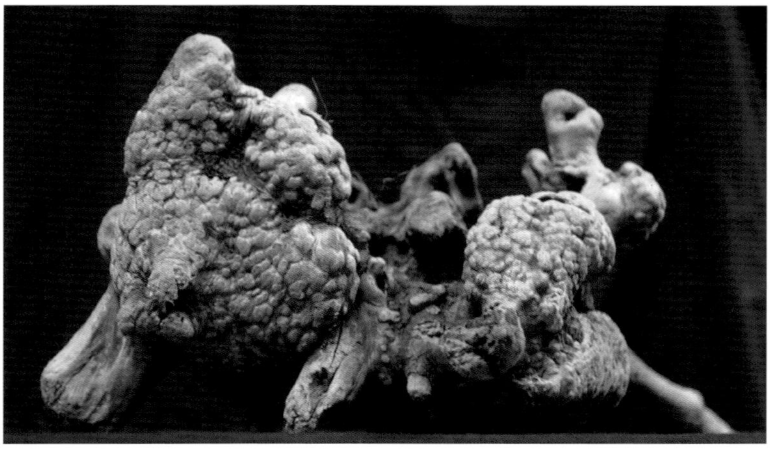

This page:
Photograph of burl in Junko's studio

Opposite:
BURLS, No. 9 (1988)
Acrylic and charcoal on paper
40 x 32 in.
(101.6 x 81.3 cm.)

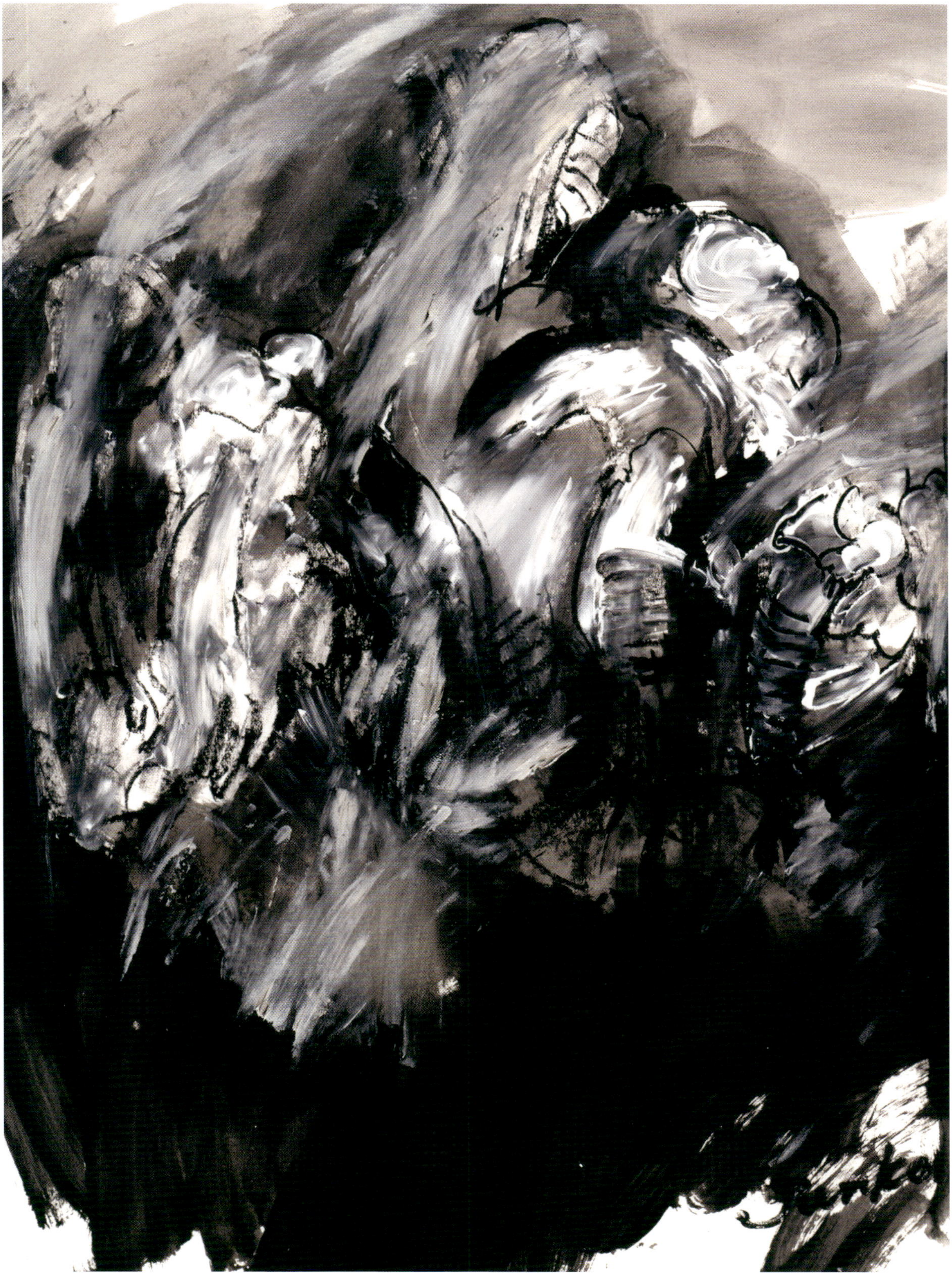

Junko has many, many burls in her studio. Unlike the root, which is a single unique object, the burls are a type of object—and Junko often finds new ones that inspire her.

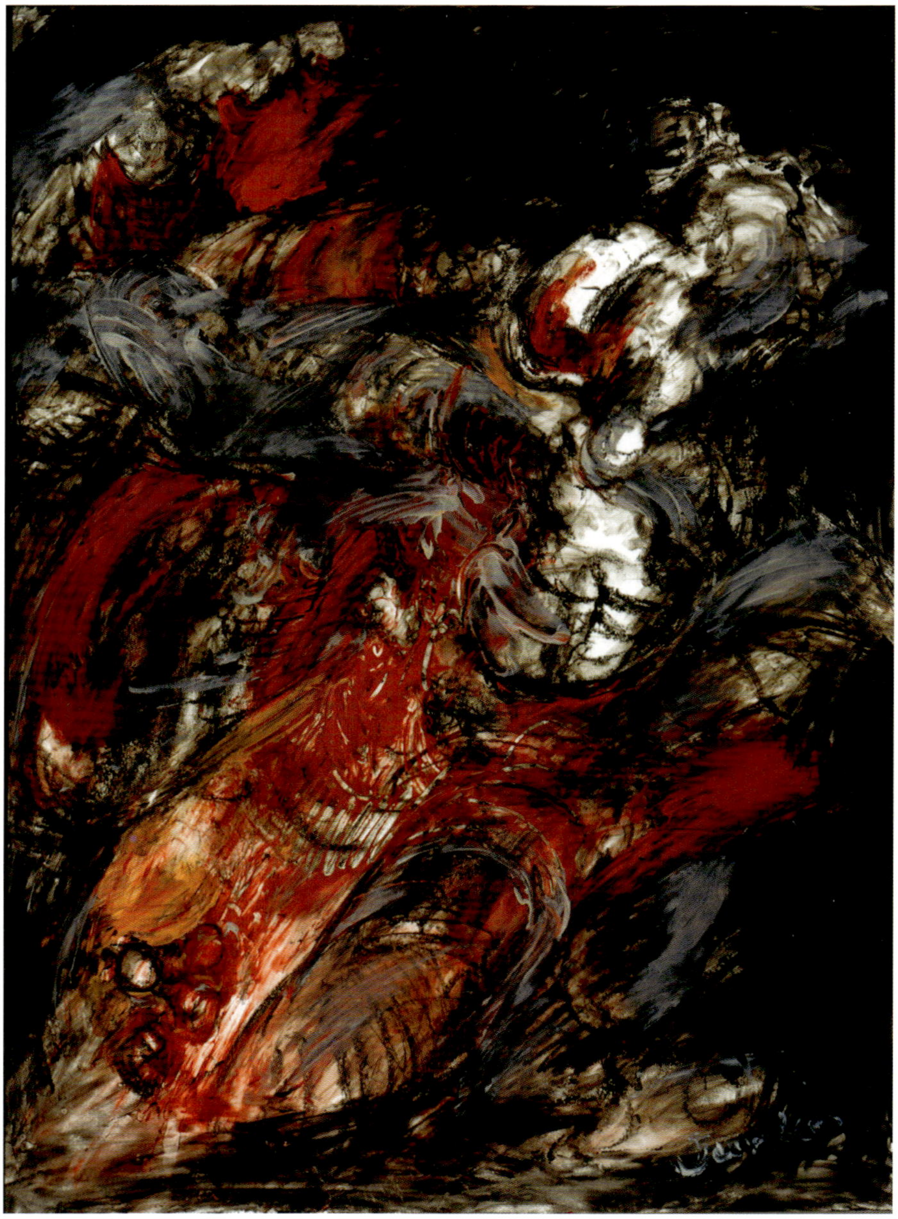

This page:
TREE SPIRITS,
No. 9 (1989)
Charcoal and
acrylic on paper
42 x 32 in.
(106.7 x 81.3 cm.)

Opposite:
INTERPLANETARY
ICON, No. 25
Mixed media on paper
Irregular shape:
26 x 25 in.
(66.0 x 63.5 cm.)
Here we see a falling figure underneath the burl, foreshadowing some of Junko's later works.

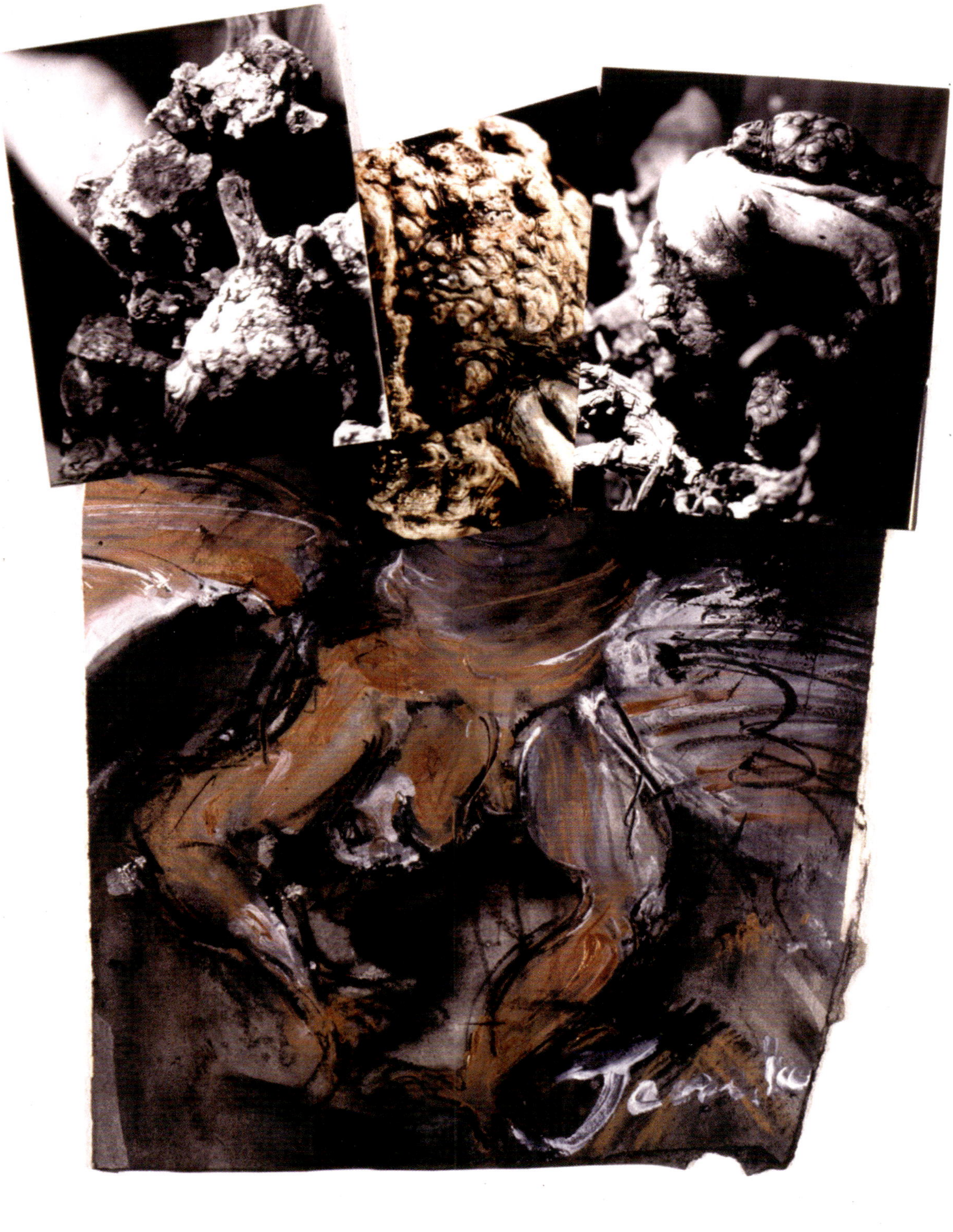

BIRDS AND THE DECANTER

Studio Notebook, 1987

Today I bought the most beautiful thing. It is a handmade arch-shaped object about one foot high. On the top and both sides, stuck into it there are roses made of tin, whose ugly pink had turned into the color of rotten meat through age and the accumulation of dust; and equally ugly leaves which are also made of tin are sticking out from the arch. So it becomes clear that the whole thing is meant to be a tree of roses. But whatever it is, the main theme of this weird object is the bird that hangs inside the arched tree, supported on both sides by wire running to the arch. Here is a bird which seems to have been made of plaster, engraved by some sharp instrument to make it look like the surface is feathered (and apparently this effort failed), painted dark green, almost black, like burned chicken just come out of the oven. And there is no head for this bird. When I looked at the part of the neck where the head should be, I saw a glass bottle buried inside of the bird. This is a wine decanter! But instead of wine, packed with Darkness up to his neck, this bird was round and swollen. The wire which supports the bird is actually stuck into both sides of his fat belly, so that the bird can turn his neck down when you want to pour wine from this decanter. And in fact right under him, there is a slight shallow hole made by a mayonnaise cap buried face up in order to hold a wine glass.

It is a coarse, ugly object from every conceivable aspect, however, one thing hit me deeply. There is a subtle tone of yellow which is the background of the arched rose tree, and it was obviously made from the flat bottom of a bucket, which was cut in half in order to fit inside the arch. On its tin surface, there was some cheap amateur painting of a house and a few trees. Behind the houses and trees is something that must have been intended as the sky, but it is painted yellow. It is a most unusual phenomenon for yellow to recede into the background so quietly: isn't it like a halo for the bird? But of course, it is just the ugly color of the gray tin appearing underneath and through the yellow. And the paint is aged, covered with dust, so the yellow has lost its glittery quality and gained a special subtle tone. The shape of the half circle looks like a celestial chart with some circled lines on it, which come from the grooves of the bottom of the bucket, and look like the orbits of the planets in the chart. Because of this yellow this bird, ugly as it is, has gained

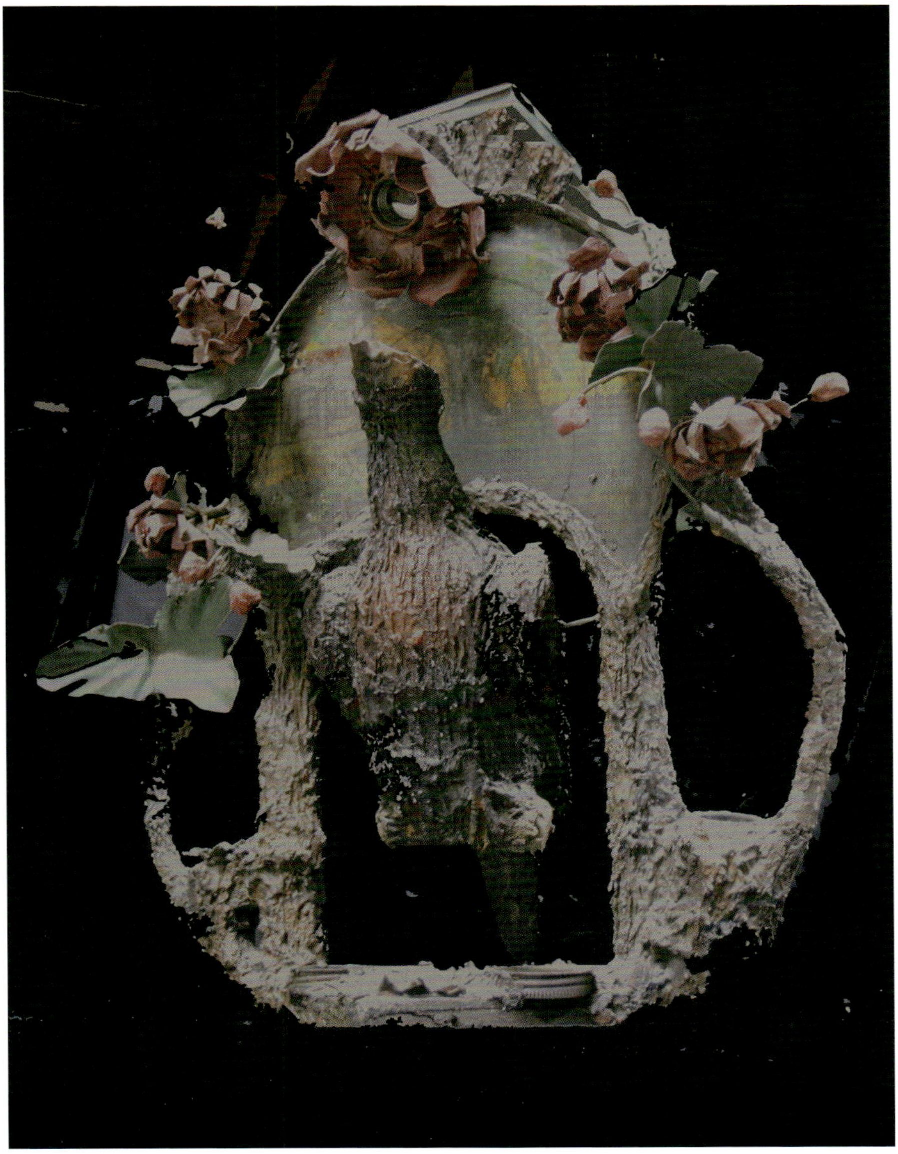

Photograph of the incredibly ugly decanter that Junko found at a junk store

a profoundly tragic tone. I saw Torcello, *Virgin and Child with the Apostles*, in this object, standing solemnly in the eternal light, embracing unfathomable sorrow in her arms.

The old man in the store, seeing me paying attention to this, said it was made for a wedding gift. If I dust it or wash it, it will come back to its original bright colors. Unfortunately the cap, which is the chopped bird's head itself, is missing: he would sell it to me at a discount.

A half century had passed since I witnessed the execution of a bird in my faraway homeland during the war. I re-encountered him today, in this sick shape, under the bright sky, in a beach town in California. When I put this in my studio, though, the whole studio seemed to darken slightly.

The experience Junko mentions of witnessing the execution of a bird in Japan during the war is related at greater length in Chapter Two. The experience developed into one of her most significant series of works, *Requiem for an Executed Bird*, discussed at great length in Chapter Four. But in order for the forty-five works in that series to come out, another four years were required after encountering this decanter. Meanwhile the image of the bird appeared on and off all her life long even in her childhood works, like magma boiling underneath a volcano, foreshadowing the big eruption to come. But even after the *Requiem* series was completed the bird kept appearing in Junko's work. In this chapter I show you only one of the works from the *Requiem* series: one in which part of the decanter is visible. But I show you also the same bird taking on the figure of a sorcerer in *FATHOM*, a series of giant mylar panels created in 2006, fifteen years after the *Requiem* series was completed.

Opposite:
REQUIEM FOR AN EXECUTED BIRD
No. 19 (1991)
Mixed media on paper
40 x 32 in.
(101.6 x 81.3 cm.)

Next pages:
FATHOM: THE SORCERER ENTERING HIS FOREST
(2005)
Collage of computer prints on mylar
Foreground: three panels
120 x 42 in.
(304.8 x 106.7 cm.)
Background: four panels
144 x 42 in.
(365.8 x 106.7 cm.)

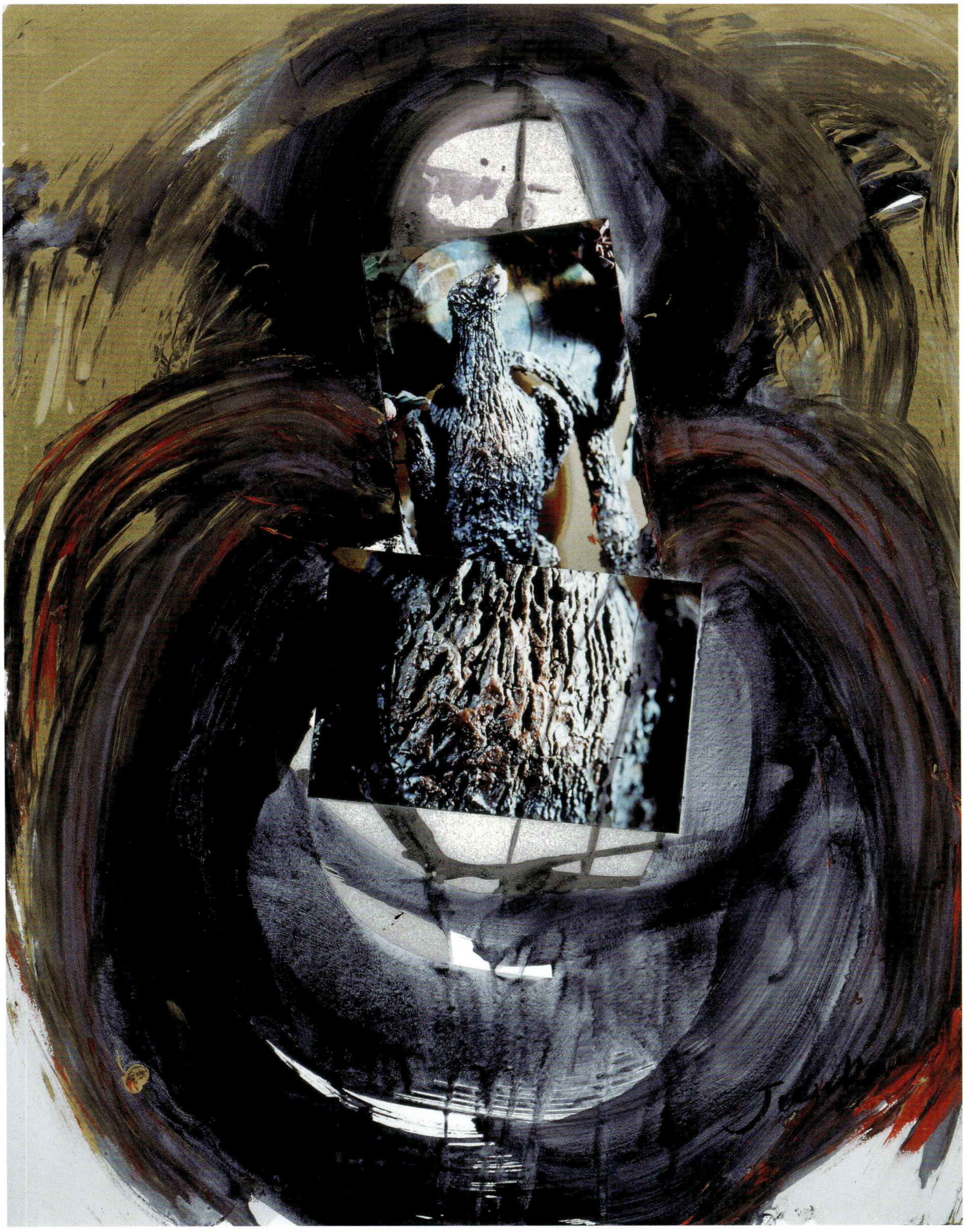

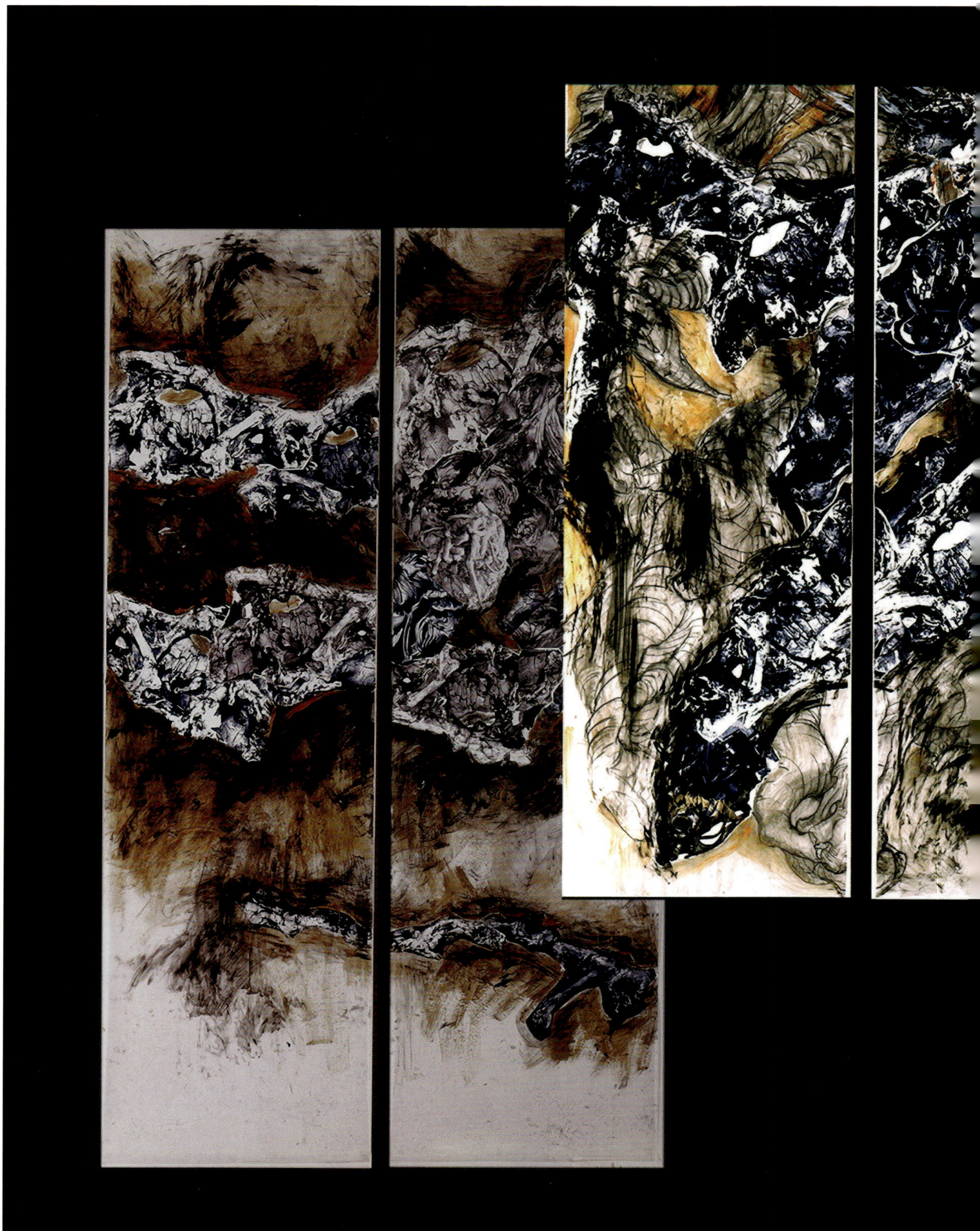

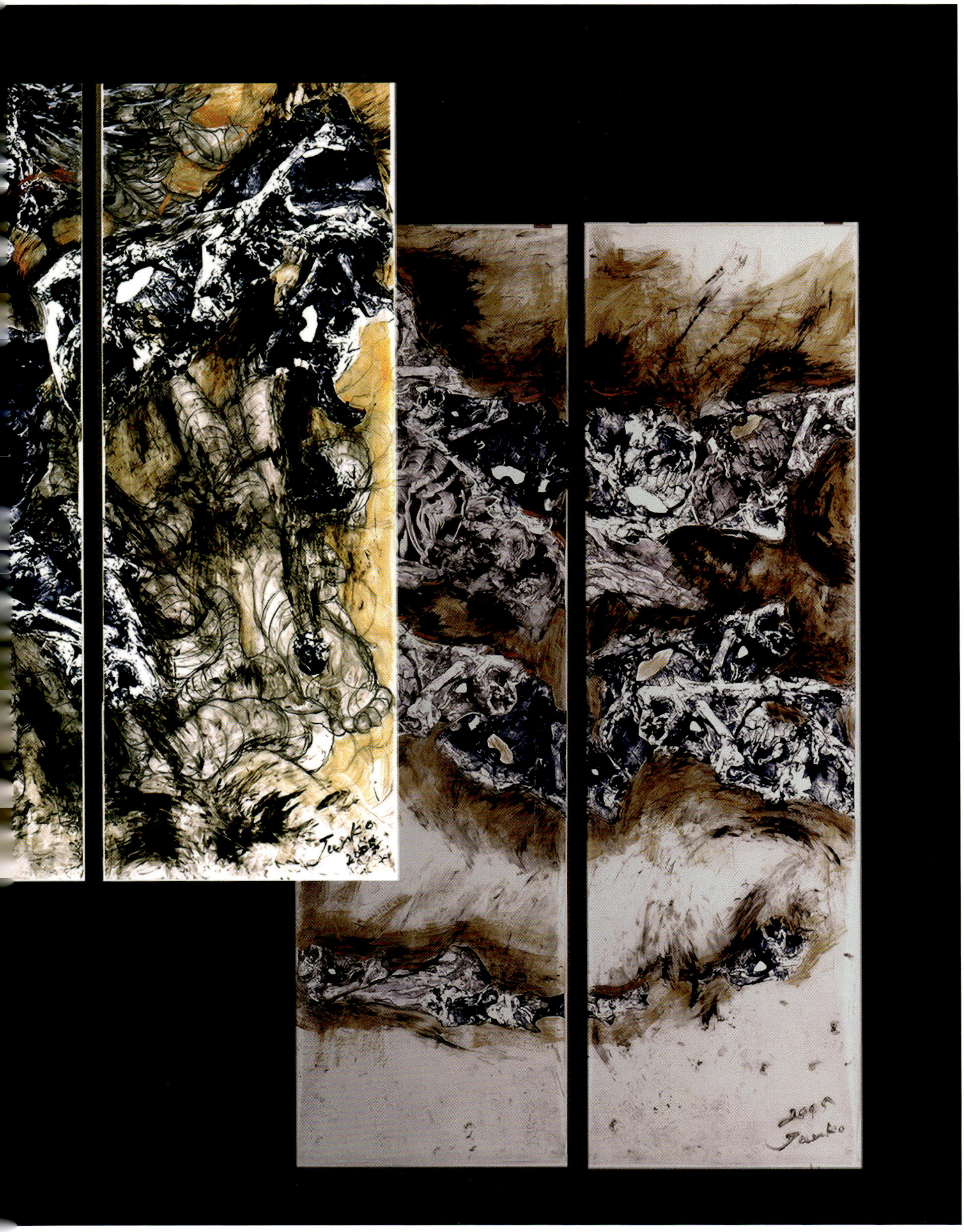

HUMAN FIGURES AND DANCE

Series Statement "Universe Moves and Humans Dance," 1984

The force which moves the universe moves us, and animates us, and makes us dance. Through dance, spirit takes form as body and body gives form to spirit. Through dance we become one with ourselves. Through dance we become one with the force which moves the universe. These works are the trace on paper of my own dance.

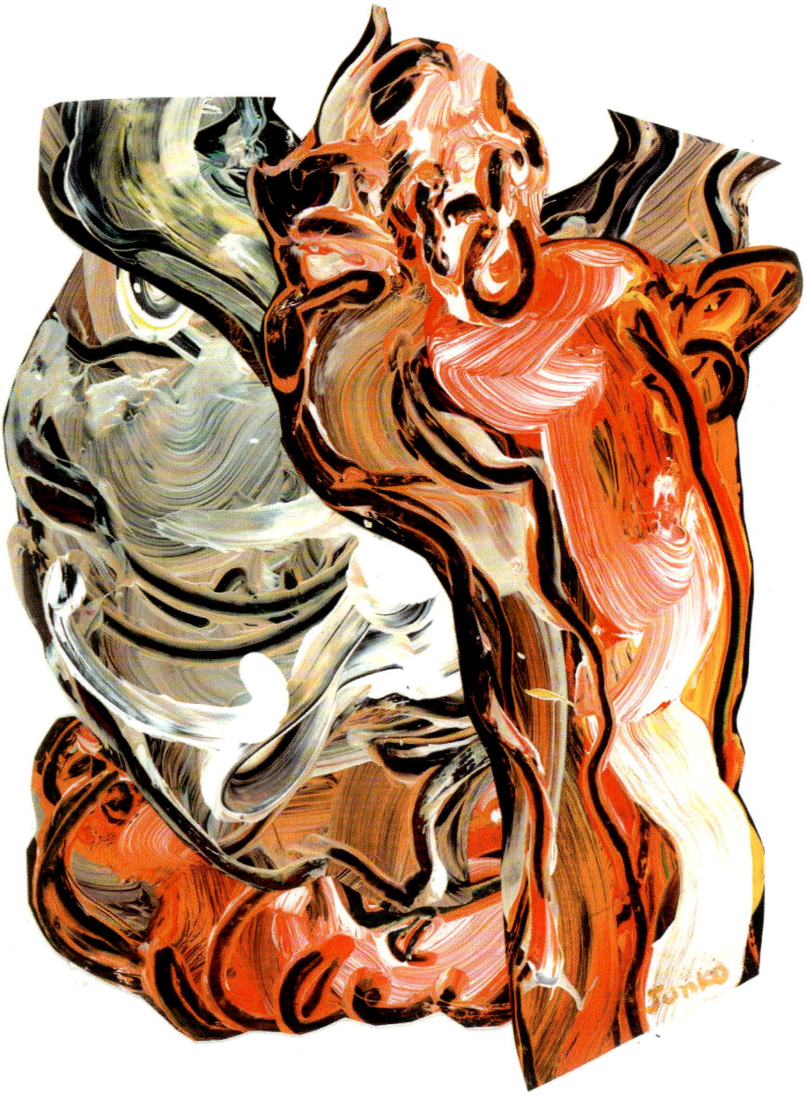

This page:
MEDITATIONS ON DANCE, No. 1 (1987)
Acrylic on coated paper
30 x 28 in.
(76.2 x 71.1 cm.)

Opposite:
DANCE IN GREEN AND RED (1984)
Mixed media on paper
15 x 10 in.
(38 x 25.4 cm.)

Following pages:
FIVE DANCING FIGURES (1984)
Mixed media on printed paper
20 x 48 in.
(51.8 x 121.9 cm.)

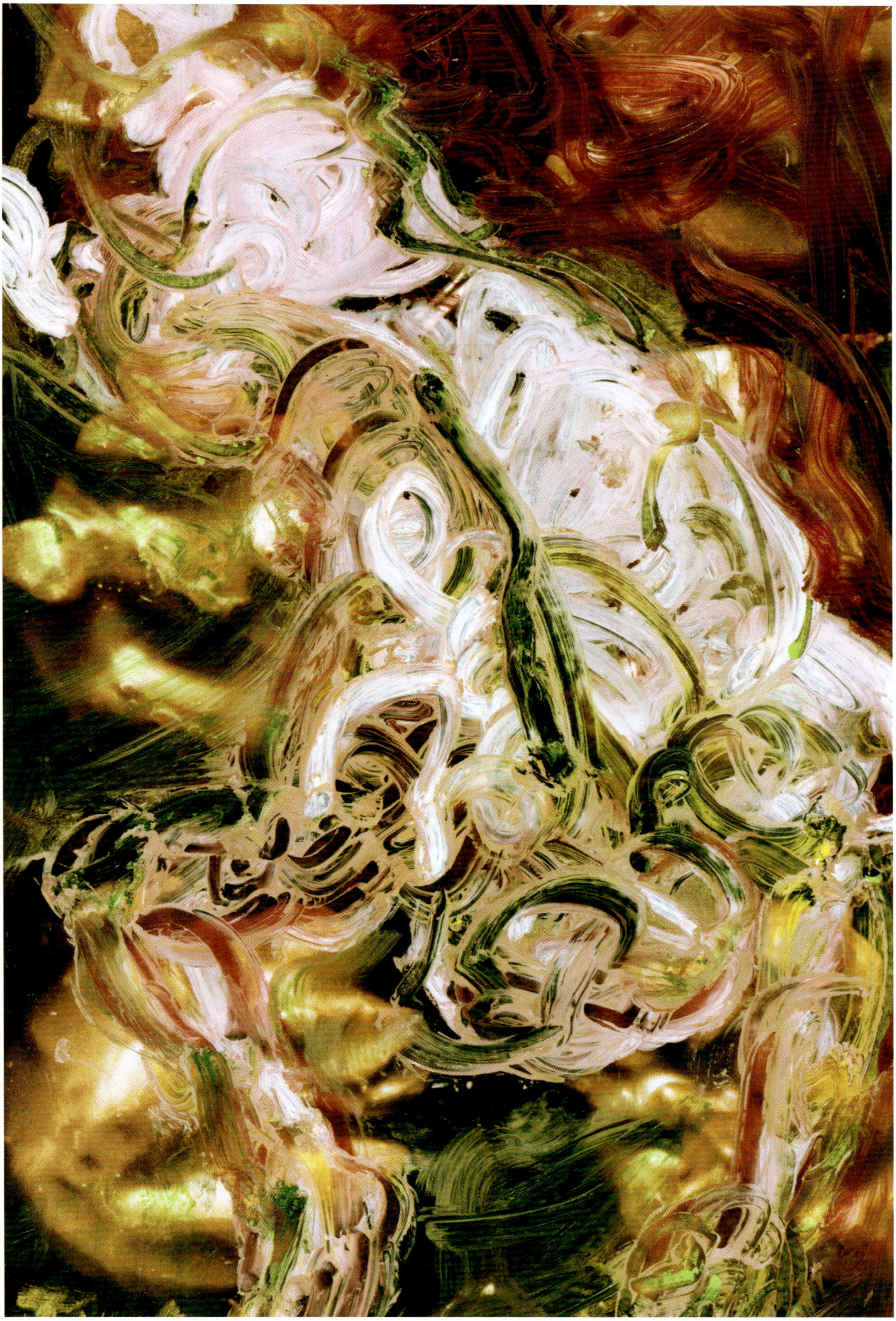

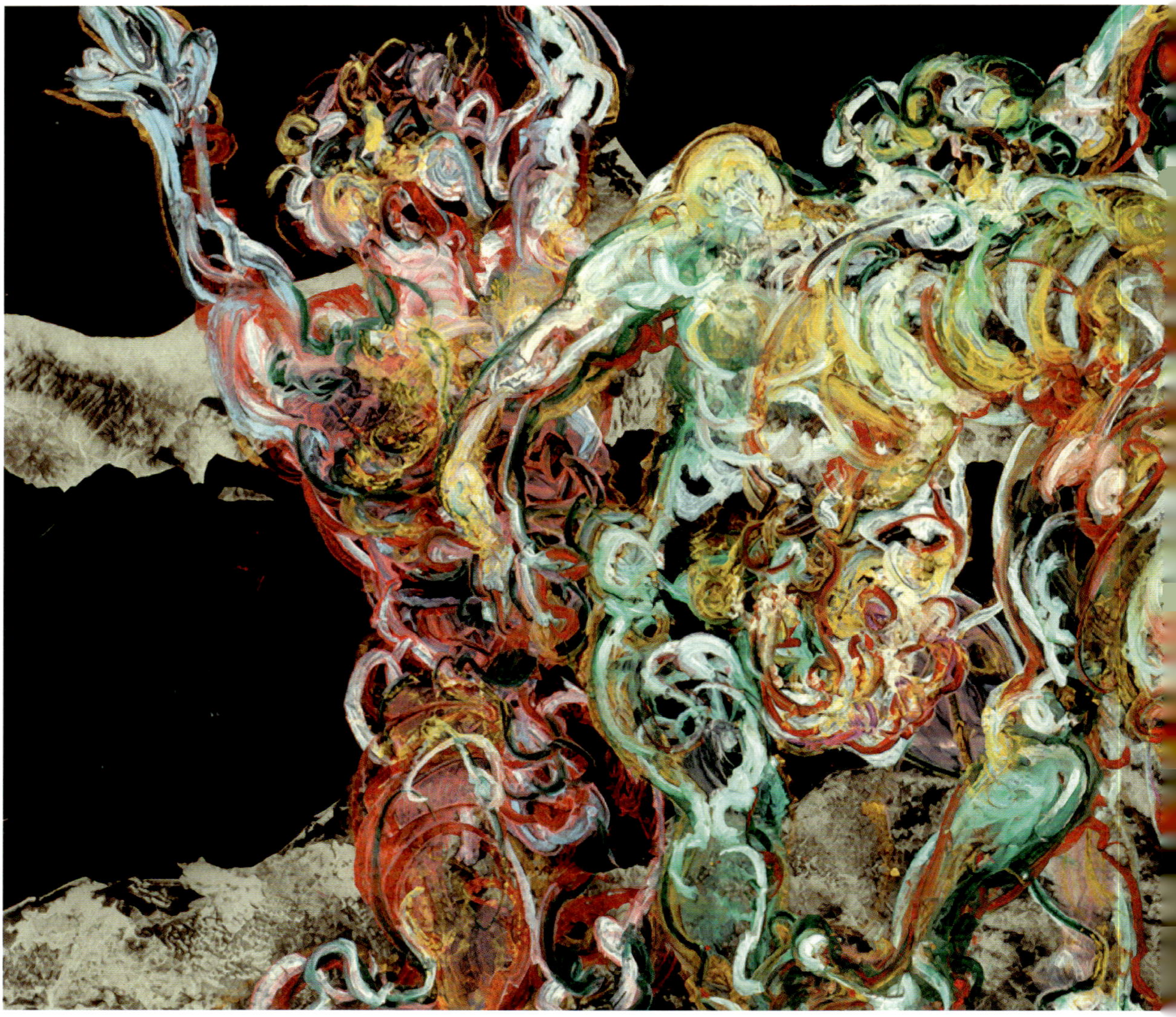

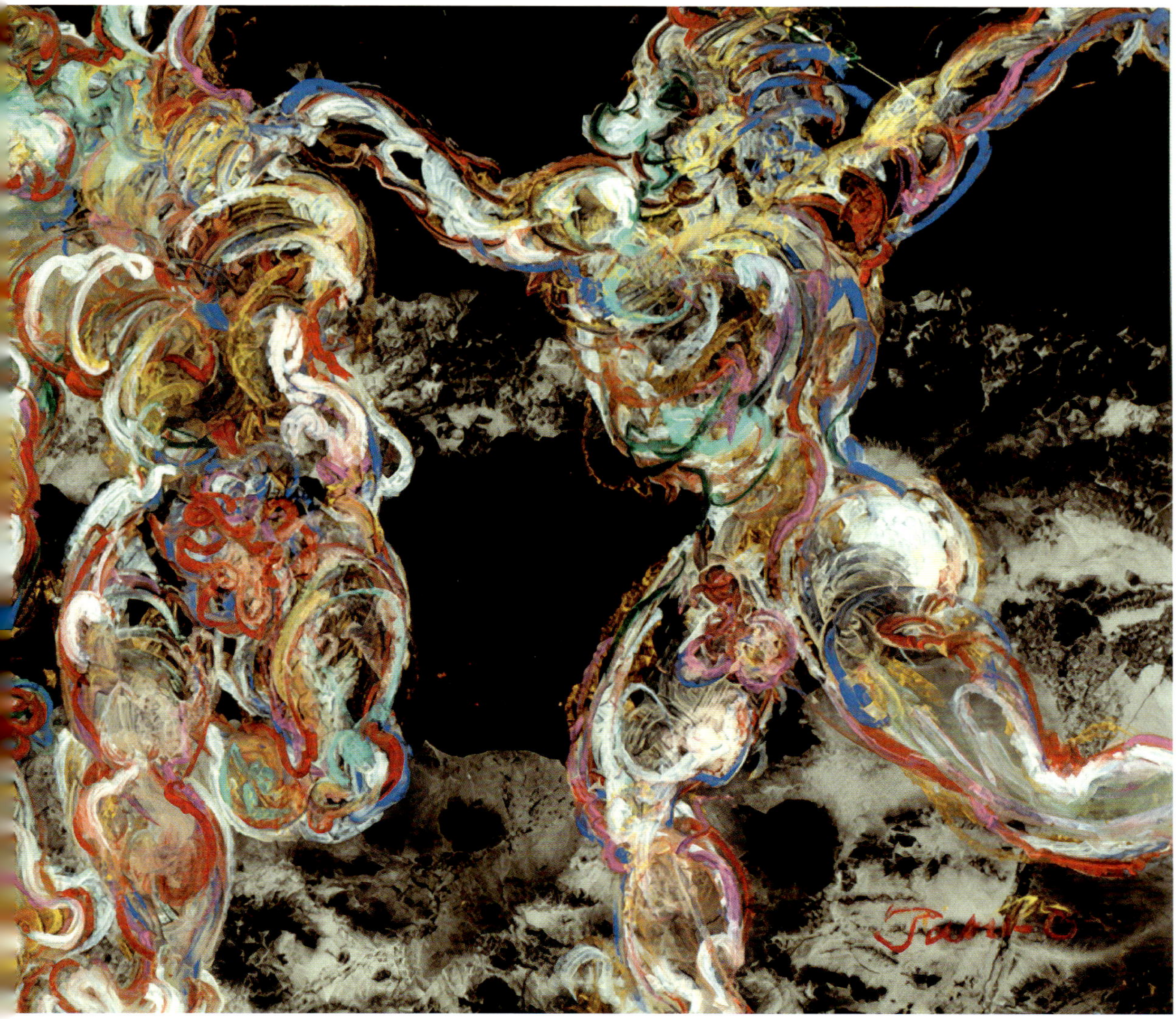

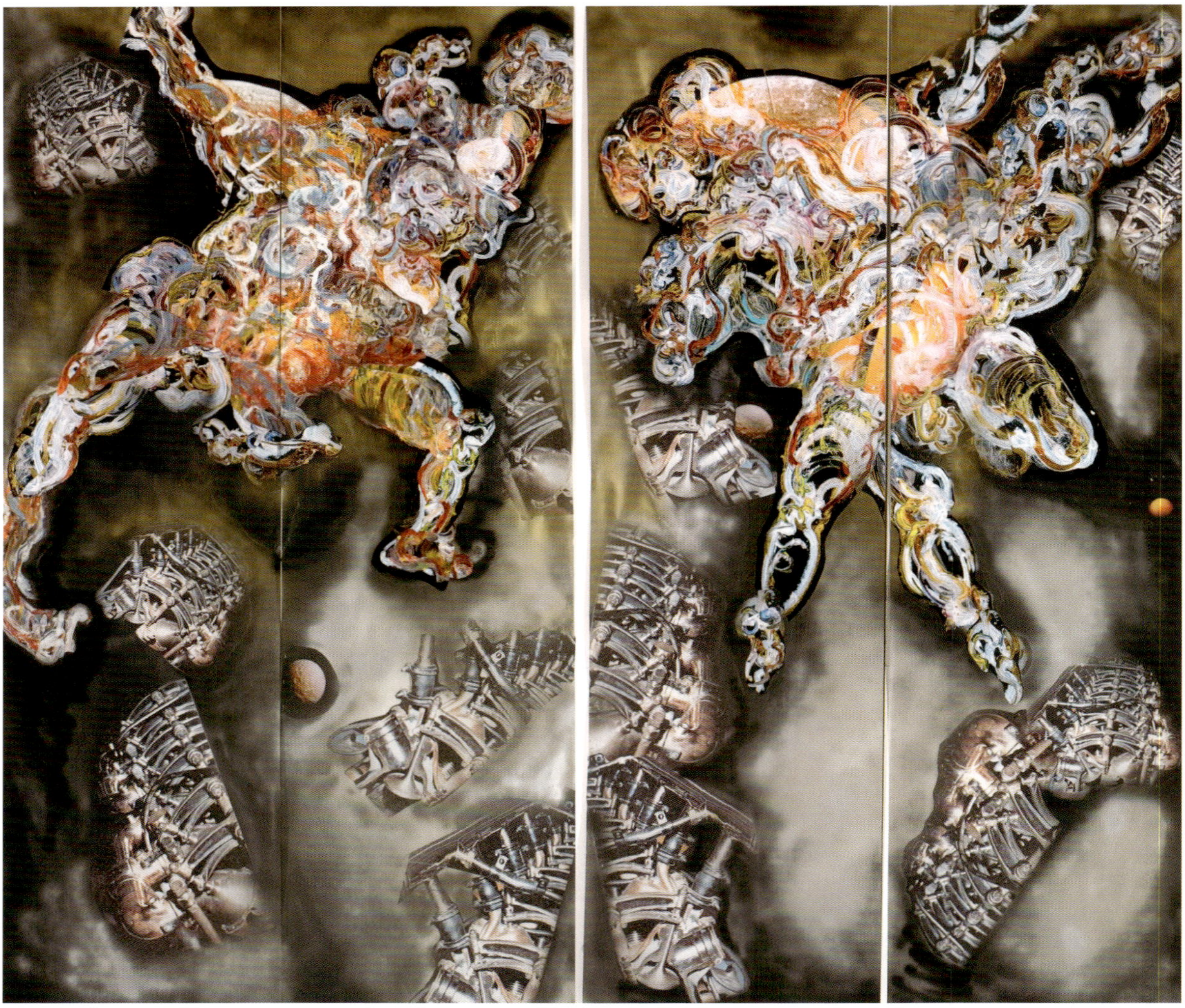

FROM *FATHOM*:
TANTRIC DANCE (2006)
Four background panels
Collage of computer
prints on mylar support
Overall dimensions:
144 x 168 in.
(365.8 x 426.7 cm.)

Figures and engines
dancing in space.

Opposite:
Junko's enounter
with the human figure
includes what she calls
"deformed babies."

DEFORMED BABIES

Studio Notebook, 1998

When I was invited to a special effects house on the outskirts of Hollywood, I saw two babies' figures—or to be precise, two deformed babies' figures—hanging on the wall. They were made to be used in a science-fiction

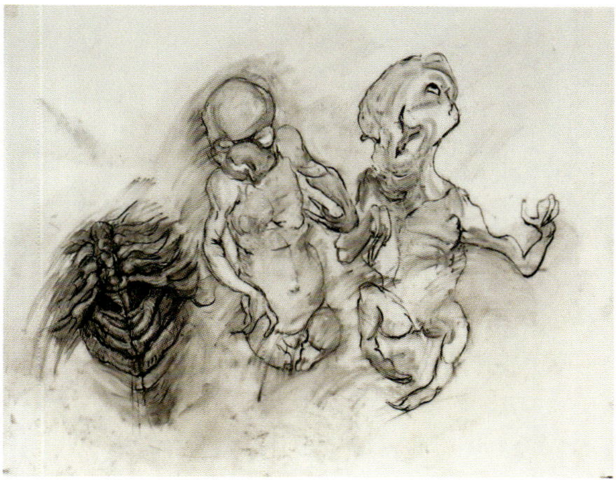

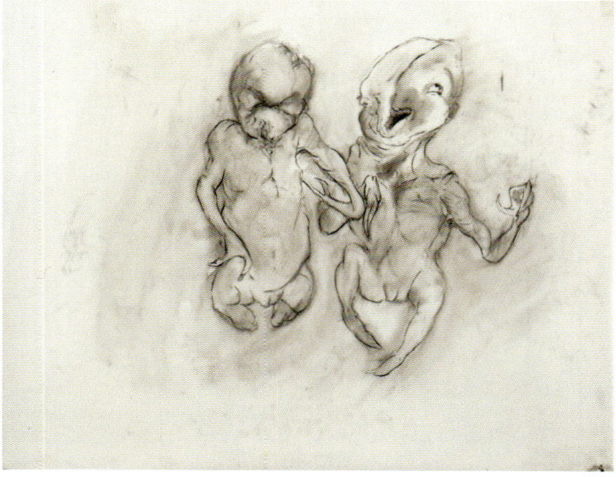

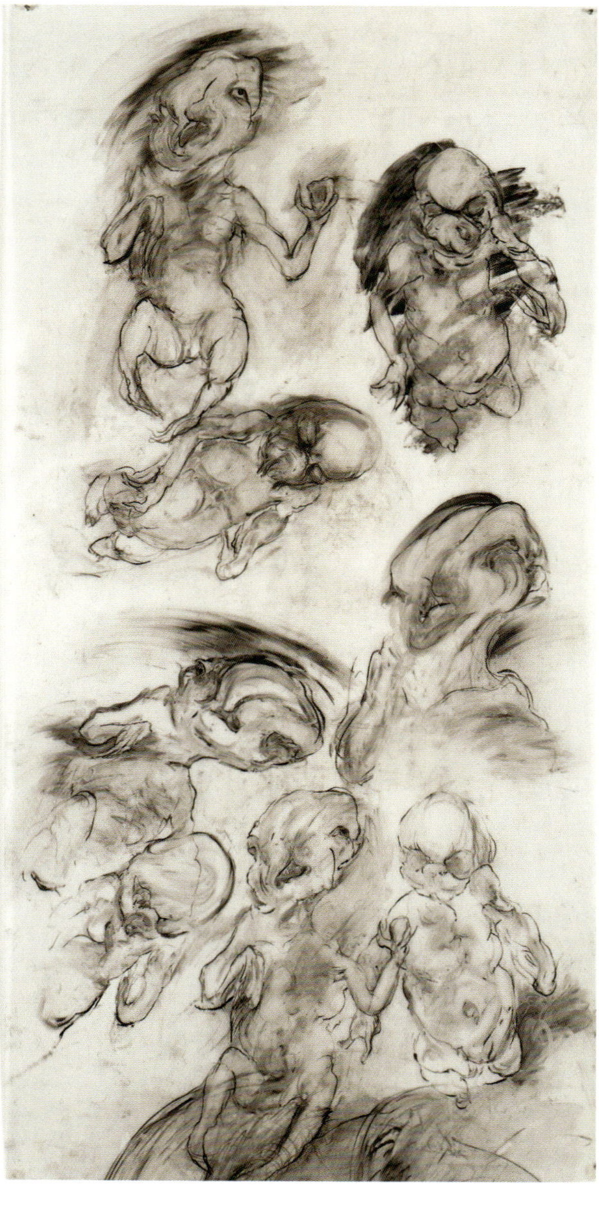

GIANT SKETCHBOOK
SACRED DEFORMITY (1999)
Charcoal on mylar
Left: 32.5 x 42 in.
(82.6 x 106.7 cm.)
Right: 83.25 x 42 in.
(211.5 x 106.7 cm.)

movie as characters of monstrous babies. They hit me so deeply at first sight that I expressed a desire to sketch them, which was warmly welcomed. After a few days of sketching them, they became important members of my circle of visitants. What hit me at that time was not pain, nor disgust, nor sympathy. I did not feel an urge to embrace them as I had felt for the horseshoe crab, the burls, or the painful broken engine from the first moment I encountered them. Instead, I fell into a serious silence and was overcome by a sense of the numinous.

These figures are myself—my true self. After all, we all are deformed in one way or another, and we all have monsters inside of us. But what really hit me was something deeper. The distant memory of an old story faintly revived in me, a story of Saint Christopher who carried people on his shoulders across the river. One stormy night a little boy appeared and asked Christopher to carry him to the other side of the river. He accepted, thinking that this child would be the easiest customer to carry. But when he started walking in the river the child on his shoulders became heavier and heavier. Finally as he approached the other shore the weight became unbearable. A voice came from atop his shoulders, "It is not strange that you feel heavy for you are carrying the whole world on your shoulders." Then Christopher realized that the little child he was carrying was Christ.

The image of your Self, when it appears to you, often takes the shape of a child and often it takes an imperfect shape of children or even of miserable animals. And yet when this image appears, it is a epiphany of the sacred and gives rise to a numinous emotion. In Christopher's story, the Self appeared first as a little child and only later did it become Christ. I saw some incredible potentialities, dignity, beauty, and strength in these vulnerable babies. When they develop through the process of individuation and self-realization, they will reveal the truth of themselves gradually. But at the same time, I was overwhelmed to have foreseen the enormous difficulties and heaviness of this child I have to carry: the cost of self-realization is high. It is a journey of suffering filled with dangers and the burden becomes heavier as time goes by. And yet the burden that made Christopher feel as if he were carrying the whole world had seemed to him at first the easiest thing to do. It is true: it feels that way. It was this strong sense of reality that made me silent.

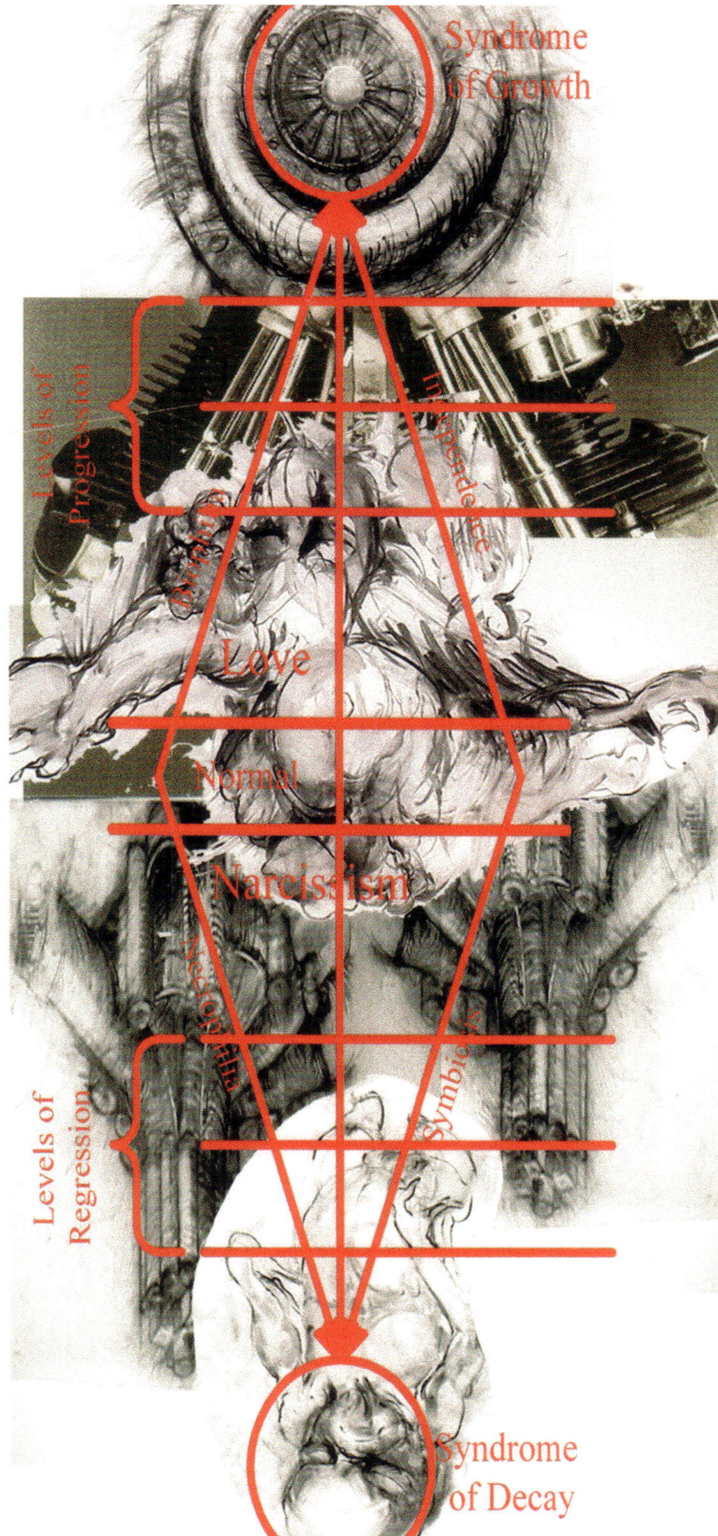

The most vicious and dangerous form of human orientation are: love of death, malignant narcissism, and symbiotic-incestuous fixation. The three orientatic when combined, form the "syndrome of decay," that which prompts men to destroy for the sake of destruction, and to hate for the sake of hate. In opposition ...is... the "syndrome of growth". This consists of love of life (as against love of death), and love of man (as against narcissim) and independence (as against symbiotic-incestuous fixation).

Sketchbook, Oct. 27, 1998
The redine diagram is by Erich Fromm: the image behind is Junko's.

See also *Birth* on page 42.

SECTION TWO
VISITANTS TRANSFORMING:
BURLS BECOMING HORRIFIC GODS

It is not possible to understand the real nature of Junko's encounter with her visitants without understanding how the visitants themselves develop in interaction with Junko's art. It is not merely that they reveal themselves in different contexts as we have seen in Section One above. In some cases, the visitants actually *transform* themselves from one thing into another.

This transformation is often "subterranean" in the sense that even Junko is not aware of it until it has already happened. And it is subterranean also in the sense that it is vegetative and slow: in the case I will show you, it took twenty years. It started in 1986 with Junko's first encounter with burls, and it continued in her sketchbooks and in her art through 2006, by which time the burls had been transformed into images of "horrific gods." But what are these?

Many images that seem grotesque, deformed, or monster-like appear in Junko's art. Some of them clearly take on the form of human figures or figures of deities. These images represent powers so vast that they cannot be confined in any normal form of life. They are the god figures which Joseph Campbell called "horrific" or "horrendous." They are destroyers of the world who burst out of the confines of all harmony, beauty, order, and ethical concern. They represent the side of nature that is irrational, unexplainable, cruel, terrifying, and destructive. They appear with offensive, frightening expressions on their faces, and they often carry threatening objects with them such as skulls, swords, and fire. In Japan, they are the *fudōmyōo*, the angry gods.

Opposite:
Sketchbook Page
Nov. 3, 1986

Oct. 24 '86
長い日々だった. start → 失敗

Nov. 3 '86
ねむられない夜がつづく. ~~berge~~ verge of tears だ 目をつぶると
私の前に巨大な壁のようなものがそびえる. もうまわり道
も抜け道もない. まっすぐに壁にぶつかるだけだ
絶対絶命の窮地に追いこまれる. 絵を描くしかない.
start するしかない 全身をいたみがかけめぐり. 身体が
くだけそうだ. しかし壁は demand する
「啓示を受けて神より使わされたものは. 精神の目の中に
神の姿をみる」というブレークの言葉を読みつづける
神は私の前に壁のようにそびえている. 絵をかくしかない

今朝. イメージがやって来た. ラオコーンのような figure が
画面の上部にあらわれる. 胸の中に涙がいっぱいだ—
— start しよう. 神の力が私と共にありますように

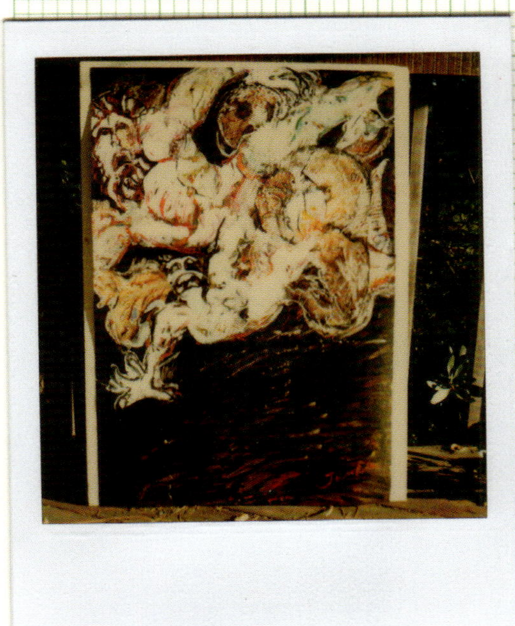

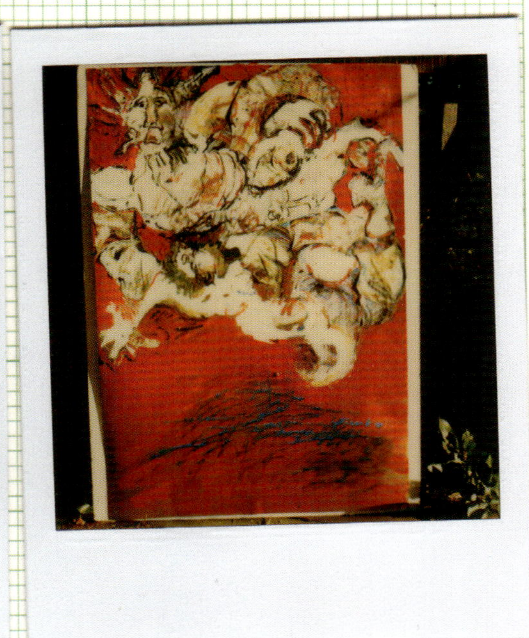

46 0700

K+E 10 X 10 TO THE INCH • 7 X 10 INCHES
KEUFFEL & ESSER CO. MADE IN U.S.A.

And yet they are not "devils," not evil, independent entities standing against the ultimate good. They are instead the wrathful aspect of the deity. Joseph Campbell talks about two aspects of meditation Buddhism in Tibet: "one peaceful and other wrathful. If you are clinging fiercely to your ego and its little temporal world of sorrows and joys, hanging on for dear life, it will be the wrathful aspect of the deity that appears. It will seem terrifying. But the moment your ego yields and gives up, in that same meditation Buddha is experienced as a bestower of bliss."[4] Those wrathful deities are indispensable visitants in Junko's art: they invest it with their prodigious energy, with dignity, and with a sense of awe. And yet it took many years for Junko to invite them fully into her world. It was only after the moment came, to borrow Campbell's words, "when the ego yields and gives up," that they appeared in Junko's pictorial space as the most dignified deities.

Here I present a sequence of images which traces the arrival of that "moment." Of course it was not really one moment. Most spiritual and psychological developments take many moments and many deep realizations which are only gradually assimilated and ultimately empower the self to break through the walls that confine it.

We can trace Junko's struggle toward that moment partly through the pages of her sketchbooks. But because she did not know where her path was leading, her writings were far from goal-oriented documents. To see her images and to read the fragments of her writing is like seeing leaves of grass in a field leveled by the wind and trying to figure out from where and how the wind blew.

Studio Notebook, 1986

Sleepless nights continued. When I closed my eyes, a huge wall loomed up in front of me. There is no way out, no escape route, nor is there any detour, I am driven into a corner. "When you are sent forth, God remains a presence for you; whoever walks in his mission always has God before him: the more faithful the fulfillment, the stronger and more constant the nearness." I keep reading Buber's book.[5] But today God stands as a huge wall before me. It seems that the only thing I have to do is to get down to work. I went to the studio and started working right on the paper. An image just like a figure from *Universe Moves and Humans Dance* appeared on the paper, and immediately it turned into a Laocoön-like figure. A big snake even came out and coiled and twisted its long body around the figure just as it did in Laocoön. Many study works continued: the images became more abstract, the figures kept changing their tone drastically towards something more demonic; innocent dancing is over. Something tremendously huge is behind the wall, something I had never expected to see, never wanted to see, is going to be revealed.

In 1987, Junko created her series, *Topological Deformations of the Cross* (twenty-three works), *Figures on Black Background* (forty-seven works), and *Meditations on Dance* (eight works), but burls in "Laocoön style" did not come up to the surface of her work until later.

Studio Notebook, 1987

The drawing of the horsehoe crab which I started a few days ago is expanding on and on to the point that it is my own body size. I feel I can finally afford the big space in my work; I feel my inner space is so vast and intense, I can expand my pictorial space to any size it wants. I will fulfill it with power and intensity from corner to corner. I have finally reached the experience of sublime space from inside to outside; I feel I am ready to receive anything into this space.

Something completely new is happening in me. I feel it very clearly, but how can I manifest that into any visible form? I followed my urge to draw

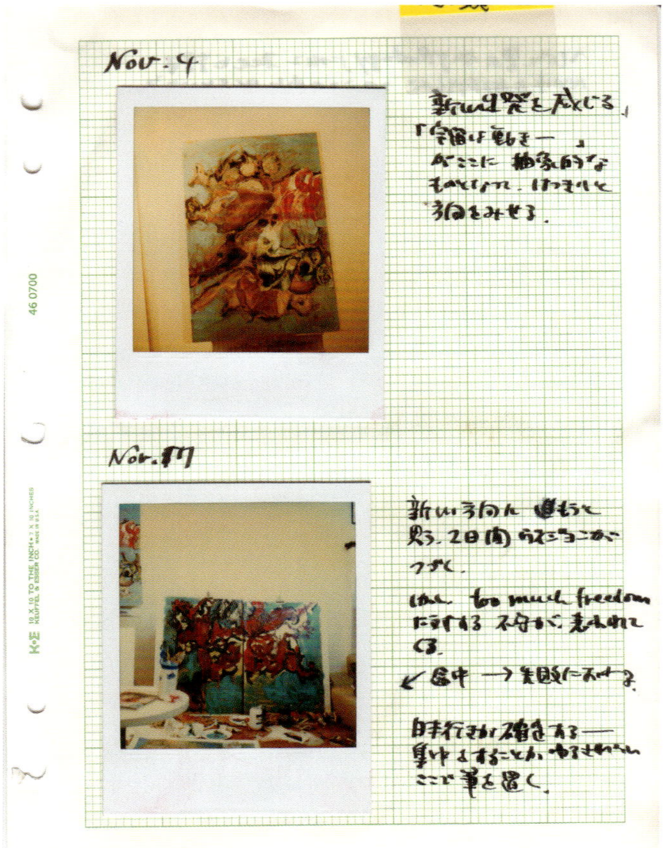

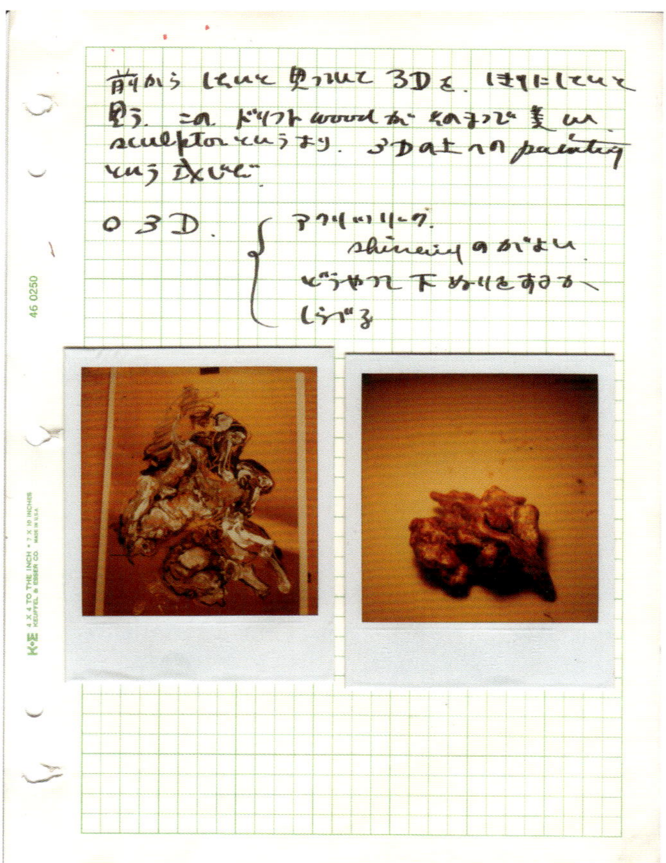

Top:
Sketchbook Page, 1986

Bottom:
Sketchbook Page, 1987

Opposite:
DANCE No. 1
SATURN AND ITS SIX MOONS (1984)
Mixed media on printed paper
27 x 20 in.
(68.6 x 51.4 cm.)

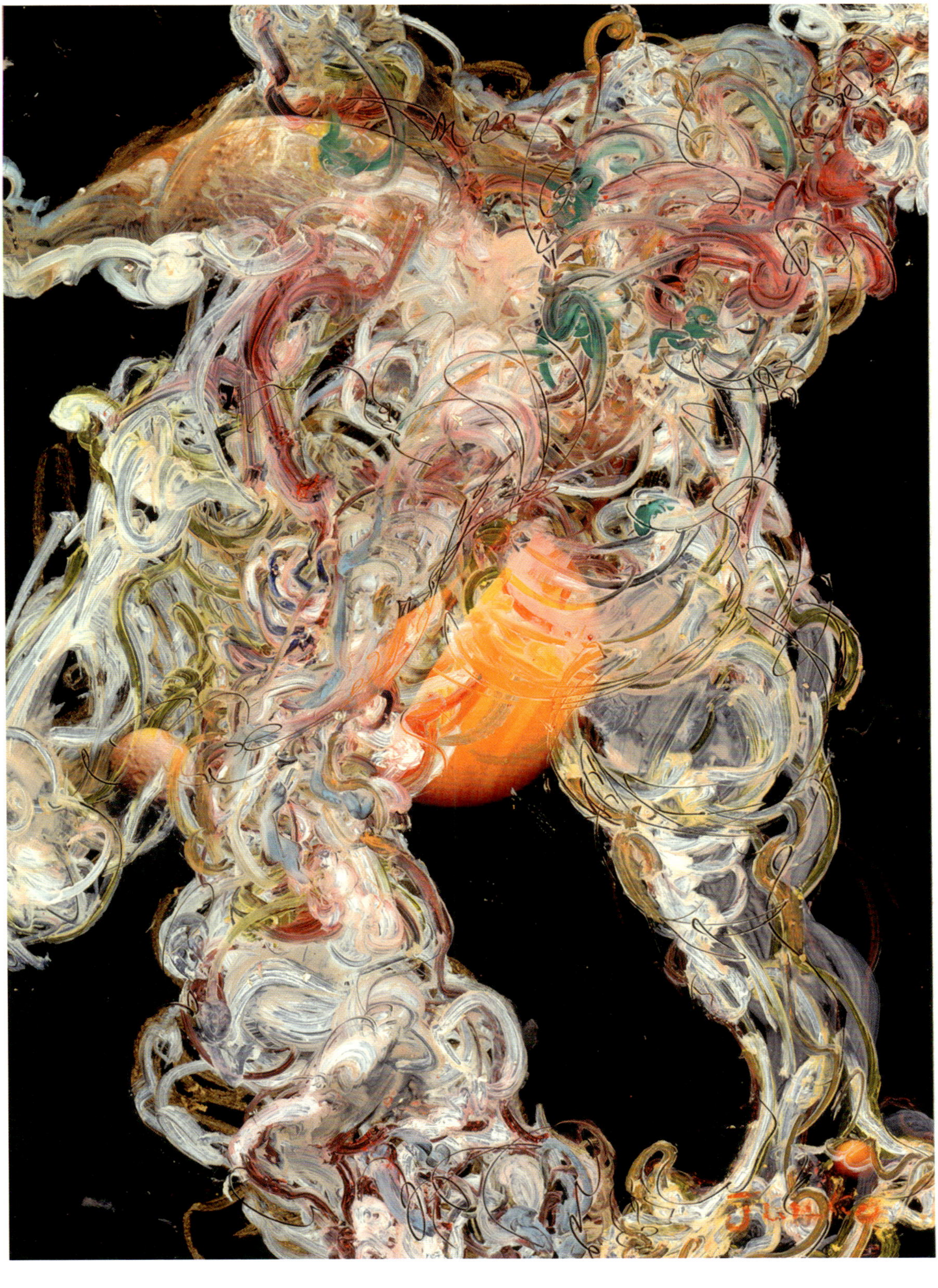

burls again, started a study piece on gold coated paper this time; it is just a very first step. This first step of a study work developed dramatically into a long series of works. In the year 1988, the series of *Burls*, twenty-one works, were created and five works of the *Giant Burls* series followed. All the works were on burls. Throughout those stormy days of creation, one desire, one prayer was always there: "not existence but the presence." It comes from Martin Buber[5]: "The presence and strength that man received through revelation—how do they become a content?"

Studio Notebook, 1989

Saturday and Sunday, I had to go to parties that wore me out. And many endless tasks which form the base of my life, tasks that cannot afford to be ignored, some of them I finished up and many I pushed away. Finally I am in my studio. I know exactly what I want to do. For more than two months, it has occupied the center of my mind, it has already started illuminating the studio. It is a big burl and a figure which looks exactly like the burl, they are aligned next to each other. The figure is a Tibetan deity—two images on one paper. I wanted to show exactly how one grows into the other. I wanted to do an objective drawing of the burl first, but the moment my hand touched the paper, the image immediately exploded.

Studio Notebook, 1989

All invitations for Christmas dinners were declined. Rafael gets all the credit for this. I am finally safe here in the studio on this Christmas day. I can go down to my inner world to be with God alone all day and all night. "Oh God!" I exclaimed in my mind, tears of delight and gratitude spring up my chest. "May the meaning of the encounter with the burl be realized through me to the world." — The Tibetan deity: it has been a few years since any material object has ceased to appear to be solid to me, so these heavy burls do appear to me as vibration and a kind of rhythm. I want to express that. What I want to draw is not existence, but Presence. I keep thinking, it can be reached only through inspiration. The study piece I did today caught this Presence. It is still very immature as a work, in fact it won't become a work as it is. And yet I already feel a premonition that this work will conjure up long generations of new works.

Junko's premonition came true two years after she wrote those words. Her *Tree Spirits in Gold* series, eight works, was completed in 1991. In that series, burls take on the shapes of human-monster-deity figures: powerful, horrific, and yet divine. In these works we can see the Laocoön-like figures which had appeared for the first time in her study piece five years earlier—but then they were only a sort of underground movement in her art. Everything she experienced during the following five-year period, during which time she created more than fifty works and countless study pieces concentrating on burls, not to mention 165 works on other themes—all of that experience contributed to the transformation of burls into horrific gods.

Series Statement "Tree Spirits in Gold," 1991

My recent series, *Tree Spirits in Gold,* I reached only after many years of encouraging the spirits imprisoned in roots under the ground, and in twisted burls, to come out into the world. I always saw those spirits as radiant, even though they were locked in the darkest places. I always grieved with them. I showed them in many series of works over the years and gradually I began to see light in the midst of their pain. Now I am astonished to see them free, standing strong and tall in the universe, starting to dance powerfully and exuberantly before me, bathed in a golden light.

This horrific deity appeared again as a ninth-century Esoteric Buddhist priest, as the figure of Kuukai on the stage of *FATHOM* in 2006. In the first scene of the dance he appeared as a sorcerer who went into the forest to train and cultivate himself leaping from tree to tree, eating rocks and stones to absorb their energies. And in the last scene, he appeared as a spirit of the mountain.[6]

You will notice that his figure in the final scene comes directly from *Tree Spirits in Gold, No. 1,* only his lower part has become the mountain itself (see pp. 82-83). That monstrous spirit is the figure of Kuukai: he appears as a deity of "the bestowal of bliss," a deity far beyond good and evil.

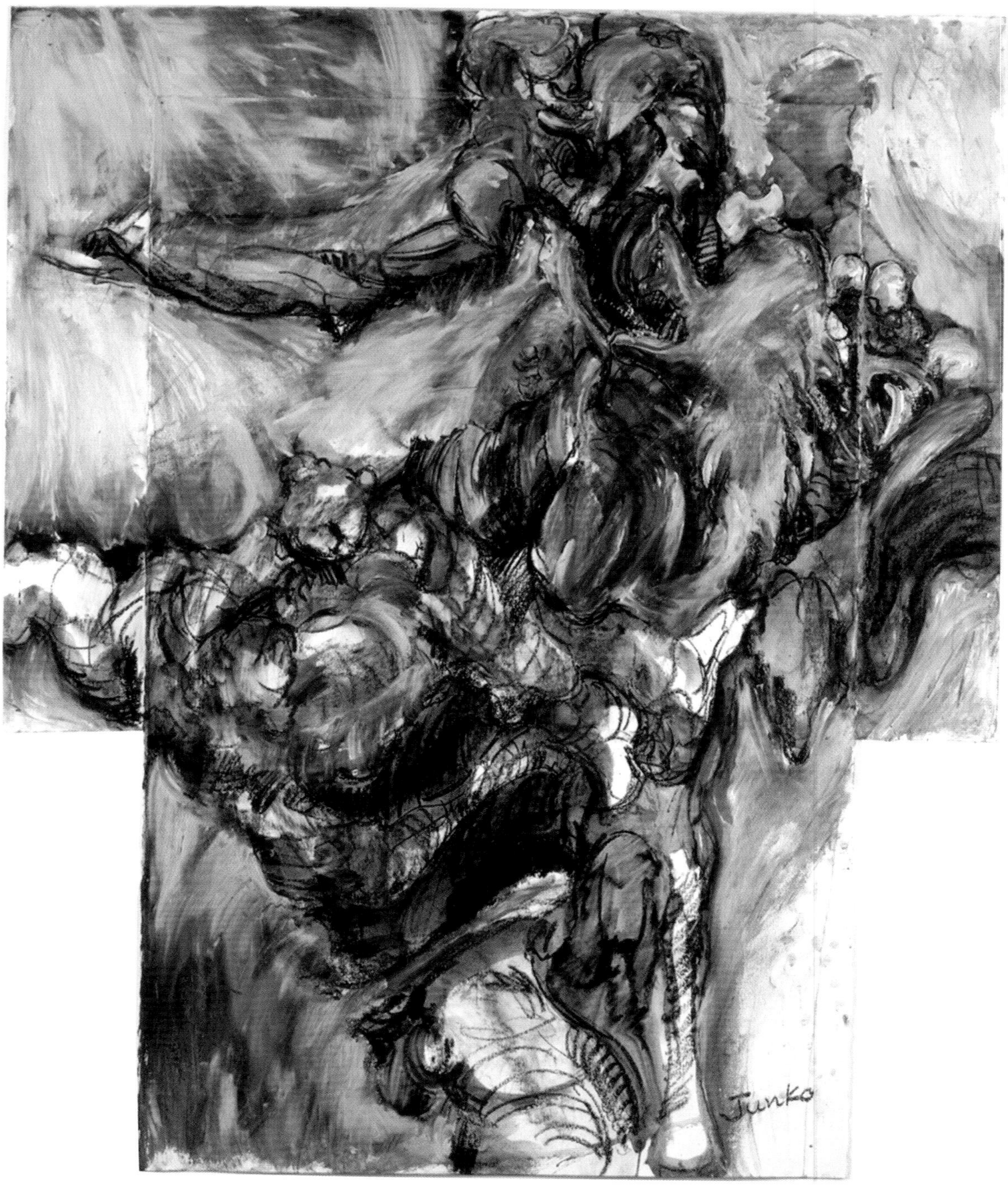
Junko

The intensity of Junko's relationship with the things she paints, the persistence with which she pursues her encounter with them over years and decades, and her development of the themes they represent, are part of what makes her centripetal art powerful. For Junko's own encounter with her visitants is a model, or a schema, which each of us may adapt in creating our own histories, our own encounters, our own realities. We must remember that the horseshoe crab which Junko actually sketched and painted is not the one she saw while she was visiting the aquarium (pg. 35), and the decanter which launched her *Requiem* series (pg. 56) was just an emblem of the bird—not the executed bird itself. Her act of responding to the particular visitants by creating her art is available to each and every one of us. For any given visitant, each viewer might create his own narrative. One hundred viewers might create one hundred different stories and we could not say which story told the truth. This is because artistic truth is something different from forensic truth, and the artwork is not a document of an experience: it is rather a response to the world and a deliberate construction of an aspect of reality.

Opposite:
GIANT BURLS
No. 2 (1989)
Acrylic and charcoal
on paper
60 x 56.25 in.
(152.4 x 142.9 cm.)

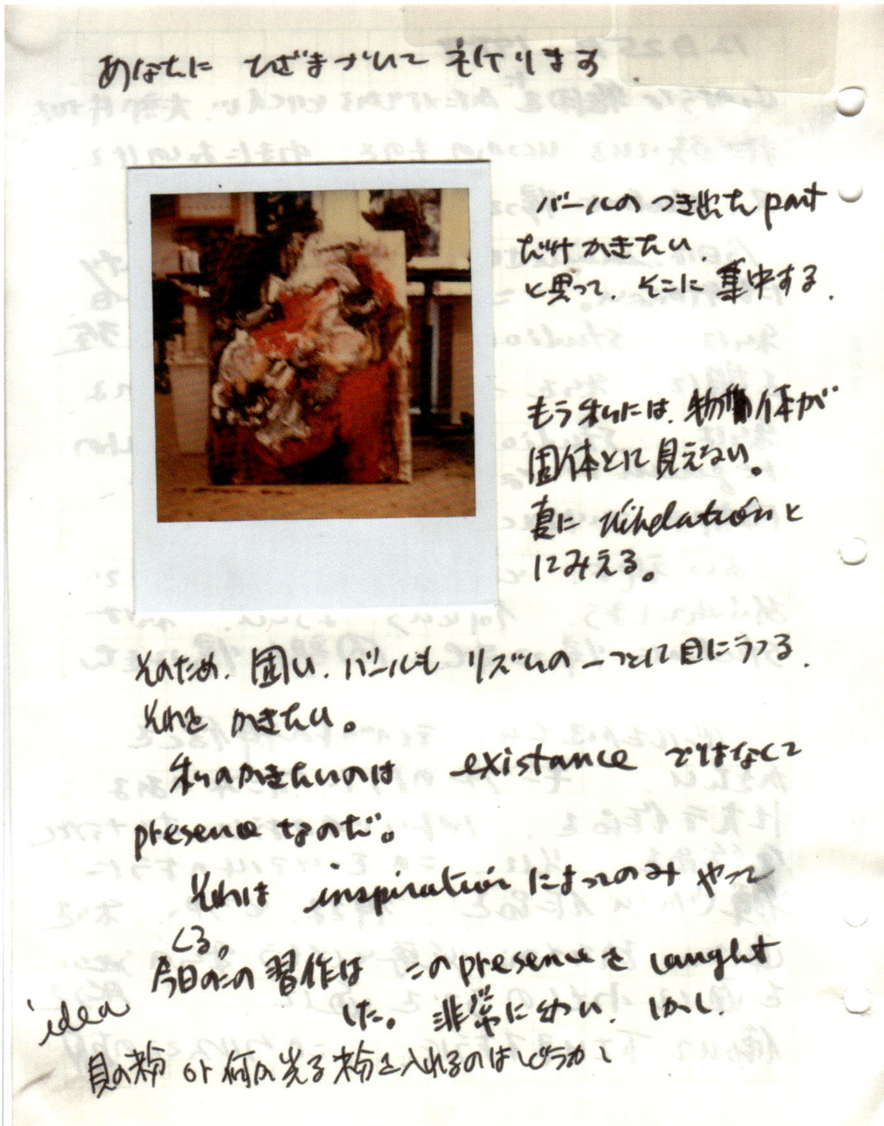

あなたに ひざまづいて 祈ります

バールのつき出た part
だけかきたい。
と思って、そこに集中する。

もう私には、物体が
固体として見えない。
更に vibration と
にみえる。

そのため、固い、バールも リズムの一つとして目にうつる。
それを かきたい。
私のかきたいのは existance ではなくて
presence なのだ。
それは inspiration によってのみ やって
くる。
今日の習作は この presence を caught
'idea' した。非常に弱い。しかし、
貝の粉 or 何か光る粉を入れるのはどうかし

Sketchbook Page,
Dec. 25, 1989

Opposite:
TREE SPIRITS IN GOLD
No. 1 (1991)
Acrylic and
charcoal on canvas
66 x 56 in.
(167.6 x 142.2 cm.)

Following pages:
FATHOM, MEDITATION
ON THE MOUNTAIN
(2006)
Collage of computer
prints on mylar
Four panels
Overall 12 ft. x 168 in.
(365.76 x 426.72 cm.)

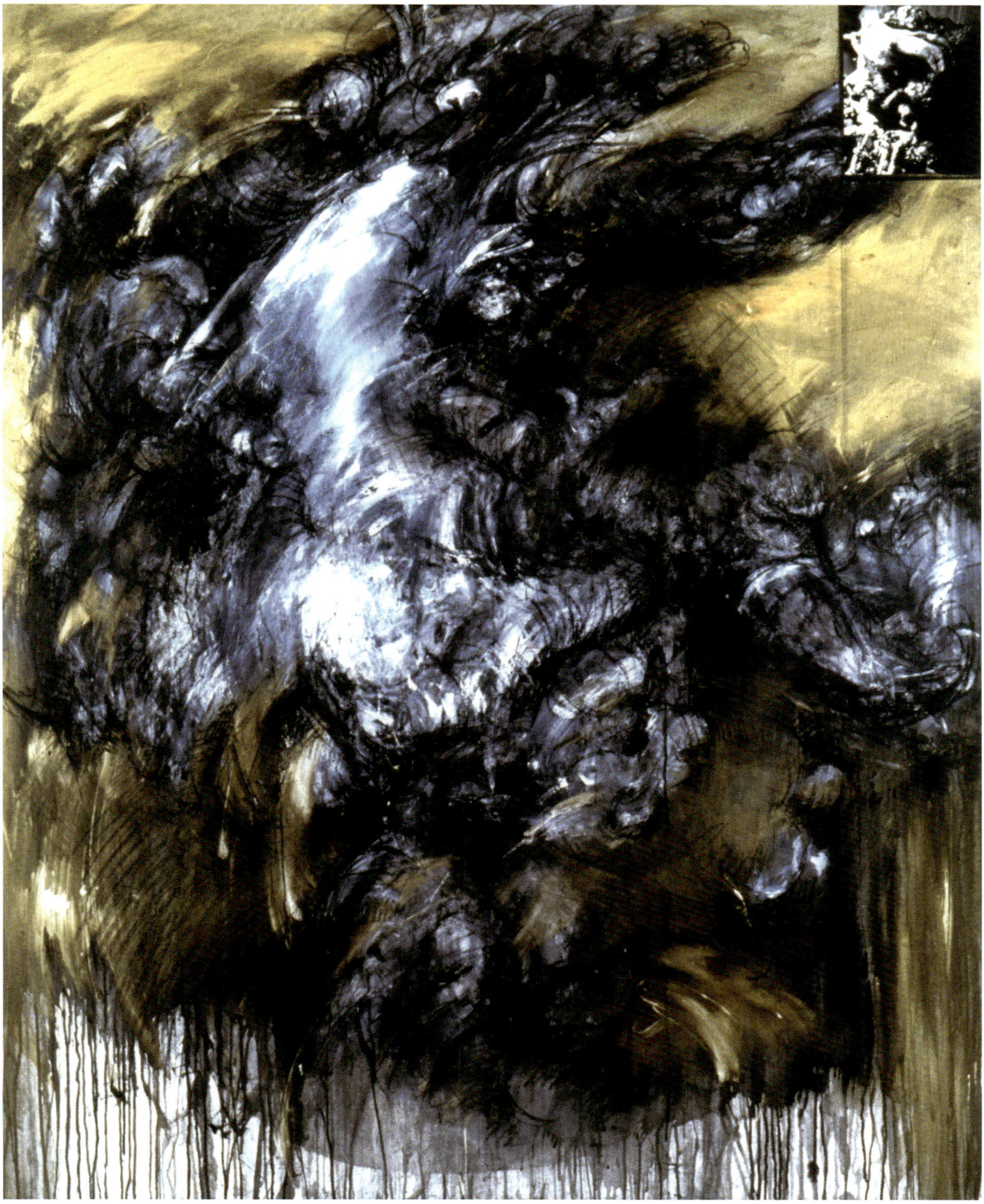

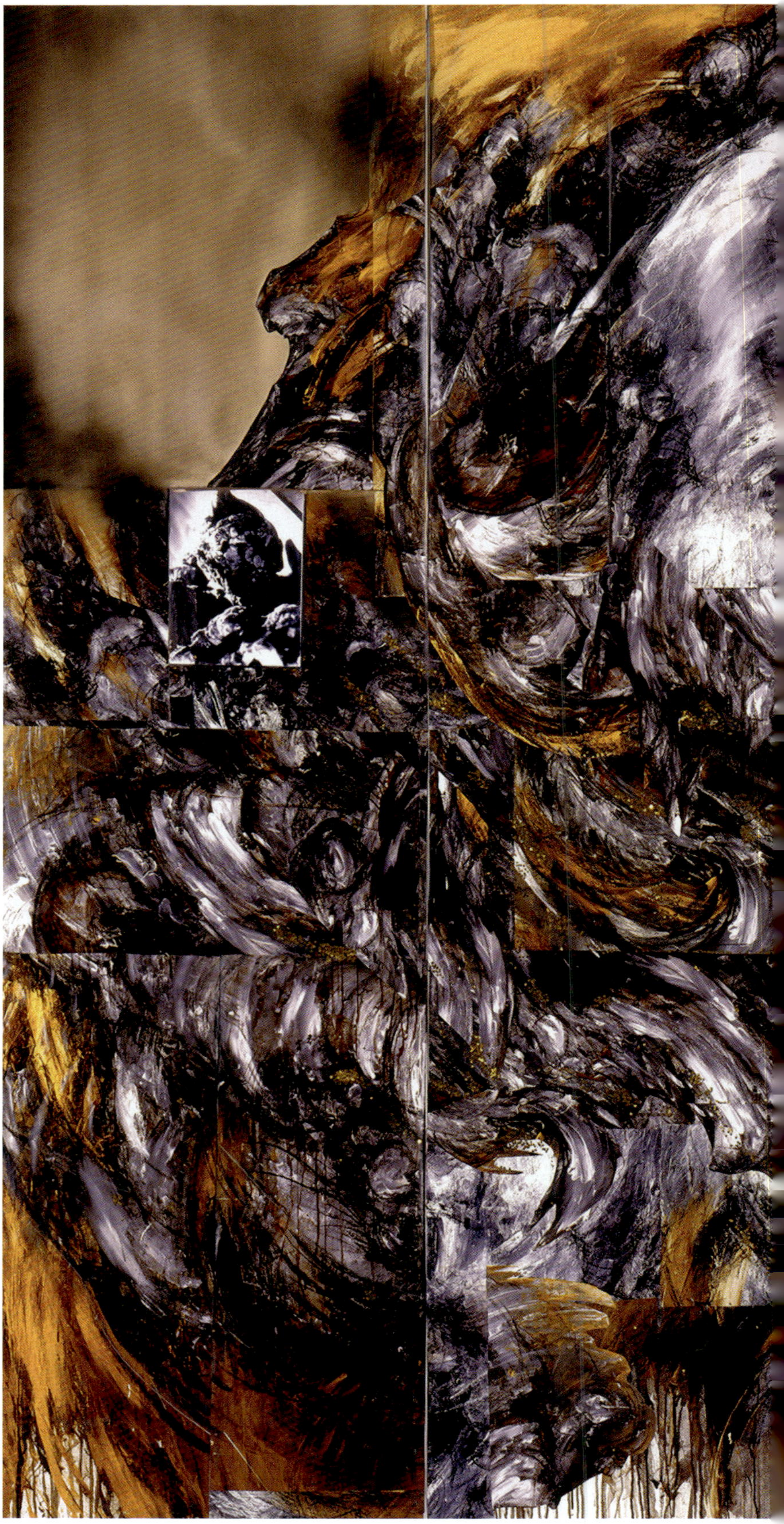

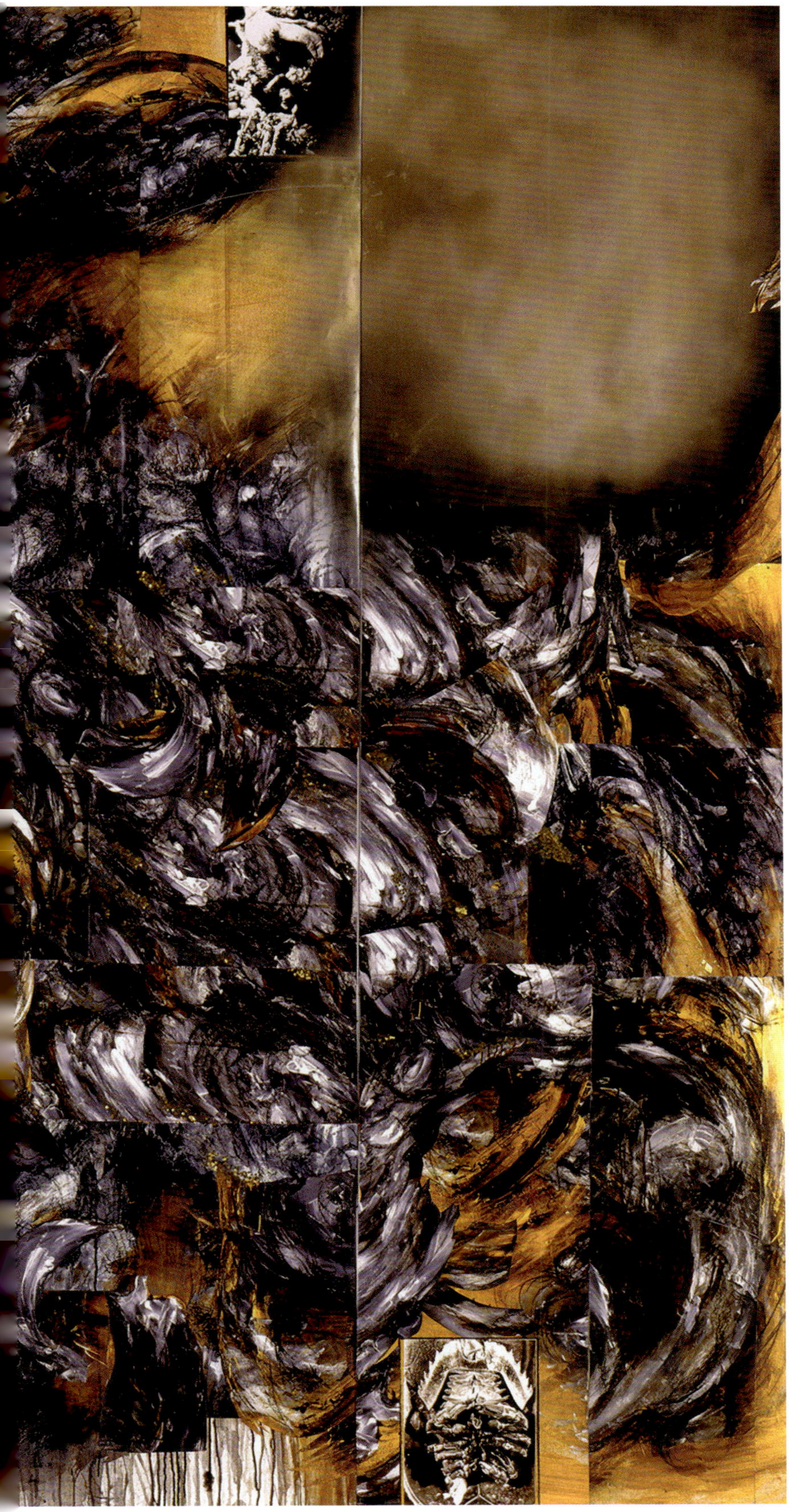

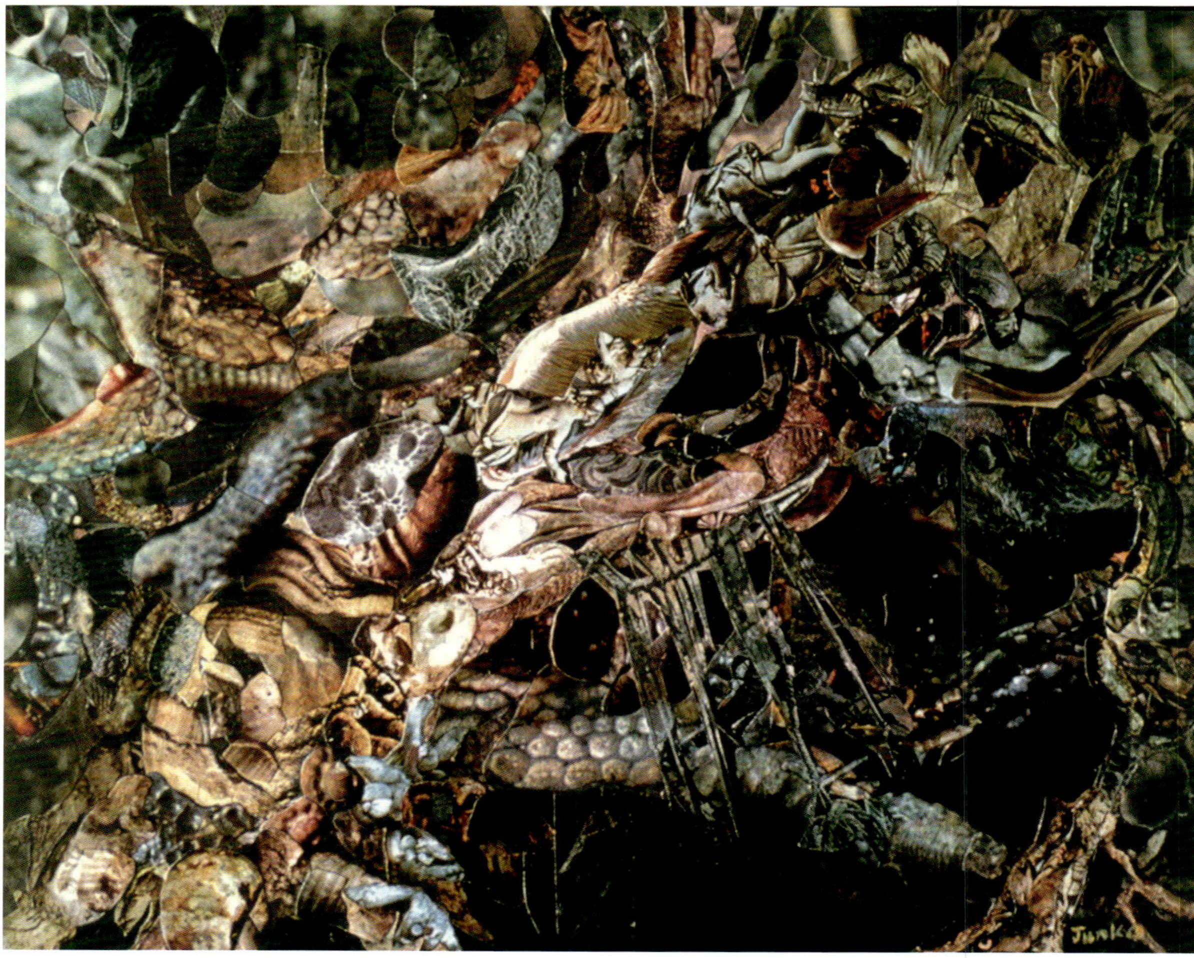

ROOT SERIES No. 9,
The Emergence of Buddha (1975)
Mixed media collage
on paper
84 x 82 in.
(213.4 x 106.7 cm.)

CHAPTER TWO
BIOGRAPHY AND CULTURAL INFLUENCES

JUNKO CHODOS (her maiden name was Takahashi) was born in 1939, in Tokyo, Japan. This was at the midpoint of the period between 1937, when Japan launched all-out aggression against China, and the 1941 attack on Pearl Harbor. It was a turbulent time throughout Japan. Junko's father was a doctor. Her mother was trained in Western classical music and taught piano—something which was very unusual for that time especially since she was descended from a family of doctors who had ministered to the Tokugawa Shogun[1] for seventeen generations. Junko's father came from a background of both Buddhism and Shinto—a traditional mixture in Japan. Her mother was raised in a Christian family, and was interested in things Western. Junko grew up in both of these religious and cultural traditions.

Junko was born in wartime and was just four years old when her family lived through the Allied bombings of Japan during World War II. Junko remembers being rushed into underground bomb shelters night after night; she remembers watching the carpet bombings of the big cities from the small village to which she had been evacuated; she remembers that the sky was almost obscured by the hundreds of B29 bombers and fighter planes that flew overhead in chessboard formation. She remembers that Shinjuku, now an urban center in Tokyo full of skyscrapers, was just a burnt field after the war, covered with debris all the way to the horizon. She remembers the underground hallways of a ruined subway station in Tokyo: filled with children who had lost their parents and their homes, some lying on the dirty concrete floor, some hobbling around like ghosts, hundreds of hundreds of them as far as her eyes could reach in the dim light that came through the broken windows, all of them in rags, skinny, covered with lice. The memory of their wide-open eyes and of the ominous silence of fear and desperation that tensely filled the entire hall never left her.

In that war almost three million Japanese had been killed, and another million were injured, sick, or severely malnourished. Junko saw death, cruelty, hunger, and desperation everywhere during the war and for many years after the war. At the same time she witnessed the miraculous postwar healing, the intense vitality of cities being rebuilt, and she saw a new life rising from the ashes. These experiences of total destruction and vibrant reconstruction both became formative elements in Junko's personality and in her art.

By 1942, at the peak of its imperial expansion, Japan had become the first and only non-white, non-Christian imperial power. Its "Greater East Asia Co-Prosperity Sphere" included Manchuria, China, Korea, the Dutch East Indies, French Indochina, Burma, Malaya, and Hong Kong. Inside of Japan, a rampant fascistic totalitarianism escalated and raged. The essential characteristic of totalitarianism is hatred of what is different and a determination to eradicate it. Even as a child, Junko feared this totalitarianism almost more than she feared the enemy attacks.

During this dark period of time Junko, who was just four years old, happened upon a bird which had just been killed. She and her family had left Tokyo to escape the bombing, and they stayed at a hospital that her uncle owned. Because of the spread of epidemics, the rest of Junko's family was quarantined in special wards of the hospital and she stayed alone with her uncle's family in the hospital's living quarters. Death was everywhere: sirens would sound day and night, people would huddle in bomb shelters, and many died of the epidemics quietly in the hospital wards. One day Junko walked into the living room and saw a chicken that her uncle had just slaughtered. Its head had been chopped off and it had been hung upside down from the ceiling, its blood dripping into a bucket which had been carefully placed on the straw-matted floor below.

Opposite:
REQUIEM FOR AN EXECUTED BIRD, No. 13 (1991)
Mixed media on paper
40 x 32 in.
(101.6 x 81.3 cm.)

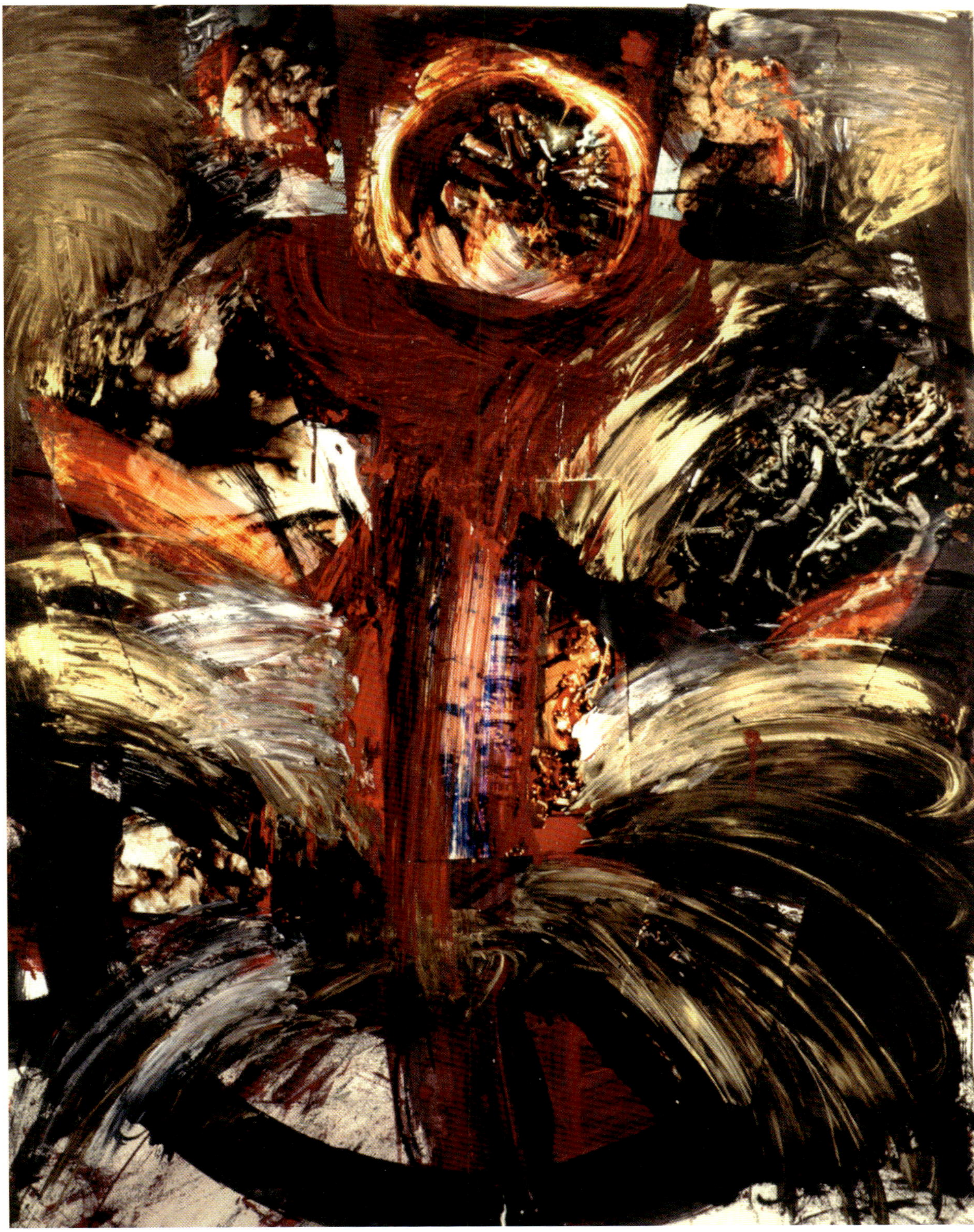

For Junko, this scene concretized all the horrors of war and fascism. To the little girl it was an execution, a punishment. This bird had to suffer just because it wanted to fly, just because it wanted to be as a bird should be. From that day on she had an intense phobia of birds, which lasted nearly half a century.

This trauma formed the base of important themes with which Junko had to struggle all her life: the abuse of authority, the repression of freedom, the taboo against being who you are. When she experienced this little incident she was too young to articulate those themes intellectually. But quite early, and long before she ever dreamed of emigrating to America, she began to think of herself as a "spiritual refugee." The conflict between the tribalistic, totalitarian tendencies of society and Junko's urge to individuate and her strong empathy with those who had to repress their own aspiration for freedom—with all those who feel deeply their own vulnerability—became important aspects of her "centripetal" art.

One year after the war was over, in 1946, Junko was accepted into the *Gakushûin* elementary school. This was the Imperial School which formerly only Japan's royal family and the aristocracy had been allowed to attend. It was immediately after General MacArthur democratized Japan's aristocratic system and institutions and just after the emperor made the historical declaration that he was a human being and not God—as he had been believed to be during the war under the state religion, Shinto. Thus the authority of the emperor system, which had become the core of Japan's fascistic totalitarian movement, was destroyed and eradicated from the *Gakushûin's* educational system. But the ancient spirit of nature worship that hovered over Japan for thousands of years, since long before Shinto became the state religion during the Meiji period, was still there, moving in the ancient forests. Junko was a member of the first generation of "commoners" allowed to attend the *Gakushûin*, and there she was trained in many of Japan's oldest traditions: how to walk, how to bow, how to speak in the ancient language. And there she also witnessed and lived through repressive totalitarian tendencies. They were more subtle and hidden than they had been during the war but her suffering and the difficulty she faced in trying to be herself deepened. Even though she became an honor student at *Gakushûin* she had to leave it after staying there for seven years. She transferred to *Seijôgakuen*, a school known for its liberal tendencies, and she was enrolled there until she graduated from high school.

Junko was already creating art as a child during the war—using the cardboard medicine boxes her father discarded because paper was too scarce. When she was in her early teens she would often work all through the night in her small upstairs room, passionately and secretly. When she was thirteen years old, in 1952, the American postwar occupation finally ended and Western things—which had been forbidden up till that point—were allowed into Japan. It was then that Junko saw reproductions of some works by Paul Klee for the first time.

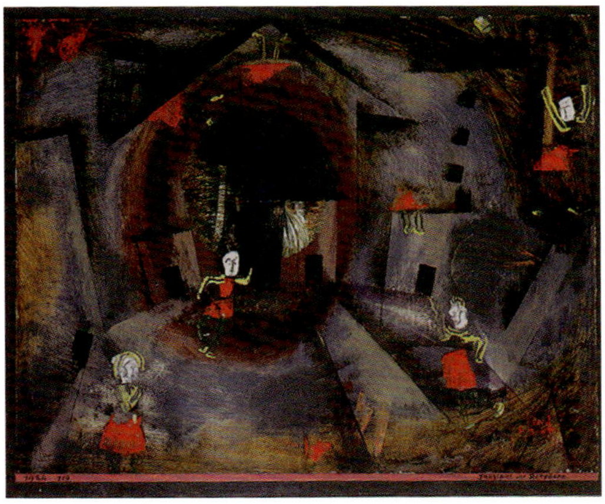

PAUL KLEE, *DANCEPLAY OF THE RED SKIRTS*

She saw only tiny reproductions and the prints were poor, but they changed her life. The painting she remembers best was titled *Danceplay of the Red Skirts*. It is a painting of many women in red skirts scattered all over the paper. Each woman is not even a complete figure—they are almost like fragments. Then you suddenly realize that these women are just reflections of one woman. She is alone in a little town at night. Behind her there is a big dark circle —it looks like an empty vacuum, a black hole—and this circle looks like it is spinning in the center of the work. In fact the whole town looks as if it is spinning—just like the image you see when you look through a kaleidoscope. The whole space looks like the stage of a theater: isolated from the world and from the air we breathe. Seeing this work, Junko was greatly moved. Later on she wrote about it.

From Lecture "Transcending Ethnicity: The Creative Process," Long Beach Museum, California, 1996

Strong feelings swept over me when I saw this painting. Using a vocabulary I know now, I can say this was the first time I saw the existential abyss in a painting. I identified deeply with the sadness, fear, and suffering which the work rather quietly expressed, and I saw my own suffering more clearly and sharply than ever before. And yet suddenly, I noticed that my suffering had been shifted already towards the much larger context of human suffering, the suffering that leads to a universal meaning that I had not known before I saw this work. It was dark and solemn; I was stricken by a sense of awe.

I was thirteen years old at that time, suffering with the strong feeling that I was walking along a ridge every day and night. On one side of the ridge there was the dark swamp where I grew up, a place of destruction and slaughter without meaning, a dark empty vacuum; if I stepped into that swamp, I would be sucked in. And on the other side of the ridge, there were a bunch of people—just about everyone who surrounded me at that time—all complacent and confident, giving me suggestions and advice which secretly I detested. This painting was quietly telling me that here is a man who chose his own path: a difficult narrow ridge, on one side of which is the depth of nihilism, and on the other side is the deep swamp of complacency. Klee was walking alone on this narrow ridge. I was humbled. I think I could say that I was awakened to the real meaning of my own suffering. I determined that I would walk on this narrow ridge myself, and that I would carry this suffering all through my life. This whole process of thought happened inside of a few seconds when I saw this painting. This painting abated in me all desire to commit suicide; when I saw it, I determined to live. This is the painting that made me realize that I was destined to be an artist.

It was during this same period, when she was fourteen years old, that she stumbled across a book of Rilke's poetry in the shelves of her junior high school library.

From Mansion of the Motoyasu, 1999

The moment I touched Rilke's words all my turmoil, chaos, pain, and groans aligned themselves in a lightning flash to point in one certain direction. The whole thing happened in one second, there was no need to think or examine it. The direction they all pointed to now was the world I had been aware of when I was painting, and yet I could not define it until I touched these poems of Rilke. It was the world of my art that had not yet been fully realized. I was fourteen years old and I was a very unhappy child. Whatever happened in the daytime, I was painting every night in my little room sitting at the desk at the window facing east. I sensed that beyond my stormy emotions, which I was dealing with through creating art, there was a world—the world of nihilism: human beings are thrown into this world without having any purpose or any reasonable structure to rely on. I saw it with a strong sense of reality.

But when I went further there was another world, filled with an absolute quietness, with a pure solitude which is different from the feeling of nihilistic isolation. That world is filled with meaning instead of being empty as the nihilistic world is. And then, I saw another completely different space beyond it; it took a transparent architectural form, made of complicated layers in tiers, solid and yet luminous. Filled with awe I called it the *sacred cathedral*. I saw it rising up in the eastern night sky from my window, but only very rarely. Rilke suddenly talked to me from that cathedral;

> *Who, if I cried, would hear me among the angelic orders? And even if one of them suddenly pressed me against his heart, I should fade in the strength of his stronger existence. For Beauty's nothing but the beginnings of Terror we're still just able to bear, and we adore it so because it serenely disdains to destroy us. Every angel is terrible.*

These words shook me violently because I realized that Rilke pointed to another world even further beyond the sacred cathedral. This is what Rilke called "terror"! If you see that world with your naked eyes, you will be destroyed and you will vanish. There is no other word for it than "terror." And yet this is a dazzlingly brilliant space, so bright that we can recognize it only as darkness. One cannot bear it. Rilke was pointing out this brilliant space to me.

This passage might be read as a memoir of an experience of literature, of art, or even as an early form of religious experience. But in fact it is a memoir of an early form of centripetal experience. In Junko's world, art, religion, literature, and philosophy are all intertwined. Each element—the transparent architectural form in the sky which can be understood as a symbolic figure of the divine, the world of Terror as the gateway to mystical irony, the journey through nihilism as the base of encounter with the divine—all are tightly connected to each other. All of these elements are developed later on and they form the solid base of Centripetal Art.

All those elements were strong in Junko but strong as they were, the people around her were oblivious to them. All through school she felt distinctly isolated. She encountered Klee and Rilke while she lived at home with her parents and her two sisters, one of whom is two years older than she and the other is one year younger. In accordance with their mother's desire, Junko's two sisters had already established glorious professional careers performing throughout Japan as child prodigy concert pianists. Junko refused to allow her life to be owned by her mother's desire and that was viewed as incompetence and rebelliousness. Junko became the "black sheep" of the family. Furthermore, there was an extremely inward, mystical, meditative quality to her personality as well as some developing psychic tendency. These became distinguishing characteristics of her art and her personality later on, but at that time they were seen as *laziness*. Furthermore the fact that at fourteen years of age she still had not established her own career was considered an undoubted sign of *failure*. In her mother's community of music professionals, Junko was always referred to as "the daughter who is not doing anything." At home with three

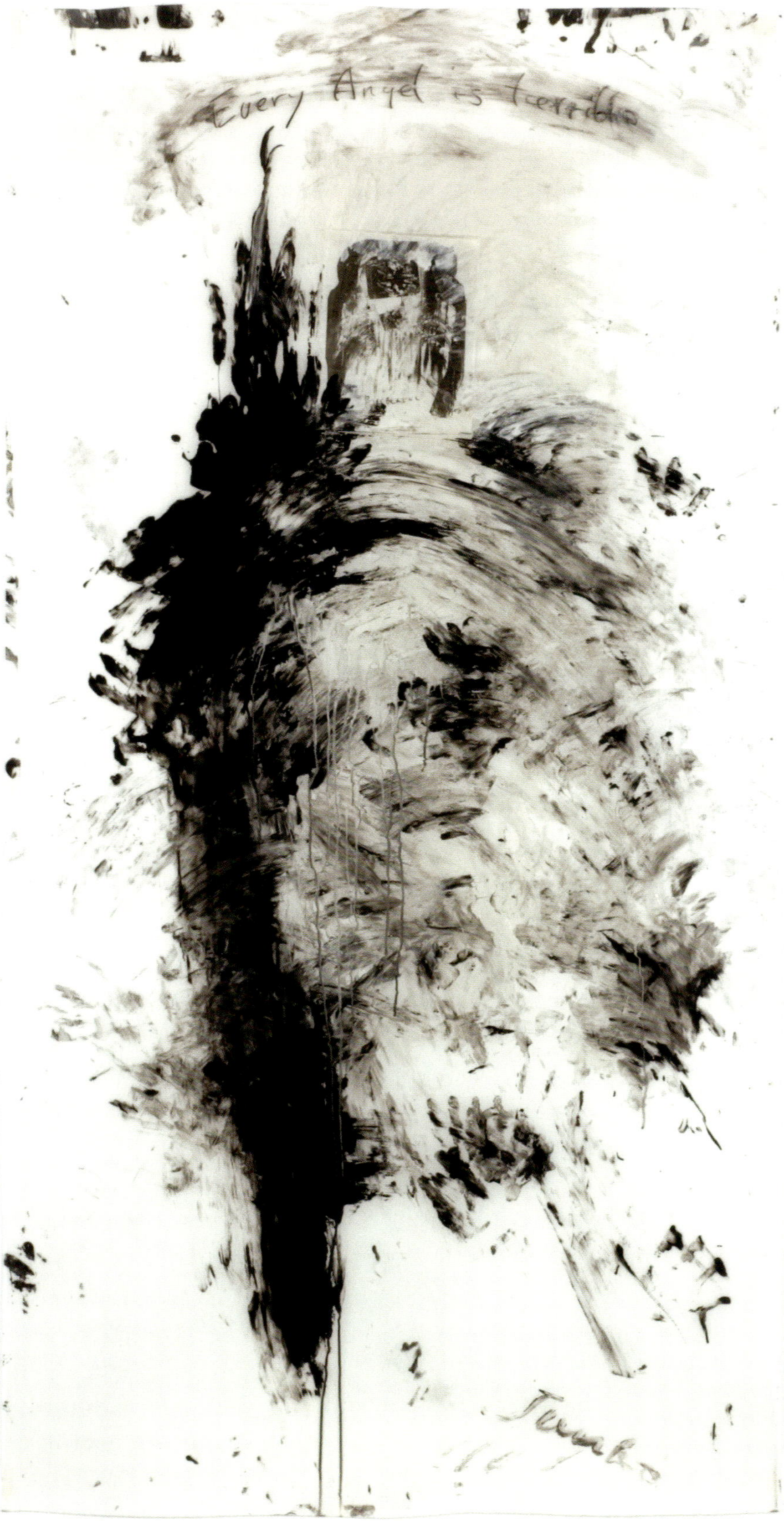

INDIVIDUATION JOURNAL, No. 1: RILKE (1995) "EVERY ANGEL IS TERRIBLE"
Acrylic and sumi ink on mylar
80 x 42 in.
(203.2 x 106.7 cm.)

grand pianos, filled with the sounds of young musicians practicing and rehearsing on pianos, violins, violas, and cellos, Junko's sense of isolation from the world was greatly reinforced.

At this time, after she finished middle school, Junko started attending a Christian church. This was unusual for a young Japanese girl in those days because Christianity was not a mainstream religion in Japan. Even after the American occupation, fewer than one percent of Japanese identified themselves as "Christian." The church Junko started attending was called the Liberal Christian Church, and it was not connected to any other missionary church in Japan. The founder was a prominent scholar, Shigetaro Akashi. Long before the war he had translated Greek mythology and some of the works of Friedrich Schiller into Japanese for the first time, believing that it was important to understand Christianity in the light of comparative mythology and that Japan should become familiar with Western thought in general. His wife too was well-known in the congregation and in the wider community in her own right, as a highly educated and capable woman and as one of the first women who graduated from university in Japan.

The congregation was composed of intellectuals who had been influenced by Akashi and who had worked with him. They all wanted to contribute to building a modern Japan in the Meiji period, before and after WWII, by introducing and spreading Christianity and other Western thoughts. Many of them were over eighty years old by then. Their students were part of the congregation, too—the next generation of professors, along with their young students, and other professionals, all of whom shared these aspirations of the older generation. Junko was by far the youngest but she felt excited to be there, and she started absorbing new thoughts enthusiastically.

During the war, while Shinto was the state religion, all Christian churches were required to register with the state as one Christian group outside of the state religion. But Akashi insisted that his church was independent from the others and for this he was thrown into prison for a period. Ultimately Akashi's church survived and became the only one in Japan to be recognized by the American Unitarian Church.

After attending his church for three years, and becoming involved in its activities, when she was eighteen years old Junko married Akashi's second son. Akashi's modest residence stood on the church grounds and Junko lived there with her husband and her parents-in-law.

Akashi was already very old and it was his older son, Junko's brother-in-law, who was designated to succeed to the minister's position. But Junko was still seen as a "Bride of the Church." In this role, not only did Junko attend regular services that often included sermons by guest professors from many different religious groups, she also attended lectures which the church sponsored. She was responsible for other operational and programmatic requirements of the congregation and she participated in all the church functions: attending funerals as her father-in-law's representative, serving meals, and helping to entertain the guests of her father-in-law and his sons. In this way she met many prominent religious thinkers who came to visit their home, some of them from divinity schools and churches in America, and she absorbed Akashi's open-minded attitudes toward religion.

One important role she accepted was teaching and managing the church's Sunday School. She took this work very seriously. The church happened to be located on the borderline of two economically different neighborhoods: one was middle- and upper-class and the other was dirt poor and most of those residents depended on welfare. The congregation of the church consisted almost exclusively of the middle class, and only six students were enrolled in the Sunday School, all of them children of university professors. Junko decided to reach out to the poor district.

From Memoir, 2005

The only time I could talk to the parents of the children was early in the morning, before they went out to their physical labor and it was still dark. Sometimes I visited them and saw how they lived. I invited them to church and the children started coming to Sunday School. My brother-in-law, the minister, assured us that we would have complete freedom to design the Sunday School programs, but there was no budget so all the activities in that church had to be run "out of pocket." We did singing, painting, story-telling, and writing scripts for a play. The only conditions we put on the script-writing were that every one of the children had to have some part in the play any time he or she attended the church, and that every part be a "speaking part" with at least one word to say, even if it was only "hello" or "yes" in unison. This made it clear that every part had to be considered equally important and that every child had responsibility for the success of the play. The children practiced and performed in the tiny theater that we set up in church. They did astonishingly well. Enrollment at the Sunday School increased drastically: four years later, there were forty-six students attending: no one stopped attending, they all just brought their new friends. At six o'clock every Sunday morning the children gathered in the churchyard: they could not wait for eight o'clock which they knew was the time I would open the church door for them. One mother visited the church and asked me if her son was telling the truth when he said that he was playing some very important part in the play in church. She could not believe such a thing was happening. She told me her son had always been a trouble-maker in school. But her son and all the other boys and girls, in spite of big age differences, brought off the whole thing remarkably.

I saw many dark things in them: the pain of not being respected, of low self-esteem, of carrying shame and fear in them, and poverty was a big part of it in their cases. I identified with their pain even though poverty did not play a major part in my own life—except for the brutal poverty during the war and just after, poverty which everyone had to go through if he survived. I was struggling with my own problems. "Junko is the shame of the family," the words I heard throughout my childhood, were ringing in my head still then. This Sunday School experience gave me a most serious opportunity for healing.

In her father-in-law's household she came to view religion, wide study, and conscious thinking as inextricably associated with one another and with the fight for freedom, the fight against repressive force even at the risk of imprisonment. This attitude carried over into her art.

During her marriage Junko also joined the Sogetsu School of Flower Arrangement. For many Japanese women, flower arrangement is just a decorative art which is thought of mainly as an adornment for brides and homemakers-to-be. But Sofu Teshigahara, the founder of the Sogetsu school, had turned flower arrangement into a radical contemporary art form and Junko found herself immediately attracted to his passionate sense of structure and movement. She passed through the standard training course in a fraction of the normal time and quickly became a certified instructor in the Sogetsu school. Although she was never interested in pursuing flower arrangement as a career, there is no question that her sense of form and structure was deeply influenced by that passionate kind of flower arrangement.

Junko's then-husband was invited to study for two years at the Starr-King School for Ministry in Berkeley, California, a graduate school for Unitarian ministers. This was a great honor for him since the Japanese government had just started to allow a very limited number of its citizens to go abroad. In 1961, Junko accompanied him on the second year of his two-year stay. Later he was ordained as a minister in the Unitarian church. His role in the United States was partly that of a student and partly that of an ambassador—the official representative of the only Unitarian church in Japan. As a future minister's wife, Junko was allowed to attend all the classes at Starr-King. She considered this a great privilege as she had nothing more than a high school diploma at the time. That year in the United States was another important one for her as she was involved there with a group of highly educated people who thought seriously about religious matters. It was important also because it gave Junko her first taste of life as an individual, outside of the social forms and rituals of Japan. She wrote of her experience much later:

From Memoir, 2005

My husband drove me to his own apartment directly from the airport. At four o'clock in the afternoon the strong California sun was still up and when we walked in, the light—refracted through the hanging shade of the window—was making a striped pattern on the cheap green carpet. I glanced at the folding sofa which probably occupied almost the entire room when it was unfolded to make a bed at night, at the small card table and folding metal chair where he must have done all his study and written all his correspondence to me and to his parents, and at the pile of reports to our church on his progress in America.

There was a knock at the door and a smiling American woman was standing there, half her face hidden behind a pot of dazzling pink azaleas which she held out towards me. The petals were huge, and it was a variety I had never seen in Japan. She was the secretary of the president of the graduate school where my husband was studying. The card on the pot said "Welcome, Junko" and the President had signed his first name.

"Welcome, *Junko*?" Do they call me *Junko* here? Am I Junko here? The thought was rushing around my head. Some years had passed since people stopped calling me "Junko" in Japan. I was called *Okusama* which is the respectful way of addressing someone's wife, or "bride of the Church," or "God–given bride," but my given name was seldom pronounced. "So here I am not a role, nor a status: I am Junko here!" That was the first freedom I felt in America.

Junko and her husband were regularly invited to weekend stays at the Northern California homes of many of the school's and church's supporters. In this way, Junko was exposed to one of the best sides of America. Although she and her husband were so poor that they could barely afford to buy groceries, they were official guests of the Unitarian Church and so they were invited to visit divinity schools throughout the United States and they attended commencement ceremonies at the University of Chicago and Harvard University as guests of honor. In order to fulfill those official functions they made a long cross-country trip from the West Coast to the East Coast by car. Coming from postwar Japan it was a great privilege for them to experience America in this way but at the same time it was a rather dangerous adventure for citizens of the defeated nation which was so recently America's enemy. Some hostility was shown to them along with a great deal of friendliness.

But in 1963, after coming back to Japan, still in her early twenties, Junko divorced her husband. It was a traumatic decision but Junko believed it had to be done. Divorce did not mean only the end of the marriage: it was also the end of all the church activities, of the obligations toward the church and of her participation in its mission. Divorce was also the end of the relationship with the Sunday School children who had now bonded to her with a strong tie. And divorce was the end of all the friends and all the networks in the congregation. It was the end of church activities after three years of attending church as a young member of the congregation, and after almost five years of fulfilling obligations towards the church and of participating in its mission during her marriage.

Divorce was also the end of the relationship with her parents-in-law who were like foster parents to her. They called Junko "a God-given Bride" and they always treated her with warmth and respect. Junko had learned many things from them, not only about being a church person but also about things that were traditional for Japanese women—like how to pick fresh green plums from the trees in the yard and ferment them into plum wine in the little hole dug under the kitchen floor decades ago, so that the family could use the wine for decades as a remedy for colds and other ailments. And she learned other things from them, too. Every morning, at her mother-in-law's request because her eyes were no longer clear, Junko read the newspaper aloud to her. She read the editorial pages, the political news, and all the coverage of international affairs. It was only after many years that Junko realized that this was one of her mother-in-law's most considerate gifts to her: Junko had given up her higher education after high school in order to marry her son, and her mother-in-law wanted to support Junko's self-education and keep her eyes open to the world in any way she could. Junko had loved to take care of her parents-in-law, often attending to them throughout the night with heartfelt affection when either or both of them got ill because of their old age. Divorce meant the end of all that.

For all these reasons, this divorce was a deeply traumatic experience for everyone involved. Junko wrote:

From Memoir, 2005

The whole thing started before I traveled to America to join my husband. It started as an overwhelmingly powerful quest to find who I really was, a quest that never gave me rest. The quest raced around my mind at full force all the time, every single second every single day. The quest was deeply related to my religious aspiration. At this period of time—living in church, living with passionate prayers every day, ministering busily to the church community and performing as a church representative to the public—those particular years of my life were the ones during which I felt furthest removed from God. I could not go into the center of myself and see Him there: God, towards whom I felt very close throughout my childhood and early teens, was lost. I was very much suffering over it.

To say what happened then I must use special, mystical language: One winter evening, I was walking out the door of my parents-in-law's quarters to the narrow path into the little yard where the private hut for me and my husband stood. I had just taken a warm bath in the parents' quarters, bowing good night to them, holding my little toilet kit in my arm, and I stepped out into the cold air. Suddenly I saw the transparent sacred cathedral which used to be so familiar to me rising up in the night sky. It soared in the narrow rift which was open between two eaves that almost overlapped. This transparent cathedral, so refined and yet so powerful, used to appear to me in the eastern sky from the window in my little room in my parents' house only when I was completely gone into the inner world and had reached the center of my self, usually when I was deeply concentrating on painting. I had lost sight of it for many years. I could not see it no matter how desperately I longed for it. But after many years of absence, there it was now. I stood on my wooden sandals with bare feet in the narrow path and looked up at it slowly beyond the eaves. Enormous joy and a sense of gratitude filled me. And yet feelings of awe and serious questions rose up in my mind.

"You will leave this place, you will pursue your aspiration towards God in your own way," I received these words from a voice without sound. It was almost like I was being given permission to pursue my own self-determination. I did not know how on earth I should pursue it, nor how I could ever bring up such a horrifying determination to my husband and his family who loved me and trusted me, how big a destruction I would bring to their lives. I had no idea whatsoever what my journey would turn out to be. And yet I was already so certain that the church—however it emphasized the freedom from denomination, and however freely all the excellent scholars discussed religion—was not the place where I should pursue my aspiration in my own way. That is not because I found anything negative in their faith: on the contrary, I found their devotion truthful, and respected them deeply for it. Only I was aware that their experiences were not my experiences, that their faith was not my expression of my own aspiration, and that it would be dishonest to myself and to them to present myself as a church person.

When I told my husband my decision, he made many serious offers and gave me serious advice: how I should compromise and find a way that everything could be smoothed out. He even offered most generously to make every effort to reduce my church work drastically in order to provide me the space and time to create art. I knew that would require enormous sacrifice from him whose life was already filled with difficulties and self-sacrifice. But it became very clear that no matter how I changed the situation I would cause total disaster to myself and to others as long as I stayed there. Because I can create art only if I have the inner freedom to be honest to myself.

In those days in Japan, divorce at the woman's request was legal but still it was viewed as something diabolical and formidable. A woman who was divorced by her husband was considered to have brought disgrace upon his family, something similar to the primitive psychological mechanism at work when a woman who was raped is labelled as the shame of the community, regardless of her innocence. But a woman who initiated a divorce was something beyond all conception, something unthinkable. Her actions brought shame on the family similar to the shame that the family of a sex offender might suffer. Occasionally Junko would find a policeman visiting her parents saying, "We understand that one of your daughters divorced and is staying with you in your house now, which is located in the district for which I am responsible. This is our community, and I have to keep an eye on this." It did not take long for Junko to see how the mechanisms of society worked: the community did not allow for the existence of individuality, and the effort to become an individual invited suspicion and persecution.

Promptly after her divorce, Junko applied to one of Japan's foremost universities, Waseda. Returning to university after divorce was another unthinkable thing in Japan—and it was nearly impossible too, because the growing number of young, ambitious students from all over Japan made the entrance examinations brutally competitive. But Junko was accepted to Waseda—a considerable accomplishment in itself and especially under those sociological conditions. She majored in art history and Western and Eastern aesthetics and she graduated from Waseda with a B.A. at the age of twenty-seven. One of her most important professors at the university was a philosopher named Shigeo Ueda who specialized in the mysticism of Christianity and Buddhism.

From Memoir, 2005

Mysticism is not a denomination of any particular religion, nor is it a dogma nor a theory. Instead we must see it as the essence of all the great religions of the world. We find it in Eastern and Western religions and in all eras of history. It is an attitude of seeking direct unity with the absolute and of a refusal to be in relationship with anything less than the absolute. It requires a form of practice more than any theory or philosophy. Those essential qualities of mysticism evoked my own mystical experiences which had caused me so much suffering because I could not explain them to people. And I was deeply stricken by the dark painful passionate struggle of the mystics throughout history to seek direct unity with the Absolute and their refusal to be satisfied with anything less than that. I was keenly aware at that time that I was in a tiny boat in a perilous ocean far from the shore where the secure and respected religious life was assured and that I had thrown all that away deliberately. I secretly identified myself with those mystics.

Among many mystic ideas, one attracted me particularly: the idea of the divine darkness. There is a divine light so dazzling, so brilliant that we humans, not awakened, see it only as darkness. This ancient Christian mystical thought immediately reconnected me to Rilke's "terror" and synthesized many fragmentary experiences in my early life and the experience I sometimes had during the process of creating art: darkness became light as it is. I thought these experiences might have a deeper meaning than I had originally suspected. Later these ideas became one of the main elements of my concept of Centripetal Art.

At the time that Junko studied with him, Prof. Ueda was translating the works of Martin Buber into Japanese. Junko read his translation of *I and Thou* as each section was completed, and she became immersed in Buber's thought at the same time that she was studying art history and aesthetics. Junko completed her graduation thesis, "Spirituality in Line: The Interrelationship of Art and Religiosity," under Ueda's guidance while he was a visiting professor at the University of Bonn in what was then West Germany. During the year he spent abroad, countless letters, draft translations, and manuscripts passed between them. The association of mystical, existentialist religious ideas with art, which Junko learned about during her five-year relationship with Prof. Ueda, remains an important aspect of her cultural background.

During elementary school at *Gakushûin*, and at both her middle and high schools at *Seijogakuen*, Junko was taught basic skills of art as part of the curriculum. After all, art training was part of the standard Japanese curriculum all the way through high school. But outside of school, all through her childhood and adolescence, Junko painted in her own way, and she was already a self-taught artist.

While she was preparing to attend Waseda Junko pursued extracurricular studies at an institute of *dessin* (the Japanese called it by this French name), where she learned a whole system of drawing plaster replicas of Greek and Roman sculptures. At the same time she studied oil painting privately with professors at Tokyo University of Art. That classical training based on the European art tradition stems from Renaissance education: it was very strict, it involved hours of standing in front of the easel every day, sometimes continuing very late into the evening, and Junko's fingernails were worn away from scraping against paper.

This Renaissance way of training was the first training for professionals that Junko ever took and she learned enormously from it and excelled at it. And yet this was the time that serious questions and doubts arose in her—about what she was doing and how it was connected to what she wanted to do in art. She realized even more clearly than ever that what she wanted to do in art was utterly foreign to those professors, even though they were young and excellent artists themselves. It caused deep philosophical turmoil in her. She sought resolution in wider fields: art history, the philosophy of art, and the history of ideas in both the East and the West.

Among the many philosophers of art that Junko studied during her student time at Waseda, Herbert Read, Ernst Cassirer, R.G. Collingwood, and Hans Sedlmayr occupied a special place in her mind and have remained an important source of ideas throughout her life. Their notion that art is "a primary act of dealing with reality and a way of forming consciousness" have animated her work and later became one of the most important elements of Centripetal Art.

From Memoir, 2005

"What man always desires is a firmer grasp of reality. This is a direct consequence of his insecure existence, his cosmic anxiety. Art, as the primary process of definition, provides essential language for this affirmation of being." When I encountered these statements of Herbert Read in his book, *Icon and Idea: The Function of Art in the Development of Human Consciousness*, my own memory of seeing Klee's work *Danceplay of the Red Skirts* which I saw first in my early teens, suddenly came back to me vividly. "That is what happened to me at that time!" I realized. I was a lonely insecure little girl, who did not know how to express herself in language yet through sense perception I gained a new language, a new affirmation, a new strength, and I survived.

Hans Sedlmayr, another author and philosopher who influenced me deeply, in his book titled *Art in Crisis: The Loss of the Center,* warned us that contemporary art's tendency to lose the center can lead to an analogous loss in human beings in general, that art can function as a powerful force that might lead to a form of internal destruction.

From those authors and philosophers I learned that art is one of the most serious ways to contribute to the development of human consciousness. I started to realize that philosophical thinking together with deep visual experience can build some kind of structure of thought which helps further the development of human consciousness. My own thinking at that time was vague, fragmentary, and still far from resolution on account of the turmoil in the *dessin* school. But instead of a resolution, I formulated a new question, "What can art do to help mankind gain a higher consciousness?" and that question grew in me and became urgent.

During this same five-year period, Junko became involved with a young man who was a serious, active Marxist, a fiery young leader who organized labor unions in factories and at construction sites. Although Junko did not believe in any politically established form of Marxism and had never been interested in any of the Communist movement's activities, she was attracted to Marx's disclosure of the falsehood and conspiracy built into our society's power structure. She felt drawn towards his uncompromising sense of ethics and towards his compassion for the victims of that power structure: the poor. Through this young man, she met people who had fought and survived extreme torture during World War II because they had worked to bring about the ideal world they believed in so wholeheartedly, a world in which the exploitation of the poor would end. It was a complicated, even weird life that Junko led then—going back and forth between her religious surroundings and the world of Marxism. But she saw Judaeo-Christianity and Marxism as the two heads of a double-headed eagle: the eagle of Western idealism. She says now that she had to walk a tightrope between those two huge ideas in order to keep her integrity and search for her own truth.

That tightrope aside, all the human relationships that Junko was involved in during that period seem to have had one thing in common: they sent a distinct message to Junko which was exactly the same message that Junko observed everywhere in society. "Don't dare to be yourself. If you want to be yourself you will be persecuted." This message was so deeply rooted in society that most people seemed to be completely unconscious of it. Instead of being themselves they were extremely keen to play the roles that everyone agreed they were supposed to play. The relationships built on those messages and those roles inhibited the spiritual growth of all the people involved. But for Junko, being herself and being individuated is the base of her honesty and of the creation of her art. It was the reason she had to divorce and it became a more urgent issue as she grew older. Six years had already passed since she began her stormy spiritual journey across the perilous ocean (see pp. 152-153) but her own psychic, mystic tendency, which had become noticeable and caused her so much suffering, still remained unresolved at that time.

In 1968, when Junko was twenty-eight years old, she emigrated to America. A few years later she married me—who am Jewish and the son of a rabbi; and so Junko's social involvement with religious matters did not quite end when her first marriage ended. Junko had been an artist before I met her: she was enrolled at the time in the Art Department of the State University of New York at Buffalo. But she was also already working ten hours a day in her studio, and her creative urge was so strong, so overwhelming, so out of proportion to everything else in her life that it often brought her to a deep altered state of consciousness and manifested itself as various kinds of undiagnosable sickness.

Also there were the huge difficulties involved in the process of adjusting to a new land: the sense of grieving for her own language and culture was overwhelming. During that chaotic and agonizing period, Junko tried to understand, and find the significance of her difficulties. Later she looked back and described them:

From Lecture "Following the Pillar of Fire: From Language to Artistic Expression," Getty Museum, 2001

I saw myself hanging from the cliff of America by both hands, craving for Japan like a drowning person gasping for air. I kept asking myself: What is the intrinsic meaning of learning English if I have to spend all my energy my whole life long just to master the language, without ever starting to address my real purpose in being here, which is to become individuated? But the answer always came: Never go back to Japan, nothing is worth having if you have to lose yourself.

Deep emotions, sharp insights, and fragmentary thoughts were gradually growing and forming into her own philosophical ideas. Those ideas became her base and later on her structure of thought, and her idea of "Spiritual Refugee" was established.

Later the idea of "Spiritual Refugee" became an important part of the much bigger concept of Centripetal Art.

From Lecture "Following the Pillar of Fire: From Language to Artistic Expression," Getty Museum, 2001

There are some people who leave their native land only in order to preserve their integrity and live with honesty towards themselves. One must have, after all, a certain amount of freedom to be honest as an individual. Without this freedom there is no way for one to take responsibility for his own actions and thoughts and therefore there is no inner life, no place where one experiences himself as an ethical being. Without that private place, others are merely strangers and one is a stranger even to himself.

In a society that does not allow for the existence of individuality, the effort to become an individual invites persecution. Although this sort of persecution is not as visible as political persecution, it is nevertheless fatal to one's spiritual being, so the persecuted person becomes an exile—a spiritual refugee. One usually goes into this sort of exile only after a sustained battle against the cultural system in which his whole life is wrapped up. The battle is painful. Wounded and bleeding, one becomes an exile. These people I call "spiritual refugees" and I consider myself one of them.

Living in exile has required and continues to require enormous effort from Junko. The loss of her native language was the loss of her most important communication tool, of her weapon against the world and her shield against it. This undermined her self-confidence in ways that native speakers cannot understand. In Japan, Junko is immediately perceived by everyone who meets her as a brilliant, well-educated, cultured, and strong person. But in America, to English speakers, she often seems at first sight unsure of herself, not particularly well-educated, and not strong. In Japan she was a member of the privileged class, a member of the proud majority; but here she feels herself always a member of a disadvantaged minority. And losing her language impacted much more than just those everyday social communications. In order to be an individuated person in this English-speaking society—something that has been important to her throughout her life—she has had to rebuild the inner structure of her psyche and put herself into the context of this new language and society. Even though she was a scholarship student and on the Dean's list at the State University of New York at Buffalo, now she had to go far beyond the level of merely adjusting to a new culture. This required great competency in reading and writing as well as in discussion and speech. Restructuring her whole psyche has been a difficult, complex, and, most of all, a dangerous task.

The difficulties of language which Junko had to overcome are deeply rooted in cultural, historical, and sociological differences, and struggling with them required Junko to step out of her whole social matrix. First, she was required to step out of monologue and into dialogue. Japanese is a language where the subject of the sentence is suppressed, or only implied. The use of the pronoun "I" is very rare. This promotes a self-effacing attitude. And there is no tradition anywhere in Japanese history of dialogue—of debate or public speaking. In order to live in America, Junko had to confront the difficulty of standing up, confronting, explaining, persuading, convincing; and for this, a radical transformation was required.

Then, she had to re-engage with words as part of a process rather than as the final product of a process. In Japan, one speaks only when the conversation is finished, when the conclusion is reached, when doubts have been resolved. In America, words are part of a process, a conversation, an effort to reach a result.

And she had to step out of a world of "vertical" relationships into a world of "horizontal" ones. In Japan, the language itself reinforces the role hierarchy. Just as Americans know that they have to address the Judge as "Your Honor" and the Queen as "Your Majesty," in Japanese, not just the forms of address, but the verbs, the pronouns, and even the nouns to be used, all of them have to change depending on the complicated hierarchical relationships among the parties to the conversation. A familiar type of question on college entrance examinations in Japan involves a reading from the *Genji Tales* where no pronouns are used. The students are required to identify the parties to the conversation, and their roles, from other cues in the passage, such as the use of the respect forms of nouns and verbs.

In struggling to live in a new language context the constant temptation for any Japanese person is to add the role of the foreigner to the other roles her culture imposed on her, in order to meet the expectations of the people around her. The greatest challenge for Junko was to make the transition from role-playing to authenticity: language itself had to become a medium of authentic self-expression—just like her art. Restructuring her whole psyche has been like an on-going surgery for her and the pain she endured during that period was deep. She wrote:

From Lecture "Transcending Ethnicity: The Creative Process," Long Beach Museum of Art, California, 1996

Your commitment to live here takes a long time to sink into your own mind and accepting it requires a complicated process, even though you came as a determined spiritual refugee. The language which you have missed since you left the land of your birth will be once more roaring inside of you. It has been a secret which no one knows nor cares to know. But for you it has been your secret lover. You thought you could keep it a secret in your mind forever, but you are not sure if you can repress it any longer. It is roaring loud and you are gasping for expression, you feel it might erupt like a volcano, gushing magma out into the sky, and reveal everything you have hidden, the love, sorrow, and pain for your mother tongue Japanese.

She wrote about "love, sorrow, and pain" but soon a deep desperation came over her. During this most critical period, Junko's strongest support came from an unexpected place: from Masahisa Goi, a Japanese spiritual/religious teacher whose thought and teaching were original but strongly influenced by a mixture of Pureland Buddhism, Shinto, and a touch of Christianity, and who was known also for his extraordinary psychic ability. In 1972 he made contact with Junko out of the blue, and offered her some words of powerful encouragement relating to her art that allowed her to bring many of her lifelong complex problems to a resolution. He told a mutual friend, "God is painting through Junko!" Hearing these words, Junko's psychic energy became directed and confined to the activity of creating art as a constructive power instead of being scattered in various areas of her life as before. Through these words she came to see the depth of her own art and realized the significance of it. She finally came to a thorough acceptance of her creativity as her destiny much more deeply than she ever had before. And that led her to a deeper commitment to her art. After receiving Goi's words, Junko's doubts and desperation over her English writing and speaking ability were replaced with a commitment to do her best—as part of her deep commitment to her art. Goi died in 1981. Although Junko and he had never met each other in person, and had contact only through a series of letters which went back and forth across the Pacific Ocean for nine years, it was largely through his powerful, continuous encouragement of her art and his view of the meaning of human life that she was able to build a solid base for what she has to do on this planet.

I encouraged Junko to be an artist and I helped her to bring her works to the world. In 1973, the year after Master Goi came in contact with her, I found the courage to arrange her first solo show. It was at a gallery on Newbury Street, which was Boston's fancy "arty" district. The show was very favorably reviewed in the *Boston Herald* (a major Boston paper in those days) and the gallery was filled with visitors who came holding the review, which they had cut out from the paper. The following year, she was in a group show in New York. In 1978 we traveled to Japan to see Junko's parents; it was Junko's first trip back after ten years of living in America. While we were in Tokyo, Junko showed photographs of her work to one of Japan's foremost artists who was an acquaintance of her family. After taking one look at those photographs he immediately arranged exhibitions in prestigious venues in Japan. In 1979, solo shows were held at the Tokyo Central Museum and at a gallery in Osaka. These shows were attended by hundreds of people every day, and they were extremely well reviewed in several major Japanese newspapers. Junko was surprised to see how deeply her art was understood by the Japanese. Later, she talked about the viewers' reactions:

From Metamorphoses: The Transformative Vision of Junko Chodos (2001)
Interview by Noriko Gamblin

Many of the viewers waited in line to talk to me about their own suffering and struggle during the shows in both Tokyo and Osaka. They understood my art as an expression of my struggle towards individuation rather than in purely stylistic terms. It was surprising to me that the culture that I had to leave in order to become myself could understand my art so well. But the truth is that if I had not left Japan, I could not have attained what I did.

Junko's parents realized during this trip that their view of Junko up to that point had been inaccurate and inappropriate. To their great credit, they recognized the kind of artist she had become and they felt genuine respect for it. They also appreciated my role in supporting Junko's work and they were grateful for it; they told Junko that they could not sleep with their feet toward me ever again—which is a Japanese expression of deep respect. For my part, I felt great affection for them, and gratitude for the many good things they had done for Junko. I told my father-in-law, in broken Japanese, that I was enjoying my visit to the "factory" where this very high quality product had been designed and produced.

But although Junko's childhood tensions with her parents had come to a certain level of resolution (a deeper resolution was to come decades later, after hundreds of letters had passed between her and her mother) and although her first Japanese shows were extremely successful, her determination to live in America never changed. In 1988 Junko was naturalized as an American citizen.

Junko has lived as an exile at two levels: at the innermost level, feeling herself a spiritual refugee since childhood even in her native Japan; and at the external level, becoming an émigré and a naturalized U.S. citizen. Having been exposed to many different cultural influences, Junko always felt that her art would go beyond what was traditionally Japanese. Junko's art does indeed transcend cultural boundaries and does achieve something universal, but it still integrates the many cultural elements to which she was exposed in Japan and this is an important part of what makes it attractive.

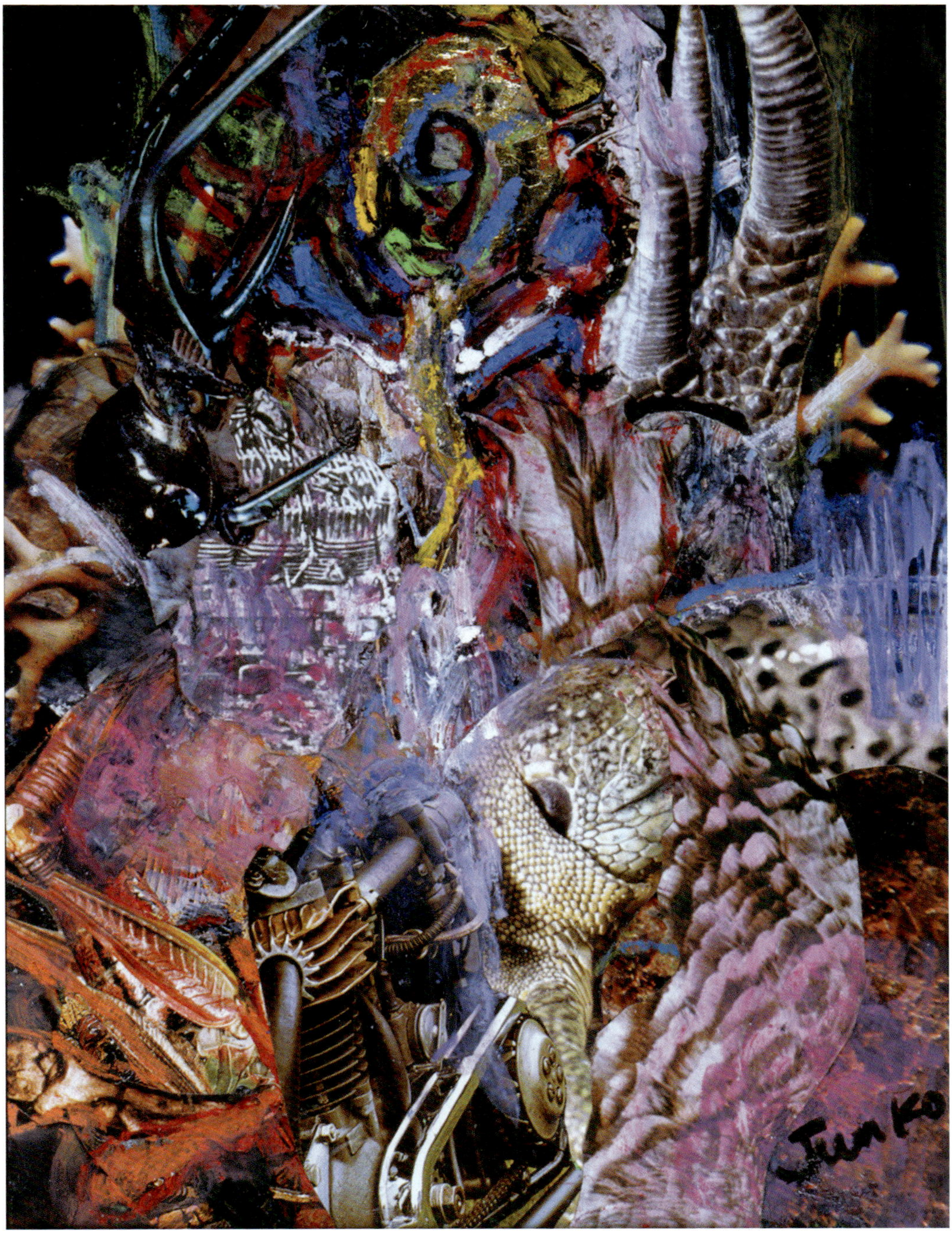

WHAT IS JUMPING OUT HERE? (1983)
Mixed media collage on paper
8 x 6 in.
(20.3 x 15.2 cm.)

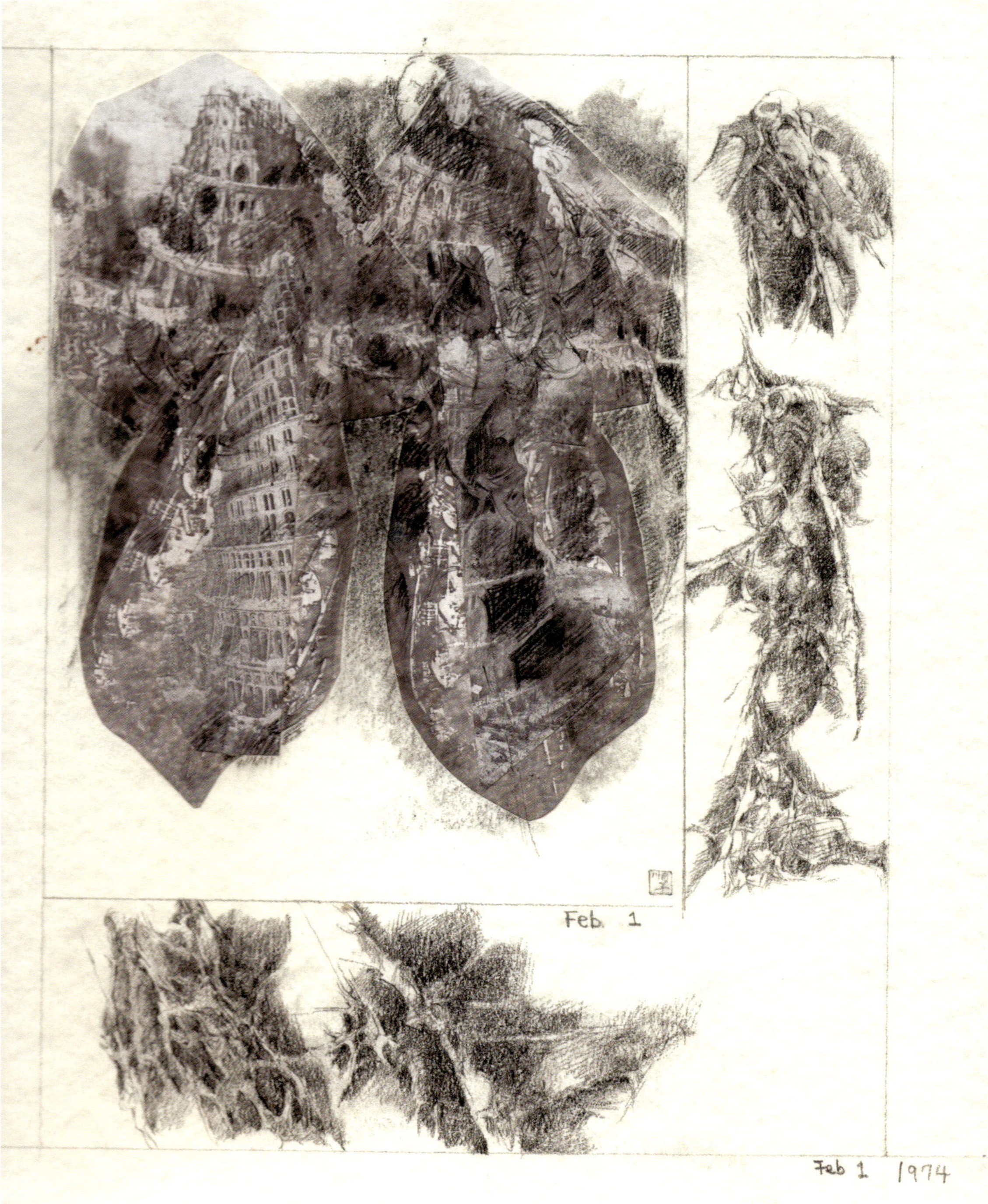
Feb 1
Feb 1 1974

CHAPTER THREE
TECHNIQUES AND STYLES

Style and technique play a central role in the art of any artist, but in the case of centripetal art they play a special kind of role. Part of Junko's encounter with her visitants is a struggle toward the truth each visitant wants to reveal. Style and technique have always been an important part of that struggle. That is why Junko has employed so many different styles and techniques over the years: dead flowers could not be encountered in the same medium in which the root presented itself, and burls, engines, figures—all required different materials and different techniques. That same struggle is also why Junko has found it necessary to invent techniques. Many of the techniques which other artists adopted, and in which she was offered training from a very young age, did not suit her vision of the truth toward which she was struggling. So she had to find new materials and new ways of using them.

Yet Junko's techniques do not clamor for our attention. Unlike Jackson Pollack's "action paintings," for example, or early cubist works by Picasso and Braque, whose impact derives partly from our consciousness of the rebellious techniques employed to create them, Junko's techniques fade deliberately into the background and allow us to confront the finished images without forcing us to focus on how the works are made.

Opposite:
SKETCHBOOK
FEB. 1, 1974
Pen and ink, charcoal, and Xerox on paper
11 x 8.5 in.
(27.9 x 21.6 cm.)

When she was studying art in Japan, Junko blamed herself because she never felt comfortable with many of the techniques that she was being taught. Her teachers encouraged her to work in oils, a "must" for students of Western art in Japan in those days; but even though she excelled in that class, she felt that oil-painting technique was not true to her inner necessity. She did well in flower arrangement, which she pursued as an extracurricular activity, but she never wanted to pursue it as a career. And she was the worst student in her Japanese calligraphy class, showing up for many sessions having "forgotten" to bring her sumi ink block and brushes.

This is all one aspect of Junko's role as a lonely seeker. When we think of people who are excellent at what they do, we imagine a life story that begins with training, then continues to mastery and, in some cases, invention. So a painter would go to art class as a youth, learn oil-painting technique, and then become a master oil painter; and perhaps he would invent some variation of oil-painting technique that he would pass on after his death. This is not Junko's life story—far from it. Her techniques are mostly things that she invented, and it is not at all likely that she can pass them on. For who else would have the desperate need to employ such techniques, particularly when standard alternatives are readily available?

But I jump ahead of myself. In this chapter, I will present examples of all the techniques Junko has used over the last forty years, and tell you what was required in order to create works using those techniques. And more important, I will try to explain why Junko needed those particular techniques at the time—that is, how her search for technique became one with her search for artistic truth.

PEN AND INK

In her first major series, *Dead Flowers* (1973, eight works) Junko used pen and ink with wash to build up the image. The technique is unusual because all the pen strokes are deliberately straight: the sense of curves and three-dimensionality is created entirely by applying many rectilinear strokes. So the works do not convey a strong sense of line; instead they convey a strong sense of soft-edged texture and surface. These qualities of the work emerge mysteriously from the detailed pen strokes.

Opposite:
DEAD FLOWER SERIES, No. 1 (1973)
Pen and ink with wash
on Arches paper
22 x 16 in.
(55.9 x 40.6 cm.)

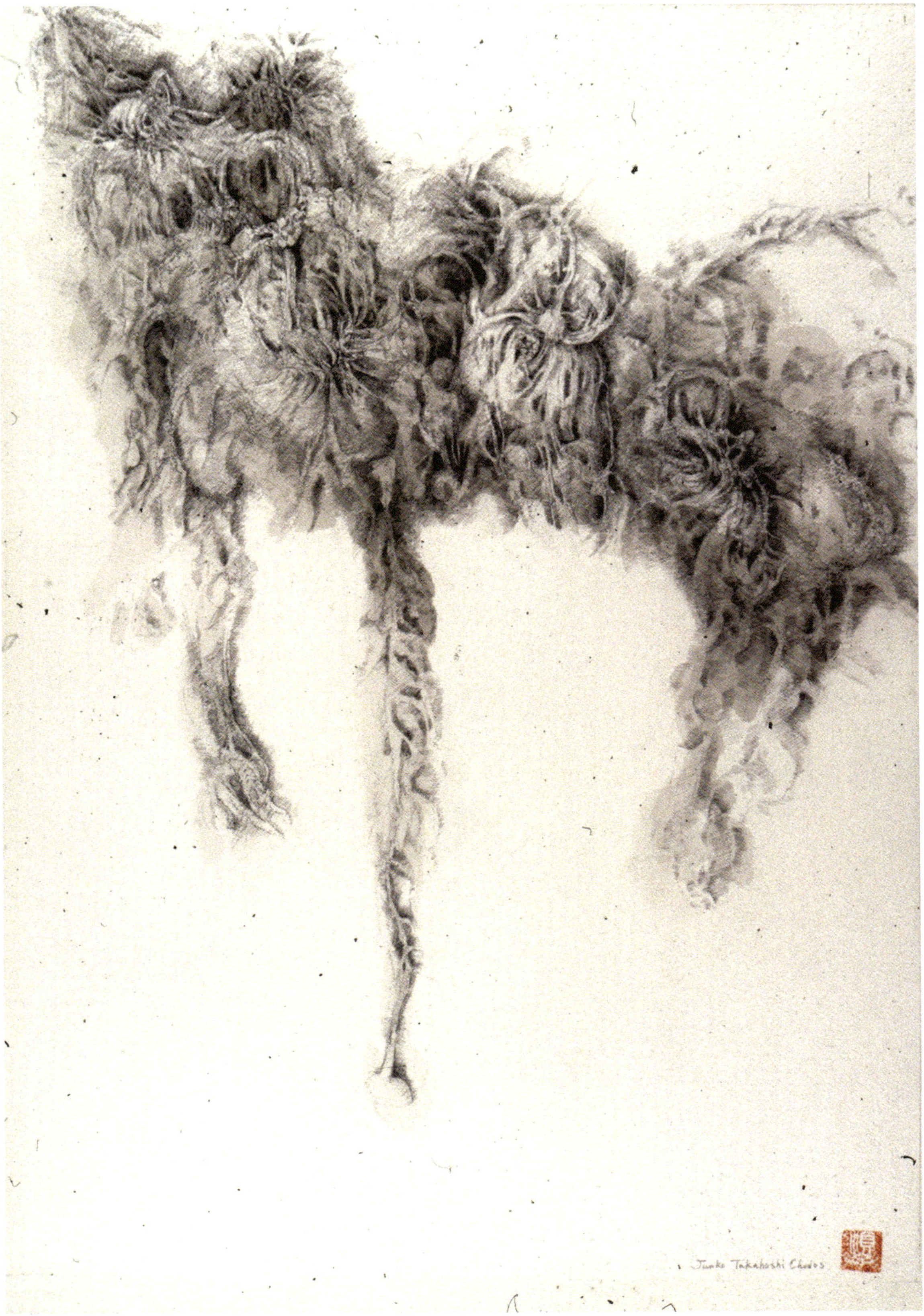
Junko Takahashi Chodos

The pen and ink technique involves deliberate, repetitive, meditative work; each of the first seven works in this series took a month of long days to create, and the three-panel *Byoobu* took even longer. It seemed to me while she was working that Junko had become almost obsessive; but I soon realized that her state of mind was very controlled, and I concluded that "meditative" was a much more accurate word. In fact, the repetitive, kinetic movement is a kind of chanting, very well suited to Junko's encounter with the *Dead Flowers* (Chapter One, pp. 15-19); it allowed Junko to become part of the flowers, and to become, as she said, death staring down at earth.

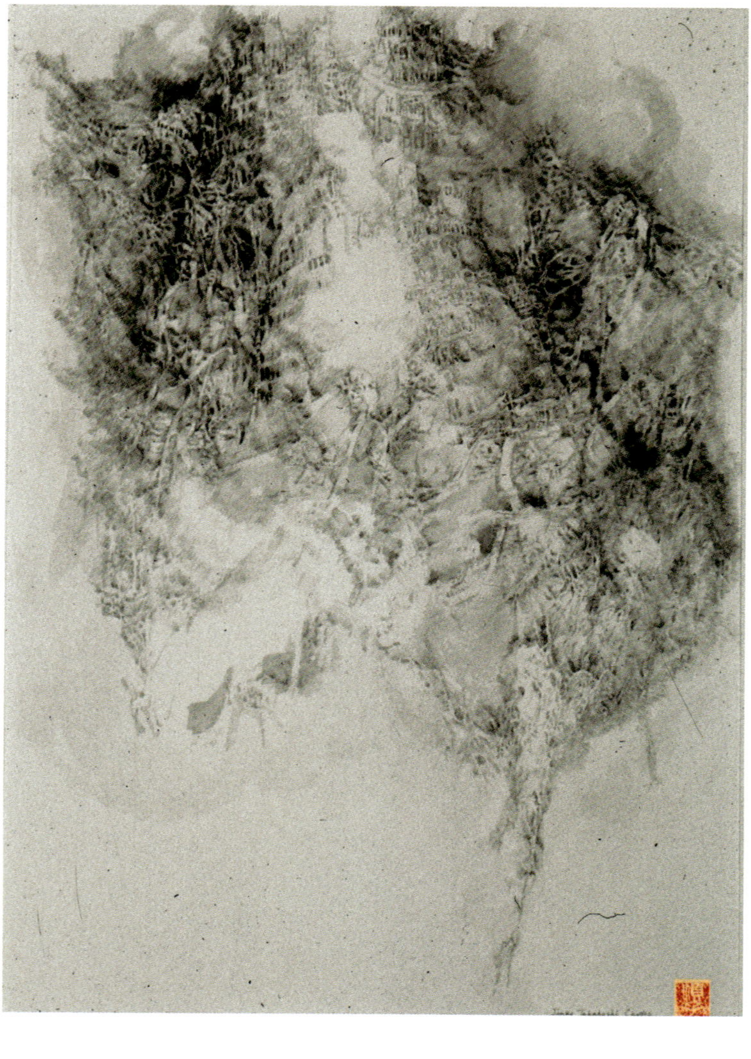

DEAD FLOWER SERIES, No. 6 (1973)
Pen and ink with wash, on Arches paper
22 x 16 in.
(55.9 x 40.6 cm.)

PENCIL AND CHARCOAL PENCIL

After she completed the *Dead Flowers* series, Junko began to sketch the root described in Chapter One. Her first two studies used pen and ink in a style very similar to the *Dead Flowers*. But soon she switched to pencil, and in those sketches there was a deliberate attempt to create the image through decisive lines whose complicated interaction was intended to represent the root accurately. When she made a study for the most elaborate work in the *Root Series*, the *Mandala* (No. 16, 1979) she began by making a complete pencil study of the work (below), before creating the collage. Also, among her early sketches of the root we can find technical drawings done in pencil that have no sense of emotional lines but use small squares to build up the surface and describe the relationships of distance and structure again, accurately.

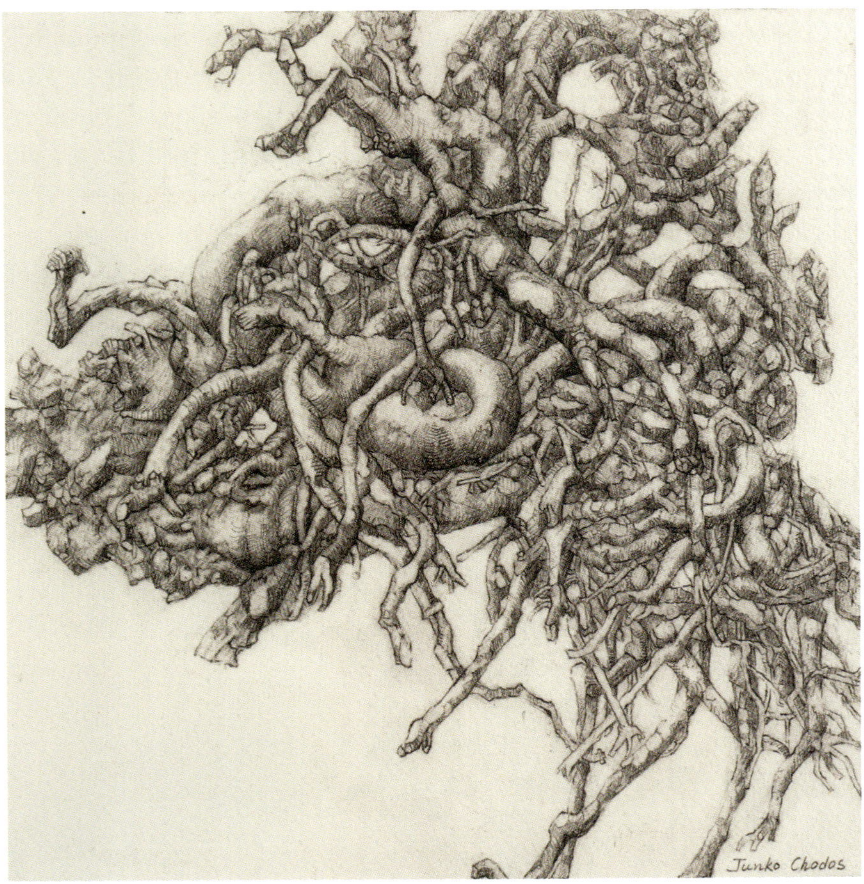

ROOT SKETCH (1975)
Pencil on paper
8 x 8 in.
(20.3 x 20.3 cm.)
Small squares used to
build the structure

In 1969, Junko created her first serious collage: *Altarpiece after Grünewald*. That image is composed of photographs which Junko cut, but which she left by and large recognizable, and assembled into a new image which has its own proper "reading." Quoting the *Concert and Nativity* scene from Grünewald's famous Isenheim Altarpiece, this collage technique involves witty paraphrase and deliberate modernization: a bottle of scotch stands at the base of one of the columns, an old motorcycle wheel replaces the infant Christ, a hand dressed in Renaissance clothing displaces the haloed saintly figure in the original, and the angel playing the viola da gamba is replaced by a jumble of colors and textures.

Of course collage, in its modern art usage, had been invented by Picasso, and used by Braque, Rauschenberg, and countless others. The themes of deliberate spatial fragmentation and displacement of images from their original context to serve new uses—this was old hat by the time Junko started painting. But Junko's *Altarpiece after Grünewald* is a combination of both a very classic way of using collage skill, where the wittiness comes from image replacement and the image itself is still important, and a new way of using it where the image is used to build a clear overall structure, and the visual properties of the images are more important than their subjects.

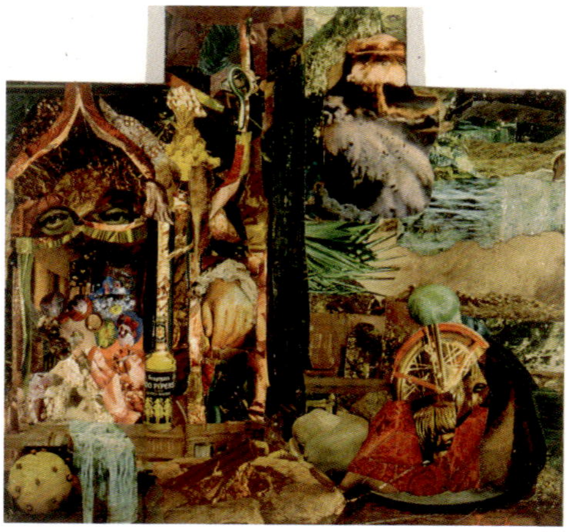

Left:
ALTARPIECE AFTER GRÜNEWALD (1969)
Collage on paper
11 x 10 in.
(27.9 x 25.4 cm.)
Junko's first collage.

Opposite:
ROOT SERIES,
No. 11 (1975)
FASTING BUDDHA, No. 2
Mixed media
collage on paper
20 x 16 in.
(50.8 x 40.6 cm.)

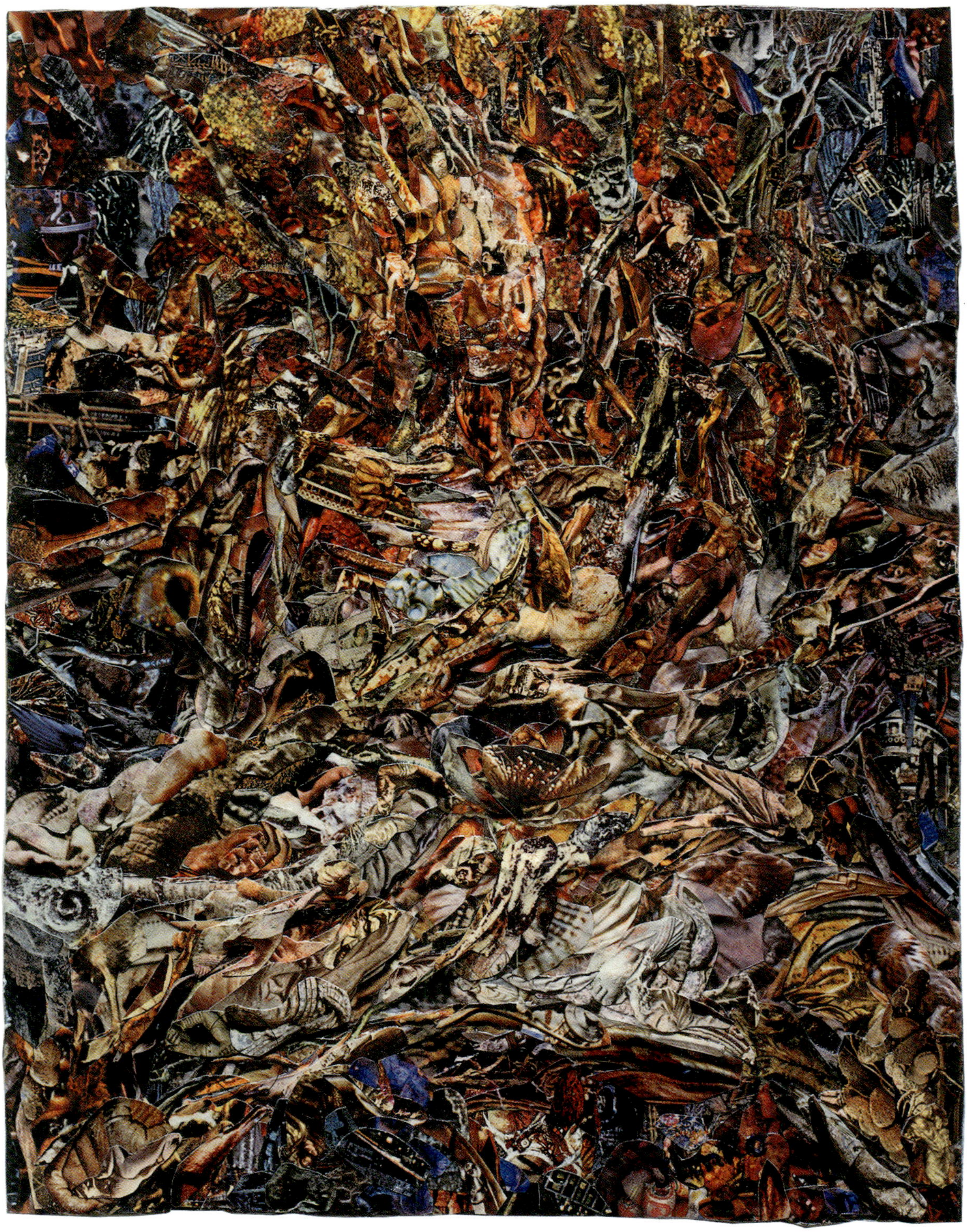

In her *Root Series* (1975-1979, eighteen works) Junko invented a new kind of collage: she cut out very small images from high-quality printed books—art books, nature photography books, medical books, technology books—and picking these tiny pieces up with tweezers she applied them to the surface of the work with glue. The individual pieces are so small and cut in such a deliberate way, and often are layered on top of each other so thickly that the images are often not recognizable. Junko uses them instead like brush strokes, for their color, hue, and texture—their *valeur*—carefully controlled in order to create a perfectly coherent depth of space. It is true that every once in a while she used a piece just big enough to allow us to see the image on it (see *Devil Escaping*, pg. 159), but for the most part the images from which the fragments came are unimportant and play at most only a subliminal role. The collages that Junko creates remind us of oil paintings. Indeed, the individual pieces that she cut to use in her collages are like individual brush strokes in an oil painting, and the thick layering often feels like *impasto*.

This kind of collage technique, like the pen and ink technique, also required meticulous, careful, repetitive work and in order to work in this technique Junko had to be in a similar meditative state. But there is something different here: there is an element of image destruction followed by reconstruction. The pen and ink technique started with nothing and ended with an image. And pen drawing has the quality that once the stroke is laid down, you cannot re-do it. But the collage technique started with images and broke them down to almost nothingness leaving them merely their visual values—hue, color, texture—and then gave them a new life in the ultimate work. And collage technique allows Junko to go over and over the same work many times until she is satisfied with it—similar to what can be done in oil painting.

Junko sees the root as "struggling in a dark place." There is a muscularity and solidity to the root that required a constructive technique. The collage technique answered the need which the encounter with the root created.

Opposite:
ROOT SERIES,
No. 15 (1976)
Mixed media collage
on paper
10 x 8 in.
(25.4 x 20.3 cm.)

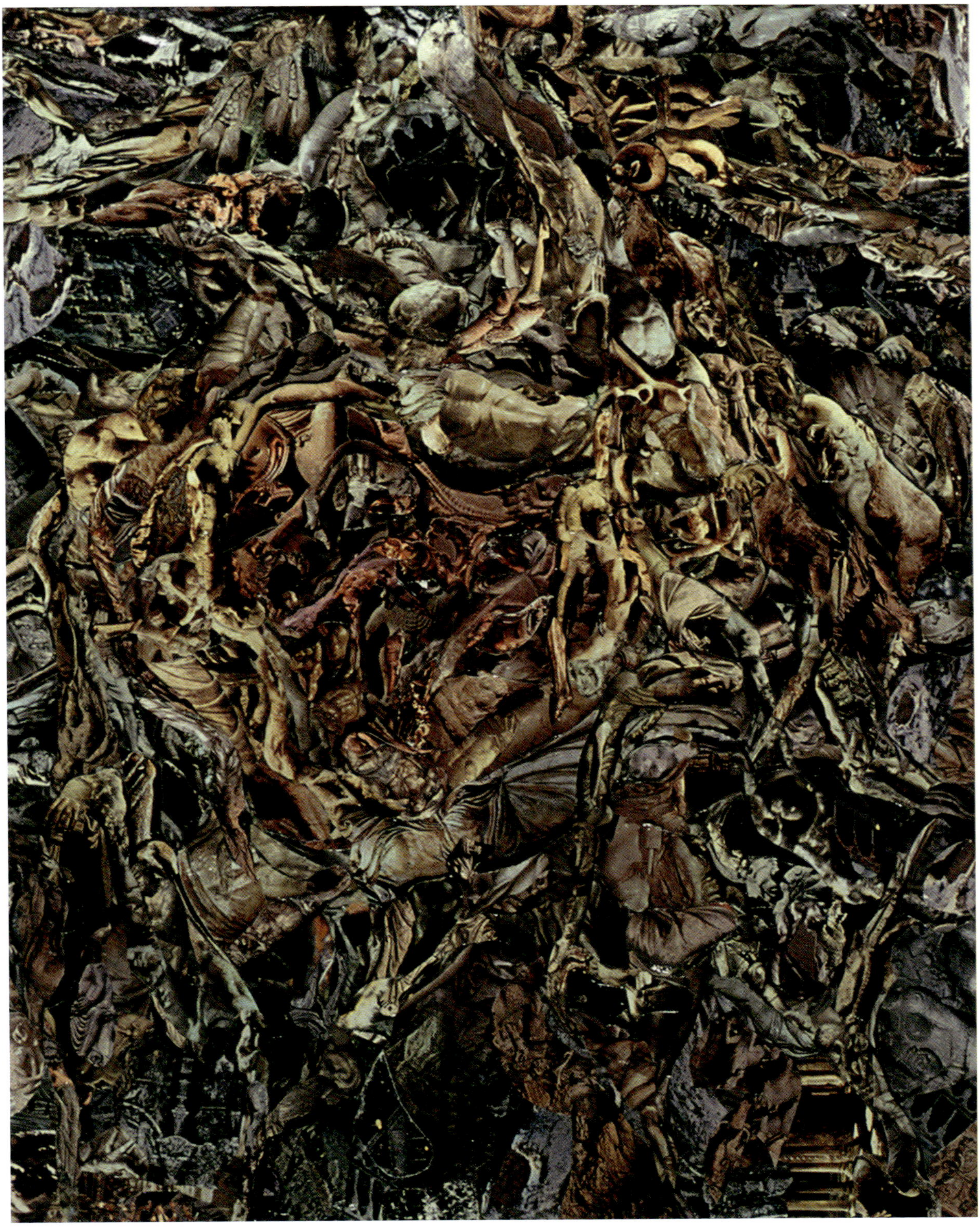

XEROX

In the early 1980s, Junko gained access to a Xerox machine, and started to experiment with it as an art medium. In her *Mysterious Paper* series (1983, six works), she began by crumpling up Kleenex tissues and making Xerox copies of them. She would then copy the copy itself, and repeat that process until the lines had precisely the degree of shadowiness that she liked. And then, using the copy as a page from a coloring book, she applied color pencil to make the final work.

This technique enrolled technology in the production of Junko's work for the first time. The Xerox machine was capable of producing a fascinatingly complex image, with wide tonal variations—but only if used imaginatively. Junko's desire to present commonplace objects in totally unthinkable ways—a desire which gave rise to the *Dead Flower* series and the *Root* series—found a new avenue of expression here. But this technique was a kind of play because there was no "visitant" toward which Junko was struggling through this technique.

Bottom:
MYSTERIOUS PAPER, No. 1 (1983)
Color pencil on Xerox on paper
5 x 10 in.
(12.7 x 25.4 cm.)

Opposite:
MYSTERIOUS PAPER, No. 4 (1983)
Color pencil on Xerox on paper
6.5 x 8 in.
(16.51 x 20.32 cm.)

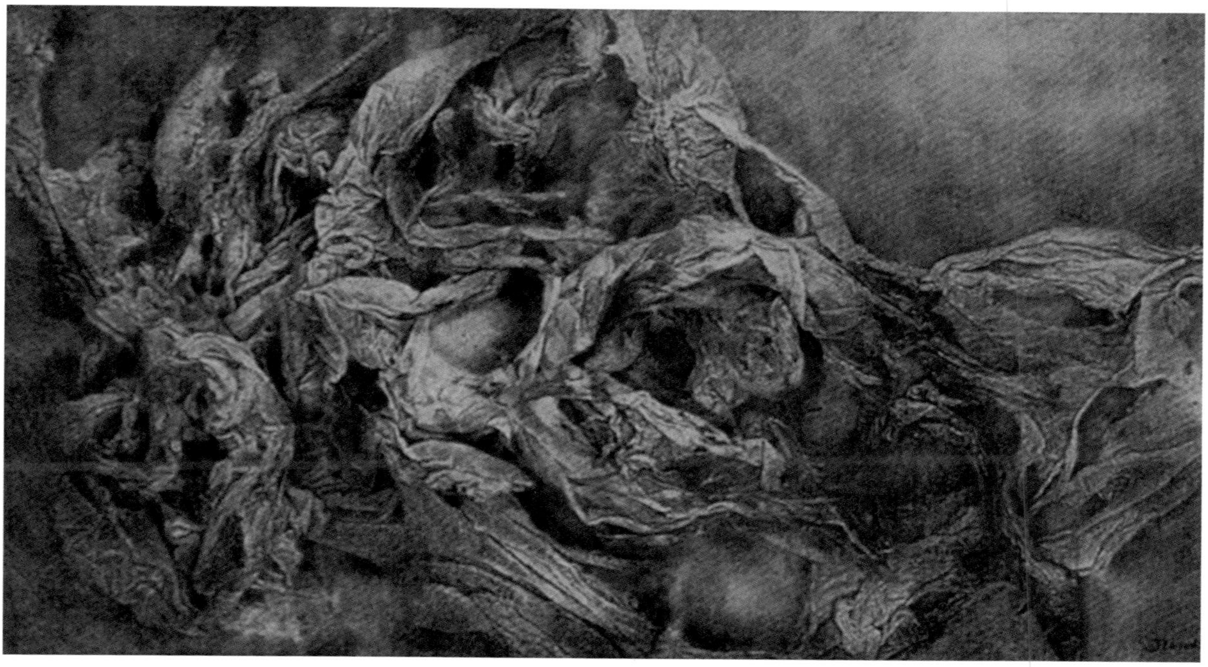

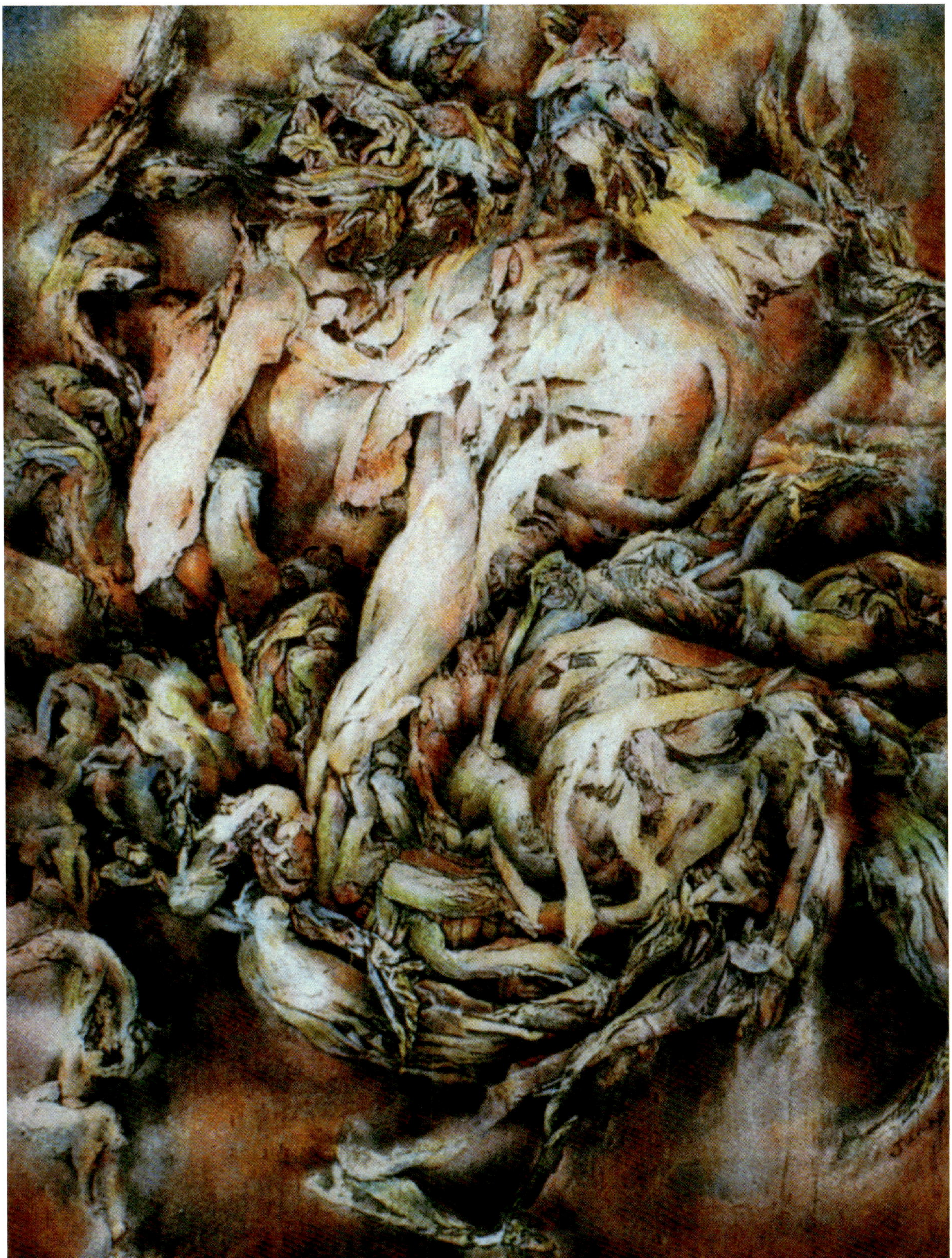

SMEARS

In the early 1990s, in the course of experimenting with different kinds of papers and paints, Junko invented a "smearing" technique in which she deliberately smears acrylic paint between two pieces of coated paper, giving the surface an eerie, outer-space feeling. There is no trace here of "brushwork"; the smear is not made by hand moving on paper, but by the hand forcing the paper to move.

This technique appears in many of the *Compact Universe* pieces from 1991 as well as in the *Interplanetary Icons* from 1990 (see *Icon No. 11*, at pg. 30).

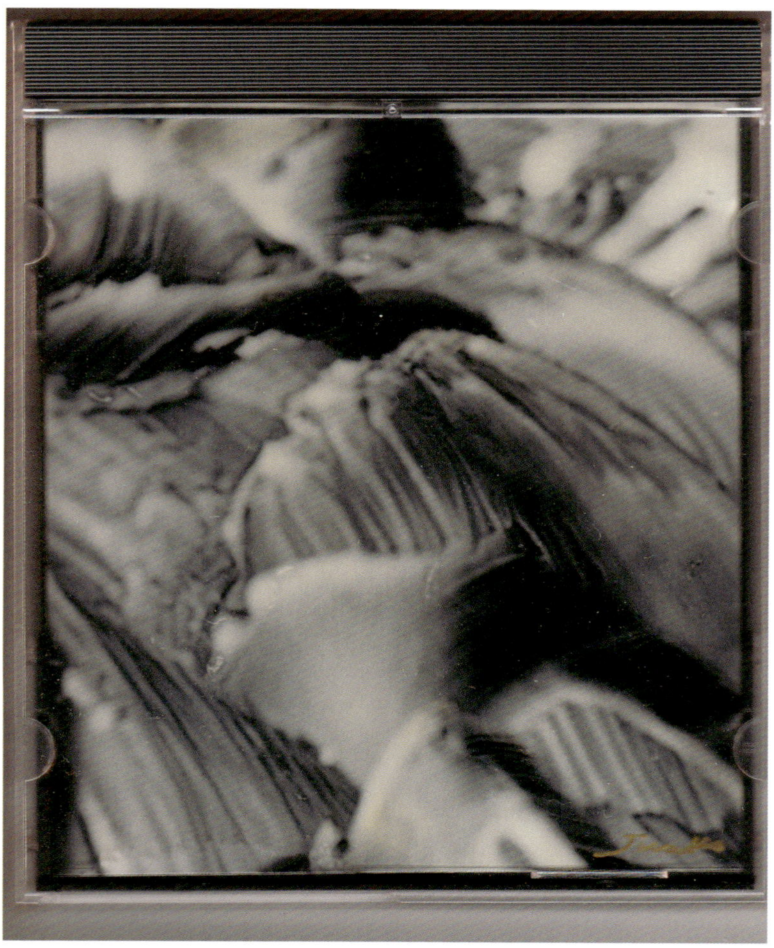

This page:
COMPACT UNIVERSE,
No. 44 (1991)
Mixed media
on Kromekote
5 x 5 in.
(12.7 x 12.7 cm.)

Opposite:
INTERPLANETARY
ICON, No. 4 (1990)
Mixed media on paper
Irregular shape:
22 x 19 in.
(55.9 x 48.2 cm.)

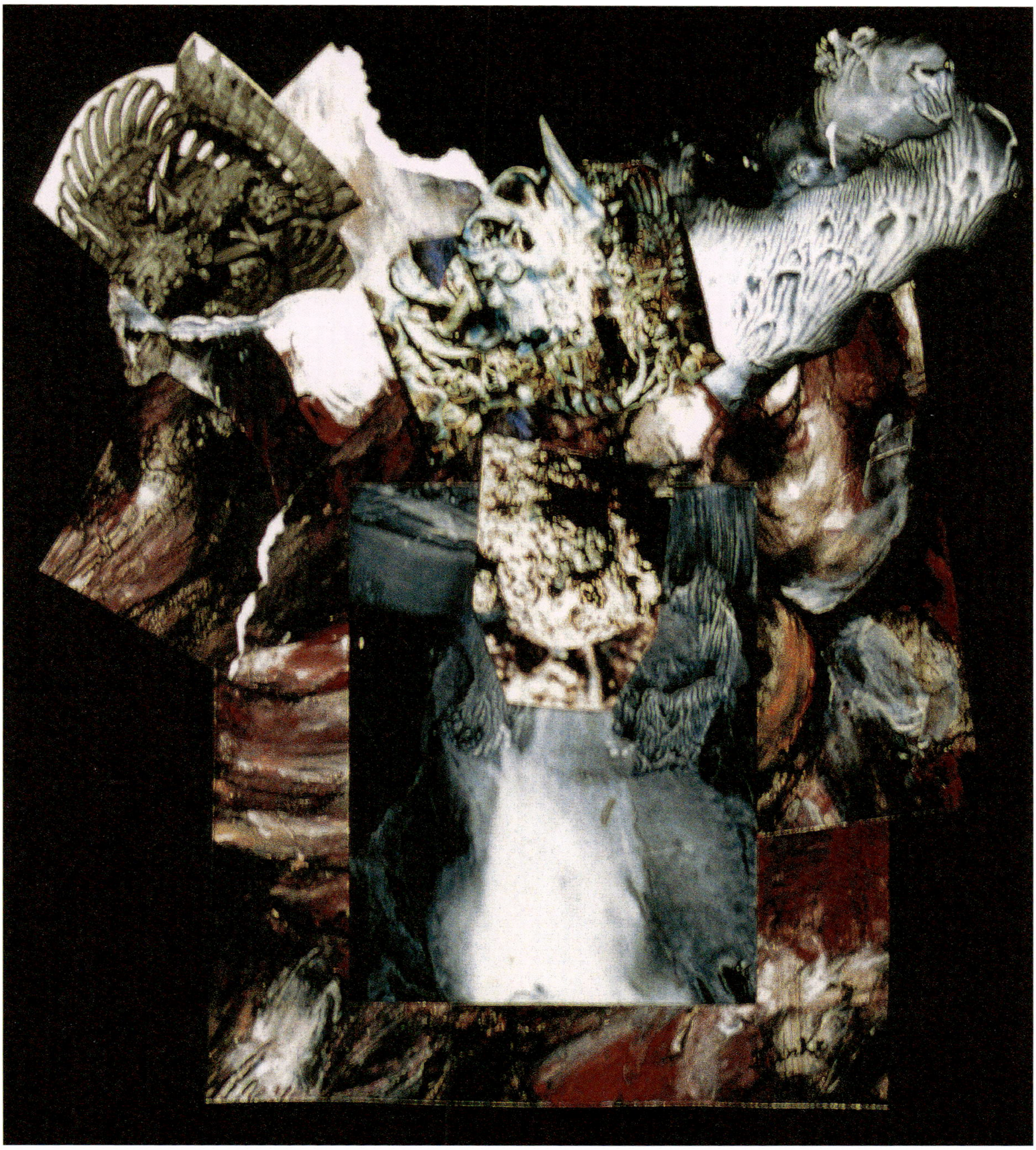

CLOROX

In the 1991 series, *Requiem for an Executed Bird,* Junko used photographs as elements of some of the works. But she destroyed the images on these photographs—not by cutting them, but by applying Clorox which partly washed them out. This technique was driven by Junko's desire to present an image falling down—showing its vulnerability and powerlessness, diluted with water and Clorox.

CANNIBALIZATION/RECYCLING

In the *Meditations on Dance* (1987, eight works) Junko found a way to cannibalize and recycle her own work. Beginning with her figure drawings, she cut them up and used parts of them to create more abstract compositions. What appears in the final work is reminiscent of legs and muscles—but the images have been so "deconstructed" that the main thing we see is the strength of the lines and the weight of the masses.

This technique was used again in Junko's recent *FATHOM* series (2005–2006, forty giant panels). Here Junko used several of her earlier works intact, but blew them up through a process of digital enlargement and then replicated them to create brand-new works which transform the originals.

MYLAR

In 1993, Junko started working on industrial mylar: .05-inch thick rolls of mylar purchased in forty-two-inch widths were cut into lengths of six, seven, or eight feet and used as a sort of canvas. Her 1993 series, *In the Forest of Amida Buddha* (see Chapter Four), was the first to use this new medium. She has continued to use it since then and has created many mylar panels over the last twelve years.

Opposite:
REQUIEM FOR AN EXECUTED BIRD, No. 3 (1991)
Mixed media on paper
40 x 32 in.
(101.6 x 81.3 cm.)

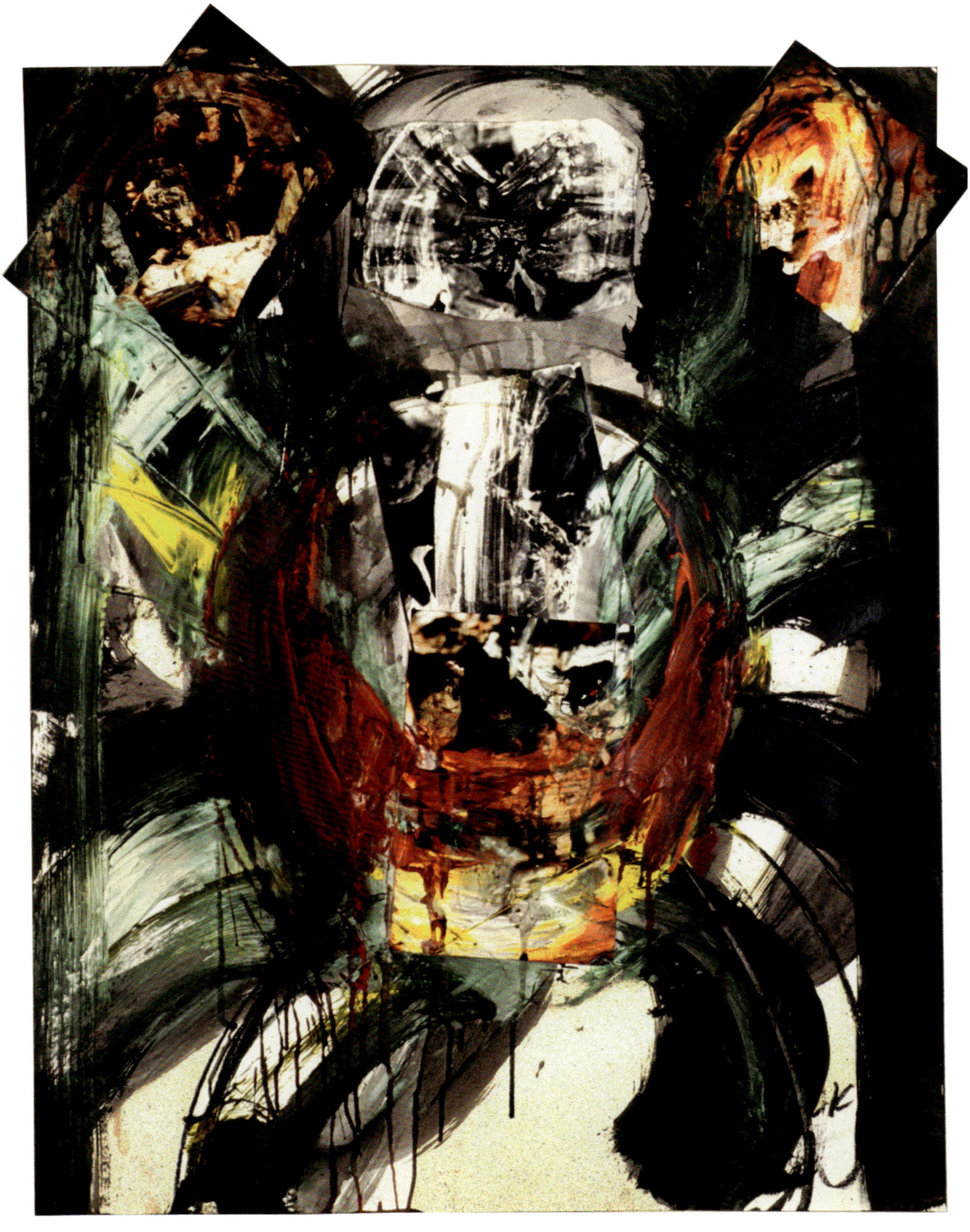

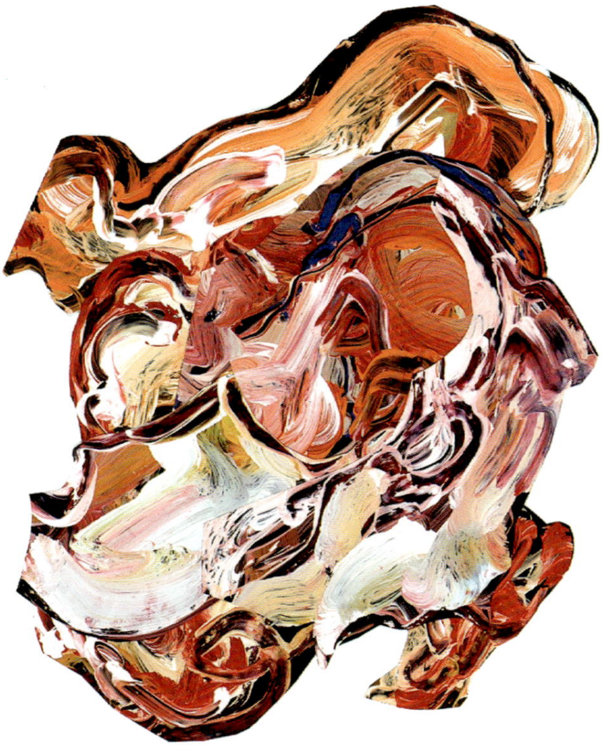

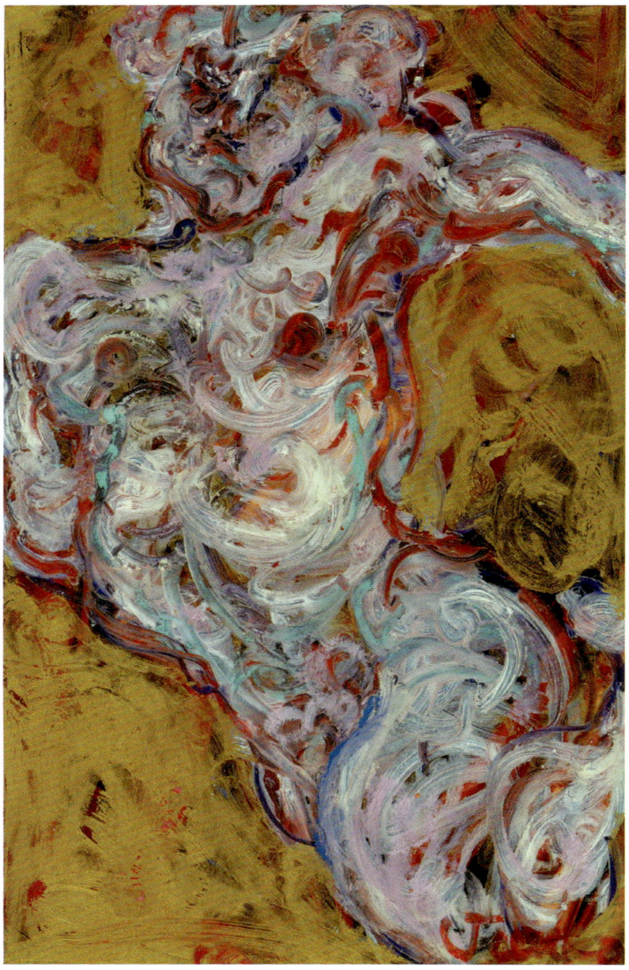

This page top:
MEDITATIONS ON DANCE, No. 5 (1987)
Acrylic on coated paper
30 x 28 in.
(76.2 x 71.1 cm.)

This page bottom:
DANCING ON GOLD BACKGROUND (1984)
Mixed media on paper
15 x 10 in.
(38.1 x 25.4 cm.)

Opposite top:
FATHOM: TANTRIC DANCE (FOREGROUND) (2006)
Collage of computer prints on mylar
Overall 10 x 10.5 ft.
(304.8 x 320.0 cm.)
This work incorporates portions of the one below it.

Opposite bottom:
UNIVERSE MOVES AND HUMANS DANCE
DANCE: ECLIPSE (1984)
Acrylic on astronomical poster
20 x 27 in.
(50.8 x 68.6 cm.)

Some works arise out of other ones.

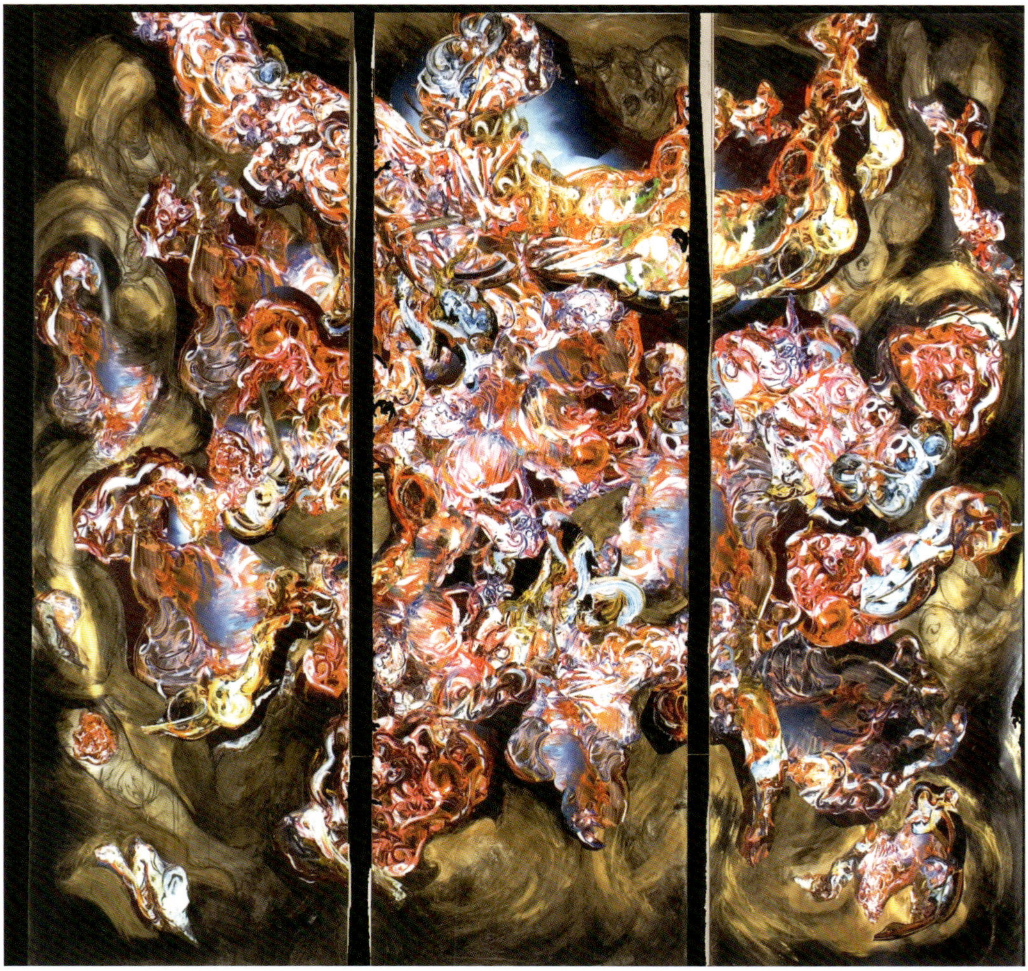

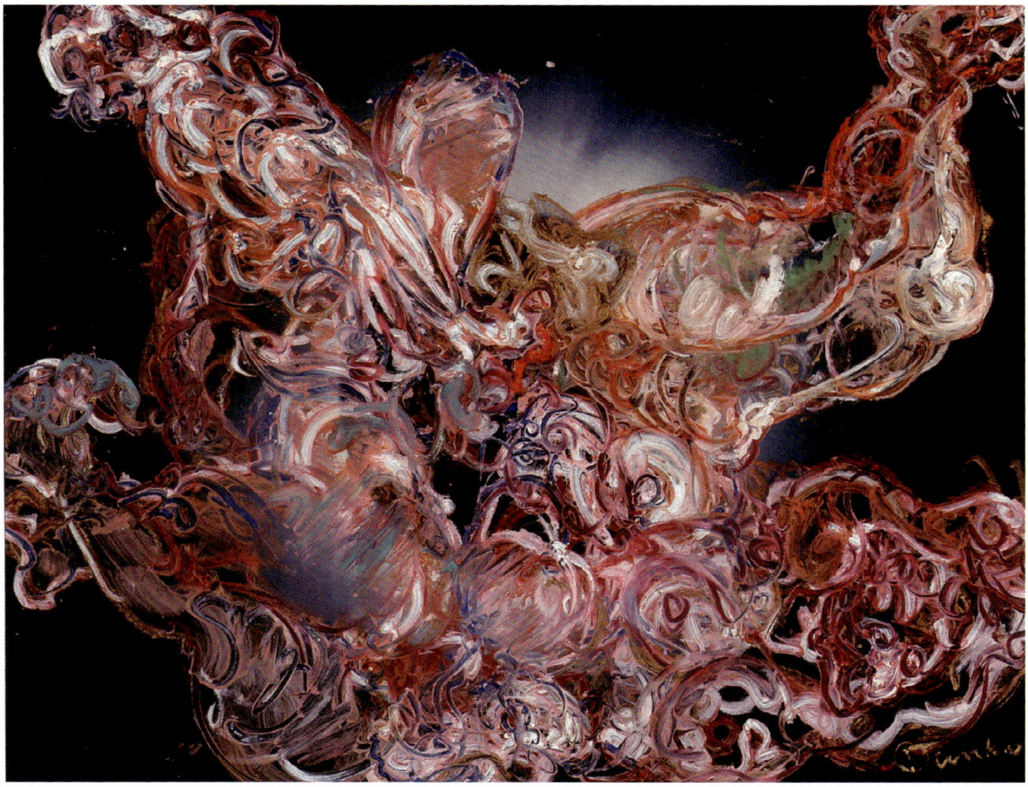

Junko likes the mylar for its translucency, and for the fact that, being nonporous, it allows her to use "drips" of acrylic that flow like blood or rain on the image. See the frontispiece to this book, *Concerning Art and Religion, No. 7, In the Beginning Is the Image* (2003). The translucency of mylar is important: Junko realized at a young age that oil painting is an expression of Western art which arises out of a long tradition—a Christian tradition—of seeing things as occupying a space which has a perfect order and structure. Things in this space have weight and mass; and oil paints are a way of representing their weight and mass in a space that is governed by scientific perspective. This tradition has governed Western art with absolute authority for five hundred years. As a result of this long tradition, even divine figures (which for Junko are not part of this world) appear material and have palpable weight.

But Junko sees things "hanging in front of her as if she were watching a screen"—a *kakejiku*, the sort of screen that you will see hanging in the *tokonoma*, that special space in a Japanese room where art is allowed into daily life and offers the inhabitants of the room access to another world. On this screen, things have different weight: they hang down at different heights, with different intensities, not because they are governed by rules of perspective or the laws of gravity, but because they have different meanings and vibrations in the other world from which they come. (See Chapter One, pp. 46-47, regarding ancient cave paintings.)

In the authoritative Japanese educational system, the teaching of Western art involved an unquestioning acceptance of scientific perspective. To question that, to be in self-doubt for decades about what that set of techniques meant to her own self-expression, was not easy for Junko. The mylar medium she found in the mid-1990s offered her a new way to paint and she was able to develop a new set of techniques around it.

Opposite:
IN THE FOREST OF AMIDA BUDDHA, No. 5 (1993)
Sumi and acrylic on mylar
81 x 42 in.
(205.7 x 106.7 cm.)

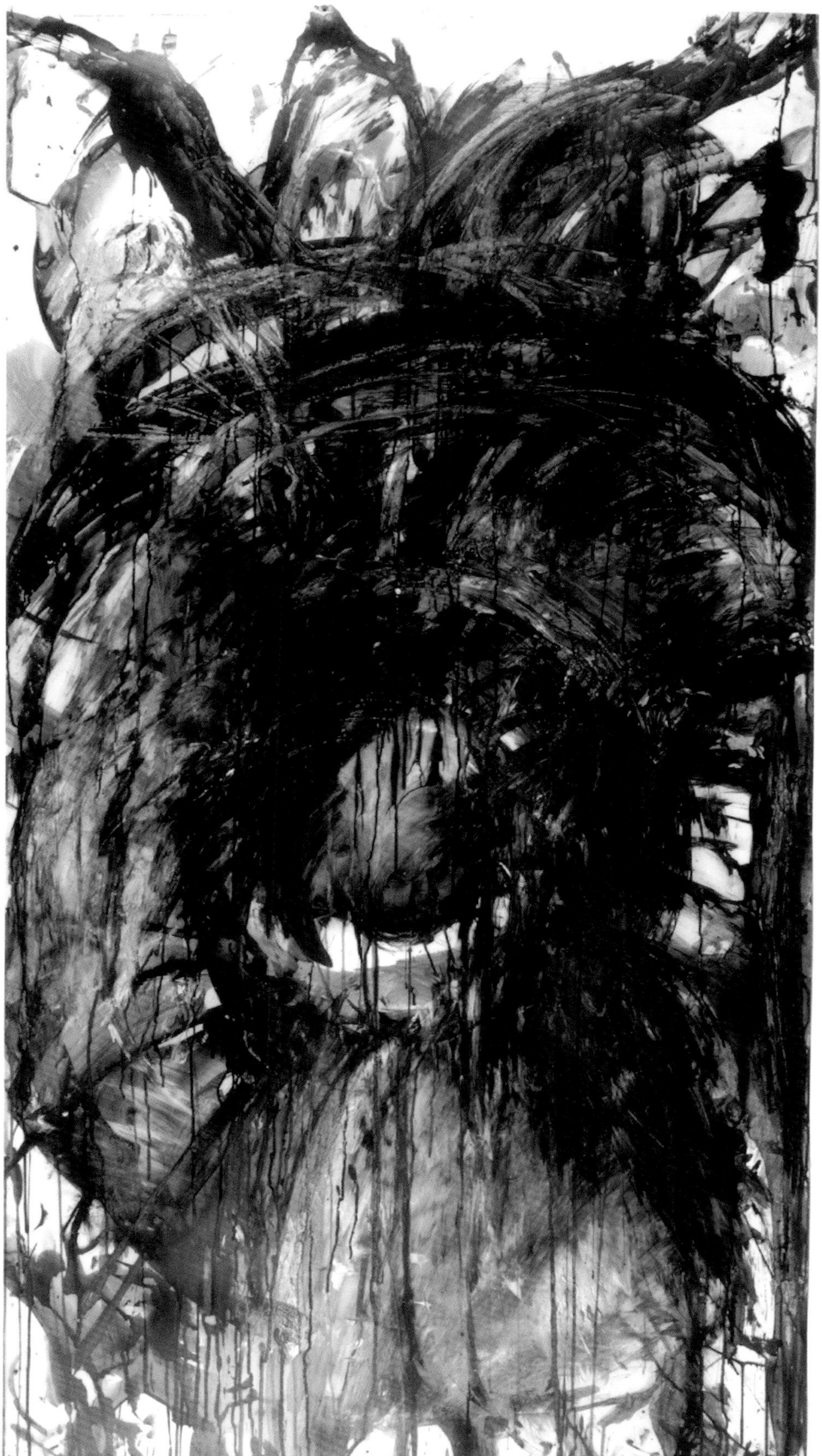

Junko's use of photographic images was an important stage in her search for a satisfactory technique. The photograph represents an ultimate sort of realism: who can doubt that the image which is photographed is "accurate"—at least, if it is not doctored? So Junko started to use images of burls, crabs, and some of her found objects, and these were mingled in with free-form brushwork and collage.

She used such photographs in *Interplanetary Icons* (1990, nineteen works), and again in *Tree Spirits in Gold* (1991, eight works). They appear also in *Requiem for an Executed Bird* (1991, forty-five works). The use of photographs in each of these three series is distinct: In *Interplanetary Icons*, we see virtual collages of photographs. In *Tree*

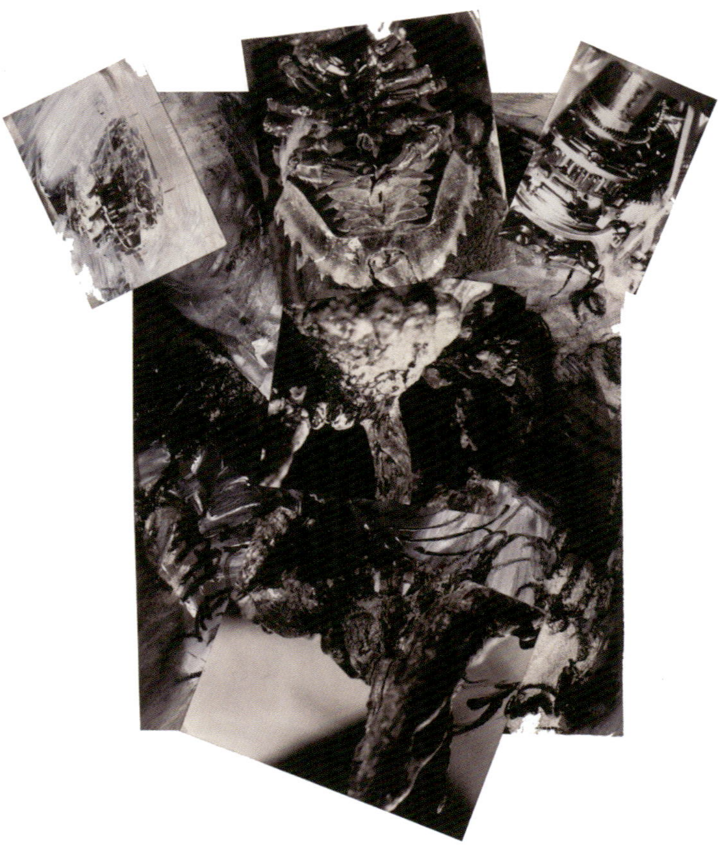

INTERPLANETARY ICON, No. 26 (1990)
Mixed media on paper
Irregular shape:
25 x 22 in.
(63.5 x 55.9 cm.)

Spirits in Gold, crisp photographs in the corners of the work, or off-center, form a striking contrast with the acrylic brushstrokes on the canvas which forms the works' support. And in *Requiem for an Executed Bird*, the photographic images are washed-out and broken down with Clorox.

Junko's relationship with photography is a chapter in her struggle to integrate left-brain and right-brain perceptions of reality: the left-brain objectivity which the photograph represents

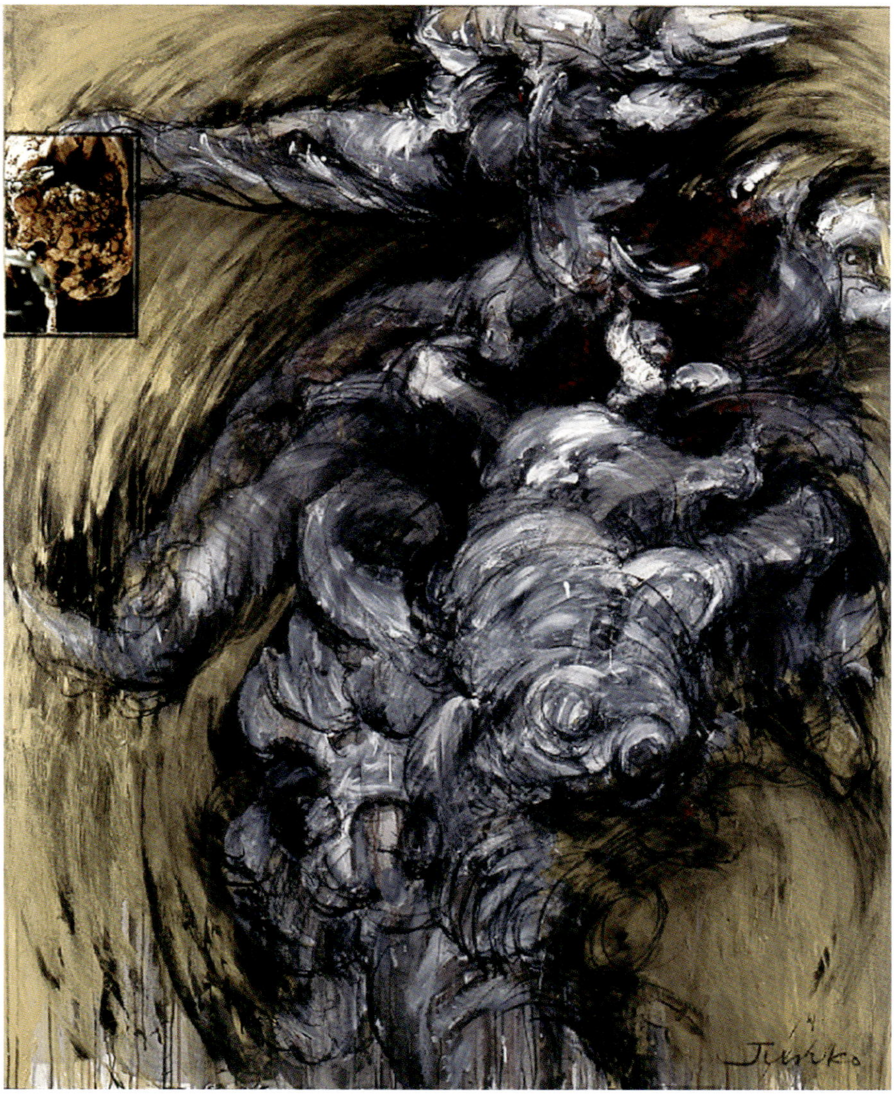

TREE SPIRITS IN GOLD, No. 8 (1991)
Mixed media on paper
66 x 56 in.
(167.6 x 142.2 cm.)

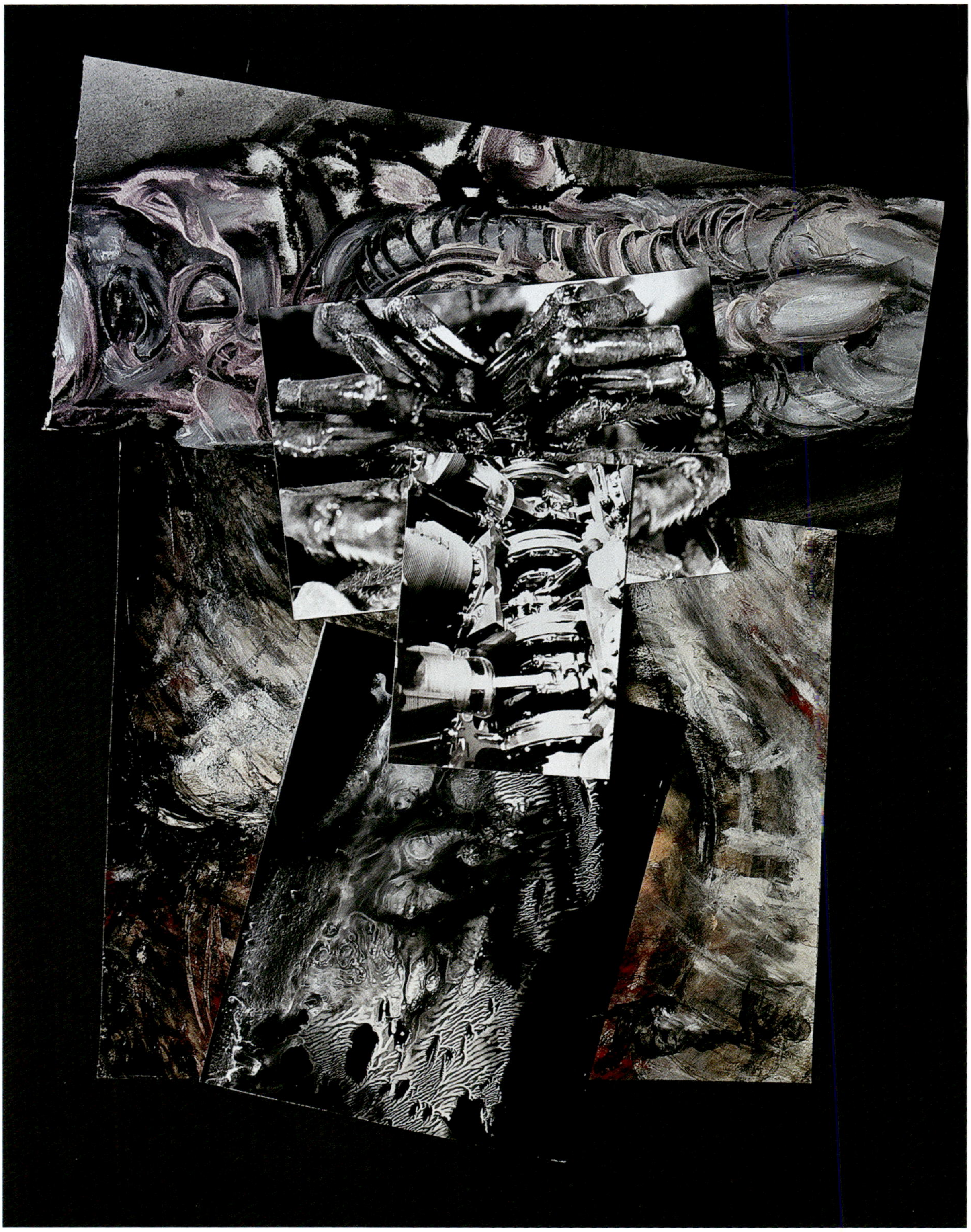

is impressed into the service of the underlying right-brain vision which is always the focus of her work. And breaking up the pictorial space with painting and photography, the artist wants to disrupt the viewer's assumption that the surface of the painting is the world, and force the viewer to realize that this is not a coherent space. Two spaces now co-exist in the same space, and the viewer realizes that he is confronting a deliberate illusion. This is another expression of Junko's strong desire to shatter complacency.

COMPUTER MANIPULATION

I spoke in the Foreword about how married people learn from each other—not in formal training sessions, but by absorbing small bits of learning regularly over the course of many years. Just as I learned from Junko to see art that way, Junko learned to integrate computers into her life and art from me.

Until the mid-1990s, Junko was uncomfortable with computers and viewed them as things that other people would touch—but not herself. But by the mid-1990s, she was using word processing to help her write, and soon after that she learned how to use email. These text-based functions of the computer freed her from a great deal of the drudgery—erasing, cutting and pasting, making small revisions—associated with generating speeches and essays in English. However, it was another couple of years before she came to feel that the computer could play a role in the generation of her art.

In those days, although I already identified myself as a lawyer and writer, I often spent fifteen hours a day writing complicated computer programs and testing them. I tried to reconcile what others saw as a "mismatch" between my announced calling and my actual activities, by arguing that computer science should be part of every liberal arts curriculum—not because computers were useful, but because they embodied styles of thinking that were essential to any form of rational activity. When I decided to leave the computer business and become a lawyer, I argued again that

Opposite:
INTERPLANETARY ICON, No. 27
Computer print and craypas on paper
Irregular shape:
25 x 22 in.
(63.5 x 55.9 cm.)

legal contracts should be designed along the same lines as the large-scale computer programs I had been writing: with definitions and common "subroutines" at the beginning, and major procedural elements in the body of the contract. I talked often with Junko about these ideas, even though she was not really familiar with what it was like to sit at a computer desk or to write an actual program.

Junko would ask me from time to time whether computers could be used to perform certain visual operations that she wanted to carry out. The fact is, she felt enormous frustration at not being able, sometimes, to translate her inner visions of enormously complex images into concrete paintings and she had urgent needs that she hoped the computer could satisfy. For example, she wanted to use a given image many times in a single work—flipping it, inverting it, distorting it, and resizing it. There are enormous piles of what must be called "preparatory Xeroxes" behind each of her finished works. Could computers help her do that? The *Root Series No. 16, Mandala* (see pg. 3), for example, shows the root in sixty-three rotations in three-dimensional space. Those rotations were done by Junko by hand: first in her pencil drawing, and then in collage. She wondered if it would be possible to do at least part of that work on a computer. I told her that the day would come when such things would be available but when we married, and through the 1980s, they were still far in the future.

But in the summer of 1997, a friend and client of mine invited Junko and me to attend a computer graphics convention at the Los Angeles Convention Center where his company would have an exhibit booth. This was a convention of the Association for Computing Machinery's "special interest group" that focused on computer graphics. There she saw for the first time, up close and in person, large drum printers and graphics software doing exactly the kind of image manipulations she had dreamed of for years. Within a few days, we had purchased a special computer and printer for her studio, along with the then-current version of Photoshop, and the two of us sat in front of that computer for sixteen hours a day, experimenting and struggling with the

Opposite left:
ESOTERIC BUDDHISM, PREPARATORY DRAWING No. 4 (2000)
Charcoal on scanned image
Virtual size

Opposite right:
GREYSCALE IMAGE (1997)
The first image Junko created using the computer.

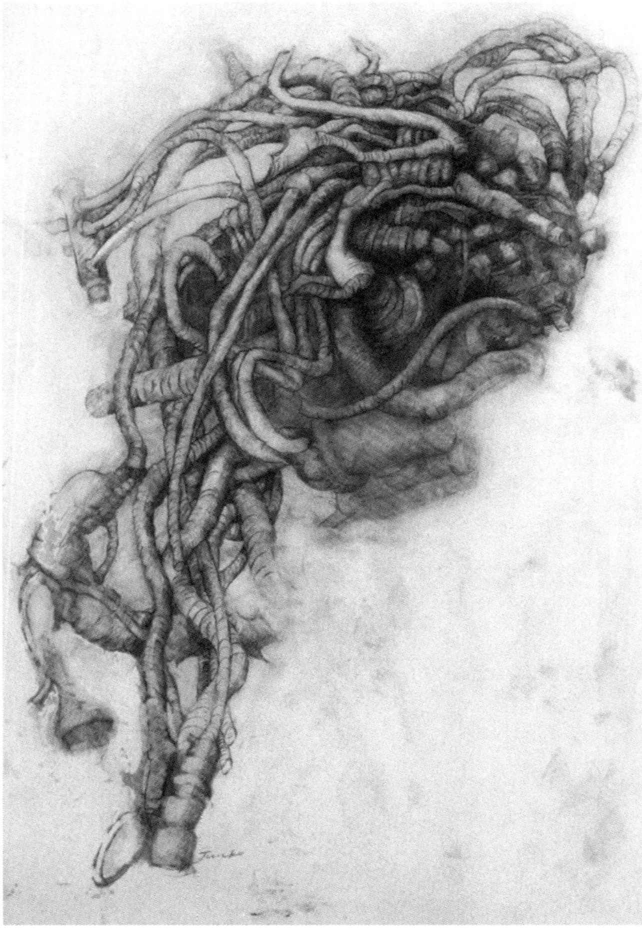

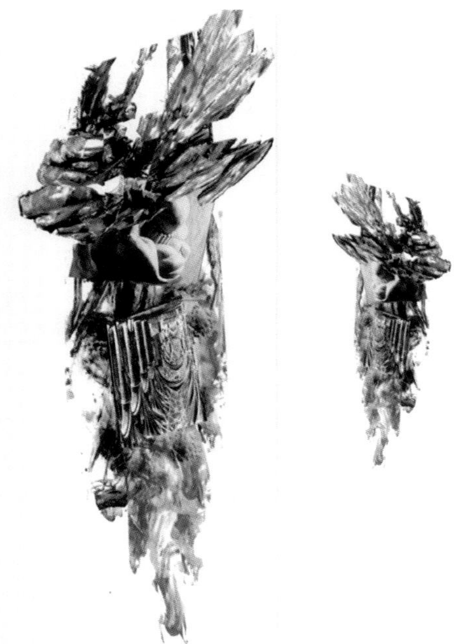

computer until we finally were able to create one image that Junko had dreamed of: *Sketchbook - Grayscale* (1997).

The task of learning how to use the computer for these purposes continued since then, and continues even now. As the one of us who is the more comfortable with computers, it is I who attend the training classes and read the manuals, and I sit at the keyboard and move the mouse. But it is Junko whose graphic intuition and specific desires drive the whole process. She tells me what she wants to do—and then it is easier for me to scan the manuals and the "Help" screens to find out how that particular task is to be accomplished.

The surprising thing is that she knows exactly what she wants to do. The computer is not a vehicle of exploration for her: it is a tool to concretize images and processes she has already conceived with amazing clarity. For years she wanted to transform images in the ways that are now so readily available in Photoshop: altering the colors, the transparency, the sizes, the orientations —these processes are now easy, and for years she had to do them by hand, or simply dream of doing them. In this way I feel she was familiar with the computer long before she even knew of computers: the graphic processes are already built into her, and she has adapted to using them most comfortably, integrating them with her other skills.

This integration appears in an interesting way in the *Preparatory Drawings* for her *Esoteric Buddhism series*. Made in the year 2000, these drawings began as pencil sketches. The sketches were then scanned into the computer and enlarged, distorted, and printed out on mylar. Then

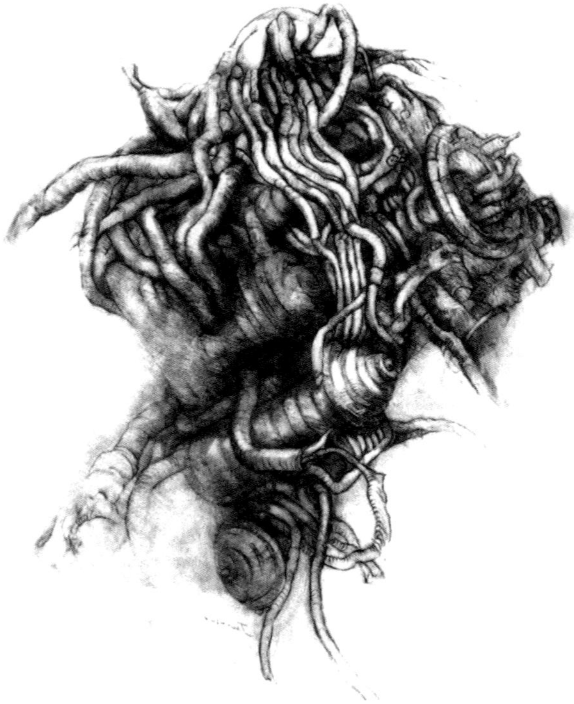

ESOTERIC BUDDHISM, PREPARATORY DRAWING No. 2 (2000)
Charcoal on computer print
Virtual size

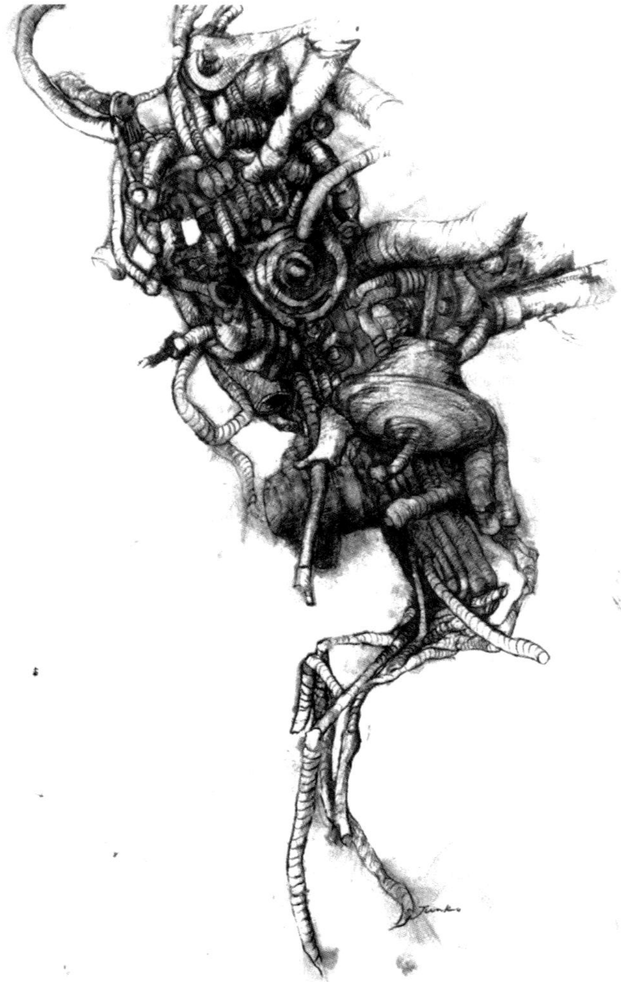

Junko went over the prints with charcoal pencil, working the drawings by hand until she was satisfied with them. This technique integrated computers and hand drawing. In the *Esoteric Buddhism* works themselves, the same technique was used again—only then, the prints were cut and used as collage. That same collage technique appears in full form again in the *FATHOM* series—except that instead of beginning with drawings, Junko began there with scans of her own earlier art works.

The fact that Photoshop includes so many of the functions that Junko wanted for so many years was also a kind of validation for Junko: there was some pathway between her private, visual world and the outside world. Programmers had worked, without having heard of her, to create the very things she needed. Her visual desires had some intrinsically reasonable qualities that were shared with others. Junko writes of her own relationship with the computer:

ESOTERIC BUDDHISM, PREPARATORY DRAWING No. 3 (2000)
Charcoal on computer print
Virtual size

Studio Notebook, 2005

I can create the images I received while I was in an altered state of consciousness. The image hangs in front of me, or above me, huge, complicated, powerful, and subtle. With the help of the computer I can transfer it on to the paper as quickly as it demands. So the computer functions as a part of my sensitive visual receiver, and as a drawing tool in my trembling hands. There are many things I wanted to handle with the computer which I had not done before the computer became available; but also, there must be many things I am doing with the computer that have never been done before me. Once more, I am standing in front of a huge new door in my life!

CHARCOAL AND ACRYLIC

Most of the techniques described here were either invented by Junko or so radically developed by her that we see them as unique. But she has created some works using a more conventional technique. Her paintings of burls and tree spirits are made with charcoal and acrylic on paper, using a brush.

Remembering that she encouraged the spirits to "toss themselves in the air and dance with her" (see Chapter One, pg. 52), a gestural technique allowing for direct hand movements was required: the meditative techniques of collage and pen and ink would not do. And although she did not invent either the materials or the overall technique, the combination of acrylic and iridescent paints with charcoal was unusual.

Her *Giant Burls* series, again, uses acrylic and charcoal; and so does her *Tree Spirits in Gold* series (1991, eight works) where she worked on canvas and included photographs.

Her *Emerging Consciousness* series, twelve works created in 1988, again use acrylic—this time on kromekote; and they are finger paintings, made with Junko's eyes almost closed. (See discussion under "Altered States" in Chapter Six.)

Opposite:
BURLS, No. 3 (1989)
Collage and
acrylic on paper
40 x 32 in.
(106.3 x 81.3 cm.)

Page 144:
TREE SPIRITS,
No. 14 (1989)
Acrylic and
charcoal on paper
32 x 40 in.
(81.28 x 101.6 cm.)

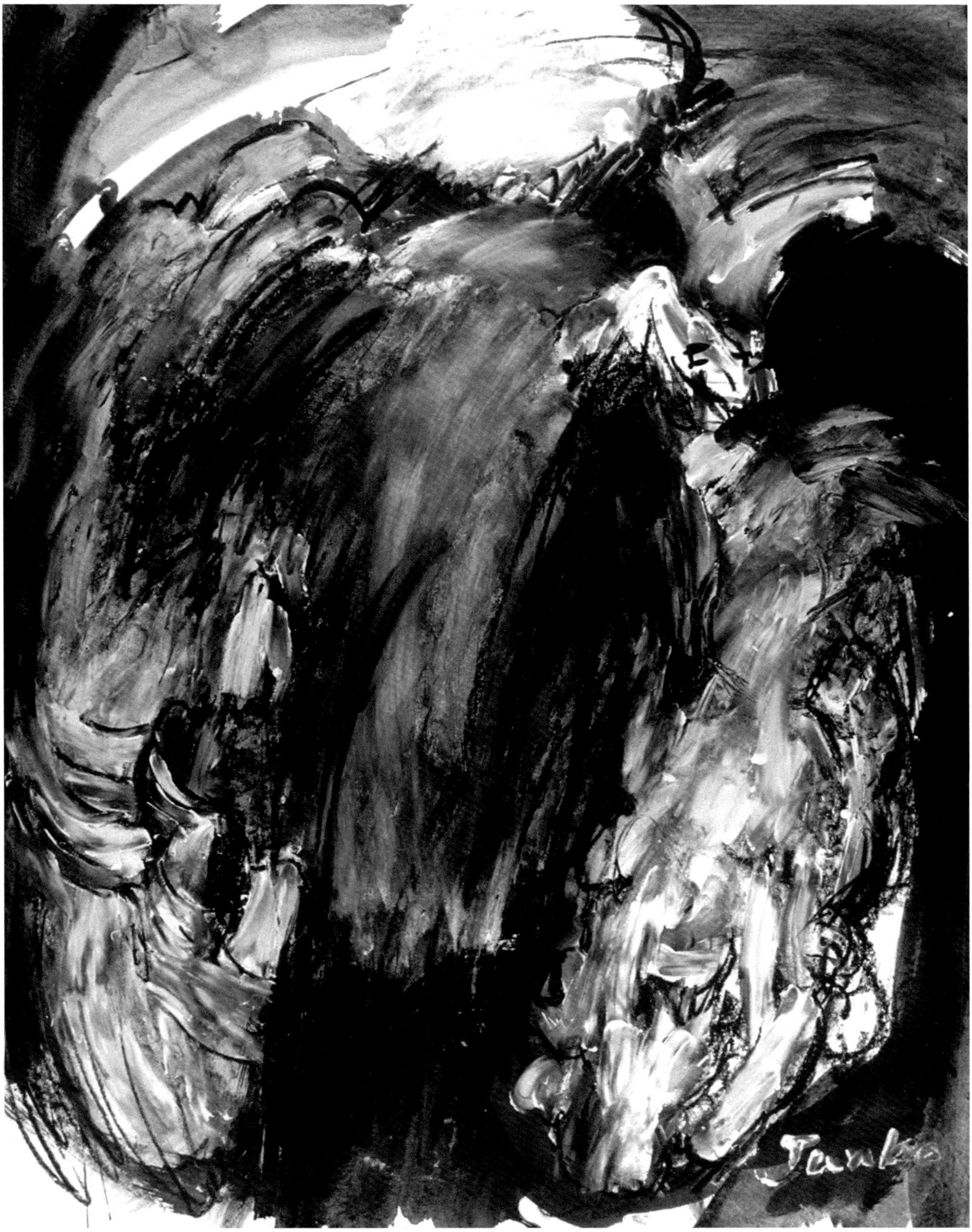
Tanaka

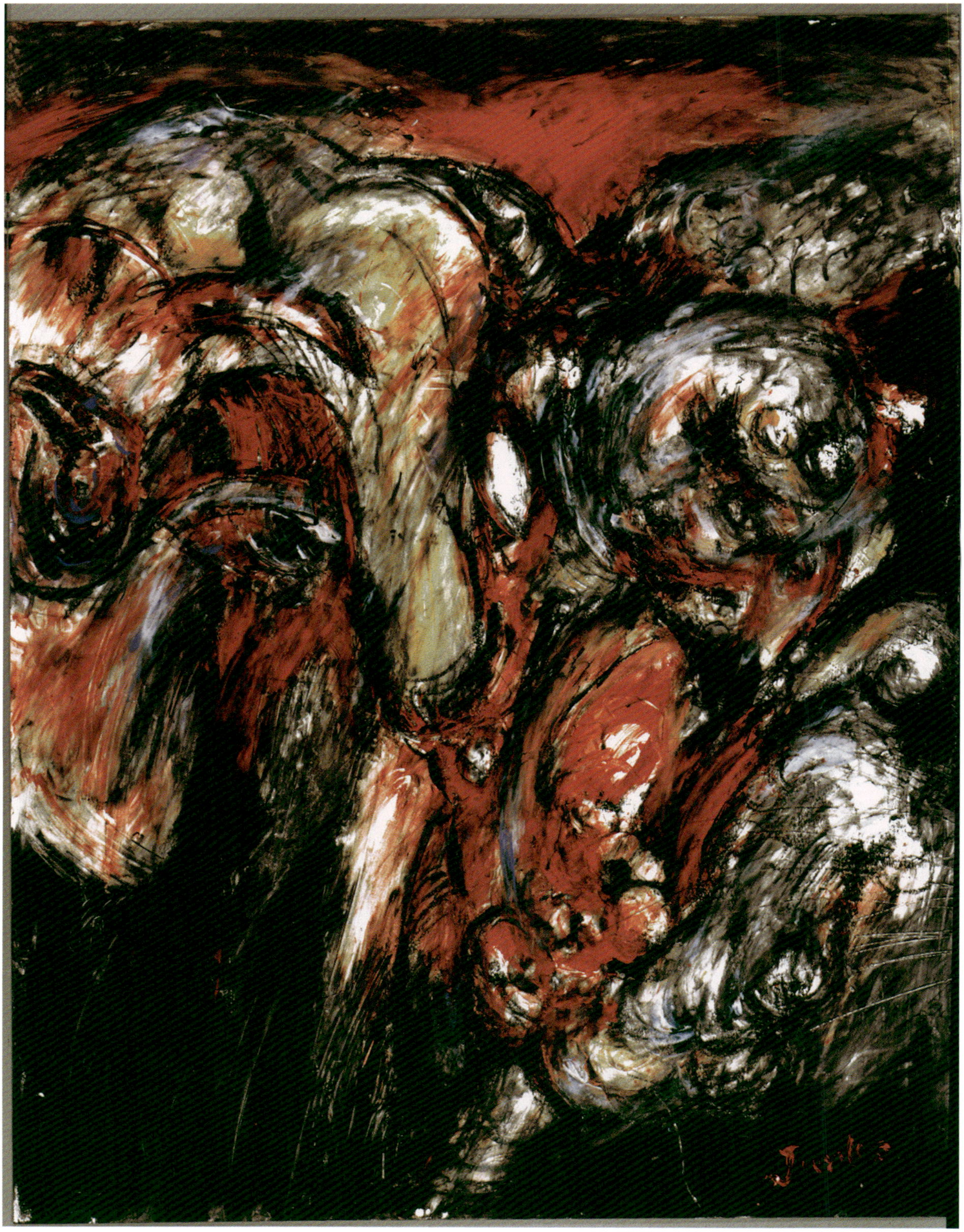

STYLES

By "style" I mean objective features of Junko's works that are not tied directly to her choice of technique.

Orientation: Vertical and Horizontal

With only a few exceptions, Junko's works are vertically oriented. That is to say, they are taller than they are wide. If you give Junko a blank piece of paper, she will turn it vertically before working on it. This is because the vertical orientation induces a sense of aspiration in her: the eye moves upward and carries the spirit with it. "I will lift up mine eyes unto the hills, whence cometh my help!"[1] But of course, Junko's works all struggle with upward/aspirational movement and downward movement—and it is the tension between these that often gives the works their strength. See for instance, *Individuation Journal, No. 7,* at pg. 260 where the "falling man" contrasts with the upward movements of the letters and the black wings.

But starting from the early 1970s, Junko has put several vertical pieces of paper together to create multi-panel works which are wider than they are tall. The earliest of these is *Dead Flower Series, No. 8, Byoobu* (1973, pp. 18-19). That work is composed of three panels, and while each panel is vertical, the whole work is horizontally oriented. In the *Esoteric Buddhism* series, Junko flanked a three-panel work which is nearly square (fourteen feet wide, twelve feet tall) with two clearly vertical panels (eight feet tall by 3.5 feet wide). This series reveals a tension between the two orientations.

Most recently, in *FATHOM*, Junko set out to create wide works which could fill a huge stage—and so even though each panel is just 3.5 feet wide, the works themselves were always conceived as horizontal. They include three-panel foregrounds and four-panel backgrounds, for an overall width of 25.5 feet, as against a height of just twelve feet maximum. But despite their objectively horizontal orientation, their size and overall composition still evoke a sense of aspiration and looking upward.

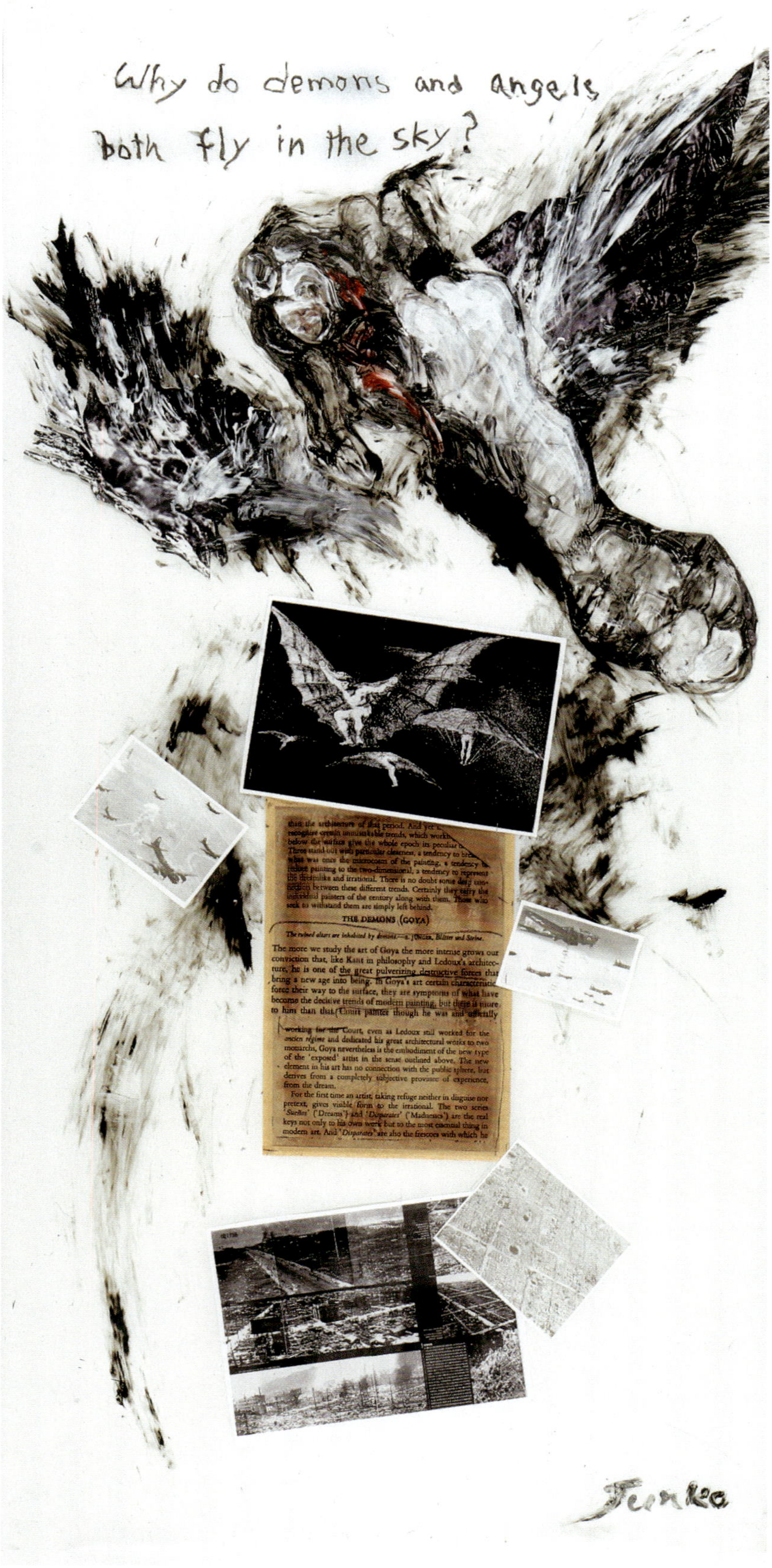

CONCERNING ART
AND RELIGION, No. 1
(2003)
"WHY DO DEMONS
AND ANGELS
BOTH FLY IN THE SKY?"
Acrylic and collage
on mylar
80 x 42 in.
(203.2 x 106.7 cm.)

Time—Gesturality

I am often asked by admiring viewers, "How long did it take Junko to create that work?" This question comes up particularly when people look at the *Root* series collages whose intricate, detailed, layered quality often intrigues them. But also, recently, viewing Junko's huge mylars in the *FATHOM* series, many viewers have asked me the same question.

The question is a natural one, but it turns out not to have a simple answer because there are three kinds of time involved in creating any work: the preparation time, the time spent in the studio specifically on that work, and the time spent returning from the studio to normal life after the work has been created.

These kinds of time arise in other settings, where they are easier to see. There is a story of a nobleman in Japan who owned a wooden screen used as a room divider. At different times, two different artists had painted very beautiful scenes on the two sides of the screen, and now the nobleman wanted to separate those two art works and use them in different rooms in his palace. He called his carpenters and craftsmen but they all told him that the wooden screen was too thin to slice apart and if they tried, they would damage the art. One day the nobleman heard that a great samurai was staying in the nearby village and that he was also a carpenter and an artist. The nobleman asked him if he could slice the images apart and he said he could. Then the nobleman said, "If you succeed, I will give you a great fortune; but if you fail, you must die!" and the samurai nodded his assent. He then told the nobleman and all his courtiers to leave him alone in the great room where the screen stood. He sat there motionless before the screen for three days and three nights, not eating, sleeping, or drinking. And then, just before dawn on the third day he leaped up, drawing his sword, and slashed the screen apart into two perfect halves in the twinkling of an eye. The nobleman and all his retainers had watched in amazement from outside the room, and gave the samurai his great chest full of gold bars as he walked out of the palace.

Would you say that the work of slicing the screen took two seconds or three days?

And if you have ever watched a martial artist practice his movements, the *kata*, you will see that after he finishes the sequence his arms still twitch and his breath still moves for minutes after he has stopped moving. This is the sign that his *ki*, his energy, is still circulating vigorously and that he must wait for it to quiet down.

These are the same kinds of time that Junko spends. The relative lengths of these three spans of time have indeed changed for Junko over the years. In the *Dead Flower* series and *Root* series, for instance, the preparation time and the in-studio time were merged: the repetitive, meditative style of these works, coupled with Junko's ability to go over the same work many times, adding strokes to it and "re-balancing" it, meant that the time in the studio overlapped the preparation time. Each of those works required approximately one month of long days in the studio to create. And then, after they were created, Junko was able to move on to the next one of them—again, because of the special characteristics of those techniques.

Later series required a longer preparation time, and then a shorter "in-studio" time. The *Requiem* series, in 1991, required at least four years of preparation, but once she was in the studio Junko created as many as three works in a single day. After working she was exhausted and would have to sleep, or drive up the coast to feel the ocean and see the mountains, before she could go back to the next works.

In the Forest of Amida Buddha was similar: Junko prepared for many weeks, but once she was ready, she created the whole series within a few weeks, often creating more than one work in a single day. Here again, the time she had to spend after the work was longer, the studio experience was intense, and very much separated from her daily life. In order to return to daily life, a longer time was needed.

Opposite Top:
DETAIL FROM ROOT SERIES No. 16, *Mandala* (1979).
The full image appears on pg. 3. The work took a year to create. The individual pieces were picked up with tweezers and layered on to the paper. The artist went over the work time and time again until the whole work was complete.

Opposite Bottom:
REQUIEM FOR AN EXCUTED BIRD, No. 33 (1991)
Mixed media collage on paper
40 x 32 in.
(101.6 x 81.3 cm.)

These works poured out of Junko three or four per day. The whole series of forty-five works was completed in less than two months. But after each day of working, Junko had to lie in bed for many days.

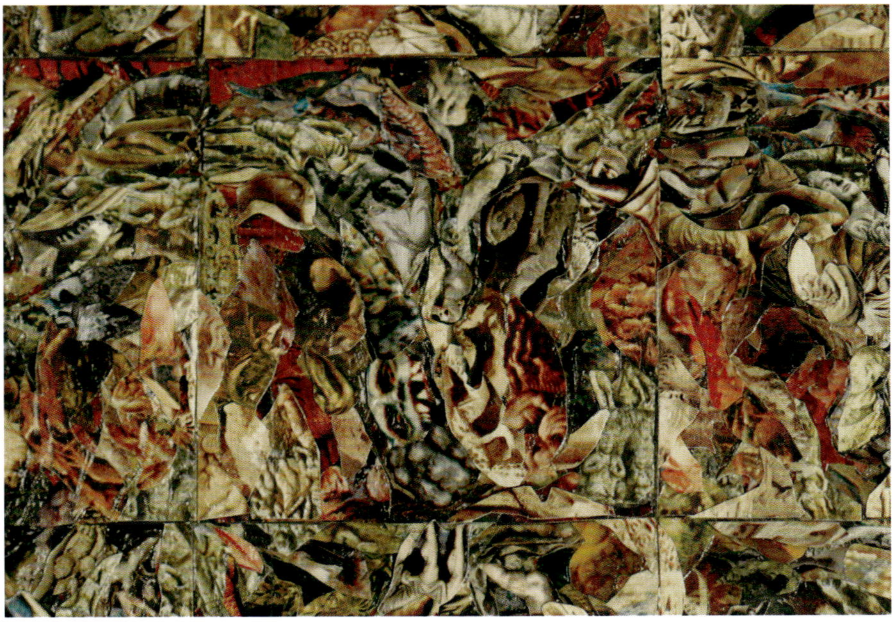

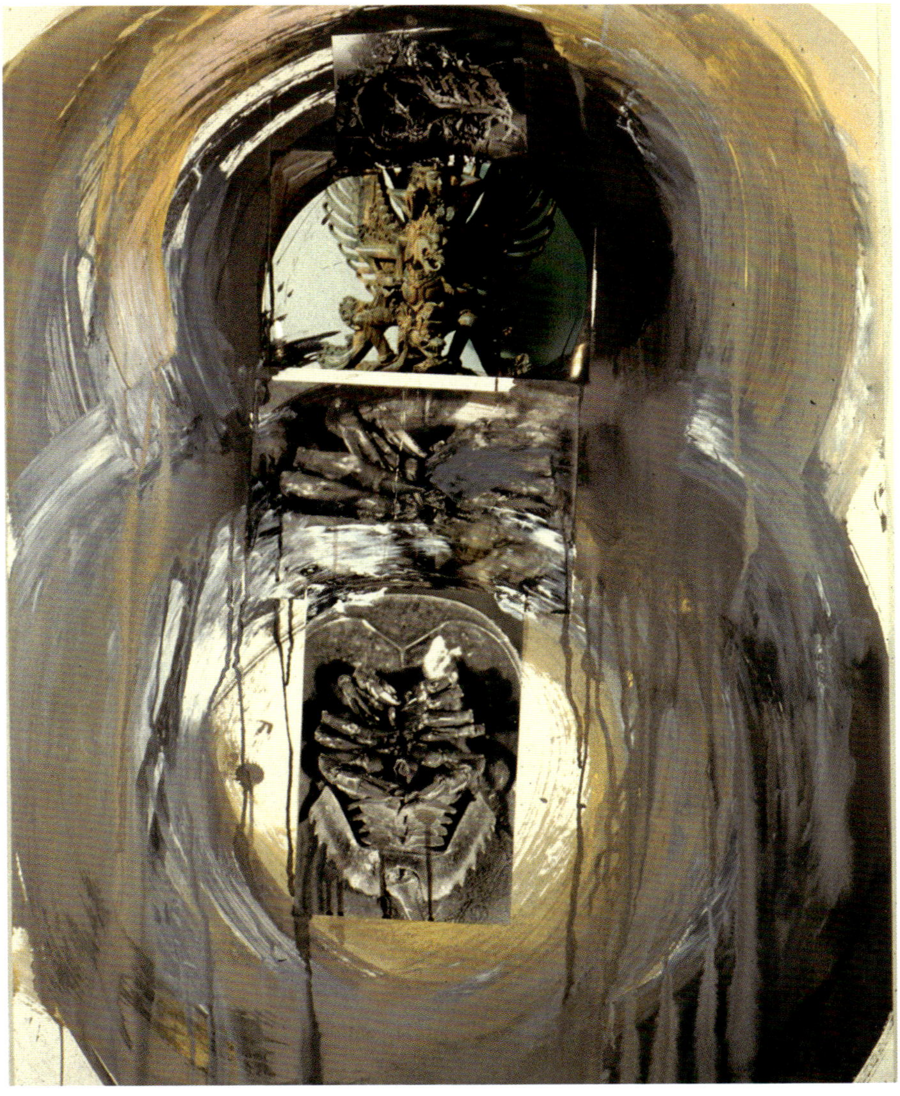

Of the three kinds of time, what I have called "preparation time" is the hardest to understand—and yet it is the most important because it is during the preparation time that the deep experience which lies at the heart of the work makes its journey from Junko's innermost heart to the painting surface. A good example is the scene called "Perilous Ocean" in the *FATHOM* series (see pp. 152-153). This is the scene of the dance where Kuukai, the ninth century Buddhist priest, crossed the ocean to China in order to study Esoteric Buddhism and bring it back to Japan. Japanese shipmaking craft was still primitive in those days: the boats had flat bottoms instead of hulls, and they were sealed with seaweed glue instead of pitch. As a result many of the boats the emperor sent to China broke up in the harsh seas and their crews perished. Kuukai knew this and went on this journey at the risk of his life. His boat was in fact shipwrecked, but he survived and was able to reach his destination. The ocean he crossed was a spiritual ocean as well as a physical one; his journey was intended to be a life-changing event for him.

Junko was particularly eager to create this scene first among all the eight scenes of the *FATHOM* program. Fifty years earlier, she herself had crossed the Pacific Ocean when she and her first husband returned from their first year in America. Japan was still a poor country in the postwar period, and Junko and her husband booked passage on a tiny, ill-equipped Japanese cargo ship. The boat was struck by storms and it was partially damaged, but after a dangerous two-and-a-half week trip it finally arrived at the pier of Yokohama Harbor. Junko's memory of that trip across a stormy ocean is still very vivid in her—and yet, she required five years of "preparation time" to begin the work in the studio. Here is what she wrote about that five-year period after it was over:

Studio Notebook, 2006

I can identify with the feeling of powerlessness at feeling the huge waves knocking on the bottom of the boat and monstrous waves standing up in front of you reaching to the sky, bathed in flashes of lightning and swallowing up the entire mast of the little boat; at hearing the squeaky, crushing, banging sounds of the boat and the growling voice of the wind—like an animal's voice. I can even identify with the feeling of oneness with the raging storm itself—all of which were things Kuukai must have experienced.

But what exactly did this stormy ocean look like to Kuukai—to the man who was thirty years old, a metaphysical thinker, and an archaic mystic, who already had direct contact with the universe and who already knew his destiny? How did he see this fury of the ocean at the very starting point of his new spiritual journey? I was twenty-one years old on my boat trip, and the decision I had already made, to divorce my first husband the moment I set foot on Japanese soil, weighed heavily on my mind. I too knew that this storm was the start of my own new spiritual journey. This stormy ocean which I experienced as a young woman, however humble my experience may have been in comparison with Kuukai's, this is what I had to use as the base to go into Kuukai's inner world in order to visualize the stormy ocean he saw in his inner eye. I needed five years for this task.

The *FATHOM* works, consisting of forty panels grouped into seven scenes, took nine months to create, but the series required more than five years of thinking and specific preparation. Because those works are heavily dependent on computer output, we might not want to call them "gestural." Yet the time spent in the studio "per square inch" was remarkably short. Junko would often have me create all the computer elements before she began putting the fragments onto the mylar, so the works might be seen as gestural after all. After she finished that series, Junko was again exhausted, and more than a year of "after time" was required before she could return to the studio.

Next Pages:
FATHOM: PERILOUS OCEAN (2005)
Collage of computer prints on mylar
Four panels
Overall: 12 x 14 ft. (365.8 x 320 cm.)

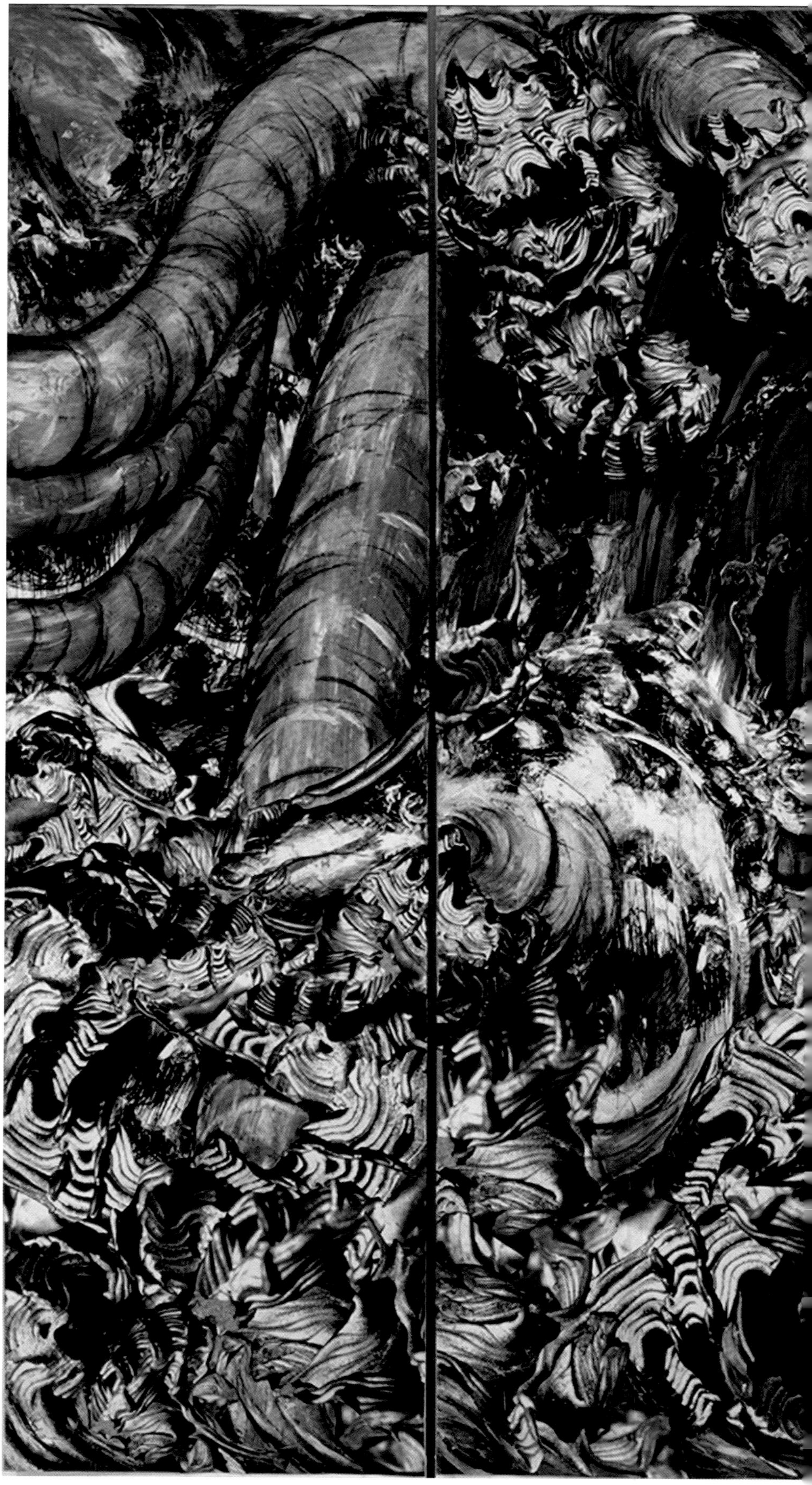

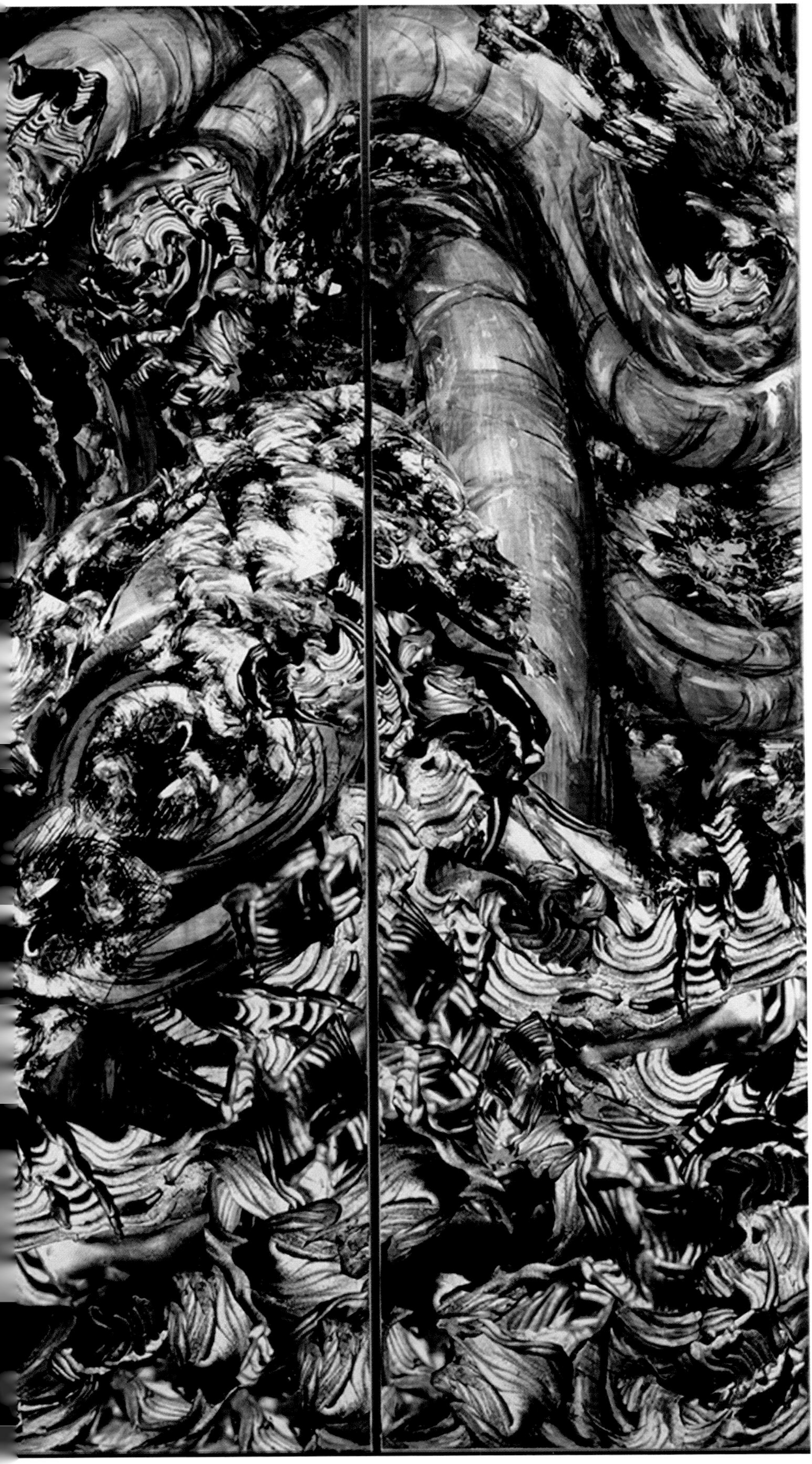

I find it useful to think of three rough periods in the development of Junko's art and I call the styles associated with these periods "images," "narratives," and "reflections."

Images. For over fifteen years, Junko drew objects, which she set before her and studied and then drew—over and over again, in series, until she felt the images had been fully apprehended and resolved. In most cases, she drew "studies" or sketches of the objects until she felt ready to create real works; and then she created a series of works. This was the pattern with the *Dead Flowers* series (1973–1974, eight works), the *Root* series (1974–1979, sixteen works), the *Horseshoe Crab* series (1983, three works), the *Burls* (1988 and 1989, twenty-one works) and *Tree Spirits* (1989–1991, twenty-seven works), the *Engines* (1981, four works), and the figure drawings (1983, 1987, fifty works).

Narratives. In 1991 Junko created a series that tells a story: *Requiem for an Executed Bird* (forty-five works, created over just six weeks in June and July of that year, see Chapter Four). In the *Requiem* series, Junko went through a painful journey which began with a traumatic childhood encounter with a bird whose head had been chopped off (see pg. 86). This encounter generated a phobia in her, and for fifty years she could not stand to look at a bird of any kind. But in 1991 she had the courage to paint a series of forty-five works featuring the executed bird, and the series itself proceeded through resolution of the phobia to a sense of redemption and transcendence. Each painting in the series is the trace of one step or milestone of that journey.

That series remains Junko's most full-bodied narrative. But two years later she created *In the Forest of Amida Buddha* (1993, twenty-four works) which tells the story of Amida Buddha passing through the forest in our back yard, as if he were coming to collect the soul of someone dead. This series was made while I myself was sick with a life-threatening illness. The last works in the series show the forest in flames—cremated. I recovered from my illness; and the trees in our forest grew back. The whole series of twenty-four works is a narrative.

Opposite:
REQUIEM FOR AN EXECUTED BIRD,
No. 24 (1991)
"The Bird is Dying"
Mixed media on paper
40 x 32 in.
(101.6 x 81.3 cm.)

This is part of a narrative series. While the image is capable of standing by itself, it has another dimension that can be understood only with reference to the other works in the same series.

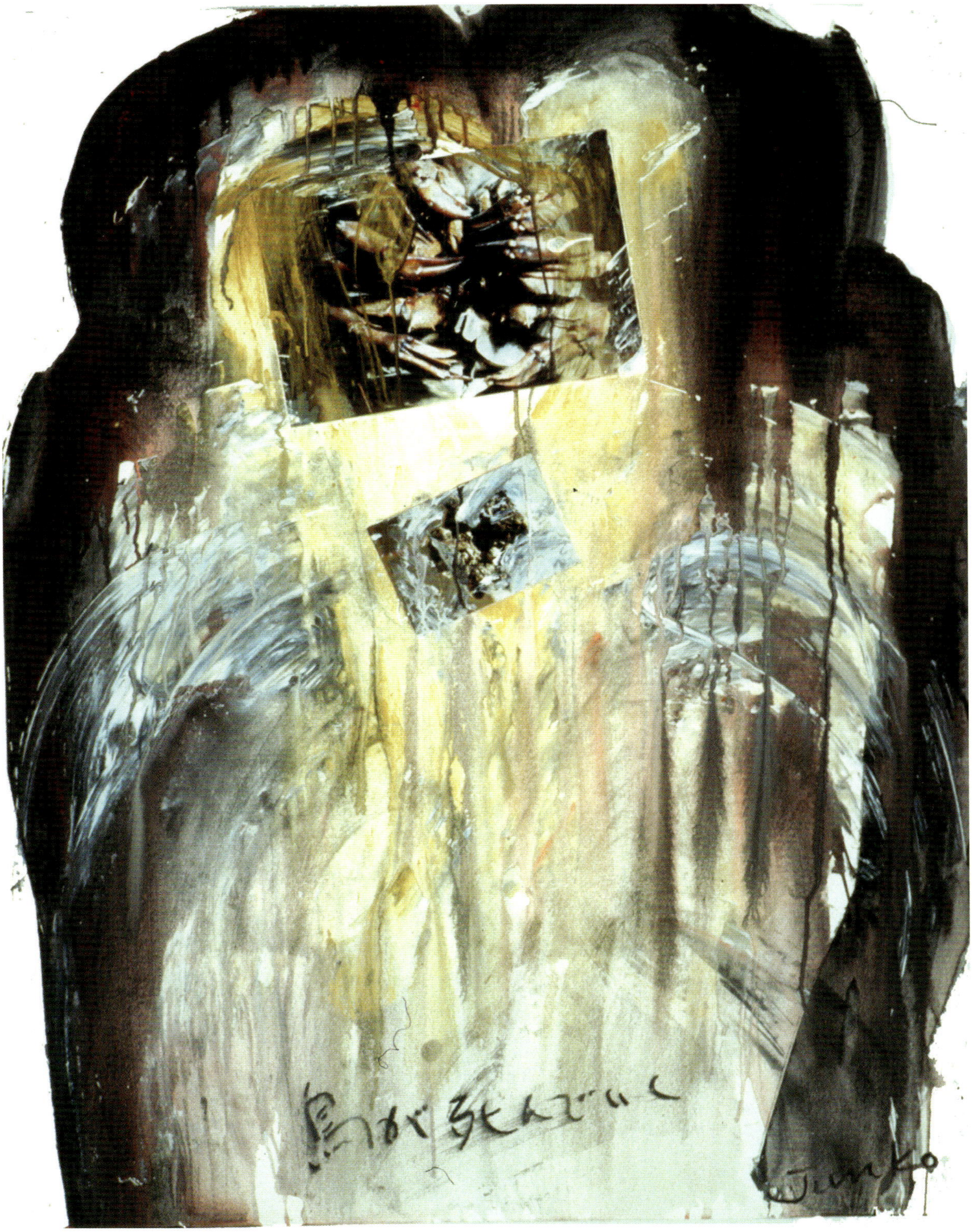
鳥が死んでいく
Junko

And in 2006, Junko created her *FATHOM* series of sets of giant mylar panels to serve as backdrops for a dance program. Each of these sets of panels depicts a major scene in the life of Kuukai, a ninth-century Japanese priest.

Junko's narrative works are best seen in a series: even though each work stands on its own, another dimension of the meaning of each work reveals itself only when we view it in relation to the earlier and later works in the same series.

Reflections. After she completed the Forest series, Junko started a new kind of painting: images that include some kind of discourse about themselves. Most of these works include text which comments on them or extends their meaning. The clearest early examples are to be found in the *Individuation Journal* (1995, thirteen works). But the *Esoteric Buddhism* series (2001, three works) also consists of images with related texts, and *Concerning Art and Religion* (2003–2004, nine works) carries this style to its limit.

The relationship of Junko's texts to her works is something different from what is found in other contemporary artists. For example, her texts are not brand names such as we find in the works of Andy Warhol (the Campbell soup can) or Jean-Michel Basquiat (Zydeco/Westinghouse), nor mere messages such as we find in some conceptual works (e.g. John Baldessari (1971), "I will not make any more boring art"), nor are they comic book captions such as we find in the works of Roy Lichtenstein, nor are they cynical or mocking messages such as we find in Ben Vautier's 1971 canvas which reads (in English translation) "Art is Useless: Go Home" or in Ed Ruscha's *Noise* (1963). Instead, Junko's texts promote the enterprise at the heart of all her work: seeking the center. Even though she sometimes uses deliberately puzzling questions as her text, her purpose is to amplify the message of the image and remind the viewer of the world of thought behind it. For example, the text for *Concerning Art and Religion, No. 1* (2003) is, "Why do demons and angels both fly in the sky?" The image includes a quote from Goya but in the twenty-first century, angels and demons are not accepted as opposites—at least, not in the naïve way they were in Goya's time.

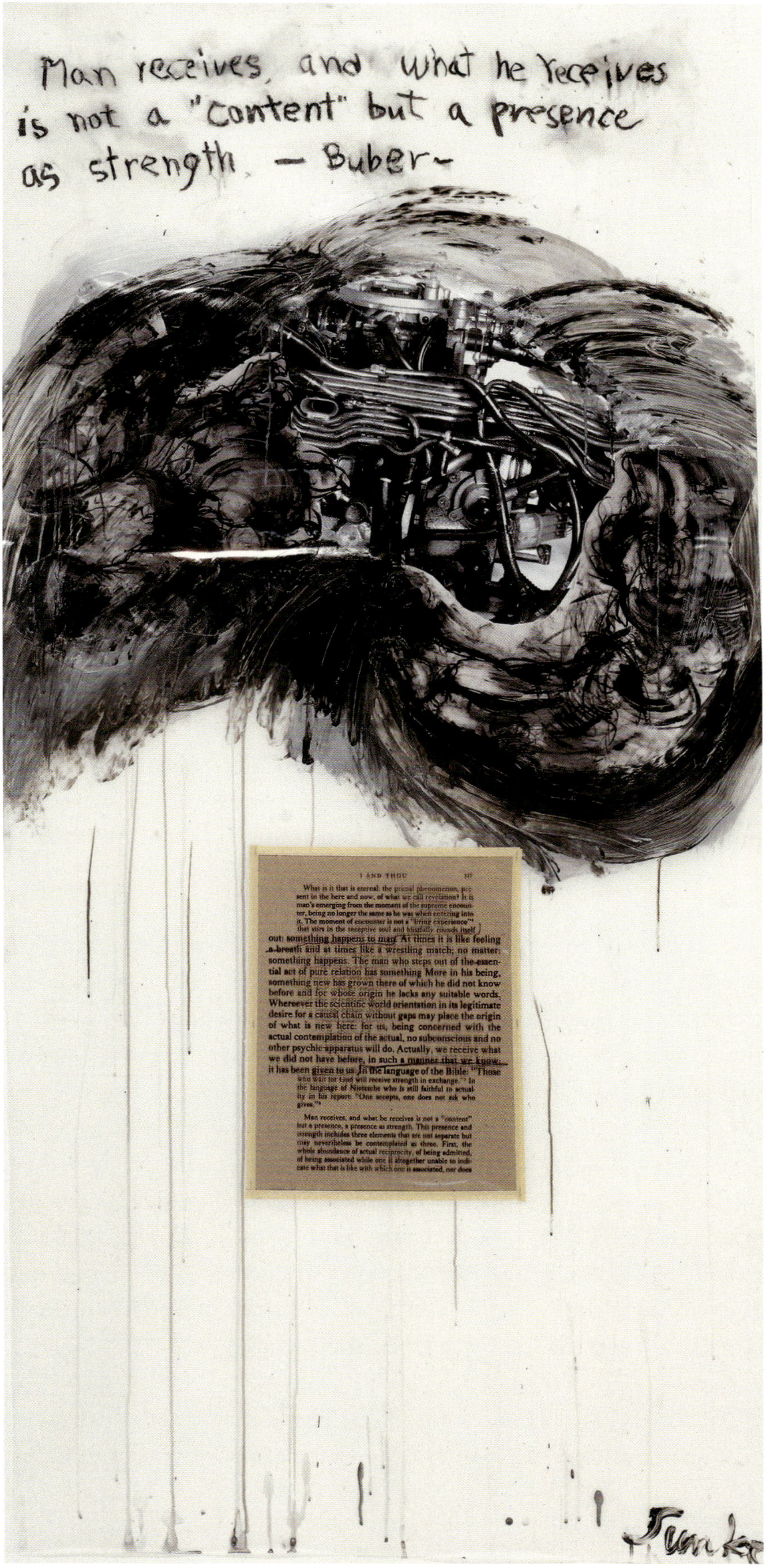

CONCERNING ART AND RELIGION, No. 6 (2003)
Acrylic and collage
on mylar support
84 x 82 in.
(213.4 x 106.7 cm.)

Sometimes the texts underscore the meaning of the images themselves which might otherwise seem more abstract than Junko intended. For instance in *Individuation Journal, No. 7, The Fall of Man* (1995, at pg. 260), the words come from Erich Fromm:

> The paralyzing effect of power does not rest only upon the fear it arouses but equally upon the implicit promise—the promise that those in possession of power can protect and take care of the "weak" who submit to them, that they can free man from the burden of uncertainty and of responsibility for himself by guaranteeing order and by assigning the individual a place in this order which makes him feel secure. Man's submission to this combination of threat and promise is his real "fall."

The image shows a man falling out of the sky. The letters curve away from him and the streaks of acrylic require us to move our eyes up and down, contributing to the sense of discomfort which the text is intended to provoke.

These three periods are not exactly chronological. For example, I classify both the *Dead Flower* series and *Root* series as "images," but there is a narrative element to the *Dead Flowers* series: after drawing images of the dead flowers over and over again, Junko finally saw Buddha heads appearing from the flowers (see pg. 17). Some of the *Root* series collages have narrative force: No. 9, *Emergence of Buddha*; No. 11 and 12, two images of the *Fasting Buddha*. And Junko has a long history of making "reflective" titles for her works. In her *What is Jumping Out Here?* and *Whatever is Coming, I am Ready for it!*, the titles are reflections on what was going to become a new direction in her art; and in *Devil Escaping* Junko included an image of the devil carrying her away from the image.

DEVIL ESCAPING (1983)
Mixed media
collage on paper
11 x 9 in.
(27.9 x 22 cm.)

But the fact remains that these three major styles permeate Junko's corpus, and they generally grew in chronological sequence.

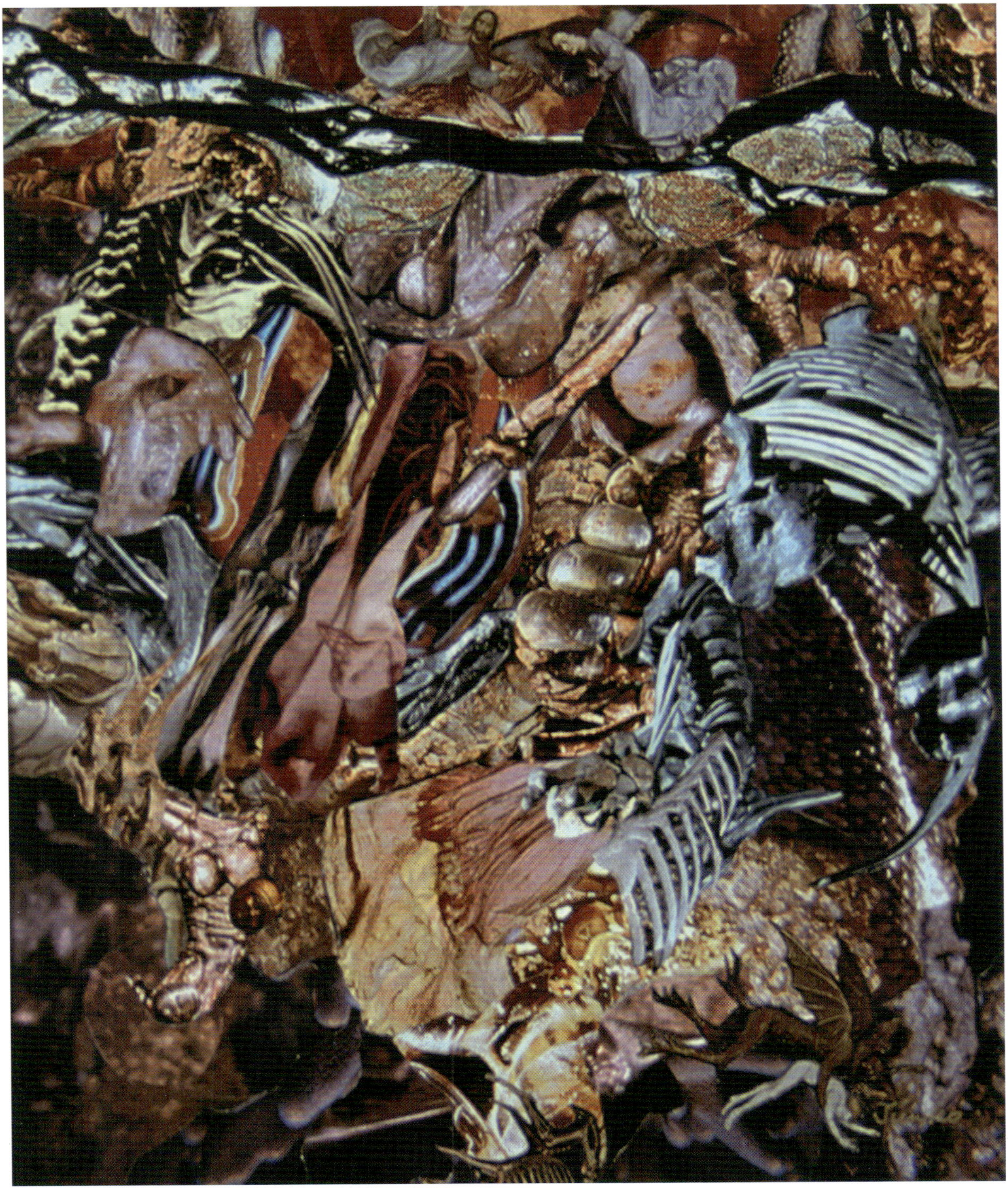

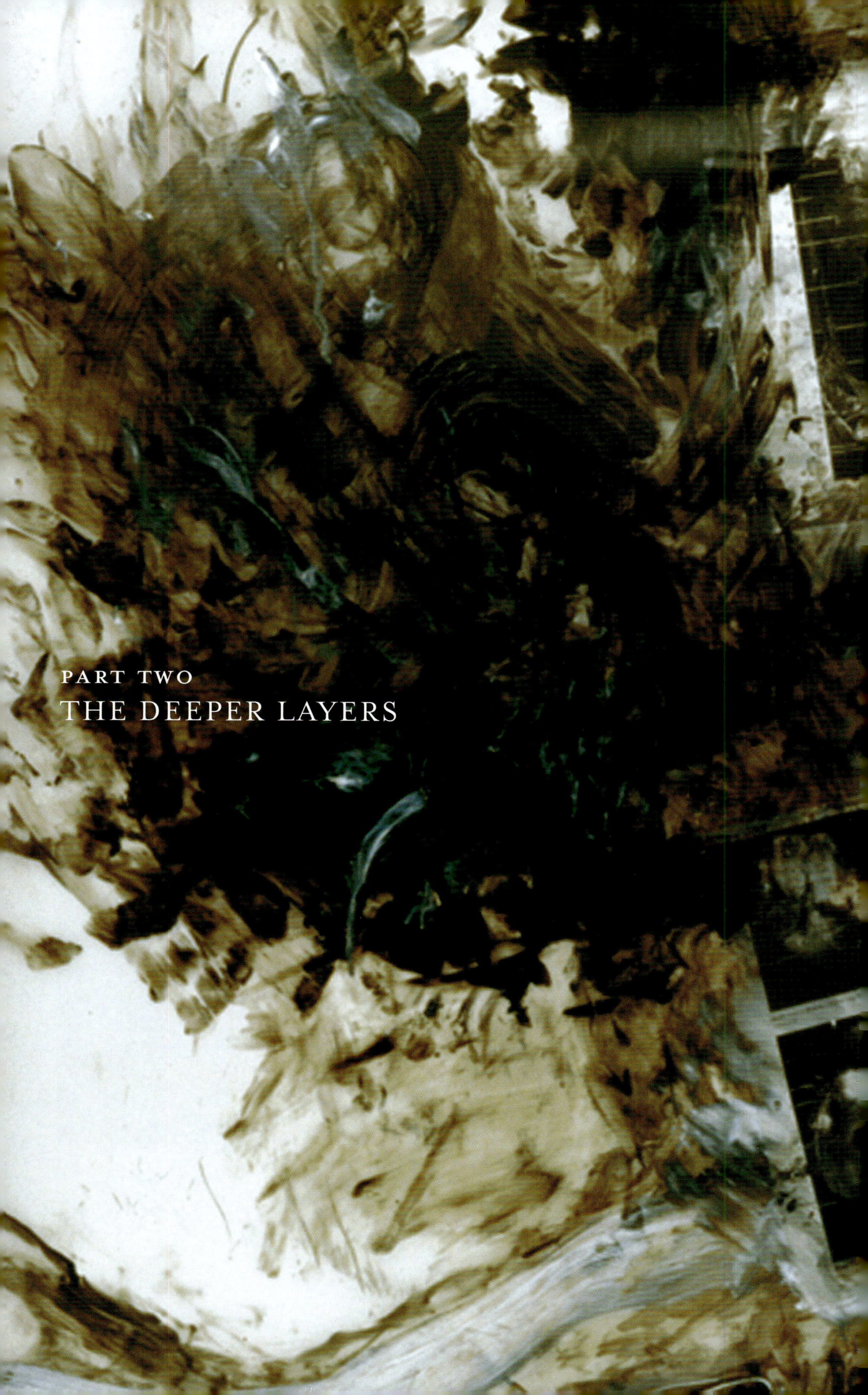

PART TWO

THE DEEPER LAYERS

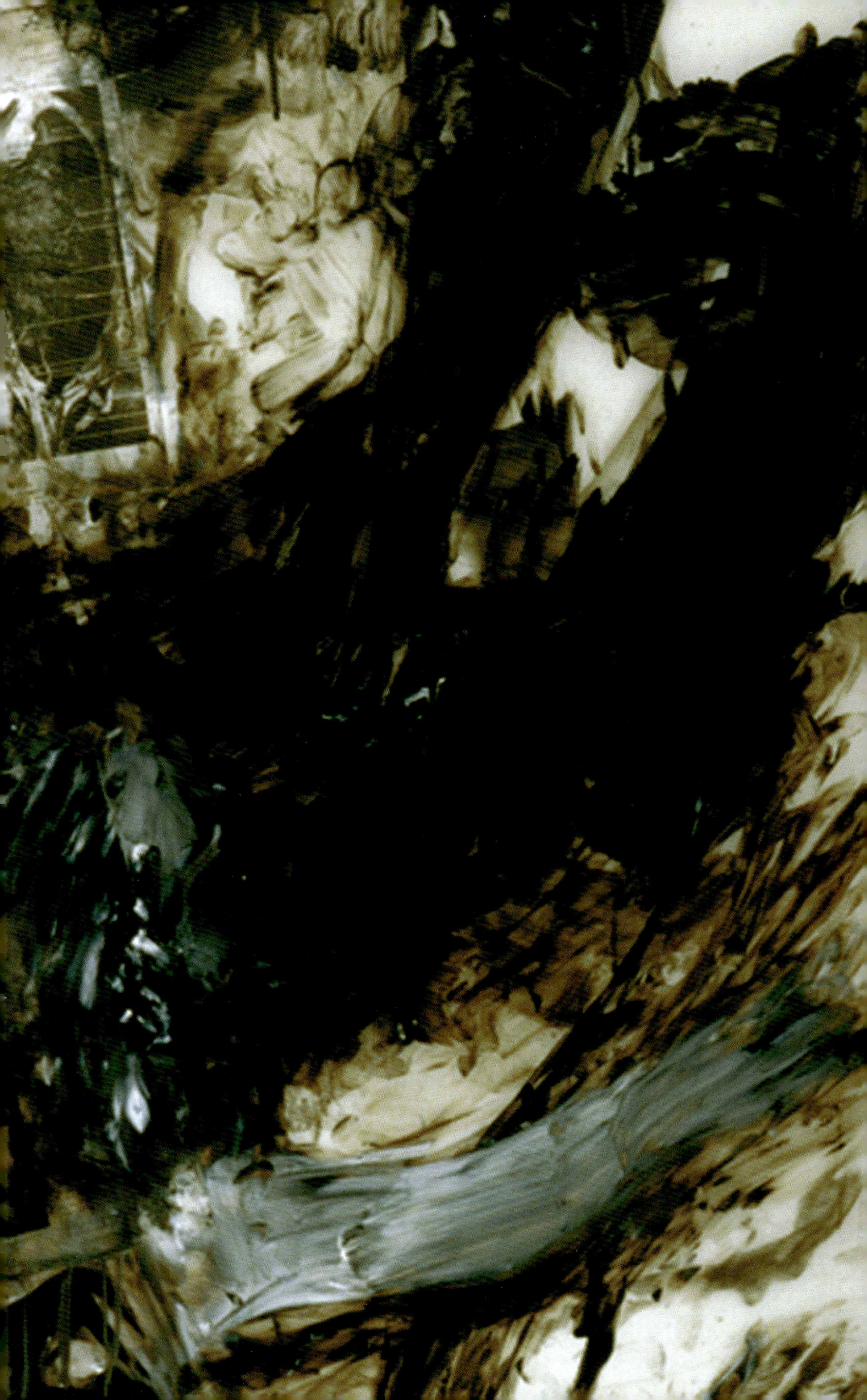

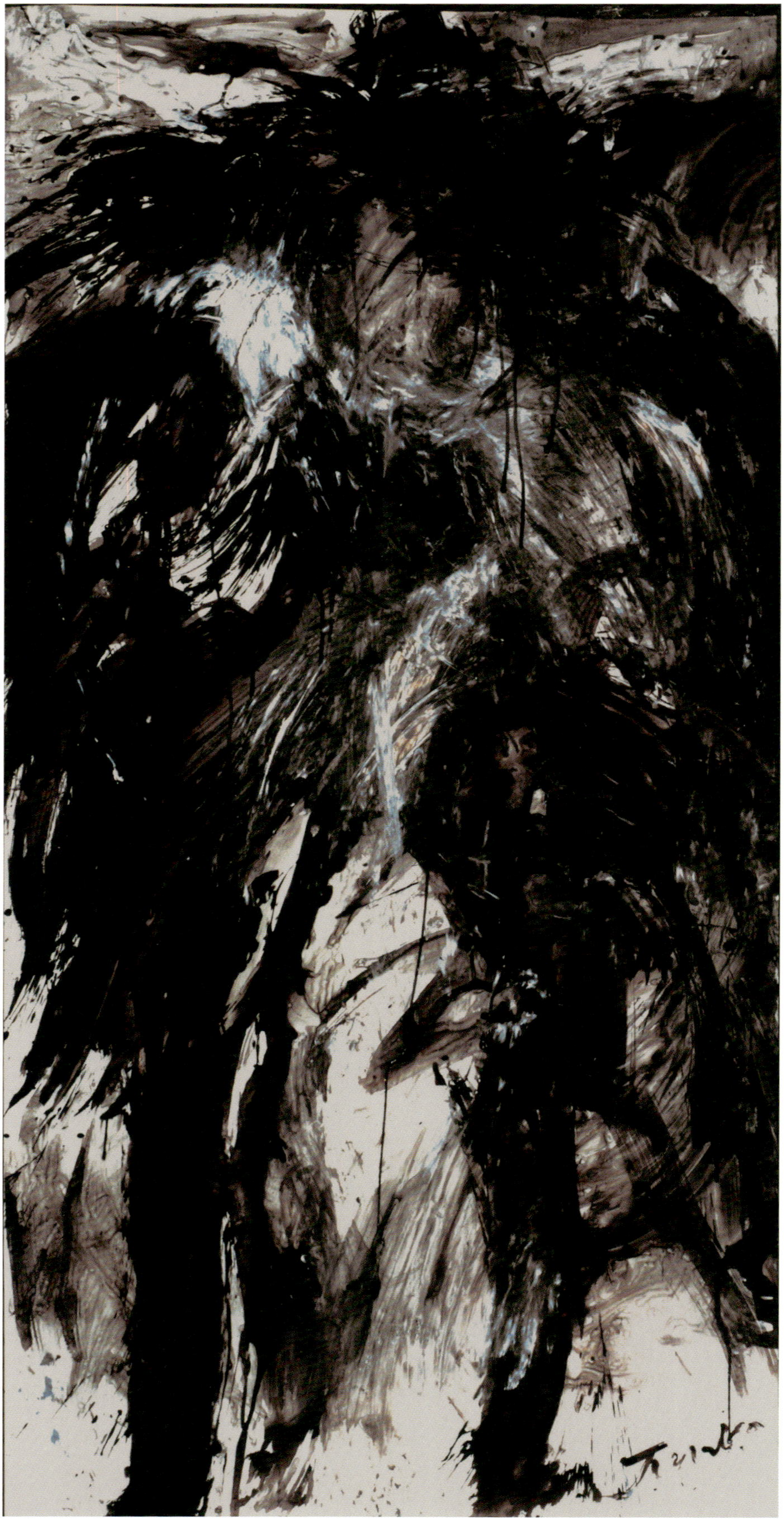

IN THE FOREST OF AMIDA BUDDHA, No. 2 (1993)
Sumi ink and acrylic on mylar support
80 x 42 in.
(203.2 x 106.7 cm.)

CHAPTER FOUR
NARRATIVE: RESOLUTION AND TRANSCENDENCE

What is the difference between the images the centripetal artist shows us in her works of art, and the images she sees in her dreams? Like the dream image, the image in the work of art comes to her; it arrives as a form of revelation and it arrives as a mystery. But she interacts with it and responds to it and creates it in a state of mind that is not entirely passive. In her interaction with the image she remains open to it, sensitive to its mystery, and honest to it—she refuses to turn it into something other than it is. This requires courage because it demands that she abandon all convention, all expectation, and all the armory of skill and calculation that artists acquire through their training. Yet it requires the highest kind of discipline: the ability to remain on the knife-edge between active and passive, often for extended periods of time.

When the work is finished, it remains as the trace on paper of the artist's struggle with the image that came to her. Then the process of understanding the work begins—both for the artist and for her viewers. Where did the image come from? How did the artist fare in her struggle with it? What did it all *mean*?

One time-honored way to answer that sort of question lies in narrative. When we see the image as part of a story, then and often only then do we think we understand it. This is the way we have sought to understand most things throughout our history: wars, floods, cataclysms, prophesies, births, deaths—we spin stories around them all and once their place in those stories is clear, we think we understand them. This is the function of myths and religious narratives and those are the templates for our dreams. A narrative work is one that cannot be fully understood without knowing the story line of which it is a part. Even though each work is valid and powerful on its

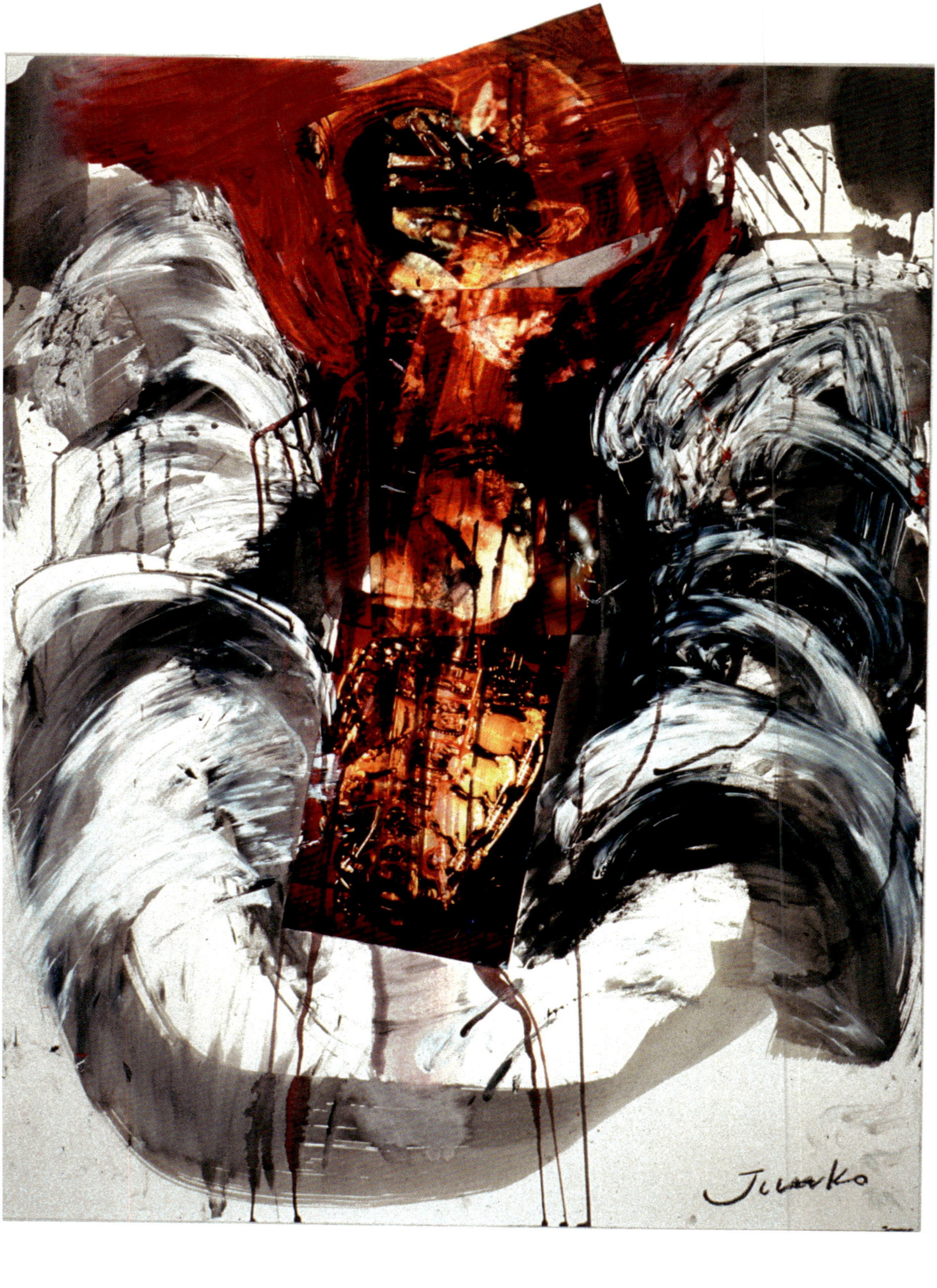

own, a full understanding of it requires us to know the whole story line.

When the images arrive in series, when they reveal themselves to the artist one after another demanding that she encounter them and respond to them in uninterrupted sequence, when she enters the altered state and creates all of the works in a series without leaving that state—then the works themselves become a special kind of narrative. The encounter with the series of images becomes a story all in itself, and each image is a scene from that story. Even if the story is not yet understood, still the artist experiences it as tension, then as resolution, then as a form of transcendence.

Most of Junko's art is narrative in this sense, and I call this kind of narrative "centripetal." The resolution and transcendence are experienced along the journey to the center of the self, and so this kind of narrative is part and parcel of centripetal art in general.

Centripetal narrative is very different from the more well-known kinds of narrative art which we call "illustration." The illustrator begins with a story and constructs images in order to present the story effectively. The centripetal artist does not know the story in advance; she must respond to images that come to her and the story unfolds through her own struggle with the images. The illustrator is constrained by the basic requirement of consistency: the same figure in the story must be recognizable in each of the story's scenes. The centripetal artist transforms the subject through her art as the story develops, so there is no requirement of consistency. The illustrator is fundamentally objective, that is, the art, even when it is abstract, corresponds to the object outside itself. The centripetal narrative has an entirely different relationship with its subject.

Opposite:
REQUIEM FOR AN EXECUTED BIRD, No. 4 (1991)
Mixed media on paper
40 x 32 in.
(101.6 x 81.28 cm.)

Junko's entanglement with narrative began in her early childhood, when she worked as a special kind of illustrator. It evolved into the kind of centripetal narrative we see in the series, *Requiem for an Executed Bird*, and *In the Forest of Amida Buddha*. And then it evolved still further into a mixed genre, exemplified by her

FATHOM series, in which elements of illustration are combined with the centripetal narrative of the earlier series.

CHILDHOOD ILLUSTRATION: *KAMISHIBAI*

There is a style of children's art in Japan called *kamishibai*, literally, "paper drama," to which Junko was exposed at a very early age. The storyteller usually rode into a neighborhood on a bicycle on which he had constructed a small wooden frame, about 15" x 20" designed to imitate a theater's stage. He would signal his arrival by clapping together two blocks of wood. Children would hear and gather in front of his bicycle, partly to buy candy from him and partly to watch the theater. Key scenes of his story were painted on thick boards and on the back side of those boards the text was written, arranged in such a way that the text associated with the picture currently in front (that is, the one the audience was looking at) was at the back so the storyteller could read it aloud. He would withdraw the boards one by one as he told his story, showing each picture to his audience in sequence. In this way, the story would progress from scene to scene, and by the time the final scene had been shown, the deck was again in order ready to repeat the story.

Junko, like thousands of other Japanese children, was fascinated by this art form. The construction of the *kamishibai* deck is not as easy as it sounds. Not only must the key scenes be identified and attractively drawn, but the sequence of images and text has to be carefully worked out so that the story deck flows properly. Junko translated several stories into this format, some of them requiring as many as twenty "key scenes," and she performed these stories in front of her whole class.

This childhood experience ingrained in Junko the idea that an art work can be related to a story line, and that part of the skill of the artist was to identify the important turning points in the story. Indeed, part of the illustrator's skill is similar to that of the movie-maker: he must segment the story into convincing

From Junko's Childhood Catalog (1953, when Junko was fourteen years old)

HAMLET SPEAKS TO THE GHOST
Acrylic on paper
8 x 10 in.
(20.32 x 25.4 cm.)

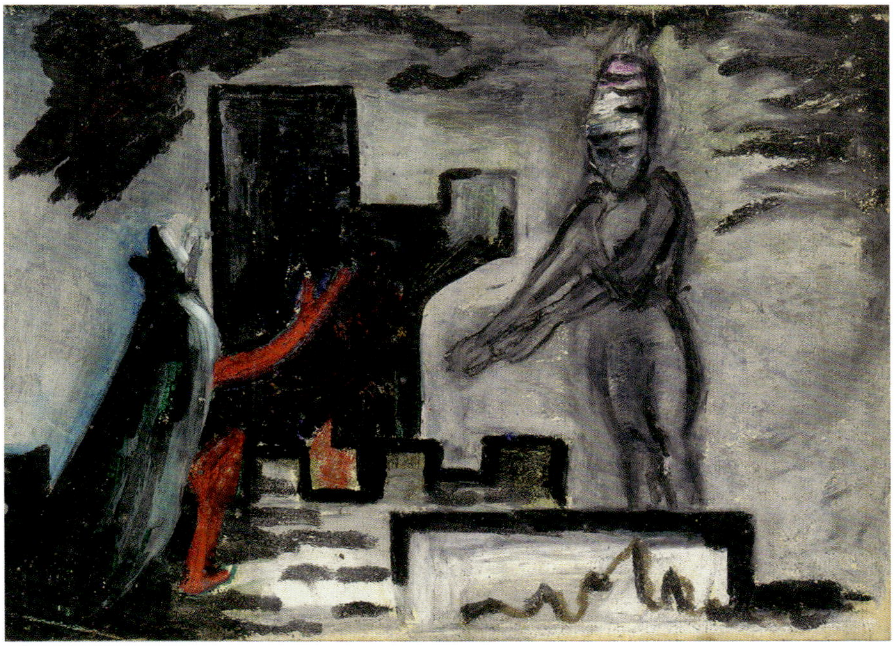

scenes which he then illustrates. But the *kamishibai* artist must also live inside the other constraints of the illustrator: objectivity and consistency. Junko learned these skills at an early age.

A great deal of what we call "sacred art" is illustration of this type. The artist begins with the story, and even knows the scene; his skill is to portray the scene faithfully and evoke in the viewer all the associations of the scene—both those in the original text and those that have accumulated over the years. Illustrations of Jesus on the cross, or of the Virgin Mary, or of the Magi—all these begin with a story and the art is deliberately subordinate to that story. How different that is from centripetal narrative.

CENTRIPETAL NARRATIVES: REQUIEM AND FOREST

From the time she started to paint, Junko's narrative works fall into the "centripetal" category. The emergence of Buddha from the *Dead Flowers* (*Byoobu*, pp. 17-19) and from the *Root* (*Emergence of Buddha*, pg. 84) represents a narrative element suggested by the images, but it is the images themselves that opened up the narrative.

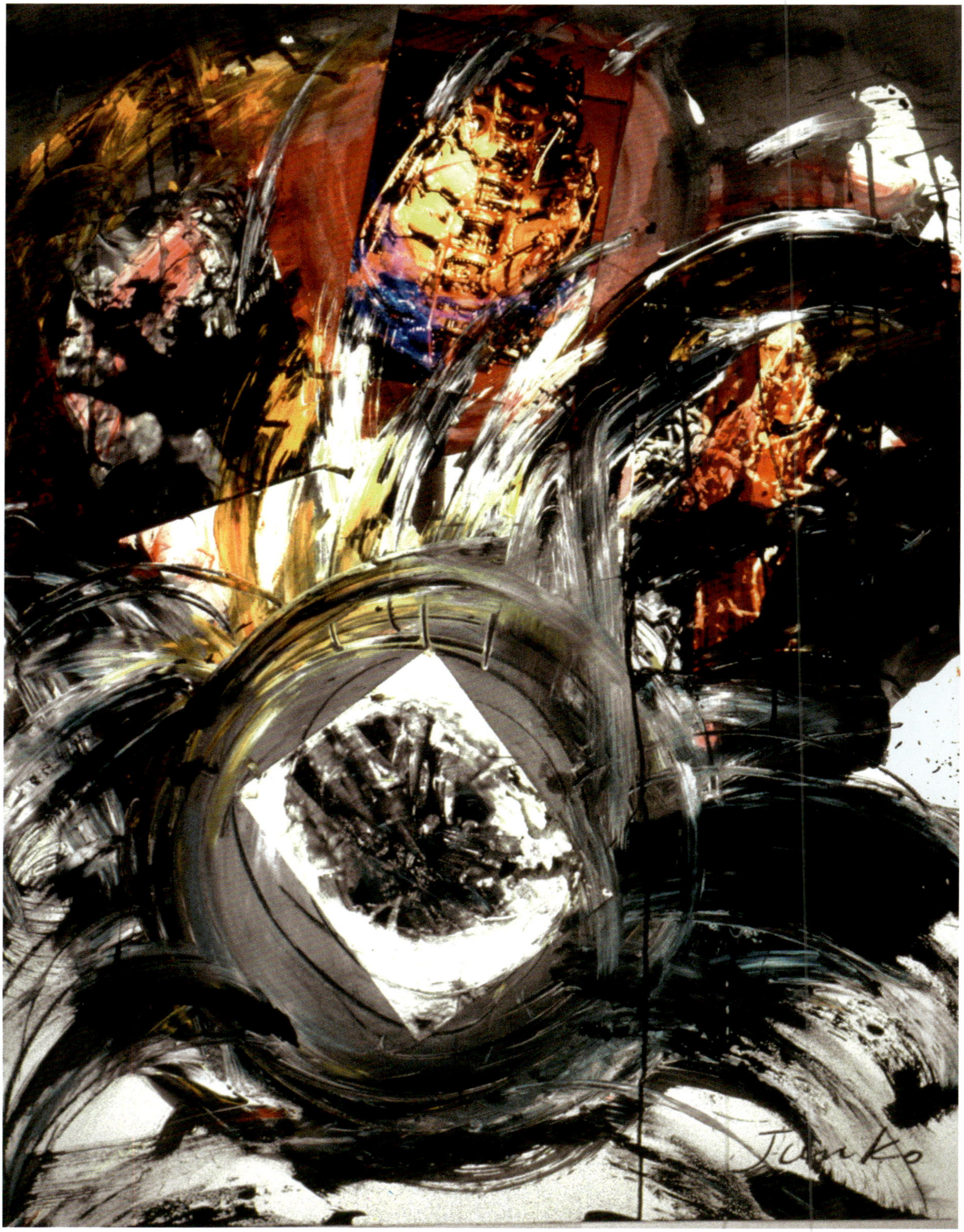

And to the extent that all of Junko's works are created in "series," usually from out of the same altered state of consciousness, they are all centripetal narratives.

REQUIEM FOR AN EXECUTED BIRD

But the best example of centripetal narrative is Junko's 1991 series, *Requiem for an Executed Bird*. That series of forty-five works, which poured out of Junko in the space of just six weeks, progressed from image to image according to a story line. But it was not an existing story line; instead, the story arose from the images themselves. The "real life" story, the external story, is the one told in Chapter Two (pg. 88). While she was staying at her uncle's hospital to escape the bombing in Tokyo, Junko saw a bird whose head had been chopped off. The sight of it traumatized her because she empathized with that bird; but by painting it, she overcame her own trauma and restored the slaughtered bird to a higher kind of life.

That is the outside story, the external narrative. But the "centripetal" narrative exists in the unfolding of the images as Junko painted the series of forty-five works: it consists in her inner struggle, in her emotional encounter with each image as it rose up from the depths. The whole series began with a material object, the decanter described in Chapter One, on page 56. It was the encounter with this "visitant" which evoked the memory of the slaughtered bird and launched the series. As she went into the studio, Junko wrote:

Opposite:
REQUIEM FOR AN EXECUTED BIRD,
No. 6 (1991)
Mixed media on paper
40 x 32 in.
(101.6 x 81.28 cm.)

Studio Diary, May 1991

Today is the only day I can start; for two weeks the suffering time has continued. Finally last week I went through the "death." But now I am feeling the strength in me. Today is the only day. It is completely open for me as a perfect day without any disturbance, schedule, or obligation. Last night, I was watching a blue-white light splashing up from my fingers just like steam from a boiling kettle. I feel the presence of God in me very strongly. Please lead me to my work. Please give me the strength to do your work.

I start painting looking at the ugly wine decanter. I still did not know what direction I was going in, only a deep feeling flooded over me. Suddenly, a completely unexpected idea came into my head. I went to the kitchen and got a bottle of Clorox and poured it on one of the photographs I had prepared for collage materials over many years. The image broke and liquidated. This is great! This works! It transforms a clear image into something liquid running down. I wanted that manneristic style because it conveys "doubt and inner conflict, anxiety, and a profoundly intimate relationship with death" (Hans Sedlmayr, *Art in Crisis*). But I did not want the manneristic style itself in my art, instead I wanted an element of that style to appear just as an ironic and casual accidental gesture. It was perfect. But casual as it might look, I felt as if my chest was splashed with Clorox: the pain and vulnerability are exposed. Perfect! I am ready to receive any images that come.

Studio Diary, May 1991

I was picking up photographs from the pile on the studio floor. I quickly picked up one of them, an airplane engine photo which Rafael took for me in the science museum in Boston years ago. For me it has always symbolized a glorious function of life and vitality. I picked it up thinking to use it in collage sometime but I had not yet thought about any of its particular visual effects. But suddenly now the shape of the engine reminds me of the bird's spine and it accelerates my emotion for the bird so rapidly. Then I added the white feathers using a brush and my fingers around it. That image frightened me (*No. 4*, pg. 162). Now I know what kind of world I have already stepped into.

These two images, the liquidated image and the bird spine which comes from a glorious airplane photo, are the key images that prepared Junko for the journey into the centripetal narrative of the "Bird execution," the bloody reality of her childhood traumatic experience. But she still had no idea how her childhood memory would unfold in front of her nor where it would lead her. The creative process continued:

REQUIEM FOR AN EXECUTED BIRD
No. 20 (1991)
Mixed media collage on paper
40 x 32 in.
(101.6 x 81.3 cm.)

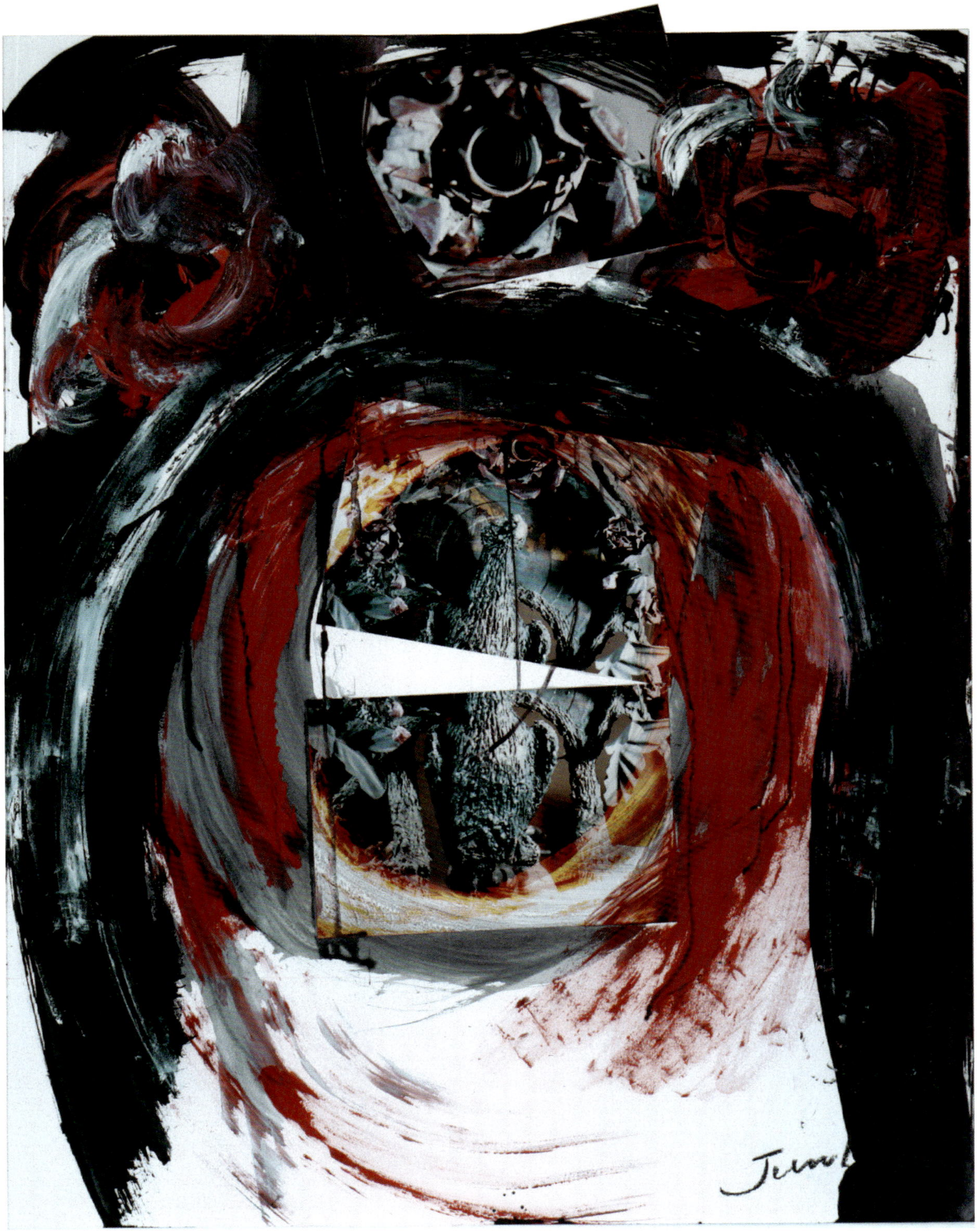

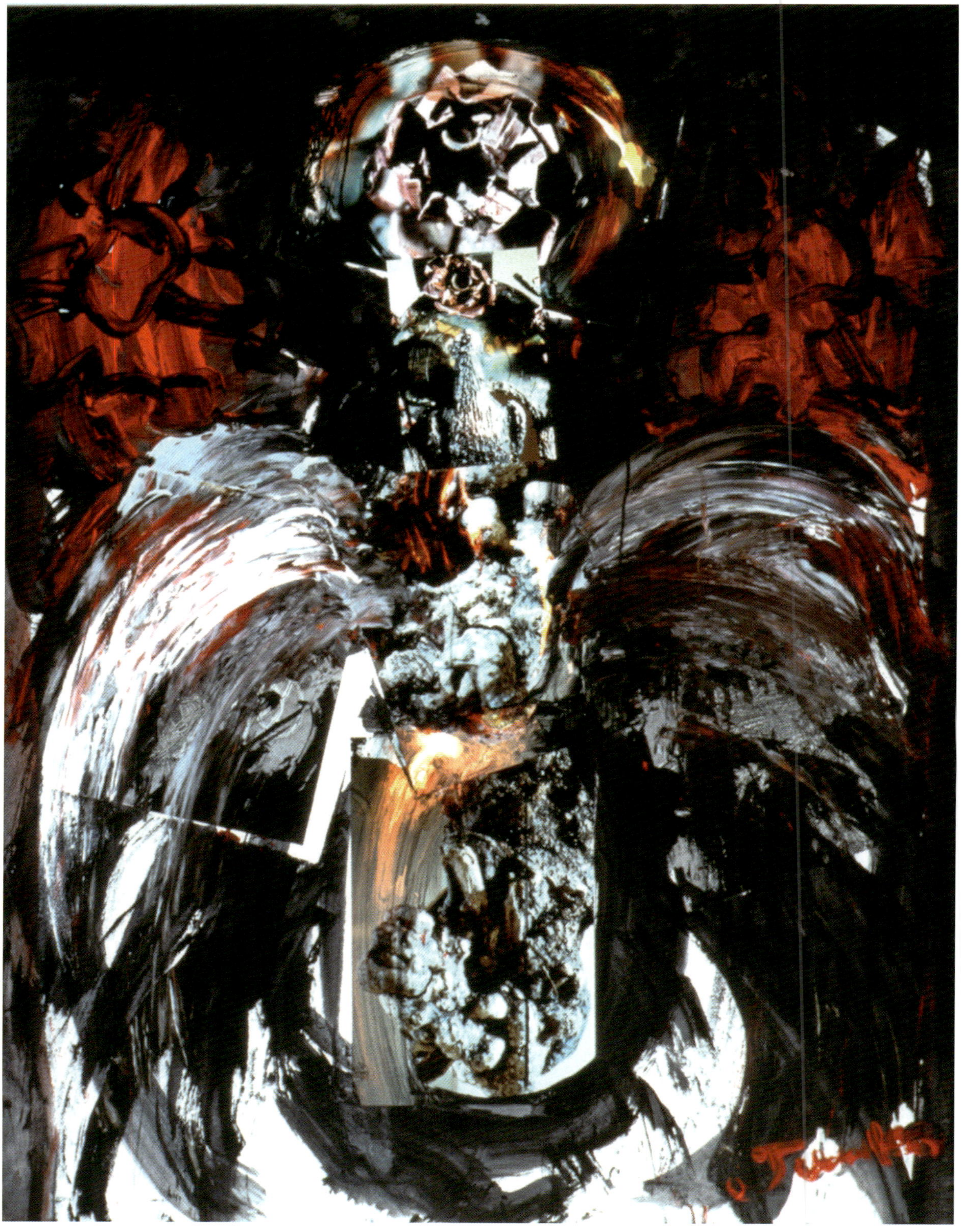

Studio Diary, May 1991

With bursts of crying in my chest I enter the studio this morning. Just like a flood, art rushed into me. I was crying in my mind. It rushed at me so fast, my hand couldn't catch up with it. I was crying in my mind. I hear my own loud crying voice burst and it echoes in my bones, and yet my horror and pain are circling wild as if it were joy. All at once the first six works are completed.

The bird represents freedom, aspiration, and transcendence. This bird was created to fly and be free. It had been slaughtered not for anything it had done but because of what it was. I saw it as a punishment—a cruel and unjustified execution. I was overcome by a phobia of birds of all kinds for nearly fifty years. Later on, the many experiences I had of abuse of authority, of violence against the individual, of the taboo against being who you are, became part of this experience. My journey towards freedom and individuation became a struggle against this phobia.

Another old terror came back; the terror of the Japanese fascistic government authority which we lived with all through the war. I was afraid of our neighbors because we were all forced to spy on each other. As little as I was, I saw very clearly the essence of totalitarianism without any intellectual knowledge of it whatsoever. It is the hatred and destruction of freedom. By commanding blind obedience to an irrational authority, and by torture and execution, they accomplished their goal. I was in terror all through my short life of revealing who I was. The slaughtered bird crystallized this terror for me instantly. When my uncle killed a beautiful bird my whole terror of fascism took a most realistic shape.

Opposite:
REQUIEM FOR AN EXECUTED BIRD
No. 22 (1991)
Bird in the Cathedral
Mixed media collage on paper
40 x 32 in.
(101.6 x 81.3 cm.)

During this state, her altered state of consciousness runs deep. In Work No. 22, the red roses which she was already putting next to the bird in Work No. 20, presented themselves to her as stained glass, and all of a sudden she realized that this bird was in a cathedral and that in painting this series, she was singing a requiem for him.

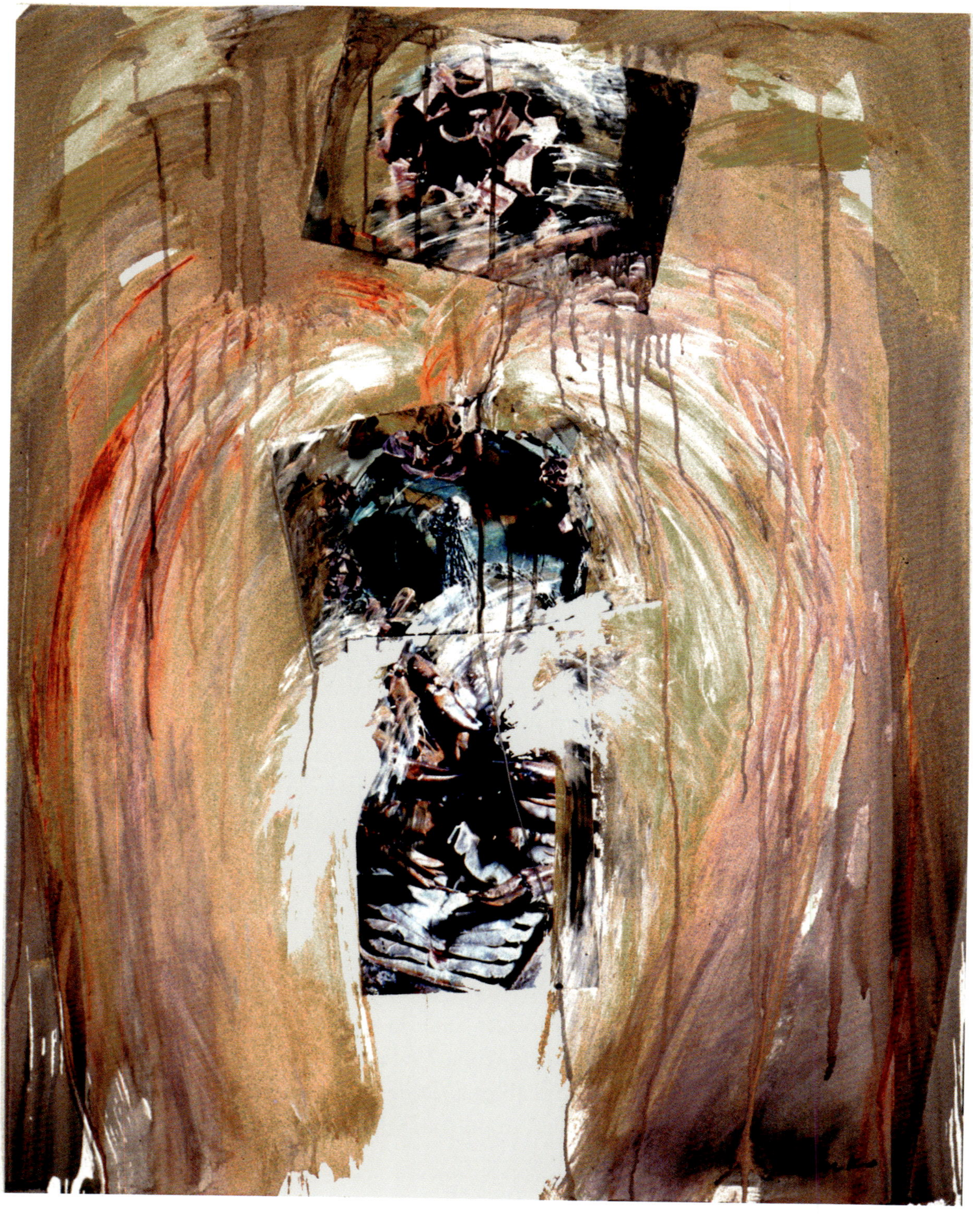

Studio Diary, June 1991

This (*No. 22*) is a requiem for the Bird! This is a requiem for the executed Bird! One after another, the Bird looms up from the depths in the painful figures. However I try to comfort him, however I try to save him with red roses, the Bird shows his most helpless figure. Oh God only you can comfort him! One after another, the cry comes up from the depths. This is a requiem for my Bird!

With tears of gratitude, I am writing this. My hands are trembling. God let me work through this. I feel God is in my body, and my body is almost exploding.

Opposite:
REQUIEM FOR AN EXECUTED BIRD
No. 29 (1991)
Mixed media collage on paper
40 x 32 in.
(101.6 x 81.3 cm.)

The violent tone is fading and a glorious gold tone is appearing. Transcending has started and Junko senses it clearly. For the first time she added Japanese letters (Work No. 24, pg. 155) saying "The bird is dying." Two circles almost appeared. Suddenly her consciousness level shifts deeply and she wrote:

Studio Diary, June 1991

"The Bird is dying. The Bird is dying. The helpless Bird, the wings that are made to fly into the expanse of the sky, are bent down and hang down powerlessly. The Bird is dying. Being executed, deprived of freedom, wailing, weeping; the world is listening. The world cries bitterly. The Bird is executed. The Bird who wanted to fly to the broad sky of freedom, has been executed...

Then her consciousness level shifted even deeper. She was pulled into a darkness darker than any darkness she ever experienced. She felt unknown, urgent danger to her psyche lay ahead of her. Her hand started writing on a piece of paper on the floor nearby:

Studio Diary, June 1991

Don't be afraid of this melody. Bring this singing into the light, then you will know that this darkness is the light. Light is gushing up everywhere, light is gushing up everywhere.

She followed those words, she continued working to break through the darkness, the danger. She wrote:

Opposite:
REQUIEM FOR AN EXECUTED BIRD No. 42 (1991)
Mixed media collage on paper
40 x 32 in.
(101.6 x 81.3 cm.)

Studio Diary, June 1991

What a freedom I feel now (Works Nos. 25-28). I am singing the requiem for my wounded ego which was filled with pain and fear, and You are celebrating me, a newly born me. I am writing this with deepest gratitude.

Work continued for the next two weeks. Many circles and half-circles appeared, some were swinging, some were standing high, a circle is completed with quiet dignity and the bird exists in that circle. His feathers are now spotted with gold—not red; golden air, golden space, and he exists there. He is finally free. The transcending process has happened and is almost completed (Works No. 29-41).

Studio Diary, July 1991

I feel my mind is so empty, I realize this series is coming to an end. I thought it had ended yet still I felt something—not emotional, different from the earlier feelings that I had. So I thought I had to paint one more. I went to Sycamore Beach and walked for about an hour and then I went to Malibu and had coffee alone, then my mind was decisive. I came back to my studio and finished four works; strong, not emotional. This is it! I came to the end. Looking at the four beautiful works, I felt extreme happiness.

Work No. 44: the circle is completed quietly with dignity. In the middle of it is the Clorox-blurred image of the Bird standing like the Virgin and Christ with the Apostles in the Mosaic in the main apse of the cathedral at Torcello, which is the image I saw in the ugly wine decanter four years ago.

Thank you very much, God, for letting me work such a long time. I am extremely grateful. I have to go back to the world and the time to study my work will begin. I will think about this work, I will write about it in order to understand your mystery much more deeply than I do now.

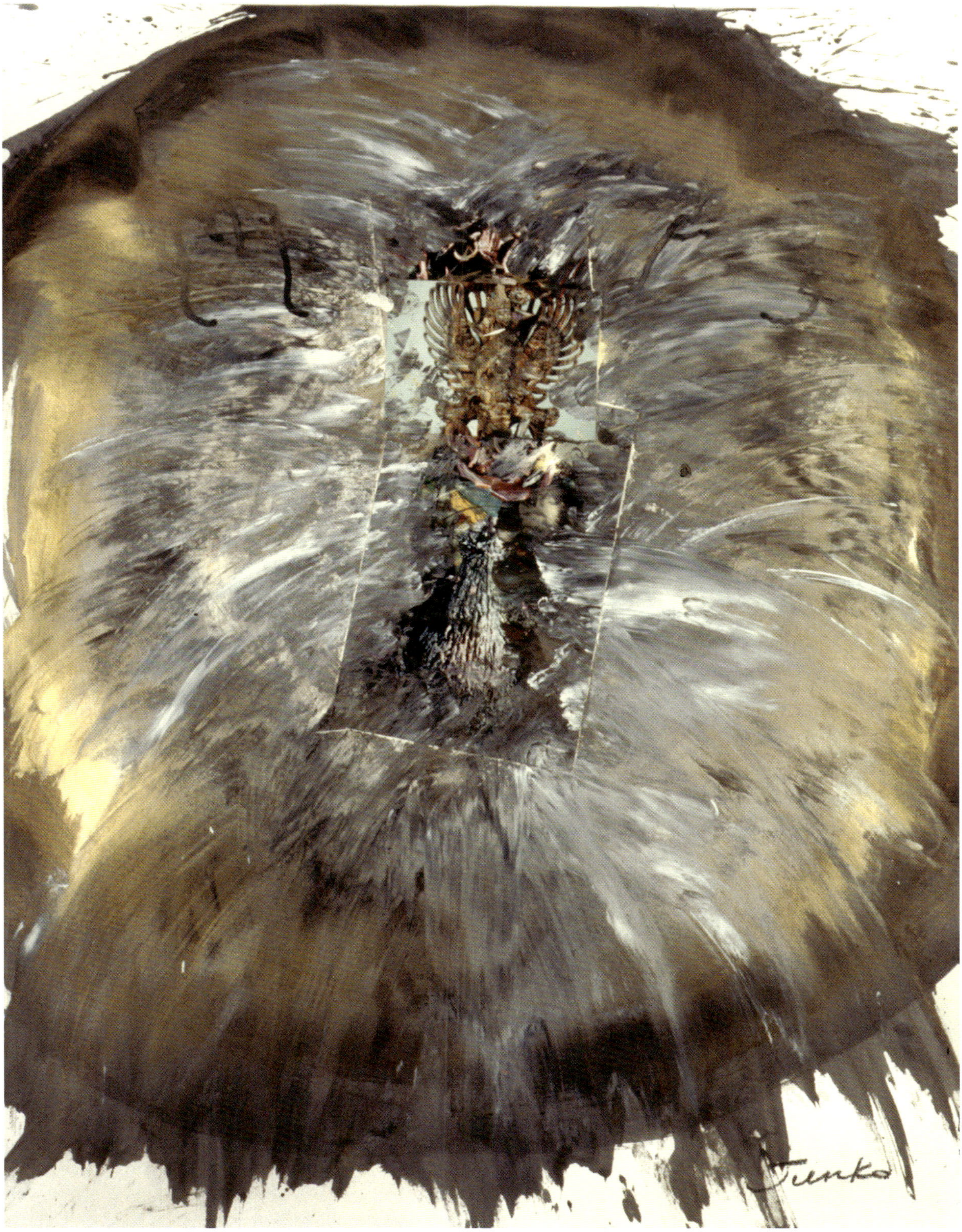
Junko

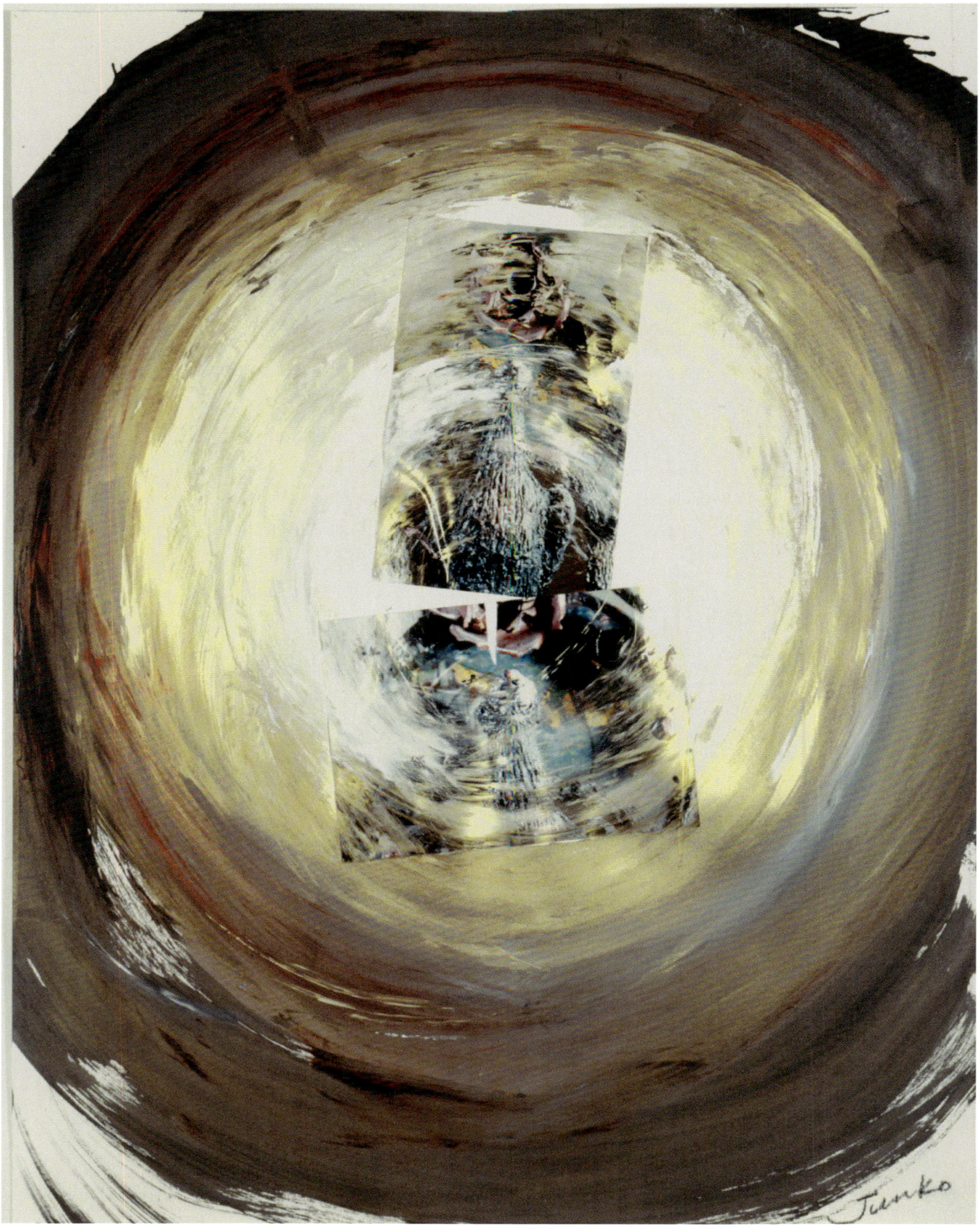
Junko

The images at the early part of the series have bloody colors, and violent brush strokes depicting the bird's torn feathers, and the works tend to burst the confines of the pictorial space. Later, the bloody reds turned into the red of stained glass as in a cathedral, and an archetypal circle arose in the images which finally achieved full presence at the end of the series. The mid-series images became more nearly symmetrical and contained within the pictorial space. Then, toward the end of the series, the bloody reds disappeared and turned to gold, and the earthly setting of the bird—whose blood dripped at first into a bucket placed on a *tatami* mat—was transformed into a heavenly setting, and the bird is shown existing in golden circles of heavenly air.

After Junko finished this series we found that her phobia of birds from which she had suffered severely for almost fifty years had disappeared. As she wrote at this end of the diary, she has continued to think about this experience and study it. She wrote about it extensively, lectured about it, and showed these works in many places. This effort continues still now after seventeen years have passed. And yet Junko and I both feel the mystery deepens every time we look at the works.

In creating this series, Junko had no idea what images were coming to her. She followed the narrative which arose from the images themselves and it was only years later that she realized the full meaning of the narrative. Later she said that while she was in the studio, she felt like the children of Israel in the Old Testament Book of Exodus following the "pillar of fire" through the barren desert—never knowing where it would lead but following nevertheless. She understood that through creating the series she had reached a deep resolution of a childhood experience that had lain unresolved in her innermost heart for more than fifty years. She understood that she had overcome a phobia that the early experience had planted there, and she understood that her work had something to do with transcending fascism and seeking a high form of individuation. But even she did not understand the full meaning of her own work and when the series was finished, she vowed solemnly that she would study it and reflect on it until she understood it fully.

Opposite:
REQUIEM FOR AN EXECUTED BIRD No. 44 (1991)
Mixed media collage on paper
40 x 32 in.
(101.6 x 81.3 cm.)

THE VIEWER'S PARTICIPATION

Part of the meaning of any artist's work is the impact it has on the viewer. Centripetal narrative offers the viewer an opportunity to *participate* in the unfolding of the narrative in a way that is not available with illustration. Of course, when we see a painting of St. George slaying the dragon, we know the story and we recognize the figures and we might identify with St. George. But real participation in a story is more than merely recognizing the figures and identifying with the hero. It involves becoming the main figure in our imaginations and undergoing, if only vicariously, the suffering and resolution which that figure undergoes in the story. It is in this way that a devout Christian participates in the story of Jesus' crucifixion and resurrection. It is not just that he knows the story: he feels that Jesus suffered for his sins and that because of Jesus' suffering, he has been redeemed. In a similar vein, my father taught me that the reason we celebrate the Passover is so that every Jew should feel that he too was a slave to Pharaoh in Egypt and that God brought him out of that slavery with a mighty Hand and an outstretched Arm.

When we see images of the Stations of the Cross, which illustrate key scenes in the life of Jesus, we are reminded of the narrative and this may bring our sense of participation in it to the foreground. But those images are illustrations. Centripetal art invites the viewer to participate in a more direct way, for he can see the unfolding of the images in front of his eyes and he can trace the artist's struggle with them from the beginning of the series to the end. By looking at the works seriously, he can participate in the narrative that unfolded through them.

In 2003, Junko was invited to exhibit some of her work at the Graduate Theological Union in Berkeley, California, as part of the school's focus that term on the crucifixion and resurrection. The curator at the school had asked Junko to lend pieces from her *Topological Deformations of the Cross* series, but I told Junko that the *Requiem* series was better suited. It was, after all, the story of the crucifixion and resurrection of the executed Bird, was it not?

This view of the matter opened both our eyes to another possible meaning of that original narrative, a convincing meaning that had remained hidden from us for more than ten years. It was the meaning from the viewer's side: it was the invitation the works extend to participate in the centripetal narrative.

IN THE FOREST OF AMIDA BUDDHA

In 1993, Junko created her second centripetal narrative series: *In the Forest of Amida Buddha*. In 1994, looking back on this series of twenty-five mylars, Junko wrote this account of the narrative:

From Memoir, 2005

In the summer of 1993, I saw the Amida Buddha in my back yard. My back yard was a forest: big oak trees spread their branches touching each other, creating a warm dark shade underneath. Eucalyptus trees arched their long, slender bodies far above them and swayed in the wind. The forest stretches without any fence into the Santa Monica Mountains beyond. It was there in the forest of my back yard that I saw the Amida Buddha. He showed his figure behind the trees, moving swiftly like a wind, as if he were playing hide-and-seek throughout the forest.

Amida Buddha is the Buddha who governs the "Pureland" hundreds of millions of miles beyond the place where the sun sets. All Buddhists dream of being reborn on one of the petals of the lotus that grows in the pond in Pureland. But as time went by, around the eleventh century in Japan, people believed that the world had arrived in its last period, in which Buddha's teaching no longer had the power to enable humans to go to Pureland by their own effort and in which the cosmic law was in decline. In fear and desperation, people started to portray Amida speeding down to earth on a jet of clouds to pick up the dying souls, instead of sitting on a lotus waiting for them to find him.

"But what is he doing in our back yard? Is it because the time has come!" Both the question and the answer hit me at the same time. It was a time when a serious illness struck my husband, Rafael, and the possibility of his

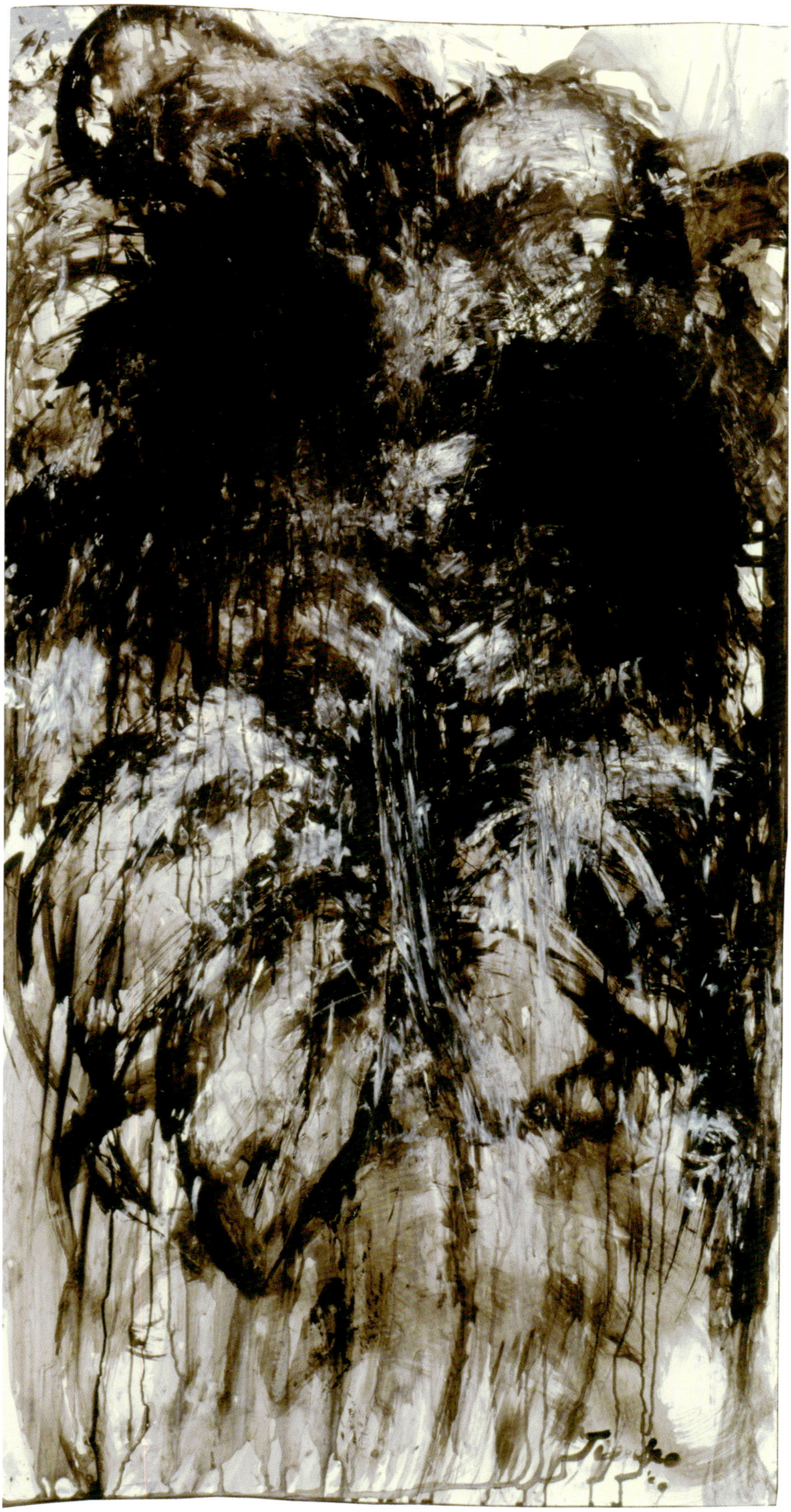

death was within the range of reality. I put my hands on the bark of the trees and put my arms around them and asked each of them to give his vitality to Rafael. And I started to paint the powerful but mysterious figures of the trees using black acrylic on sheets of mylar taller than I was. They came out intense and dark. I painted twenty-one of those works.

And then suddenly I saw that the forest in my painting turned red instead of black and seemed to be flaming up like fire. I painted three works like that, but I was puzzled and disturbed by the flaming image of the red forest.

Opposite:
IN THE FOREST OF AMIDA BUDDHA
No. 6 (1993)
Sumi ink and acrylic on mylar
80 x 42 in.
(203.2 x 106.7 cm.)

This narrative began in response to a vision, not to a particular "visitant." The tension that had to be resolved was the vision itself: Why was it there? What did it mean? Junko pursued the images as they drew her further and further into the narrative, and then, after three late works in which reds replaced blacks, the series ended with works in gold. But the tension still was not resolved until later:

From Memoir, 2005

Rafael underwent his surgery and it was successful. A few months later, the Malibu fires of November 1993, which had destroyed thousands of acres of wild forest along the California coast, finally reached our back yard. The fire stood high in the sky behind the mountain and swiftly came down to our Amida Forest. It lapped at the edge of our house for four days. Amida's forest became part of the area declared to be a national disaster. We had to evacuate to a nearby hotel and on the TV set in our hotel room, we glimpsed our own house which was standing at the edge of the burning forest, looking small and vulnerable. Then, in a second, our view of our house was blocked by a curtain of fire: the camera showed only the flaming forest and the images of trees falling in the flames over and over and over. The images were exactly like what I had painted just a few months earlier.

So had the visions been a premonition? But where was the resolution? Where was the transcendence?

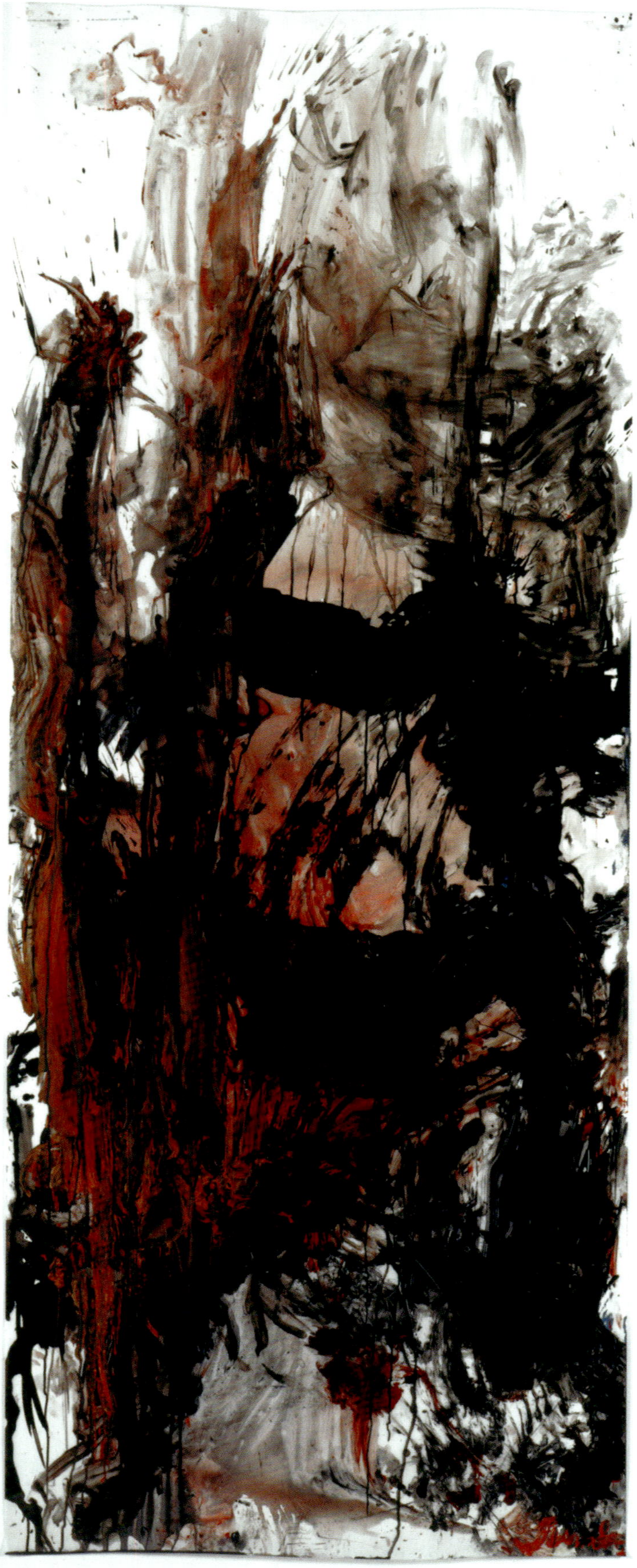

IN THE FOREST OF
AMIDA BUDDHA,
No. 22 (1993)
Sumi ink and
acrylic on mylar
80 x 42 in.
(203.2 x 106.7 cm.)

From Memoir, 2005

Our house remained unburned but the forest had disappeared entirely from this earthly plane and left only a burnt hillside as its trace. The trees that I had embraced and asked to give their vitality to Rafael were lying—some blackened, one on top of another, some still standing but burned. I was stunned. Did these trees sacrifice themselves in the purifying flame in order to give their vitality to Rafael in response to my prayer? Where did the Amida Buddha go? No answer came. Only the birds who had lost their nests in those trees were frantically making circles above the embers with sharp, shrieking cries, as if they were mourning the dead trees. Rafael recovered from his illness and the shadow of death which had fallen over our life passed on.

Incidentally, green shoots and leaves started sprouting from the trunks of the black trees the very next spring and those trees are now higher than the roof of our three-story house. They have formed a new forest—not exactly thick and dark like before, but the trees are vital and beautiful again.

The last works of the series still evoke memories of our trees standing tall in those flames, being consumed by them. So it was possible to understand the whole centripetal narrative series as a kind of premonition—but that would not be the whole truth. The works were another kind of revelation, something having to do with air and matter, fire and spirit, death and rebirth.

But the full meaning of that narrative has yet to be understood and as with the *Requiem* series, it has to do with the viewer's participation. The resolution began to come gradually, as the new forest grew.

The power of the narrative which Junko had created in 1991 transformed both our lives, even though we did not fully understand it at the time. Watching Junko pursue a compelling narrative by following images she had herself created with utter honesty and faith, had repercussions in my own life. About eighteen months later, I was diagnosed with a life-threatening form of cancer and I had to decide whether I wanted to undergo the violent treatment which was required or whether I preferred to let my life come to an end at that time. Following Junko's lead—without fully understanding it yet—I decided to live. The reality of my own death and the recognition of my body's vulnerability had made me revise the inner narrative of my life: a narrative which I determined at that point to follow, rather than to abandon. Even though I did not know where it would lead, something in that narrative attracted me and motivated me—compelled me to follow it *by creating it*. It was while I was in the hospital that I began to write my most ambitious book to that point, a major lawbook which took me seven years to complete. It was only from that point that I began to live consciously as an adult.

A few years after the fires, I was able to build a small deck at the lower story of our house: this deck is at the level of the forest and standing on it early in the morning, I can often see fog in the trees and I can hear the birds singing, now peacefully. Many mornings, before the sun rises over the hills in the State Park, I go out on to that deck to practice *tai chi*. I think about the cancer that might have ended my life, I think about my decision to live. Soon after I started using that new deck, I found a small statue of one of Buddha's disciples in an antique store in Claremont. I put that statue in the corner of the deck, and as I practice, I think of the Amida Buddha moving through the trees. And I am thankful that I still have the strength to move with him—and I try to move as he moves, silently, forcefully, like a wind.

MIXED GENRE: FATHOM

More recently, Junko created yet another kind of narrative series which combines aspects of illustration and centripetal narrative.

In the year 2000, Junko started to read some of the poems of a priest named Kuukai. This priest is well known in Japan as the founder, in the ninth century, of a form of "Esoteric Buddhism"—a

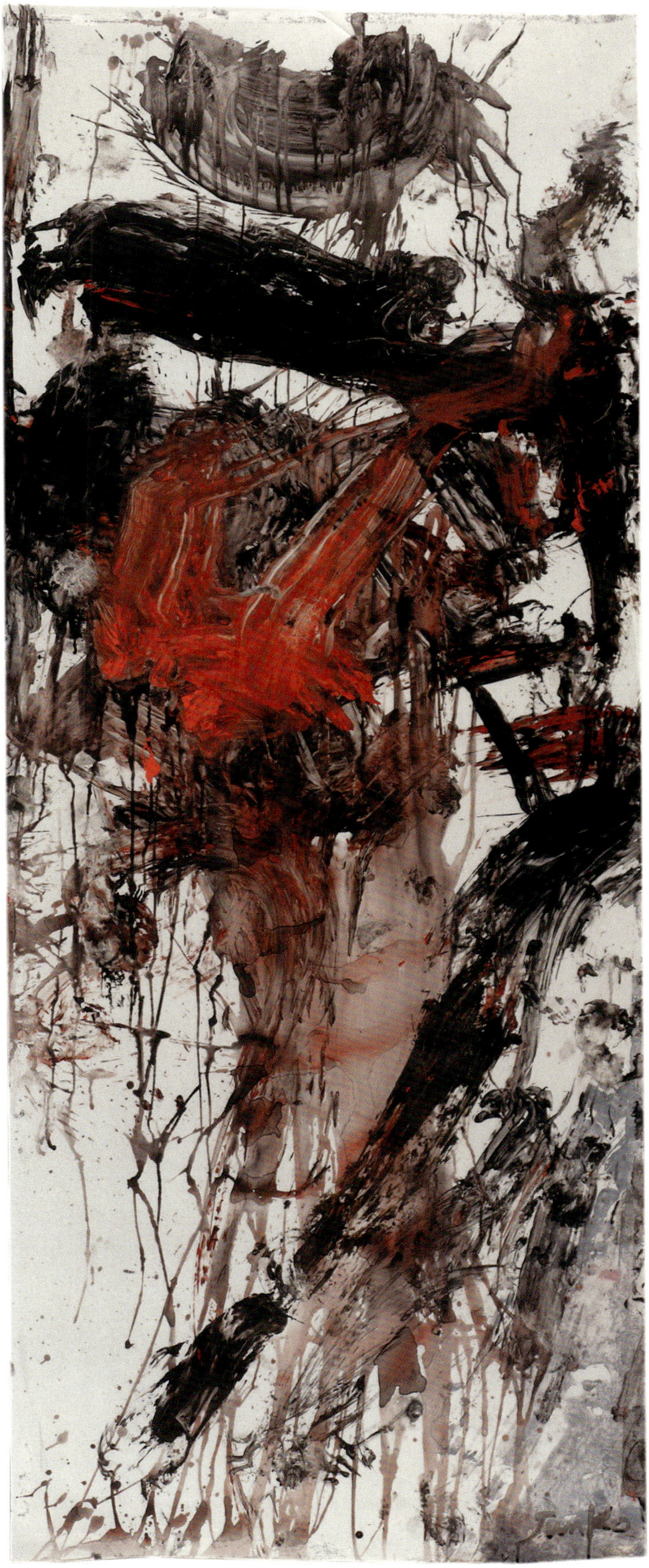

IN THE FOREST OF AMIDA BUDDHA, No. 24 (1993)
Sumi ink and acrylic on mylar
103 x 42 in.
(261.6 x 106.7 cm.)

form of Buddhism that comes from Tantric sources and forms a stark contrast to the minimalist, intellectual "Zen Buddhism" with which most Westerners are familiar. Kuukai's religion is mystical and full of life.

Kuukai is an attractive figure for Junko because he was able to integrate a range of qualities that we think of as incompatible. He was a mystic who spent several years in the forest training and meditating, eating rocks (it is said, in order to ingest their magical powers) and leaping from tree to tree. Yet he was worldly enough to raise money from the emperor and the aristocracy to build a string of temples all across Japan, and in that way he established his new religion, which he called "The True Word" (*Shingonshu*). He combined an archaic sensibility with a very modern, high-tech one. Late in his life when he built an Esoteric Buddhist monastery on Mt. Kooya, he was asked why he chose that particular mountain from among all the mountains where he had trained in his youth. He answered, "Mt. Kooya is covered with snow and when it melts it provides an abundance of water for people to drink, for vegetation and fish, and for the Dragon to live in." He also designed and built several irrigation systems which are still in use today, eleven hundred years later. He is the author of over nine hundred scrolls, whose topics include engineering, poetry, religion, cosmology, and the attainment of enlightenment.

In 2001, Junko created a series of five large mylars which she titled *Esoteric Buddhism*, and two of the works include texts by Kuukai: *Birth*, "Born, reborn, and born yet again, in the cycle of reincarnation, in darkness..." and *Death*, "Dying, dying, and dying yet again, in the cycle of reincarnation, in darkness" (pp. 42-43).

Junko's works and her passionate talk about Kuukai caught the interest of a leading choreographer in San Diego, the founder and director of MalashockDance; and in 2002, he and Junko agreed that they would create a dance program based on the life of Kuukai. That program, named *FATHOM,* opened at a major theater in San Diego in mid-2006 and ran for seven nights to crowded audiences. It was a collaboration among Junko, the choreographer, and the composer (there was an original score). Junko created art that formed the backdrop for the eight scenes of the dance. But it was difficult for her to commit herself to this kind of project. Here is what she wrote, before she had actually started to create the works:

Studio Notebook, 2005

Kuukai's life narrative deeply moved me and that is the reason I agreed to work on the dance production. Yet the fact that there was a narrative already existing before my process of creation was the most difficult thing I had to handle.... Because of that difficulty, over the course of the four years I was preparing to create the works, I came to the edge once or twice of abandoning this project entirely.

In my turmoil I generated a tremendous number of studio diary entries, sketches, and essays: fragmentary thoughts and dreams were piled up. I actually created a few giant works, and two of those were even displayed in a museum but I destroyed them after they came back to my studio. Sketches, mockups, scene planners, and charts were piled up in my studio; some were stored, some were discarded. And after all, the resolution of the difficulty came from this very pile.

I had written in the entries in the pile, over and over again, that going deeply into my own center and going deeply into Kuukai's center are one and the same thing. When you reach the deepest center of yourself the sense of sharing experience with others becomes strong. The center is universal: nothing is limited or tethered to anything, everything is connected to everything else and changes form—metamorphosizes: everything is like liquid, running to all corners instantly and flowing, and you feel enormous freedom.

The scene of the sorcerer entering his forest is the first scene of the story; when the curtain rises I wanted the whole audience to gasp at it. Kuukai went into the forest at the top of Mt. Kooya and there he mastered all magic, the mystery and wisdom of nature. But how did he fight against the power of the unconscious? For the dark forest is the place of the unconscious. How did Kuukai struggle with the terror that comes from his inner, deepest place, that comes with the fear of being born out of the womb as one independent being? I know that he expanded his own territory of consciousness to something vast. I have to reach his inner world through my own inner route: not by illustrating his life, but by following its centripetal narrative. No matter how small and poor the result I might be able to reach, this is the way I wanted to do it.

This is what I realized and after all this is what I had written over and over in my documents. And yet, it took me a long time to accept it deeply.

Junko sees centripetal narrative as a determination to follow the narrative created by the images, rather than to press the images into the service of the narrative. And so a tension was created at the outset, a tension between the existing story and the inner narrative. We can get a glimpse of Junko's process of trial and error, which she went through in order to reach a fusion of illustration and centripetal narrative:

Studio Notebook, April 2002

My head is dim, as if it is filled with fog, but I am thinking that this is the only time to start...

Old memories arose in me so vividly last night that I could not sleep until 2:00 in the morning: memories of crossing the Pacific Ocean from America to Japan, in winter, during a severe storm. All night through, until 6:00 in the morning, I spent the time following images with my eyes of that storm that whirled and stampeded our small boat along the black swell of ocean. At 8:00, I fell asleep and now I finally stuck out my head and peeped over the ocean waves.

Now I am in contact with the core that resonates with the intense terror and sense of isolation I experienced at that time on the sea. ...

I am looking up at the images which spread on the screen in my mind. What a pleasure I feel now. Since I saw these images I can go straight ahead. Suddenly one image divided into two images in my dream last night and later divided into multiple images just like the division of cells.

The first image is the image of the waves in the ocean moving, rustling, rolling, and sharply reflecting lightning, but at the same time, it turned into the image of a dense forest, as if it were an impenetrable jungle. This image developed into more chaotic images, entangled like a gigantic beard that is not well groomed. This image is the most chaotic form of mandala, rather like a mandala in the mother's womb.

The second image divided from the first image, it developed into a wilder image, roaring, growling, and howling. This is also an image of flames, anger, terror and of the spirit which fights against terror. From here, the image of *Fudômyoô* appeared. Is it possible for this image of a *Fudômyoô* to develop into a mandala? Or must it become a more independent image of a huge *Fudômyoô* hovering over the ocean, his eyes glittering and the flames he carries on his back burning red, spreading to the night sky?

The third image is again an image divided from the first image. Each image of waves of the ocean has become 3D, each holds a Buddha in the center and hangs in the air just like a gigantic hanging plant. When it is arranged in a certain way, it creates a 3D Mandala world.

The fourth image was a jumble of images of gigantic plants hanging close to each other to create a dense forest: they were buzzing, rustling in the dark and under sudden changes of stage light, the whole scene became the inside of a human body. When these images are all spot-lighted in different colors suddenly they will appear as an incredible three-dimensional mandala universe since after all, the human body is a mandala of the cosmos.

Studio Notebook, May 2003

What on earth had I been thinking? I was thinking that I had to follow each scene of Kuukai's narrative as something I had to paint—as if it were a landscape that I had seen somewhere. Forget it! I want to start from the inside: I want to start from a very small work. I want to pour only my absolutely honest images, my honest emotions which rise up from my own unconsciousness, into that small pictorial space no matter how frightening they are. The images must be just like drops of my blood on the paper. I want to watch how that first smallest trace of blood develops.

Studio Notebook, September 2005

Rafael and I went walking in a redwood forest near Santa Cruz as we often do whenever we can take some time off. We encountered a huge fallen tree there. Its roots were forced out of the earth by the leverage of its heavy trunk and were spread wide as if a hand were open and each of the fingers pointed to the sky: these roots looked like animals howling at the heaven. We took pictures of the roots and I made sketches of them. I decided to go into the *FATHOM* project by working on "The Sorcerer Entering His Forest" scene.

"The forest is the place where Gods dwells." The ancient Shinto words came back to me. But ancient Gods are not kind, and the forest is not pretty. In reality we should rather say, "The forest is the place where unknown dark forces and evil dwell." It is a dark terrifying universe: filled with roaring ferocious animals and shrieking strange birds, severe winds, rain and snow soaks you and drenches you, tangled ivy and coiled snakes are underneath your feet....

On August 12th I started my studio work, and on August 23rd I completed the three panels of the foreground piece. I sent this new piece which was barely dried, flattened on the floor of the truck sent by the museum where my solo show was just about to open, along with the older works I had already sent. In addition to those works this newest one was displayed as a focal piece of the show: not just as a stage back drop, nor just as an illustration for *FATHOM*. This work was shown as the trace of my own spiritual struggle and of the transcendence inspired by the narrative of Kuukai's life. The years-long narrative problem was finally solved. The first work of Mixed Genre was born.

After Junko had created this first scene of the Mixed Genre narrative, the other scenes came more naturally: Communicating with Nature, Shipwreck, Chang An, Tantric Dance, the Mandalas. And in the last scene, Meditation on the Mountain, Junko showed Kuukai as he reached his own transcendence: her art resonated and the series reached its transcendence in that image.

This narrative was not provoked by any material object: there was no visitant like the decanter as in the *Requiem* series; no such vision as initiated the *Forest of Amida Buddha* series. But there were visions, as Junko tells us: memories, dreamlike visions that evoked deep-lying energies. There was tension—then there was resolution, and then there was transcendence.

The *FATHOM* series required an integration of the two kinds of narration I mentioned above. Junko was constrained to present the scenes which had been agreed upon. Each scene was based on an episode in Kuukai's life, so the works had to depict those scenes in a recognizable way: although they are abstract, they are still "objective" in that sense. But like all of Junko's art, these works came to her while she worked in an altered state. She was not content merely to "illustrate" the scenes from Kuukai's life: instead, she identified herself with Kuukai and only then could she receive the works that arose from her own experience.

RESOLUTION AND TRANSCENDENCE

Next page:
FATHOM:
THE FINAL SCENE,
WITH DANCERS:
MEDITATION
ON THE MOUNTAIN
(MAY 2006)
See the work without
dancers at pp. 82-83

The role of narrative in Junko's art is bound up with her search for resolution and transcendence. "Resolution" means that the artist begins with a sense of profound disquiet: there are competing forces to which she is responding and they create conflict which she must struggle to resolve. When she finds the resolution—which expresses itself in the image she creates—she thereby achieves a kind of transcendence. The greater the conflict, the more powerful is the resolution and the greater is the transcendence. Of this, Junko wrote:

Essay "Altered States of Consciousness and the Process of Creating Art," 1999

The experience of transcendence is deeply numinous and overwhelming to the artist when it happens. It happens in a painting and the artist sees it coming: it becomes unmistakably clear to the artist that every stroke of her brush, subtle as it is, points towards the firm definite moment. The parts of life which have not been integrated, go beyond and cross over the limit

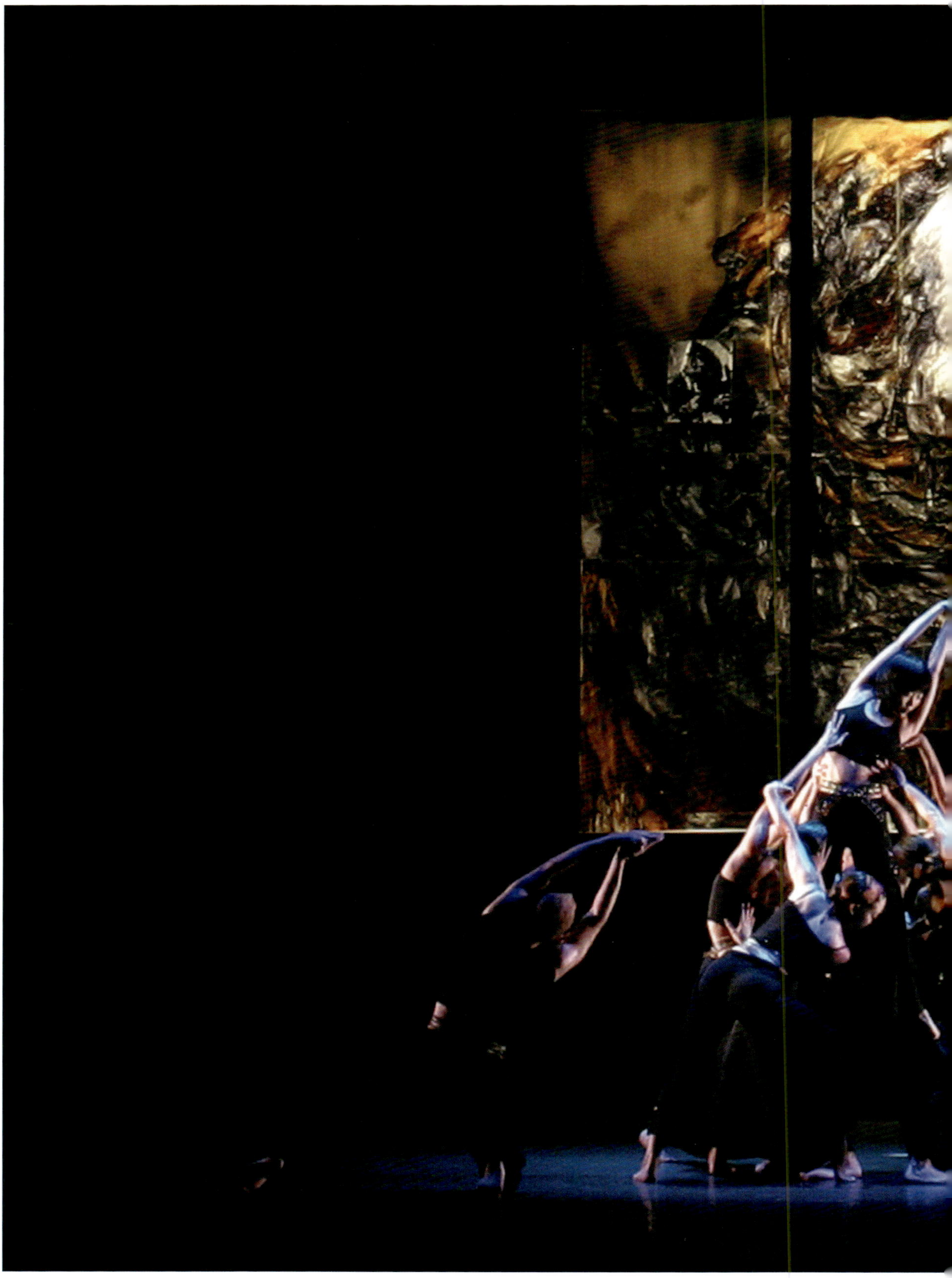

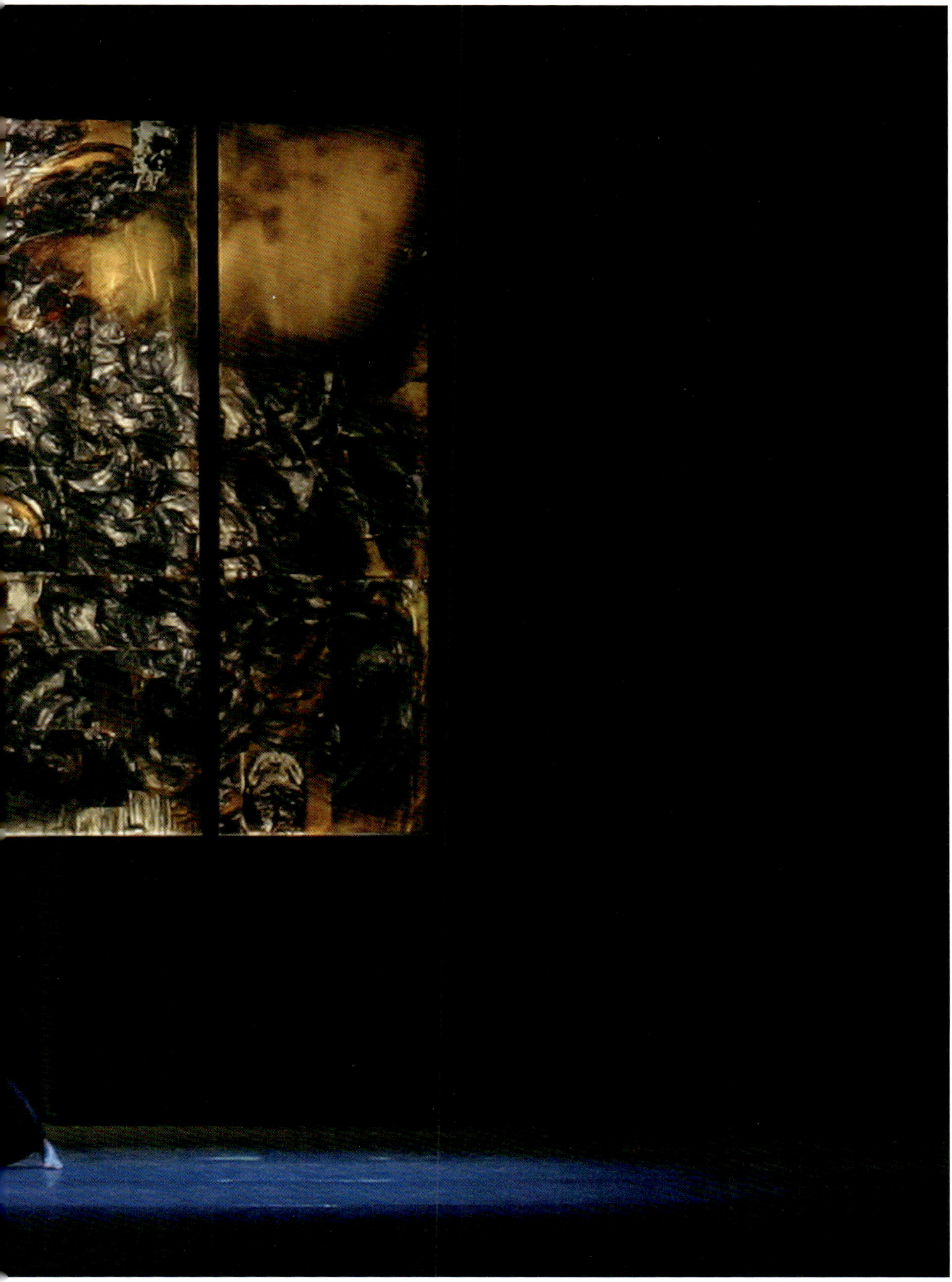

and become a part of you during this process. All facts, thoughts, or concepts may not be resolved practically and yet their significance will be altered and emotionally resolved. They are no longer attached to the ego part of you. Then there is an epiphany and the painting becomes a Presence. It assures the whole meaning of the work. The artist suddenly realizes that in this act of creating art, talking to God and receiving from God have become one. The experience will soon be over, but the artist will never be the same as before. The Presence might be sealed in the artwork for a long time but every time a viewer stands in front of the work with an open soul, the Presence quietly reveals itself to him.

Opposite:
BURLS, No. 18 (1988)
Acrylic and
charcoal on paper
40 x 32 in.
(101.6 x 81.3 cm.)

Collection of the Long
Beach Museum of Art

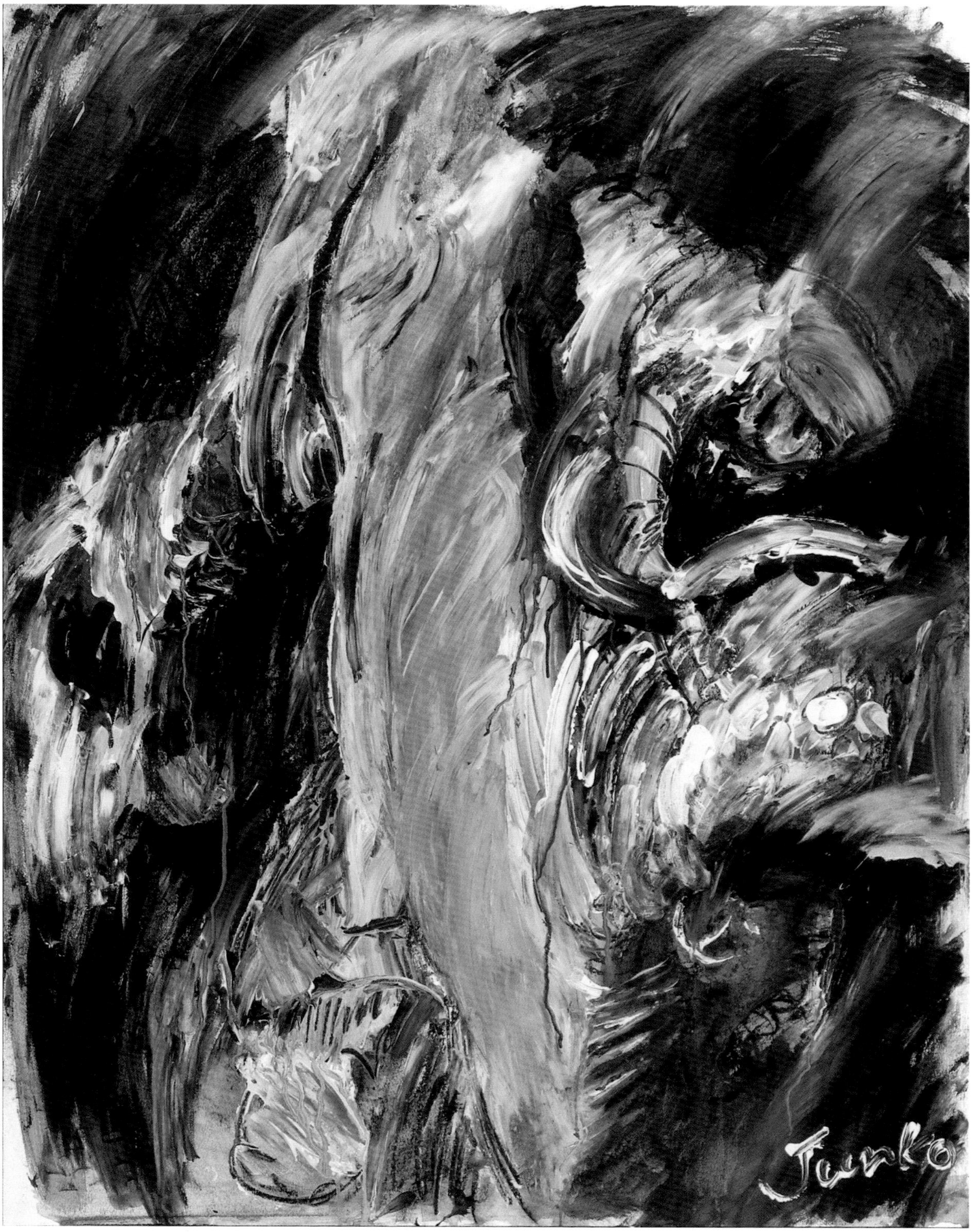
Junko

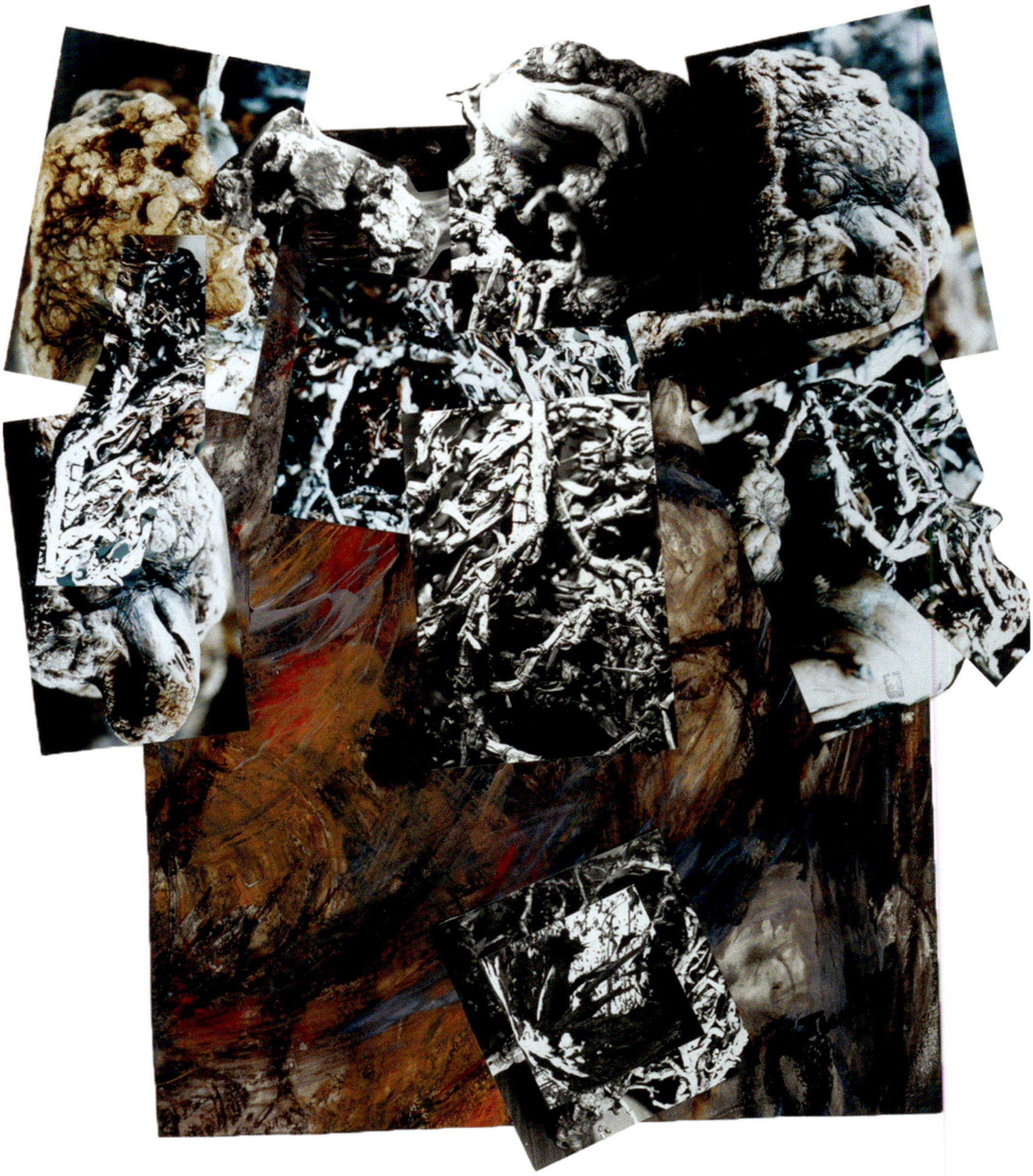

CHAPTER FIVE
A VITAL SPIRITUALITY

Junko is a spiritual artist for the twenty-first century. I do not say this to praise her: after all, it might be said of many artists that their art is "spiritual." The question to be asked about a body of art is not, "Is this work spiritual?" but rather, "HOW is this work spiritual? What is its unique kind of spirituality?" And Junko's work exhibits a unique kind of spirituality which grows out of the shared experience of the twentieth century and is honest to our age. Yet it has its roots deep in the spirituality of an earlier period. It is a vital spirituality.

My readers may hear echoes throughout this book of a discourse that flourished a hundred years ago, from the late nineteenth century through the 1930s, around "the Spiritual in Art."[1] Ideas that van Gogh had expressed in his letters, about the need for the artist to pursue his "inner necessity" and to "disentangle" the object from nature so that its eternal essence could be perceived[2]; Kandinsky's notion that the artist's job is to raise the consciousness of the viewer, and that the artist's talent is society's only road to "the spirit of the future"[3]; Worringer's identification of "empathy" as a more advanced stage of art than "abstraction"[4]—all those ideas have discernible echoes in Junko's own writing about her art and they echo throughout this book.

And there is more. The influence on the thinkers and artists of the early twentieth century of "spiritualism" in the form of Theosophy and the writings of Mme. Blavatsky seems to be felt also in Junko's art and thinking.[5] This influence, which was combined with a new respect for Indian thought and culture that piggybacked on the burgeoning distaste for colonialism and for the arrogance that went with it[6] spread to many of the artists whose work Junko admires: Kandinsky, Klee, Picasso, and Mondrian.[7]

INTERPLANETARY ICON,
No. 14 (1990)
Mixed media on paper
Irregular shape:
22.75 x 20.5 in.
(57.8 x 52.1 cm.)

The deliberate dissociation among the Theosophists of the sphere of the truly "spiritual" from any form of organized religion, and their notion that an apprehension of true spirituality would form an "international brotherhood" that would transcend cultural and religious boundaries—these ideas also echo in Junko's insistence that her work and her mission go "beyond ethnicity" and "beyond denomination," and in her notion that to the extent her art is honestly *personal*, and only to that extent, does it become truly *universal*.

There is no question that all these ideas, which enjoyed such currency in the salons and art centers of Europe and North America in those days, have had a profound influence on Junko—so much so that we might be tempted to include Junko in a catalog of spiritual artists of the twentieth century. But she does not belong in such a catalog because her brand of spirituality and the characteristics of her artistic output place her squarely in the present day, outside the accomplishments and the consciousness of the artists and thinkers of seventy-five to a hundred years ago. This is why I say that Junko, who calls herself a centripetal artist, is a spiritual artist for the twenty-first century.

This earlier wave of spiritual painters lived before World War II, and their art and thought reflect a kind of innocence which was lost in the tumultuous events of the mid-twentieth century. Five different social and intellectual developments occurred after those earlier artists died, which have combined to form Junko's unique and very contemporary kind of spirituality: psychology, multiculturalism, the experience of fascism, existentialism, and the atomic bomb.

THE IMPACT OF PSYCHOLOGY

Van Gogh, Kandinsky, and Klee died (or finished working) before World War II. Although they were Freud's contemporaries[8] it does not appear that any of those artists read his works nor did his central ideas penetrate into their art. His conception of the

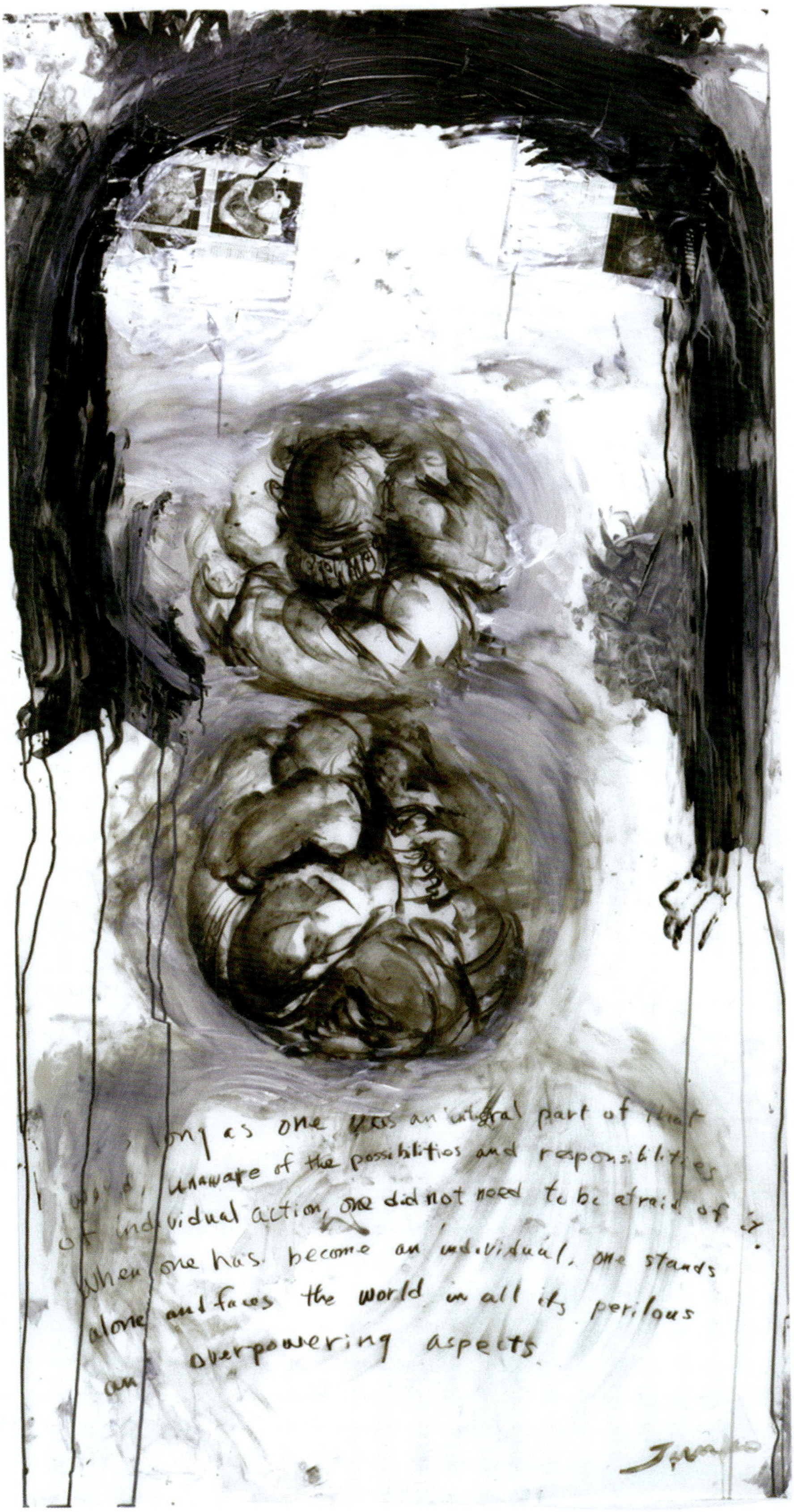

INDIVIDUATION
JOURNAL, No. 2
(1995)
"As long as one was an integral part of that world, unaware of the possibilities and responsibilities of individual action, one did not need to be afraid of it. When one has become an individual, one stands alone and faces the world in all its perilous and overpowering aspects."
Acrylic and photographs on mylar
80 x 42 in.
(203.2 x 106.7 cm.)

personality as comprising a subconscious, an ego, and a superego, and of the many forces that act upon the ego from above and below to influence behavior and belief, led to a basic distrust of the self that has influenced all late twentieth-century thinkers. But neither van Gogh (who had to struggle with his own personal demons) nor Klee nor Mondrian nor Kandinsky—none of them had to struggle with the view of the normal self as potentially misshapen or distorted. Such distortions, to the extent they were recognized, were associated instead with "genius" or with "madness" or with "tragedy"—never with normalcy.

Nor did any of the artists of that earlier period have any model of developmental psychology outside the church or the academy. All of them conceived of the individual's life as a journey toward God, or toward excellence, or both. The notion of "individuation," articulated by Jung in the early decades of the century but not well circulated until the 1950s and 1960s, was unknown to them.

Freud's work was focussed primarily on mental illness but his associates and students—Jung and Adler, later Karen Horney and Erich Fromm—applied his theories to a much wider range of social and cultural concerns. They evolved a new conception of what it means to become a healthy individual and their work is central to Junko's conception of her own path of development. Junko's concern with issues of developmental psychology reveals itself most directly in the *Individuation Journal* series (1995), but it shows up throughout her work because the whole notion of a "series" is itself an expression of Junko's struggle toward individuation and the "truth" associated with it.

Without a modern psychological awareness, centripetal art could not have stood on as firm a philosophical basis as it does. The notion of the "center" of the "self" is a contemporary notion, and the whole project of seeking that center is a notion explored in developmental psychology. This point is discussed further in Chapter Six, under "Individuation."

THE IMPACT OF MULTICULTURALISM

The early spiritual artists were very much European, and their acquaintance with cultures outside Europe was generally superficial. As a consequence, their incorporation of "primitive," or Egyptian, or "Eastern" images into their art is often sentimental: a kind of exoticism. All those artists lived in the days when Europeans assumed that Europe was the center of culture, and when cultural exchange was essentially a voluntary thing. For us, having lived through the last half of the twentieth century, cultural exchange is not optional: we live shoulder to shoulder with other cultures and sometimes, as Junko and I have done, we intermarry and face the gap between cultures every single day. There are families in our large cities in which three different languages must be spoken: one in which the husband communicates with his wife, another in which he communicates with the children, and yet another in which the wife communicates with their children. That is the world we live in, and the "Eurocentrism" of those earlier artists seems now to be nothing more than a set of childish prejudices.

But there are other aspects to multiculturalism that the earlier generations never appreciated: its difficulty and the pain it causes. Right up to the 1960s, openness to other cultures was seen as a positive, happy thing: it was associated with an affirmation that we are all members of "The Family of Man."[9] Even in today's world, for many people who live in developed countries, travelling and visiting other cultures, or witnessing local public displays of foreign cultural identity (such as Cinco de Mayo or the Chinese New Year celebrations), are seen as a form of recreation analogous to visiting a museum. But Junko's experience of multiculturalism is deep, personal, and painful.

Every culture has a strong tendency to make the people who are born into it believe that there are absolute values in it, and that those values are universal. The process of accepting cultural relativity involves shaking one's faith and identity, and when representatives of two different cultures live together the encounter can be painful for both parties: it often arouses anger and hostility. Junko's struggle with multiculturalism brought her to a completely new and unexpected level of understanding of what it involves. In Japan she was a member of the elite. Although she had to struggle hard to individuate herself in that totalitarian society, she still was unquestionably a member of the powerful social majority. But once she came to America and started to live here as an immigrant, almost overnight she found herself to be a member of an under-privileged minority. Not only were there ethnic and cultural differences: as a person who has a handicap in expressing herself in our language, she became a member of a powerless minority. Life turned upside down. At a lecture she gave in 2001, at a conference on Exile sponsored by the Getty Museum, Junko said this about what she felt:

From Lecture, "Following the Pillar of Fire: From Language to Artistic Expression," Getty Museum, 2001

The world had turned 180 degrees around me and I had become a minority—not only in respect of race but also because I had to become a member of a less intellectual minority group. Not only my language—everything I had learned about how I should behave as a well brought-up lady, all my self-effacing training worked bitterly against me. I realized that no matter how deep my sense of isolation was, at least in Japan I was in every other way unmistakably a member of the majority.

I started noticing the groups of people here who are minorities for one reason or another; because of language or ethnicity or age or because of some physical difficulty. All of them were living in the pain of not being accepted or respected in this society. I heard their unspoken cry of aspiration like the howling of a wolf, everywhere I saw them. I identified myself with them and with their cries. I began to realize how much I had taken my own language ability for granted. How proud I was of being an expert in Japanese writing and speaking—which language remains within me still intensely in my mind, like a secret. I had to accept my new reality, just like a former athlete who is now confined to a wheelchair has to accept the new reality and focus his efforts on rehabilitation. But no matter how miserable he looks now, his identity is still that of an athlete. And it is that way also with the immigrant.

This aspect of her experience of multiculturalism raised her consciousness in unexpected ways. She started to be aware of the dark side of the power structure that exists in every society: of the prejudice, the distortion, the arrogance, and the lies which are taught and ingrained in societies all over the world. She started seeing sharply how the elite in any society write history to suit themselves; how the stories of massacres, slavery, colonization, and of other tremendous humiliation and violence are never clearly revealed nor recognized. And she came to realize that unless we see these truths clearly we build only a dishonest multiculturalism based on those lies. The happy, innocent multiculturalism in which the artists of a hundred years ago believed is not at all true to her very contemporary experience.

Junko has written at length about her status as a "Spiritual Refugee" (see Chapter Two, pg. 107). Her experiences are personal, and yet they reach the raw, vulnerable essence of what multiculturalism involves. Junko's insistent struggle towards honesty and integrity was amplified by her experience of multiculturalism, and the tendency of her art to empathize with things that are vulnerable, became even deeper. Her identity as someone who suffers a repressed pain, already deeply rooted in her, was reinforced by her experience of living as an exile. She expresses this identity in her work: you can feel it and hear it, like the howling of a wolf. When viewers in the museums stare at her works with tears in their eyes, this identity is an important part of what they see there.

THE IMPACT OF WORLD WAR II AND FASCISM

In the decades leading up to World War II, waves of fascism swept over the world and enveloped countries that had considered themselves models of high culture and civilization. This was something new in the twentieth century. It was not just the Nazis in Germany: fascism flourished in Spain, Portugal, Italy, Romania, and Hungary, and communism in Russia and China had much in common with it. Fascism and totalitarianism also flourished in

Japan in the very place where Junko grew up. Fascism was part of what prepared the way for World War II and all the destruction that came with it. At its deepest level Junko's centripetal art represents a response to these mid-twentieth century experiences.

In fascist societies, fundamental respect for the individual is lost. The individual who wants to be free in order to be himself, who wants to act as a rational ethical being—that individual is crushed and overwhelmed in a turbulent current of group identity, an insistence on blind obedience to an irrational authority whose power over the group depends on the darkest elements of the human psyche. What elements? Erich Fromm has written about them: the refusal to separate from the primal Mother and become oneself, which is a form of *incestuous attachment*; the attraction to death rather than to life, a form of *necrophilia* which allows the fascist regime to use people like machines and to kill people en masse; and a kind of *malignant narcissism* which requires those who believe in it to see the group and its activities as glorious and angrily stamps out any voice that whispers against the shared illusion.[10]

We tend to think of fascism as a social and political phenomenon—and of course it is. But it also has deep psychological aspects; it appeals to the individual's fear of facing the responsibilities of freedom. It offers him a ready-made, group-approved substitute for real self-respect. It offers him a counterfeit kind of security by inviting him to remain unseparated from the blood and soil from which he sprang. If he attorns to the fascist group and subscribes to its underlying narcissistic mythology, the individual is relieved of self-doubt and of the need to struggle towards his own individuation. This is what makes it possible for fascism to flourish in the first place. It is these deep-lying aspects of the human psyche that remain even after the mid-century fascist regimes were toppled. Fascism and its related pathologies threaten to surface even today in so-called democratic societies.

Junko reacted strongly against the fascism she experienced in Japan. She refused, even from the age of four, to be obedient to an authority she sensed was irrational. The whole terror of

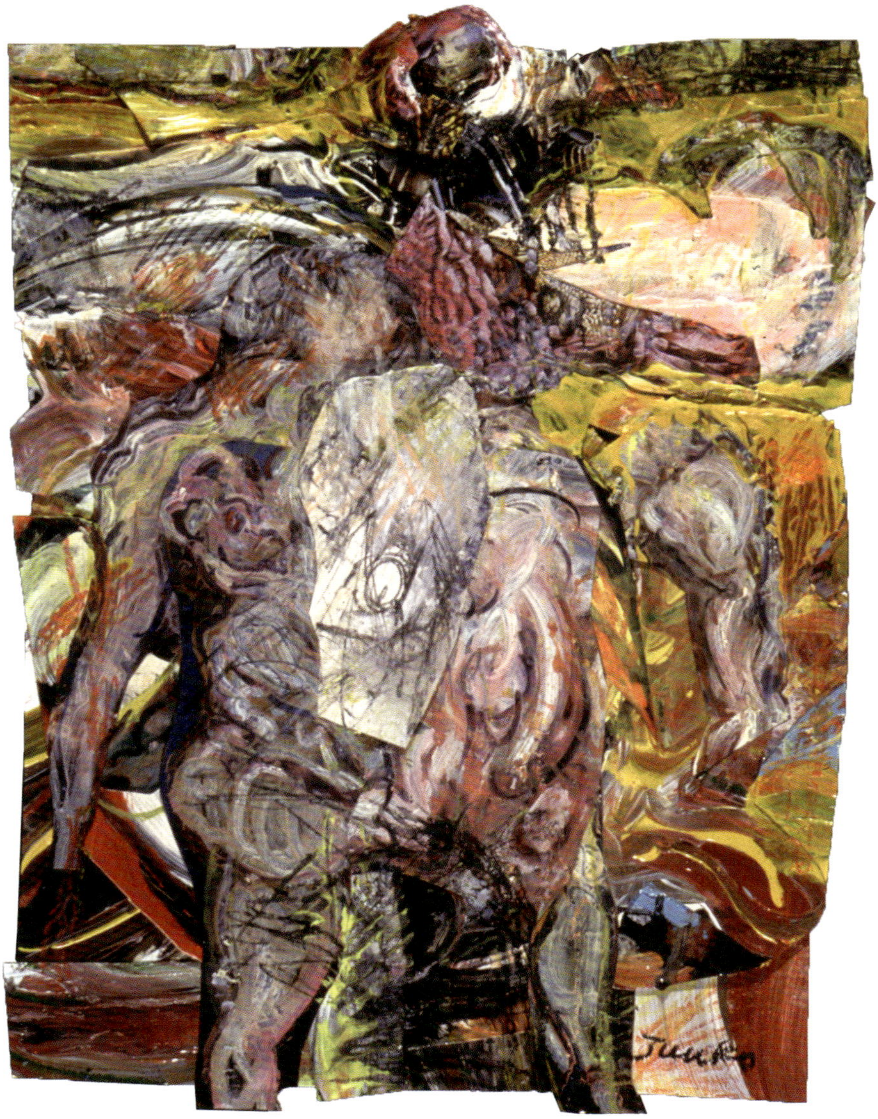

TOPOLOGICAL DEFORMATIONS OF THE CROSS
No. 18 (1987)
"KNOW BEFORE WHOM YOU STAND"
Collage and acrylic on paper
21 x 16 in.
(53.3 x 40.6 cm.)

These words are written on the Ark in most Jewish synagogues: Junko was moved by them.

fascism—its fascination with death and its cruel suppression of the individual—was crystallized for her in her encounter with the executed Bird. This was an experience she had as a small child, and she could not verbalize it or understand its impact at the time. So the experience internalized itself in her as a phobia of birds. But when Junko was an adult, the experience reenacted itself and in her powerful series, *Requiem for an Executed Bird*, discussed in Chapter Four, Junko overcame her phobia. That series is her transcendent response to fascism and is an example of centripetal art that could not have been created earlier in history.

Junko's experience of the destruction of war also had profound repercussions in her art. Because she grew up in a world that was being destroyed in front of her eyes, and saw that world reconstructed after the war, the fragility and "deconstructed" essence of the world is something Junko never forgets. So when van Gogh said of his trees, skies, and seas that he found them all in nature but that he felt he needed to "disentangle" them from nature, he still left them where he found them: his trees are on the ground, in forests where they belong; and their "essence" struggles from there (van Gogh's *Olive Trees*, 1889, *Mountains at St.-Remy*, 1889). But Junko draws roots and trees which are already torn up from their contexts. In her *Interplanetary Icons*, her burls float in outer space, already deconstructed. Her root is not just disentangled from nature: it sat for five years on her studio table while she drew it. Even her engine parts, which are human constructions, are torn out of their contexts and "disentangled" from the engines which are their natural place.

Because Junko encounters the world this way, her art is uncomfortable to look at. And this brings us to another aspect of it.

THE IMPACT OF EXISTENTIALISM: THE TOTAL ABSENCE OF COMPLACENCY

When Kierkegaard wrote in *Fear and Trembling* of Abraham's "leap of faith" and when Buber spoke of an "I/Thou" relationship with God, they ripped apart large pieces of the fabric in which religion had been wrapped. By emphasizing the quality of the individual's religious experience, these thinkers undermined the notion that mere membership in a religious group, or mere adoption of an official credo, could guarantee either salvation or any authentic relationship with God. The existentialists' notion that we construct our world through our own actions and that "reality" is not anything "out there" for us to see, or to paint, but something we construct—these notions were not familiar to the early spiritual painters.[11]

Junko's connection to Existentialism did not start with her intellectual interest. The first reality she experienced in her early life was the terror of war: running away from air raids night after night; the fear of losing her parents and being deserted; the awareness of dark, irrational authorities and people who were slaughtered by them; the terror and apathy that come from the total destruction of the values people had believed in throughout history. The world in which she found herself was nothing but "absurd"—the very word the existential philosophers and writers used to describe the world as irrational.

When Junko was fourteen years old, Camus' *Stranger* was translated into Japanese for the first time—eleven years after it was published in France. Junko read it and was shocked to find that it was so close to her own mind, and she was moved by the fact that Sartre and other philosophers and writers who went through World War II as she did had established the new movement named Existentialism. The idea that this world is meaningless, and that only through living with this awareness, holding up this "absurdity" in front of you, can life be lived meaningfully, sounded like an expression of her own mind.

Seeing Klee's art was Junko's first encounter with existentialism in visual art: this is the incident she wrote about (Chapter Two, pg. 89). That was a year before she started reading Camus and other existential works such as Dostoevsky, Nietzsche, and Kierkegaard. Some years later, she read Freud and Buber. The central ideas of existentialism are woven into Junko's art and are conspicuous there. Junko's art aims toward a high kind of resolution and transcendence but Junko does not see those things as existing in the world outside of her; they are something toward which she has to struggle, and they exist only by virtue of her struggle toward them. We see the sense of struggle in all of her images: even the most nearly peaceful ones are still full of ambiguities and internal conflict.

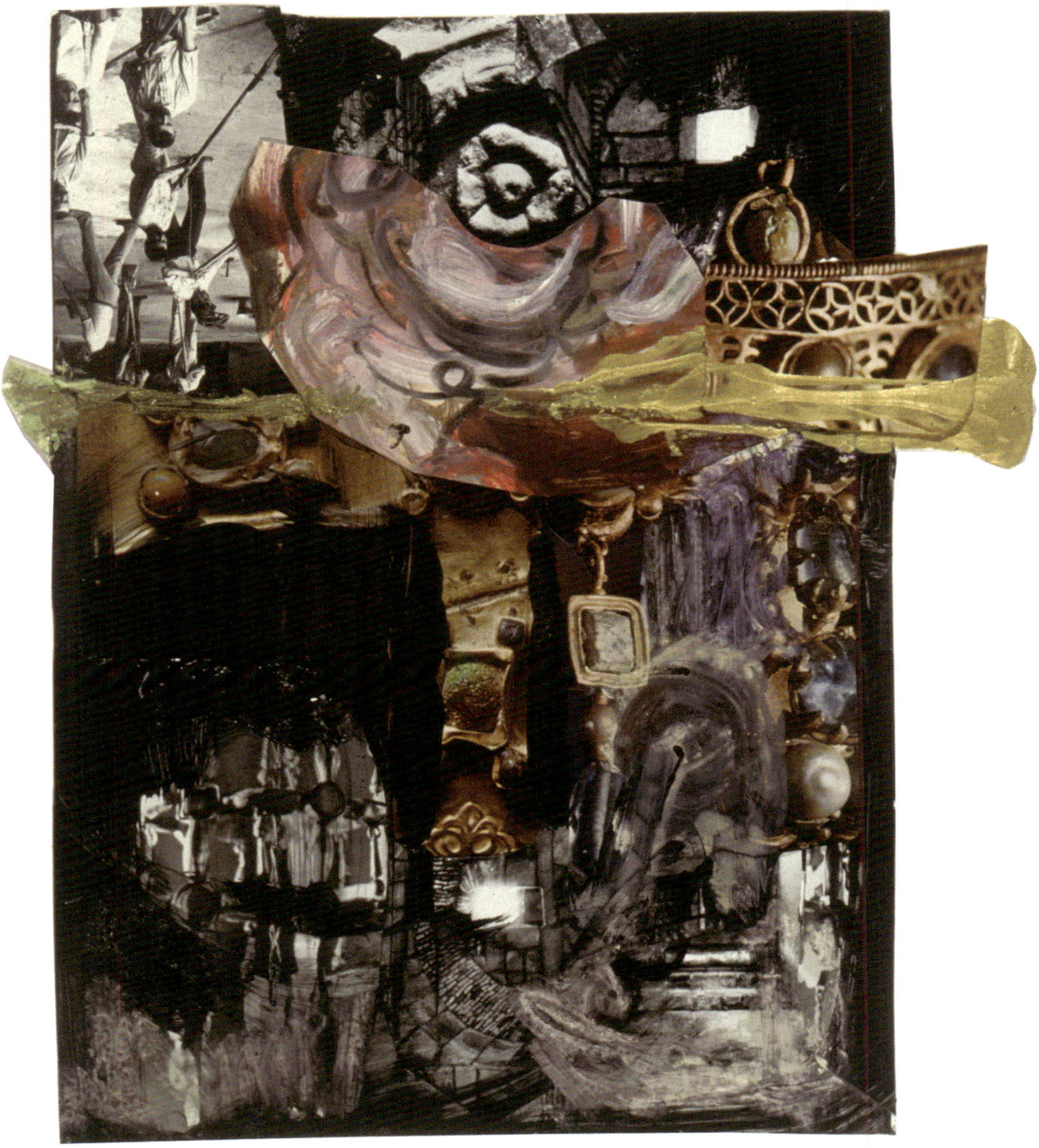

THE IMPACT OF THE ATOMIC BOMB; ECOLOGICAL CONCERNS

Japan became the first victim of this new kind of weapon of mass destruction. The atomic bomb did not cause only the physical destruction of the cities on which it was dropped: it caused kinds of chemical and biological destruction whose effects lasted over many generations. While Junko was not personally a victim of the bomb, she grew up in the country that had to deal most directly with its effects.

The atomic bomb brought a permanent end to the innocent optimism that the earlier spiritual artists had felt about technology. To a degree unparalleled in earlier history,[12] people came to realize the destructive effects of technology. And the atomic bomb also changed the view of war radically: people saw for the first time in history that the new kind of war would bring devastating consequences not only to human targets but also to all creatures and to the globe itself. The radiation harms the DNA of humans and of all other living things on the earth; its effects last for generations. When massive doses of radiation spread through the air and water all over the globe, it is impossible to localize the harm. So basic concepts of war had to change: the categories of ally and enemy, victor and vanquished—all the concepts used to justify sacred wars and patriotism were deeply shaken. War itself came to be considered a crime against mankind and the earth. And this shook the belief of Junko's generation in the Judaeo-Christian view of mankind as the "crown of creation," above nature. For we came to realize that mankind could become an adversary to both itself and to the whole of creation. This in turn reinforced a distaste for the notion that nature is there for man to conquer and exploit. Instead, the experience of the atomic bomb made all of us more receptive to ecological concerns. And this led to a distrust of the views which underlay and promoted the industrial revolution: economic prosperity and growth came to be seen as just one aspect of a more complicated picture, and not as an entirely positive aspect.

Opposite:
TOPOLOGICAL DEFORMATIONS OF THE CROSS
No. 1 (1987)
Mixed media on paper
21 x 16 in.
(53.3 x 40.6 cm.)

Private Collection.
In the early works of the series, the cross is clear and the impression is almost sacramental. But see what happens to the cross in the middle and later works.

Since the atomic bombs fell, it has become urgent for us to find ways for man and nature to live together in harmony. This urgency goes beyond the merely practical idea that in order to extract more resources from nature over a longer time we have to restrain ourselves and husband nature's resources more carefully. It is instead an effort to form a new relationship between humans and the natural world of which humans are a part. "New" for many of us, but not for all of us. The idea that we are born out of the earth, that we all—animals, trees, and plants—are spirits, that humans are the caretakers of nature, and that by respecting the spirits, the rules, and harmony of nature, we will reach oneness with it; these are ideas with which the American natives lived and these ideas are part of the Shinto world view. The Japanese say that in the West, people cut down the forest to make an open space and build a church there, but that in Japan wherever a shrine is built a deep forest grows around it. The forest is the source of all life, and an asylum for all living things, so they gather there and make the forest bigger. Every single tree is a ladder on which God comes down to us. That ancient Shinto sensibility has started to take root even in the Western heart.

All these sensibilities are palpable throughout Junko's work, which does not "glorify" mankind and empathizes with life in plants, in roots, and even in inanimate things.

These five influences combined to move the art world away from "modernism" and into "postmodernism;" let me call them the "Five Motivations." The postmoderns reacted against the innocence of the moderns and, eager to clean their philosophical house, they swept the baby out with the proverbial bathwater. Because the moderns still believed in the grand narratives of the past, the postmoderns rejected the whole concept of a narrative: they did not think of the possibility that there might be another kind of narrative. Because the moderns still believed in excellence and truth, the postmoderns rejected the whole concept of standards: they did not think of the possibility that there might be another kind of truth. Because the moderns still believed that art could speak seriously to the community of man, the postmoderns rejected the whole notion of such a community and instead insisted that art is ultimately a matter of pure self-expression. Junko lives and works after the postmodern age and her work reflects a vibrant consciousness of the Five Motivations; but her art represents a radically alternative response to them.

MARKERS FOR SPIRITUALITY

There are many "markers" for spirituality in Junko's work.

One of these markers is her entry into what she calls an "altered state of consciousness"—a state which is beyond the ego, higher than everyday consciousness. The acceptance of this state of mind is something fostered by Jung as well as by age-old Eastern ideas to which Junko was exposed from earliest childhood. I discuss the altered state of consciousness as it applies to Junko's art in Chapter Six.

Another marker is her frequent use of religious themes. For example, she has painted altarpieces and a whole series of works on the cross. She sees Buddha emerging from dead flowers and the root, and she has painted a whole series called *In the Forest of Amida Buddha*. She names one of her series *Interplanetary Icons* (nineteen works, 1990), and a pivotal piece in her series of forty-five works, *Requiem for an Executed Bird*, is subtitled, *Bird in the Cathedral* (see pg. 170). Her most recent works, the *FATHOM* pieces, are a series of scenes from the life of Kuukai, a ninth-century Buddhist priest; and her *Esoteric Buddhism* series incorporates quotations from Kuukai's poetry. Junko often makes it clear that she has spiritual and religious themes on her mind, even though her handling of these themes is not pious or in any way orthodox.

Another marker for spirituality is Junko's preoccupation with the spiritual essence of her visitants. This is evident from her own series statements presented in Chapter One: she wants to paint the horseshoe crab's "vulnerability"; she wants the spirits of the trees to "dance" with her; she wants the engine parts to be "reconnected" to the cosmic forces from which they have been ripped. She sees everything, in other words, with an inner eye.

These three aspects of Junko's art are markers for spirituality as distinct from religion. For Junko, the distinction between the realm of the spiritual and the realm of organized religion is not something that has to be proven or argued for: it is taken for granted in her work. This is partly because of the "built-in multiculturalism" I just mentioned: during her adult life, Junko has never felt it necessary to identify herself with any one religion—not with the Shinto or Buddhism or Christianity that she found in her family of origin; not with the Unitarianism she experienced in her first marriage; and not with the Judaism she encountered in me. Instead, Junko has viewed all these religious worlds as sources of material to be appropriated and woven into her own original expression of spirituality.

CENTRIPETAL ART OVERFLOWS THE STUDIO

Junko's struggle with these five major developments of the mid-twentieth century—psychology, multiculturalism, fascism, existentialism, and the atomic bomb—took place in her studio, of course; but it overflowed her studio and spilled into our marriage and also into our religious views, and I myself was drawn into that struggle.

When we were in our forties, Junko started seeing a therapist, and soon after she started, it became clear to me that I had to start seeing a therapist of my own. I was surprised that Junko, being Japanese, could tolerate the kind of open, candid interchange that therapy requires because the cultural chasm between Japan and America was widest at that point. After all, the Western tradition of the "confessional" faiths, built on the notion of a relationship with a personal God, is not part of Japanese culture. But Junko's multiculturalism, characterized by her insistent struggle toward integrity and individuation, showed itself capable of bridging even that chasm.

By that time, we had both read Freud, Karen Horney, and others—but I must say that Junko had read them more deeply than I had. Her understanding of what neurosis meant and how it might be cured was already deeply ingrained in her, and through therapy she was able to reinforce the foundation of her centripetal art. She said that therapy was one of the best things that American culture offered her.

The commitment to therapy is in fact the same commitment that is at the foundation of Junko's centripetal art: a commitment to go deep into her center, a commitment to a sharp, introspective, analytical view of the self, a commitment to complete honesty, and a commitment to avoiding complacency. This commitment is a strong weapon against narcissism, and Junko, who had suffered as a victim of the malignant narcissism of her family, was already comfortable with it. It gave her confidence and became an important part of the philosophical basis of her centripetal art. In spite of the general belief that subjectivism leads inevitably to narcissism, Junko's art is deeply anti-narcissistic. Later on, she came to view her art as something entirely outside of subjectivism.

Junko's refusal to be complacent about what I was ready to see as minor problems in our marriage gave her the courage to confront them—and to force me to confront them.

Because of Junko, I was forced to reconsider my relationship to Judaism and to law, at the deepest levels. This did not take place through any kind of confrontation between Junko and me. Instead, Junko asked me quite earnestly, when we had been married nearly seven years, "What contribution does Judaism have to make to the twenty-first century?" It was a fair question, asked in a very constructive spirit—much in line with other questions we asked each other about our sense of mission and the contribution we wanted to make to the world. But it took me seven years of thinking to come up with an answer that satisfied us both—and this answer I wrote down in my first book.[13] It was then that I came to realize the meaning that law had for me: *law is society's on-going search for integrity* and by being a lawyer, I was helping society to find its own center and its own deepest kind of integrity. In this way, Junko's passionate commitment to her mission awakened me to aspects of my own mission.

Meanwhile, Junko had taught me that Japanese people think it is quite normal to be a member of one religion when you are young, another when you are adult, and still a third when you reach old age. When census forms are passed around in Japan asking people to identify themselves as members of this or that religious group, the total number of check marks is regularly nearly twice the total number of questionnaires: a religion is not viewed as a lifelong affiliation, but is rather a stage along life's path. It took me a long time to understand this idea and then to accept it and this was just part of my own very local experience of the insistent multiculturalism which is transforming us in the twenty-first century. I return to this subject in the Afterword.

A NEW KIND OF SPIRITUALITY

One of the artist's functions is to raise expectations and then force us to confront them and realign them. If the art does not force us to realign our expectations, it is mere flattery, or communal art—affirming values and ideas that are already accepted. But if it does not raise any expectations in us at all, then it cannot speak to us. I will give you an illustration of this aesthetic idea drawn from music. The great composer moves from chord to chord in ways which are just slightly beyond our expectations: otherwise the music would be trivial. In his setting of *Ave Verum Corpus*, Mozart's departure when he repeats the last line of the text—"*in mortis examine*"—takes our breath away: without that progression, the piece might be just another nice piece of choral church music but the surprise progression, the betrayal of our complacent expectations, raises the piece to divine heights. The same idea can be applied to visual art—particularly to centripetal art. Junko can be understood as an artist who forces us to revise our expectations about spirituality with high consciousness and deliberateness.

Many of us are brought up to believe in a dichotomy between what is spiritual and what is material and we have in our minds a list of qualities associated with these two stereotypes: The spiritual, we tend to think, is associated with the eternal and permanent (not with the transient and the time-bound); with the otherworldly (not with things pertaining to this world); with what is quiet (not with anything turbulent); with what is refined (rather than coarse); with what is simple (rather than complex); with what is perfect and complete (not with anything imperfect or broken); with higher things (not with lower things).

This dichotomy and its associated expectations have very ancient roots, particularly in Western thought. Its sources can be traced to Sumerian ideas of the holy and the sacred which go back at least to the third millenium B.C., and it is deeply ingrained in Western culture. But it is not only a Western idea: the Buddhist conception of escape from the endless cycle of dying and rebirth and the Indian notion of Nirvana, which includes Cessation and Complete Purity, both imply a similar set of stereotypes surrounding a similar dichotomy.

Yet Junko's art flies in the face of most of these stereotypes and deliberately disappoints most of these expectations. It is true that Junko's art concerns itself with what is eternal rather than what is transitory: her roots, her dead flowers, her engine parts, her burls—all of them exist in a timeless space. This is so because her works are never "transactional": they do not show people walking on roads or fighting or meeting or saying goodbye; and when she deals with sexual energy (*Ecstasy* at pp. 42-43, *Tantric Dance* at pg. 66) the sexual energy is on a universal rather than a personal scale. So the time depicted in her works is always eternity—never a particular moment. But this is the only expectation associated with "spirituality" which Junko does not disappoint.

Most of her works are not at all "otherworldly": instead, they are bound up with very earthly, even mundane objects, such as the roots, dead flowers, burls, and engine parts presented in Chapter One. Nor are her works at all "quiet": instead, they are turbulent in the extreme and any sense of quiet they convey is a sense of quiet after a storm rather than a quiet from the outset. Her *Forest of Amida Buddha* is not a still, dark forest but a tempestuous, wild forest in which branches and flames whirl around. The sense of spirituality consists precisely in that whirling—not in the stillness or grandeur we see in the paintings, say, of Albert Bierstadt, a Hudson River School painter often associated with "spiritual" landscapes, or of Mark Rothko whose space is sometimes filled with depth and quietness. The quiet in her *Root Mandala* is the quiet of multitudinous complexity resolved, rather than the quiet of simplicity or minimalism.

Nor are Junko's paintings "refined" in the usual sense: she often prefers them to be coarse—particularly in her later works. This is something we explore more fully in Chapter Six below under the heading of "destruction." But even at first glance we can see that she loves to disrupt images, destroy them, cut them, tear them, and leave her works deliberately rough-edged—and this is an important aspect of her special kind of spirituality (see *Concerning Art and Religion, No. 5*, following page; and *FATHOM: Meditation on the Mountain*, pp. 192-193). And as we have just said, she eschews "simplicity" and "minimalism" and prefers a boisterous complexity in all her works, and yet this very complexity is part and parcel of her style of spirituality. As for "perfection" and "completeness," she prefers things that are broken and incomplete to things that are perfectly made: her "icons" show parts of broken engines floating in space, and her roots are torn and tangled. And as for her attitude towards "higher" things, it is clear that she sees the highest radiance and loftiest energies in the very lowest things; this is part of the core of her spirituality.

So in all these ways, Junko's spirituality expresses a cluster of ideas and appeals to a sensibility which formed only recently. It surprises us because it is not at all what we expect—and this is an important part of its value. It is a *vital* spirituality, not anything relaxed, or quiet, or peaceful, or bloodless. It is also a complex spirituality—and that is a matter I address in the following chapter.

Opposite:
INTERPLANETARY ICON, No. 19 (1990)
Mixed media on paper
Irregular shape:
26 x 25 in.
(66 x 63.5 cm.)

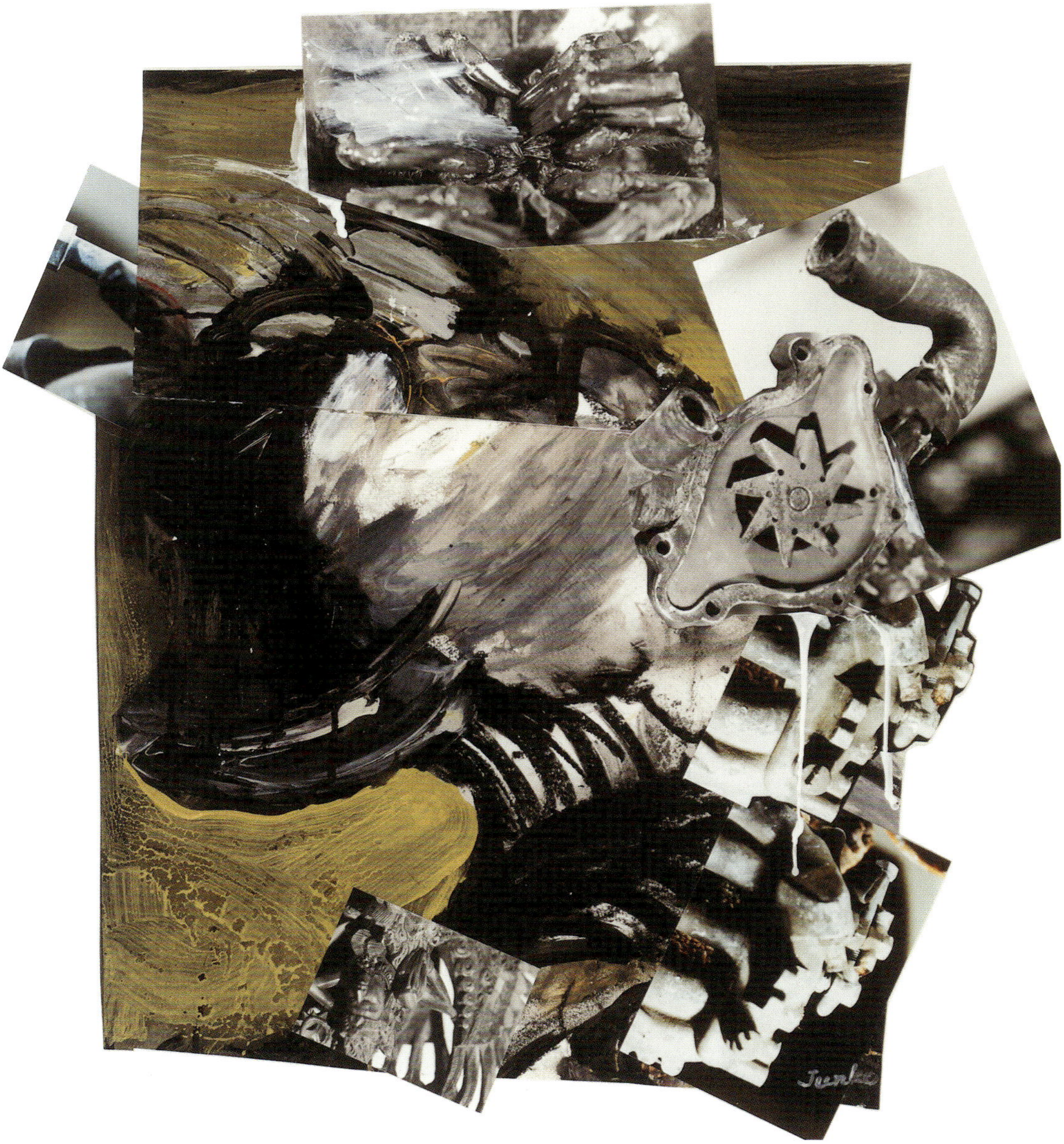

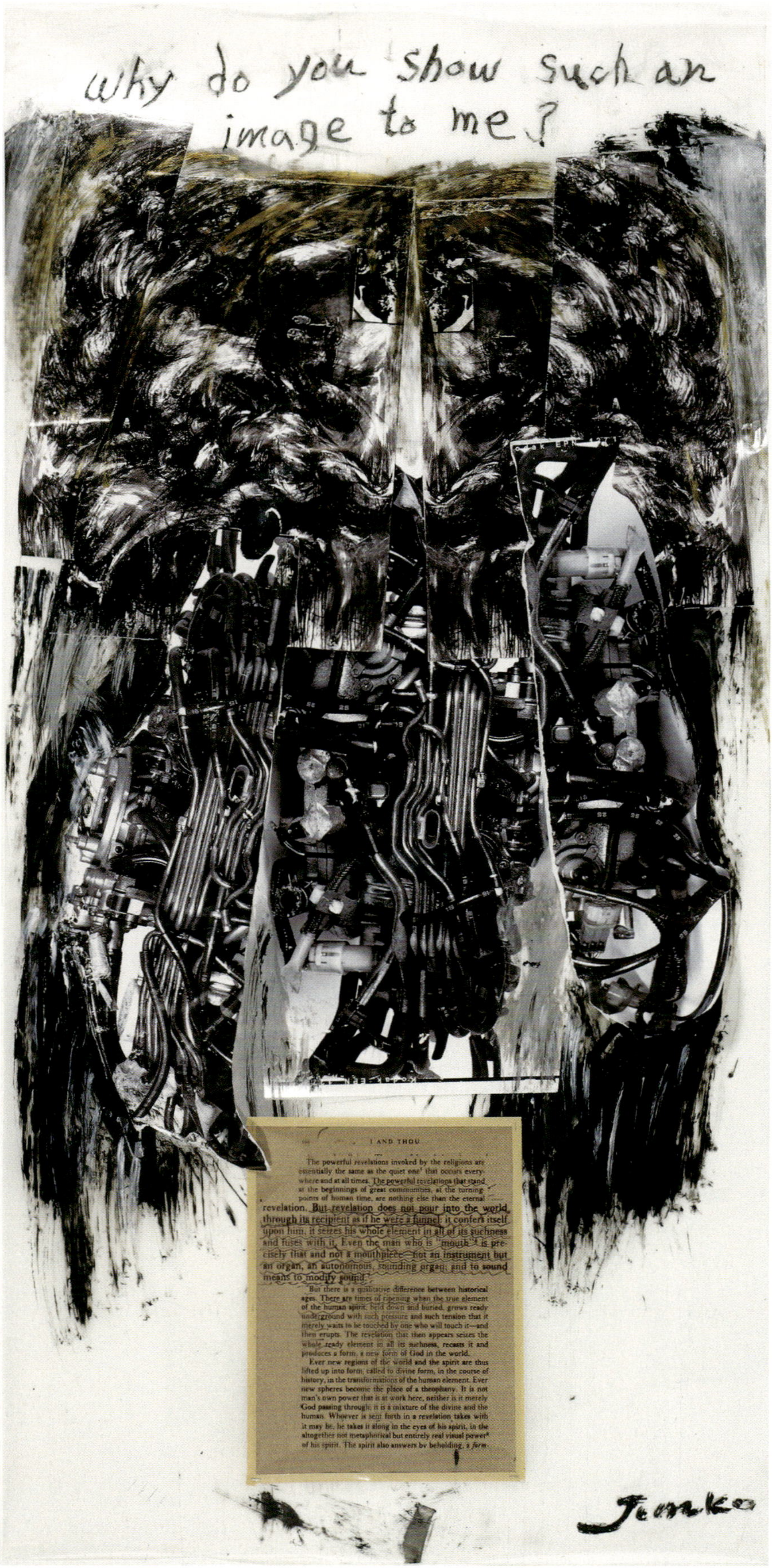

CONCERNING ART AND RELIGION, No. 5 (2003) "WHY DO YOU SHOW SUCH AN IMAGE TO ME?"
Collage of film and paper, with charcoal and acrylic on mylar support
84 x 42 in.
(213.4 x 106.7 cm.)

CHAPTER SIX
A COMPLEX SPIRITUALITY

To all of us who have believed through the years that the world is too much with us and that our true spirit will emerge only when we have shaken off the flesh and the desires of the flesh, and ascended beyond the transient concerns of our everyday lives; who believe that in order to reach the realm of the spiritual we must leave the everyday world behind us; who believe that when we reach the realm of the spiritual it will be perfectly quiet or filled with only heavenly music, and that the sounds of the city will never reach it; who believe that in the realm of spirit all things that are not-spirit will be left behind and we will be able to confront and contemplate Pure Spirit undisturbed by anything else—to all of us who were taught to believe that, Junko's art sends a strong message: "No, it is not like that. The world of Pure Spirit is here, and it is not necessary to leave this world in order to reach it. Spirit forms the world and because we are in the world, we are already in the realm of Pure Spirit. All the issues and all the complexities that we must deal with in this world have to be dealt with in that realm as well. Our task is to raise our consciousness high, and then the world will take on a different aspect for us and we will see it as the realm of Pure Spirit. And my art is my way of raising my own consciousness high."

In the twenty-first century, it is sentimental to dream of a realm of pure spirit which is far away from the world: our real spiritual task is to transform this world—not by rising above it, but by raising it to a higher place. It is merely nostalgic to look at the Japanese temple standing in the quiet mountain forest and to think, "That is my destination": it is the small saint who lives in the mountain and the big saint who lives in the city. In today's world, the spirituality we need is not anything we can reach through a process of denial, escape, or isolation: in order to reach it, we have to fill our lungs with the air we have to breathe, we have to dirty our hands with the soil on which we have to stand, and we have to accept this world in all its complexity. Having accepted it, the task is to bring order back into the world, to reconfigure the soil and the dust into structures that will call us to our highest selves.

Junko's centripetal art exhibits a complex spirituality, a spirituality woven of many threads, a spirituality that does not require, or pay obeisance to, any notion of simplicity. It is thickly layered: it is a tangle of concerns and aspirations that seem to have little to do with each other but which, in her art, are convincingly conjoined. I call your attention to the most important of them, one by one.

FORMATIVE EXPERIENCE: DESTRUCTION

Look again at Junko's *Esoteric Buddhism* series (pp. 42-43). What do we see? Something fascinating but disconcerting. It is thickly layered and each piece of film was obviously carefully cut and then pasted onto the finished work. There is acrylic paint applied; there is handwriting. This appears to be something constructed, something built up out of nothing. But listen to what Junko wrote about it as she was crawling around on her studio floor in 2001, creating these works:

Letter to a Friend, 2001

Now all the images for these five panels are laid out on the wall and floor, powerful and beautiful as they are. But the real task starts from here; after perfectly constructing the images, which is hard work but fun, I am going to destroy them. I have to break their completed perfect looks: they look just like a self-righteous man and I have to destroy the complacency of their illusional beauty. I will slash them, tear their skin literally, twist them, liquefy them by splashing Clorox on them. Then they will bounce back and fight against me, if they are real, they will grow stronger in the fighting with me. I can see this clearly in my pictorial space. But some of them are destroyed by me, and they have to go. This is the most frightening but the most exciting part of creation.

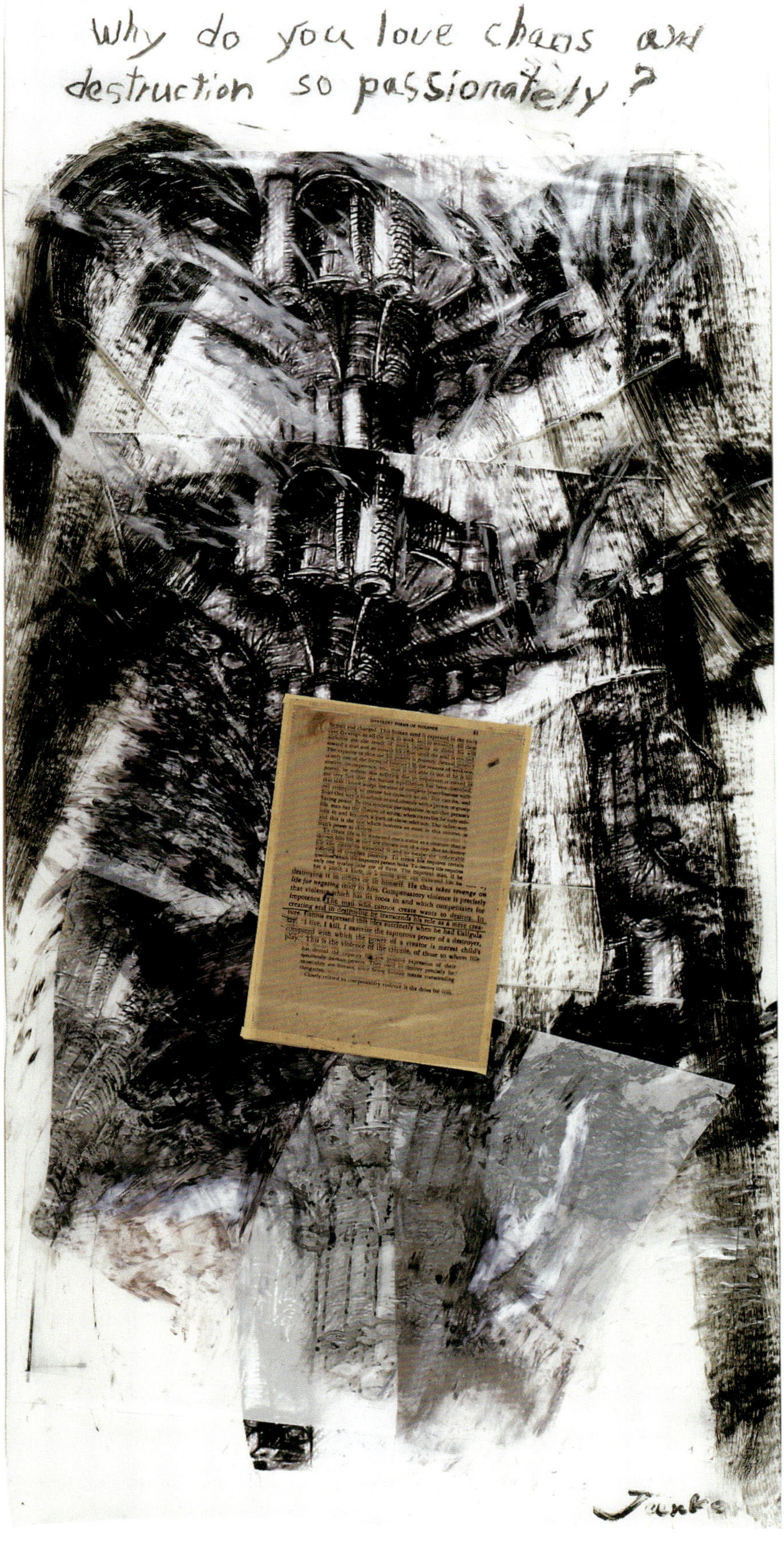

CONCERNING ART AND RELIGION, No. 2 (2003)
"WHY DO YOU LOVE CHAOS AND DESTRUCTION SO PASSIONATELY?"
Acrylic and collage on mylar
102 x 42 in.
(213.4 x 106.7 cm.)

So now we see what it is about these images that is so disconcerting, and so contemporary: destruction is part and parcel of the construction.

Destruction—but not destructiveness. These are very different. Destruction is often necessary for growth and is part of the cycle of life, death, and rebirth. But destructiveness springs from hostility, from the inability of the destroyer to individuate. It is one of the three "escape routes," three systemic responses to feelings of anxiety and inadequacy, that Erich Fromm identified in *Escape from Freedom*:[1] through destructiveness the weak individual seeks to overcome his feeling of insignificance by destroying others. That negative sort of destructiveness has nothing to do with Junko's art. Instead, her destruction is a force of creation: it is like the Refiner's Fire (Malachi, 3:3), or like the Sword of Shiva; it is the life-giving fire *In the Forest of Amida Buddha* (see pg. 185). This kind of generative destruction is one aspect of Junko's hyper-contemporary spirituality, and it finds its source in one of the formative experiences I have already hinted at.

When Junko was a girl of just four years old, often she and her family had to hide from the Allied bombings which carpeted the major cities in Japan in the last years of World War II. Junko, her mother, and her sisters would sit in a darkened room as the bombs fell. Junko remembers that at those times, her mother would open the phonograph and play a recording of Beethoven's *Ninth Symphony* which was on a tall set of "standard play" wax records. Junko remembers that her mother would lower her voice and say to her and her sisters, "Before you end your short lives, you must hear the most beautiful thing which human beings have ever created." And she would play the *Ninth Symphony*, this most sublime expression of joy, but at the lowest volume, for under that fascistic government everyone was surrounded by spying eyes and ears and they had to keep the listening volume down to the lowest level. Junko listened to the *Ninth Symphony* more than once against the cacophonous background noise of bombs dropping.

At other times, it was necessary for Junko and her sisters to leave their home and huddle in dark bomb shelters. She would often carry crayons and cardboard—paper was too rare, but she could use her father's discarded cardboard medicine boxes over and over as a drawing surface—and she would draw in the darkness. This activity was her refuge and her strength. She has said many times that it saved her sanity—just enough so that she could survive in that most insane world.

These experiences turned out to be formative for Junko, they have had repercussions throughout her life and her art. For Junko, art is a very serious business—a matter of life and death. Most of her works have an urgent quality, as if Junko is saying to herself, "Before I die, I must create this work." Throughout her life, Junko has felt that if her art cannot send this intense message as a final statement it is not worth creating. This inevitably requires her works to have a certain scale and philosophical ambition—like Beethoven's music. Even if some of the works are tiny in size they must still have a gigantic scale.

This sense of urgency makes Junko seek a path towards transcendence and reintegration in every work. So her first major series, *Dead Flowers* (1973-1974), starts with a bowl of dead flowers and then finds its way to images of Buddha emerging from the dead flowers (see pg. 17). The *Root* series (1974-1979) also focuses on a dead root—something pulled up from the ground, long forgotten, not flowering or growing. Yet as Junko drew it and created her special kind of collages from it, the root too appeared as Buddha coming out of the ground (*Root Series No. 9, Emergence of Buddha*, pg. 84) or as *Fasting Buddha* (pg. 121) or as a living *Mandala* (pg. 3) which radiates a special light that seems to emanate from the center of the world. And even single works incorporate into themselves images of destruction and reintegration. For example, in *Interplanetary Icon, No. 8* (following page) the elements are all fragmented and scattered but they are reassembled into a balanced figure which projects a higher kind of stability and integrity.

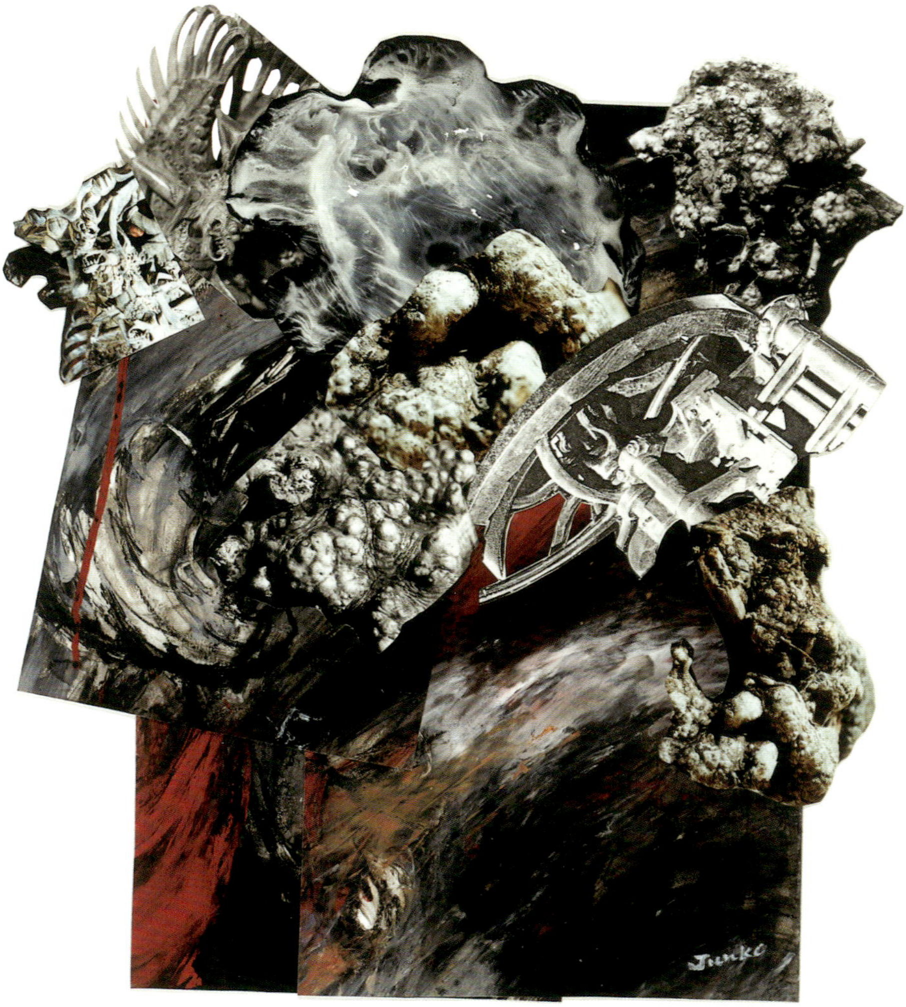

INTERPLANETARY ICON, No. 8 (1990)
Mixed media on paper
Irregular shape:
22 x 20 in.
(55.9 x 50 .8 cm.)
...the elements are all fragmented and scattered but they are reassembled into a balanced figure which projects a higher kind of stability and integrity

Junko has even gone so far as to say that if her artwork does not include destruction it cannot be profound. It seems to me that the passion for destruction comes from her deep-seated desire to see the world in its essence, in its reality. This applies even to the world of thoughts; she does not trust any thoughts that have not gone through the severe test of existential doubt and destruction. This is probably the essence she drew from her formative experience of listening to great music against the background of the sound of bombs, and of drawing in the darkness of the sheltering cave. She must have asked herself, What will still be able to give assurance of human dignity after everything has been destroyed? For what was lost in that war was not only human lives. What was destroyed was not only buildings and cities. Thoughts, beliefs, trust, dignity, and hope were also destroyed. Japanese state religion had taught the divinity of the emperor and the glory of dying in a holy war; those ideas were crushed in front of Junko's eyes. Her first husband, the son of a Unitarian minister, had been drafted into military service when he was eighteen and was forced to train himself to jump in front of an enemy tank, with explosives tied on his back. This training, which lasted every day until the war was actually over, left deep scars in his psyche—which Junko saw at close range. So what could redeem the dignity of life? Only the things that have gone through that most severe test of destruction. Even though those things are injured and bleeding, broken or fragmented, only in them does Junko see the dignity of life and it is them that she embraces. Because for Junko, to draw them means to embrace them in her arms.

FORMATIVE EXPERIENCE: PERFORMANCE VERSUS CREATION

In the Introduction to Chapter Two, I have already told you about Junko's two sisters—one two years older and the other a year younger—who were both so talented at music. Junko's mother was a piano teacher and saw very early that she had two potential prodigies in her home. She resolved to become a "stage mother": as soon as the war was over she became passionately involved in the ambitious project of building the first world-class school of music in postwar Japan so that her daughters could have a base from which to develop and gain recognition in the world. And that project succeeded: Toho Gakuen School of Music trained a long list of conductors and violinists, many of whom became world-famous in the decades after the war. Both of Junko's sisters were recognized early as prodigies, and both of them went to Juilliard on scholarships after they had enrolled in Toho. The younger one was the first full Fulbright scholar from Japan; she gave frequent concerts and was often the subject of newspaper articles because she had become a national figure of glory in the defeated nation.

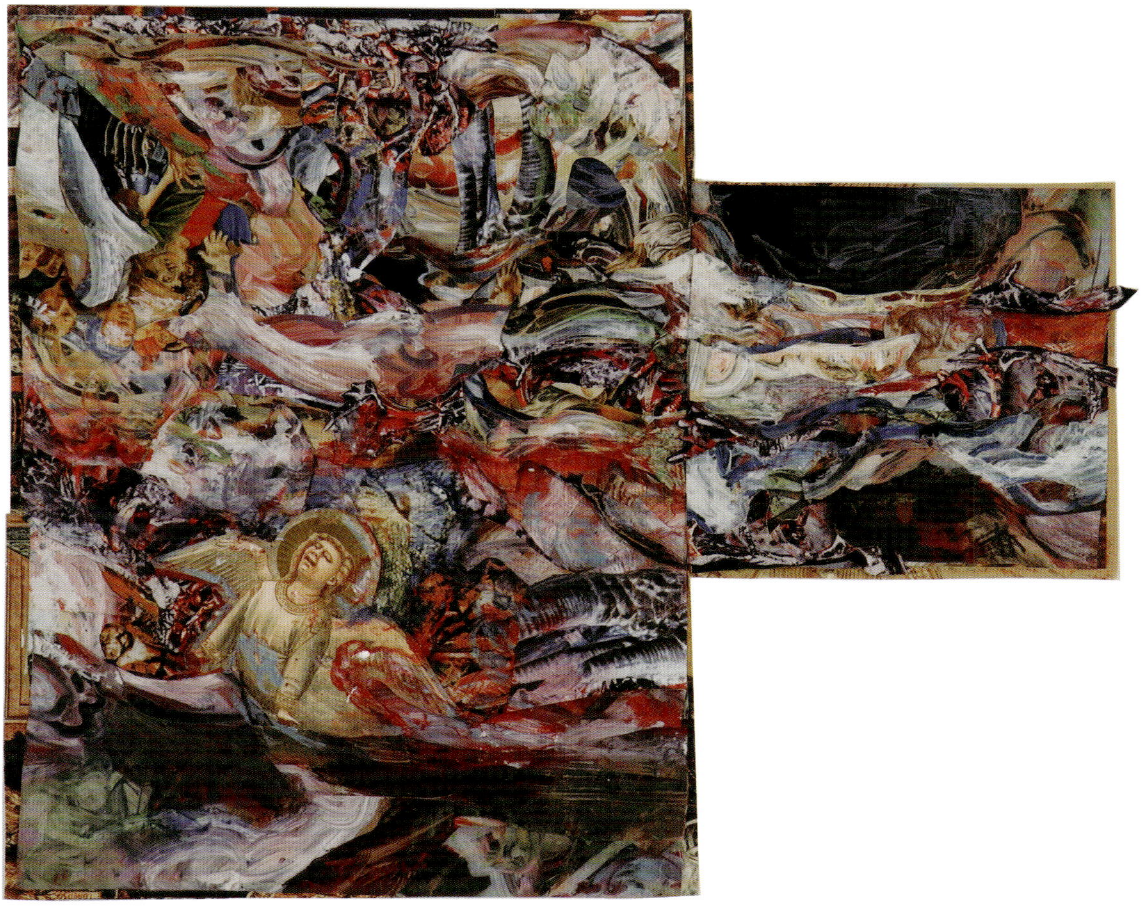

Junko also was offered training in violin and singing—but she abandoned those pursuits early on. She sensed, even as a child, that there was a bargain being offered to her: if she chose to pursue the career path which her mother would approve, she would lose her own life. She chose her own life. Part of this choice involved a clear recognition of the difference between the destiny of the performer and the destiny of the composer, and reinforced Junko's identity as a "composer." For Junko's mother, the highest aspiration conceivable was to play Beethoven's music in order to bring it to audiences around the world. But Junko's aspiration became to create art in the same way and at the same scale as Beethoven composed his music.

ALTARPIECE II,
AFTER GIOTTO (1998)
Collage on paper
(Irregular shape)
12 x 15 in.
(30.5 x 38.1 cm.)

This early choice which Junko made has had effects throughout her work. There is a continuum that runs from total freedom and unconstrained innovation on one side, to rote repetition on the other side. It is possible to be close to the "rote repetition" end of the continuum and still be a credible performer; it is harder to be at that point of the continuum and still be a composer. Of course, the great performer is close to being a composer in that he innovates and brings something original even to an existing work. But many performers, no matter how accomplished they are, set out to do what someone else thinks ought to be done. At first and for many years it is the teacher who tells the student how to play the piece, and finally, when the student has achieved maturity and no longer needs a teacher, it is the composer who tells the performer how to play. No matter how honest, how disciplined, how earnest he is in his search for the truth of the piece he is performing, the less-than-great performer is inevitably involved in seeking someone's approval: the approval of the teacher, or the audience, or of the hypostasized composer.

But the composer starts out with a commitment to bring something brand new into the world—something of whose value he and he alone must ultimately be the judge. Of course he will prefer it if the audience appreciates his creation, but if he is a real composer he will create whether they appreciate it or not. He will compose anyway because he is driven to compose. This is a kind of courage that is not required of the performer.

It is the kind of courage that Junko exhibits in creating her art. There is something overwhelmingly idiosyncratic about it: although she makes occasional references to the works of earlier artists (Grünewald, pg. 120, and *Altarpiece II*, quoting Giotto, opposite), she does not really work in any earlier artist's style. And her choice of subject matter, and her free-thinking quotations of religious themes (see pg. 211)—these are a direct consequence of her thinking of herself as a composer rather than as a performer.

This has important implications for her kind of spirituality: it is original, it is not affiliated with or born of or confined by any

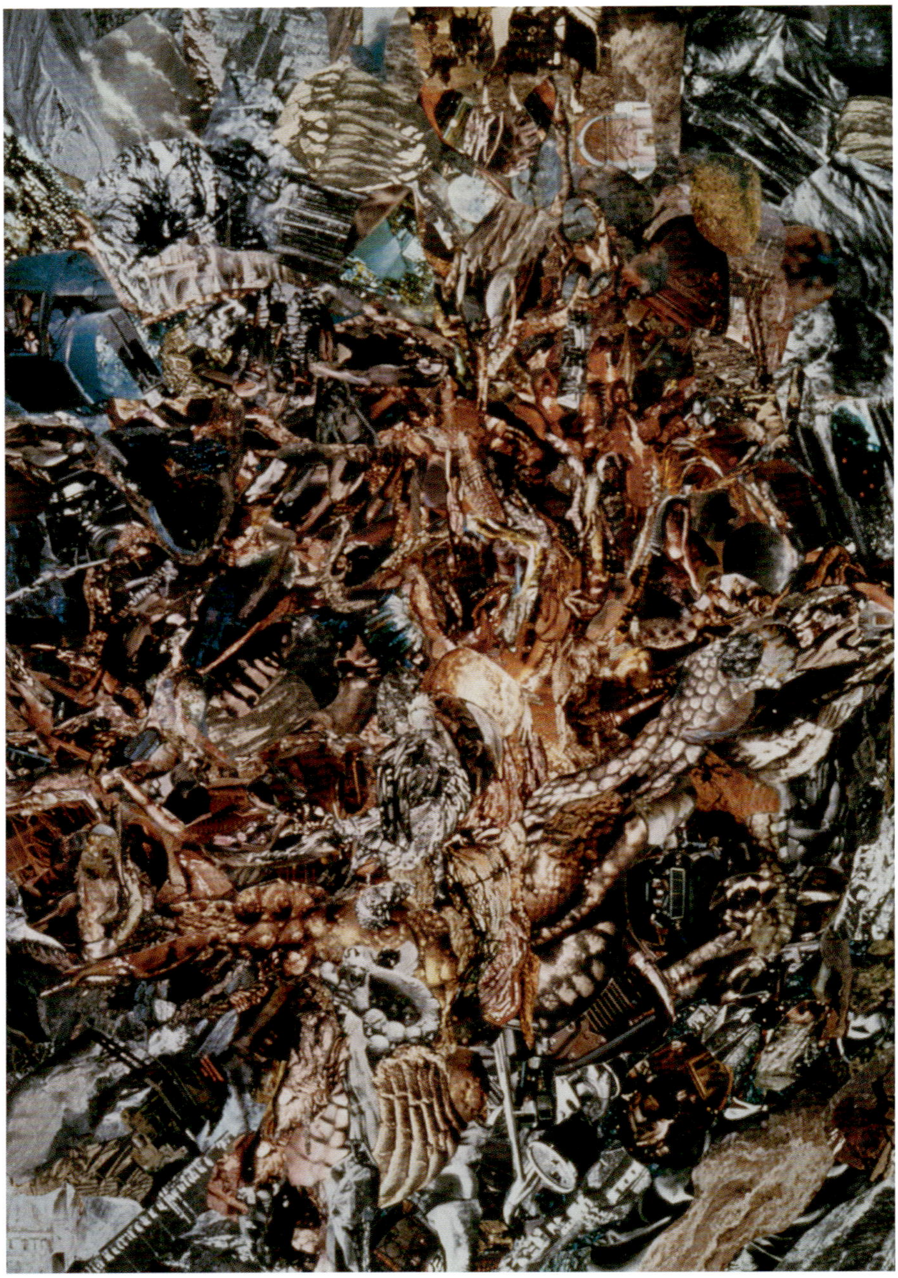

ROOT SERIES,
No. 7 (1975)
Mixed media
collage on paper
22 x 16 in.
(55.9 x 40.6 cm.)

particular dogma or organized religion, it is the very opposite of complacent (see discussion of complacency at pg. 206). This again is a very contemporary kind of spirituality: not a smiling face nodding its head in endless affirmation of ancient values, but a modern face with open eyes and earnest intent, struggling to see the highest kind of vitality and nobility in the midst of the complexity of today's world.

INDIVIDUATION

One of the most important things about Junko's art is the role that creating art plays in her own process of individuation. The term comes from Jung, and a very similar idea was articulated by Abraham Maslow as "self-actualization."[1] But it is in the work of Erich Fromm that Junko found the most satisfying discussion of individuation and of its connection to her art.

Before saying anything else about individuation I must caution my readers not to confuse it with individualism, with which it is often confused. Actually, the two ideas pull in opposite directions: individualism focuses on the individual by concerning itself with his rights, liberties, and prerogatives; while individuation focuses on the preconditions for healthy membership in the community. When we talk about individuation, we are not talking about the rights of the individual as against those of the community, nor about the liberty of the individual to be different—to speak his mind, to wear distinctive clothing, to express himself. Instead we are talking about issues that precede these things: we are talking about how the individual becomes himself. He cannot express himself before he becomes himself; he cannot speak his mind before he knows his own mind. The process of individuation is the process by which he becomes himself, and it is a process that takes place—when it does take place—at the very deepest layers of the personality. And not only that: the process of individuation is a necessary precursor to love, for until the individual has become himself he is not capable of love and a healthy relationship with his fellow-man.

Fromm's work can be seen as a response to his experience of fascism and totalitarianism: he asked himself, as so many other intelligent people did during and after World War II, How could such a thing have happened? And right here in Europe? How could so many people have supported the Nazi regime and participated in its atrocities? He found the answer in his study of human developmental psychology.

The human being starts out his life connected to his mother: nourished in her womb, the child forms "primary ties" with her—a figurative "umbilical cord" which it requires courage to break. That cord gives the child a sense of a security and of belonging, even though it restricts his freedom. Primitive societies are built on the foundation of this umbilical cord, on the strong tie to the mother—and by extension, to the family and the tribe, to blood and soil. The relationship of the individual to the world is thus symbiotic: he needs the cord in order to survive and he perceives the womb and its cluster of symbiotic relationships as a "paradise."

The process of individuating is a process of getting out of this symbiosis and this "paradise," of reaching a stage where the individual can be free and yet not alone, critical and yet not filled with doubt, independent and yet a productive integral member of the human community. This freedom can be attained only by man's becoming himself and actuating his spontaneous, integrated personality.[2] In order to reach that stage, each of us has to go through a separation from the mother and has to stand alone and face the overwhelming reality of the world. This induces a painful feeling of insignificance in the face of the world, and it leads to enormous fear and anxiety.

The process of separation is expressed in mythology as "killing the Great Mother," a subject discussed by Erich Neumann in *Origins and History of Consciousness*. He says that one must kill the terrifying Great Mother who swallows him up into the chaos out of which he was born. If he lacks the courage to kill the mother, he

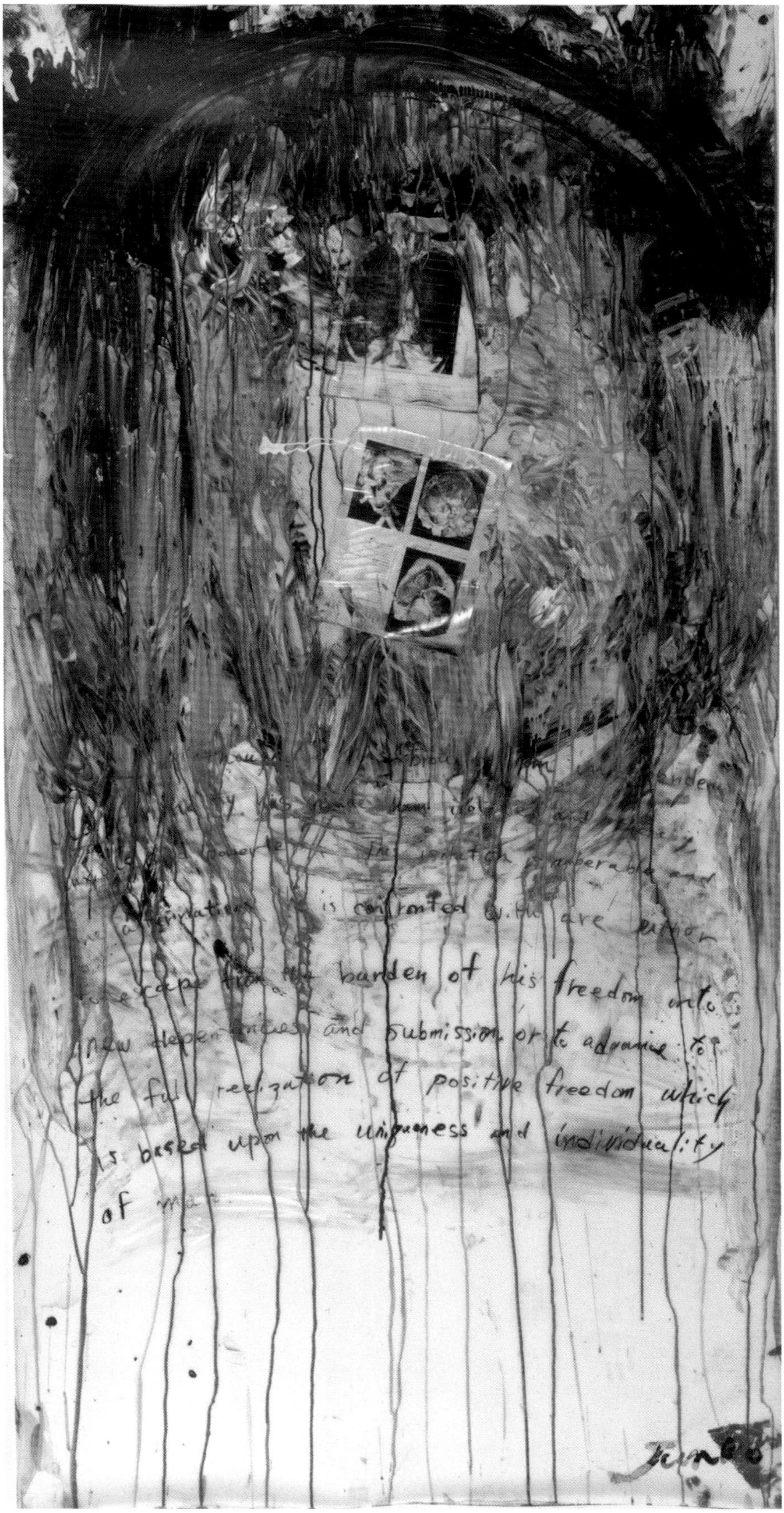

INDIVIDUATION JOURNAL, No. 1: FROMM (1995)
Freedom, though it has brought him independence and rationality, has made him isolated and, thereby, anxious and powerless. This isolation is unbearable and the alternatives he is confronted with are either to escape from the burden of his freedom into new dependencies and submission, or to advance to the full realization of positive freedom which is based upon the uniqueness and individuality of man.[3]
Acrylic and collage on mylar
80 x 42 in.
(203.2 x 106.7 cm.)

will remain tied to her forever, figuratively bound by the incestuous tie. That tie frustrates the natural course of human growth and so the incestuous attachment causes tremendous confusion, terror, rage, and guilt, and the unindividuated man begins to exhibit pathological symptoms. He remains imprisoned in a maternal-tribal-racial-national-religious fixation.

In order to escape the acute fear of separation and its associated anxiety, Fromm observes that people may choose one of three recognized "escape routes"—all of which lead in the opposite direction from individuation and end up exacerbating the unresolved terror, rage, and sense of guilt:

[1] Submission to authority. By submitting to authority, the weak individual clothes himself with the semblance of power and gains an illusional superiority over less powerful people.

[2] Destructiveness. The individual may seek to overcome his feeling of insignificance in the face of the outside world by destroying others. This too makes the outside world seem less threatening to him, and the more the drive towards real life—toward becoming an individual—is thwarted, the more intense becomes the urge towards destruction.

[3] Automaton conformity. The person who gives up his identity and becomes an automaton, identical with millions of other automatons around him, need not feel anxious or alone any more but the price he pays is the loss of his self.

All three of these "escape routes" lead ultimately to sadism and masochism, and to totalitarianism and fascism, for all of them are ways of exaggerating the power differential between the subject and the split-off "other," ways of aggrandizing authority, and ways of evading individual responsibility. So Fromm explains the phenomena of the Holocaust and mid-twentieth-century fascism as the consequence of millions of individuals lacking the courage to individuate.

INDIVIDUATION JOURNAL, FREE WILL – BUBER (1998)
Fate is encountered only by him that actualizes freedom… It is not his limit but his completion (Buber)
Virtual work
See companion work at pg. 292
Text is from *I and Thou*.

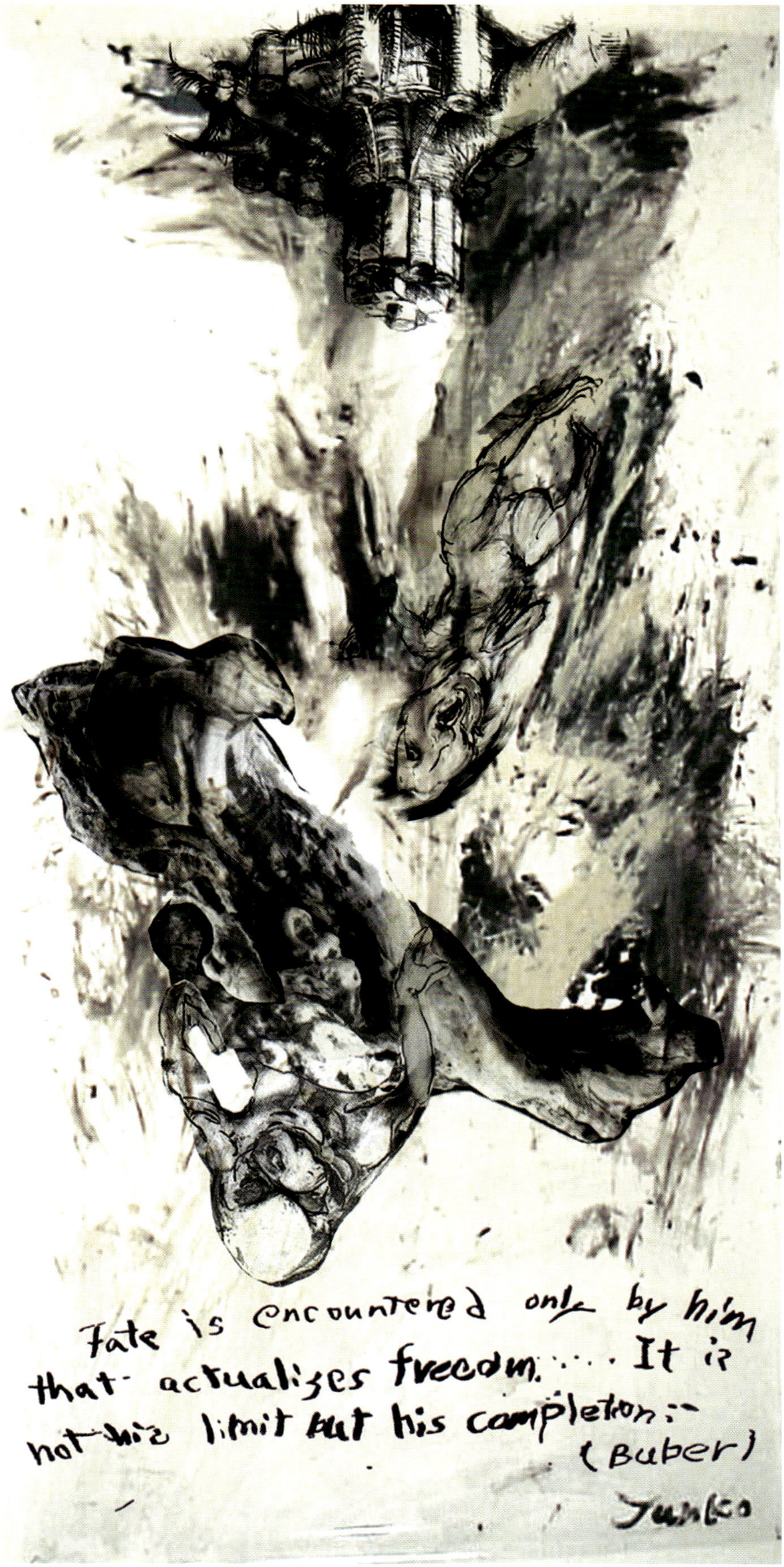

But Fromm wrote[4] that there is another path—a way to realize individuality without falling into any of these three traps: a way which involves a spontaneous relationship to man and to nature, a relationship that connects the individual with the world, that is rooted in the integration and strength of the total personality and whose most complete expressions are love and productive work.

Here is where centripetal art can play a strong role—if it is successful—for such art is an expression of love and productive work. In ways that Fromm never wrote about, centripetal art involves both the artist and the viewer in a process of individuation. The artist undertakes a solemn responsibility toward her subject matter, vows to eradicate everything that might be called "the corruption of consciousness,"[5] and vows to pursue complete honesty toward her vision.

She invites the viewer to participate in her process, to see the art deeply, to read the work, to follow the lines and experience the movement of the artist's own breath—this is already to share in the work's vibrations and to participate in the process that led to its creation. In this way, we may say that the viewer approaches the image from the front, and the artist stands behind the image, and the two of them encounter each other in the plane of the image. In this encounter, all three—the artist, the viewer, and the image—take a step toward completion and self-realization.

All of Junko's works are part of her struggle toward individuation: they are the traces of that struggle on paper. But it was not until 1995 that she began to think explicitly about the relationship between her process of creating art and her process of individuation. In that year she created a series of ten works which she titled *Individuation Journal*. One of these works quotes the words of the poet Rainer Maria Rilke (see pg. 93), And the remaining seven works quote the words of Erich Fromm. Three years later, she added two virtual works to the series—works dealing with the related issues of free will and determinism (see pp. 233, 292).

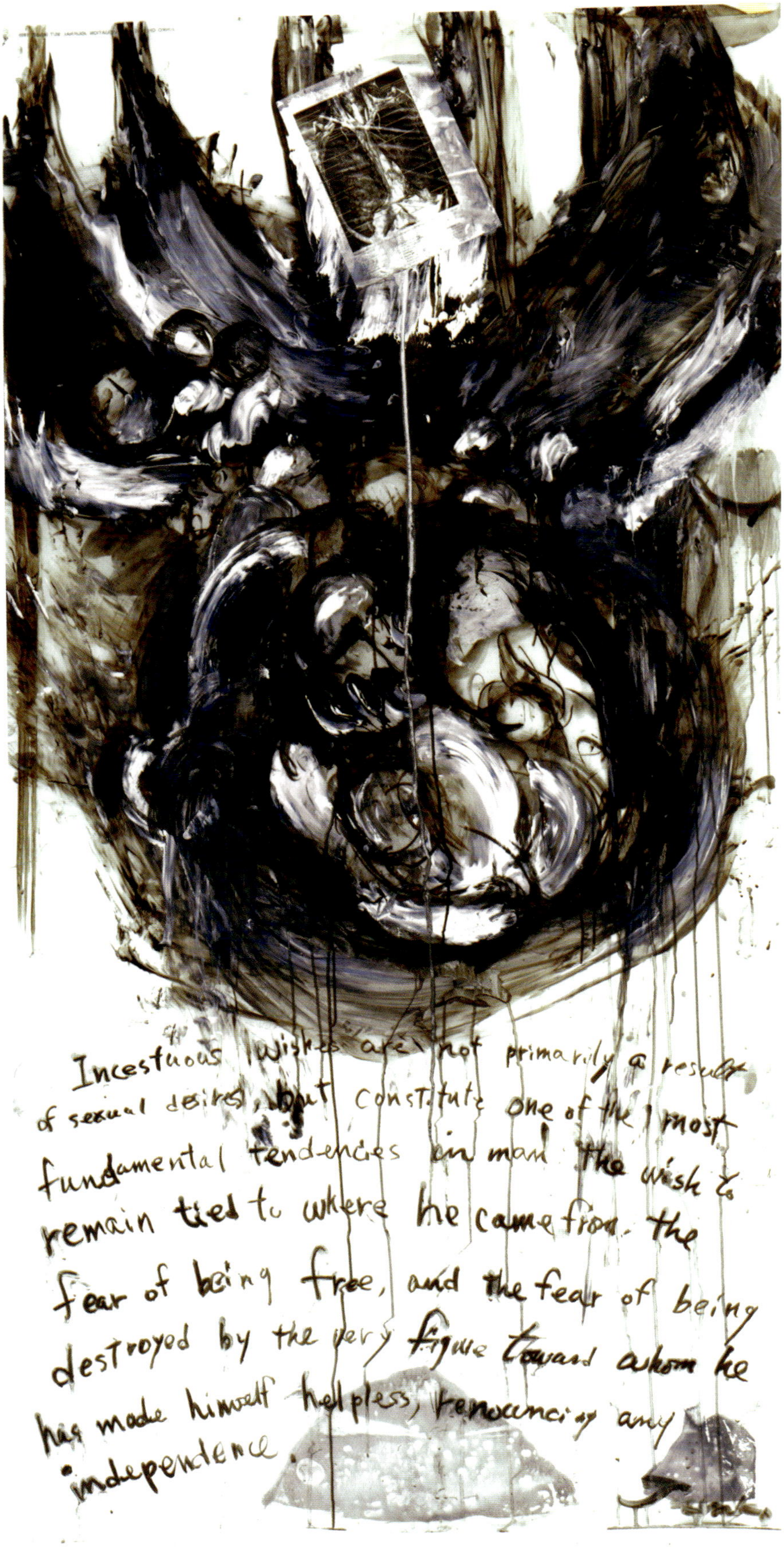

INDIVIDUATION JOURNAL, No. 5: FROMM (1995)
Incestuous wishes are not primarily a result of sexual desires, but constitute one of the most fundamental tendencies in man: the wish to remain tied to where he came from, the fear of being free, and the fear of being destroyed by the very figure towards whom he has made himself helpless, renouncing any independence.
Acrylic and collage on mylar
80 x 42 in.
(203.2 x 106.7 cm.)

Individuation through a Legal Dispute.

In 1992 Junko's commitment towards individuation was intensified when she was drawn into a dispute with one of her sisters in Japan. Rather than allowing her own rights to be ignored and abused, Junko decided to bring her dispute to court. She appointed a Japanese lawyer in Japan and she appointed me as her American lawyer. The dispute lasted more than three years and that period was emotionally draining both for Junko and for me. The legal fight was waged in the courts of different countries and states, and required a great deal of international legal and cultural collaboration. Junko wrote hundreds of letters and several essays in those days, both in English and in Japanese, about the legal and philosophical issues which surfaced during this dispute.

This was one of the most vivid occasions on which we both saw clearly how the process of creating art creates the artist in the same way that the artist creates the art. The dispute arose just one year after Junko had completed the *Requiem for an Excecuted Bird* series. Had she not created that series, Junko would not have had the sharp insight into this matter that she did, nor would she have had the courage to confront her sister and bring her dispute to court while pursuing her highest aspiration: her earnest fight for her own integrity. But the hard work of her Japanese lawyer, and my own work, and finally the justice she received in a Japanese courtroom, assured Junko that she did not have to allow her Bird to be executed a second time.

This legal victory that came in 1995 severed almost all of Junko's ties with her family: her parents were already gone but now she was cut off also from her sisters, from her life-long family friends, and from her homeland itself. This was the final cutting of the "umbilical cord," the end of all ties to tribe, to blood, and to soil. Not everyone's separation and individuation process needs to take this drastic form but there are people who do have to renounce the whole world in order to gain it. Traumatic as this dispute was, Junko remade the experience into the birth of her new individuated self. It was in that same year, 1995, that the *Individuation Journal* series was born.

We might say that Junko immigrated to America physically in 1968, and that it was 27 years later when she completed the process of immigration internally. But the truth is much more than that: after living as an exile, and as a spiritual refugee, and as an immigrant in diaspora, Junko finally started to live more free from cultural and ethnic boundaries, to take on a more universal identity and to live as something that might be called a citizen of the world. And in this new role, the concept of centripetal art found solid ground in which to take root.

Junko's thinking about "individuation" and "separation" at that time was stimulated and intensified partly by me. It was about then that a couple of major cases I was handling came to a head. During that period, law and the principles of justice became an everyday topic of conversation for us. This was at the same time that I was working hard on my second book, a 1,700-page treatise on the law of fiduciary duties. I would read the sections to Junko one by one as I completed them, and we would talk about the underlying principles of fairness and justice. Junko and I talked constantly about the law as a way of ordering interpersonal contacts consciously and rationally.

But the litigation taught us more painful lessons. During and after the three years that this dispute lasted, one of the most frightening realities we witnessed was the way what seemed to be the most beautifully harmonized community revealed its weakness and turned into a totalitarian community almost overnight when it was forced to confront an unpleasant reality. In Japan, harmony is believed to be the most important social principle. Adopted from Confucian thought, it is established in the first constitution in Japanese history in the sixth century. Since then, its legitimacy and importance have been taken for granted—similar to the way the Ten Commandments function in the West. The community often appears to manifest this principle: they take care of each other, they are peaceful, and orderly. But once people are challenged to face certain realities and required to stand up for the truth, the fear of breaking the harmony of their little community overcomes them, and they turn into the worst kind of totalitarian, fascistic

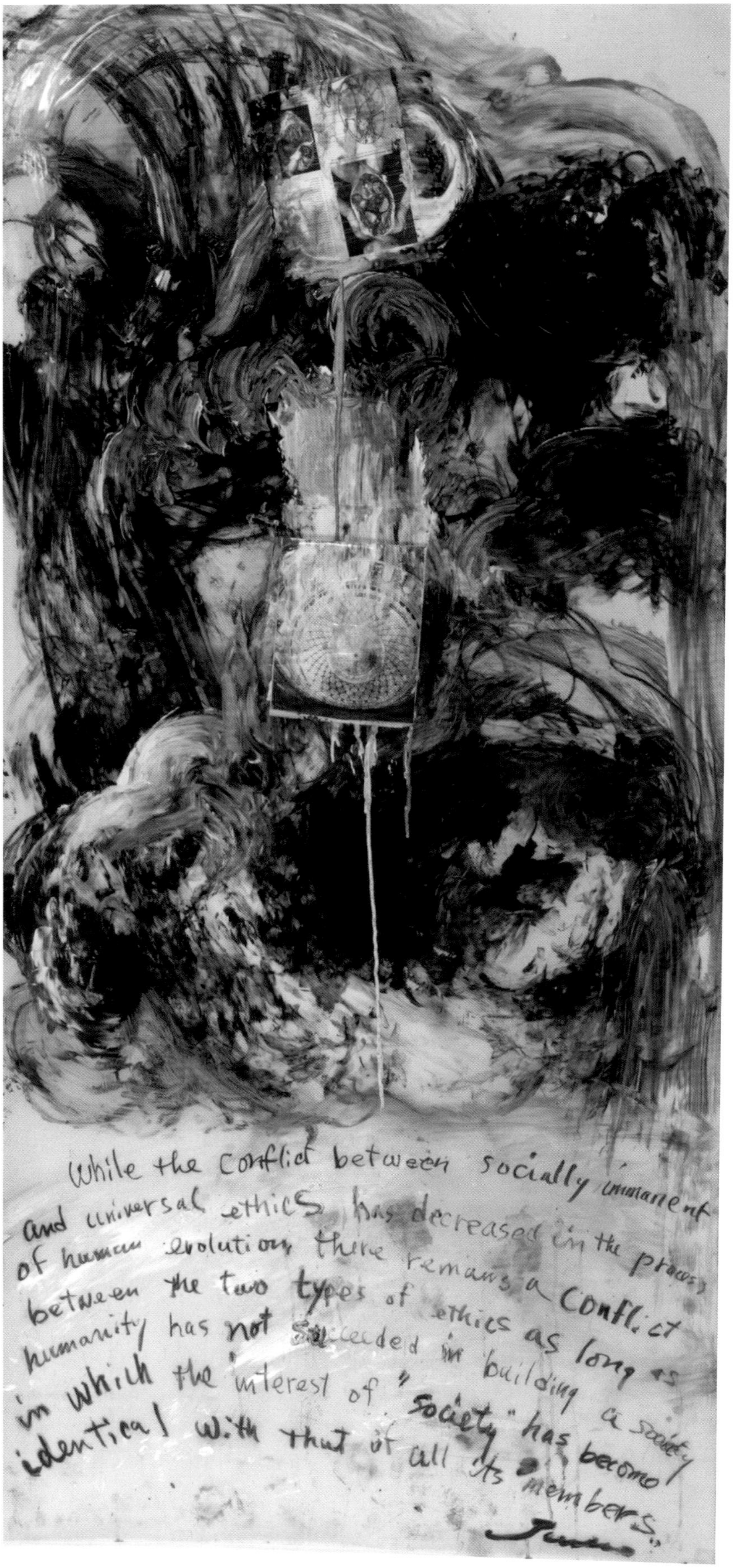

INDIVIDUATION JOURNAL, No. 8: FROMM (1995)
While the conflict between socially immanent and universal ethics has decreased in the process of human evolution, there remains a conflict between the two types of ethics as long as humanity has not succeeded in building a society in which the interest of "society" has become identical with that of all its members.
Acrylic and collage on mylar
80 x 42 in.
(203.2 x 106.7 cm.)

community. However small their communities may be, they still exhibit all the symptoms of those totalitarian fascistic societies. The harmony they experience is the harmony of being together in the mother's womb: they are not yet separated, and so it is not the harmony that was reached by separate individuals, not spontaneous, not the result of each member of the community accepting individual responsibility.

Both of us saw, and had to face this frightening form of harmony; both of us had to accept the fact that no matter how peacefully such a community seems to function most of the time, unseparated, unindividuated individuals cannot reach real harmony. Many of them became victims themselves in their own little community, but they repressed their own feelings and refused to face the truth for the sake of the illusional harmony of their community. Through the lens of the litigation, which involved the small community of Junko's family and close friends, we thought we saw exactly Erich Fromm's world. No wonder Junko left this society. The difference can never be emphasized too much between the harmony built by pre-separated consciousness and the harmony built by separated individuals.

This phenomenon is by no means restricted to Japan. I have been an American trial lawyer for over thirty years, and I have found that legal disputes often arise out of the psychological problems of one or more of the disputants. This is particularly true in disputes between partners or between family members—that is, between people whose relationship is personal and therefore offers an opportunity for psychological problems to make themselves felt. Such relationships are very different from the relationships we tend to have with manufacturers, retailers, credit card companies, and other drivers on the road: those "arms-length" relationships may give rise to a major part of the litigation that fills our courtrooms, but they tend not to have complicated psychological dimensions. But business disputes between people with close relationships are often driven by psychological problems. When such disputes are brought to court, the litigants are required to conform their behavior to rational standards; this requirement is often painful for them as it tends to disrupt the whole basis of their close relationships up to that point. To go through this kind of radical disruption of close relationships takes courage and this, I have found, is why the legal process is often a kind of healing for the litigants—even for the ones who lose their cases. By being forced to adjust their behavior to rational norms, they make progress toward their own individuation. Junko's *Individuation Journal* series is the record of this very kind of courageous healing. The works in the series seem to be discursive and intellectual. But if you look carefully at them you will see that their intellectual message is always embedded in a highly emotional visual presentation.

ORGANIC/INORGANIC

In Junko's art, there is no real boundary line between what is dead and what is alive, between what is inorganic and what is organic: everything that seems dead and inorganic ends up being organic and alive. Many of Junko's works focus on the processes by which spirit moves from places underground, from machines, from torn roots and burls, to manifestations of transcendent life. Particularly in her treatment of engines and engine parts, Junko imbues seemingly lifeless things with life. While engines are indisputably "inorganic" Junko treats them as alive and even as erotic figures. The engine block became the beating heart of *Ecstasy* (see pp. 42-43, and detail on pg. 270), and it curves sensuously in *Concerning Art and Religion, No. 3* (pg. 33) and in *FATHOM: MANDALA 2, The Engine Embraces the Flame* (pg. 32).

Where does this quality come from? We might say that this sensibility, which sees the boundary between life and death as something permeable, is traditionally Japanese. But Junko's own personal experiences have helped to integrate that sensibility into an artistic style that is mainly Western: the fact is that this quality of her art is yet another response to her early experience of fascism. For what lies at the root of fascism is the desire to transform the organic into the inorganic: the desire to approach life mechanically as if all living persons were things, as if their feelings and thoughts were merely there to be used and manipulated. This is a desire that

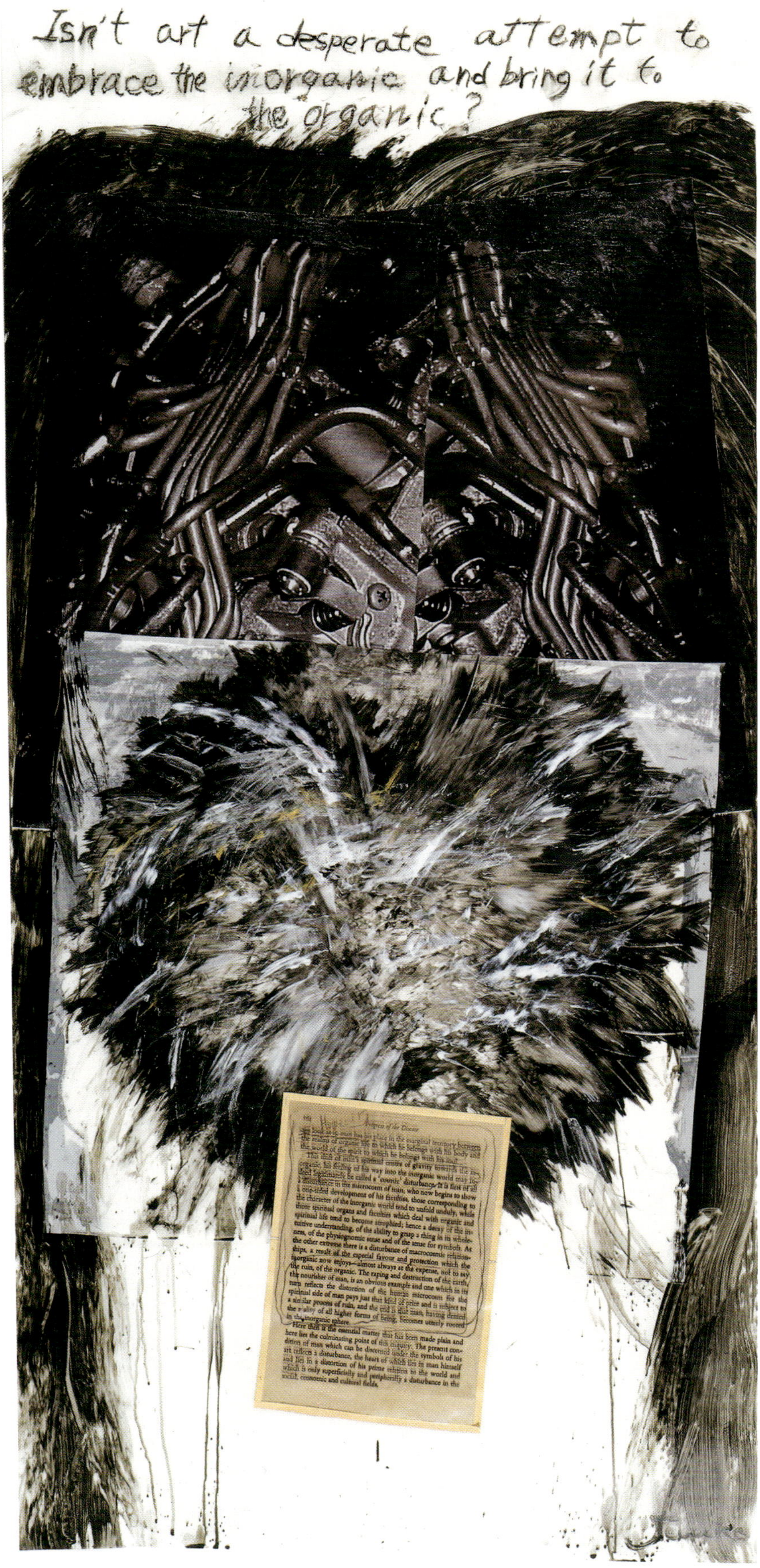

CONCERNING ART AND RELIGION, No. 4 (2003)
"ISN'T ART A DESPERATE ATTEMPT TO EMBRACE THE INORGANIC AND BRING IT TO THE ORGANIC?"
Sumi, acrylic, and collage on mylar support
84 x 42 in.
(213.4 x 106.7 cm.)

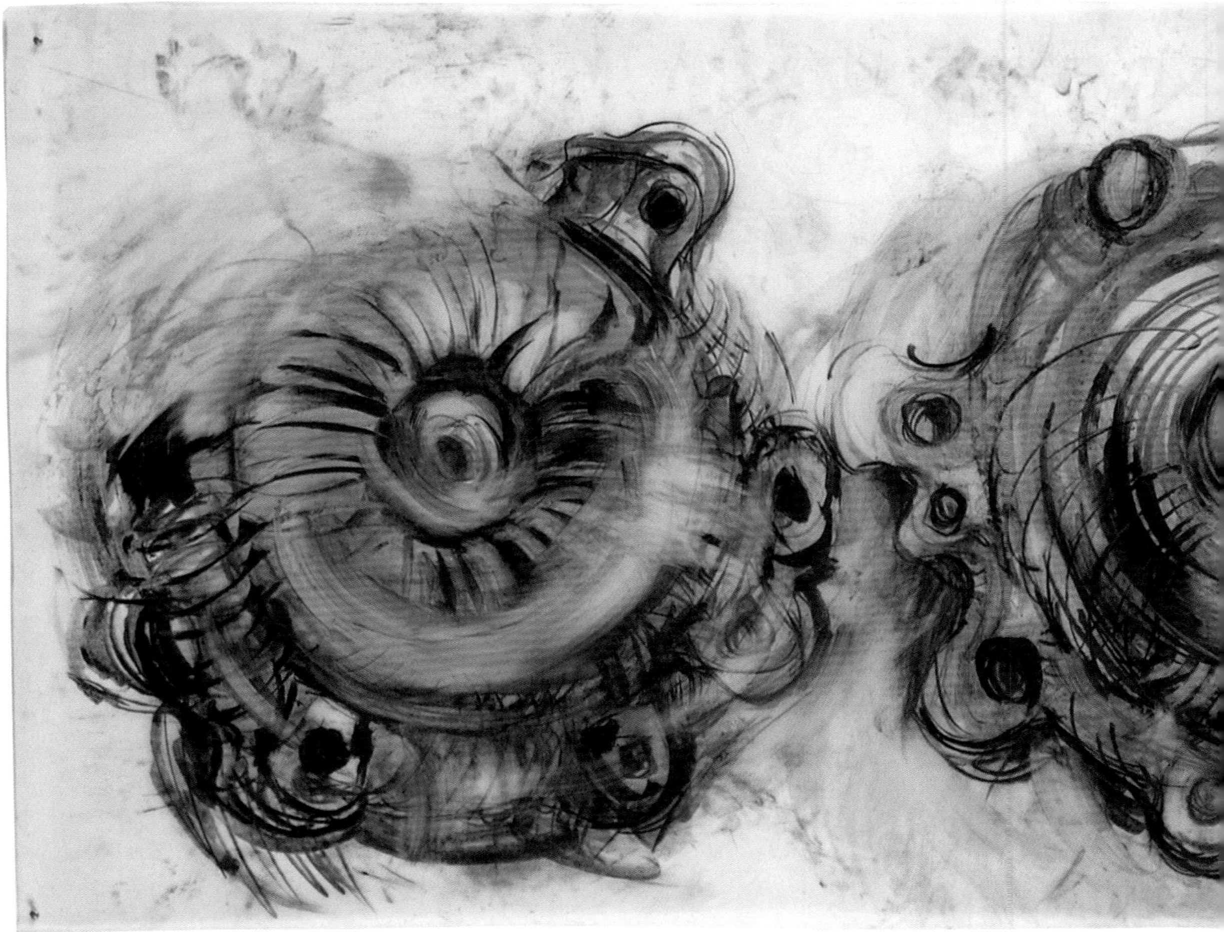

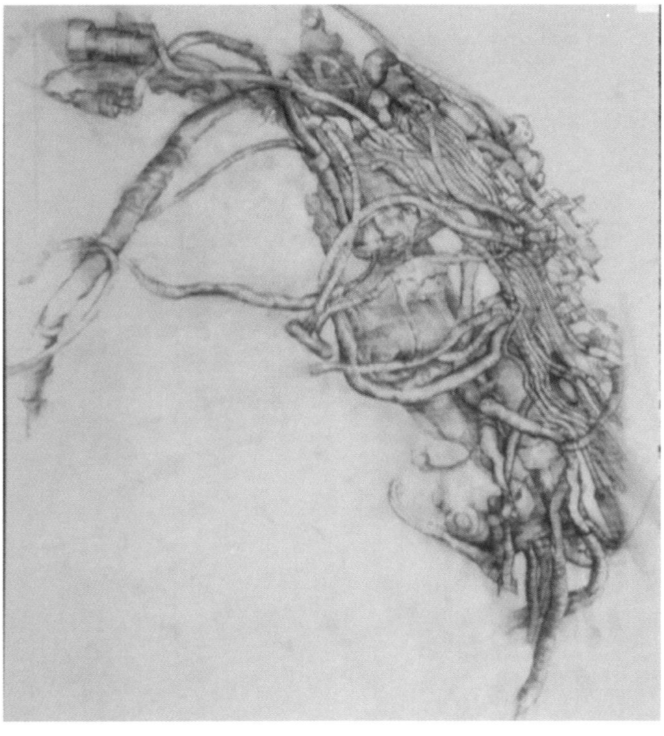

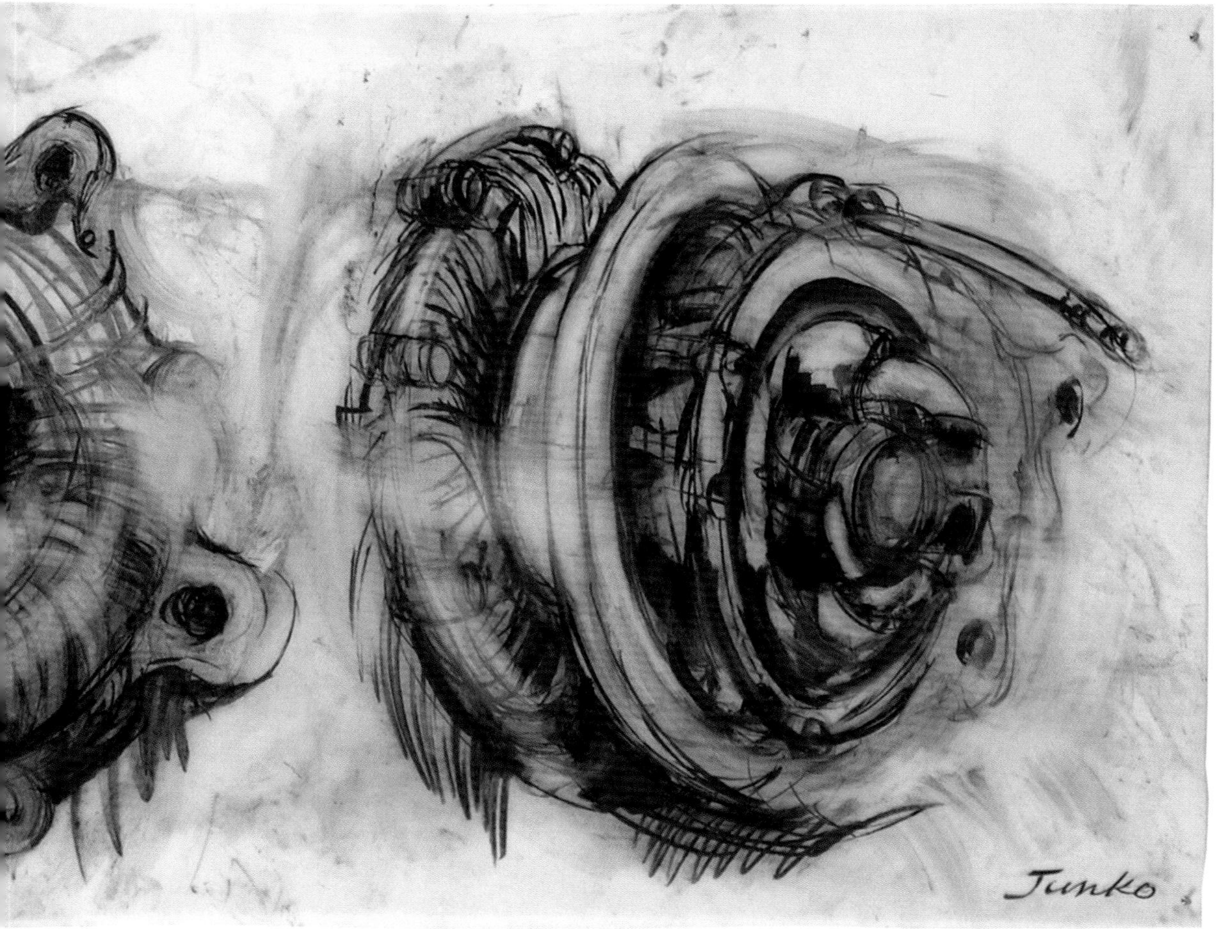

Bottom left:
ESOTERIC BUDDHISM, PREPARATORY DRAWING No. 1 (2000)
Charcoal on computer print on mylar
Virtual size

Above:
GIANT SKETCHBOOK, No. 2 (1997)
Charcoal on mylar
42 x 118 in.
(106.68 x 299.72 cm.)

finds expression not only in governmental settings today, but also in the world of commerce and marketing, which treats everyone as a consumer and which commodifies even human attention.

The attachment to the inorganic expresses itself also as an attachment to memory, which is dead, rather than to experience, which is alive. This attachment is part of what inhibits the individual's separation and individuation, as I just explained. It is also something that makes itself felt in our religious and academic communities, which often value tradition and doctrine over original authentic thought and revelation.

The attachment to the inorganic expresses itself also as the desire to have rather than to be. This too is a dangerous aspect of the modern world that many commentators have already observed.

Of course the boundary line between the living and the dead is something very much on our contemporary mind, and very important for the spirituality of the twenty-first century. Issues surrounding this boundary line make their way into our newspapers almost every day: birth control, abortion, artificial insemination, preimplantation genetic diagnosis, dying with dignity, prosthetics, stem cell research, human cloning; all of these issues are at the center of highly emotional debates and policy conflicts. But around this boundary line much deeper battle lines have been drawn and we can still see forces arrayed on either side of them: these are the lines between the destructive, negative qualities that foster fascism, and the life-affirming qualities of love which resist fascism and seek transcendence.

After all, the fact that inanimate matter assembles itself into living beings and that those living beings ultimately become disassembled and fall again into the undifferentiated mass of inanimate matter—this is one of the great mysteries of our time. There are many artists who focus their attention on the life-to-death aspect of this mystery: they show living bodies as machines, or as incorporating machines, or they present images of brutality, of sadism, or of lifelessness. In contrast to those deeply negative tendencies, we find in Junko a centripetal artist who takes the opposite view and focusses on the movement from apparent death to life: who wants to show Buddha emerging from dead flowers, and pulsating sexual energy radiating from a broken engine block.

ALTERED STATES

When Junko is painting, she is in an altered state of consciousness. The "complex spirituality" I see in Junko's art, the sort of spirituality that I think rings so true for us today, has much to do with the fact that it comes from, is filtered through, and is formed by this altered state of consciousness. I will describe that state of consciousness as best I can, and tell you how Junko moves into it, in just a moment.

But before I do I want to tell you that of all the "layers" of Junko's art, this is the one I must describe from the greatest distance, and yet it is the deepest and the most complicated. It is the layer at which the vulnerability that makes Junko's work so special is most clearly exposed. It is also the aspect of her art which has had the most direct impact on our marriage: while she is in that altered state, Junko needs protection from the everyday world and it falls to me to give her that protection. So I have always been sensitive to when the altered state is coming over her, and I am ready to let her go into her studio and work there free from all disturbances until she emerges with new works. But both Junko and I have had a difficult relationship with this altered state.

Almost from the beginning days of our marriage I was aware that when she withdrew into her studio, Junko was passing away from this world and entering a very different world. At first I felt concerned that she was sick; I did not know whether the illness was physical, or mental, or both. She would seem distracted and sometimes had trouble breathing. I would find her crawling on her studio floor unable even to sit in a chair; she could not sleep. Several times in those early years, I actually called an ambulance

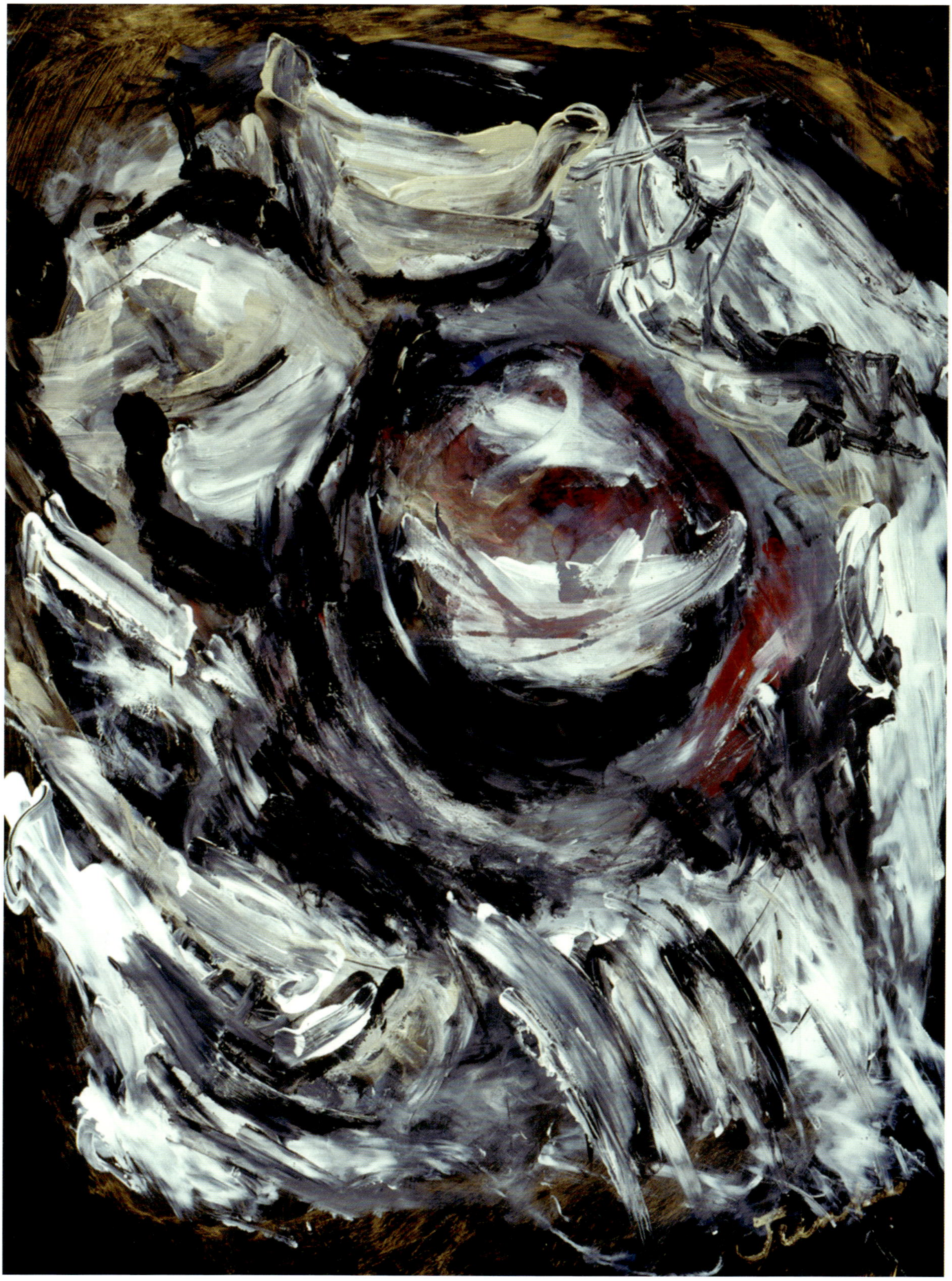

to our house and she was taken to the emergency room. But the doctors never found anything wrong with her. By the time we came back home, whatever it was that had caused us to call the ambulance had passed.

So I became irritated by this altered state: if there was nothing medically wrong with Junko, why did we have to go through these dramatic episodes? I saw it for a while as a kind of abandonment, as if Junko were leaving me alone in violation of the spirit, if not the letter, of our marriage vows. But soon I realized that Junko always came back from this altered state, carrying new artworks she had just created; so there was no abandonment. Then, still later, I thought I saw in it something potentially sinister: images of *The New Melusina*[6] floated through my mind, and I wondered whether I had not married a magical creature who would ultimately draw me away from my own life and entice me into a closed-in world where normal, healthy interaction with my fellow man was not possible. But those were just my first ideas.

Later Junko told me a Japanese fairy tale about a young man who was walking along a path by the side of a swamp and came upon a group of unruly boys throwing stones at a crane (*tsuru*, in Japanese). The crane was crying and trying to get away. The young man quickly dispersed the boys and allowed the crane to fly away. The next day a beautiful young woman appeared in his village whom nobody there had ever seen before. She said her name was "Tsu" and she was trying to find this young man. The moment he saw her he fell hopelessly in love with her, and they married. One evening, after the sun had set, Tsu went into her private room where she kept a loom. She told her husband that he must never come into that room while she was weaving, and she closed the door behind her. A few days later, she brought him the most beautiful fabric that he had ever seen. He took it to town and sold it at a handsome price. This happened again and again, until the couple became wealthy. Soon the man told his wife, "Tsu, you must go into your weaving room again tonight and make another beautiful fabric. I have customers waiting in

Opposite:
EMERGING CONSCIOUSNESS, No. II (1988)
Acrylic on coated paper
26 x 20 in.
(66 x 56.8 cm.)

town." And she did. Night after night the man sent his wife into her private room, and saw the light shimmer behind the screen as he heard the sounds of her weaving. He hardly noticed that she was growing weak and thin, and that her skin which had been so beautiful now appeared pale and wan. One night he was overcome with a curiosity he could not restrain: as Tsu was at her loom, he slid the *shoji* screen open a crack and saw, to his shock, that his wife was a crane, and that she was plucking her feathers from her own body to weave them into the fabrics he had been selling. Tsu saw him looking at her through the crack in the door. "Now you have seen me," Tsu said to him, "and you realize that I have almost no feathers left. If I pluck one more feather from my body, I will not be able to fly again." The man fell back in shock and surprise, and watched helplessly as Tsu flew out of the open window—and he never saw her again.

When I heard that story, I wondered whether I was not like that man: protecting Junko from the outside world, sending her into her studio, encouraging her to pluck all the feathers from her body in order to create the beautiful works we hung on our walls, and which she exhibited in galleries, and sometimes sold.

But the archetype of the female figure who must keep her real identity secret from her lover, and who must disappear forever from this world once she has been seen—this archetype which appears in the story of Orpheus and Eurydice, and again in the Roman story of Cupid and Psyche—never fit Junko. In fact, she is the very opposite: her withdrawal into the altered state—her going into her studio and shutting the door behind her—was always a first step toward the production of new art that she always intends to bring back from her studio and give to the world; so it is a way of revealing her identity most clearly, not keeping it secret. Nor do these periods of withdrawal eat away at her: instead, they transform her and nourish her, though not in an obvious way.

My initial distrust of Junko's altered state of consciousness is not anything that should surprise you. We in the West tend to

Opposite:
EMERGING CONSCIOUSNESS, No. 15 (1988)
Acrylic on coated paper
26 x 20 in.
(66 x 56.8 cm.)

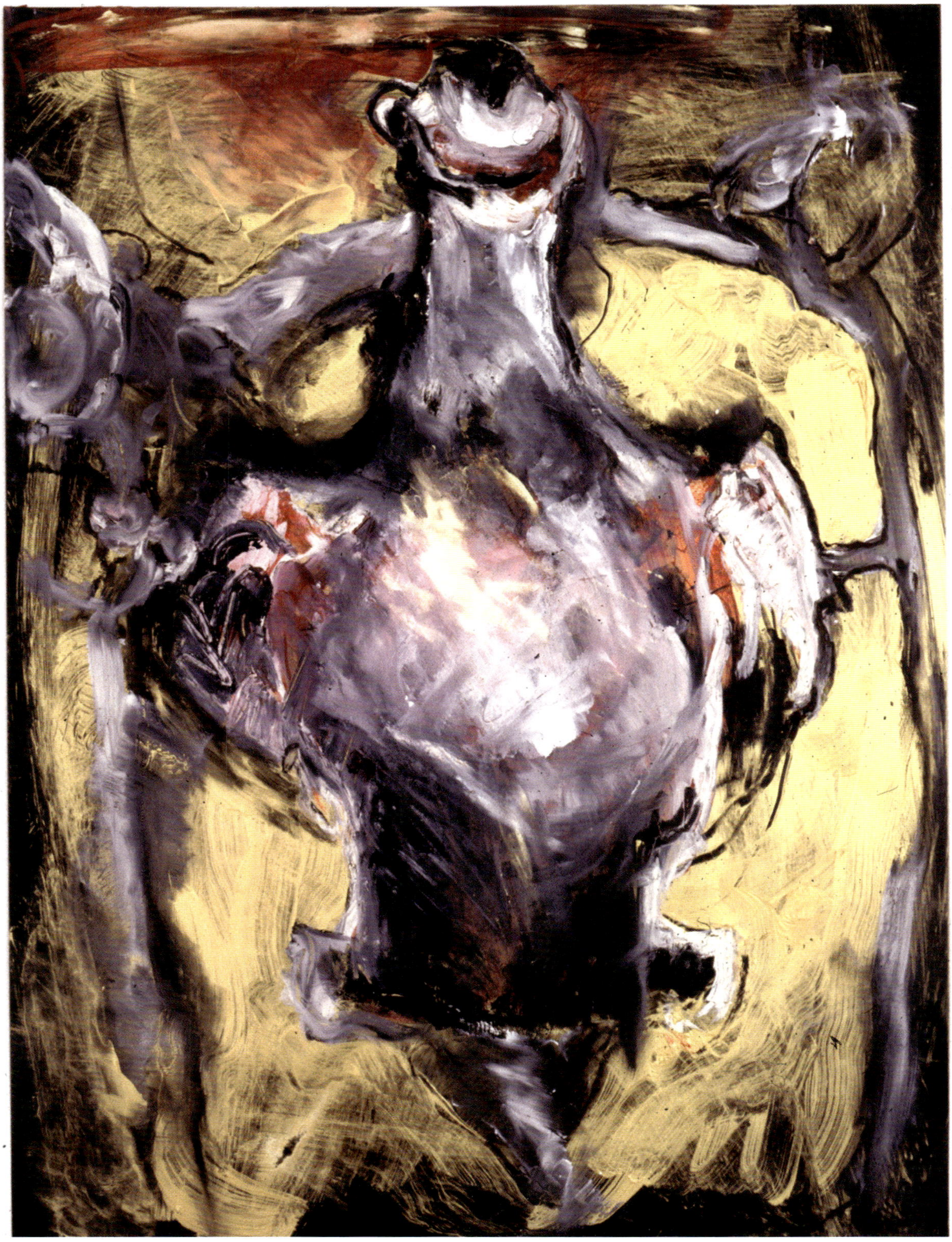

regard the ordinary waking state as the optimal state of consciousness and we view any deviation from that state as a kind of illness or debility. But in other systems of thought, something called a "higher consciousness" is admired and sought after. Such a state of consciousness may be reached through prayer or meditation, and some say they reach it through drugs. Even dance, and certain kinds of music, can induce such states. In those states, the mind comprehends aspects of the world and relationships among them that are hidden from the ordinary view.[7] It may well be mere propaganda to label one state of mind as "higher" than another: suffice it to say that there are different states, and some of them are not accessible to all of us. But Junko has the ability, and the determination, to reach that altered state:

Studio Diary, 1989

All my art rises up from the deepest part of my inner world. I go down to that world, catch the images that I encounter there, and bring them back to my pictorial space. I can make that journey only when I am in the altered state of consciousness. I had a long history of experiencing this altered state since my childhood, and it seemed to me a negative, dark element—others called it pathological, malignant, narcissistic, or at best, lazy. Only after it became focused, and limited its function in my life to the area of creating art, could I finally start accepting it as a positive force in my own psyche and as a powerful element in my art. Finally I was able to learn how to integrate this altered state into my personality and cherish it, and respect it as one of the significant gifts I have received in my life.

The world into which Junko descends so deeply during the periods of altered state of consciousness is experienced by her as a dark, dense forest, an unexplored region of a mountain, a cave, or the bottom of the ocean. Those are the very places that Erich Neumann describes as the places to which people make a "night voyage."[8] They are the places at the deepest part of the unconscious world and the purpose of the night voyage is to confront the terrifying powers of darkness that come from those places. Neumann talks about this night voyage, followed by a dragon fight, as the "Hero Journey"—the most significant process of human consciousness development. Neumann, and Jung before him,[9] have written about the structure of the unconscious world and the numinous feeling that occurs in people when they encounter images that arise from the unconscious. But they have written also about the dangers that people encounter when they descend into their unconscious world: unless one has a strong sense of the boundary between this world and that other one, and unless one has a strong spiritual base from which he can stand on the edge of these two worlds, the journey to the unconscious world would result in the destruction of the psyche.

Junko's transition to an altered state has much in common with this sort of "Hero Journey." While she was creating her *Emerging Consciousness* series (1988, sixteen works) she wrote this in her studio diary:

Studio Diary, 1988

Dark suffering days have continued. Finally I was overcome by some strong desire: my consciousness level had changed, the inside of my consciousness and the outside had turned around and my consciousness became inside out. I closed the studio door and started working.

Mysterious works started: my eyes were almost closed. I could not tell if they were open or closed. In my dimmed sight I saw only that both my hands were moving slowly, one with a brush, the other with wet paint on my fingertips sliding smoothly on black coated paper. Only one desire was in my mind: to transfer the inner movement to the outside as it is, to the surface of the paper. I listened to the inner movement: my hands follow it, but if my hands move against it and if they are moved by their own will for even one second, my hand takes a paper towel and wipes out that trace. I put the engine and burls on the table in front of me but my eyes are not following their forms. I need them only because they are solid, they are located on the edge of the material world, which I can rely on, to pull the material essence out of it in order to create a solid thing in this overwhelming non-solidity world.

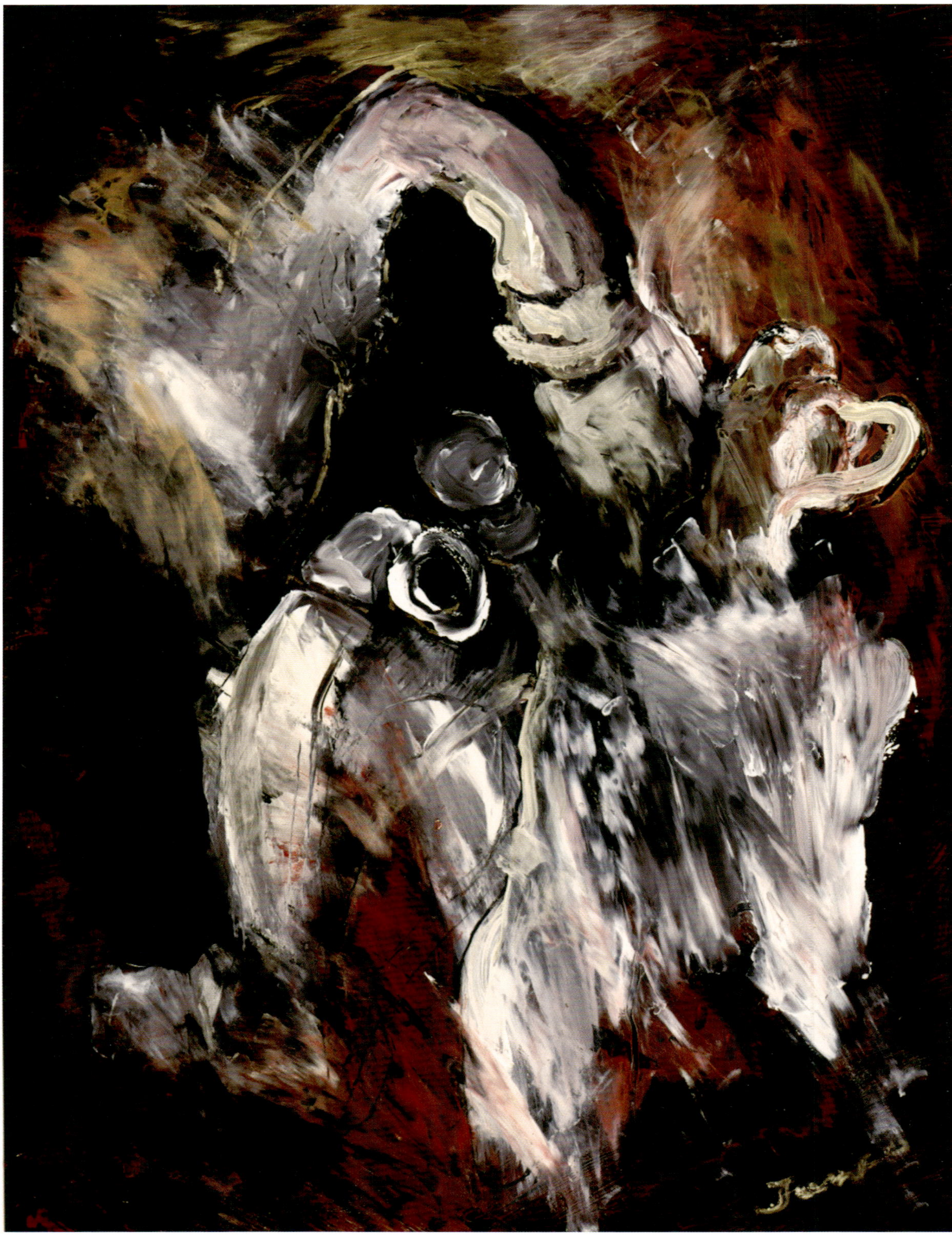

"God," I whisper, "What am I doing? I am throwing away all that I have learned, all technique to build a strong structure in the painting, to make every part of it alive from corner to corner. I am throwing away the sharp eye which judges instantly if the relationship between the part and the whole is real, and I am painting now with my eyes almost closed, without using my reason, my judgment, my intellect. How can I be an artist?" A huge lump moved up my windpipe and came up to my throat, a shocking sensation moved through my body, and my hands are still continuing the movement.

When my hands stopped—it had lasted less than fifteen minutes altogether—a strange irresistible sleepiness came over me and I slept in my chair at the working table. A second drawing continued then, just like the first one.

Junko worked this way for a month and the series of eighteen works was born. A month later, a new set of works, titled *Circles*, started.

Studio Diary, 1988

The works that I have just finished—I don't even know if I am allowed to call them "works"—are so different from all the other works that I created before, even more so than the *Emerging Consciousness* works. There is no shape, no form, no existence, further no more intention to suggest such things. A strong whitish aura gushing out from the tips of my fingers—I see it now; I dip them into the iridescent paint jar and put them on the paper, I let them slide, dance on the paper: it is like a mediation of fingers, of arms and hands, and the whole body.

Opposite:
EMERGING CONSCIOUSNESS, No. 5 (1988)
Acrylic on Kromekote paper
26 x 20 in.
(66.0 x 50.8 cm.)

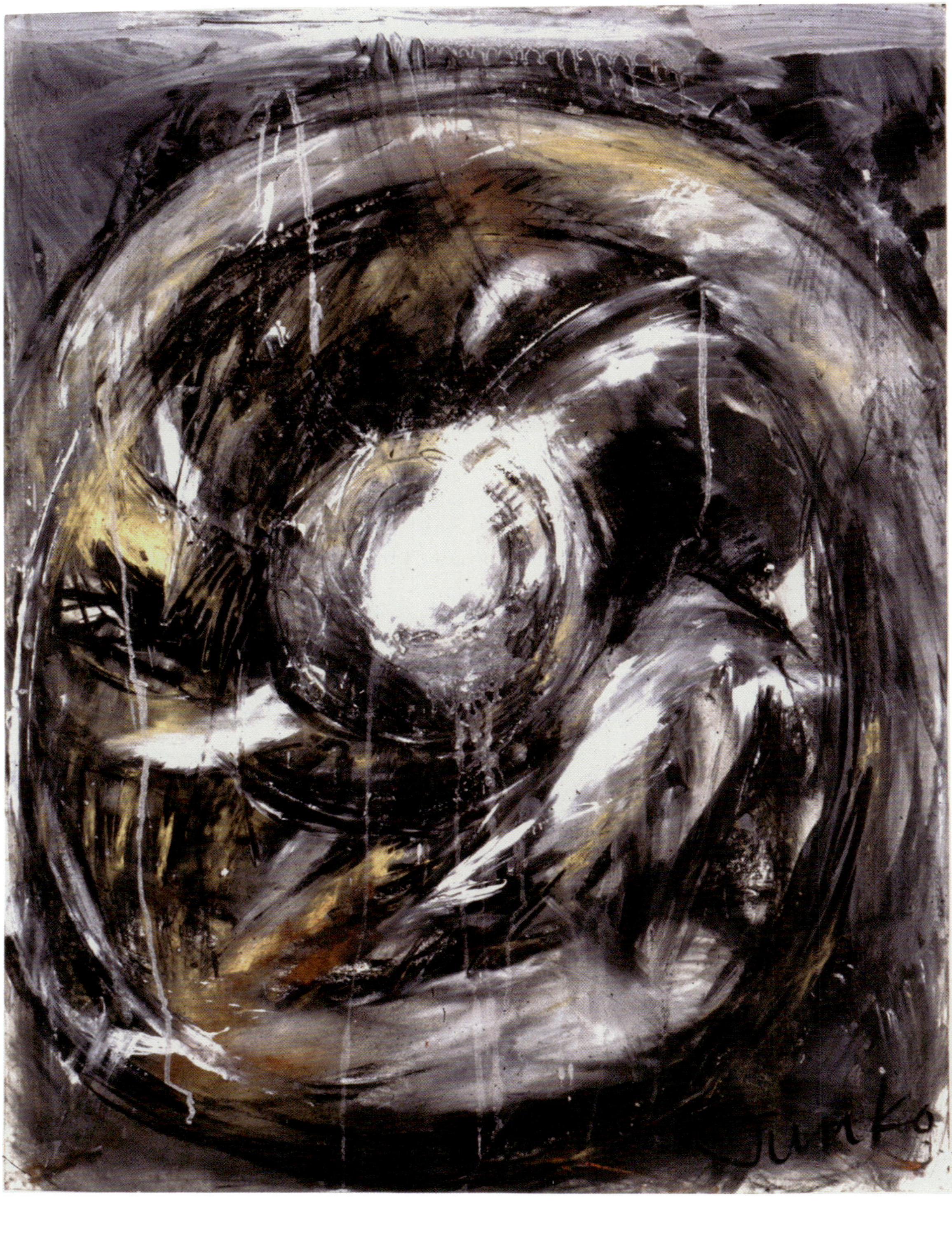
Junko

The idea that I am no longer an artist had flashed often in my mind. The fear was strong, my vulnerability was deep. If I cannot integrate my thoughts, my intellect into my work—something for which I have worked hard all my life—what does my work mean to the world? What message can it possibly convey? And how can I possibly take responsibility for it? But then some overwhelming thoughts swept over me: You are not like an empty pipe. Messages come through you, the whole you, everything about you comes through with it. No matter what you do during your altered states of consciousness, you are yourself. The idea that I am in training followed: training to make contact with the unknown territory located in a much deeper, much darker, much more dangerous place that I had ever gone. I probably have to descend even further: that is the most important thing I have to train myself to do.

These entries in Junko's studio diary show that she too, at first, was suspicious of her own "altered states" and she was the last person to be convinced of their authenticity and their value. Her own doubts and suspicions played a significant role in her history of building her own confirmation and affirmation of her altered state: those doubts and suspicions were very much part of her desire to avoid illusion and complacency. But gradually she came to realize that her transition from ordinary consciousness into altered consciousness is not a passive process: it requires her active commitment. And once she came to that realization, her trust in the altered state was confirmed:

Opposite:
CIRCLES, No. 1 (1988)
Acrylic on paper
40 x 32 in
(101.6 x 81.3 cm.)

Studio Diary, 1989

The reality which I reach in that state of consciousness is firm and substantial—it is never like an illusion. My journey to the dark unconscious world is made by me alone. I have never used substances of any kind to help me on the journey, nor to ease the pain which comes with it—nor have I used them at any other time of my life. This is in spite of the widespread usage of psychedelics and conciousness-altering techniques among researchers on consciousness during the 1960s.

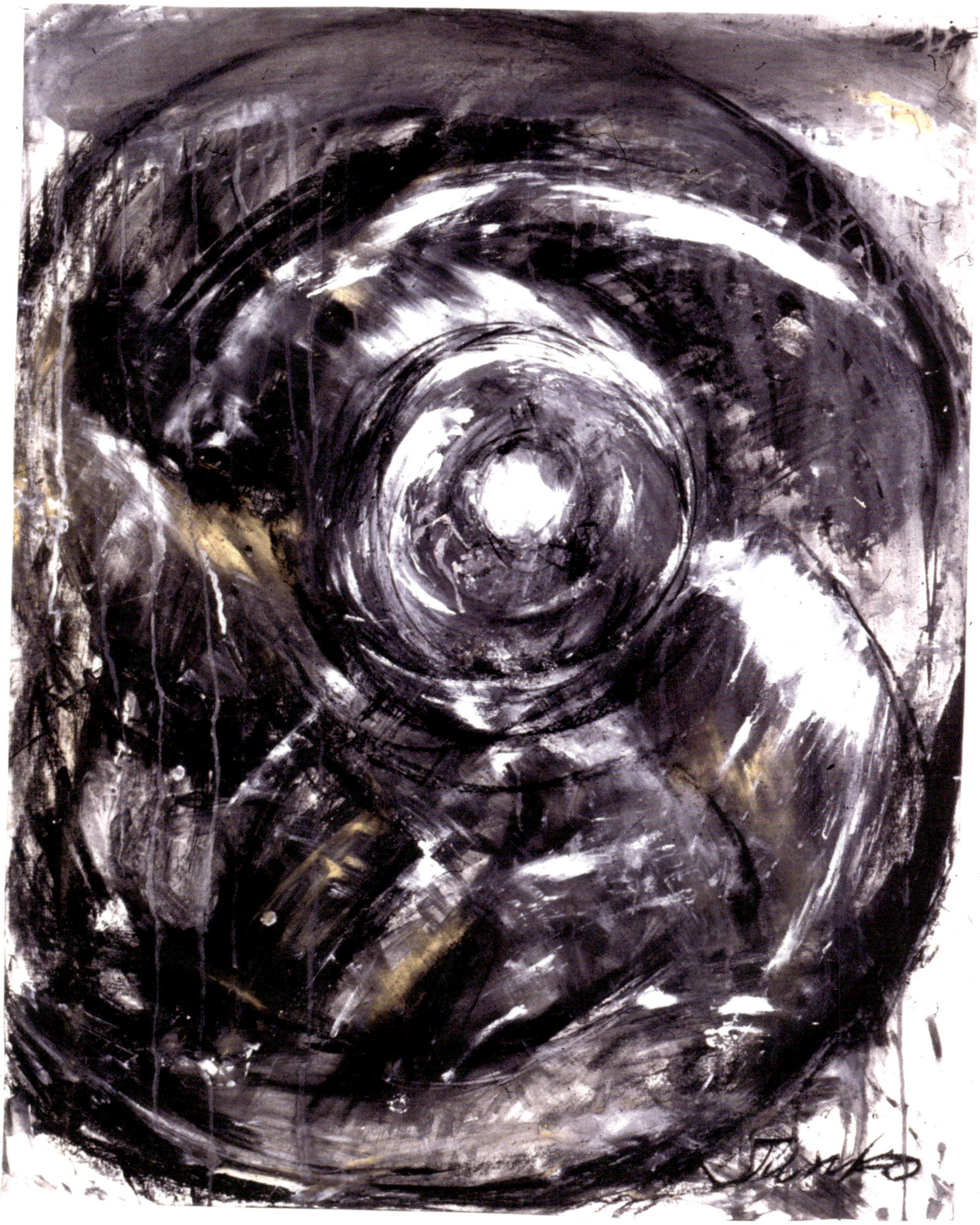

The journey into the altered state has many stages and I can exercise only a little control over the time when the journey occurs, or how long it takes, or the depth to which I can descend. Each stage of the journey has its own danger, which can be considerable.... I descend deeper and deeper through my own contemplation, concentration, through my own disciplines and with my own risks. My sincere quest and my prayer to reach the Truth—those are my only guide. That is the way all the images in my art become my responsibility, and that is the way creating art becomes a severe spiritual training for me. The ancient Japanese idea that artists are ascetics is still strongly alive in me.

But this intense awareness of your own active attitude does not cause conflict with the overwhelming passive feeling you experience while you are in the altered state of consciousness. The power experience of receiving the image passively and the active expression of the image—these two become one in the act of creating art, and this is the essential quality of Revelation.

The resolution of the tension between the passive and the active states that Junko mentions here is something that she strives for also outside the altered state. She has often said that in creating her art, she plays three roles at the same time: artist, scientist, and guinea pig. The scientist records the art and the process of creating it, while the guinea pig takes risks by journeying to new places while the scientist watches. She keeps her studio diaries and notebooks out of a sense of responsibility to that scientist. Her life, she says, is actually part of God's file, so she has a responsibility to maintain that file and preserve it for future students who want to study the mystery of artistic creation, just as a doctor keeps his patients' files believing that his records may contribute to future medical research. Junko's transitions into and out of the altered state are part of the file.

Opposite:
CIRCLES,
No. 4 (1988)
Acrylic on paper
40 x 32 in
(101.6 x 81.3 cm.)

In the early days of our marriage, whenever I would express distrust, or irritation, at Junko's evident movement into the altered state, Junko always answered, "We have to judge this state of mind by its fruits." And that turned out to be true. If the altered state is sick, or unreal, it prevents the artist's real growth: the art remains compulsive and repetitious and the artist's personality never grows toward real love and productiveness. But when the altered state is real, the artist's personality grows ever more cohesive and the rational relationship with the artist's inner necessity is deepened. This shows itself in subtle and sometimes revolutionary changes in the art, and then the artist's personality grows toward more love and productiveness.

By the time she created her series *Requiem for an Executed Bird* in 1991, Junko had come to see her altered state of consciousness as a positive thing and she realized that she had to be in the altered state in order to create her works. The series consists of forty-five works, all made in six weeks' time, from late May to early July. She worked almost constantly, spending twelve to fourteen hours a day in her studio and sleeping the rest of the time. But there was a pause after she finished the forty-first work. Finally she was just barely able to drive again; her concentration and descent into the altered state had been so deep up to that point that driving was out of the question. But at that point she wanted to see the ocean, and so she made the effort to drive, and this is what she wrote in her diary:

Studio Notebook, 1991

Sycamore Beach is a state park where you have to pay to get in. It is quieter than other parts of the beach along the Pacific Coast Highway. Being afraid that a sudden change of scenery might make my altered state of conciusness fade away, I walked on the sand as if I were carrying my body in a big container filled with liquid up to its brim, being careful not to spill even one drop from it. The sea looked different from the way I see it in everyday consciousness. It was vivid; every edge of each wave looked sharp and bright. The sound of the waves rising far away from the beach reached my ear with clarity. The light dancing on the top of each wave, which moved constantly, was brilliant, delicate, and overwhelmingly complicated. But overall, the thing that struck me most was the undoubted feeling of assurance that I understood the meaning of this whole scene. The whole sky and the sea, the air and the light, had tremendous meaning for me. I had a sudden realization: that the most serious Divine process of Creation is in progress right now, in this moment, and through creating my art, I was participating in that process in no matter how small a way. It was a most solemn realization that moved me to awe.

The altered state, which had seemed—to both of us, in different ways—so sinister, was now part of our life. Junko's ability to feel comfortable with that altered state helped me to move in and out of a near-death state when I was sick two years later. The visions which came to me then felt generative rather than ominous. The peace Junko came to feel with this state helped her to integrate "left-brain" and "right-brain" elements in her *Individuation Journal* in 1995. And its affinity with forms of religious mysticism led her to create her *Esoteric Buddhism* series, and nourished her interest in Kuukai, the ninth–century mystic who founded that religion in Japan. And so much had her altered state become a natural, healthy part of her life—and of mine—that fifteen years after her walk on Sycamore Beach, Junko and I were both able to work together in her studio every day for half a year, creating the works for *FATHOM*.

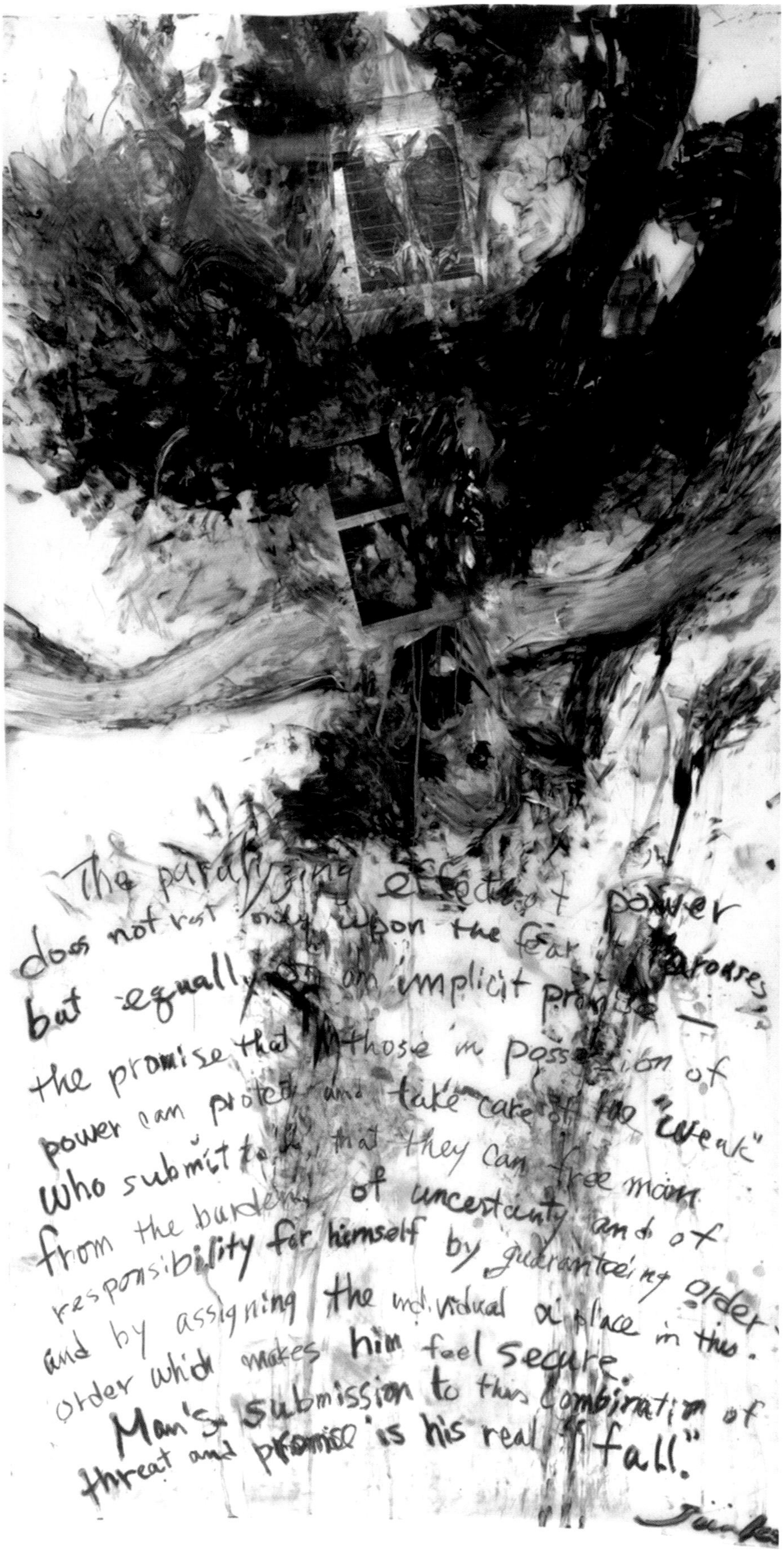

INDIVIDUATION
JOURNAL
No. 7 (1995)
THE FALL OF MAN
(ERICH FROMM)
The paralyzing effect of power does not rest only upon the fear it arouses, but equally on an implicit promise – the promise that those in possession of power can protect and take care of the "weak" who submit to it, that they can free man from the burden of uncertainty and of responsibility for himself by guaranteeing order and by assigning the individual a place in this order which makes him feel secure. Man's submission to this combination of threat and promise is his real "fall."
Acrylic and collage
on mylar
84 x 42 in.
(213.4 x 106.7 cm.)
Collection of the
Central European
University, Budapest

CHAPTER SEVEN
THE ROLE AND MISSION OF THE ARTIST

Who needs the centripetal kind of art that Junko creates? What good is it? What worthwhile contribution does such an artist really make to the community?

Junko has taken these questions quite seriously, and in an essay she wrote a few years ago, which she read as a lecture, she offered this answer:

From Lecture "Spirituality and the Process of Creating Art," Graduate Theological Union, Berkeley, California, Oct. 9, 2003

Just like the shaman, the artist sets off on his frightening journey alone. He struggles and fights, he does not know what he will encounter until he embraces the image in his arms, then he has to crawl back to the pictorial space where the images are transcended. This little space is the artist's universe in which everything happens and in which the artist is the creator. The artist wants nothing more than this little universe, and this little universe is all he offers to society.

But why to society? And why does society care for these images—if it does care? Because the viewer will see his own mind in them, the things that are so dark, so ugly, that he had denied them and forbidden himself to see them. And just like I went through the wall of phobia during my process of creation, the viewer will break his own preventive wall and see what he had been afraid to see. His own journey will start.

If the artist's journey has reached the extraordinary depths and taken him to the divine world, it is possible that the viewer will also glimpse that world through the art work and there he will see the divine presence at his own center. There he will see something beyond gender, beyond all ethnicity, and beyond all religious denominations, prejudices, and restrictions. For what he saw first as fences he will come to see as curtains, and he will lift these curtains and see what lies behind them.... Because it is the function of art to make us see what it has been prohibited to see ... great art often makes us uncomfortable. But at the risk of the viewer's displeasure, the artist keeps offering his work. And the images the artist brings forth, as ironical as they are, can come to be accepted as a part of society's constructive consciousness.

Junko sees her role as similar to that of the shaman. Her role is similar also to that of the prophets of the Old Testament: like those ancient prophets, she goes into the desert to encounter truth and then comes back to the community to proclaim that truth. Even at the risk of the community's intense displeasure, she proclaims the truth she has encountered. But the artist is different from the prophet because she speaks to each viewer individually rather than to the community as a whole. And unlike the prophet, who urges the community to accept his message as true and to act in accordance with it, the artist does not urge any particular action: she is not a propagandist. The artist's only purpose is to awaken each viewer to his own truth—a truth that need not be the same for every viewer—and what is important is that the art should encourage each viewer to find a pathway to his own deepest center.

Essential to the role of both the shaman and the prophet is the quality of being a constructive outsider. To be an outsider requires one to scrape away everything that is external to his core: one leaves behind the whole matrix of social interactions which seemed to define the self, which determined rank, status, and merit, and which seemed to offer security and a path to follow; and one commits to live as what is left after all those things have been scraped away. The artist too, in searching for what is essential, scrapes away everything that is external and superfluous to the image, and determines to encounter the essence of the image that remains.

But if Junko is a shaman, she is a distinctly twenty-first century shaman. Instead of using drums and magic potions,

Junko uses computers and drum printers. Instead of crawling into a dark cave, Junko withdraws into her studio and into her inner world. Instead of intoning magical incantations, Junko studies and writes and speaks clearly about her art. And Junko's focus is psychological rather than sociological, as we have seen.

We might see the artist's journey also as a sort of "hero's journey." She starts out on her journey alone, and her contribution has to do with opening the viewer's mind and raising society's consciousness. She identifies herself as a person who has lived apart from the community and then returns to it with a contribution. The contribution could never have been made unless Junko had the courage to leave the community in the first place: to live as an exile and as a spiritual refugee (Chapter Two); to be individuated and an outsider, and then return to the community as an individual (Chapter Six).

Although the notion of the hero's journey as a lonely journey is very ancient, it has been very much out of fashion during all of Junko's adult life.[1] We live in a time when people want to identify with groups and when "culture studies" in one form or another permeate academic discourse. But Junko's concerns are intensely personal and remind us that only what is authentically personal can also be universal. It is no accident that Junko has never been on the faculty of any art school and has never identified herself as a member of any group of artists—not "women artists" or "Asian artists" (even though her works are sometimes included in those sorts of shows)—or of any movement. She has had the courage to confront her inner world, and the battles she fights as an artist are always inner battles.

THE ARTIST'S MISSION IN THE TWENTY-FIRST CENTURY

Junko's idea that the viewer will see her art and be transformed, and then start on his own journey—this too is an idea that marks her as an artist who could not have lived before the twentieth century. For the recognition that the viewer

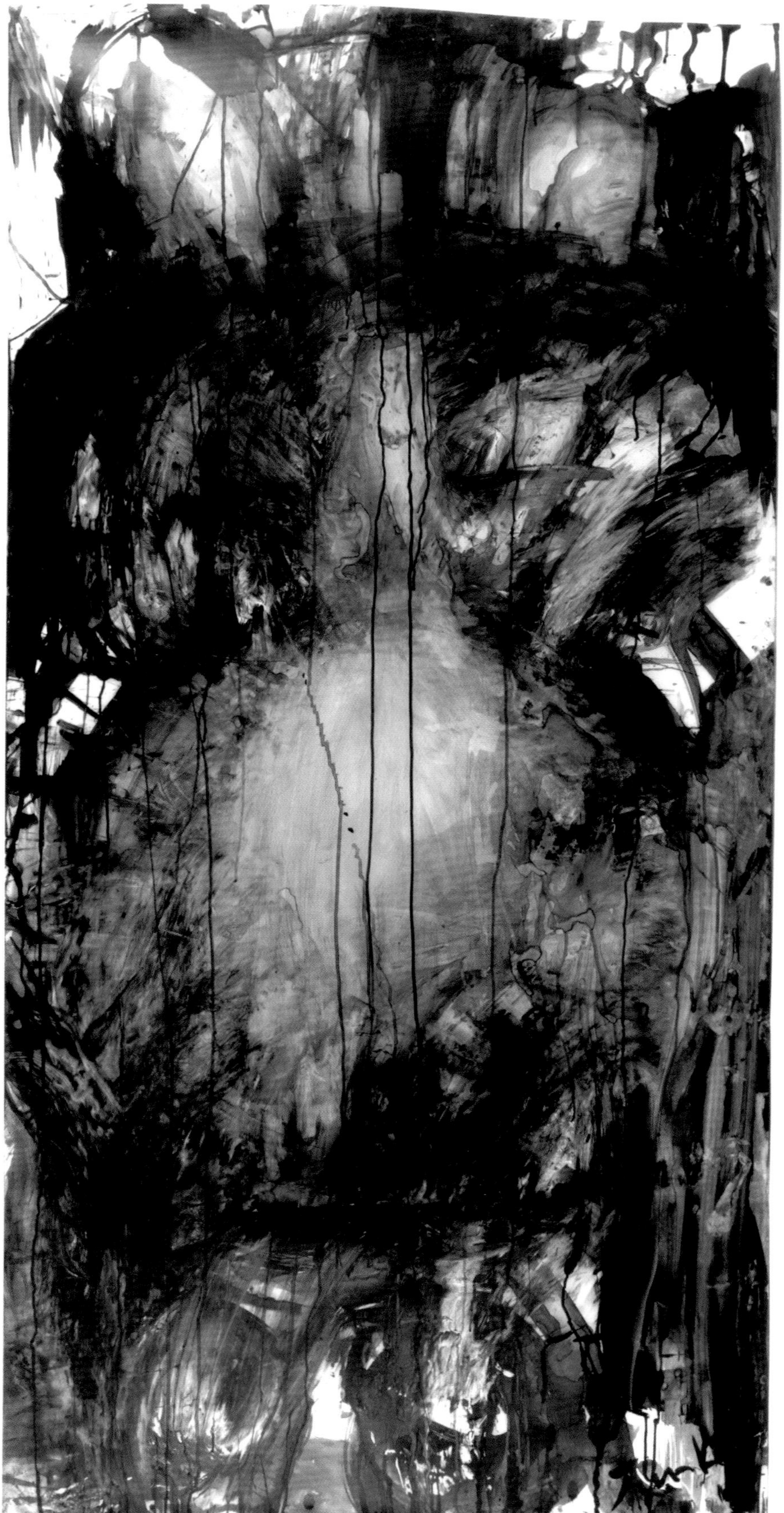

IN THE FOREST OF
AMIDA BUDDHA
No. 1 (1993)
Sumi ink and acrylic
on mylar support
80 x 42 in.
(203.2 x 106.7 cm.)

has phobias, things he is afraid to see, and that the artist has a responsibility to make him see these very things—that is a notion that could never have occurred to any pre-twentieth century philosopher. How different it is from Aristotle's notion of "catharsis," for example: a purging, or purification, which can be experienced and re-experienced every time the viewer sits through the tragedy and identifies with the characters on stage.[2] Unlike catharsis, transformation cannot be repeated: if it is real, it is a one-time event and the viewer is changed by it forever.

The notion that the viewer might be transformed by seeing images requires more thought. It is an idea with a different history in the East and the West. In China and Japan, an art work is judged excellent to the extent that it holds the artist's life-force, what in Japan is called his "*ki*." If you can feel the emanations of that life-force rising from the work, then the work has value; otherwise, no matter how skillful the artist, no matter how beautiful the work, it is merely craft. Under that view, the viewer is literally touched by the life-force in the work of art, and it is that touch that transforms him.[3] But the transformation itself is unexplained.

For us in the West, our attitude toward the image is more polarized. In the Old Testament, prophets often heard God's voice and spoke with God but not even Moses was permitted to see God's face, for "no man can see my face and live."[4] Why was it that seeing God was terrifying and even fatal, while hearing His voice was allowed? Just a few hundred years after Exodus was written down, and just a few hundred miles to the west, Plato and Aristotle had a much more complacent view of what seeing images meant. In their view, images give us pleasure to the extent that they accurately imitate reality. Such notions, evolved as they were without the benefit of contemporary psychological awareness, seem shallow to us today. Junko's notion that the viewer might be transformed by seeing her art is more compelling. And this is her mission as well: to transform the viewer through the images she creates.

"This little pictorial space"—that is all the artist has to contribute. By encountering this space, the viewer may be transformed. But what is the mechanism by which such a transformation might take place? The answer is that the artist teaches by example, but she does this in a way which is not obvious.

We begin by observing a distinction between "honesty" and "integrity"—two qualities we value highly, and which are sometimes confused. Honesty is a relationship between our words and the world, while integrity is a relationship between our words, our actions, and the world. It is much harder to reach integrity than honesty, and sometimes integrity even requires that we be dishonest. For instance, if you are hiding Jews in your basement and the Gestapo knocks on the door and asks, "Are there any Jews here?," the honest answer is "yes" but the answer with integrity is "no." For that is what it means to be hiding the Jews. If you say "yes," why did you put them in your basement in the first place?

Now generally speaking, mere honesty is easy to achieve. Sometimes we may have to take unpleasant consequences by disclosing truths we would rather hide, but except in unusual cases, we all know how to be honest and we can all do it. In fact, as a general rule, most of us are honest. But integrity is something excruciatingly difficult to achieve, and this is partly because we do not control the world. We may act a certain way intending a certain result, and we may find that our actions had an unintended result—or that the actions we had intended to carry out cannot be carried out. Or we may lack the imagination to envision a world with sufficient accuracy to formulate clear intentions; because the complexities of including all the relevant considerations in our calculations are beyond us, we often act with limited focus and intention.

And it is here that the centripetal artist plays a role, for the artist constructs a world over which she exercises complete control. In that world, the artist sees all, and is capable of all. When the art is successful, the artist models complete integrity for us, we see it in the work, and we respond to it. This "modeling" is beyond mere imitation[4] because the world of the art is consciously constructed. It is not imitated, it is not borrowed: it is original and created. Yet it incorporates elements from the real world, and it transforms them, and shows us aspects of the world and possibilities in the world that we had not imagined. Seeing these things modeled for us, we are inspired to an integrity of our own—and this is the contribution that the artist makes to us.[5]

When Junko says that the viewer's own journey will start, that is what she is talking about. The viewer senses the artist's journey, and is invited to participate in it, and he is inspired to go on a similar journey of his own. The journey need not involve the production of imagery, for each viewer has his own life-path to follow. Junko's works are merely the traces on paper of her struggle and her journey. They give the viewer who sees them deeply the courage to carry on his own struggle.

This is the function of centripetal art and it is a hyper-contemporary function, imbedded in a very modern awareness of the viewer's vulnerability and of his earnest search for meaning. This art arises from a kind of respect for the viewer, and love for him, that the artists of former times did not feel. For many of them, the "viewer" was after all, the patron: the nobleman, or the church; and the desire to please them, to flatter them, to glorify them was an expression of only superficial respect for them. And for most of the twentieth century, beginning with the age of "modern art," it may be said that the artist painted mainly to express himself.

Next page:
CONCERNING ART AND RELIGION No. 9 (2004) "WHO WILL SHATTER THE ILLUSIONS? THE PROPHET? THE ARTIST?"
Computer prints and acrylic on mylar three panels
Overall 84 x 126 in. (213.4 x 320 cm.)

But Junko's centripetal art is something quite different. It is an invitation to the viewer to participate in the search for truth, and in this way it is one of the highest expressions of love: for to love the viewer is to call him to his highest self.

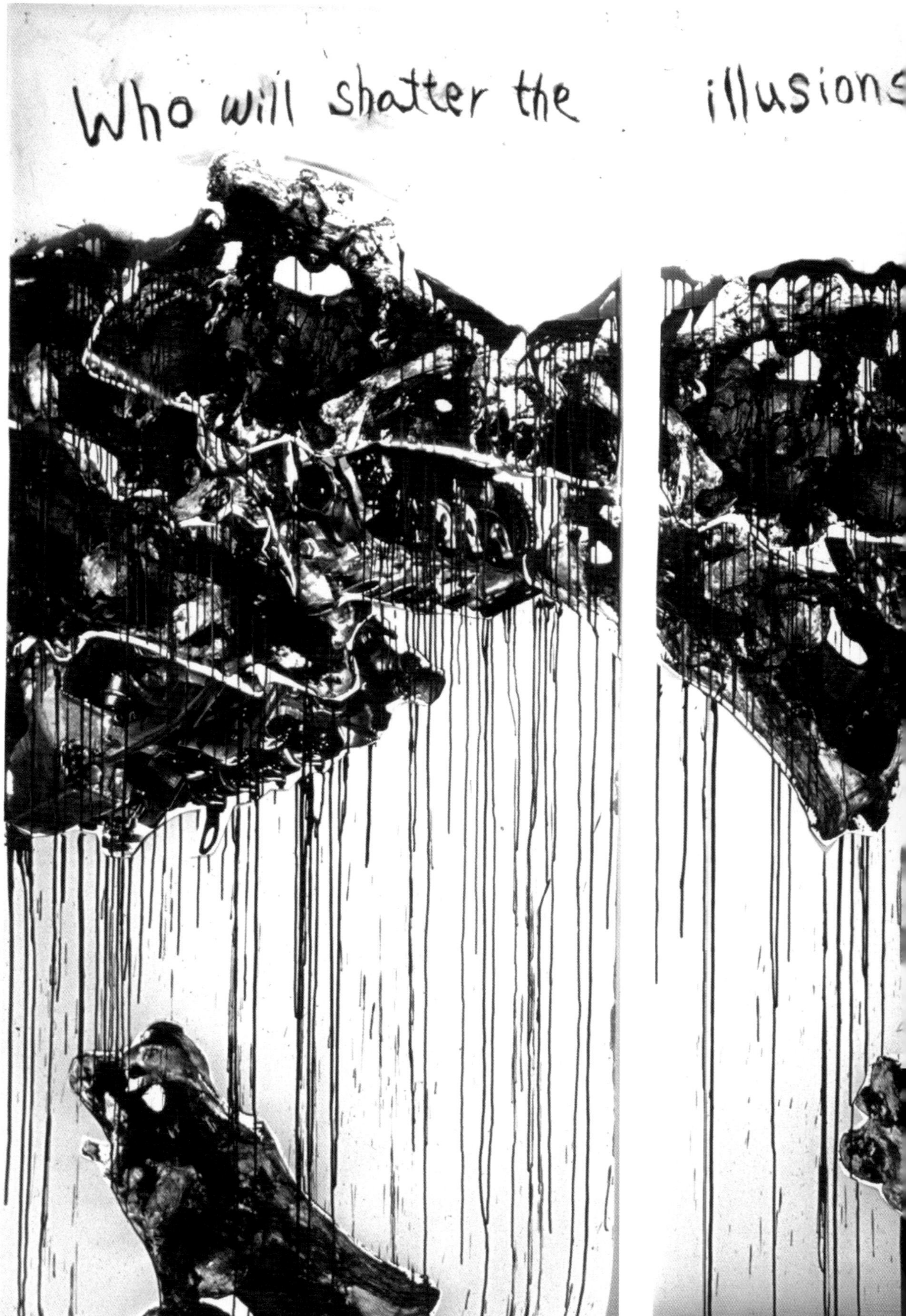
Who will shatter the
illusions

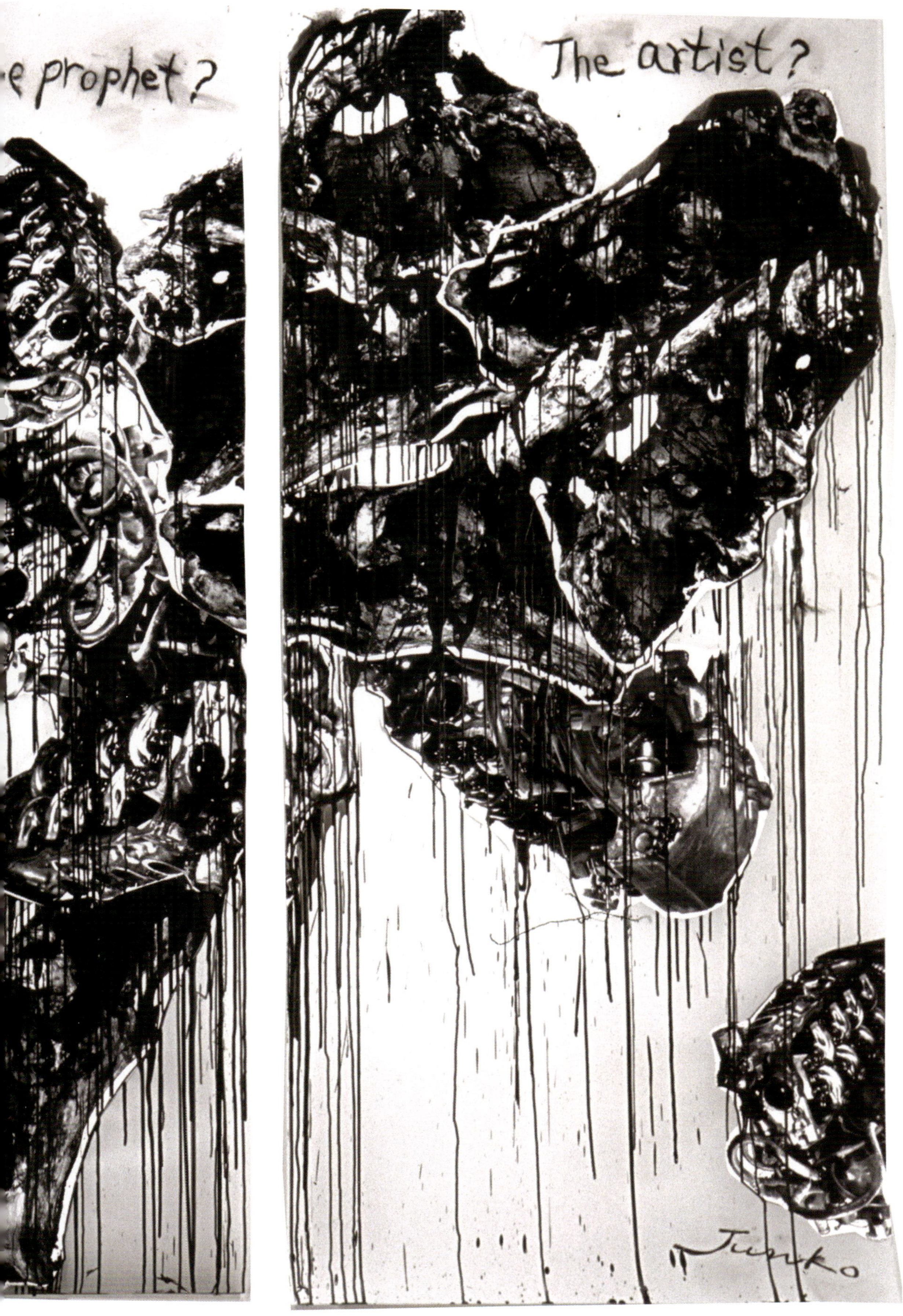
e prophet ?
The artist ?
Junko

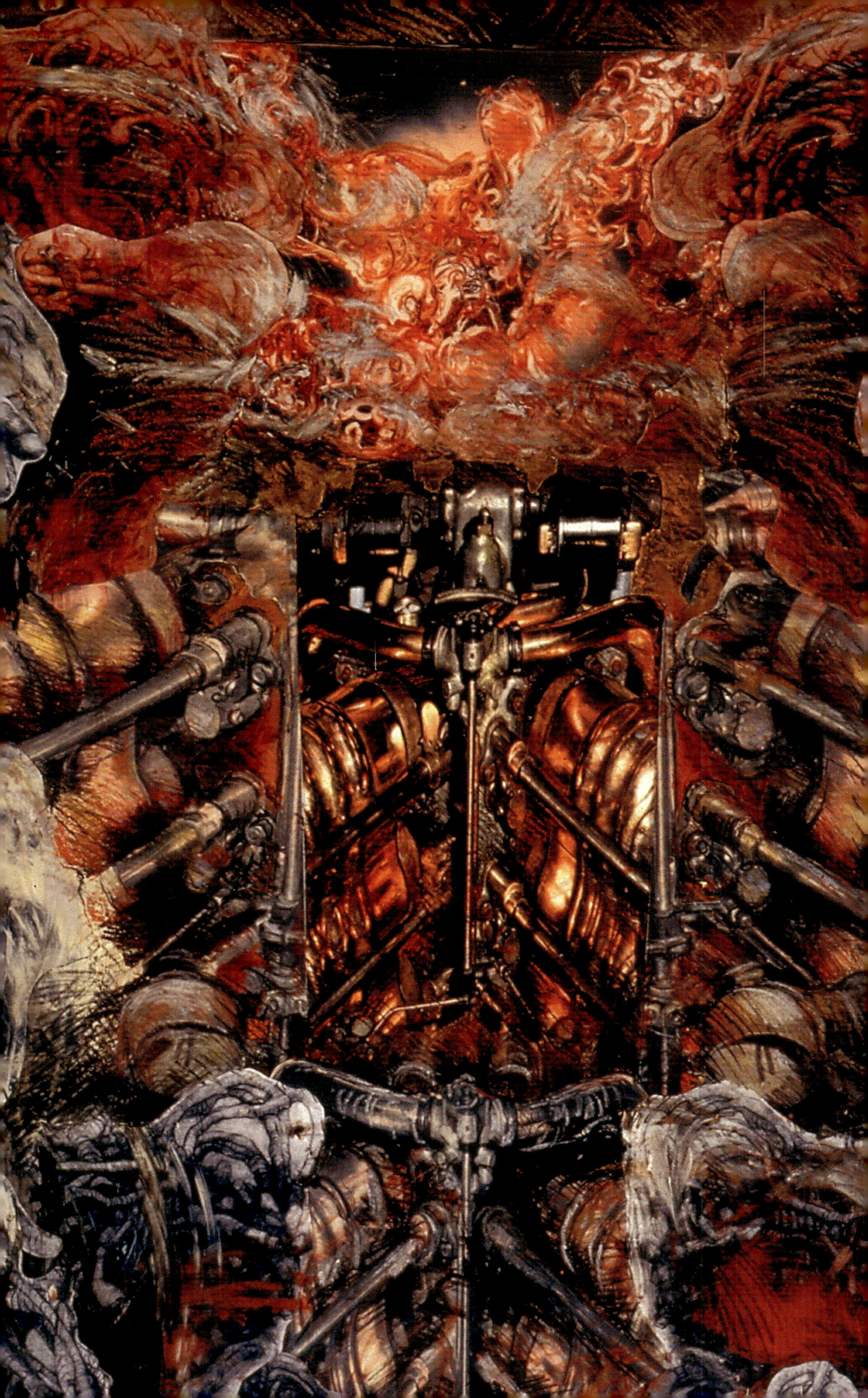

AFTERWORD: THE FURNACE

Seven years ago Junko invited me into her studio to show me the works she had just completed: the *Esoteric Buddhism* series. *Ecstasy*, the main piece in this series (see pp. 42-43), is a three-panel work so huge that it could not even hang on the wall of the studio she had in those days: the bottom of it draped along the floor. I found the whole series overwhelming and after looking at the works for several minutes, I told Junko that I found them to be the most disturbing works she had ever created. She asked me why, and I said, "Because they are so clearly polytheistic."

I was surprised to hear myself say such a thing. Even though Junko and I come from very different religious backgrounds, our household has never been the scene of religious disputations. To the contrary: it seemed to me from the day I met her that Junko understood what I found beautiful and essential in Judaism—more so than any of my so-called Jewish friends whose relationship to their religion is based in obedience, or in nostalgia, or in tribalism; Junko's perception of Judaism was colored by none of those things. And for my part, I have always felt moved by the refined purity of Shinto, and even in my college days I had found Buddhism to be an attractive "dietary supplement" to the Western monotheistic religions.

When we went to Japan together for the first time after our marriage, Junko's father woke me up early in the morning to take me to Meiji Jingu, the Shinto shrine dedicated to the Meiji Emperor. Set in a dense evergreen forest in the middle of Shibuya, one of Tokyo's insanely hectic business districts, Meiji Jingu is a gateway from the urban, everyday world into the quiet world of nature. Not the nature of hiking and camping and all-terrain vehicles: in that shrine no one speaks above a whisper,

Opposite:
DETAIL FROM
ESOTERIC BUDDHISM,
No. 2, ECSTASY (2001)
See full image, p. 42-43

and when you walk through this forest you can hear your own footsteps on the swept gravel stones. My father-in-law and I walked silently through the *torii*—the tall Japanese gate made of two trees and two cross-beams—along the walkway which leads through the dark forest to the shrine in the center of the park, and I watched as he bowed his head and clasped his hands and stood silent for a few minutes. We said nothing to each other until we were back on the busy streets of Shibuya. From that experience I think I learned the true nature of prayer more deeply than I had learned it in years of going to synagogue and reciting the time-hallowed texts. So why did the notion of "polytheism" occur to me, and why did I find it so disturbing?

Of course, the works are disturbing: if they were not disturbing they could not be great art.[1] And the central work, *Ecstasy*, is in fact outrageously and emphatically polytheistic. It depicts a bird, but this is no bird that Jehovah could ever have imagined when He created the flying things on the fifth day. It is too enormous to be a bird, and its heart is made of steel, an engine—and there is fire in the center of it. And it is at the same time a giant female sexual organ. It hovers over a script, the *risshukyô*, the sutra recited daily, with great solemnity, in esoteric Buddhist services in thousands of temples across Japan[2] that reads, "Sexual ecstasy, clean and pure, this too is the realm of the boddhisatva": the notion of sexual ecstasy being "clean" and "pure," and the idea of reciting such a proposition daily in church, is about as far from the Judaeo-Christian tradition as it gets. Although this bird derives from the slaughtered chicken, it shows more the aspect of tyrannosaurus rex and the fierce predatory dinosaurs from whom it is descended. It is an epiphany of the Bird Junko had painted in her 1991 *Requiem* series, but this bird is not about to be executed. No, quite the opposite: it feels as if it might leap off the gallery wall and devour the viewer. But it could not leap: it is too heavy. Its mode of locomotion is mysterious. It might waddle, or it might move simply by willing itself from one place to another; or if it could fly, it would not fly toward heaven but would flap its leafy wings over whole cities and terrify the residents—or so it seemed to me when I first looked at it.

But still, my words troubled Junko for a couple of reasons. First of all it was because she realized that I had expressed, involuntarily, certain prejudices shared by all Westerners.

The first prejudice was the notion that monotheism is some kind of an advance over polytheism, and that "nature religions" are "lower" in the Great Hierarchy than the religions that revolve around a personal God.[3] This prejudice, which has supported Western missionaries and colonists in their global enterprise, has far-reaching ramifications. For the Japanese, to the contrary, the notion of a personal God seems unrefined: the higher one's spiritual state, the closer he comes to nature and to the impersonal forces that govern it. The idea that one might talk to God, that God might have any interest in such conversation—that idea provokes only polite smiles in Japan: for them, it is the idea of a child who is not yet ready to perceive the higher truths. Every tree has its spirit, its *kami*; yet to argue over monotheism versus polytheism is itself a childish kind of rigidity, for nature cannot be counted. While for us, the history of religion is bound up with the biographies of great personalities—Moses, Jesus, Muhammad—such matters have no counterpart in the Eastern religions. Buddha taught that we should follow the universal order and that his own life was of little importance. One points at the moon to draw our attention toward the moon—not toward the index finger he raises toward the moon. The spirit should move from the personal toward the impersonal. My remark had brought this whole cluster of differences in our backgrounds to the fore.

And the second prejudice has to do with the Western attitude towards sexuality. In the West sexuality is generally considered a negative thing: the "fall of man." Western people assume that if sex is encouraged it will inevitably lead to immorality, lechery, and violence. But Esoteric Buddhism carries the Tantric tradition which sees sexual energy in nature and respects it. When this kind of sexual energy is harmonized with the personality man becomes part of the Great Desire of the universe—and this is one of the most powerful, solemn, and sublime forces that humans can make use of. In order to reach that high state of being, Tantric traditions have all kinds of disciplines, meditations, and rituals. This very ancient precursor to the idea of "sublimation" has been well known in Eastern traditions for thousands of years before Freud.

Junko had worked very hard to reach this state of mind. Before creating this painting, she had written a long essay on the Tantric aspects of Esoteric Buddhism. She had deliberately brought fragmentary images of engines cut off from the cars—not functioning, not connected to the universe any longer, wounded and bleeding—into her pictorial space to revive them and make them function as a vital part of the little universe she had created, until they radiated oxidized gold light and illuminated the whole painting with their glow. I had not seen it: I had missed the whole point of the work. Because of my Westerner's prejudices against polytheism, against nature religion, and against sexuality I had been prevented from seeing the solemnity and refinement of this powerful painting.

And there was still another reason: the remark was a little bit of a betrayal because it cast Junko and me in the roles of representatives of different religious backgrounds. Western monotheism fosters a certain personality type, which is quite different from the Eastern personality type: it is a complicated, tangled personality type which relishes conflict and contradiction, whose notion of spiritual striving is restless and anguished.[4] It is very different from the "Eastern" personality type, which strives towards peace and quiet. The Eastern seeker strives for escape from the circle of karma, and imagines Nirvana as a still lotus pond. For the Western seeker, "heaven" is a place full of life, a heavenly court, with angels playing background music, where one can hold conversation with God and with all the souls that have ever lived—a place from which the activities of this world can be monitored and even perhaps influenced.

But Junko herself has strong aspects of that Western type of personality combined with deep layers of the Eastern personality type. For Junko, as for me, the spiritual quest has an inherently tumultuous quality, and if it reaches a resolution it is a resolution through climax—like sexual activity, or like the climax of a piece of music or of a work of art. It will never be a resolution through increasing quietude. That shared personality type is an important part of our marriage: it is part of what we find attractive in each other. So my remark had failed to acknowledge this most important shared aspect of our personalities and in that way it was an involuntary betrayal.

After our conversation this strong Western aspect of Junko's personality manifested itself again in the form of her series of works titled *Concerning Art and Religion*, created in 2004 and 2005. In those nine works Junko articulated fundamental ideas which are implicit in all her works: "*In the beginning is the image*" (frontispiece)—which means that image precedes even narrative and myth; that the artists who painted the cave drawings at Lascaux are Junko's ancestors because the encounter with the image precedes and is more important than the adoption of any dogma. "*Why do angels and demons both fly in the sky?*" and "*Why do you love chaos and destruction so much?*"—those works advert to the destructive aspects of monotheism which has shown itself, throughout its history of "holy wars" and colonialization, to foster a kind of hostility and rigidity leading often to destructiveness. Creating those works, partially in response to my remarks, prepared Junko for the *FATHOM* series two years later, a series which begins, again, with "*The Sorcerer Entering His Forest*"—another appearance of the Bird but this time as a sorcerer in almost human form.

As for me, our conversation made me start to think. Gradually the *Esoteric Buddhism* works grew on me: their dignified lines, and the solemn, powerful energy they display, made me start to think more deeply about their underlying themes and this made me confront religion and my relationship to it more directly. I finally remembered that there is a spiritual realm beyond monotheism and polytheism, and pantheism and panentheism, a realm in which disputes over doctrine and dogma seem petty and inconsequential, in which many of the Western ideas associated with monotheism seem small and recede from view: a realm in which the divine process of creation really takes place. To insist on apprehending God as a personal agent rather than merely as an aspect of the world, to insist on a divinity which is male or female, or one or many—these matters arise from the human mind and grow out of human cultures: they are not aspects of the divine presence itself. The divine presence which Junko seeks in her art moves like a wind through Christianity and Buddhism, through monotheism and polytheism, through forests of trees and forests of bamboo, in a realm beyond gender, beyond ethnicity, and beyond dogma. This is the realm in which centripetal art is born and Junko's art, dancing freely in that realm, drew even me into it.

In an often-quoted remark, Goethe said that he was a pantheist when it came to science, a polytheist in art, and a monotheist in ethics.[5] His statement has provoked much discussion for it summarizes in a quotable capsule many ideas we Westerners take for granted. Science is a matter of study, entirely unemotional; in carrying it out, we must accord respect to everything we study, nothing should be beneath our attention, and everything should be seen as equally important. In art, we must be polytheists in order to abandon ourselves to the passions and appetites which, in Goethe's view, are art's special province. But in ethics, he thought, we must be monotheists.

Yet this quotation, as attractive as it is, is anathema to Junko because it abandons the quest for integrity and elevates the lack of integrity to a principle. The real task after all is to integrate the scientist, the artist, and the moralist and to be one whole person whose honesty and integrity inform all our thoughts, our actions, and our social interactions. This is the project of the centripetal artist, and it is what distinguishes her from other kinds of artists. In order to achieve this kind of integration, the rigid categories into which we are educated have to be transcended and we must be transformed.

I would not say that Junko and I learned how to compromise and live with each other, I as a monotheist and she as a polytheist; I as a Western Jew, she as a Japanese Christian-Shinto-Buddhist; I as a lawyer, she as an artist. Instead, we both became transformed so that I am no longer the kind of Jew, monotheist, or lawyer that I was before, and she is no longer the kind of Japanese, Shinto, Buddhist, Christian, polytheist that she was before. Our identities have become fluid—not fixed. The intermixing of cultures, backgrounds, and identities goes far, far beyond "cohabitation" or "accommodation": in the quest for integrity, the coarse matter with which we began has been refined and purified and sublimated and recombined, and something brand new has come out. It is as if we have leaped into a furnace—the kind of furnace the alchemists used in their unceasing efforts to turn lead into gold: the furnace called the "*athanor*"—an Arabic word, cognate to "*tanur*" in Hebrew, meaning "furnace."[6] Things are put into this furnace and left there for a prescribed time, and then pulled out—and they are changed.

What is marriage after all, but such a furnace? Of course it is many things. It is an apotheosis of romantic love, and of friendship. It is the locus of intimacy made possible by the process of separation and individuation: "therefore shall man leave his father and his mother and cling to his wife, and they shall become one flesh." It is the union of opposites when it is between man and woman, and it is the formation of the matrix in which children can be raised. It is a contract and an exchange of vows, and a commitment so deep that it can be called a sacrament. And it is a fertility rite which gives joy to the community which it helps to perpetuate. It is of course all these things.

But I see it also as the *athanor*, the furnace into which we leap every day and from which we emerge always changed and ennobled.

And this brings me back to the question with which Junko and I struggled so hard for so many years: *Why on earth does God have to paint?* Each of us has arrived at an answer—but you will not be surprised to hear that our answers are slightly different.

For me, the answer comes with the observation that Junko's studio is another *athanor* all by itself. In her centripetal art, all the things I have spoken of in this book—the memories, the cultural influences, the psychological, philosophical, and religious ideas, the narratives, the courage, and the altered states of the mystic—all are thrown together, and transformed and refined, and out come the art works. This I would say is an authentic process of creation similar to God's own process, and this, I think, is why God has to paint. His creation is not and never was the making of something out of nothing, but it is rather the process of encountering the world in utter honesty, and transforming it by making it manifest to us.[7] This process is never complete: God requires our participation to complete it.[8] And centripetal art is one of the highest forms of participation.

For Junko, this participation is something that happens between the artist and the viewer: it is the special quality of centripetal art. As she has written:

Essay "Altered States of Consciousness and the Process of Creating Art," 1999

Art has the power to help penetrate and crumble down the viewer's own defensive wall, to help him become a whole person and to step even further towards the divine presence in himself. What is required of the artist here is not to create "religious figures" or "mythological symbols." Instead the artist dives into his or her deepest personal abyss—to the depth where the most personal thing has become the most universal. If the artist succeeds in going through this most difficult, dangerous process truthfully, only then, encountering the art, the viewer might follow a journey to his or her own transcending. God needs to use this deepest personal abyss where the most personal thing has become the most universal because this is the mystery of art. It is through this mystery that God reveals Himself at the center of each of us.

May this book move you to ask this question for yourself, and to formulate the answer that is most convincing to you.

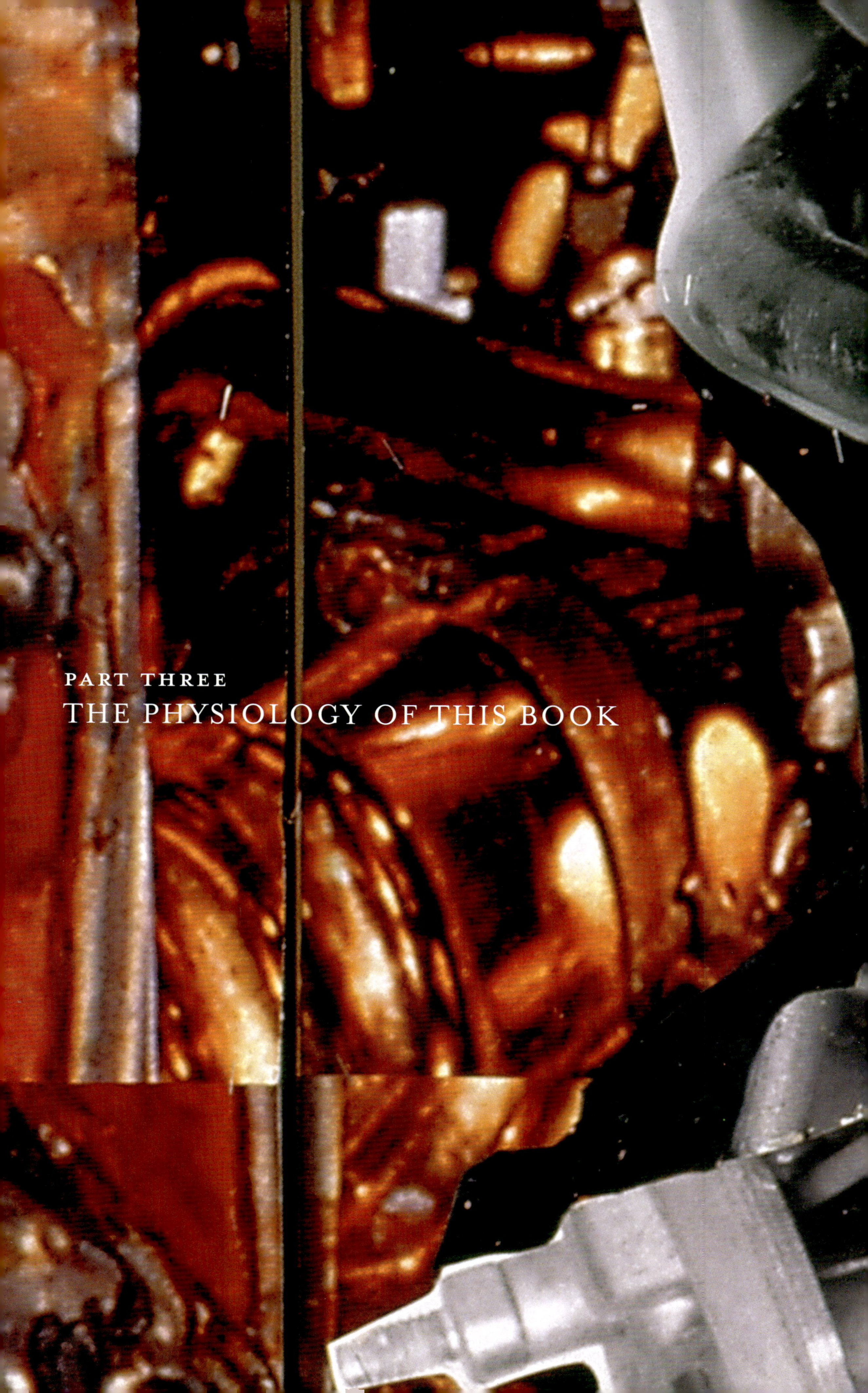

PART THREE
THE PHYSIOLOGY OF THIS BOOK

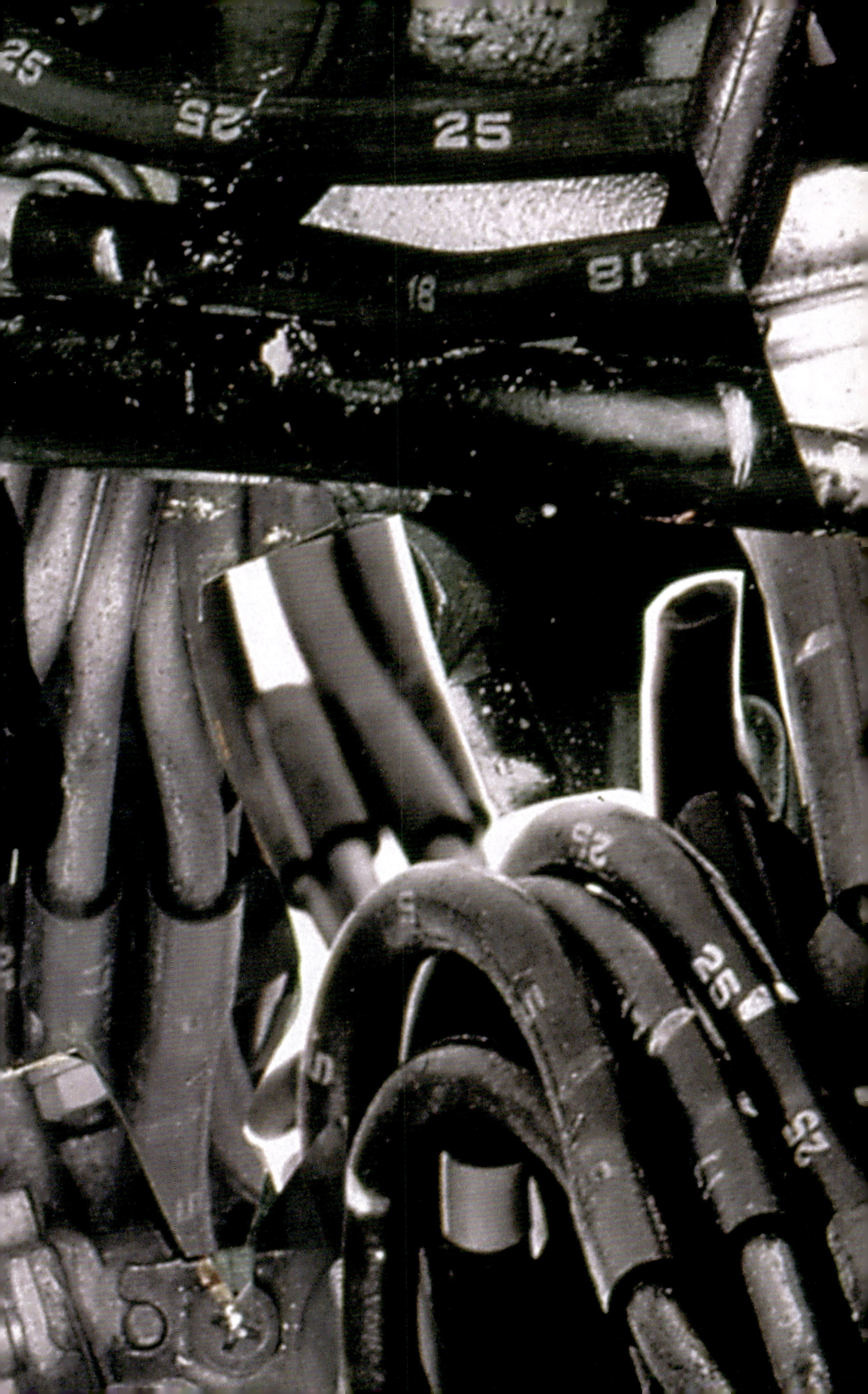
25
18
18
25

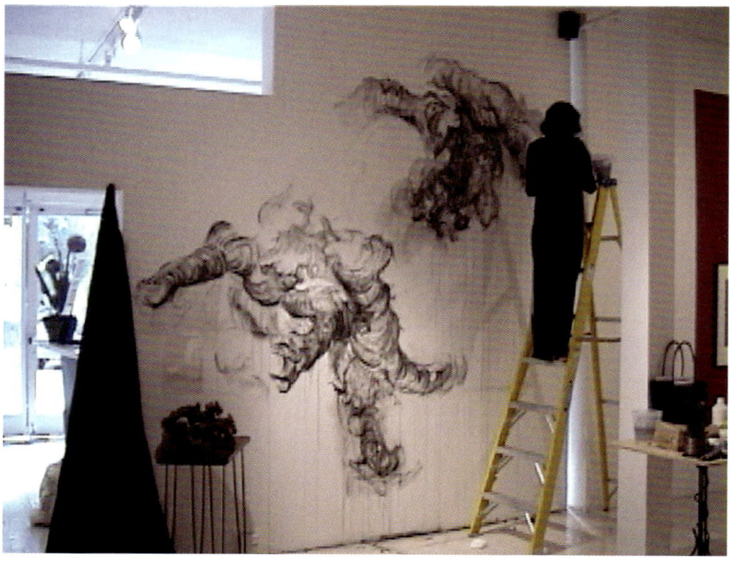

Toss yourselves into the air
and I will dance with you

The day before Junko's one-person exhibit at the Boulder Museum of Contemporary Art was t
open, the director of the museum asked her to fill a large wall in the exhibit space, 12 feet high an
12 feet wide. Using just charcoal, paper towels, a step-ladder, and a bucket of water, Junko mac
this graffiti in the space of a few hours.

The Wall from
Junko Chodos: A Passionate Witness
BMOCA, June 27 - August 31, 2002

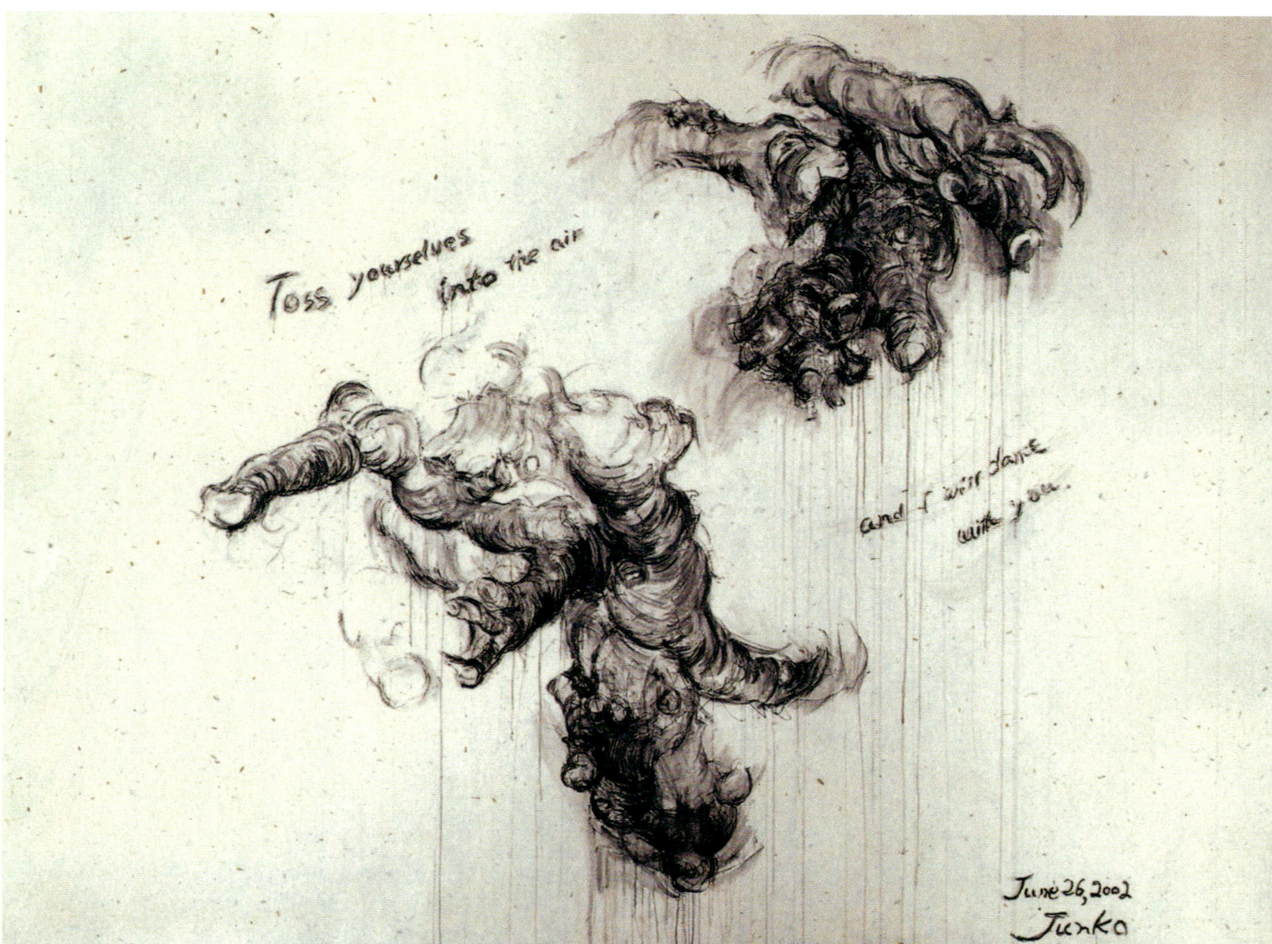

CURRICULUM VITAE Junko Chodos

BACKGROUND AND INTERESTS

1939 Born in Tokyo, Japan. Spent her childhood during and after World War II.

1961 - 1962 First visit to the United States. Attended classes for one academic year at Starr-King School for the Ministry (Unitarian), Berkeley, California.

1966 • Graduated from Waseda University. B.A. in Eastern and Western Art History, and the Philosophy of Art.
• Studied Mysticism and the philosophy of Martin Buber with Prof. Shigeo Ueda, noted translator of Buber into Japanese.
• Graduation Thesis, "Spirituality in Line: Interrelationship of Art and Religiosity."

1968 Moved to the United States.

1969 - 1970 Studied on a scholarship at State University of New York-Buffalo, Art major.

1971 Married Rafael Chodos, Lawyer, Author.

1972 Masahisa Goi made contact; deep influence received.

1981 Masahisa Goi died.

1988 Became naturalized U.S. citizen.

1995 With her husband, began supporting and participating regularly in seminars at Claremont Graduate University co-sponsored by the Institute for Antiquity & Christianity and the Medieval Studies Department, building the philosophical basis of her art and developing a relationship with other intellectual endeavors such as religion and philosophy, in the context of the history of ideas.

2004 With her husband, began supporting the Center for the Study of the Hellenistic Tradition, based at the Central European University in Budapest, and began a deep communication with scholars from all over Europe relating to the exchange of ideas between East and West.

2005 - 2006 Deeply involved in collaborative *FATHOM* project with MalashockDance in San Diego. Besides studio work, developed translations of Kuukai's texts, wrote her own poem for use in choral work composed by Ariel Blumenthal, and gave several talks to the dance company's supporters.

SELECTED SOLO EXHIBITIONS

2006 North Park Theater, San Diego, California, *FATHOM: The Body as Universe*. Stage art for dance production: 40 panels grouped into seven scenes, each group 15 feet high by 35 feet wide.

2005 Fresno Art Museum, *Junko Chodos: Translucent Meditations*, one-person show given as part of Council of 100 Distinguished Woman Artist of the Year award.

2005 Museum of Contemporary Religious Art, St. Louis, Missouri, *Junko Chodos: The Breath of Consciousness*.

2003 Graduate Theological Union, Berkeley, California, *Requiem for an Executed Bird*, at the Flora Lamson Hewlett Library.

2002 Boulder Museum of Contemporary Art, Boulder, Colorado *Junko Chodos: A Passionate Witness*.

2001 Long Beach Museum of Art, Long Beach, California *Metamorphoses: The Transformative Vision of Junko Chodos.*

1995 Pacific Asia Museum (Foyer Gallery), Pasadena, California, *In the Forest of Amida Buddha.*

1992 • L.A. Artcore Annex, Curated by Rafael Chodos. Los Angeles, California, *Art, Mysticism and Psychology*
• Space Gallery, Los Angeles, California, *Junko Chodos - Painting*

1988 Frank Bustamante Gallery, New York, New York, *Junko Chodos Recent Works on Paper*

1984 Fujii Garo Art Salon, Tokyo, Japan, *The Universe Moves and Humans Dance: Junko Chodos One-Person Show.*

1979 • Gallery Nakatsumi, Osaka, Japan, *Staring at Inner Light: Junko Chodos One-Person Show.*
• Tokyo Central Museum, Tokyo, Japan, *Staring at Inner Light: Junko Chodos One-Person Show.*

1973 Alibrandi Bottega of Art, Boston, Massachusetts, *First One-Person Show of the Artist Junko Chodos.*

SELECTED GROUP EXHIBITIONS

2006 Fresno Art Museum, Fresno, California, *Eighteen Profiles: Distinguished Women Artists of California.*

1997 Long Beach Museum of Art, Long Beach, California, *Roadmaps: Structure, Process and the Collection*

1996 Asian American Arts Center, New York, New York, *"Passion and Compassion: Five Artists' Reflections on Buddhism,"*

1995 Long Beach Museum of Art, Long Beach, California, *Crossing Currents (Permanent Collection Show)*

1994 Long Beach Museum of Art, Long Beach, California, *New Acquisitions Show*

1993 Couturier Gallery, Los Angeles, California, *Present Art*

1992 • Olga Dollar Gallery, Curated by Edward Lau. San Francisco, California, *Collage/Assemblage,*
• Gensler and Associates, Curated by Francine Ellman. Los Angeles, California, *One Square Foot*
• Long Beach Museum of Art, Long Beach, California, *New Acquisitions,*.

1991 Fleck-Ellman Gallery, Aspen, Colorado.

1990 • Space Gallery, Los Angeles, California, *Accretions, Collage and Assemblage*
• Gallery SHO, San Francisco, California.
• Grand Canyon College, A.P. Tell Gallery, Phoenix, Arizona, *Expressions of Faith IV*

1989 • Lancaster Museum/Art Gallery, Lancaster, California, *California Collagists*
• Grand Canyon College, A.P. Tell Gallery, Juried by Bruce D. Kurtz. Phoenix, Arizona, *Expressions of Faith III*

1988 • New York University, New York, New York, *Twelfth Annual Small Works Competition*
• Appalachian State University, Boone, North Carolina.
• Grand Canyon College, A.P. Tell Gallery, Phoenix, Arizona, *Expressions of Faith II.*

1987 Art 54 Gallery, International Art Competition winner, New York. Juried by Janet Salz.

1984 Laguna Beach Museum of Art, Laguna Beach, California. Juried by Henry Hopkins. All California winner.

1981 Galeria Artica, Cuxhaven, West Germany.

SELECTED PUBLIC COLLECTIONS

2008 Central European University, Budapest, Hungary, *Individuation Journal, No. 7, "The Fall of Man"* (1995).

2005 Fresno Art Museum, *Giant Burls, No. 5* (1989)

1998 Long Beach Museum of Art, *Celestial Curtain, No. 1* (1988)

1995 Pacific Asia Museum, *Dead Flower Series, No. 8* (1974)

1994 Long Beach Museum of Art, *Interplanetary Icon, No. 9* (1990)

1991 Long Beach Museum of Art, *Burls Series, No. 18* (1988)

SELECTED LECTURES / PUBLIC SPEAKING ENGAGEMENTS

2006 Symposium at Fresno Art Museum, Fresno, California: *"American Originals: A Lifetime of Art"* Sep. 9, 2006.

2005 60-minute Auditorium Lectures at Fresno Art Museum, Fresno, California

Sep. 9, 2006, *"Artistic Experience as Religious Experience"*
Sep. 10, 2006, *"Spiritual Refugee"*

2005 Radio Interview KWMU—FM (Local NPR Station, St. Louis) Live 45 minutes, with Revd. Terrence Dempsey, Director, Museum of Contemporary Religious Art. Interviewer: Stephen Potter. March 18, 2004.

2004 • Lecture. Claremont Graduate University as part of the conference, "Visions and Dreams", Nov. 13, 2004 (60 minutes) *"Artistic Experience as Religious Experience"*

• 30-minute lecture followed by discussion on Art and Spirituality at Graduate Theological Union, Berkeley, California, Feb. 7, 2004. Symposium jointly sponsored by GTU and the Society for the Arts, Religion, and Contemporary Culture, *"Art and Spirituality."*

2003 Lecture at Graduate Theological Union, Berkeley. California, Oct. 9, 2003, *"Spirituality and the Process of Creating Art"* (60 minutes)

2002 Lecture, Claremont Graduate University, as part of the conference, THE EMPIRE OF TRANSLATION, Nov. 9, 2002 *"Following the Pillar of Fire: From Loss of Language to Visual Expression,"* (60 minutes)

2002 Lecture, Naropa University (Boulder, Colorado) – Summer Writing Workshop, *"Spiritual Refugee."* (60 minutes)

2001 Lecture, Getty Museum, as part of the conference on EXILE, *"Following the Pillar of Fire: From Loss of Language to Artistic Expression,"* Dec. 8, 2001 (30 minutes)

1999 • Lecture, Claremont Graduate University, Conference on Exile, *"Spiritual Refugee,"* Nov. 13, 1999 (30 minutes)
• Lecture and slide show, Long Beach Museum of Art, March 14, 1996, *"Transcending Ethnicity: The Creative Process"* (90 minutes)

1996 Lecture and slide show, Long Beach Museum of Art, March 14, 1996, *"Transcending Ethnicity: The Creative Process"* (90 minutes)

1992 Lecture and slide show, Association for Transpersonal Psychology, Annual Conference, Asilomar, California, August 28-30, 1992, *"Transcending Suffering Through the Artistic Process"* (90 minutes)

SELECTED BOOKS, ARTICLES, AND MULTIMEDIA PRODUCTIONS

2005 DVD, *Cry of Ecstasy!*, A film by Robert Primes, ASC. Violinist Malcolm Goldstein responding to nine works by Junko Chodos. Produced by Giotto Multimedia.

2002 Article, *"Spiritual Refugee" CrossCurrents,* Winter 2003.

2001 Hardcover book, *Metamorphoses: The Transformative Vision of Junko Chodos* Published collaboratively by Giotto Multimedia and the Long Beach Museum of Art. Winner, 2002 Independent Publishers Award, 1st Prize in Art category.

1999 Interactive CD-ROM, *Requiem for an Executed Bird* produced by Giotto Multimedia and designed by Aswan Karapetian.

1992 • Videotape *Junko Chodos: A Spiritual Artist for the New Renaissance Age* produced and directed by William Barnett, c. 20 minutes.
• Videotape *Junko Chodos: Art, Mysticism and Psychology* produced and directed by Rafael Chodos, c. 18 minutes.

SELECTED REVIEWS

2006 Janice Steinberg, "*FATHOM* Contains Complex Ideas," *San Diego Union-Tribune*, May 12, 2006, review of collaborative dance program produced by MalashockDance.

2005 Ivy Cooper, "The Breath of Consciousness," *Riverfront Times*, St. Louis, Missouri, April 26, 2005.

2004 Patrice Wagner, "Junko Chodos at the Graduate Theological Union", *Artweek*, March 2004 and COVER

2002 Cara Hopkins, "Painting with Sound," *Colorado Daily*, August 20, 2004.

1995
- William Wilson, "Junko Chodos Finds a Way 'In the Forest'," *Los Angeles Times*, April 14, 1995.
- Peter Frank, in "Art Pics of the Week", *L.A. Weekly*, May 12-18, 1995

1993 Mac McCloud, "Stuff and Presence", *Visions*, Los Angeles, California, Summer.

1992
- James Scarborough, "Junko Chodos," *Visions*, Los Angeles, California, December, pp. 52-53.
- Peter Frank, "Art Pick of The Week," *LA Weekly*, Los Angeles, California, October 23-October 29th.
- James D. Williams, et al., *The Interdisciplinary Reader*, Harper Collins Publications , pp. 621-624

1991 Noriko Gamblin, "Junko Chodos," *Visions*, Los Angeles, California, Summer 1991.

1990
- Suvan Geer, "Art Reviews," *Los Angeles Times,* Calendar section, July 13th.
- Suzanne Lummis, "Into the Mystic: Junko Chodos' Interplanetary Icons," *Los Angeles Downtown News*, July 9th.

1988 • David Pagel, "Lifting the Curtain: Junko Chodos," *Visions*, Los Angeles, California, Fall 1988.
• Cynthia H. Craft, "Century Gallery Showcases Art, the Environment," *Los Angeles Times*, June 17th, 1988.
• *Bijutsu Techo*, Japanese nationwide monthly art magazine, June 1998 issue, "News from Abroad."
• "Staring at the Light Beyond the Darkness", *Asahi Shimbun* satellite edition, New York and Los Angeles, April 8, 1988.

1984 • Amaury Saint-Gilles, "Art: People and Places," *Mainichi Daily News*, Tokyo, Japan, September 20, 1984.
• "Junko Chodos One Person Show," *Mainichi Shimbun*, Tokyo, Japan, September 20, 1984.
• "The Globe of the Earth is the Canvas", in *People*, *Asahi Shimbun*, September 6, 1984.

1980 "Junko Chodos Collage," *Geijutsu Shincho*, Japanese monthy nationwide art magazine, June 1980 Issue.

1979 • "Junko Chodos' Show," *Mainichi Shimbun*, Osaka, Japan, December 5, 1979.
• "Rich, Dense Beauty," *Kobe Shimbun*, Osaka, Japan, December 4, 1979.
• Amaury Saint-Gilles, "Art: People and Places," *Mainichi Daily News*, Tokyo, Japan, November 17, 1979.
• "Exhibition: Junko Chodos' One-Person Show," *Mainichi Shimbun*, Tokyo, Japan, November 16, 1979.
• "Finding Self in Encounter with Root: Japanese Woman Who Lives in America has One-Person Show," *Asahi Shimbun*, Tokyo, Japan, November 15, 1979.

1973 "It's the Way of the Devil," Bob Garrett, *Sunday Herald-Advertiser*, Boston, Massachusetts, January 21, 1973.

CURRICULUM VITAE Rafael Chodos

Rafael Chodos is a business litigation attorney who has been in private practice in Los Angeles for 30 years. He specializes in cases and transactions involving the construction and deconstruction of business entities and projects. He became an attorney in his mid-30s, earning a J.D. from Boston University in 1977. He is the author of *The Law of Fiduciary Duties* (2000, Blackthorne Legal Press, 1700 pages), an authoritative treatise found in major law libraries across the country. He published this book in both hard-copy and CD-ROM formats. He is also the author of *The Jewish Attitude Towards Justice and Law* (1984, 101 pages, dist. by E.J. Brill), a book in which he characterizes law as "society's on-going quest for integrity in interpersonal affairs."

Planning in his youth to become a rabbi like his father, he earned his way through college teaching Hebrew, Latin, and Greek, and working as a cantor in various synagogues. He received his B.A. in Philosophy from UC-Berkeley in 1964.

Upon graduating he worked at a wide variety of jobs: as a fisherman in Alaska, as a construction worker in Alaska and Oregon, as a researcher in artificial intelligence in Eugene, Oregon, as a programmer at a major clothing manufacturer in Portland, Oregon, as an assistant editor on a 3-volume set of philosophical writings at McGill University in Montreal, and as a systems programmer at a defense contractor in Hartford, Connecticut.

In the late 1960s he entered the then-fledgling computer software field, in which he remained active for 15 years. During the 1970s he founded and operated an advanced computer software company which developed and marketed "expert systems" used to design very large-scale communications networks for fifty of the largest companies in the United States.

He has published a range of articles and essays on a variety of subjects, including a series of "legal fairy tales" in *The Law of Fiduciary Duties, supra*; an essay titled "God Does Not Require Obedience: He Abhors It" in *The Destructive Power of Religion* (Greenwood Press, J. Harold Ellens, ed., 2004); "Protecting the Righteous Employer Against Abusive Sexual Harassment Claims" (*American Journal of Trial Advocacy*, 1995, reprinted in *The Defense Law Journal*, Fall 1996); "Co-ownership of Copyright and Fiduciary Duty: The Poverty of Preemption" (*New Matter*, Summer 1997, reprinted in *Entertainment and the Arts Handbook*, 1999); and "Law as Dance, Theater, or Music: Legal Procedure and Ritual" (in the Summer 2002 issue of *CrossCurrents* reprinted in *Procession, Performance, Liturgy and Ritual* (Inst. of Medieval Music, Ottawa, 2007). He has also lectured frequently on subjects relating to law and the history of ideas at Claremont Graduate University, Graduate Theological Union, several meetings of the Calfornia State Bar, and at the Museum of Contemporary Art in Los Angeles.

Seven years ago he founded Giotto Multimedia, which is the publisher and producer of several books and videos featuring his wife's art, including *Metamorphoses: The Transformative Vision of Junko Chodos* (co-published with the Long Beach Museum of Art, 2001) and *Cry of Ecstasy* (DVD, 2005).

He recently accepted an invitation from the Peter F. Drucker and Masatoshi Ito Graduate School of Management at Claremont Graduate University to design and teach a course in the Executive MBA program. The course he designed, titled "Law, Ethics, and the Enterprise," was given for the first time in Spring 2008. His website is **chodos.com**.

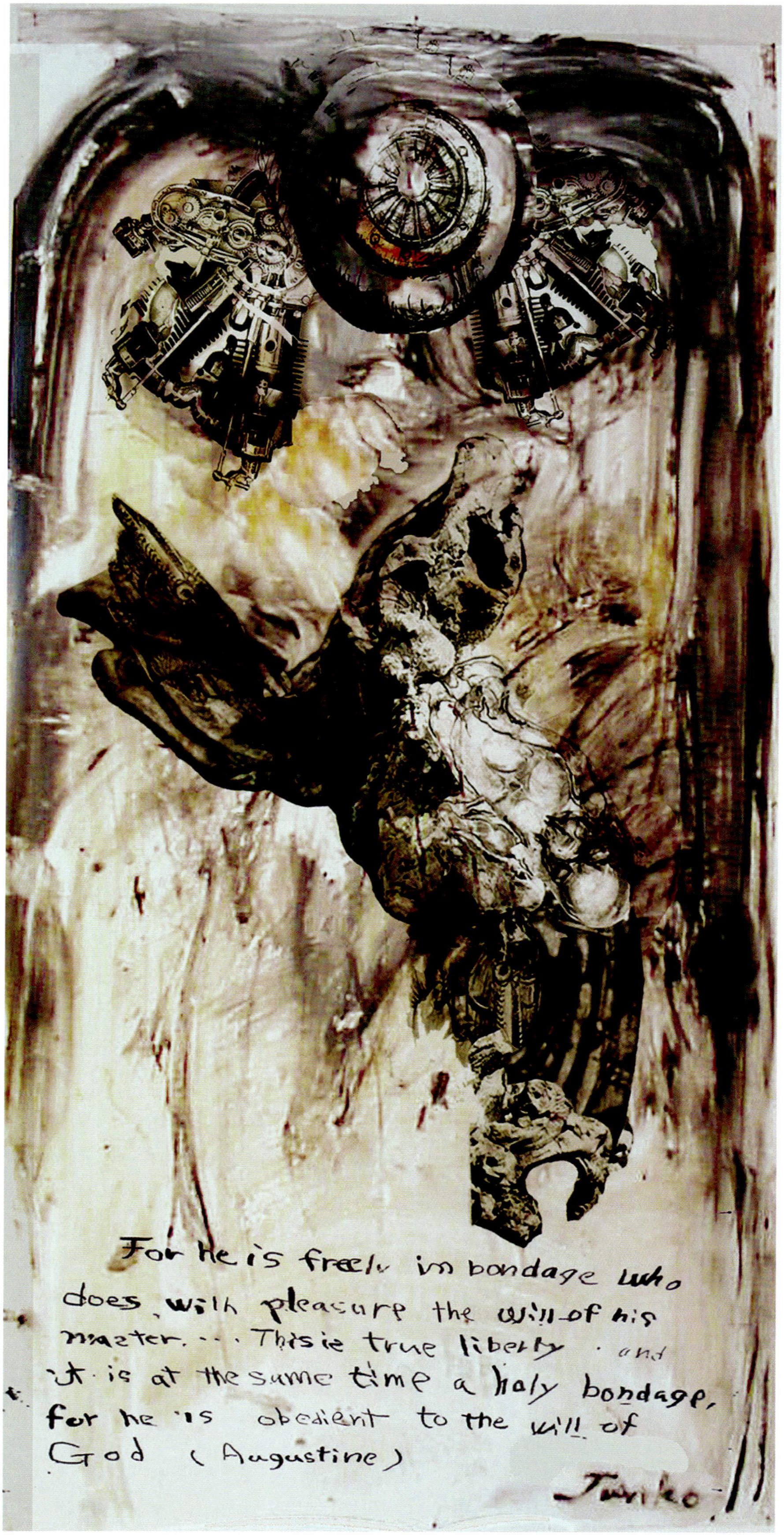
For he is freely in bondage who
does with pleasure the will of his
master. . . This is true liberty . and
it is at the same time a holy bondage,
for he is obedient to the will of
God (Augustine)
Juriko

ENDNOTES

PREFACE

1/ii In order to understand this kind of art we will have to use its native terminology. Recognizing that terms like "center" of the "self", "encounter", and "divine presence" are as evocative as they are denotative, we nevertheless must use them and have trust that we will understand them as they appear and reappear in the discussion that follows.

I speak deliberately of "divine presence"—and not of "the Divine Presence" (using capitals and the definite article), which is a Judaeo-Christian expression tied to monotheism; nor of "a divine presence," which is a polytheistic expression. Without either "a" or "the," the phrase denotes an aspect of the self, or of the world. See *kami* in the Index of Japanese terms. That word was used by Japanese translators of the Bible, to translate "God" —but that is because Japanese had no word for "God" and so they took a familiar word and used it in an unfamiliar way.

Opposite:
Individuation Journal
FREE WILL—AUGUSTINE (1998)
For he is freely in bondage who does with pleasure the will of his master.... This is true liberty and it is at the same time a holy bondage, for he is obedient to the will of God (Augustine)"
Acrylic and charcoal on mylar.
Virtual work
See companion work pg. 233.
Text is from Augustine's Enchiridion.

2/ii That is, from the formalists, structuralists, conceptualists, and minimalists, as well as the "appropriation/simulation" artists of the earlier decades of the past century. See for instance, a collection of essays by Donald Kuspit, *The New Subjectivism: Art in the 1980s*, UMI Research Press, 1988. In the "Foreword," Dianne Waldman distinguishes formalist criticism from subjectivist criticism. In the "Introduction," Kuspit distinguishes the art he is discussing from "appropriation/simulation" art, and there as well as in the essays, he characterizes this sort of art as a "New Expressionism" centering on the subjectivity of the artist himself. But Kuspit's essays demonstrate the rarity of the centripetal artist because for Kuspit, "subjectivity" is hopelessly bound up with narcissism and has little to do with the notion of divine presence. As I discuss in Chapters Four and Six, centripetal art is strongly anti-narcissist by nature, and actually offers a cure for narcissism.

3/iii The death of God: Nietzsche, *Thus Spake Zarathustra*. The death of Art: Arthur C. Danto, *After the End of Art*, A. W. Mellon Lectures in the Fine Arts, (Bollingen Series 44, Princeton University Press, 1995). Also, Hans Belting, *The End of the History of Art?* (1983, Christopher & Wood, 1987)

FOREWORD

1/5 The notion of the "divine darkness" is very much part of Junko's thinking. It is traceable to the writings of the fifth-century mystic, pseudo-Dionysus, sometimes called "Dionysius the Areopagite."

2/6 *Visions*, Summer 1993. Review by Mac McCloud, commenting on the fact that I hung the paintings high on the ceilings, on the structural pillars in the room, on easels away from the wall—as if the images of the bird were flying out towards the viewers.

3/9 See Louis Breger, *Dostoevsky: The Author as Analyst*, New York University Press, 1989. Part of what makes the author great is his ability to maintain an "observing ego" with regard to the events related or imagined so intensely in the novel. This makes the author more like the analyst than the patient. The same applies to the artist, as she maintains distance and objectivity with regard to the things she paints so passionately. See also Chapter Six, pp. 245 ff., discussing Altered States.

CHAPTER ONE

1/24 Ryotaro Shiba, The Japanese title is *The Landscape of Kuukai* but the book was published in English as *Kuukai the Universal: Scenes from His Life* (ICG Muse, 2003).

[2/33] Marinetti wrote, in article 4 of the Futurist Manifesto, "We declare that the splendor of the world has been enriched by a new beauty: the beauty of speed. A racing automobile with its bonnet adorned with great tubes like serpents with explosive breath ... a roaring motor car which seems to run on machine-gun fire, is more beautiful than the Victory of Samothrace."

[3/46] J. David Lewis-Williams, *The Mind in the Cave* (Thames & Hudson, 2002).

[4/72] Joseph Campbell, *The Power of Myth* (1988), PBS Series with Bill Moyers, Companion volume at 222. See picture of *fudômyoô*.

[5/73] Martin Buber, *I and Thou*, trans. Walter Kaufman (Scribner's 1970), p.164.

[6/77] For a fuller description of *FATHOM*, see pp. 184 ff.

CHAPTER TWO

[1/85] The Shogun had unified Japan's feudal system and had ruled over the country for more than two-and-a-half centuries. His rule ended when Commodore Perry appeared from America and demanded that Japan open its country to the world. It was only then, in 1868, that Japan began its modernization and joined the world's industrial capitalistic competition as a latecomer.

CHAPTER THREE

[1/145] Psalm 121:1.

CHAPTER FIVE

[1/197] I speak of the 1930s. But see the excellent catalog accompanying the 1986 exhibition at the Los Angeles County Museum of Art, titled *The Spiritual in Art: Abstract Painting 1890-1985*, ed. Maurice Tuchman. Although the art works represented there were created into the 1980s, the "discourse" had died down by the end of the 1930s.

2/197 Letter to Emil Bernard, Oct. 7, 1888, from Arles.

3/197 Kandinsky, *Concerning the Spiritual in Art*, Trans. M.T.H. Sadler, (Dover Publications, 1977), pg. 12

4/197 Wilhelm Worringer, *Abstraction and Empathy*, trans. Michael Bullock (Elephant Paperbacks, Ivan R. Dee, Inc., 1997).

5/197 Not that Junko ever read Mme. Blavatsky: her ideas come from other sources. But it appears that the earlier group of "spiritual artists" did in fact read Mme. Blavatsky's writings, and treated them as a principal source of the ideas they espoused.

6/197 For example, E.M. Forster's novel dealing with this subject, *A Passage to India*, was published in 1924.

7/197 The nature of each of these artist's involvement with theosophy was different. Picasso was interested in many things and took inspiration from a wide variety of sources—including alchemy and, tangentially, theosophy. Mondrian actually joined the Theosophy Society early in his career; and Kandinsky mentions Blavatsky's ideas with approval in *Concerning the Spiritual in Art* (pp. 13-14). Klee knew of theosophy, but did not identify himself with it. But he nevertheless seems to have agreed with some of the movement's central tenets.

8/198 Van Gogh (1853-1890), Klee (1879-1940), Kandinsky (1866-1944), Freud (1856-1939).

9/201 Edward Steichen, ed., *The Family of Man* (Museum of Modern Art, 1955) contrib. Carl Sandburg.

10/204 Erich Fromm offers what is probably the deepest analysis of the psychological aspects of fascism. See for example *Escape from Freedom* (1941), Chapter VI; and generally, *Heart of Man* (1964).

11/207 Of course, these ideas have been traced to the highly influential eighteenth-century philosopher, Immanuel Kant, whose notion of the "synthetic a priori" can be seen as the epistemological precursor of existentialism. But Kant, influential as he was, does not seem to have had a direct influence on the early twentieth-century artists.

12/209 The invention of gunpowder was also viewed with alarm by thinkers of the time, since it allowed killing at a distance, whereas up till then, killing took place mainly in hand-to-hand combat. [Roman catapults and other means of propelling rocks and explosives into castles and fortresses were not "personal killing" technologies.] But gunpowder did not pollute the environment or disrupt the gene pool.

13/213 Rafael Chodos, *The Jewish Attitude Towards Justice and Law* (1984, dist. EJ Brill). The answer to Junko's question that this book articulates is this: Judaism is the last surviving mystery religion, developed during the rabbinic period on the model of the mystery religions of the Alexandrian Age. But in Judaism, the central mystery is Justice and Law is the techné or secret art. So in Judaism, striving for justice is the way to come closest to God – and this is the contribution that Judaism may make to the twenty-first century.

CHAPTER SIX

1/229 Individuation: Jung, Jung's Collected Works, Vol. 9, *The Archetypes and the Collective Unconscious*, Bollingen Series No. XX, pg. 275, "Conscious, Unconscious and Individuation"; Maslow' "self-actualization" is similar, but places less emphasis on the process of separation which is important to Jung. See also Karen Horney's discussion of neurosis in *Neurosis and Human Growth* (Norton Paperback, 1970).

2/230 Fromm, *Escape from Freedom*, pp. 256-257.

3/231 The quote in the image comes from Fromm, *Escape from Freedom*, pp. 256-257.

4/234 Fromm, *Escape from Freedom*, pp. 266 ff.

5/234 R. G. Collingwood, in *The Principles of Art*, at 282-285

6/247 Goethe, "*The New Melusina*," in *The Sorrows of Young Werther and Selected Writings*, (Signet Classics collection, paperback, 1962).

7/250 See Ken Wilber, "The Spectrum of Consciousness" in *The Eye of Spirit* (Shambhala 2001),; also essays collected in *Beyond Ego*, eds. Roger N. Walsh and Frances Vaughan (1980, J. P. Tarcher), particularly Secs. 1 and 2. And of course William James, *The Varieties of Religious Experience* (Simon and Schuster, 1997), based on James' Gifford lectures at the end of the nineteenth century which awakened Western audiences to the idea that there is more than one kind of authentic religious experience.

8/250 Erich Neumann, "night sea journey", in *The Origins and History of Consciousness* (Bollingen Series XLII, Princeton University Press 1954), pp. 408, 415. More generally, Neumann's notion of the "dragon fight" as part of the later-stage development, the notion of the Hero.

9/251 Jung, "numinous feeling" discussed at pg. 544 and ff. of *Mysterium Coniunctionis* (trans. R.F.C. Hull, *Collected Works on Jung*, vol. 13, Princeton University Press 1963).

CHAPTER SEVEN

1/263 The journey: see Campbell, *supra*, Chapter V. Otto Rank, *The Myth of the Birth of the Hero* (trans. Richter and Liebermann, original German edn. 1909, Johns Hopkins University Press 2004). But I say the journey is out of fashion because in the last decades of the twentieth century, there was a greater emphasis placed on sociology than on psychology. Even though the last century saw the birth of both these two major intellectual developments, it was sociology that ended up becoming the dominant intellectual force and psychology has receded. I think this is largely due to the ascendance of media, who find it both easier and more profitable to focus on the sociological aspects of the world than on its psychological aspects. Groups, once formed, tend to be interested in the same things, and so one can sell multiple copies of the same article to all members of a group—if they believe they are part of a group. The hero's journey, though, is fundamentally a psychological notion—not a sociological one.

2/265 Aristotle's *Poetics*, 1449b28, discussing catharsis. And the whole book discusses "imitation." Of course, Aristotle is discussing tragedy—not visual art, but he believes that the arousal of "pity and fear" through "imitation" is common also to the visual arts, and that the "purging" of these feelings is the point of the art.

3/265 This theory of aesthetics is expounded in a Chinese classic text, the *Kogahinroku*, fourth century, which lays out the six canons or principles thought to be essential for the appreciation of Chinese painting. The first of these is "spirit resonance" which is translated into Japanese as "*ki*".

4/265 Exodus 33:20.

5/267 Modelling is different from imitation. In fact, the notion of "modelling" turns the classical idea that "art imitates life" on its head. The truth is that when the art is successful, the artist models something for us and we are inspired to imitate the art.

AFTERWORD

1/272 This aesthetic principle is fundamental to centripetal art, and is part of what defines it. For many artists, though, who do not consider themselves "centripetal," great art does not have to involve any kind of pain or displeasure at all—or any effort on the part of the viewer.

2/272 Esoteric Buddhism has many more adherents in Japan than Zen Buddhism—which is the kind of Buddhism most familiar to Westerners. Esoteric Buddhism derives from tantric sources, and instead of the cool, restrained, minimalist mood of Zen, it is characterized by an enthusiastic affirmation of the life force in all its forms.

3/273 The notion that religions can be arranged in a hierarchy is widespread, particularly among Western religions. The idea that "our God" is "higher" than "the gods of the other peoples" is expressed often in the Old Testament (Genesis 35:2; Exodus 12, 20, 23; Deuteronomy 6:14, 12:12) and is ingrained in Western religious thought. The idea was enshrined in the work of the nineteenth-century anthropologist, Edward Burnett Tylor, who saw animism and nature worship as lowest in the ranking of religions, and Christianity as the highest manifestation of religion. But of course, the "Great Hierarchy" of religions was as much a social and political construct as a scientific idea. Western colonialists needed to believe that they were bringing the "higher" religion to the peoples they were subduing, whose indigenous religions they wanted to see as "primitive" and "lower."

4/274 See *God: A Biography*, by Jack Miles (Knopf, 1995) at pp. 4-7.

5/276 Goethe, Letter to Jakobi (1813). See Jaroslav Pelikan, *Faust the Theologian* (Yale University Press, 1995), in which he applies this 3-part structure to Faust.

6/277 *Athanor.* See Herbert Silberer and Smith Ely Jelliffe, *The Problems of Mysticism and Its Symbolism* (Kessinger Press, 1917). Also Jung, *Alchemical Studies* (Bollingen Series XX, Princeton University Press, 1967), at pp. 137 ff. for the development of the idea of the "furnace" as a transformative environment.

7/278 An idea adopted by the Kabbalists, that God's act of creation was not a creation of something out of nothing, but an act of revealing that which was hidden. See recently, Adin Steinsaltz, *The Thirteen Petalled Rose* (Basic Books, 2006), pg. 26.

8/278 The idea that the act of creation is on-going and that God requires our participation to complete it, is a cornerstone of Jewish mysticism. See for instance, Talmud Shabbat 10a, "Every judge who judges a case with complete fairness for even a minute participates with God in the act of creation." Also, Abraham Joshua Heschel, *Man Is Not Alone* (Noonday Press, 1951) pg. 144.

BIBLIOGRAPHY

Aristotle, *Poetics*. Revised Oxford Translation, Princeton: Bollingen Seriews LXXI v. 2, 1984.

Augustine. *The Enchiridion on Faith, Hope, and Love*. Washington, D.C.: Regnery Press, 1961.

Belting, Hans *The End of the Hsistory of Art, 1983,* translated by Christopher S. Wood, Chicago: University of Chicago Press, 1987

Blavatsky, H.P. *Isis Unveiled.* 1877. Reprint. Pasadena, Calif.: Theosophical University Press, 1999.

Blavatsky, H.P. *The Secret Doctrine.* 1888. Reprint. Pasadena, Calif.: Theosophical University Press, 1999.

Breger, Louis *Dostoevsky: The Author as Analyst,* New York University Press 1989.

Buber, Martin *I and Thou.* Translated by Ronald Gregor Smith. New York: Scribner, 1970.

Campbell, Joseph, *The Power of Myth.* New York: Doubleday, 1988.

Chodos, Rafael. *The Jewish Attitude Towards Justice and Law,* Dist. E. J. Brill, Leiden, 1984.

Cohn, Norman, *The Pursuit of the Millennium: Revolutionary Millenarians and Mystical Anarchists of the Middle Ages.* New York: Oxford University Press, 1970.

Collingwood, R.G. *The Principles of Art.* Oxford: Clarendon Press, 1938.

Danto, Arthur C. *After the End of Art.* The A.W. Mellon Lectures in the Fine Arts, 1995. Bollingen Series, 35:44. Princeton: Princeton University Press, 1997.

Forster, E.M. *A Passage to India.* New York: Harcourt, Brace, 1924.

Fromm, Erich. *The Anatomy of Human Destructiveness.* New York: Holt, Rinehart & Winston, 1973.

———. *Escape from Freedom.* New York: Farrar & Rinehart, 1941.

———. *Man for Himself.* New York: Rinehart, 1947.

———. *The Heart of Man: Its Genius for Good and Evil .* New York: Harper & Row 1964

Goethe, Johann Wolfgang von. *The New Melusina.* In *The Sorrows of Young Werther and Selected Writings,* tr. Catherine Hutter. Signet Classics 1962

Goldenberg, Naomi. *The Changing of the Gods.* Boston: Beacon Press, 1979.

Heschel, Abraham Joshua. *God in Search of Man.* New York: Noonday Press, 1951.

———. *Man Is Not Alone.* New York: Farrar, Straus & Young, 1951.

Horney, Karen, *Neurosis and Human Growth.* New York: W.W. Norton & Company, Inc. 1950.

Huizinga, Johan. *The Waning of the Middle Ages.* Garden City, N.Y.: Doubleday, 1954.

James, William. *The Varieties of Religious Experience.* New York: Simon and Schuster, 1997 (paperback edition).

Jung, Carl Justav. *Alchemical Studies.* Bollingen Series, XX. Princeton, N.J.: Princeton University Press, 1967.

———. *The Archetypes and the Collecxtive Unconscious,* Bollingen Series, XX. Princeton, N.J.: Pantheon Books, 1959.

———. *Psychology and Alchemy* 2d ed. Bollingen Series, XX. Princeton, N.J.: Princeton University Press, 1968.

———. *Mysterium Coniunctionis,* 2d ed., Bollingen Series, XX, Princeton, N.J.: Princeton University Press, 1963

Kandinsky, Wassily. *Concerning the Spiritual in Art.* Translated by M.T.H. Sadler. 1914. Reprint. New York: Dover Publications, 1977.

Klee, Paul. *The Thinking Eye.* 2 vols. New York: G. Wittenborn, 1961.

Kuspit, Donald, *The New Subjectivism: Art in the 1980s,* UMI Research Press, 1988.

Lewis-Williams, J. David. *The Mind in the Cave.* New York: Thames & Hudson, 2002.

Lipsey, Roger. *An Art of Our Own: The Spiritual in Twentieth-Century Art.* Boston: Shambhala, 1988.

Marinetti, F.T. *The Futurist Manifesto.* First published in *Le Figaro* (Paris), 20 February 1909.

McBrien, Richard, ed. *The HarperCollins Encyclopedia of Catholicism,* s.v. "Relics." New York: HarperCollins, 1995.

Miles, Jack, God: *A Biography,* New York: Knopf, 1995.

Neumann, Erich. *The Origins and History of Consciousness.* Princeton, N.J.: Princeton University Press, 1954.

Nietzsche, Friedrich Wilhelm. *The Genealogy of Morals. In The Birth of Tragedy and The Genealogy of Morals.* Translated by Francis Golffing. Garden City, N.Y.: Doubleday, 1956.

———. *Thus Spake Zarathustra.* Los Angeles: Gateway Editions, 1957.

Pelikan, Jaroslav. *Faust the Theologian.* New Haven, Conn.: Yale University Press, 1995.

Read, Herbert. *Icon and Idea.* Cambridge: Harvard University Press, 1955.

Regier, Kathleen J., ed. *The Spiritual Image in Modern Art.* Wheaton, Ill.: Theosophical Publishing House, 1987.

Rilke, Rainer Maria. *The Duino Elegies.* Translated by C.F. Macintyre. Berkeley: University of California Press, 1961.

Sedlmayr, Hans, *Art in Crisis: The Loss of the Center,* original English edition 1957, now available from Transaction Publishers, 2006.

Shiba, Ryotaro. *Kukai the Universal: Scenes from His Life.* Translated by Akiko Takemoto. New York: ICG Muse, 2003.

Silberer, Herbert, and Smith Ely Jelliffe. *Problems of Mysticism and Its Symbolism.* New York: Moffat, Yard, 1917.

Steichen, Edward, ed. *The Family of Man.* New York: The Museum of Modern Art, 1955.

Talmud, Babylonian. Shabbat 10a.

Tuchman, Maurice, ed. *The Spiritual in Art.* New York: Abbeville Press, 1986.

van Gogh, Vincent. *The Letters of Vincent van Gogh.* New York: Atheneum, 1963.

Walsh, Roger N., and Frances Vaughan, eds. *Beyond Ego.* Los Angeles: J.P. Tarcher, 1980.

Wilber, Ken. *The Eye of Spirit.* 3d ed. Boston: Shambhala, 2001.

Worringer, Wilhelm. *Abstraction and Empathy.* Translated by Michael Bullock. Chicago: Ivan R. Dee, Inc. 1997.

LIST OF CITATIONS TO WRITINGS OF JUNKO CHODOS

PAGE	TYPE	TITLE
P.15	Series Statement	Dead Flowers, 1973
P.15	Studio Notebook	1983
P.21	Series Statement	Roots, 1979
P.24	Letter to a Friend	2001
P.26	Series Statement	Engines, 1982
P.28	Studio Notebook	2000
P.28	Letter to a Friend	2001
P.31	Essay	"Esoteric Buddhism," 2001
P.35	Series Statement	Horseshoe Crab, 1983
P.35	Studio Notebook	2003
P.39	Series Statement	Curtains, 1988
P.40	Letter to a Friend	2001
P.46	Studio Notebook	2003
P.48	Series Statement	Relic, 1984
P.50	Studio Notebook	2001
P.52	Series Statement	Burls, 1989
P.52	Studio Notebook	1989
P.56	Studio Notebook	1987 (Decanter)
P.62	Series Statement	Universe Moves and Humans Dance, 1984
P.67	Studio Notebook	1998 (Deformed Babies)
P.73	Studio Notebook	1986
P.73	Studio Notebook	1987 (Decanter)
P.76	Studio Notebook	1989 (Deformed Babies)
P.76	Studio Notebook	1989 (Deformed Babies)
P.77	Series Statement	Tree Spirits in Gold, 1991
P.90	From Lecture	"Transcending Ethnicity: The Creative Process," Long Beach Museum, 1996
P.91	From Mansion of the Motoyasu	1999
P.96	From Memoir	2005

PAGE	TYPE	TITLE
P. 98	From Memoir	2005
P.100	From Memoir	2005
P.102	From Memoir	2005
P.104	From Memoir	2005
P.107	From Lecture	"Following the Pillar of Fire: From Language to Artistic Expression," Getty Museum, 2001
P.109	From Lecture	"Transcending Ethnicity: The Creative Process," Long Beach Museum of Art, 1996
P.111	Metamorphoses	From Interview by Noriko Gamblin, 2001
P.142	Studio Notebook	2005
P.151	Studio Notebook	2006
P.167	Studio Diary	May 1991
P.168	Studio Diary	May 1991
P.171	Studio Diary	May 1991 (continuing)
P.173	Studio Diary	June, 1991
P.173	Studio Diary	June 1991 (continuing)
P.174	Studio Diary	June 1991 (continuing)
P.174	Studio Diary	July 1991
P.179	From Memoir	2005
P.181	From Memoir	2005
P.183	From Memoir	2005
P.187	Studio Notebook	2005
P.188	Studio Notebook	April 2002
P.189	Studio Notebook	May 2003
P.190	Studio Notebook	September, 2005
P.191	Essay	"Altered States of Consciousness and the Process of Creating Art," 1999
P.202	From Lecture	"Following the Pillar of Fire: From Language to Artistic Expression," Getty Museum, 2001
P.220	Letter to a Friend	2001
P.250	Studio Diary	1989
P.251	Studio Diary	1988

PAGE	TYPE	TITLE
P.253	Studio Diary	1988
P.255	Studio Diary	1989
P.258	Studio Notebook	1991
P.261	From Lecture	"Spirituality and the Process of Creating Art," Graduate Theological Union, Oct. 9, 2003
P.278	Essay	"Altered States of Consciousness and the Process of Creating Art," 1999

JAPANESE TERMS USED IN THIS BOOK

BYOOBU A screen, sometimes used as a room divider, but more often used to separate a room to mark some space as special or holy. Junko's *Dead Flower Series, No. 8*, is subtitled "Byoobu" because it is intended to mark the space in which it is displayed as holy and special.

FUDŌMYOŌ A "horrific deity," mentioned in Chapter One, Section Two. Usually shown holding a sword, with hugely angry eyes and prominent musculature, and flames in back of him. His function is to destroy every obstacle to enlightenment.

GAKUSHŪIN A school established in 1877, during the Meiji era, to teach the children of the aristocracy. The Emperor's family was educated there (Emperor Hirohito was an alumnus). After WWII, the school opened itself up to commoners, and Junko was one of the first generation of these to attend. See Chapter Two.

JINGU A Shinto Shrine, literally "god palace." See description of Meiji Jingu in the Afterword.

KAKEJIKU, KAKEMONO A Japanese vertical scroll painting, usually hanging unrolled in the *tokonoma* (see below). Many of Junko's paintings are like these scroll paintings: vertically oriented, sometimes integrating texts and images, with lots of white space and the sense of energy reminiscent of brushwork.

KAMI A divine spirit. The Japanese believe that there is a *kami* in every tree, every river, every mountain—everywhere. This word might be translated "divine presence" (see Preface). When, in the nineteenth century, Japanese scholars set about to make an official translation of the Bible they were unfamiliar with the word "God" and the notion of monotheism, and they had no concept of an almighty masculine authority. After much trial and error, they used *kami* as the translation. In Junko's notebooks and diaries, which are written originally in Japanese, she uses *kami*. Throughout this book, we translate that into "God" and because of that, this translation might be a little awkward.

KAMISHIBAI Literally, "paper theater." A story told, often to children, with the key scenes illustrated on cardboard cards which the story teller displays in a small stage as in a frame, one by one as he tells the story. See the careful description in Chapter Four.

KI Life force, or spiritual energy. It is *ki* which the martial artist masters and directs where he will. Oriental medicine is based on the idea that sickness comes about when *ki* stops circulating properly throughout the body, and the doctor's skill is to release the blockages. The artist, also, leaves the trace of her *ki* on the paper or scroll. See discussion in Chapters Six and Seven. According to the *Kogahinroku*, mentioned in Chapter Seven, the fourth-century tractate on aesthetics, this quality of art is one of its most important elements.

NOREN A curtain which commonly hangs at the entrance to retail stores or restaurants. It is cut into three sections to allow people to pass through it easily. Junko's Giant Burls, with a large central section and two smaller side sections, are reminiscent of this form

SHOJI A sliding screen or door made of rice paper on a wooden grid. It is interesting to us Westerners because even when it is closed, it is possible to hear what is going on behind it, and even to see shadows cast on it. But for the Japanese, when the shoji screen is closed, the space behind it is private. See mention in the story of "tsu" in Chapter Six.

TATAMI Mats made from the *igusa* plant, thickly woven, and used in Japanese rooms as floor coverings. A room's size is usually designated in the number of tatami it takes to cover its floor. See the mention of it in Junko's original encounter with the slaughtered bird, in Chapter One.

TOKONOMA A special area in a Japanese room, with a raised platform, usually decorated with a flower arrangement and a *kakemono*. This alcove is a special space, which serves as a sort of gateway from the everyday world into another world. See discussion in Chapter Three.

TORII The gate to a Shinto shrine: a gateway to a divine space. Constructed of two tall wooden beams and two cross beams. Below is a picture of the *torii* at Meiji Jingu. You can see how tall it is from the figure passing under it (not me). See description of the path to Meiji Jingu in the Afterword.

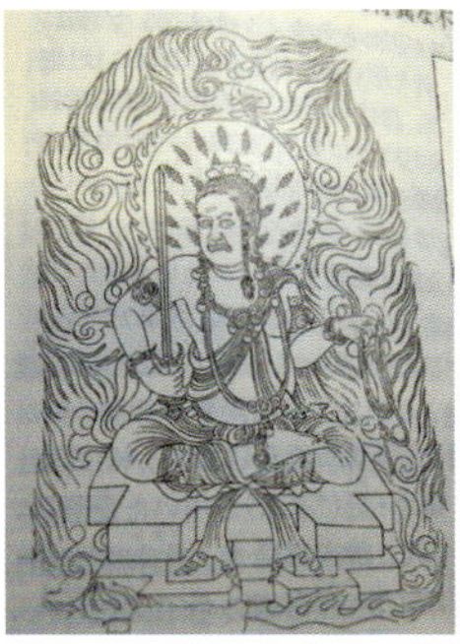

Fudômyoô

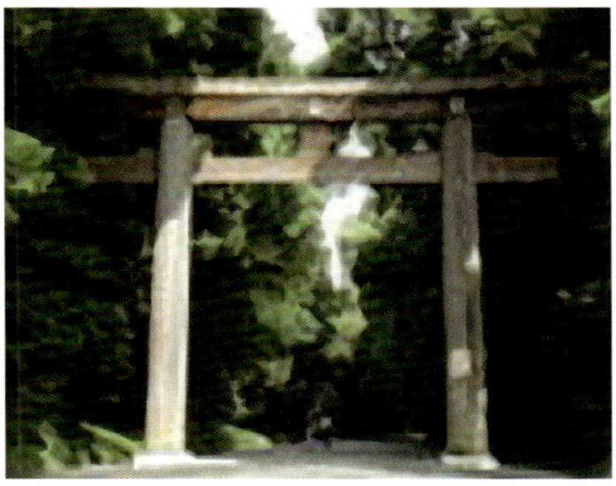

Toriî

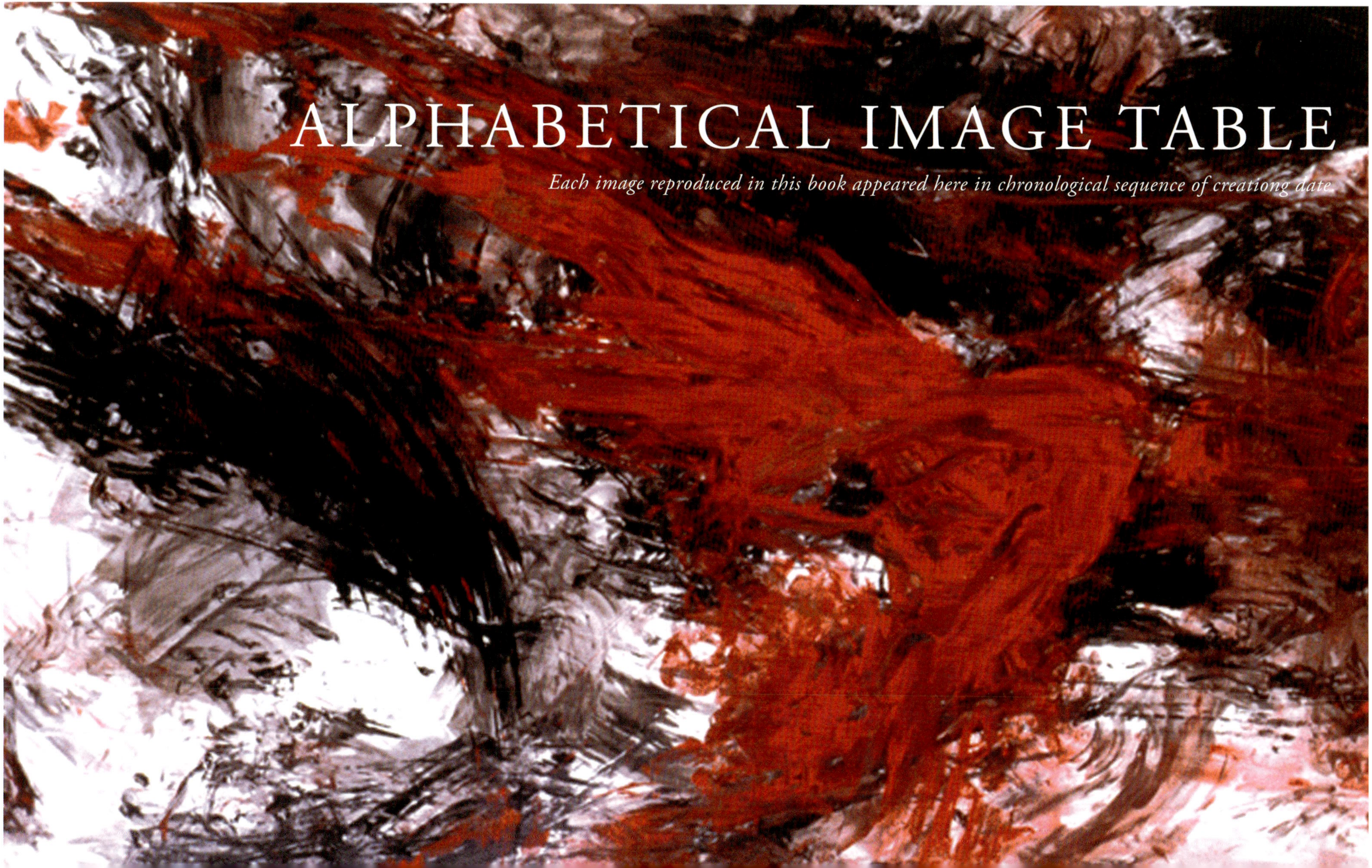

ALPHABETICAL IMAGE TABLE

Each image reproduced in this book appeared here in chronological sequence of creationg date.

A - Z

▸ *Image Index is sorted in alphabetical order left to right then down*

ALTARPIECE AFTER GRÜNEWALD (1969)
Collage on paper
11 x 10 in.
(27.9 x 25.4 cm.)
Junko's first collage.
p.120

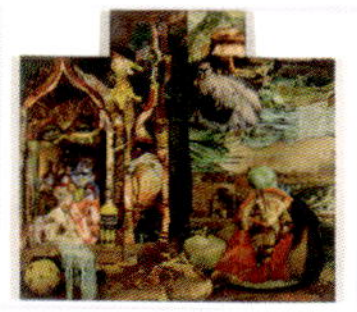

ALTARPIECE II, AFTER GIOTTO (1998)
Collage on paper
Irregular shape:
12 x 15 in.
(30.5 x 38.1 cm.)
p.226

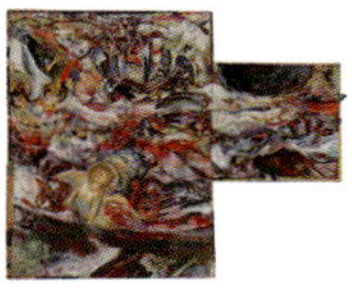

BURL PHOTO (1988)
Photograph of burl in Junko's studio
p.52

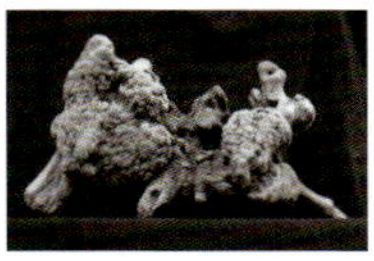

BURLS, No. 3 (1989)
Collage and acrylic on paper
40 x 32 in.
(106.3 x 81.3 cm.)
p.143

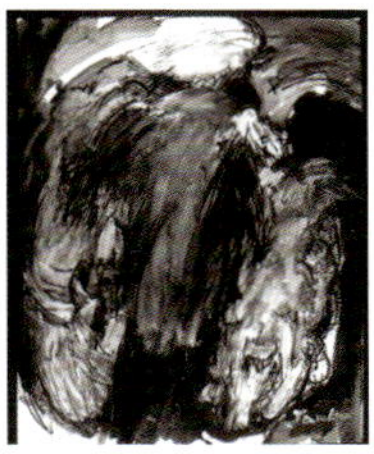

BURLS, No. 9 (1988)
Acrylic and charcoal on paper
40 x 32 in.
(101.6 x 81.3 cm.)
p.53

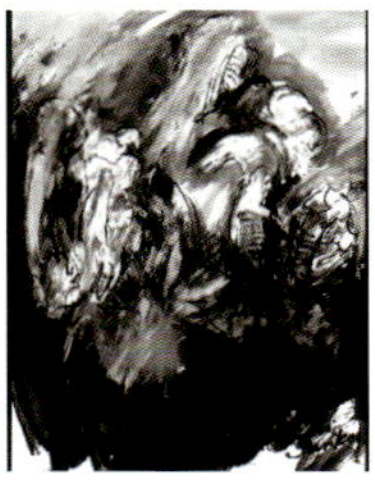

BURLS, No. 18 (1988)
Acrylic and charcoal on paper
40 x 32 in.
(101.6 x 81.3 cm.)
Collection of the Long Beach Museum of Art
p.195

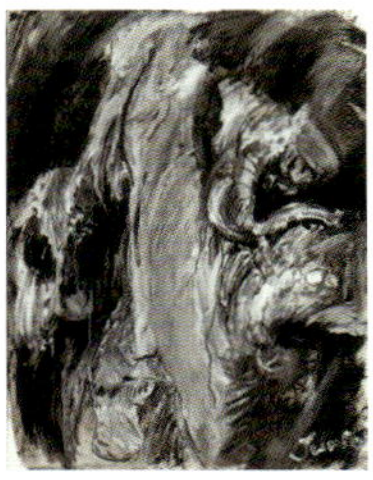

CELESTIAL CURTAIN, No. 1 (1988)
Mixed media on paper
77 x 64 x 3 in.
(195.6 x 162.6 x 7.6 cm.)
Collection of the Long Beach Museum of Art
p.41

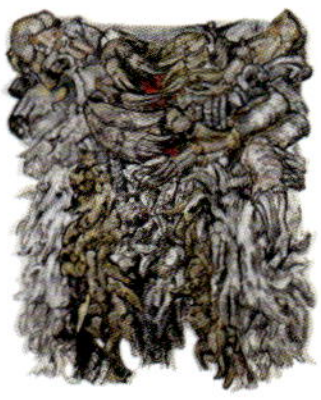

CIRCLES, No. 1 (1988)
Acrylic on paper
40 x 32 in
(101.6 x 81.3 cm.)
p.254

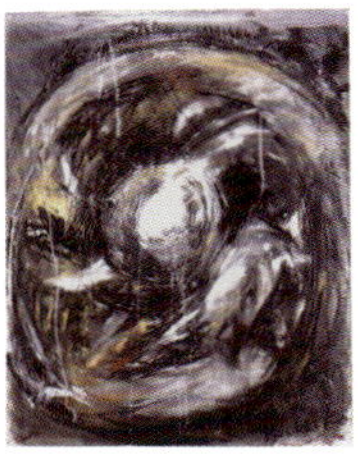

CIRCLES, No. 4 (1988)
Acrylic on paper
40 x 32 in
(101.6 x 81.3 cm.)
p.256

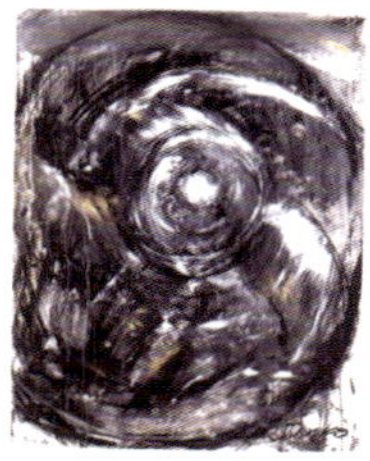

COMPACT UNIVERSE, No. 44 (1991)
Mixed media on Kromekote
5 x 5 in.
(12.7 x 12.7 cm.)
p.126

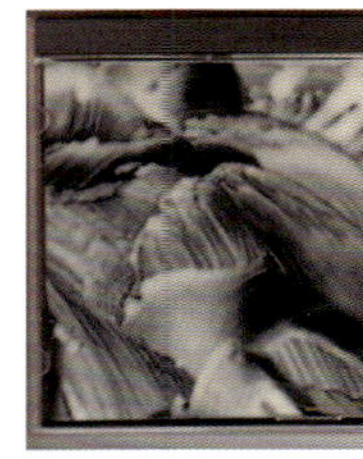

CONCERNING ART AND RELIGION, NO. 1 (2003) "WHY DO DEMONS AND ANGELS BOTH FLY IN THE SKY?"
Acrylic and collage on mylar
80 x 42 in.
(203.2 x 106.7 cm.)
p.146

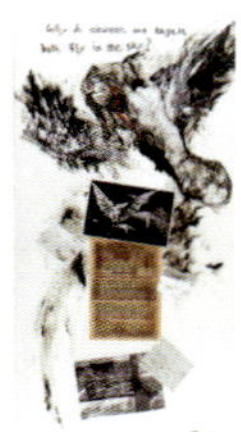

CONCERNING ART AND RELIGION, NO. 2 (2003) "WHY DO YOU LOVE CHAOS AND DESTRUCTION SO PASSIONATELY?"
Acrylic and collage on mylar
102 x 42 in.
(213.4 x 106.7 cm.) p.221

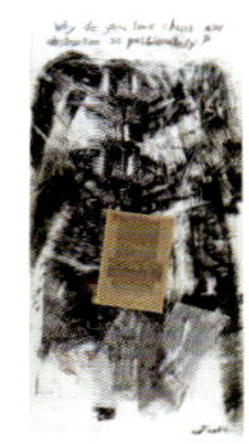

CONCERNING ART AND RELIGION, NO. 3 (2004) "IS THE NIKE OF SAMOTHRACE MORE BEAUTIFUL THAN A BROKEN ENGINE?"
Computer prints and collage on mylar.
80 x 42 in.
(203.2 x 106.7 cm.) p.33

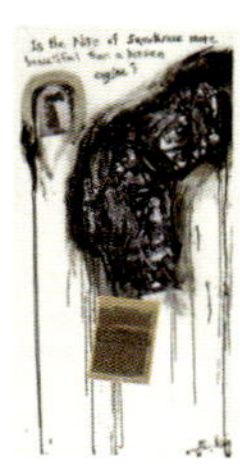

CONCERNING ART AND RELIGION, NO. 4 (2003) "ISN'T ART A DESPERATE ATTEMPT TO EMBRACE THE INORGANIC AND BRING IT TO THE ORGANIC?"
Sumi, acrylic, and collage on mylar support
84 x 42 in.
(213.4 x 106.7 cm.) p.241

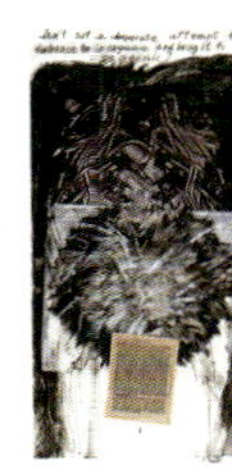

CONCERNING ART AND RELIGION, NO. 5 (2003) "WHY DO YOU SHOW SUCH AN IMAGE TO ME?"
Collage of film and paper, with charcoal and acrylic on mylar support
84 x 42 in.
(213.4 x 106.7 cm.)
p.218

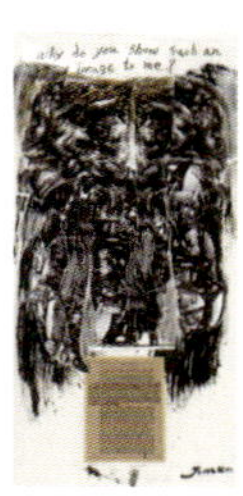

CONCERNING ART AND RELIGION, NO. 8 (2003) "EMBRACE ME IN THE MOMENT OF ETERNITY!"
Collage of computer prints on mylar
84 x 42 in.
(213.36 x 106.68 cm.)
p.51

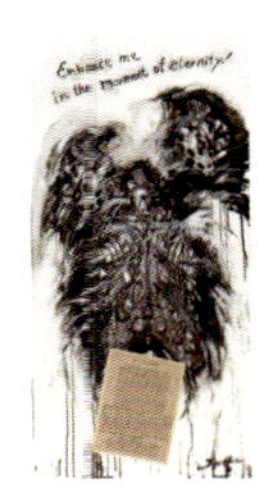

CONCERNING ART AND RELIGION, No. 6 (2003)
Acrylic and collage on mylar support
84 x 82 in.
(213.4 x 106.7 cm.)
p.157

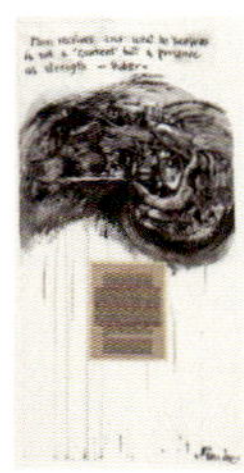

◂ DETAIL
Cover

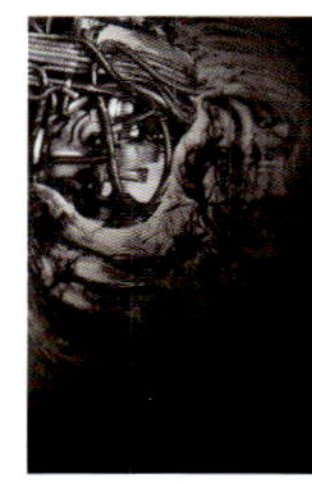

CONCERNING ART AND RELIGION, NO. 7 (2003) "IN THE BEGINNING IS THE IMAGE"
Paper, acetate and acrylic on mylar
84 x 42 in.
(213.4 x 106.7 cm.)
Opening and closing spreads: details from this work.

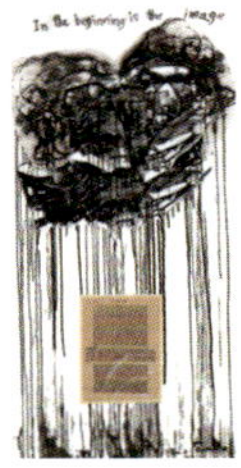

◂ DETAILS
Opening and closing spreads.
p.3

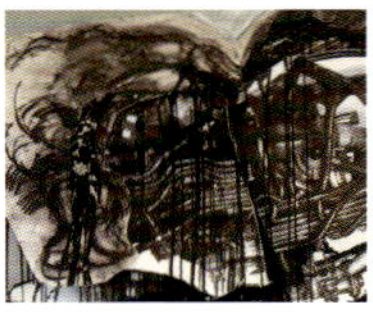

CONCERNING ART AND RELIGION NO. 9 (2004) "WHO WILL SHATTER THE ILLUSIONS? THE PROPHET? THE ARTIST?"
Computer prints and acrylic on mylar.
Three panels, overall
84 x 126 in.
(213.4 x 320 cm.)
p.268 - 269

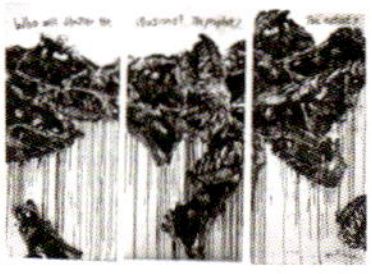

DANCE IN GREEN AND RED (1984)
Mixed media on paper
15 x 10 in.
(38 x 25.4 cm.)
p.63

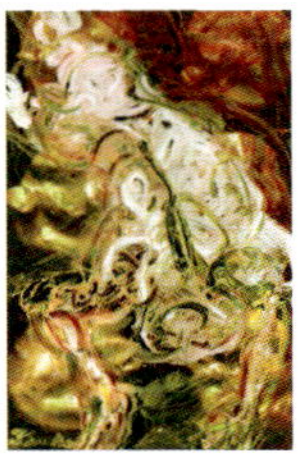

DANCE No. 1 SATURN AND ITS SIX MOONS (1984)
Mixed media on printed paper
27 x 20 in
(68.6 x 51.4 cm.)
p.75

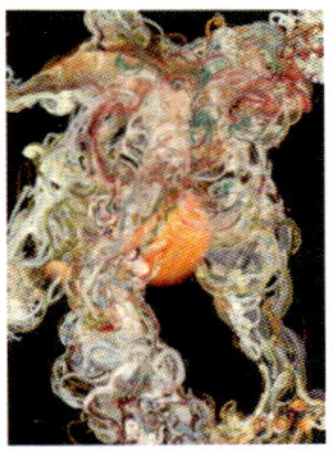

DANCE PLAY OF THE RED SKIRTS
Paul Klee,
p.89

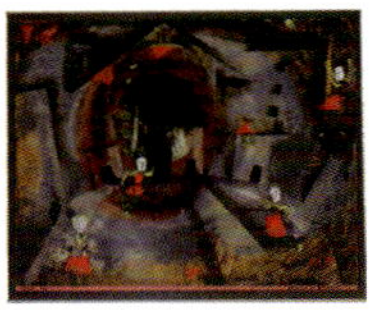

DANCING ON GOLD BACKGROUND (1984)
Mixed media on paper
15 x 10 in.
(38.1 x 25.4 cm.)
p.130

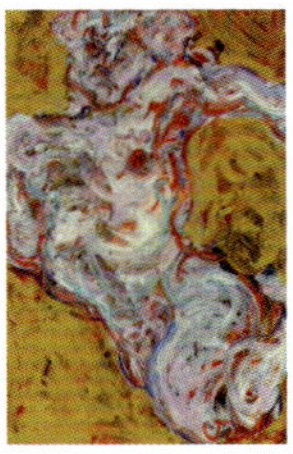

DEAD FLOWERS PHOTO (1973)
Dead flowers sitting on Junko's studio table
p.14

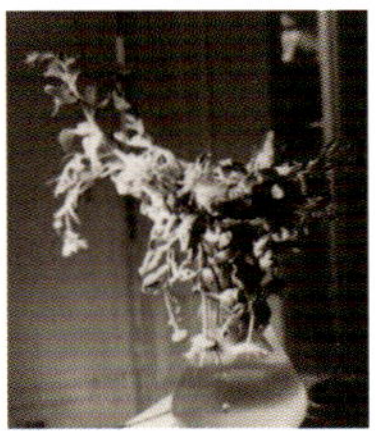

DEAD FLOWER SERIES, No. 1 (1973)
Pen and ink with wash, on Arches paper
22 x 16 in.
(55.9 x 40.6 cm.)
p.117

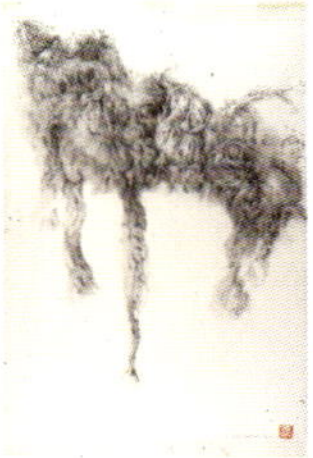

DEAD FLOWERS SERIES, No. 5 (1973)
Pen and ink on paper, with wash
22.5 x 16 in.
(57.2 x 40.6 cm.)
p.49

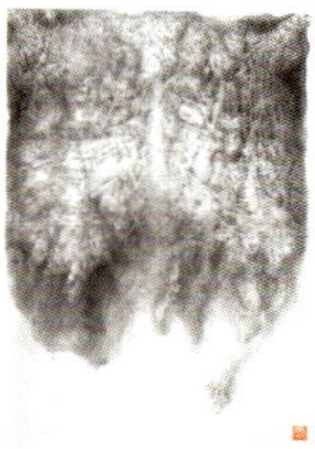

DEAD FLOWER SERIES, No. 6 (1973)
Pen and ink with wash, on Arches paper
22 x 16 in.
(55.9 x 40.6 cm.)
p.118

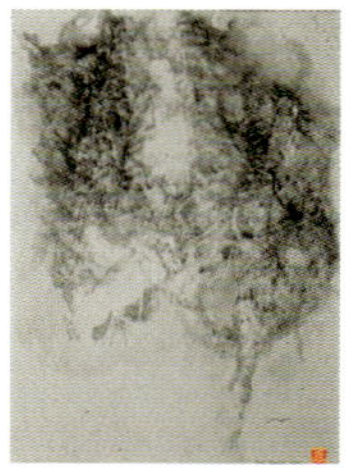

DEAD FLOWER SERIES No. 7 (1973)
Pen and ink with wash on Arches paper
Overall 40 x 66 in.
(101.6 x 167.6 cm.)
Collection of the Pacific Asia Museum
p.16

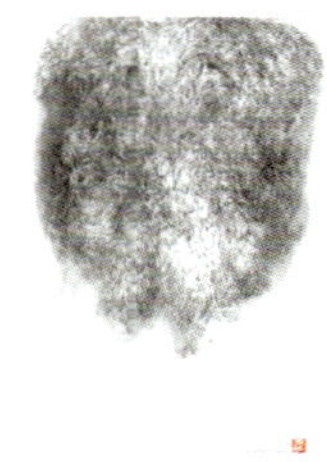

DEAD FLOWER SERIES, No. 8, *Byoobu* (1973)
Pen and ink with wash on Arches paper
Overall 40 x 66 in.
(101.6 x 167.6 cm.)
Collection of the Pacific Asia Museum
p.18-19

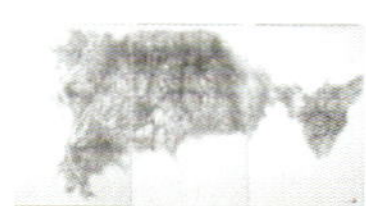

◂ DETAIL
p.17

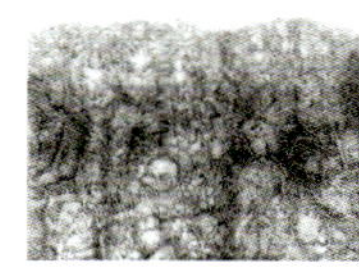

DEAD FLOWERS SKETCH (Sept. 25, 1973)
8 x 10 in.
(20.3 x 25.4 cm.)
p.14

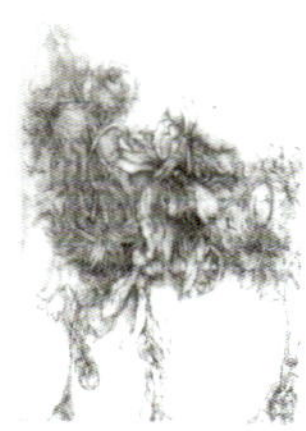

THE DECANTER
Photograph of the incredibly ugly decanter that Junko found at a junk store
p.57

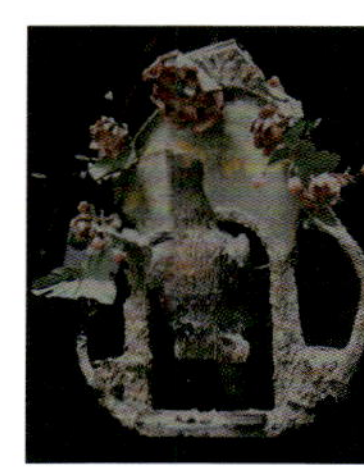

DEVIL ESCAPING (1983)
Mixed media collage on paper
11 x 9 in.
(27.9 x 22 cm.)
p.159

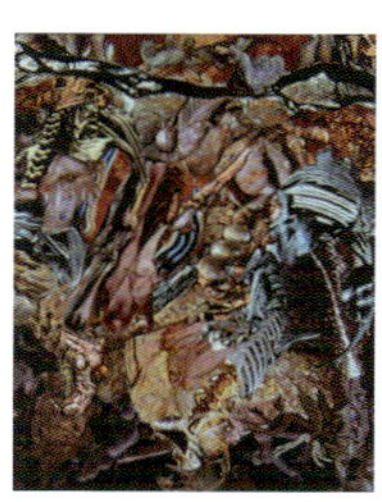

EMERGING CONSCIOUSNESS, No. 5 (1988)
Acrylic on Kromekote paper
26 x 20 in.
(66.0 x 50.8 cm.)
p.252

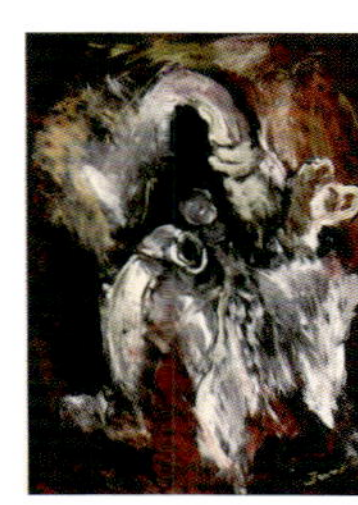

EMERGING CONSCIOUSNESS, No. 11 (1988)
Acrylic on coated paper
26 x 20 in.
(66 x 56.8 cm.)
p.246

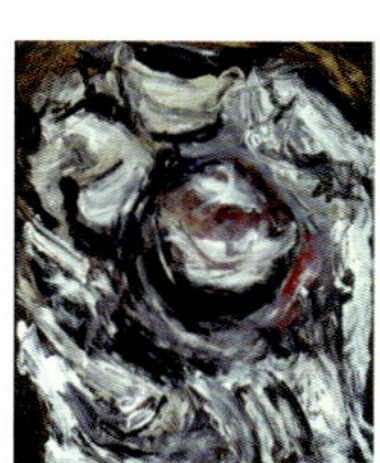

EMERGING CONSCIOUSNESS, No. 13 (1988)
Acrylic on coated paper
26 x 20 in.
(66 x 56.8 cm.)
p.249

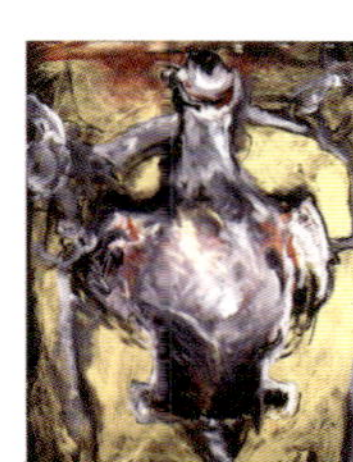

ENGINE PHOTO (1995)
Photograph of an engine part in Junko's studio
p.26

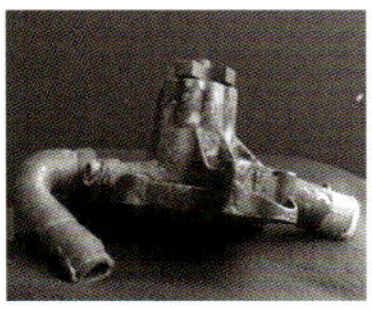

ENGINE PHOTO (1995)
Photograph of used engine purchased from an auto parts store
p.28

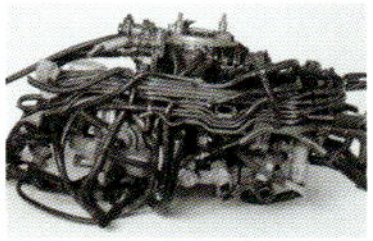

ENGINE SERIES No. 2 (1981)
Pencil on paper
10 x 8 in.
(25.4 x 20.3 cm.)
p.27

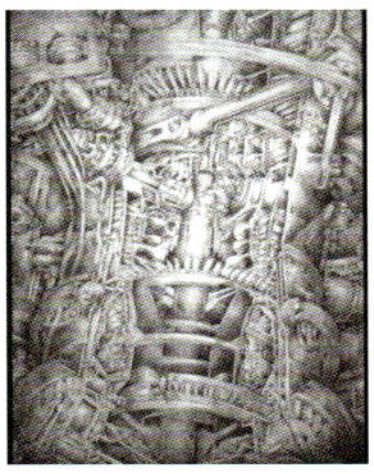

ENGINE SERIES, No. 4 (1983)
Pencil on paper
13.25 x 10.5 in.
(33.7 x 26.7 cm.)
p.36

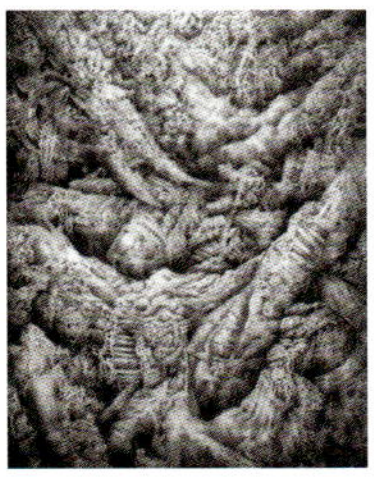

ESOTERIC BUDDHISM PREPARATORY, No. 5 (2000)
Charcoal on industrial mylar, computer processed
Virtual size
p.29

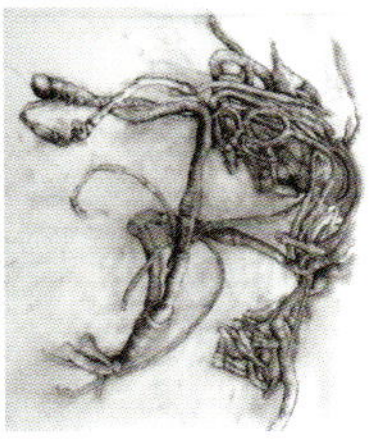

ESOTERIC BUDDHISM, PREPARATORY DRAWING No. 1 (2000)
Charcoal on computer print on mylar
Virtual size
p.242

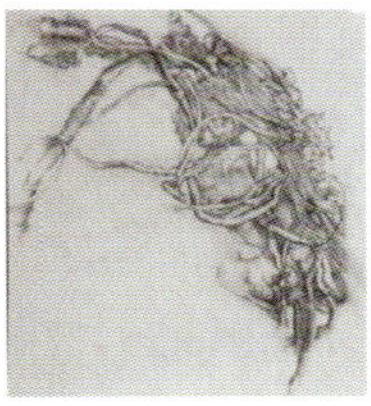

ESOTERIC BUDDHISM, PREPARATORY DRAWING No. 2 (2000)
Charcoal on computer print
Virtual size
p.140

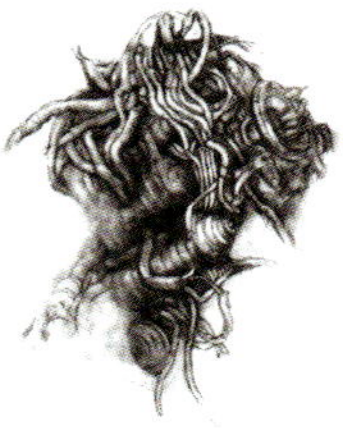

ESOTERIC BUDDHISM, PREPARATORY DRAWING No. 3 (2000)
Charcoal on computer print
Virtual size
p.141

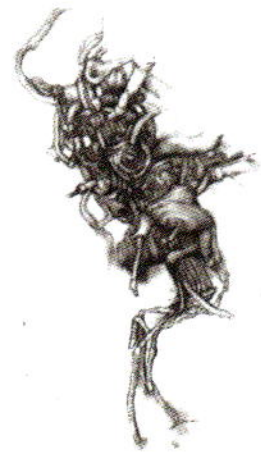

ESOTERIC BUDDHISM, PREPARATORY DRAWING No. 4 (2000)
Charcoal on scanned image
Virtual size
p.139

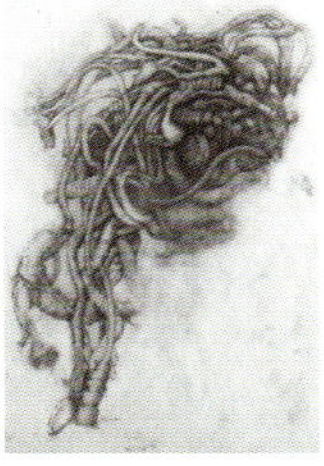

ESOTERIC BUDDHISM SERIES No. 1, *Birth* (2001)
Mixed media collage mounted on mylar
90 x 42 x 1 in.
(228.6 x 106.7 x 2.5 cm.)
p.42

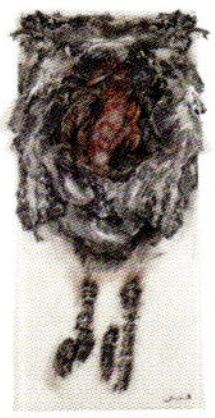

ESOTERIC BUDDHISM SERIES No. 2: ***Ecstasy*** **(2001)**
Mixed media collage on film mounted on mylar
Three panels,
overall 132 x 126 x 1 in.
(325.3 x 320 x 2.5 cm.)
pp.42-43

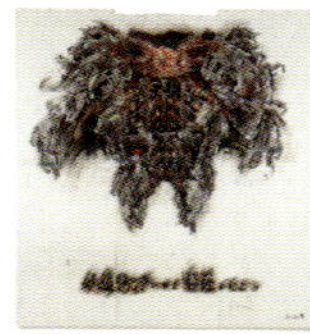

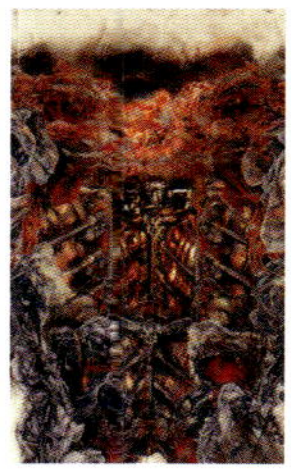

◀ DETAIL
p.270

ESOTERIC BUDDHISM SERIES No. 3: ***Death*** **(2001)**
Mixed media collage mounted on mylar
90 x 42 x 1 in.
(228.6 x 106.7 x 2.5 cm.)
p.43

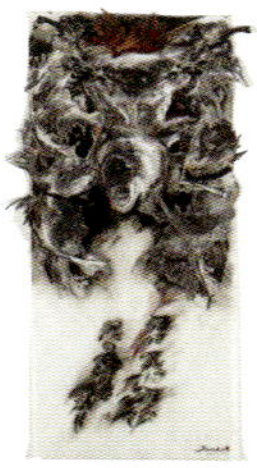

FATHOM: **MANDALA No. 2 (2006) THE ENGINE EMBRACES THE FLAME**
Collage of computer prints on mylar
12 ft. x 84 in.
(365.8 x 213.4 cm.)
p.32

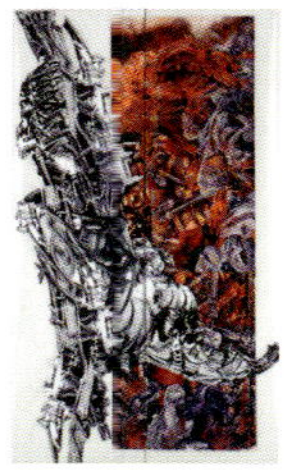

FATHOM: **COMMUNICATING WITH NATURE, DETAIL. (2006)**
Collage of computer prints on mylar
Each 10 ft. x 42 in.
(304.8 x 86.7 cm.)
p.25

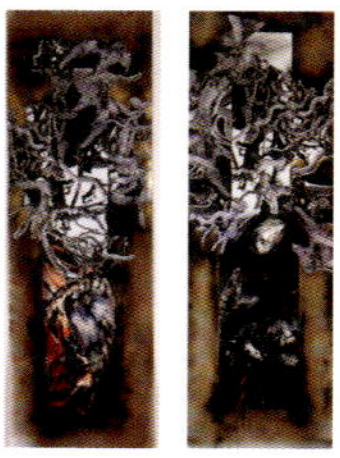

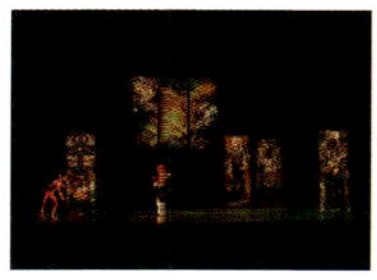

◀ WITH DANCERS
p.44-45

FATHOM, **MEDITATION ON THE MOUNTAIN (2006)**
Collage of computer prints on mylar,
Four panels,
overall 12 ft. x 168 in.
(365.76 x 426.72 cm.)
p. 82-83

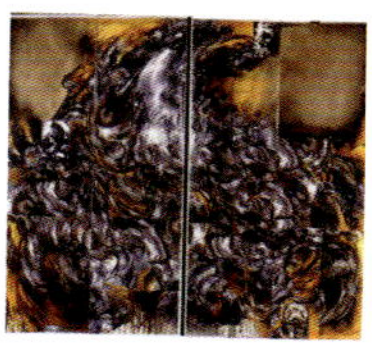

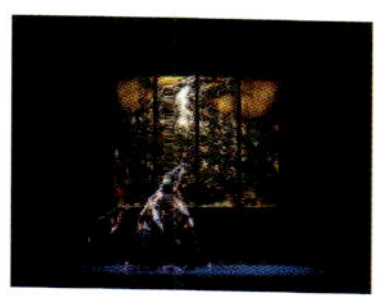

◀ WITH DANCERS
p.192-193

FATHOM: **PERILOUS OCEAN (2005)**
Collage of computer prints on mylar
Four panels.
Overall: 12 x 14 ft.
(365.8 x 320 cm.)
pp.152-153

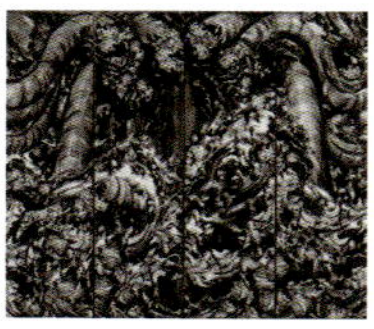

FATHOM: **THE SORCERER ENTERING HIS FOREST**
Collage of computer prints on mylar
Foreground: three panels
120 x 42 in.
(304.8 x 106.7 cm.)
Background: four panels
144 x 42 in.
(365.8 x 106.7 cm.)
pp. 60-61

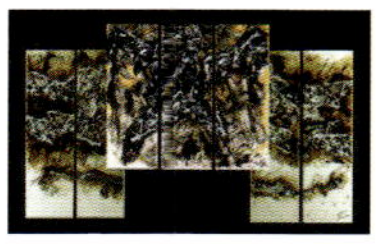

FROM *FATHOM:* TANTRIC DANCE (2006)
Four background panels
Collage of computer prints on mylar support
Overall dimensions:
144 x 168 in.
(365.8 x 426.7 cm.)
p.66

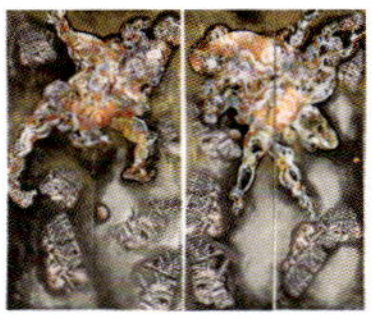

***FATHOM:* TANTRIC DANCE (FOREGROUND) (2006)**
Collage of computer prints on mylar
Overall 10 x 10.5 ft.
(304.8 x 320.0 cm.)
This work incorporates portions of the one below it.
p.131

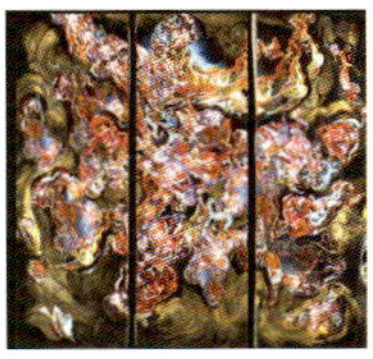

FIVE DANCING FIGURES (1984)
Mixed media on printed paper
20 x 48 in.
(51.8 x 121.9 cm.)
p. 64-65

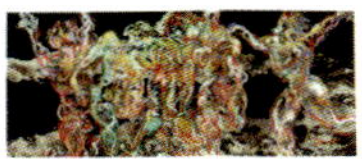

GREYSCALE IMAGE(1997)
The first image Junko created using the computer.
p.139

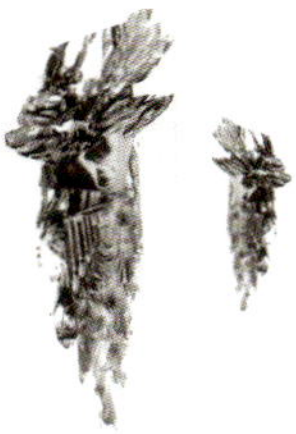

GIANT BURLS No. 2 (1989)
Acrylic and charcoal on paper
60 x 56.25 in.
(152.4 x 142.9 cm.)
p.78

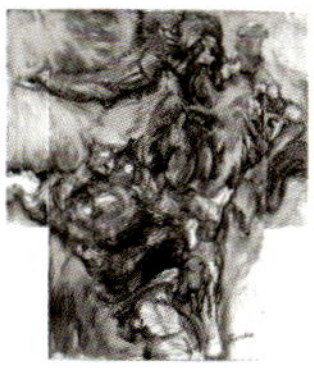

GIANT SKETCHBOOK, ENGINE DRAWING No. 1 (1997)
Charcoal on mylar
42 x 118 in.
(106.7 x 29.7 cm.)
p.26

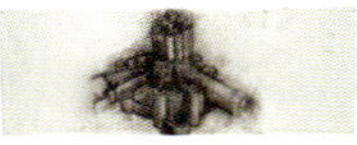

GIANT SKETCHBOOK, (1999) *SACRED DEFORMITY*
Charcoal on mylar
32.5 x 42 in.
(82.6 x 106.7 cm.)
p.67

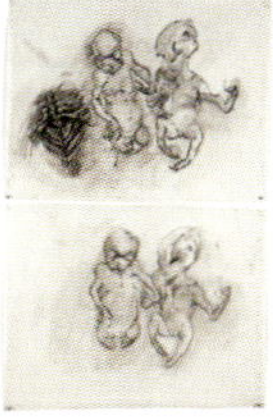

GIANT SKETCHBOOK, (1999) *SACRED DEFORMITY*
Charcoal on mylar
83.25 x 42 in.
(211.5 x 106.7 cm.)
p.67

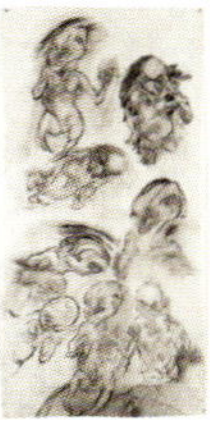

GIANT SKETCHBOOK, No. 2 (1997)
Charcoal on mylar
42 x 118 in.
(106.68 x 299.72 cm.)
p.242-243

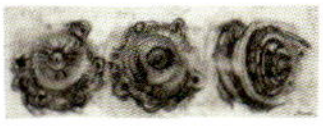

HAMLET SPEAKS TO THE GHOST
From Junko's Childhood Catalog (1953, when Junko was 14 years old)
Acrylic on paper
8 x 10 in.
(20.32 x 25.4 cm.)
p.165

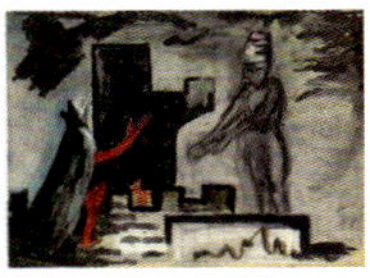

HORSESHOE CRAB SERIES No. 1 (1983)
Charcoal on paper
9 x 7 in.
(22.9 x 17.8 cm.)
p.34

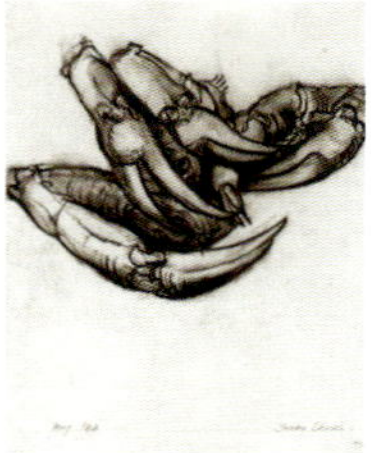

HORSESHOE CRAB PHOTO (1983)
Photograph of horseshoe crab
p.34

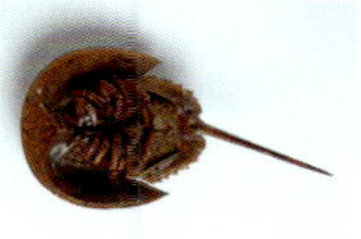

IN THE FOREST OF AMIDA BUDDHA No. 1 (1993)
Sumi ink and acrylic on myler support
80 x 42 in.
(203.2 x 106.7 cm.)
p.264

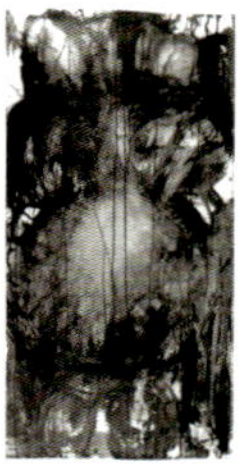

IN THE FOREST OF AMIDA BUDDHA No. 2 (1993)
Sumi ink and acrylic on mylar support
80 x 42 in.
(203.2 x 106.7 cm.)
p.160

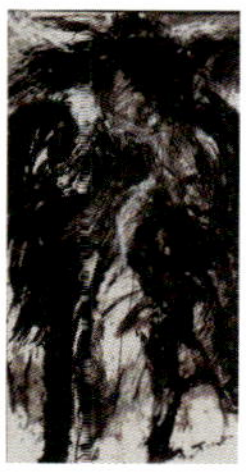

IN THE FOREST OF AMIDA BUDDHA, No. 5 (1993)
Sumi and acrylic on mylar
81 x 42 in.
(205.7 x 106.7 cm.)
p.133

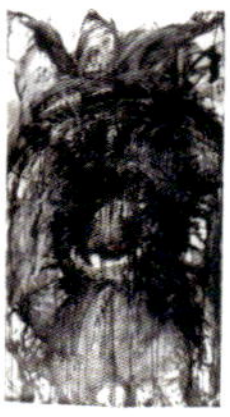

IN THE FOREST OF AMIDA BUDDHA, No. 6 (1993)
Sumi ink and acrylic on mylar
80 x 42 in.
(203.2 x 106.7 cm.)
p.180

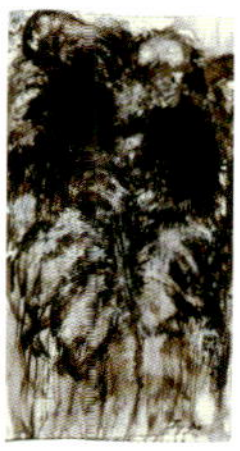

IN THE FOREST OF AMIDA BUDDHA No. 22 (1993)
Sumi ink and acrylic on mylar
80 x 42 in.
(203.2 x 106.7 cm.)
p.182

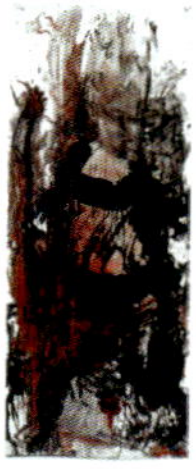

IN THE FOREST OF AMIDA BUDDHA, No. 24 (1993)
Sumi ink and acrylic on mylar
103 x 42 in.
(261.6 x 106.7 cm.)
p.185

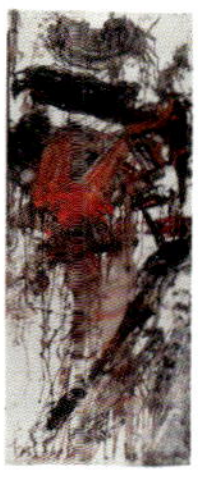

INDIVIDUATION JOURNAL, No. 1: RILKE (1995) “EVERY ANGEL IS TERRIBLE”
Acrylic and sumi ink on mylar
80 x 42 in.
(203.2 x 106.7 cm.)
p.93

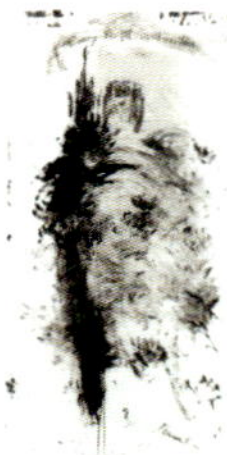

INDIVIDUATION JOURNAL, No. 1: FROMM (1995)
Acrylic and Collage on mylar
80 x 42 in.
(203.2 x 106.7 cm.)
p.231

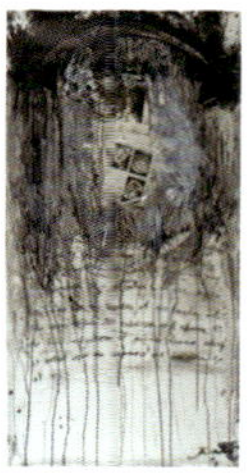

INDIVIDUATION JOURNAL, No. 2 (1995)
Acrylic and photographs on mylar
80 x 42 in.
(203.2 x 106.7 cm.)
p.199

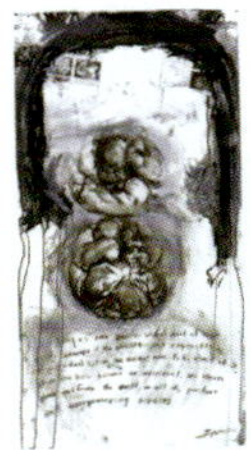

INDIVIDUATION JOURNAL, No. 5: FROMM (1995)
Acrylic and collage on mylar
80 x 42 in.
(203.2 x 106.7 cm.)
p.235

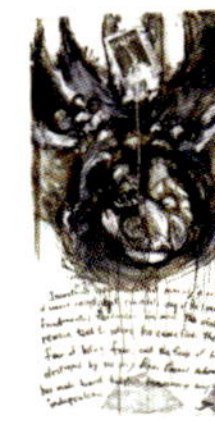

INDIVIDUATION JOURNAL No. 7 (1995) *"THE FALL OF MAN"*
(Erich Fromm)
Acrylic and collage on mylar
84 x 42 in.
(213.4 x 106.7 cm.)
p.260

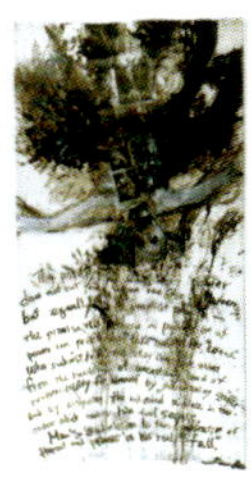

INDIVIDUATION JOURNAL, No. 8: FROMM (1995)
Acrylic and collage on mylar
80 x 42 in.
(203.2 x 106.7 cm.)
p.238

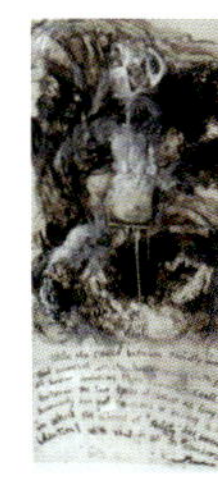

INDIVIDUATION JOURNAL, FREE WILL—AUGUSTINE (1998)
Acrylic and charcoal on mylar.
Virtual work
See companion work at pg. 233
p.292

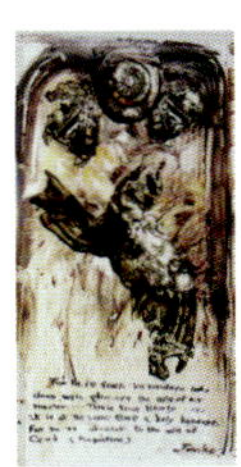

INDIVIDUATION JOURNAL, FREE WILL—BUBER (1998)
Virtual work
See companion work at pg. 290
p.233

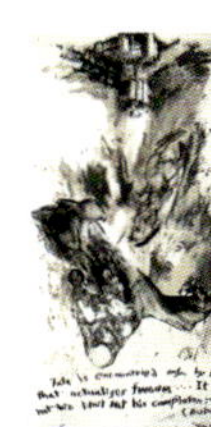

INTERPLANETARY ICON, No. 4 (1990)
Mixed media on paper
Irregular shape:
22 x 19 in.
(55.9 x 48.2 cm.)
p.127

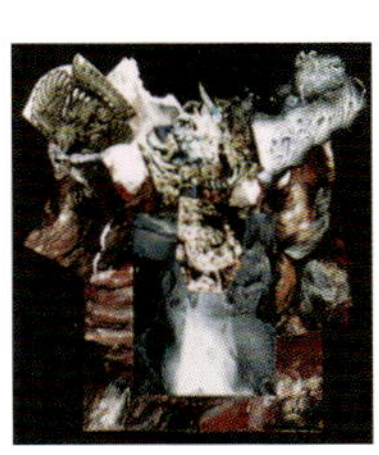

INTERPLANETARY ICON, No. 8 (1990)
Mixed media on paper
Irregular shape:
22 x 20 in.
(55.9 x 50 .8 cm.)
p.224

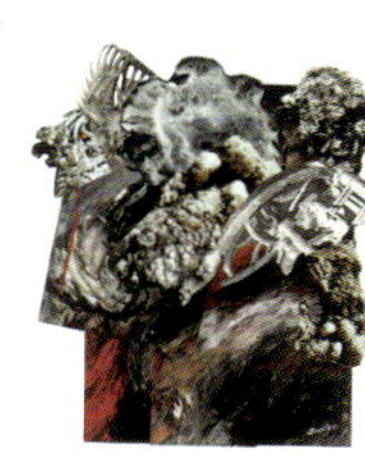

INTERPLANETARY ICON, No. 11 (1990)
Mixed media on paper
Irregular shape:
23 x 19.5 in.
(58.4 x 49.5 cm.)
p.30

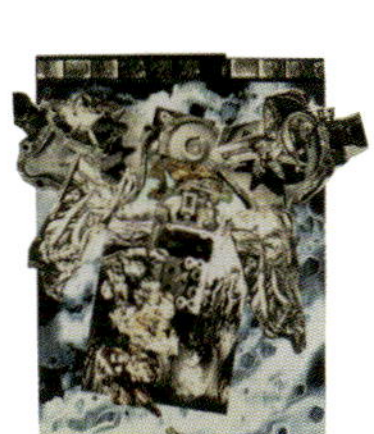

INTERPLANETARY ICON, NO. 12 (1990)
Mixed media on paper
Irregular shape:
21.5 x 21.25 in.
(54.61 x 54.0 cm.)
p.38

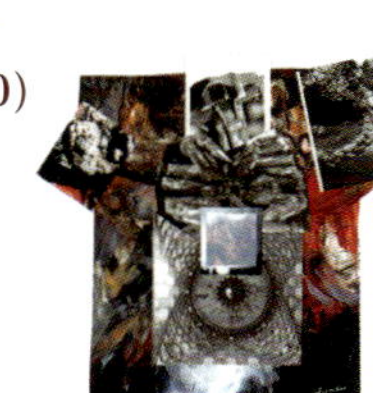

INTERPLANETARY ICON, No. 14 (1990)
Mixed media on paper
Irregular shape:
22.75 x 20.5 in.
(57.8 x 52.1 cm.)
p.196

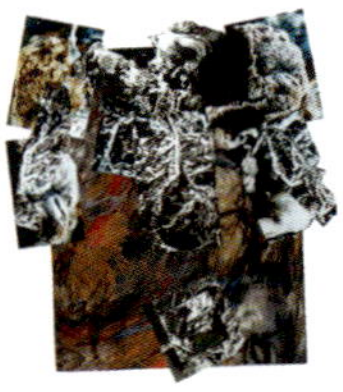

INTERPLANETARY ICON, No. 19 (1990)
Mixed media on paper
Irregular shape:
26 x 25 in.
(66 x 63.5 cm.)
p.217

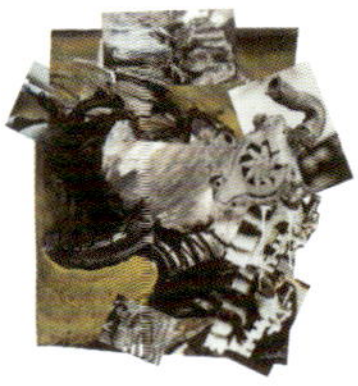

INTERPLANETARY ICON, No. 25
Mixed media on paper
Irregular shape:
26 x 25 in.
(66.0 x 63.5 cm.)
p.55

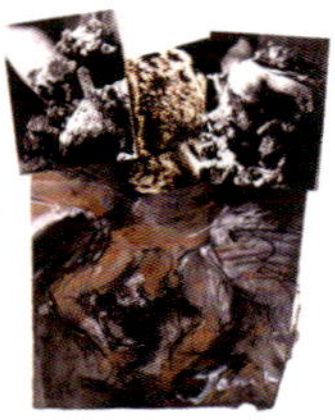

INTERPLANETARY ICON, No. 26 (1990)
Mixed media on paper
Irregular shape:
25 x 22 in.
(63.5 x 55.9 cm.)
p.134

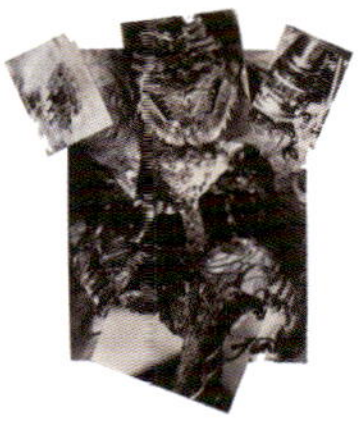

INTERPLANETARY ICON, No. 27
Computer print and craypas on paper
Irregular shape:
25 x 22 in.
(63.5 x 55.9 cm.)
p.136

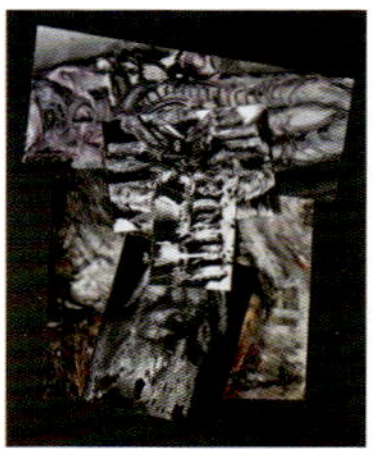

MEDITATIONS ON DANCE, No. 1 (1987)
Acrylic on coated paper
30 x 28 in.
(76.2 x 71.1 cm.)
p. 62

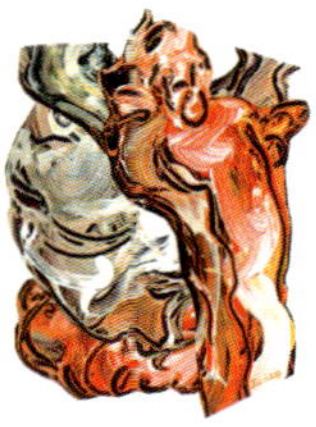

MEDITATIONS ON DANCE, No. 5 (1987)
Acrylic on coated paper
30 x 28 in.
(76.2 x 71.1 cm.)
p.130

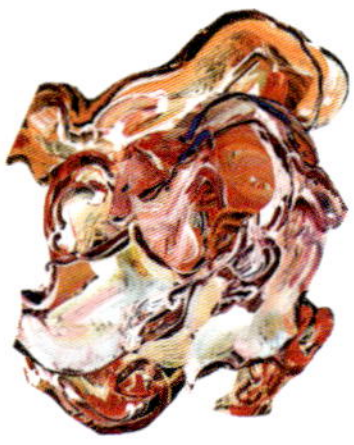

MYSTERIOUS PAPER, No. 1 (1983)
Color pencil on Xerox on paper
5 x 10 in.
(12.7 x 25.4 cm.)
p.124

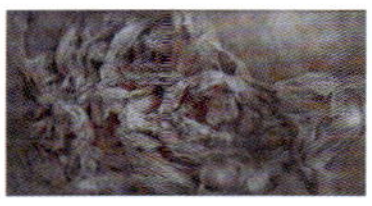

MYSTERIOUS PAPER, No. 4 (1983)
Color pencil on Xerox on paper
6.5 x 8 in.
(16.51 x 20.32 cm.)
p.125

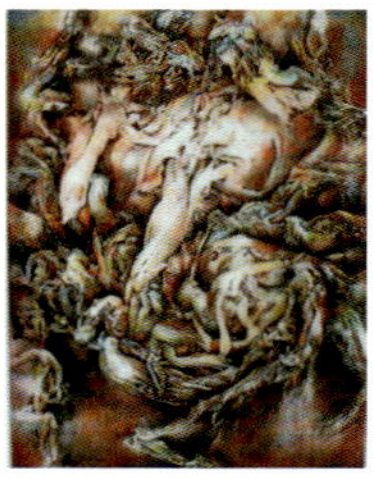

RELIC (1984)
Collage and acrylic on paper
3-dimensional
11 x 9.125 x 2 in.
(27.9 x 23.2 x 5 cm.)
p.48

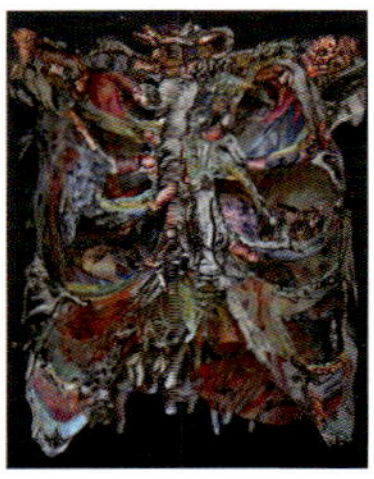

REQUIEM FOR AN EXECUTED BIRD, No. 23 (1991)
Mixed media on paper
40 x 32 in.
(101.6 x. 81.3 cm.)
p.37

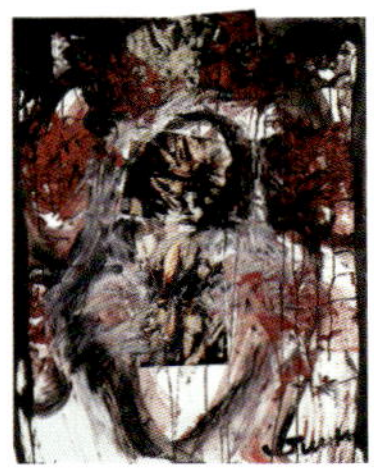

REQUIEM FOR AN EXECUTED BIRD, No. 24 (1991)
"The Bird is Dying"
Mixed media on paper
40 x 32 in.
(101.6 x 81.3 cm.)
p.155

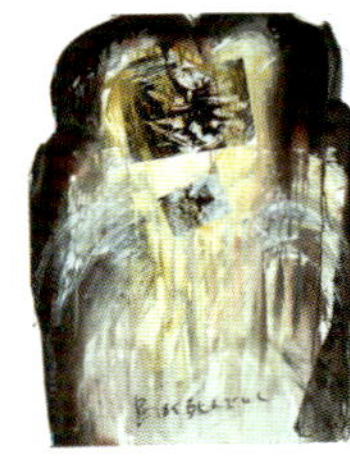

REQUIEM FOR AN EXECUTED BIRD, No. 3 (1991)
Mixed media on paper
40 x 32 in.
(101.6 x 81.3 cm.)
p.129

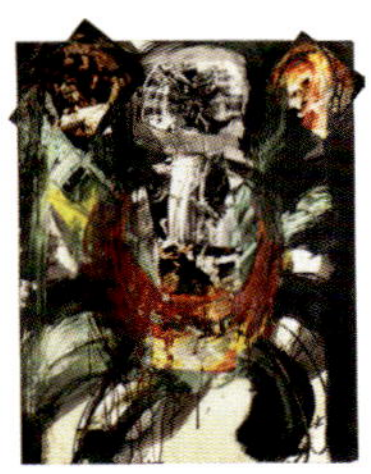

REQUIEM FOR AN EXECUTED BIRD No. 6 (1991)
Mixed media on paper
40 x 32 in.
(101.6 x 81.28 cm.)
p.166

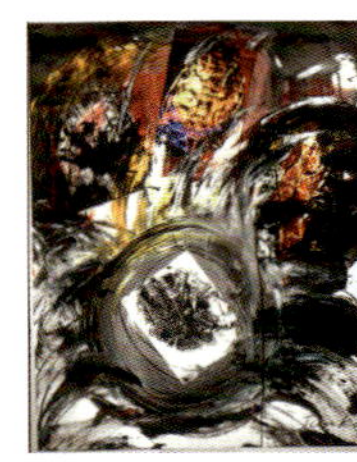

REQUIEM FOR AN EXECUTED BIRD, No. 4 (1991)
Mixed media on paper
40 x 32 in.
(101.6 x 81.28 cm.)
p.162

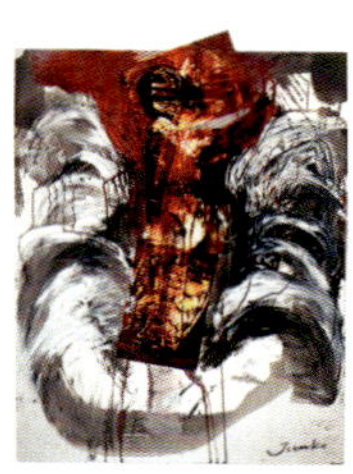

REQUIEM FOR AN EXECUTED BIRD No. 13 (1991)
Mixed media on paper
40 x 32 in.
(101.6 x 81.3 cm.)
p.87

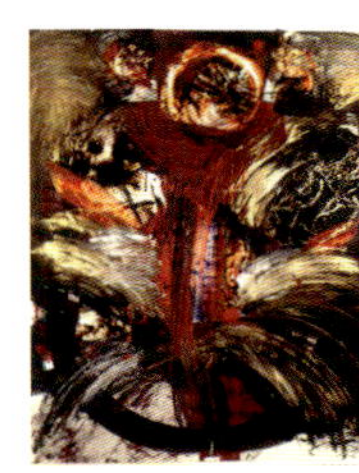

REQUIEM FOR AN EXECUTED BIRD, No. 19 (1991)
Mixed media on paper
40 x 32 in.
(101.6 x 81.3 cm.)
p.59

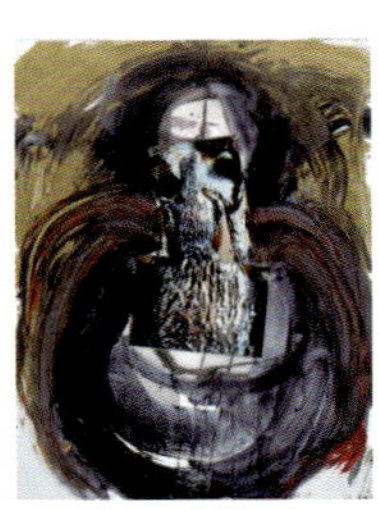

REQUIEM FOR AN EXECUTED BIRD, No. 20 (1991)
Mixed media collage on paper
40 x 32 in
(101.6 x 81.28 cm.)
p.169

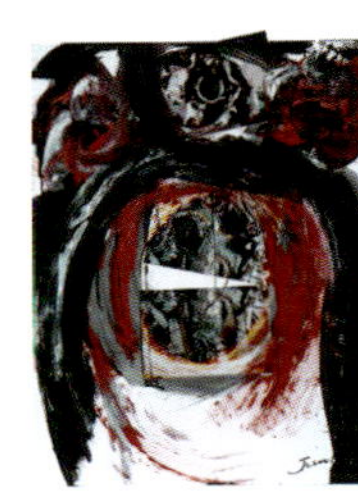

REQUIEM FOR AN EXECUTED BIRD, No. 21 (1991)
Mixed media on paper
40 x 32 in.
(101.6 x 81.3 cm.)
p.10

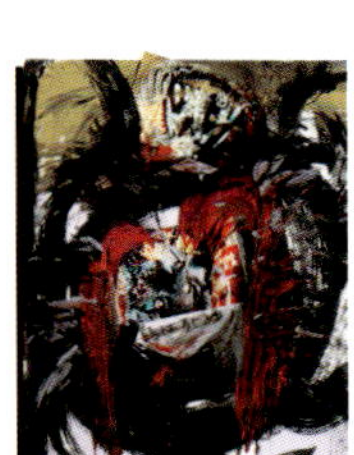

REQUIEM FOR AN EXECUTED BIRD, No. 22, *Bird in the Cathedral* (1991)
Mixed media on paper
40 x 32 in.
(101.6 x 81.3 cm.)
p.170

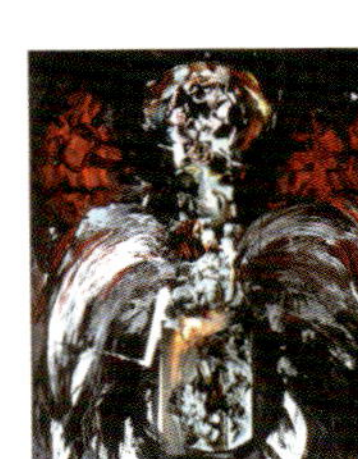

REQUIEM FOR AN EXECUTED BIRD, No. 29 (1991)
Mixed media collage
on paper
40 x 32 in.
(101.6 x 81.3 cm.)
p.172

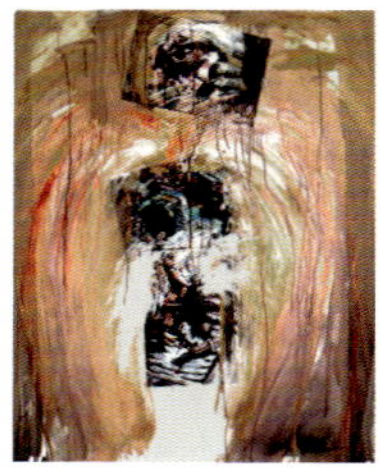

REQUIEM FOR AN EXCUTED BIRD, No. 33 (1991)
Mixed media collage
on paper
40 x 32 in.
(101.6 x 81.3 cm.)
p.149

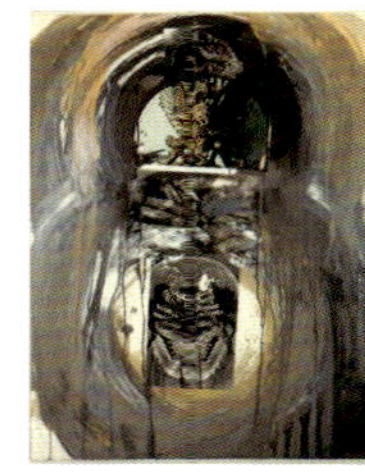

REQUIEM FOR AN EXECUTED BIRD, No. 42 (1991)
Mixed media collage
on paper
40 x 32 in.
(101.6 x 81.3 cm.)
p.175

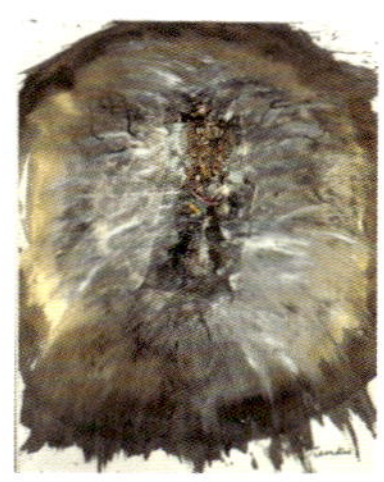

◀ DETAIL
Facing page 1

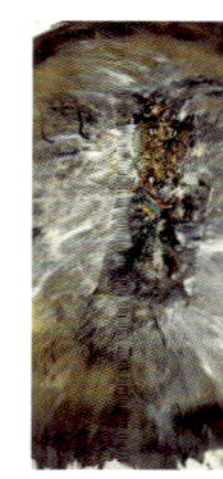

REQUIEM FOR AN EXECUTED BIRD, No. 44, (1991)
Mixed media collage
on paper
40 x 32 in.
(101.6 x 81.3 cm.)
p.176

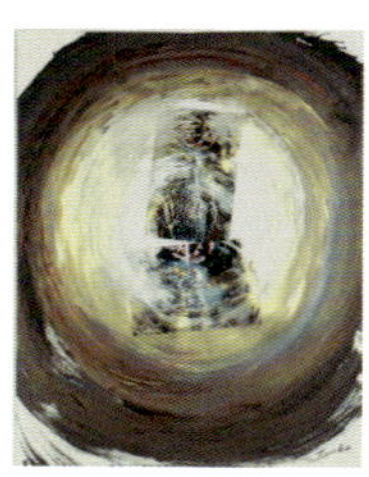

ROOT PHOTO (1974)
Photograph of the
root sitting on Junko's
studio table
p.21

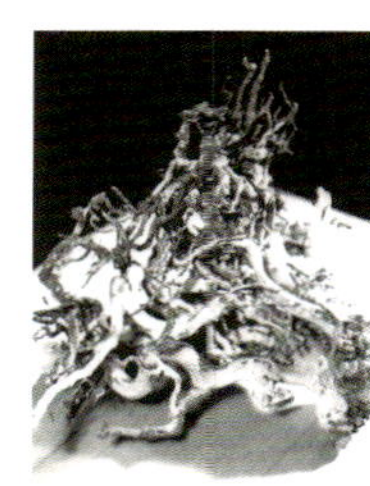

ROOT SERIES No. 1 (1975)
Mixed-media collage
on paper
22.5 x 16 in.
(57.2 x 40.6 cm.)
Also preparatory pencil
sketch
p.22

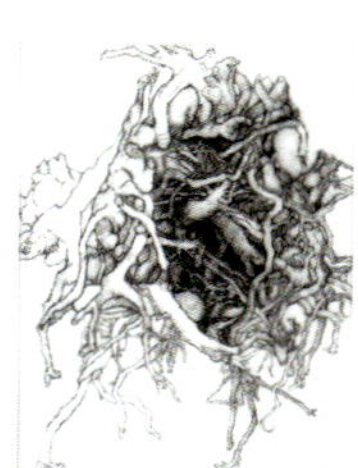

ROOT SERIES No. 1 (1975)
Mixed media collage
on paper
22.5 x 16 in.
(57.2 x 40.6 cm.)
This is the collage based
on the sketch on the
preceding page.
p.23

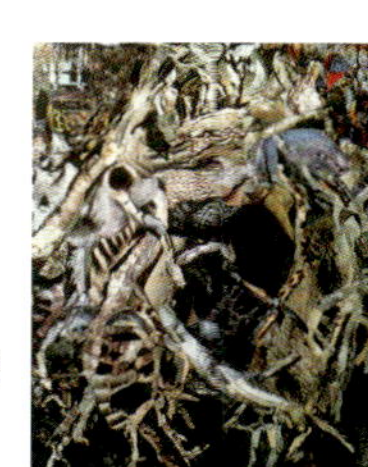

ROOT SERIES, No. 7 (1975)
Mixed media collage
on paper
22 x 16 in.
(55.9 x. 40.6 cm.)
p.228

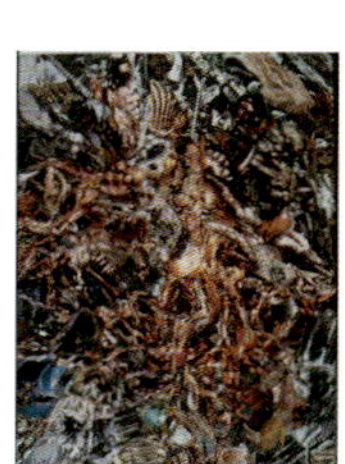

ROOT SERIES No. 9, *The Emergence of Buddha (1975)*
Mixed media collage
on paper
84 x 82 in.
(213.4 x 106.7 cm.)
p.84

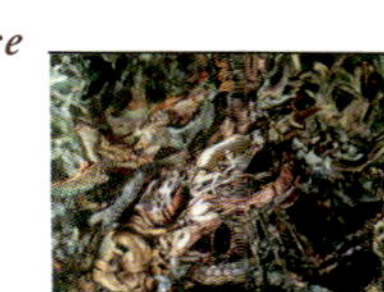

ROOT SERIES, No. 11, FASTING BUDDHA, No. 2 (1975)
Mixed media collage
on paper
20 x 16 in.
(50.8 x 40.6 cm.)
p.121

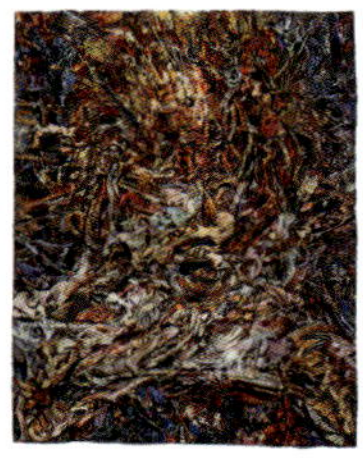

ROOT SERIES, No. 15 (1976)
Mixed media collage
on paper
10 x 8 in.
(25.4 x. 20.3 cm.)
p.123

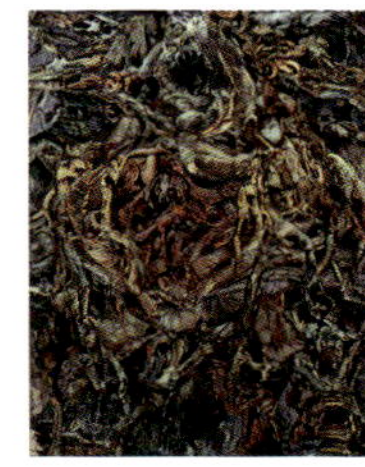

ROOT SERIES No. 16, *Mandala* (1979)
Mixed media collage
on paper
21 x 16.5 in.
(53.3 x 41.9 cm.)
p.3

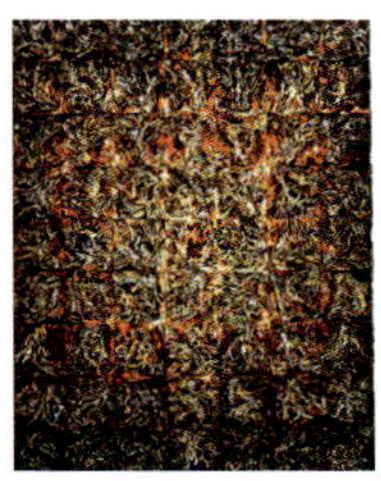

◂ DETAIL
p.149

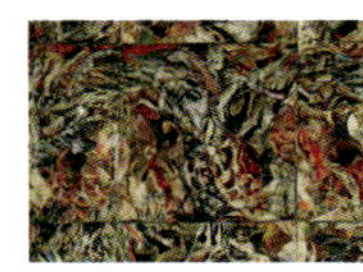

ROOT SERIES No. 16, *Mandala* (1979)
Preparatory work
p.20

ROOT SKETCH (1975)
Pencil on paper
8 x 8 in.
(20.3 x 20.3 cm.)
Small squares used to
build the structure
p.119

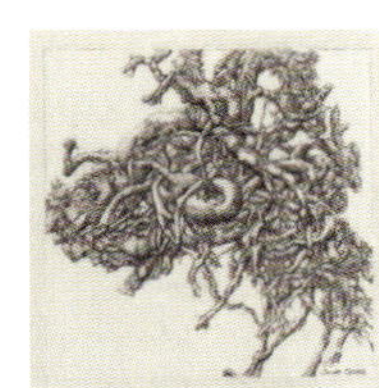

ROOT STUDY (1975)
Pen and ink on paper
22.5 x 16 in.
(57.2 x 40.6 cm.)
p.21

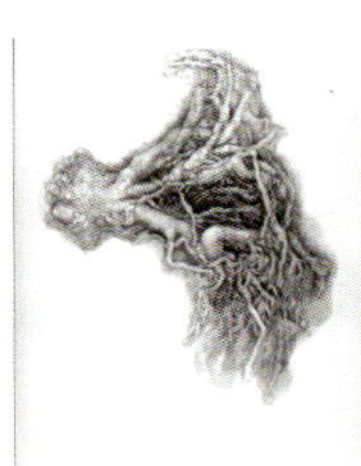

SKETCHBOOK PAGE, (1986)
p.71

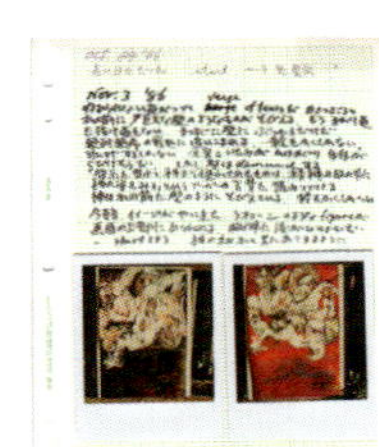

SKETCHBOOK PAGE, (1986)
p.74

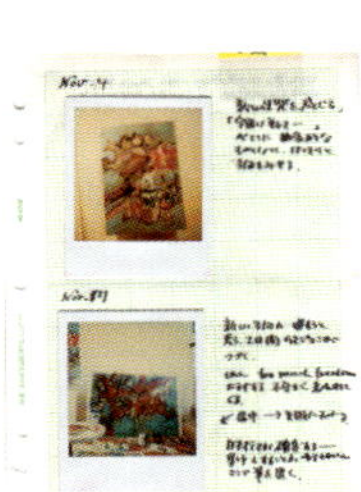

SKETCHBOOK PAGE, (1987)
p.74

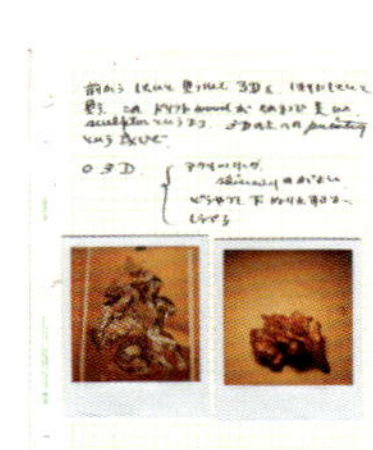

SKETCHBOOK PAGE, (1989)
p.80

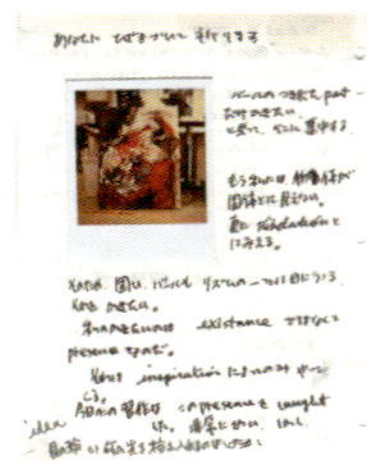

SKETCHBOOK (1974)
Pen and ink, charcoal, and Xerox on paper
11 x 8.5 in.
(27.9 x 21.6 cm.)
p.114

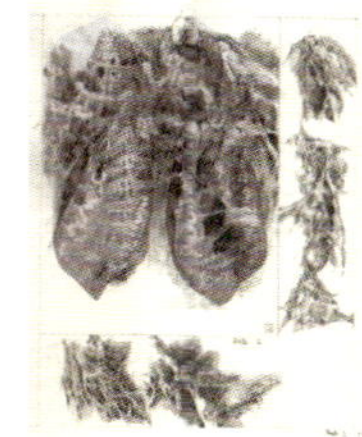

SKETCHBOOK (1998)
Oct. 27, 1998
The redine diagram is by Erich Fromm: the image behind is Junko's.
p.69
See also Birth at pg. 42

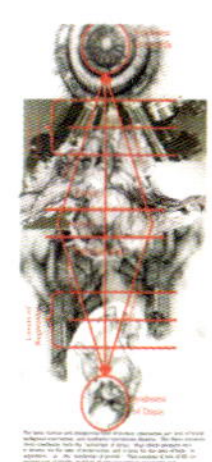

TOPOLOGICAL DEFORMATIONS OF THE CROSS No. 1 (1987)
Mixed media on paper
21 x 16 in.
(53.3 x 40.6 cm.)
p.208

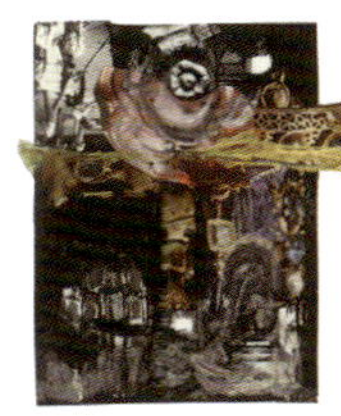

TOPOLOGICAL DEFORMATIONS OF THE CROSS No. 18, "KNOW BEFORE WHOM YOU STAND" (1987)
Collage and acrylic on paper
21 x 16 in.
(53.3 x 40.6 cm.)
p.205

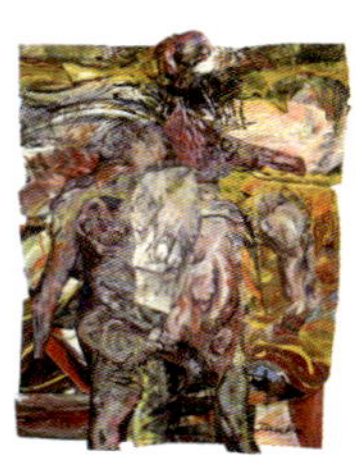

TREE SPIRITS, No. 9 (1989)
Charcoal and acrylic on paper
42 x 32 in.
(106.7 x 81.3 cm.)
p.54

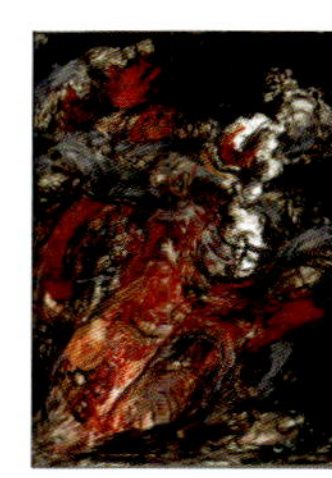

TREE SPIRITS, No. 14 (1989)
Acrylic and charcoal on paper
32 x 40 in.
(81.28 x 101.6 cm.)
p.144

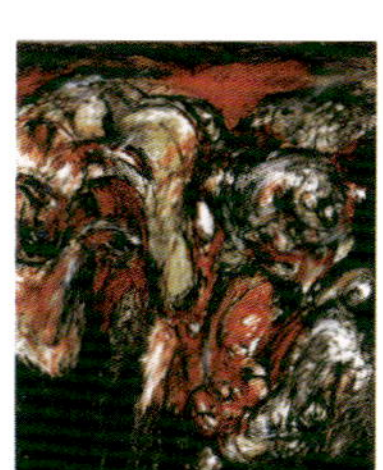

TREE SPIRITS IN GOLD, No. 1 (1991)
Acrylic and charcoal on canvas
66 x 56 in.
(167.6 x 142.2 cm.)
p.81

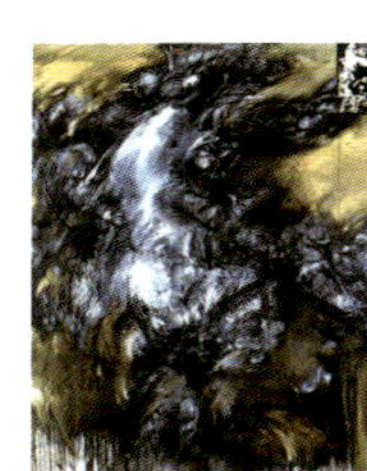

TREE SPIRITS IN GOLD, No. 8 (1991)
Mixed media on paper
66 x 56 in.
(167.6 x 142.2 cm.)
p.135

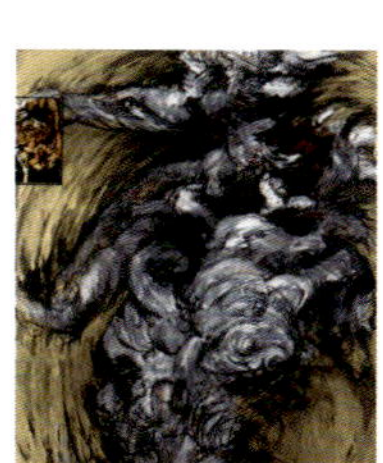

UNIVERSE MOVES AND HUMANS DANCE *DANCE: ECLIPSE* (1984)
Acrylic on astronomical poster
20 x 27 in.
(50.8 x 68.6 cm.)
p.131

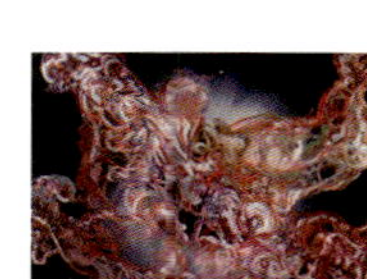

WHAT IS JUMPING OUT HERE? (1983)

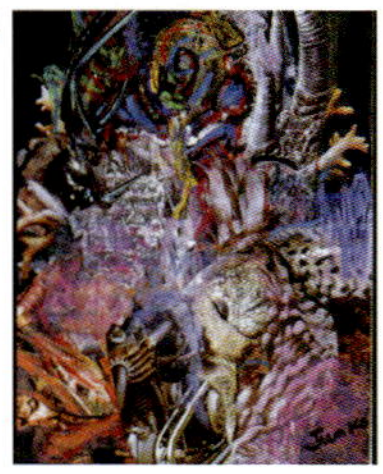

Mixed media collage
on paper
8 x 6 in.
(20.3 x 15.2 cm.)
p.113

SERIES LIST: CHRONOLOGICAL

Individual works and sketchbooks not included.

	ABBREV.	SERIES TITLE
1	Hmlt	Hamlet
2	eBird	Early Bird
3	Altr1	Altarpiece after Grunewald
4	DFS	Dead Flower Series
5	Root	Root Series
6	Micro	Microscopic World
7	Engn	Engine Series
8	Myst	Mysterious Paper
9	Crab	Horseshoe Crab Series
10	UNIV	The Universe Moves and Humans Dance
11	Altr2	Altarpiece after Giotto
12	Topo	Topological Deformations of the Cross
13	Medn	Meditations on Dance
14	Clst	Celestial Curtain
15	BCC	Behind the Celestial Curtain
16	Emrg	Emerging Consciousness
17	Brls	Burls
18	CRCLS	Circle Series
19	GBRL	Giant Burls
20	FigsBB	Figures on Black Background
21	TreeSP	Tree Spirits
22	Icon	Interplanetary Icon
23	TGLD	Tree Spirits in Gold
24	Reqm	Requiem for an Executed Bird
25	CMPU	Compact Universe
26	FRST	In the Forest of Amida Buddha
27	Indiv	Individuation Journal
28	GSKT	Giant Sketchbook
29	EBPrep	Preparatory Drawings for Esoteric
30	EB	Esoteric Buddhism
31	FthmSt	*Fathom* Studies
32	CAR	Concerning Art and Religion
33	FTHM	*FATHOM* Series

# PANELS	MEDIUM	YEAR
4	Craypas on paper	1953
1	Craypas on paper	1954
1	Collage on paper	1969
8	Pen and ink on paper with wash	1973-1974
18	Collage	1975-1980
4	Collage	1980-1981
4	Collage, pencil	1981-1982
6	Color pencil on xerox paper	1983
3	Mixed media	1983
37	Oil stick on paper	1983-1984
1	Collage, mixed media	1984-1985
21	Collage, mixed media	1987
8	Mixed media	1987
2	Mixed media	1988
3	Mixed media	1988
12	Mixed media	1988
17	Acrylic and Charcoal on paper	1988
18	Acrylic and Charcoal on paper	1988
4	Acrylic and Charcoal on paper	1989
47	ESTIMATE	1989
19	Acrylic and Charcoal on paper	1989
19	Mixed media	1990
8	Mixed media on canvas	1991
45	Mixed media on paper	1991
175	Mixed media collage on Kromekote	1991-1992
24	Acrylic on mylar	1993
9	Mixed media on mylar	1995
6	Charcoal on mylar	1997
7	Charcoal and pen on mylar	2000
5	Mixed media on mylar	2001
2	Backlit film, with acrylic on mylar (Destroyed)	2002
9	Backlit film, with acrylic on mylar	2003-2004
40	Collage of computer prints on mylar	2005-2006

GENERAL INDEX

References to Series and to Individual Artworks are in Italics.
See Series List for Abbreviations, then Image Table for Page References
Use Table of Contents for Primary Navigation

A

Aesthetics, theories of 46-47, 103-104, 261 ff.
Akashi, Shigetaro 94-95
Artist, role of 116, 261 ff.
Athanor, 277. See also Furnace
Atomic Bomb 209 ff.

B

Beethoven 222-223, 226
Buber, Martin 73, 76, 103, *206-207, Indiv(Buber)* 233
Buddha, Amida 154, 179 ff., *FRST*
Buddhism, Esoteric 184 ff., 220, 271 ff., *EB*

C

Campbell, Joseph 70-72
Catharsis 265
Cave paintings 46-47, 132, 224, 262, 275
Centripetal ii-iii, 12, 13; —narrative 163 ff.
Christ, 11, 68, 120, 174, *Reqm*
Christopher, St. 68
Complacency 90, 135-137, 206 ff., 219-220, *CAR9*
Computers 6, 137 ff.
Consciousness —altered states of 8, 46 ff., 142, 191 ff., 211, 245 ff.; —Corruption of 234; —higher/lower 46, 105, 211, 250
Crab 35 ff., 68, 73, *Crab* see also vulnerability
Crucifixion 28, 31, 178, *Topo*

D

Dead Flower Series 2, 15, *DFS*
Death 15, 31, *EB* 43, 50, 86, 167-168, 179 ff., 204-205; —of God and of Art, iii

Decanter 12, 56 ff.
Destruction 86 ff., 122, 220;
—destructiveness distinguished 222
Divine Darkness 5, 91-92, 103, 173, 186, *EB*
Divine Presence ii-iii, 167, 194, 259, 275 ff.

E

Ecology 209 ff., *Brls, TreeSP*
Empathy 12, 197
Encounter ii, 12, 68, 70 ff., 92, 115, 163, 278
Engine 26 ff., *Engn*
Ethnicity ii, 90, 109, 201, 271 ff.
Existentialism 206 ff.

F

Fascism 86, 88, 171, 203 ff., 232
Flower arrangement 97
Free Will see *Indiv(Augustine)* 292, *Indiv (Buber)* 233
Fromm, Erich 158, 204, 229 ff., *Indiv (Fromm)*
Furnace 277 ff., *Ecstasy Detail 270*

G

Gakushuin 88-89
Gesturality 147 ff.
God iii, 4, 70-73, 190, 265, 273, 278;
See also Divine Presence, *kami*
Goethe 247, 276
Goi, Masahisa 4, 110

H

Horrific gods 70 ff.

I

Identity 4, 226, 247-248; —cultural 201 ff.
Individuation 204, 229 ff., 236, 277, *Indiv*;
—individualism distinguished 229
Integrity, 107, 212, 276 ff.; —honesty distinguished 264 ff.
Irony 4, 31, 92

J
Japan 50, 85 ff., 107 ff.
Journey 106, 150-151, 163;
—artist's journey ii, 68, 150, 154, 261, 278
—hero's journey 250
Judaeo-Christian tradition 4, 209, 271 ff.
Judaism, 212 ff., 271 ff., *Topo18*
Jung, C. G. 12, 200, 211, 229, 251

K
Kami 273 (see list of Japanese terms)
Kamishibai 164 ff. (see list of Japanese terms)
Kandinsky 11, 197 ff.
Ki 148, 265 (see list of Japanese terms)
Kierkegaard 206, 207
Klee, Paul 4, 89-90, 104, 197-198
Kuukai 150-151, 156, 184 ff., *Fthm*

L
Laocoön 73, 77
Law and Litigation 5, 236 ff.

M
Marinetti 33, *CAR Nike*
Marriage iii, 1, 4-5, 35, 95 ff., 212 ff., 274-277
Meiji Jingu 271-272
Monsters 67-68, 70 ff.
Multiculturalism iii, 201 ff.
Mysticism iii, 6, 102, 259

N
Narrative 15 ff., 154, 161 ff., *FRST, Reqm*
Nietzsche iii, 207

O
Organic/inorganic 240 ff., *CAR4*

P
Performer vs. composer 225 ff.
Picasso 11, 47, 115, 120, 197
Prophet 262, *CAR9*
Psychology iii, 6, 198 ff., 212 ff.

R
Recycling 128
Reflections 154
Religion i-ii, 186 ff., 197-198, 206, 212 ff., *CAR*;
—monotheistic/polytheistic 271 ff.
Requiem for an Executed Bird 12, 56, 86 ff., 148, 165 ff., *Reqm*
Resurrection 178
Rilke 91-94, *Indiv (Rilke)*

S
Sexuality 28 ff., 273-274, *EB;*
—Dance 62 ff., 77, B*rls, UNIV,*
Medn, Tantric Dance
Shaman 9, 46, 261 ff.
Sogetsu School 97
Shinto 85, 110, 190,210, 271-272
Spirituality iii, 7, 9, 197 ff., 211 ff.

T
Technology 33, 122, 124, 134 ff., 209
Theosophy 197 ff.
Tokugawa Shogun 85
Transcendence 154, 161 ff., 177, 191 ff.
Tuberculosis 48 ff., *DFS5, Relic*

U

Ueda, Shigeo 102 ff.
Unitarian 94-99, 225

V

Van Gogh 11, 197, 198, 200, 206
Visitants 11 ff.
Vulnerability 34-35, 48, 88, 128, 168, 184, 245, 267

W

World War II ii, 85 ff., 198, 203 ff., 222, 230

NOTES

NOTES

For further information:
Giotto Multimedia
P.O. Box 995
Malibu, CA 90265
USA

An internet version of this book is available at
www.centripetalart.com

More information about Junko Chodos is available at
www.junkochodos.com

Designed by Hsu Design, Jeanette Hsu-Zamora

Text printed on 80# Garda Silk White
Hardcover printed on Sierra over 100pt. board
Jacket printed on 100 lb. Gloss C1S White
Printed by Friesens in Canada
CENTRIPETAL ART™

CentripetalArt™

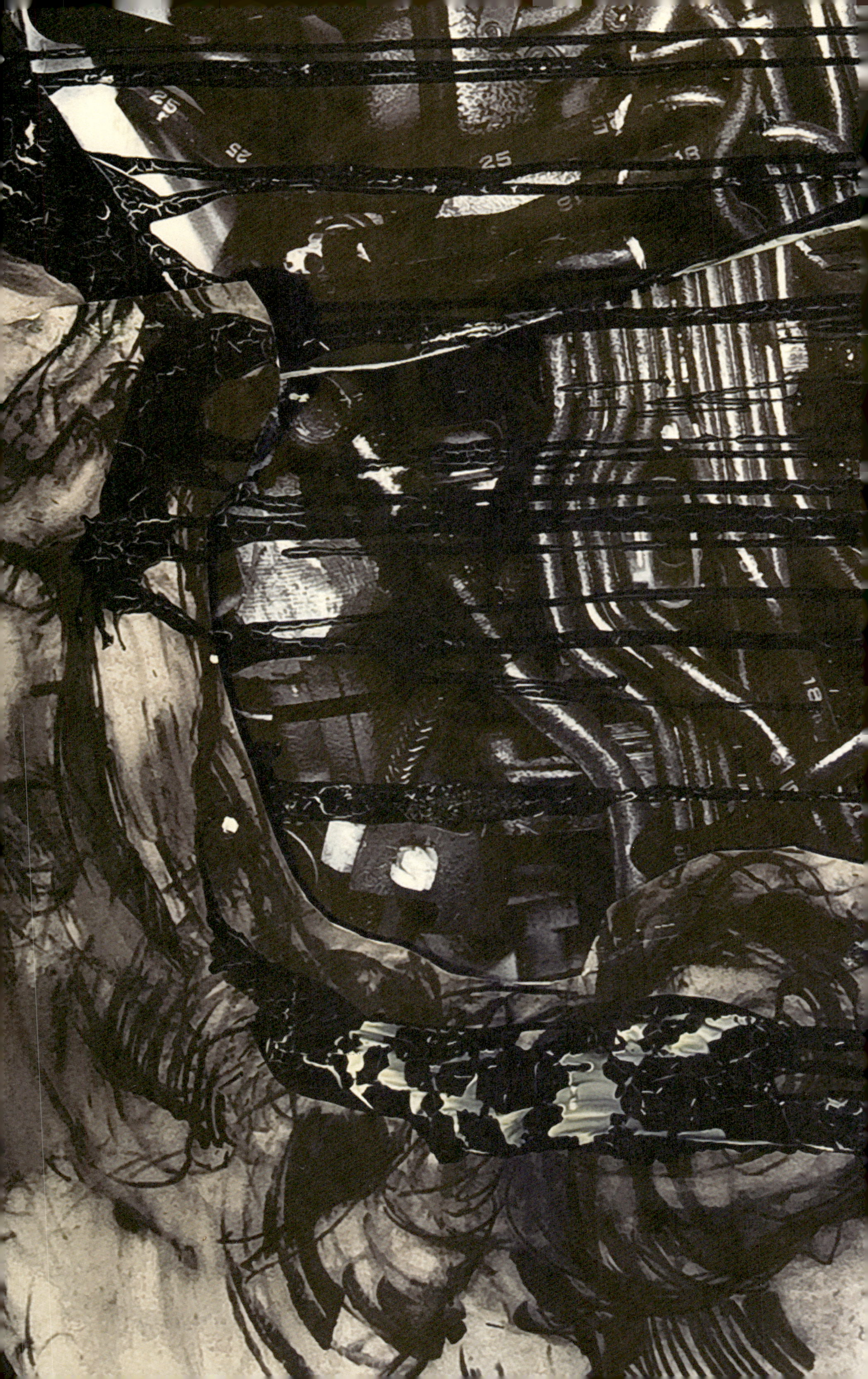